World Gazetteer
and
Geographical Dictionary

World Gazetteer
and
Geographical Dictionary

VOLUME – TWO

L-Z

General Editor

J. Gunn, M.A., D.Sc., F.R.S.G.S.

LOGOS PRESS

New Delhi-110 002

ISBN -13 : 978-81-7268-167-8 (Set)
ISBN -10 : 81-7268-167-4 (Set)

ISBN-13: 978-81-7268-168-5 (Vol. I) ISBN-10: 81-7268-168-2 (Vol. I)
ISBN-13: 978-81-7268-169-2 (Vol. II) ISBN-10: 81-7268-169-0 (Vol. II)

Edition 2008

Printed and Published by

LOGOS PRESS

Building No. 4788-90, Street No. 23, Ansari Road, Darya Ganj,
New Delhi-110 002 (India)

Phone : 23272187

PREFACE

THERE is more need to-day than ever before for a handy, comprehensive, and reliable Gazetteer of the World. The extraordinary changes in the means of communication, not only by sea and land but also by air and ether, have so reduced the effect of distance that the whole world lies open to our view. Almost every day, therefore, the question arises in the home, the office, and the classrooms of our schools, " Where is that place ? " The further questions are hardly less insistent, " What sort of a place is it ? " and " How should its name be pronounced ? "

The present volume has been compiled with the aim of providing answers to these and similar questions. The following are some of its chief features :

Comprehensiveness.—This Gazetteer and Geographical Dictionary contains over 10,000 entries. Its aim has been to include the name of every place in the world that is likely to be met with in the course of general reading or study, and about which any fact of geographical, historical, or other importance is known. In the interests of space, it is obvious that in the larger units only the most outstanding facts could be given. The work is intended as a book of reference for the general reader and for pupils in senior and advanced classes, and not for the specialist.

Reliability.—Care has been taken to base the facts and figures upon the latest available official or other authoritative sources of information. The populations given are those of the latest published Census figures—in the case of Great Britain, those of 1931.

Spelling of Names.—The published lists of the Royal Geographical Society have been taken as a guide in this matter, but in the main only so far as the sounds can be represented by the ordinary English alphabet. Special characters such as those adopted in certain countries of Central and Eastern Europe are of service to the specialist but not to the ordinary English reader.

Pronunciation.—In every case guidance to the pronunciation sufficient for the ordinary reader has been given. Where it has seemed necessary the name has been rewritten, so that by reference to the "Key to Pronunciation," on page vii, at least an approximation to the sound is easily obtained.

Special English Forms.—Where custom has sanctioned a special English form or pronunciation for a foreign name, this is adhered to though differing from that used in the foreign country, as, for example, the spelling of Naples, Brussels, Florence, etc., and the pronunciation of Paris, Trafalgar, etc. The function of any such book is not to prescribe what the form or pronunciation ought to be, but to record what is commonly accepted among English-speaking people. In all cases where it has seemed desirable, however, the foreign as well as the accepted English usage is given.

The Geographical Dictionary.—The Dictionary of Geographical Terms gives in handy form an explanation of the terms most commonly used in Physical Geography, Meteorology, World Commerce, and other allied topics. This will be found of service not only in the school classroom but also by the general reader, and is a distinct novelty in works of this character.

The Publishers claim that no Gazetteer has ever before been produced which contains so much information in so compact and handy a form. Every care has been taken to ensure that the information is trustworthy and up-to-date, and it is hoped that the book will be found equally valuable in the School, the Office, and the Home.

The task of compiling and editing so comprehensive a work required the services of highly qualified experts, and the staff employed included Messrs. G. S. Dickson, M.A., B.Sc., J. Hamilton Birrell, M.A., Ph.D., F.R.S.G.S., A. P. Gray, M.A., W. Carnon, M.A., and others, together with the General Editor.

KEY TO PRONUNCIATION

ä as in mar (*mär*), psalm (*säm*), hurrah (*hurä'*).
a, *ă* „ cat (*căt*), battle (*bătl*), abbot (*ăb'ot*).
ā „ mate (*māt*), pain (*pān*), weight (*wāt*).
au, *aw* as in call (*cawl*), appal (*apawl'*), brought (*brawt*).
e as in sell (*sel*), ferry (*fer'i*).
ĕ „ her (*hĕr*), fur (*fĕr*), gird (*gĕrd*).
ē „ meet (*mēt*), leaf (*lēf*), mere (*mēr*).
i, *ĭ* „ knit (*nit*), *silly* (*sil'i*), busy (*biz'i*).
ī, *ȳ* „ white (*whīt*), arise (*arīz'*), might (*mīt*).
o „ pot (*pot*), watch (*woch*), lorry (*lor'i*).
ō „ grow (*grō*), know (*nō*), loaf (*lōf*).
ö „ lord (*lörd*), resort (*rezört'*).
oo „ room (*room*), glue (*gloo*), shoe (*shoo*).
u „ full (*ful*), book (*buk*), could (*cud*).
ŭ „ shun (*shŭn*), mud (*mŭd*), above (*abŭv'*).
ū „ mute (*mūt*), few (*fū*), pure (*pūr*).
ou, *ow* as in doubt (*dout*), knout (*nowt*), aloud (*aloud'*).
oi as in coin (*koin*), buoy (*boi*), royal (*roi'al*).
ch „ chime (*chīm*), catch (*kăch*).
ch „ loch (*lo*ch), pibroch (*pē'bro*ch).
g „ good (*gud*), linger (*ling'ger*).
j „ jam (*jăm*), gem (*jem*), judge (*jŭj*).
n (nasal) as in entente (*äntä*n*t'*), savant (*sävä*n).
sh as in shove (*shŭv*), tension (*ten'shon*), action (*ăk'shon*).
zh „ leisure (*lezh'ūr*), vision (*vizh'on*).
th „ think (*think*), theme (*thēm*), health (*helth*).
th „ thine (th*īn*), wreathe (*rē*th), though (th*ō*).
wh „ while (*whīl*), somewhere (*sŭm'whār*).

When the accent is placed immediately after a vowel, that vowel is long; when the accent is placed after a consonant, the vowel of that syllable is short, as

ca'ble	cab'in	o'ral	or'ange
se'cret	sec'ond	pu'ny	pun'ish
pi'lot	pil'lar	ty'rant	tyr'anny

ABBREVIATIONS

ac.	acres.
alt.	altitude.
anc.	ancient.
bor.	borough.
Brit.	British.
c.	about (*circiter*).
cap.	capital.
cent.	century.
co.	county.
comm.	commune.
dep.	department.
dist.	district.
div.	division.
E., E.	east, eastern.
eccles.	ecclesiastical.
episc.	episcopal.
est.	estimated.
exp.	exports.
Fr.	French.
ft.	feet.
govt.	government.
I., isl.	island.
I.F.S.	Irish Free State.
in.	inches.
L.	Lake.
l. bk.	left bank.
m.	miles.
mkt.	market.
Mt., mts.	mount, mountains.
munic.	municipal.
N., N.	north, northern.
par.	parish.
parl.	parliamentary.
pop.	population.
prod.	products.
prov.	province.
R., riv.	river.
r. bk.	right bank.
rep.	republic.
rly. (jn.)	railway (junction).
R.S.F.S.R.	Russian Socialist Federal Soviet Republic.
S., s.	south, southern.
sq. m.	square miles.
str.	strait.
terr.	territory.
tn.	town.
trib.	tributary.
U.K.	United Kingdom.
univ.	university.
urb. dist.	urban district.
U.S.A.	United States of America.
U.S.S.R.	Union of Socialist Soviet Republics.
vil.	village.
W., w.	west, western.
wat.-pl.	watering-place.
yds.	yards.

L-3

L

Laaland, isl., Baltic Sea, at s. end of Great Belt; coast much indented; surface low and fertile; beech and oak forests; forms part of Denmark. Cap. Maribo. Area, 444 sq. m.

Labrador, peninsula, N. America, between Hudson Bay and Gulf of St. Lawrence; part belongs to Newfoundland (with an area of *c.* 110,000 sq. m., and pop. 4,000), and remainder to Quebec. Surface is mainly a plateau, 2,000 ft. above sea-level. Along Atlantic coast, cod, salmon, and herring fishing and sealing are important industries during summer. Area, *c.* 520,000 sq. m.; pop. *c.* 15,000.

Labuan (*la-boo-an'*), Brit. isl., Malay Archipelago, 6 m. N.W. of Borneo; administered as part of Straits Settlements; rice, coconuts, sago, rubber; excessive rainfall. Area, 30 sq. m.; pop. 6,000.

Laccadive Islands (*lak'a-dēv*), group of fourteen coral islands in Indian Ocean off W. coast of Madras; flat, low, barren; discovered by Vasco da Gama (1498); administered by Madras; produce coconuts and coir. Area, *c.* 80 sq. m.; pop. 14,000.

Lachine (*lă-shēn'*), tn., Montreal I., Quebec, Canada, at head of Lachine Rapids, 8 m. S.W. of Montreal; bridge-building works, wire-rope factory, lumber yards; favourite pleasure resort. Pop. 15,000.

Lachlan (*lach'lan*), riv., New South Wales, Australia; rises in Blue Mts.; joins Murrumbidgee; navigable only in rainy season; length, 700 m.

Lackawan'na, city, New York, U.S.A., on L. Erie; ironworks and steel foundries. Pop. 18,000.

Laconia (*la-kō'ni-a*), city, New Hampshire, U.S.A., 22 m. N. of Concord; hosiery and knitting machines. Pop. 11,000.

La Crosse, tn., Wisconsin, U.S.A., on Mississippi R.; railway centre; lumber trade; flour and grist mills. Pop. 40,000.

Ladákh, prov., E. Kashmir, between Himalayas and Karakoram Mts.; drained by Indus R.; one of the most elevated regions of the earth; cultivation confined to valleys and sheltered spots; gold found; originally part of Tibet. Cap. Leh. Pop. *c.* 37,000.

Ladoga, LAKE (*lad'o-ga*), lake between Russia and Finland, largest in Europe; coast-line of W. and N. is rocky, S. and E. low, marshy; drained by R. Neva; rich in fish; mean depth, 300 ft.; area, 7,000 sq. m. Canal constructed along S. shore (1861–6) to secure communication with Leningrad in stormy weather.

Ladrones. See MARIANAS ISLANDS.

Ladybank, burgh, Fife, Scotland, 5 m. S.W. of Cupar; rly. jn.; linen and malting industries. Pop. (including Monkston) 1,100.

Ladybrand, tn., Orange Free State, S. Africa, 80 m. E. of Bloemfontein; in rich and well-cultivated dist.; a health resort. Pop. *c.* 4,000.

Ladysmith, tn., Natal, S. Africa, 80 m. N.W. of Pietermaritzburg; coal-mining district; railway workshops. Notable defence (1899–1900) by Brit. in S. African War. Pop. 7,000.

Lafayette (*la-fā-et'*). (1) City, Indiana, U.S.A., 130 m. S.E. of Chicago; machinery, farm implements, wagons; lumber mills. Pop. 26,000. (2) Tn., Louisiana, U.S.A., 55 m. W.S.W. of Baton Rouge; sugar and cotton-seed oil. Pop. 8,000.

Lagos (*lă'gos*). (1) Cap. of Nigeria, Brit. W. Africa; has the only natural harbour on Slave Coast for distance of 1,000 m.; has been made a first-class port, and is now an important commercial town and wireless station; connected with interior by rail; engineering and repairing workshops. Pop. *c.* 100,000. (2) Seapt., s. Portugal; has good harbour; tunny fisheries and coasting trade. Pop. 10,000.

La Guaira (*la gwī'ra*), or LA GUAYRA, port, Venezuela, S. America; connected by rail with Caracas; good harbour; exports coffee, cocoa, hides, and sugar. Pop. 8,000.

Laguna (*la-goo'nă*), tn., isl. of Teneriffe, Canary Islands; oranges, raisins, tobacco. Pop. 13,000.

Lahore (*la-hōr'*). (1) Div. of Punjab, India; cereals, cotton, tobacco, opium. Area, 24,872 sq. m.; pop. 5,466,600. (2) Dist. of above. Area, 2,691 sq. m.; pop. 1,131,000. (3) Cap. of Punjab, on R. Ravi; railway centre; anc. Hindu temple, Mohammedan mosques, Anglican cathedral; Punjab Univ.; textiles, carpets, gold and silver wares, pottery. Pop. 282,000.

Lahr (*lăr*), tn., Baden, Germany, 29 m. N. of Freiburg; tobacco, cardboard, cotton and woollen goods. Pop. 14,000.

Laibach. See LJUBLJANA.

Lairg, par. and vil., Sutherlandshire, Scotland, at S.E. end of Loch Shin; has Pictish towers; centre for tourists and anglers. Pop. (par.) 1,050.

Lake Charles, tn., s.w. Louisiana, U.S.A.; rice mills, lumber trade, oil production; winter resort. Pop. 13,000.

Lake District, dist., Cumberland, Westmorland, and Lancashire, England; famed for beautiful lake and mountain scenery; includes Lakes Windermere, Ullswater, and Derwentwater; among mountain peaks are Scafell, Skiddaw, Helvellyn; rainfall heavy; associated with Wordsworth, Coleridge, and Southey, who are called the *Lake Poets*; tourist centre. Chief towns, Ambleside, Bowness, Coniston, Keswick. Area, *c.* 700 sq. m.

Lakeland, city, Florida, U.S.A., 32 m. E. of Tampa; centre of rich agricultural dist. producing much fruit; phosphate mines; winter resort. Pop. 17,000.

Lake of the Thousand Islands. See under ST. LAWRENCE.

Lakewood, tn., Ohio, U.S.A.; residential suburb of Cleveland; grapes. Pop. 70,000.

Lakhimpur (*lŭk-ēm-poor'*), dist., E. Assam, India; in Brahmaputra valley; numerous tea gardens; coal mines and petroleum wells. Chief tn., Dibrugahr. Area, 3,757 sq. m.; pop. 588,000.

Lalin (*lă-lēn'*), tn., N.W. Spain, 30 m. N.E. of Pontevedra; paper mills and tanneries. Pop. 17,000.

La Linea. See LINEA.

Lambayeque (*lam-bī-ā'kă*), mar. dep., N. Peru; sugar, rice, tobacco, cotton. Chief tn., Chiclayo. Area, 4,614 sq. m.; pop. 124,000.

Lambeth, metropolitan bor., S. London; opposite Westminster; contains Lambeth Palace, residence of Archbishop of Canterbury; pottery and chemicals. Pop. 296,200.

Lam'bourn, tn., Berks, England, 13 m. N.W. of Newbury; training stables for race-horses; trout fishing. Pop. 2,340.

Lamesley (*lāms'li*), par. and vil., Durham, England, 3 m. s. of Gateshead; coal and iron mines; grindstone quarries; chemical works. Pop. (par.) 6,800.

Lammermoors', or LAMMERMUIR HILLS, broad range, S.E. Scotland, in Berwickshire and E. Lothian. Highest summit, Lammer Law, 1,733 ft.

Lam'peter, munic. bor. and mkt. tn., Cardiganshire, S. Wales, on R. Teifi, 23 m. N.N.E. of Carmarthen; agricultural trade; contains St. David's Coll. (1827), affiliated with universities of Oxford and Cambridge. Pop. 1,700.

Lanai. See HAWAIIAN ISLANDS.

Lan'ark, royal burgh and co. tn., Lanarkshire, Scotland, 22 m. S.E. of

Glasgow; drugget and wincey; cattle, sheep, and horse sales; rich in Wallace associations; racecourse. Pop. 6,200. New Lanark, 1 m. s., has cotton mills.

Lanarkshire, co., s.w. Scotland; surface rises from N. to Lowther Hills in s.; watered by Clyde and its tributaries. In s. are sheep farms, in centre market gardens and orchards, in N. important coalfields. Lanarkshire is most populous and busiest manufacturing county in Scotland. Iron goods, steel, machinery; contains chief seats of cotton, linen, and woollen industries; shale mines, oilworks; contains Glasgow, Hamilton, Airdrie, and other industrial centres. Co. tn., Lanark. Area, 882 sq. m.; pop. 1,586,000.

Lan'cashire, or LANCS, co., N.W. England; low, flat coast is much indented; many good harbours; surface rugged and mountainous in N. and E., reaching 2,633 ft. in Coniston Old Man in N.; drained by Duddon, Lune, Ribble, Mersey, Irwell, and other rivers. Lancashire is most populous and busiest manufacturing county in England; contains large coalfield, which has become chief seat of cotton industry, with centre at Manchester. In detached portions in the N. are large deposits of iron ore which have developed great iron and steel industries at Barrow-in-Furness. Manufacture of machinery is important; other industries include shipbuilding, dye works, manufacture of chemicals, glass, soap, leather, silk and woollen textiles; oats, wheat, and potatoes are grown; cattle and sheep reared. County is crossed by numerous railways, and by several canals, including the Manchester Ship Canal. There are remains of many monasteries, the finest of which is Furness Abbey, a Cistercian foundation. Cap. Lancaster. Chief seapt., Liverpool, second seapt. in U.K. Other important tns., Manchester, Salford, Bolton, Oldham, Blackburn, Preston, Burnley, St. Helens. Area, *c.* 1,880 sq. m.; pop. 5,039,100.

Lan'caster. (1) Co. tn., Lancashire, England; anc. castle, now used as county prison; fine old church, St. Mary's; connected with Kendal and Preston by Lancaster Canal; cabinet-making, upholstery, cottons, railway plant. Pop. 43,400. (2) Tn., S.E. Pennsylvania, U.S.A.; tobacco, cottons, silks; rich agricultural dist. Pop. 61,000. (3) Tn., Ohio, U.S.A., 28 m. S.E. of Columbus; agricultural trade; flour, shoes, glass, and machinery. Pop. 15,000.

Lan'chester, par., vil., Durham, England, 7 m. N.W. of Durham; coal mines; Roman remains. Pop. (par.) 5,100.

Lanchow', cap. of Kansu, China, on R. Hwang-Ho; cloth and camel's-hair goods; centre for mineral, silk, fur, tobacco, grain, tea produce of province. Pop. *c.* 369,000.

Lanciano (*län-chē-ä'nō*), tn., Abruzzi e Molise, Italy, near Adriatic coast; seat of archbishop; grain, fruit, oil, wine; silk, linen, and hemp factories. Pop. 20,000.

Lan'cing, seaside resort, Sussex, England, 2½ m. w. of Shoreham; chemical works. Pop. 4,000.

Landes (*lond*), dep., s.w. France; watered by R. Adour; three-fifths of dep. is known as the *landes*, and consists of tracts of sand interspersed with marshes, and forests of cork, pine, and oak; produces resin, charcoal, rock-salt, iron; horses bred. Chief tn., Mont-de-Marson. Area, 3,604 sq. m.; pop. 263,000.

Landeshut (*län'des-hoot*), tn., Silesia, Prussia, 65 m. s.w. of Breslau; textile industry and shoes. Pop. 13,000.

Landsberg - an - der - Warthe (*vär'te*), tn., Brandenburg, Prussia, on Warthe R., 45 m. N.E. of Frankfurt-on-the-Oder; machinery, sawmilling, and brick making. Pop. 43,000.

Land's End, most westerly point of England, Cornwall, 9 m. s.w. of Penzance; granite cliffs, 60 ft. to 100 ft. high, fantastically eroded.

Landshut (*lands'hoot*), tn., Lower Bavaria, Germany, on riv. Isar, 38 m. N.E. of Munich; old castle of

Trausnitz (1232); machinery, breweries, and tobacco. Pop. 26,000.

Landskrona (*lands-krō'na*), seaport, Sweden, 22 m. N. of Malmö; railway centre; tanneries, flour and sugar mills; exports butter, eggs, and bacon. Pop. 18,000.

Langenbielau (*lang-en-bē'lou*), tn., Silesia, 35 m. S.W. of Breslau; woollens, cottons, chemicals. Pop. 20,000.

Langholm (*lang'um*), mkt. tn., Dumfriesshire, Scotland, on R. Esk, 21 m. N.W. of Carlisle; tweeds, tanneries. Pop. 2,400.

Langreo (*lăn-grā'ō*), tn., N. Spain, 10 m. S.E. of Oviedo; coal and iron; iron foundries. Pop. 34,000.

Langres (*lon'gr*), tn., Haute-Marne, France, 20 m. S.S.E. of Chaumont; strongly fortified; cutlery; trade in grain, live-stock, and wine. Pop. 6,000.

Lan'sing, city, Michigan, U.S.A., cap. of state, 85 m. N.W. of Detroit; Michigan Agricultural Coll.; good water-power; automobiles; agricultural implements, machinery. Pop. 78,000.

Lanzarote (*lan-tha-rō'tā*), most easterly of Canary Islands; volcanic and very mountainous; produces excellent grapes. Cap. Arrecife, on S.E. coast. Area, 326 sq. m.; pop. 17,000.

Laoag (*lă-o-ăg'*), cap., Ilocos Norte, N.W. Luzon, Philippines, on Laoag R., 5½ m. from coast; rice, corn, tobacco, sugar, and cotton. Pop. 38,000.

Laoighise. See LEIX.

Laon (*lă-on*), chief tn., Aisne, France, 87 m. N.E. of Paris; important fortress since Roman times; fine 12th-cent. Gothic cathedral; linen and metal goods. Pop. 14,000.

Laos (*lă'os*), general name for Central Indo-China, including basin of R. Mekong and upper basin of Rs. Menam, Chao Bhraya, and Salween; bordering Siam and Burma on the W., Yunnan on the N., Tongking and Annam on the E., and Cambodia on the S. Divided into (1) *Eastern* or *French Laos*, Fr. Protectorate since 1893. Area, 82,604 sq. m.; pop. 837,000. (2) *Siamese Laos*, number of semi-independent principalities. (3) *Shan States* of Lakon, Chiengmai, Nan, etc. Products include rice, maize, sugar-cane, cotton, indigo, fruits, tobacco, teak; gold, tin, lead, and precious stones are found, but little worked; cattle raising is chief industry.

La Paz. (1) Dep., Bolivia, S. America; mountainous in S., with peaks Illimani (22,500 ft.) and Sorata (23,500 ft.); produces coca, coffee, rubber, copper, tin, gold, silver. Area, 40,686 sq. m.; pop. *c.* 724,000. (2) Or LA PAZ DE AYACUCHO, cap., Bolivia, S. America; important commercial city; trade in copper, alpaca, wool, cinchona. Pop. 142,000.

Lap'land, terr. having no political existence, largely consisting of the Arctic region of Norway, Sweden, and Finland; mainly mountain, forest, and morass; inhabitants (Lapps, so named by Swedes) are mostly nomad hunters and fishers, with large herds of domesticated reindeer. Great wealth of copper, iron ore, and timber.

La Plat'a, tn., cap. of Buenos Aires prov., Argentina; trades in cattle and agricultural produce; university. Pop. 166,000.

La Porte, city, N. Indiana, U.S.A.; iron and steel goods, woollen goods, and flour. Pop. 15,000.

Larache (*la-rash'*), tn., Spanish Morocco, on Atlantic coast; exports include cork, beans, wool. Pop. *c.* 15,000.

Lar'bert, par. and vil., Stirlingshire, Scotland, 20 m. E.N.E. of Glasgow; coal mines; rly. jn. Pop. (par.) 12,400.

Laredo (*la-rā'dō*), frontier city, Texas, U.S.A., on Rio Grande; connected by bridges with Nuevo Laredo (Mexico) on opposite bank; iron, brick, foundry and machine-shop products; wool, hides; natural gas and petroleum. Pop. 33,000 (two-thirds Mexicans).

Lar'go, UPPER and LOWER, two coast villages, 1 m. apart, and par., S.E. Fife, Scotland. Alexander Selkirk, original of 'Robinson Crusoe,' a native; statue erected in 1885. Pop. 2,400.

Largs, seaside resort, N. Ayrshire, Scotland, 4 m. S. of Wemyss Bay; here Haakon of Norway was defeated by Alexander III. (1263). Pop. 6,100.

Laris'sa, name of several towns in anc. Greece, most important of which is represented by modern town, on R. Salambria, 35 m. N.W. of Volo, Thessaly; many mosques; silk and cotton goods. Pop. 24,000.

Laristan', dist., Fars prov., Persia, bordering on Persian Gulf; arid and sandy waste with salt steppes; camels reared; silk manufactured. Cap. Lar, 180 m. S.E. of Shiraz. Area, *c.* 20,000 sq. m.

Larkan'a. (1) Dist., N. Sind, Bombay, on r. bk. of Indus; greater part fertile and well-watered plain; chief products, rice, wheat, cotton, wool; carpets and leather goods are manufactured. Area, 5,053 sq. m.; pop. 598,000. (2) Tn. in above, 150 m. N. of Hyderabad; neighbourhood known as 'Eden of Sind'; cotton, silk, leather, and paper. Pop. 18,000.

Lark'hall, tn., Lanarkshire, Scotland, 3 m. S.E. of Hamilton; coal mines; brick and tile making industries. Pop. 14,000.

Lar'naca, or LARNAKA, seaport, Cyprus, on S. coast; exports grain, cotton, fruit, gypsum. Pop. 10,000.

Larne, mkt. tn. and seaside resort, co. Antrim, N. Ireland, W. of entrance to Lough Larne; bleaching, linen and woollen weaving, paper making; bauxite exported; daily communication by mail steamer with Stranraer, Scotland (39 m.). Pop. 8,000.

La Rochelle (*lä rō-shel'*), chief port and cap., Charente-Inférieure, France, on Bay of Biscay; connected with Newfoundland fishing; shipbuilding, cotton yarn manufacture, glass works, sugar refining, and distilling; commerce chiefly centred at port of La Pallice. Pop. 38,000.

La Roche-sur-Yon (*lä rosh-soor-yon'*), cap., Vendée, France, 48 m. S. of Nantes; market for agricultural produce, horses, and cattle; flour mills. Pop. 12,000.

Larvik. See LAURVIK.

Lashkar. See GWALIOR (2).

Las Pal'mas, chief tn., Grand Canary, Canary Islands, on N.E. shore; fishing; glass, hats, and leather goods; bananas, potatoes, tomatoes. Pop. 66,000.

Lasswade. See BONNYRIGG AND LASSWADE.

Latakia (*la-ta-kē'a*), seaport, Beirut, Syria; exports sponges, olive oil, and famous Latakia tobacco. Pop. *c.* 22,000.

La Tuque (*lä-took'*), tn., Quebec, Canada, on St. Maurice R., 78 m. N. of Three Rivers. Pop. 6,000.

Lat'via, rep., E. and S. of Gulf of Riga; bounded N. by Estonia, E. by Russia, S. by Lithuania, and W. by Baltic Sea. Surface generally plain, with marshy or sandy areas; chief riv. S. Dvina, flowing into Gulf of Riga; over 1,000 lakes. Pine forests cover *c.* one-third of surface. Agriculture is principal occupation; chief crops, rye, barley, oats, and flax; stock raising is important; some dairy farming and gardening. Textiles, flour, paper, oil, sawmills, distilleries, sugar refineries, leather and linseed industries. Principal ports, Riga (cap.), Ventspils, and Liepaja. Area, *c.* 25,000 sq. m.; pop. 1,895,000.

Lau'der, royal burgh, Berwickshire, Scotland, on riv. Leader, 29 m. S.E. of Edinburgh; favourites of James III. hanged over bridge (1483). Pop. 600.

Lauenburg (*lou'en-boorg*), tn., Pomerania, Prussia, 38 m. W.N.W. of Danzig; woollens, linen, leather, machinery. Pop. 15,000.

Launceston (*läns'tun*). (1) Mkt. tn. and munic. bor., Cornwall, England, 22 m. N.W. of Plymouth; ruined castle; several times besieged during Civil War. Pop. 4,100. (2) Chief tn., N. Tasmania; sawmilling, iron and engineering works. Pop. (with suburbs), 29,000.

La Union (*lä oo-nē-ōn'*), tn., Murcia, Spain, 5 m. E. of Cartagena; iron, lead, sulphur, and manganese mines. Pop. 25,000.

Laur'encekirk, mkt. tn., Kincardineshire, Scotland, 30½ m. s.w. of Aberdeen; makes handloom linens; carriage building. Pop. 1,300.

Lauren'tide Mountains, name sometimes applied to s. escarpment of Laurentian Plateau or Canadian Shield, Canada; many waterfalls; forested.

Laurvik (*lour'vik*), or LARVIK, seapt. and spa, Norway, 100 m. s.w. of Oslo; shipbuilding, glass works; saw and pulp mills; exports timber, ice, wood pulp, and granite. Pop. 11,000.

Lausanne (*lō-zan'*), cap., Vaud, Switzerland; half a mile from Ouchy, its port on N. shore of Lake Geneva; cathedral (1235–75); univ. and educational centre; rly. jn.; on Simplon route between Paris and Milan; machinery, tobacco, and chocolate; vineyards. Pop. 78,000.

Lauterbrunnen (*lou-ter-broon'en*), tourist resort, Bernese Oberland, Switzerland, 6 m. S.E. of Interlaken, on White Lütschine; most famous of its waterfalls, Staubbach, 980 ft. high; mountain railway to Grindelwald by Wengernalp; funicular and electric railway to Mürren.

Lauzon (*lō-zōn'*), tn., Quebec, Canada, on s. shore of R. St. Lawrence, 3½ m. E. of Quebec. Pop. 6,000.

Laval', cap., Mayenne, France, 45 m. E. of Rennes; 12th cent. Gothic cathedral; anc. ducal château; manufacture of cotton goods, paper, leather, and machinery; marble quarries in vicinity. Pop. 24,000.

Law'rence. (1) City, Massachusetts, U.S.A., on the Merrimac R., 26 m. N.W. of Boston; cotton and woollen and worsted goods; foundry and machine shop products. Pop. 85,000. (2) City, Kansas, U.S.A., 38 m. W. of Kansas City; state univ.; flour, paper, machinery, nails. Pop. 12,400.

Leadgate, urb. dist., Durham, England, 9 m. W. of Chester-le-Street; coal mining. Pop. 6,400.

Lead'hills, vil., Lanarkshire, Scotland, near border of Dumfries; silver-lead mines; birthplace of Allan Ramsay; alt. 1,301 ft. Pop. 815.

Leamington (*lem'ing-ton*). (1) Or ROYAL LEAMINGTON SPA, munic. bor. and health resort, Warwickshire, England, 2 m. E. of Warwick; mineral waters. Pop. 29,700. (2) Tn., Ontario, Canada, on L. Erie, 30 m. S.E. of Windsor. Pop. 5,000.

Leatherhead, tn., Surrey, England, 12 m. s.w. of Croydon; brick and tile works, breweries, and tanneries. Pop. 6,900.

Leavenworth, city, Kansas, U.S.A., 25 m. N.W. of Kansas City; coal mining; bricks, stoves, furniture, machines, flour. Pop. 21,000.

Leb'anon ('white'). (1) Two parallel mountain ranges, Syria; mts. composed of white chalk and limestone rock. Ranges are: Lebanon on W., reaching an extreme elevation of 10,018 ft.; and Anti-Lebanon on E., with outlying Mt. Hermon (*c.* 9,200 ft.). Between ranges stretches plain drained by Rs. Litâny and El-Asi (the ancient Leontes and Orontes). Cedars of Lebanon now found only in certain districts. Vines, olives, mulberries grow in lower regions; cereals, tobacco, silk, honey, coal. Greater Lebanon, extending to frontiers of Palestine, is a state under French Mandate. Cap. Beirut. Pop. 796,000. (2) City, Pennsylvania, U.S.A., 85 m. N.W. of Philadelphia; iron mining; machinery and brick making. Pop. 26,000.

Lebrija (*le-brē'ha*), or LEBRIXA, tn., Seville, Spain, 34 m. S. of Seville; grain, oil, wine, and cattle; ruined castle. Pop. 12,000.

Le Cateau (*le cä-tō*), formerly CATEAU-CAMBRÉSIS, tn., Nord, France, 16 m. E.S.E. of Cambrai; textiles; sugar refining, brewing, metal founding, and mosaic work. Scene of much fighting during Great War. Pop. 8,000.

Lecce (*let'chā*), chief tn., prov. Lecce, Apulia, Italy, 23 m. S.E. of Brindisi; ruined fortifications; dist. produces fruit and grain; castle of San Cataldo in vicinity. Pop. 39,000.

Lecco (*lek'ō*), city, prov. Como, Lombardy, Italy, on S.E. arm (Lake Lecco) of Lake Como; iron, copper, silk, and cotton. Pop. 29,000.

Ledbury, mkt. tn., Herefordshire, England, on Malvern Hills, 13 m. E. of Hereford; cider orchards and hop gardens. Pop. 3,300.

Leeds, city and co. bor., W. Riding of Yorkshire, England, on R. Aire; canal communication with Humber and with Liverpool; univ., founded 1904, includes textile and art departments; famed for triennial musical festivals; chief centre of woollen industry; locomotives, machinery, heavy iron and steel goods of all kinds, chemicals, glass, printing, leather goods, artificial silk and pottery; Kirkstall Abbey, 2½ m. distant, belongs to corporation. Pop. 482,800.

Leek, tn., Staffordshire, England, 10 m. N.E. of Hanley; manufactures silk, artificial silk, braids, laces, and covered buttons; charter dates from 1208. Pop. 18,600.

Lee-on-the-Solent, wat.-pl., Hants, England, on Southampton Water, 3 m. W. of Gosport. Pop. 4,000.

Leeuwarden (*lā'oo-war-den*), tn., Friesland, Holland, 26 m. W. of Gröningen; dairy and agricultural produce; iron, copper, and lead goods, musical instruments, boats. Pop. 47,000.

Leeward Islands, chain of islands, Lesser Antilles, W. Indies. Those belonging to Britain are Dominica, Antigua (including Barbuda and Redonda), St. Kitts (with Nevis and Anguilla), Montserrat, and the Virgin Islands. St. Thomas, Santa Cruz, and St. John in the Virgin Islands belong to U.S.A. Others of the group are owned by Holland and France, Guadeloupe being largest French possession in W. Indies. Islands volcanic with lofty peaks, highest Morne Diablotin (4,746 ft.) in Dominica. Produce sugar and molasses, cotton, citrate of lime, cacao; lime juice exported from Montserrat and Dominica. Area (of Brit. Islands), 715 sq. m.; pop. 122,000.

Legaspi. See ALBAY.

Leg'horn (Ital. *Livorno*), seaport, Tuscany, W. coast of Italy; exports hemp, hides, marble, olive oil, candied fruit, wine, soap, boracic acid, and hats; shipbuilding, glass making, and copper and brass founding are carried on; fine cathedral. Pop. 129,000.

Legnago (*len-yä'gō*), tn., Lombardy, Italy, on R. Adige, 25 m. S.E. of Verona; one of the four fortresses of the 'Quadrilateral'; centre of fertile dist.; rice, cereals, and sugar. Pop. 19,000.

Legnano (*len-yä'no*), tn., Lombardy, Italy, 17 m. N.W. of Milan; cotton, silk, thread, and machinery. Pop. 27,000.

Leh (*lā*), cap. of Ladakh, Kashmir, India, 5 m. from r. bk. of Upper Indus; in open valley, alt. 11,500 ft.; starting-place for caravans into central Asia; commands entrances to passes N. and E.; headquarters of Brit. political officer. Pop. 2,000.

Lehe. See WESERMÜNDE.

Leicester (*lest'er*), co. tn., Leicestershire, England; manufactures hosiery, boots and shoes, elastic web, and agricultural implements. Pop. 239,100.

Lei'cestershire, inland co., Midlands, England, of varied surface, rugged in Wolds (N.E.) and in Charnwood Forest (long deforested), where Bardon Hill rises to 912 ft. Chief rivers: Soar; Trent in N.W., and Avon and Welland in S.E. Cattle and sheep are reared; long noted for wool and Stilton cheese; oats, wheat, turnips, and mangolds are principal crops. Coal and iron largely worked, former in N.W.; granite and slate quarried in Charnwood. Manufactures include hosiery (Leicester, Loughborough, Hinckley), boots and shoes, silk plush, elastic web, bricks and pottery. Melton Mowbray, Market Harborough, and Loughborough are hunting centres. Co. tn., Leicester. Area, 830 sq. m.; pop. 541,800.

Leigh (*lē*), mkt. tn. and munic. bor., Lancs, England, 7 m. S.E. of Wigan; coal mining; cotton and silk; brewing; agricultural implements and iron foundries. Pop. 45,300.

Leighton Buzzard (*lā'ton*), urb. dist., Bedfordshire, England, 40 m. N.W. of London; has fine Early Eng. church;

agricultural trade and market gardening; paper making. Pop. 7,000.

Leinster (*len'ster*), or LAIGHEN, S.E. prov., I.F.S., extending from Dundalk Bay to Waterford Harbour. Other inlets: Dublin Bay and Wexford Harbour. Comprises twelve counties: Louth, Meath, Dublin, Wicklow, and Wexford, on the coast; Kilkenny, Carlow, Kildare, Leix, Offaly, Westmeath, and Longford, inland. Area, 7,580 sq. m.; pop. 1,149,100.

Leipzig (*līp'zig*), city, Saxony, Germany, on fertile plain at junction of Rs. Elster, Pleisse, and Parde. The ancient town (now business section) is separated from extensive suburbs by fine promenades, built on site of old fortifications. Seat of Supreme Court of Justice of Germany. Ranks among first cities in the world in bookselling, publishing, typefounding, and music; European fur market; also important in metal and textile industries, and manufacture of chemicals, scientific instruments, leather, rubber, foodstuffs; famous fairs held Easter, Michaelmas, and New Year since Middle Ages. Pop. 679,000.

Leiston (*lā'ston*), or LEISTON CUM SIZEWELL, urb. dist., Suffolk, England, 22 m. N.E. of Ipswich; ironworks; agricultural machinery and implements. Pop. 4,200.

Leith. See EDINBURGH.

Leitmeritz. See LITOMERICE.

Leitrim (*lē'trim*), mar. co., prov. Connaught, I.F.S., with coast on Donegal Bay; almost cut in two by Lough Allen. N. generally mountainous, with fertile valleys. E. of Lough Allen is another mountainous tract. S. more open and better suited for cultivation. R. Shannon enters county N. of Lough Allen and partly forms S.W. boundary. Many lakes. Fodder crops, oats, and potatoes; coal is worked; iron, lead, limestone, and marl occur. Co. tn., Carrick-on-Shannon. Area, 613 sq. m.; pop. 63,500.

Leix, or LAOIGHIS (*lēz*), formerly QUEEN'S COUNTY, co., Leinster, I.F.S. In N.W. are Slieve Bloom Mts., in S. and S.E. are various scattered ranges of hills; centre is mainly flat. Principal rivers are Nore and Barrow. Agriculture and dairy farming are chief industries. Coal occurs in S. Chief towns, Maryborough (co. tn.), Mountmellick. Area, 664 sq. m.; pop. 51,000.

Leman, Lake. See GENEVA (3).

Lemberg. See LWOW.

Lem'nos, or LIMNOS, one of the largest islands in N. Ægean Sea, about 40 m. W. of entrance to Dardanelles; largely mountainous; grain, tobacco, and fruits. Chief port, Kastro or Lemnos, on W. coast. Area, *c.* 150 sq. m.; pop. *c.* 4,000.

Le'na, riv. of Siberia, with drainage area of *c.* 1,000,000 sq. m.; length, 2,900 m.; rises in Baikal Mts. W. of Lake Baikal; reaches Arctic Ocean through large delta. Chief tribs.: (r. bk.) Vitim (1,200 m.), Olekma (1,100 m.), Aldan (1,300 m.); (l. bk.) Vilui (1,500 m.); sands of first two contain gold. Total length of navigable waterways, 7,110 m.

Leninakan', formerly ALEXANDROPOL, fortified tn., Erivan dist., Armenia, U.S.S.R.; important silk trade. Pop. *c.* 50,000.

Len'ingrad, originally ST. PETERSBURG, and later PETROGRAD, former cap. of Russia, and second city of U.S.S.R., at mouth of R. Neva where it enters Gulf of Finland; only outlet to Baltic remaining to Russia; climate severe, R. Neva being frozen from November to April. Many magnificent palaces. State Library ranks after those of London and Paris. There are many important educational institutions, particularly the Leningrad State University. There are thirteen cathedral churches, the most sumptuous being that of St. Isaac with its beautiful gilded dome. Industrial establishments include metal works, iron foundries, sugar refineries, distilleries, breweries, shipbuilding yards, and printing works; chemicals, tobacco, soap, crystal and glass, cotton and cloth, leather, cordage, pottery, porcelain, and machinery are also made. City is connected by riv., lake, and canal with Rs. Volga and Dnieper, and so with Caspian and Black Seas. Pop. 1,614,000.

Len'nep, tn., Rhineland, Prussia, 8 m. S.E. of Elberfeld; machinery, woollens, cottons, and silk. Pop. 14,000.

Lens, town, Pas-de-Calais, France, 10 m. N.E. of Arras; is in rich coal-field; suffered almost total destruction during Great War; iron and steel works, sugar, soap, and wire-rope factories. Pop. 30,000.

Lentini (*len-tē'nē*), anc. LEONTINI, tn., Sicily, 16 m. S.W. of Catania; founded by Greek colonists (730 B.C.); trades in oil, wine, cereals. Pop. *c.* 26,000.

Leominster. (1) (*lem'ster*) Tn., N. Herefordshire, England; par. church partly Norman; tn. dates from 658; agricultural implement works; cider and hops. Pop. 5,700. (2) (*lem'in-ster*) Tn., Massachusetts, U.S.A., 40 m. N.W. of Boston; pianos, combs, paper, jewellery. Pop. 22,000.

Leon (*lā-on*). (1) Prov., N.W. Spain, bounded on N. by Cantabrian Mts.; mountainous in N. and W.; wheat, rye, oats, barley, and maize largely cultivated; cattle, mules, coal, iron, and leather are exported. Area, 5,936 sq. m.; pop. 419,000. (2) Cap. of above, on fertile plain; fine Gothic cathedral; Byzantine church of St. Isidore; parts of Roman wall still exist. Pop. 21,000. (3) Tn., Nicaragua, Central America, on fine plain near Pacific coast; cathedral, univ., and bishop's palace; manufactures cotton and woollen goods, and boots and shoes. Pop. 23,000. (4) Tn., Guanajuato, central Mexico; gold and silver; leather, cotton, and woollen goods. Pop. 53,000.

Leonforte (*lā-on-for'tā*), walled tn., Sicily, 49 m. W. by N. of Catania; trade in sulphur, cattle, wine, and oil. Pop. 20,000.

Leopoldville, cap., Belgian Congo, Africa, on R. Congo, at entrance to Stanley Pool; station for organized steam transport on Upper Congo; connected with Matadi by railway (250 m.) to avoid cataracts. Pop. *c.* 6,000.

Le Puy (*le pwē*), or LE PUY-EN-VELAY, cap. of Haute-Loire, France, 90 m. S.E. of Lyons; 12th cent. Romanesque cathedral; thread and guipure lace. Pop. 16,000.

Lérida (*ler'ē-dä*). (1) Prov., N. Spain; northern half mountainous, watered by Segre, trib. of Ebro; chief prods. are wine, oil, wool, timber, and live-stock. Area, 4,690 sq. m.; pop. 315,000. (2) Cap. of above, on R. Segre, 80 m. W. by N. of Barcelona; leather, paper, glass, and woollen, cotton, and silk goods. Pop. 38,000.

Ler'wick, cap. of Shetland Islands, Scotland, on Bressay Sound, E. coast of Mainland, 110 m. N.N.E. of Kirkwall, Orkney; important herring-fishing station; exports fish, ponies, sheep, cattle, and knitted goods. Pop. 4,200.

Les Andelys (*lāz on-dlē'*), tn., Eure, France, 30 m. S.E. of Rouen; includes Grand and Petit Andely; site of former fortress; large trade in grain, flour, cattle, and leather. Pop. 4,000.

Les'bos, or MYTILENE, Greek isl. in Ægean Sea; early settled by Æolian Greeks. Birthplace of anc. Greek poetess Sappho; Turkish from 1462 to 1912. Surface hilly, rising to over 3,000 ft.; upper districts wooded; lower ground produces olives, grapes, figs. Chief tn. Mytilene (pop. 28,000). Area, 675 sq. m.; pop. 161,000.

Leskovac (*les'kō-vats*), tn., Yugoslavia, on R. Morava, 22 m. S. of Nish; trade in hemp and cloth. Pop. 14,000.

Les'lie, tn., Fife, Scotland, on R. Leven, 12 m. S.W. of Cupar; paper and flax mills; manufacture of fountain pens. Pop. 2,500.

Lesmahagow (*les-ma-hā'gō*), par. and vil., Lanarkshire, Scotland, 5 m. S.W. of Lanark; coal mining; fruit. Pop. (par.) 12,900.

Les Sables d'Olonne. See SABLES D'OLONNE.

Lesuto. See BASUTOLAND.

Leszno (*lesh'nō*), formerly LISSA, tn., Poland, 40 m. S.W. of Poznan;

manufactures machinery, shoes, and tobacco. Pop. 16,000.

Letch'worth, garden city, Herts, England, 2 m. N.E. of Hitchin; planned so that not more than twelve houses are built to the acre, and theoretically limited to 35,000 inhabitants; founded 1903. Pop. 14,500.

Leth'bridge, tn., Alberta, Canada, 95 m. S.E. of Calgary; coal-mining centre. Pop. 11,000.

Le Tréport (*le trā-por'*), seapt., Seine-Inférieure, N. France, 15 m. E.N.E. of Dieppe; watering-place; fisheries, shipbuilding, and glass making. Pop. 5,000.

Letterkenny, mkt. tn., co. Donegal, I.F.S., 17 m. W. by S. of Londonderry; grain, flax, and rope making. Pop. 2,300.

Leuchars (*looch'arz*), par., vil., and rly. jn., Fife, Scotland, 5 m. N.W. of St. Andrews; has 12th cent. Norman church; air station. Pop. (par.) 2,800.

Levant', eastern end and shores of Mediterranean. Greece, Egypt, Asia Minor, Syria, and Palestine lie around Levant.

Le'ven. (1) Coast tn., E. Fife, Scotland; golf links; flax spinning, linen weaving, seed crushing, and coal mining. Pop. 7,400. (2) LOCH, lake, Kinross-shire, Scotland; area, *c.* 5½ sq. m.; famous for trout; has seven islands, including Castle Island, on which are ruins of Queen Mary's place of imprisonment (1567–68).

Le'ver, LITTLE, urb. dist., Lancashire, England, *c.* 2 m. S.E. of Bolton; coal mining; cotton mills and paper and chemical works. Pop. 4,900.

Levis (*lā'vē* or *lev'is*), or POINT LEVIS, tn., Quebec, Canada, on r. bk. of St. Lawrence, opposite Quebec; has graving dock and extensive wharves; important centre of river trade. Pop. 10,500.

Levkosia. See NICOSIA (1).

Lewes (*loo'is*), co. tn., Sussex, England; trades in wool, sheep, cattle, and farm produce. In battle of Lewes (1264) Henry III. was defeated by Simon de Montfort. Pop. 10,800.

Lewis. See LEWIS-WITH-HARRIS.

Lew'isham, suburb (parl. and metropolitan bor.) of London, 4 m. S.E of St. Paul's; includes part of Blackheath and Sydenham. Pop. 219,900.

Lew'iston. (1) City, Maine, U.S.A., 25 m. N. of Portland, on Androscoggin R., at the falls, which supply water-power; cottons, wools, machinery, and foundry and lumber products. Pop. 35,000. (2) Tn., N. Idaho, U.S.A., on Snake R.; mining centre; exports fruit, grain, timber, and live-stock. Pop. 6,000.

Lewis-with-Harris, or 'THE LEWS,' largest and most northerly of Outer Hebrides, Scotland; consists of two parts: Lewis to the N. (area, 575 sq. m.), part of Ross-shire, and Harris to the S. (area, 195 sq. m.), part of Inverness-shire. General surface of Lewis is flat, greater portion unproductive moorland; Harris mostly mountainous; chief industry fishing; noted for Harris tweed, made by the cottars. At Callernish, in W. Lewis, is the most perfect Druidical stone circle in Brit. Isles. Stornoway, chief tn. of Lewis, is headquarters of a fishing fleet. Pop., Lewis, 28,400; Harris, 5,300.

Lex'ington. (1) City, Kentucky, U.S.A., 75 m. S. of Cincinnati; agricultural industries; in centre of 'blue grass country,' famed for horses and cattle; race-horses bred; tobacco; univ. Pop. 46,000. (2) Tn., Massachusetts, U.S.A., 11 m. N.W. of Boston; trade in agricultural products; scene of first bloodshed (1775) in American War of Independence. Pop. 8,000.

Leyden (*lī'den*), or LEIDEN, tn., S. Holland, Netherlands, on Old Rhine, 9 m. N.E. of the Hague; seat of famous univ. (1575); manufactures woollens, linen, leather; printing an important industry. Famous siege by Spaniards (1573–74). Pop. 70,000.

Ley'land, urb. dist., Lancs, England, 5 m. S. of Preston; cotton mills and bleach works. Pop. 10,600.

Ley'ton, urb. dist., Essex, England, on Lea, 8 m. W. of Romford, N.E. suburb of London; Roman remains Pop. 128,300.

Lhasa (*las'a*), cap., Tibet; name means 'Abode of the Gods'; sacred city of Buddhists; on fertile plain about 12,000 ft. above sea-level; encircled by mountains. Long known as the 'Forbidden City.' Principal building is the Potala, residence of Dalai Lama. The great temple, or Jokhang, contains many sacred shrines, one of which holds life-size image of Buddha. The Ramo-ché is also a celebrated temple. There are also many monasteries. Meeting-place of caravans from India, China, and Turkistan; trades in tea, silk, carpets, gold, lace, gums, porcelain, musk, rice, tobacco. Pop. *c.* 20,000.

Liaoning, formerly FENGTIEN, or SHENG KING, southmost prov., Manchuria. E. portion is richly wooded and contains valuable coal deposits; W. is very fertile. Cap. Mukden. Area, 56,000 sq. m.; pop. (est.) 15,000,000.

Liao-yang', city, Liaoning, Manchuria, on railway from Mukden to Port Arthur; scene of great Russian defeat in war with Japan (1904); in rich cotton dist. Pop. (est.) 100,000.

Libau. See LIEPAJA.

Liberec (*lib'er-ets*), formerly REICHENBERG, tn., Bohemia, Czechoslovakia, on R. Neisse, 87 m. N.N.E. of Prague; woollen and cotton cloth. Pop. 35,000.

Libe'ria, independent Negro republic, W. Africa, extending S.E. of Sierra Leone for 350 m. along coast to French Ivory Coast, and claiming the country for *c.* 150 m. inland. Was established as home for freed U.S.A. slaves in 1822. Coast is low and swampy; interior rises, and has excellent timber; watered by R. Kavalli and other streams; soil very fertile; produces coffee, palm oil and kernels, rubber, cocoa, hides, kola nuts. Iron is widely distributed and is worked. Interior little developed and in parts unexplored. Inhabitants all Negroes, mostly Christians. Cap. Monrovia. Area, *c.* 43,000 sq. m.; pop. (est.) 2,000,000–2,500,000.

Libertad', mar. dep., N.W. Peru, between Pacific on W. and dep. of Loreto on E.; mahogany, hides, cattle, rice, sugar, cotton, coffee, and cocoa; silver and copper are mined. Cap. Trujillo. Area, 10,206 sq. m.; pop. *c.* 380,000.

Liberty Island. See BEDLOE'S ISLAND.

Libourne (*lē-boorn'*), riv. port, Gironde, France, on R. Dordogne, 20 m. E.N.E. of Bordeaux; brandy, sugar, and woollen goods; vineyards. Pop. 14,000.

Libreville (*lēbr-vēl'*), cap. of Gabon Colony, French Equatorial Africa; important seaport and coaling station. Pop. *c.* 2,000.

Libya (*lib'ē-a*). (1) Anc. name for N. Africa; in Roman times applied to Libyan Desert, lying W. of the Nile; immense stony plateau (alt. 600–1,000 ft.); depressions contain oases of Kharga, Dakhla, Farafra, Bahariya, and Siwa; on W. merges into Sahara. (2) ITALIAN LIBYA, formerly TRIPOLI, lies between Egypt on E. and Tunis and Algeria on W. Divided into districts of Tripolitania and Cyrenaica. See TRIPOLITANIA, CYRENAICA.

Licat'a, or ALICATA, port, Sicily, 24 m. S.E. of Girgenti; exports sulphur; good harbour. Pop. 25,500.

Lich'field, munic. bor., Staffs, England; cathedral dating from 12th to 15th cent.; birthplace of Dr. Samuel Johnson; brewing. Pop. 8,500.

Lid'desdale, valley of Liddel Water, which flows through Roxburghshire, Scotland, to join R. Esk.

Lido (*lē'dō*), chain of sandy islets, Italy, separating lagoons of Venice from Adriatic.

Liechtenstein (*lēch-ten-stīn*), PRINCIPALITY OF, independent state, between Switzerland and Austria, some 20 m. S. of L. Constance; mountainous (Rhætian Alps); corn, vines, fruits, flax; no taxation or military service. Chief tn., Vaduz. Area, 65 sq. m.; pop. 11,000.

Liége (*lē-āzh'*), fortified tn., Belgium, on R. Meuse, 55 m. S.E. of Brussels; old town on hills on l. bk., new town on r. bk.; coal mining; important manufacturing city; the Belgian Birmingham; firearms, cannon, hardware, zinc, motor-cars, machinery, watches, linen, woollens. During Great War taken by Germans after ten days' siege (Aug. 16, 1914). Pop. 170,000.

Liegnitz (*lēg'nēts*), tn., Silesia, Germany, 40 m. W.N.W. of Breslau; cloth, machinery, shoes, pianos, tobacco, oil, and pottery. Pop. 73,500.

Liepaja (*lyā'pä-yä*), formerly LIBAU, port, Latvia, Europe, 120 m. W.S.W. of Riga; generally ice-free; coaling and oil station; exp. grain, timber, flax and linseed, dairy produce, hides and skins. Pop. 61,000.

Lierre (*lē-er'*), tn., Belgium, 9 m. S.E. of Antwerp; silks, boots and shoes, cutlery, lace, and sugar. Pop. 27,000.

Liévin (*lē-ā-vän'*), tn., Pas-de-Calais, France, 1½ m. W. of Lens; coal mines. Pop. 25,000.

Liffey, riv., Leinster, I.F.S.; flows in an arc from Wicklow Mts. to Dublin Bay; chief tn. on bank, Dublin. Length, 70 m.

Ligny (*lēn-yē'*), vil., Belgium, 13 m. W. of Namur; here Blücher was defeated by Napoleon (June 16, 1815). Pop. 2,000.

Ligur'ia, dep., N.W. Italy; comprises Genoa, Imperia, Savona, and Spezia provs.; surface mountainous; coast known as Riviera. Area, 2,097 sq. m.; pop. 1,434,000.

Lille (*lēl*), cap., Nord dep., France, near Belgian frontier; fortress; rly. jn.; important centre of iron trade; manufactures linens, cottons, damask, tulle; sugar, soap, tobacco factories; dye works, chemical works, printing establishments, and distilleries; univ.; captured and occupied by the Germans (Oct. 7, 1914–Oct. 17, 1918). Pop. 202,000.

Lima (*lē'mä*). (1) Maritime dep., Peru, S. America. Area, 15,048 sq. m.; pop. 550,000. (2) Cap. of Peru; contains tomb of Pizarro, who founded city in 1535; iron and copper works; textiles; manufactures gold lace, silver ware, stamped leather, glass, furniture; frequently suffers from earthquakes. Pop. 265,000. (3) City, Ohio, U.S.A., 90 m. N. of Cincinnati; oil refineries, railway shops. Pop. 42,000.

Limassol (*lē-mäs-sol'*), port, S. Cyprus; exp. carobs, grapes, raisins, wine; salt obtained from lakes in vicinity. Pop. 13,500.

Limavad'y, mkt. tn., N. Londonderry, N. Ireland; maize and oat milling, linen weaving. Pop. 2,800.

Lim'bach, tn., Saxony, Germany, 6 m. W.N.W. of Chemnitz; woollen, silk, and cotton goods; sewing machines; dyeing and bleaching works; serpentine quarried. Pop. 17,000.

Limbourg (*län-boor'*), prov., Belgium; flat, infertile in N.W.; E. produces beetroot, sugar, iron, coal. Cap. Hasselt. Area, 930 sq. m.; pop. 358,500.

Limburg (*lēm'boorg*), prov., Holland; drained by R. Maas (Meuse); agriculture; famous for cattle; coal mines. Cap. Maastricht. Area, 847 sq. m.; pop. 531,500.

Lim'erick (LUIMNEACH). (1) Co., W. Munster, I.F.S.; surface undulating; hills on W. and S.; watered by R. Shannon; live-stock raised; dairy farming; includes part of fertile Golden Vale. Area, *c.* 1,034 sq. m.; pop. 101,000. (2) Cap. of above, at head of estuary of R. Shannon; near hydro-electric station; important port; exp. fish and agricultural produce; headquarters of salmon fisheries; lace manufacture, bacon curing, flour milling. Pop. 39,500.

Limoges (*lē-mōzh'*), tn., cap., Haute-Vienne, France, *c.* 110 m. N.E. of Bordeaux; principal seat of porcelain manufacture; textile and paper industries. Pop. 98,500.

Limon (*lē-mon'*), or PORT LIMON, port, Costa Rica, Central America, on Caribbean Sea; exp. bananas. Pop. 16,000.

Limpo'po, riv., S.E. Africa; rises in hills S.W. of Pretoria; flows in curve between Transvaal and Rhodesia; crosses Portuguese E. Africa, and discharges into Indian Ocean, N.E. of Delagoa Bay; navigable *c.* 100 m.; length, *c.* 1,000 m.

Linar'es, tn., Jaen, Spain, 70 m. N. of Granada; silver-lead mining; manufactures sheet lead, pipes, and dynamite. Pop. 40,500.

Lincoln (*link'on*). (1) Co. tn., Lincs, England, on R. Witham; important rly. centre; has canal communication with Nottingham, the Humber, Boston, and the Wash; manufactures agricultural implements; trade in corn and wool; great horse fair annually; magnificent cruciform cathedral dating from Norman times. Pop. 66,200. (2) City, Illinois, U.S.A., 28 m. N.E. of Springfield; coal and grain. Pop. 12,000. (3) Cap., Nebraska, U.S.A., 55 m. S.W. of Omaha; rly. centre; flour mills, meat-packing factories. Pop. 76,000.

Lincolnshire, E. coast co., England; surface largely low wolds and fens; drained by Rs. Trent, Witham, Welland; co. divided for administrative purposes into three dists., called Parts of Holland, Parts of Kesteven, Parts of Lindsey; soil fertile; produces barley, wheat, turnips, and other crops; horses, sheep, and cattle raised in large numbers; iron ore, limestone, freestone, gypsum occur; important fisheries along coast. Largest tns., Grimsby, Lincoln (cap.). Area, 2,646 sq. m.; pop. 624,600.

Lindau (*lin'dou*), tn., Bavaria, Germany, at S.E. of L. Constance; pleasure resort. Pop. 14,000.

Lin'den, tn., Hanover, Prussia, adjoins tn. of Hanover; machinery, textiles, carpets, chemicals, rubber goods. Pop. 82,500.

Lind'field, par. and vil., Sussex, England, 13 m. N. of Brighton; picturesque old wooden houses; brick and tile making. Pop. (par.) 3,000.

Lin'disfarne. See HOLY ISLAND.

Lind'say, tn., Ontario, Canada, 70 m. N.E. of Toronto; lumber, grain; saw and flour mills; agricultural machinery. Pop. 8,000.

Lind'sey, PARTS OF. See LINCOLNSHIRE.

Linea (*lē'nā-ä*), or LA LINEA, tn., Cadiz, Spain, between Gibraltar and San Roque; supplies Gibraltar with vegetables and fruit. Pop. 63,500.

Lingayen (*lēn-gä-yen'*), tn., Luzon, Philippines, on Lingayen Bay; rice, fisheries; health resort. Pop. 23,000.

Lingeh. See BANDER LINGEH.

Ling'field, par. and vil., Surrey, England, in S.E. of co., on head-stream of R. Medway; Roman remains; racecourse; trout fishing. Pop. (par.) 4,905.

Linguaglossa (*lēn-gwä-glos'sä*), tn., Catania, Sicily, on N.E. slope of Mt. Etna; sulphur. Pop. 15,000.

Linköping (*lēn'chō-ping*), tn., S.E. Sweden, 25 m. S.W. of Norrköping; episc. see; tobacco, cloth, hosiery. Pop. 29,500.

Linlithgow (*lin-lith'gō*), anc. royal burgh, co. tn., W. Lothian, Scotland; ruined royal palace, birthplace of Mary Queen of Scots; paper, soap; tanning, brewing. Pop. 3,700.

Linlith'gowshire. See WEST LOTHIAN.

Linnhe (*lin'e*), LOCH, sea-loch, Argyll and Inverness shires, Scotland; extends 21 m. N.E. from junction of Firth of Lorne and Sound of Mull to Fort William.

Linth'waite, urb. dist., W. Riding, Yorks, England, partly in Huddersfield; woollen goods; stone quarries. Pop. 9,700.

Linz (*lints*), riv. port, Upper Austria, on R. Danube; rly. jn.; boat building; iron and textile industries. Pop. 102,000.

Lipa (*lē'pä*), tn., Luzon, Philippines, 90 m. S. of Manila; sugar, tobacco, maize, and cocoa. Pop. 47,000.

Lipari Islands (*lēp'ä-rē*), group of volcanic islands, Mediterranean Sea, N. of Sicily; most important are Lipari and Stromboli; former exports pumice-stone; Stromboli has constantly active volcano (3,155 ft.); grapes, figs, olives, wine, currants; sulphur and salt mines; fisheries. Pop. 21,000.

Lip'etsk, tn., S. Russia, on Voronezh trib. of R. Don; mart for live-stock, timber, honey; flour mills, tanneries. Pop. 21,000.

Lippe (*lēp'e*), rep., Germany, in basin of R. Weser; surface generally mountainous; well wooded; chief industry is agriculture; horses, cattle, and pigs reared; manufactures meerschaum pipes, tobacco. Cap. Detmold. Area, 469 sq. m.; pop. 164,000.

Lipp'stadt, tn., Westphalia, Germany, on R. Lippe, trib. of R. Rhine; tobacco, agricultural implements, tiles, ropes, brandy. Pop. 18,500.

Lis'bon, or LISBOA, cap., Portugal, on estuary of R. Tagus; cathedral built *c.* 1150, twice restored; fine aqueduct; strongly fortified; one of finest harbours in Europe; exports wines, fruits, cork, oil, salt, leather, wool, cattle, pit-props, tinned fish; manufactures gold and silver ware, tobacco, textiles, chemicals; almost entirely destroyed by earthquake (1755). Pop. 530,000.

Lis'burn, tn., Antrim, N. Ireland, on R. Lagan; linen and damask manufactures; bleaching and dye works; corn mills. Pop. 12,400.

Lisieux (*lēz-yoo'*), tn., Calvados, N. France, 25 m. E. of Caen; textiles, dairy produce, boots and shoes, machinery. Pop. 15,000.

Liskeard (*lis'kard*), mkt. tn., E. Cornwall, England; woollens, iron goods; granite quarries. Pop. 4,300.

Lismore'. (1) Tn., Waterford, I.F.S., on R. Blackwater; cathedral dates from 12th cent.; angling centre. Pop. 1,400. (2) Isl., entrance to Loch Linnhe, Scotland, 9½ m. long; fertile soil; oats, potatoes; exports lime. Pop. 350. (3) Tn., N.E. New South Wales, Australia; sugar refineries, sawmills, creameries. Pop. 9,500.

Liss, par. and vil., Hants, England, 17½ m. E. of Winchester; military camps in vicinity. Pop. (par.) 2,322.

Lis'sa. (1) Isl. See VIS. (2) Tn., Poland. See LESZNO.

Lith'erland, urb. dist., Lancs, England; residential suburb of Liverpool; manufactures matches. Pop. 16,000.

Lithgow (*lith'gō*), tn., New South Wales, Australia, 60 m. N.W. of Sydney; on coalfield; government small-arms factory; ironworks, potteries. Pop. 16,500.

Lithuania (*lith-u-ā'nē-a*), rep., on Baltic Sea, Europe; bounded N. by Latvia, E. and S. by Poland, and W. by E. Prussia and Baltic Sea; S. frontier still in dispute with Poland; surface generally plain; chief riv., Niemen; climate extreme; agriculture is principal occupation; chief crops, rye, wheat, barley, oats, flax; live-stock and dairy farming; forests; Lithuanians claim Vilna as cap.; present seat of govt., Kaunas (Kovno). Area, *c.* 22,600 sq. m.; pop. 2,317,000.

Litomerice (*lit'om-yer-zhit-se*), formerly LEITMERITZ, tn., Czechoslovakia, on R. Elbe, 36 m. N.N.W. of Prague; agricultural centre; brewing. Pop. 17,000.

Littleborough, tn., Lancs, England, 3 m. N.E. of Rochdale; cotton and woollen goods. Pop. 12,000.

Little Falls, city, New York, U.S.A., on Mohawk R.; bicycles, knitted goods, paper, leather. Pop. 13,000.

Littlehamp'ton, tn. and wat.-pl., W. Sussex, England; fine golf links; sea fishing. Pop. 10,200.

Little Hulton, urb. dist., Lancs, England, 3 m. S. of Bolton; coal mining; cotton spinning. Pop. 7,900.

Littleport, mkt. tn., Cambridgeshire, England, 5 m. N.N.E. of Ely; shirt factory; skating championships held here. Pop. (par.) 4,500.

Little Rock, cap., Arkansas, U.S.A.; machinery, cotton-seed cakes, and oil; head of navigation for large steamboats on Arkansas R.; exp. cotton. Pop. 82,000.

Little St. Bernard Pass leads from French valley of upper Isère to Italian valley of Aosta; traversed by carriage road; alt. 7,179 ft.

Liukiu Islands. See RYUKYU ARCHIPELAGO.

Liv'erpool, city and co. bor., Lancs, England, on estuary of R. Mersey; greatest seaport on W. coast, with many miles of docks; tunnels and ferry steamers cross Mersey to Birkenhead. Accounts for one-fourth of imports and two-fifths of exports of U.K.;

chief imports are raw cotton, wheat, live-stock, wool, tobacco, sugar, timber; chief exports: iron and steel manufactures, cottons, chemicals, machinery, silk, woollen and linen goods; principal industries are shipbuilding, with associated metal industries, flour and rice milling, sugar refining, manufacture of tobacco, glass, chemicals; centre of slave trade in 18th cent.; owes its importance to s. Lancs coalfield and cotton industry. Pop. 855,500.

Liv'ersedge, tn., W. Riding, Yorks, England, 6 m. S.E. of Bradford; woollen and cotton goods; chemicals, machinery. Pop. 15,000.

Liv'ingstone, cap. of N. Rhodesia, near R. Zambezi, 7 m. from Victoria Falls. Pop. (white) 800.

Livingsto'nia, mission station, Nyasaland, Africa, on N.W. L. Nyasa; mission established on s. of lake (1875).

Livny, tn., central Russia, 80 m. S.E. of Orel; trades in leather, livestock, and general agricultural produce. Pop. 21,000.

Lizard Point, or THE LIZARD, promontory with dangerous reef, s. Cornwall, England; most s. point of Great Britain; fine cliff scenery.

Ljubljana (*lyoob'lyan-a*), formerly LAIBACH, tn., Yugoslavia, 40 m. N.E. of Trieste; episc. see; tourist centre; textiles, chemicals, beer, and leather. Pop. 57,000.

Llanberis (*hlan-ber'is*), tn., Carnarvonshire, N. Wales; slate quarries; starting-point for ascent of Snowdon. Pop. 2,400.

Llandaff (*hlan-daf'*), tn., Glamorganshire, Wales; cathedral and ruined episc. palace; practically a suburb of Cardiff. Pop. 13,300.

Llanddeiniolen (*hlan-dī-ni-ol'en*), par. and vil., Carnarvonshire, Wales, 4½ m. E.N.E. of Carnarvon; slate quarrying; prehistoric remains. Pop. (par.) 4,800.

Llandebie (*hlan-deb'i*), par. and vil., Carmarthenshire, Wales, 12 m. N.E. of Llanelly; coal and ironstone mining. Pop. (par.) 8,000.

Llandilo (*hlan-dīl'ō*), or LLANDEILO, urb. dist., Carmarthenshire, Wales, on R. Towy; in neighbourhood are ruins of Dinefawr Castle; corn and woollen mills. Pop. 1,900.

Llandovery (*hlan-dov'er-i*), munic. bor., Carmarthenshire, Wales, on R. Towy; ruined castle; cattle mkt. Pop. 2,000.

Llandrindod (*hlan-drin'dod*), or LLANDRINDOD WELLS, tn., Radnor, Wales; mineral springs. Pop. 2,900.

Llandudno (*hlan-did'nō*), tn., Carnarvonshire, N. Wales, between Great Orme's Head and Little Orme's Head; summer resort. Pop. 13,700.

Llanelly (*hlan-eth'li*), mkt. tn. and port, Carmarthenshire, Wales; copper works; tinplate, chemicals, bricks, tiles; collieries; exp. anthracite and bituminous coal. Pop. 38,400.

Llanes (*lyä'nez*), port, Oviedo, N. Spain; summer resort; trade in timber, butter, and fish. Pop. 23,000.

Llanfairfechan (*hlan-vīr-vech'an*), tn., N. Carnarvonshire, Wales, at foot of Penmaenmawr mountain; seaside resort. Pop. 3,200.

Llangollen (*hlan-goth'len*), mkt. tn. and summer resort, Denbighshire, Wales; has ruined fortress; bridge over Dee dates from 1345; tourist resort; flannel. Pop. 2,900.

Llanidloes (*hlan-id'lois*), mkt. tn. and munic. bor., Montgomeryshire, Wales, on R. Severn; tourist resort; manufactures flannel; lead mining. Pop. 2,400.

Llanrwst (*hlan-roost'*), mkt. tn., Denbighshire, Wales, 10 m. s. of Conway; tanneries, breweries; flannel. Pop. 2,400.

Llantrisant (*hlan-tris'ant*), mkt. tn., Glamorganshire, Wales, 10 m. N.W. of Cardiff; ruined castle; coal mining. Pop. 22,000.

Llanwrtyd Wells (*hlan-oor'tid*), vil., Breconshire, Wales; mineral springs. Pop. 700.

Loanda (*lo-and'a*), ST. PAUL DE, port, Angola, W. Africa; exports rubber, wax, ivory, palm oil, coffee, rum, coconuts; episc. see. Pop. *c.* 23,000.

Loango (*lō-ang'gō*), port, French

Equatorial Africa, lying N. of mouth of R. Congo; formerly centre of slave trade; exports rubber, palm oil.

Loanhead (*lōn-hed'*), tn., Midlothian, Scotland, 5 m. s. of Edinburgh; coal and ironstone mining; paper mills in vicinity. Pop. 3,900.

Lobito Bay (*lob-ē'to*), port, Angola, W. Africa, 22 m. by rail N. of Benguella; large harbour works; terminus of Benguella Rly., which joins 'Cape to Cairo' Rly. at Tenke, in Katanga prov., Belgian Congo. White pop. *c.* 600.

Lob Nor. See LOP NOR.

Locar'no, tn., Ticino canton, Switzerland, on L. Maggiore, 15 m. N.W. of Lugano; Locarno Treaties signed here (1925). Pop. 5,550.

Lochgelly (*loch-gel'i*), tn., Fife, Scotland, 7 m. N.E. of Dunfermline; coal, iron. Pop. 9,300.

Lochma'ben, royal burgh, Dumfriesshire, Scotland, 7 m. N.E. of Dumfries; ruins of castle, formerly the seat of the Bruces; tourist resort. Pop. 1,000.

Lochnagar', mt. peak, Grampian plateau, Aberdeenshire, Scotland, between Balmoral Castle and Loch Muick; alt. 3,768 ft.

Lochwin'noch, tn., Renfrewshire, Scotland, on R. Calder at s.w. of Castle Semple L., 16½ m. s.w. of Paisley; makes furniture. Pop. 4,225.

Lock'erbie, mkt. tn., s. Dumfriesshire, Scotland; annual sheep and lamb sales; rly. jn. Pop. 2,600.

Lock'port, tn., New York, U.S.A., 25 m. N.E. of Buffalo; fruit, chalk, sandstone; machinery, pulp, paper, furniture, flour. Pop. 21,000.

Locle, LE (*lokl*), tn., Switzerland, 16 m. N.W. of Neuchâtel; centre of watch-making industry; first watch made here (1680). Pop. 12,000.

Lodi (*lō-dē'*), tn., Lombardy, Italy, 20 m. S.E. of Milan; manufactures majolica; dairy produce, especially Parmesan cheese; cathedral (1158). Pop. 29,000.

Lodore' Falls, waterfalls, Cumberland, England, near s. end of Derwentwater; made famous by Southey.

Lodz (*woodzh*), tn., Poland, 82 m. s.w. of Warsaw; large cotton mills; silk, wool, linen, flour, and iron industries. Pop. 452,000.

Lofoten (*lo-fō'ten*), or LOFODEN, **Islands,** large group of islands off N.W. coast of Norway; good pasturage for cattle; cod fishing important; exports fish guano and oil; contains once dreaded whirlpool Maelstrom. Area, *c.* 2,000 sq. m.

Lof'tus, urb. dist., N. Riding, Yorkshire, England, 12 m. N.W. of Whitby; ironstone and alum rock are worked. Pop. 7,600.

Lo'gan, MOUNT, peak, Cordilleras, s.w. Yukon Terr., Canada, close to Alaskan boundary; probably second highest peak in N. America. Alt. 19,514 ft.

Lo'gansport, city, Indiana, U.S.A., 90 m. S.E. of Chicago; important trade in lumber, grain, fruits; machinery, woollen goods. Pop. 21,000.

Logroño (*lo-grōn'yō*). (1) Prov., Old Castile, Spain; mountainous; produces vegetables and fruit; specially famous for red wines; iron, silver, lead are found. Area, 1,946 sq. m.; pop. 194,000. (2) Walled tn., cap. of above, on R. Ebro; centre of Rioja wine dist. Pop. 27,000.

Loire (*lwär*). (1) Longest riv. of France; rises in Cevennes, and after flowing some distance N., bends to W. and enters Bay of Biscay; chief tribs., Allier, Vienne, Sarthe; largest towns on banks, Orleans, Tours, Angers, Nantes; subject to frequent floods, and dykes constructed to prevent inundations. Length, 620 m. (2) Dep., France; mountainous; drained by Rs. Loire and Rhone; coal; iron and lead mines; manufactures iron and steel goods, machinery, textiles, glass, paper. Chief tn., St. Etienne. Area, 1,852 sq. m.; pop. 669,000.

Loire-Inférieure (*lwär-an-fā-rē-oor'*), coast dep., w. France; surface generally low and flat; drained by Loire; produces cereals, potatoes, wine, cider; dairy farming, stock raising; salt manufactured from coastal marshes; fishing; coal, iron, copper, machinery, shipbuilding. Chief tns., Nantes (cap.) and St. Lazaire. Area, 2,693 sq. m.; pop. 651,000.

Loiret (*lwä-rā'*), inland dep., France; surface rises from N.W. to S.E.; drained by R. Loire and tributaries of R. Seine; forests; wheat and oats; live-stock; manufactures woollens, leather, sugar, flour; iron and copper founding. Chief tn., Orleans. Area, 2,629 sq. m.; pop. 341,000.

Loir-et-Cher (*lwär-ā-shär'*), inland dep., France; watered by Rs. Loir and Cher; produces cereals, fruit, vegetables, timber, wine; horses and sheep bred; manufactures textiles, leather. Chief tn., Blois. Area, 2,478 sq. m.; pop. 248,000.

Loja (*lō'hä*). (1) City, s. Spain, 30 m. w. of Granada; fortified by Moors; manufactures coarse woollens, silk, paper, and leather; trade in grain and cattle. Pop. 20,000. (2) Prov., s.w. Ecuador, S. America; mountainous; cinchona bark. Area, 3,706 sq. m.; pop. 100,000. (3) Cap. of above; alt. 6,900 ft. Pop. *c.* 10,000.

Lokeren (*lok'er-en*), tn., E. Flanders, Belgium, 12 m. E. of Ghent; textile, tobacco, and chemical industries. Pop. 23,000.

Lokoja (*lo-kō'ja*), tn., Nigeria, Brit. W. Africa, at junction of Rs. Benue and Niger; military post and formerly chief commercial centre of Protectorate, but since opening of railways its importance has declined.

Lom'bardy, div., N. Italy, central part of R. Po basin; includes provinces of Bergamo, Brescia, Como, Cremona, Mantua, Milan, Pavia, Sondrio, Vanese; contains most Italian lakes; very fertile; large crops of wheat, rice, maize; vineyards; mulberry trees; chief industrial dist. of Italy; manufactures textiles (particularly silk goods), automobiles, and paper; iron, zinc, and marble worked. Chief town, Milan. Area, 9,190 sq. m.; pop. 5,400,000.

Lombok', one of Lesser Sunda Islands, Dutch E. Indies; volcanic; mountainous (highest peak, *c.* 12,000 ft.); fertile valleys; rice and coffee. Wallace's Line passes between Bali and Lombok. Area, *c.* 3,000 sq. m.; pop. 599,000.

Lomond (*lō'mond*), LOCH, between Dumbartonshire and Stirlingshire, Scotland; largest lake in Scotland; drains to Clyde by the Leven; almost entirely surrounded by mountains; picturesque scenery. Length, 24 m.; breadth, 1 to 5 m.

Lomza (*lom'zhä*), tn., Bialystok, Poland, on R. Narew, 75 m. N.E. of Warsaw; trade in grain and timber. Pop. *c.* 25,000.

London. (1) Cap. of U.K., and largest city in world; on both banks of R. Thames, at the head of navigation. Greater London (including the City of London, the Administrative County, and the 'Outer Ring') occupies parts of Middlesex, Surrey, Kent, Essex, and Hertfordshire. The following metropolitan boroughs make up the Administrative County: N. of Thames are Hammersmith, Fulham, Chelsea, Westminster, Kensington, Paddington, Marylebone, Hampstead, St. Pancras, Finsbury, Islington, Hackney, Shoreditch, Bethnal Green, Stepney, Poplar, Stoke Newington, and Holborn; on S. side are Wandsworth, Battersea, Lambeth, Deptford, Greenwich, Woolwich, Camberwell, Lewisham, Southwark, and Bermondsey. The City of London, the oldest part and chief business centre, has area of 678 ac.; Administrative County, *c.* 117 sq. m.; Greater London, or metropolitan police area, *c.* 692 sq. m.

The Bank of England may be called the central point of the City. Traffic crosses R. Thames by nineteen bridges as well as by steamers and five tunnels.

London is full of interesting buildings. Most important churches include Westminster Abbey, St. Paul's Cathedral (built by Sir Christopher Wren), Temple Church, St. Martin's-in-the-Fields, and the R.C. cathedral at Westminster. Among important public buildings are: Tower of London (built by William the Conqueror), Houses of Parliament, Guildhall, Mansion House, Royal Exchange and Bank of England, Somerset House and law courts, Brit. Museum, Victoria and Albert and Natural History Museums. Fine art collections include: National Gallery, National Portrait Gallery, the Wallace Collection, and Tate Gallery; annual exhibition of Royal Academy is held at Burlington House. Royal palaces include Buckingham Palace, St. James's Palace, Marlborough House, Kensington Palace. There are many beautiful parks, including Hyde Park and Kensington Gardens, Green Park and St. James's Park, Regent's Park (which contains Zoological and Botanical Gardens), Battersea Park, Hampstead Heath and Ken Wood, favourite Bank Holiday resorts. London is seat of univ., and has famous public schools, hospitals, and theatres.

One of the world's busiest seaports, the Port of London extends from the lock at Teddington to an imaginary line drawn from Warden Point, Isle of Sheppey (Kent), to Havengore Creek, on the shores of Essex. It has *c.* 30 per cent. of total trade of U.K.; value of imports is nearly double that of exports, owing to enormous population and distance from coal. London is important distributing centre, and is meeting-place of all the great railway systems of the kingdom. There is enormous dock accommodation—London Docks, St. Katharine Dock, East and West India, Royal Victoria, Royal Albert, Millwall, Tilbury, King George v., and other docks. It is also the largest manufacturing city in Great Britain, and its industries include those connected with food supply, clothing, shipping appliances, house fittings and furnishings, textiles.

There are many notable markets, including Billingsgate Fish Market, Leadenhall Meat Market, London Central Markets, in Smithfield, for fruit, meat, provisions, and Covent Garden for flowers, fruit, and vegetables. Pop. of City, 11,000; of County, 4,396,800; of Greater London, 8,202,800.

(2) Tn., Ontario, Canada, *c.* 100 m. s. of Toronto; centre of rich agricultural dist.; large trade in grain, live-stock; factories, foundries, railway shops, chemical works, petroleum refineries, sulphur springs. Pop. 61,000.

Lon'donderry. (1) Maritime co., N. Ireland; surface hilly in centre and s., elsewhere flat; drained by Rs. Foyle, Bann, Roe; linen manufactures, agricultural produce, fisheries. Area, *c.* 800 sq. m.; pop. 140,000. (2) Or DERRY, cap. of above, on R. Foyle; encircled by walls; Anglican and R.C. cathedrals; excellent harbour; has salmon fisheries, shipbuilding yards, linen manufactures, distilleries. Famous siege (1689). Pop. 45,000.

Long, LOCH, arm of sea between Argyllshire and Dumbartonshire, Scotland; picturesque scenery; extends N. and S. for 17 m.

Long Ash'ton, par. and vil., Somerset, England, 3 m. s.w. of Bristol; stone quarries. Pop. (par.) 2,220.

Long Beach, seaside resort, California, U.S.A., 20 m. s. of Los Angeles; lumber, fruits, oil, and natural gas. Pop. *c.* 142,000.

Longbenton, urb. dist., Northumberland, England, 4 m. N. of Newcastle; coal mining. Pop. 14,100.

Long Branch, city, wat.-pl., New Jersey, U.S.A.; market gardening; settled about 1667. Pop. 13,000.

Long Eaton, urb. dist., Derbyshire, 10 m. S.E. of Derby; lace making and rly. carriage building. Pop. 22,300.

Long'ford. (1) Inland co., Leinster, I.F.S., with extensive tracts of bog; bare hills on Leitrim border; good grazing land in centre and s.; agriculture, especially stock raising and dairy farming, is chief industry. Area, *c.* 400 sq. m.; pop. 40,000. (2) Cap. of above; agricultural centre; seat of R.C. bishop; tanning, corn milling. Pop. 3,700.

Long Island, isl., New York State, U.S.A., separated from mainland by

East R., a narrow channel which widens to N.E. as Long Island Sound; surface undulating; considerable area is woodland and sandy waste, and there are a number of lakes; at W. end of island are Queen's Borough (with Long Island City) and Brooklyn, now parts of New York City; Coney Island is popular resort. Excellent fisheries and oyster beds; market gardening. Area, 1,681 sq. m.

Long Mel'ford, par. and tn., Suffolk, England, 14 m. S. of Bury St. Edmunds; two Elizabethan moated houses. Pop. (par.) 2,700.

Long'ridge, urb. dist., Lancashire, England, 7 m. N.E. of Preston; cotton spinning and weaving, brassfounding; noted building-stone quarries. Pop. 4,200.

Long'ton. See STOKE-UPON-TRENT.

Long'town, mkt. tn., Cumberland, England, on R. Esk, 9 m. N. of Carlisle; brick and tile works. Pop. 6,400.

Longwy (*lon-vē'*), tn., Meurthe-et-Moselle, France, *c.* 90 m. N.N.W. of Nancy; ironworks; porcelain. Pop. 12,000.

Lons-le-Saunier (*lon-li-sō'nē-ā*), cap., Jura, France; salt springs; produces wine, and trades in live-stock and agricultural produce. Pop. 11,000.

Loo-choo Islands. See RYUKYU ARCHIPELAGO.

Looe, port, Cornwall, England, 17 m. W. of Plymouth; fisheries; exp. clay and granite. Pop. 2,900.

Loon, largest tn. of isl. of Bohol, Philippines, on W. coast; good anchorage. Pop. 24,000.

Loos (*lōs*), vil., Pas-de-Calais, France, 2½ m. N.W. of Lens; coal mines; scene of fierce battle (1915).

Lop Nor, lake, Sinkiang, China, in desert of Gobi; shallow and fresh water.

Lorain (*lō-rān'*), city, Ohio, U.S.A., on L. Erie; fine harbour; ships coal; steel works and shipbuilding yards; important fisheries. Pop. 44,000.

Lorca (*lor'kā*), tn., Murcia, Spain, 40 m. W. of Cartagena; porcelain, woollen goods, chemicals, leather; trade in agricultural products and live-stock. Pop. 75,000.

Lord Howe Islands, group of islands, S. Pacific, between Australia and New Zealand; vegetation abundant, especially banian trees; discovered in 1788, occupied in 1834. Belong administratively to New South Wales. Area, 5 sq. m.; pop. 112.

Loreto (*lor-ā'tō*). (1) Dep., N.E. Peru; a vast plain; thickly wooded; traversed by R. Marañon and tribs.; resources abundant but not well developed; chief export, rubber. Cap. Iquitos. Area, 163,240 sq. m.; pop. *c.* 150,000. (2) Tn., Marches, Italy, 15 m. by rail S.S.E. of Ancona; cathedral church of the Holy House is place of pilgrimage for Roman Catholics. Pop. 6,700.

Lorient (*lo-ri-on*), seapt. and fortified naval arsenal, Morbihan, France, on Bay of Biscay; important naval dockyard; exp. wine, sardines, tinned vegetables. Pop. 38,000.

Los Angeles (*ang'gel-ēz* or *an'je-lez*), tn., S. California, U.S.A.; centre of fruit-producing dist.; important petroleum industry; other industries include fruit canning, meat packing, lumbering, manufacture of flour, steel, cottons. Hollywood, the great centre for production of cinema films, was annexed to Los Angeles in 1910. Pop. 1,234,000.

Los'siemouth, tn., Morayshire, Scotland; wat.-pl.; fishing. Pop. 3,900.

Lostwith'iel, mkt. tn., on R. Fowey, Cornwall, England; railway workshops. Pop. 1,300.

Lot (*lō* or *lot*). (1) Riv., S. France; rises in Cévennes; joins Garonne near Aiguillon; length, 300 m.; 160 m. navigable. (2) Dep., S.W. France; hilly; chief rivs., Lot and Dordogne; principal products, wine, tobacco, cereals, chestnuts, truffles, and live-stock, especially sheep; iron and coal mines. Cap. Cahors. Area, 2,017 sq. m.; pop. 172,000.

Lot-et-Garonne (*lot-ā-gā-ron'*), dep., S.W. France; watered by Rs. Garonne and Lot; chief occupation, agriculture; produces cereals, potatoes, vines, tobacco, and fruit, especially plums and apricots. Cap. Agen. Area, 2,078 sq. m.; pop. 247,000.

Loughborough (*lŭf'bŭr-ŭ*), mkt. tn., N. Leicestershire, England; hosiery, locomotives, machinery. Pop. 26,900.

Loughrea (*loch-rā'*), mkt. tn., on Lough Rea, Galway, I.F.S.; remains of old fortifications. Pop. 2,800.

Loughton (*lou'ton*), tn., Essex, England; part of Greater London. Pop. 7,400.

Louisburg (*loo'is-burg*), tn., and ruined fortress, Cape Breton I., Nova Scotia, Canada; formerly important seaport and headquarters of cod-fishing industry; lobster canning and export of coal. Pop. 1,100.

Louisiana (*loo-ē-zē-ă'na*), one of Southern States of U.S.A., bounded N. by Arkansas, E. by Mississippi, S. by Gulf of Mexico, W. by Texas. Surface flat and marshy, especially towards the sea; R. Mississippi delta occupies about one-third of total area; drained by R. Mississippi, Red R., and Sabine; climate semi-tropical; state thickly wooded in parts, producing yellow pine, cypress, cottonwood, red gum, oak; a great cotton, maize, sugar-cane, and rice producing region, esp. along coast and Mississippi valley; also corn, oats, potatoes, tobacco, fruits. Horses, cattle, sheep, and pigs; important oyster fisheries. Industries include lumbering, sugar refining, preparation of rice, manufactures of machinery, cotton-seed oil, tobacco, and confectionery. Minerals include rock salt, sulphur, and petroleum. Cap. Baton Rouge; largest towns, New Orleans, Shreveport. Area, 48,506 sq. m.; pop. 1,798,000.

Louisville (*loo'i-vil* or *loo'is-vil*), tn., Kentucky, U.S.A., on Ohio R.; chief trading city in state, and largest tobacco mart in world; other industries, leather, meat packing, manufacture of machinery, furniture, metal pipes, flour, cotton-seed oil and cake; great rly. centre; important port on Ohio R. Has univ., many educational and charitable establishments, and fine parks. Pop. 308,000.

Loulé (*loo'lā*), tn., Faro, S. Portugal; basket making; leather and porcelain manufactures. Pop. 23,000.

Lourdes (*loord*), tn., Hautes-Pyrénées, France, on R. Pau; ancient castle; place of R.C. pilgrimage, on account of sacred spring, whose waters are credited with miraculous cures; marble and slate quarries. Pop. 8,000.

Lourenço Marques (*loo-ren'sō mar-kās'*), cap., Portuguese E. Africa, on Delagoa Bay; founded as trading post (1544); terminus of railway to Pretoria, carrying large percentage of Rand imports and exports; has excellent harbour; coaling port. Pop. 37,000.

Louth. (1) Co., Leinster, I.F.S., extends from Carlingford Lough in N. to riv. Boyne in S.; smallest co. in Ireland; hilly in N., flat elsewhere; rivers Fane, Laggan, Dee, and Glyde enter Dundalk Bay; is chiefly agricultural; fishing; oysters are found in Carlingford Lough; linen manufactured. Area, 316 sq. m.; pop. 63,000. Chief towns, Dundalk (co. tn.), Drogheda. (2) Mkt. tn. and munic. bor., Lincolnshire, England, 15 m. S.E. of Grimsby; agricultural centre; iron foundries. Pop. 9,700.

Louvain (*loo-van'*), or LEUVEN, tn., Brabant, Belgium, 18 m. E. by N. of Brussels. Manufactures beer, lace, starch, tobacco; destroyed in Great War by the Germans, who burnt univ. with famous library. Much rebuilding (including univ.) done since the war. Pop. 41,000.

Louviers (*loo-vē-ā'*), tn., Eure, France, 17 m. S. of Rouen; cloth manufactures, tanyards, and casting of bells. Pop. 9,000.

Lovedale, Scottish educational and mission station, Cape Province, S. Africa, *c.* 90 m. N.W. of E. London.

Low Archipelago. See TUAMOTU.

Lowell (*lō'el*), tn., Massachusetts, U.S.A., on Merrimac R., 25 m. N. of Boston; cotton, woollens (carpets, hosiery, etc.), iron goods, cartridges, machinery, chemicals, patent medicines. Pop. 100,000.

Lowestoft (*lō'stoft* or *lō'es-toft*),

munic.bor., seaport, and seaside resort, Suffolk, England, on North Sea; old town stands on cliff forming part of Lowestoft Ness, most easterly cape in England; great centre of herring fishery; net making, boat building. Pop. 41,800.

Loyalty Islands, group of coral islands, s. Pacific; included in French administration of New Caledonia, which lies about 60 m. w.; coconuts, rubber, copra. Area, 800 sq. m.

Lozère (*lō-zăr'*), dep., s. France; surface very mountainous; Cévennes Mts. in S.E.; drained by R. Lot; subject to violent rainstorms; sheep and cattle rearing and cheese making are the chief occupations; cereals, fruit, and chestnuts grown; extensive forests; culture of silkworms; valuable deposits of silver, lead, copper, and antimony. Cap. Mende. Area, 1,996 sq. m.; pop. 105,000.

Luang-Prabang (*loo-ang' pra-bang'*), chief tn., Laos, French Indo-China, on R. Mekong, at head of navigation; products include rubber, ivory, silk, indigo. Pop. *c.* 12,000.

Lübeck (*loo'bek*). (1) Republic, N. Germany, on Baltic Sea; fertile; cereals, fruit. Area, 115 sq. m.; pop. 128,000. (2) Free city, cap. of above, on R. Trave, about 12 m. from Baltic; important port, trading chiefly with Baltic countries; a picturesque old town, founded in 12th cent. Chief industries are shipbuilding, machinery, chemicals, breweries, soap. Pop. 121,000. (3) Province. See OLDENBURG.

Lublin (*loob'lin*), tn., Poland, 100 m. S.E. of Warsaw; manufactures thread, hemp, linen, and woollen goods, and trades in grain and agricultural produce. Pop. 94,000.

Lucca (*look'a*), tn., N. Tuscany, Italy, 13 m. N.E. of Pisa; seat of archbishop; has a cathedral dating in part from 11th cent., and containing fine pictures; many old churches, palaces, and educational establishments; manufactures silk, cotton, jute. Pop. 78,000.

Lucena (*loo-thă'na*), tn., s. Spain, 35 m. S.E. of Cordoba; brandy, wine; textiles, pottery, matches, earthenware. Pop. 23,000.

Lucera (*loo-chă'ra*), tn., Apulia, s. Italy, 30 m. w. of Gulf of Manfredonia; cathedral and castle; silk. Pop. 17,000.

Lucerne (*loo-sern'*), or LUZERN. (1) Canton, Switzerland; chief stream, R. Reuss; agriculture and dairy farming. Area, 575 sq. m.; pop. 177,000. (2) Cap. of above; beautifully situated on L. Lucerne; tourist resort; anc. town hall, Hofkirche, museum, arsenal, glacier garden; sewing machines, cotton goods, cheese. Pop. 46,000. (3) LAKE OF ('lake of the four forest cantons'), Switzerland, surrounded by cantons of Lucerne, Unterwalden, Schwyz, and Uri; area, 44 sq. m.; overlooked by Mts. Pilatus and Rigi; traversed by R. Reuss; subject to sudden storms; beautiful scenery; associated with William Tell.

Luck (*wootsk*), or LUTSK, river port, Volhynia, Poland, on R. Styr, 85 m. N.E. of Lwow; manufactures glass, cloth, paper. Pop. *c.* 20,000.

Luckenwalde (*look-en-vald'a*), tn., Brandenburg, Prussia, 30 m. s. of Berlin; cloth, hats; machine shops, foundries, and breweries. Pop. 25,000.

Luck'now, city, United Provinces, India, on R. Gumti; noted for heroic defence (1857) in Indian Mutiny; muslins, brassware, pottery; important railway centre with railway workshops; univ. (1920). Pop. 240,000.

Lüdenscheid (*loo'den-shīt*), tn., Westphalia, Prussia, 19 m. E. by s. of Barmen; iron foundries, metal ware. Pop. 33,000.

Lüderitz (*lood'er-itz*), formerly ANGRA PEQUEÑA, tn. and bay, S.W. Africa; good natural harbour; surrounding country desert, but rly. links up with S. African system at De Aar; important diamond centre; fisheries. Pop. *c.* 2,000.

Ludhiana (*lood-hi-ă'na*). (1) Dist., Punjab, India; wide-spreading plain producing wheat, maize, and sugar. Area, 1,452 sq. m.; pop. 568,000.

(2) Tn. in above, near R. Sutlej, 80 m. w. of Simla; trade in grain, shawls, cloths, and turbans; rly. jn. Pop. 52,000.

Lud'low, mkt. tn., s. Shropshire, England; tanning, corn milling. Here Butler wrote *Hudibras* and Milton's *Comus* was first performed (1634). Pop. 5,600.

Ludwigsburg (*lood'vigs-boorg*), tn., Württemberg, Germany, 10 m. N. of Stuttgart; iron foundry and arsenal; chemicals and textiles. Pop. 29,000.

Ludwigshafen (*lood'vigs-hä-fen*), tn., Palatinate, Germany, on R. Rhine, opposite Mannheim; aniline dyes and chemicals; iron foundries, breweries, sawmills. Pop. 102,000.

Lugano (*loo-gä'nō*). (1) Tn., Ticino, Switzerland, on Lake Lugano; tourist centre; silk, paper. Pop. 13,000. (2) Lake, Switzerland and N. Italy; length, 22 m.; breadth, 1 m.; delightful scenery.

Lugansk (*loo-gansk'*), or LUGAN, tn., Ukraine, U.S.S.R, situated on the Donetz coal basin; iron foundries and engine shops; flour milling and brewing. Pop. 71,000.

Lugar (*loo'gar*), par. and vil., Ayrshire, Scotland, 16 m. E. of Ayr; has extensive ironworks. Pop. (par.) 3,000.

Lugo (*loo'gō*), tn., Galicia, N.W. Spain, on R. Minho; chief industries are tanning and textile manufacture; hot sulphur baths. Pop. 28,000.

Luleå (*loo-lē'ō*). (1) Seapt., Sweden, on Gulf of Bothnia; exp. Gellivara iron ore, timber, tar, salmon, reindeer hides. Pop. 11,000. (2) Or LULE, riv., Sweden; length, 255 m.

Lumphinnans (*lŭm-fin'ans*), vil., Fife, Scotland, 1 m. w. of Lochgelly; coal. Pop. 2,500.

Lund (*loond*), tn., Sweden, 10 m. N.N.E. of Malmö; univ.; furniture, gloves; sugar refining, iron smelting. Pop. 25,000.

Lun'din Links, vil., Fife, Scotland, 1 m. w. of Largo; summer resort. Pop. 1,000.

Lundy (*lŭn'di*), small isl. at entrance of Bristol Channel, England; interesting ruins. Area, 1,047 ac.; pop. 48.

Lüneburg (*loon'ĕ-boorg*), tn., Hanover, Prussia, on R. Ilmenau, 27 m. S.E. of Hamburg; anc. Hanse town; old Gothic churches and interesting mediæval buildings; cement and salt; beer, chemicals, ironware. Pop. 29,000.

Lunéville (*lü-nā-vēl'*), tn., Meurthe-et-Moselle, E. France, on R. Meurthe, 18 m. S.E. of Nancy; cotton and woollen industries, gloves, hosiery, glass. Pop. 20,000.

Lungchow', port, Kwangsi, China; opened to foreign trade in 1889; is being well developed. Pop. 15,000.

Lur'gan, tn., N.E. co. Armagh, N. Ireland; manufactures cambric, diaper, lawn, and tobacco. Pop. 12,500.

Lushai Hills, dist., India, in Lushai Hills, on frontier of Assam, Bengal, and Burma; largely forest and jungle; became British in 1890. Area, 7,230 sq. m.; pop. 98,000.

Luton (*loo'ton*), mkt. tn., S.E. Bedfordshire, England, on R. Lea; straw and felt hats; dyeworks; brass, iron, and motor-car works. Pop. 68,500.

Lutsk. See LUCK.

Lut'terworth, mkt. tn., s. Leicestershire, England; Wyclif was rector here. Pop. 2,100.

Lüttringhausen (*loot-ring-hou'zen*), tn., Rhineland, Prussia, 6 m. S.E. of Elberfeld; ironmongery, cotton goods. Pop. 14,000.

Lützen (*loot'zen*), tn., Prussian Saxony, 12 m. S.W. of Leipzig; here Wallenstein was defeated by Gustavus Adolphus of Sweden, who was killed in action (1632). Pop. 4,000.

Luxembourg. (1) Grand-duchy, Europe, bordering on Belgium, Prussia, and France; surface generally tableland; iron ore; manufactures hardware, leather, beer, paper; in economic union with Belgium. Area, 999 sq. m.; pop. 285,000. (2) Cap. of above duchy. Pop. 52,000. (3) (*looks-an-boor'*) Prov., S.E. Belgium; high-lying and wooded; produces marble, fruit, timber. Cap. Arlon. Area, 1,706 sq. m.; pop. 224,000.

Lux'or, tn., Upper Egypt, on R.

Nile, 120 m. N. of Aswan; contains magnificent ruins of Thebes.

Lux'ulyan, par. and vil., Cornwall, England, 6 m. N.W. of Fowey; granite quarries. Pop. 1,000.

Luzern. See LUCERNE.

Luzon', island, Philippine Islands; largest and most northerly of group; irregular in shape, with three main mountain ranges, largely volcanic; well-watered, chief rivs. being Rio Grande de Cagayan, Agno, and Abra; vegetation is luxuriant; chief crops are rice, sugar, hemp, cotton, coffee, maize, and tobacco; chief minerals are coal, copper, gold, asphalt; industries include manufacture of silks and cottons, leather goods. Cap. Manila. Area, 40,814 sq. m.; pop. *c.* 4,000,000.

Lwow (*lvoof*), formerly LEMBERG, city, Poland, on the Peltew R., 185 m. E. of Cracow; seat of three archbishoprics — R.C., Greek Catholic, and Armenian; univ.; machinery, ironware, liquors, leather, matches, and candles are manufactured. Pop. 219,000.

Lyck, or LYK (*lik*), tn., E. Prussia, 100 m. S.E. of Königsberg; machinery, tiles, paper, leather, and flour. Pop. 15,000.

Lyd'brook, or LIDBROOK, vil., Gloucestershire, England, 14 m. W. of Gloucester; coal, iron, and tin mines; chemicals. Pop. 2,500.

Lydd, mkt. tn., S. Kent, England; 'Lyddite' shells; important military camp. Pop. 2,800.

Lydenburg (*lī'den-burg*), tn., Transvaal, S. Africa, 144 m. E.N.E. of Pretoria; gold mining; sheep farming, and growing of cotton, wheat, and tobacco. Pop. 1,500.

Lyd'ford, par. and vil., Devonshire, England, 11 m. E. of Launceston, on edge of Dartmoor; was long the chief town of the Devonshire 'Stannary.' Pop. 2,200.

Lyd'ney, par. and tn., Glos, England, in Forest of Dean, 8 m. N.E. of Chepstow; iron and tin factory; exports coal and iron. Pop. (par.) 5,000.

Lye and Wollescote, urb. dist., Worcestershire, England, 1½ m. E. of Stourbridge; coal mines; bricks, nails, vices, anvils. Pop. 12,200.

Lyme Regis (*līm rē'jis*), seaport and wat.-pl., Dorsetshire, England; 'blue lias' cliffs quarried for manufacture of lime and cement. Pop. 2,600.

Ly'mington, seapt. and mkt. tn., New Forest dist., Hampshire, England; yacht building. Pop. 5,200.

Lymm (*lim*), urb. dist., Cheshire, England, 5 m. E. of Warrington; residential dist. Pop. 5,600.

Lympne (*lim*), or LYMME, vil., E. Kent, England, 2½ m. W. of Hythe; air station; wireless station; Roman remains. Pop. 600.

Lynch'burg, city, Virginia, U.S.A., on James R., 95 m. W. of Richmond; tobacco trade; agricultural implements, boots and shoes. Pop. 41,000.

Lynd'hurst, par. and vil., Hants, England, in New Forest, 9 m. W.S.W. of Southampton; has been administrative centre of New Forest from anc. times. Pop. (par.) 2,500.

Lynn, seapt., Massachusetts, U.S.A., 10 m. N.E. of Boston; centre of boot and shoe trade; electrical machinery. Pop. 102,000.

Lyn'ton and **Lyn'mouth**, two seaside resorts, N. Devon, England; Lynton is situated on cliff 500 ft. high, with Lynmouth below; connected by water-balance lift. Pop. 2,000.

Lyons, or LYON (*lī'ons* or *lē'on*), third city of France, at confluence of Rs. Rhone and Saône; episc. see; great commercial and industrial town; centre of silk trade; first-class fortress; many fine bridges and quays; Roman remains (aqueducts, etc.); mediæval churches; 17th cent. Hôtel de Ville, Palais des Arts, Bourse, unique Musée des Tissus; univ.; Hôtel-Dieu and Hospice de la Charité, first of their kind in France. Chief industries, manufacture of silk fabrics, chemicals, motor-cars, printing, and engineering; great banking centre (*Crédit Lyonnais*). Pop. 571,000.

Lys (*lēs*), riv., France and Belgium,

rises in dep. Pas-de-Calais, and flowing N.E. past Armentières, Menin, and Courtrai, forms boundary between France and Belgium; falls into the Schelde at Ghent. Length, 120 m.

Lytham St. Anne's (*lith-am*), munic. bor., formed by union of Lytham and St. Anne's, Lancashire, England, 16½ m. S.E. of Blackpool; favourite wat.-pl.; graving dock and harbour. Pop. 25,800.

Lyt'telton, port of Christchurch, E. coast of South Island, New Zealand; artificial harbour; large graving dock; largest export trade of New Zealand; connected with Christchurch by railway tunnelled through hills. Pop. 4,000.

M

Maas. See MEUSE (1

Maasin (*mä-sēn'*), tn., Leyte I., Philippines; fishing industry; manufactures cloth, pottery; exports manila hemp and copra. Pop. 22,300.

Maasluis (*mäs'lois*), river port, Holland, on New Waterway, 10 m. W. of Rotterdam; fishing, and sail making. Pop. 10,000.

Maastricht (*mäs-tricht*), tn., cap., Limburg, Holland, on R. Meuse; manufactures tobacco, glass, pottery; distilleries, breweries. Pop. 60,000.

Ma'blethorps and Sutton, wat.-pl., Lincolnshire, England, on coast, 13 m. by rail E. of Louth; frequented by Tennyson; favourite summer resort. Pop. 3,900.

McAl'ester, tn., Oklahoma, U.S.A., 100 m. S.E. of Oklahoma City; centre of important coal region; railway stock. Pop. 12,900.

Macao (*ma-kow'*). (1) Portuguese prov., China, at mouth of Canton R.; comprises Islands of Macao, Taipa, and Colôane. Area, *c.* 11 sq. m.; pop. 157,000. (2) Tn. on Macao Is.; exp. large quantities of tea, silk, indigo, rice, fish, oil; important fisheries. Pop. 84,000.

Macarsca (*ma-kar'ska*), tn., port, Dalmatia, Yugoslavia, E. of I. of Brazza; trade in wine and grain. Pop. 12,100.

Macas'sar, port, S. Celebes, Dutch E. Indies; exports coffee, copra, spices, hides, rattans, tortoiseshell, pearls, sandalwood. Pop. 50,000.

Macclesfield (*mak'ls-fēld*), mkt. tn., Cheshire, England, on R. Bollin; chief silk manufacturing centre in England; textile manufactures; breweries; coal in vicinity. Pop. 34,900.

Macduff', port, Banff, Scotland; salmon and herring fisheries; summer resort. Pop. 3,300.

Macedonia (*ma-se-dō'ne-a*), dist., Balkan Peninsula, N. and N.W. of Ægean Sea; partly in Yugoslavia, partly in Greece, bounded on W. by Albania. Yugoslav portion is mountainous, Gr. portion hilly. Chief rivs. are Vardar, Vistritza, Struma, and Mesta. Malaria is rampant. Climate subject to extremes of cold in winter. In alluvial plains and better parts of highlands agriculture is carried on; crops include olives and cotton; rice in Struma valley; irrigation is practised. Fishing is important. In anc. times famed for gold and silver mines, and produced oil and wine. Chief products are grain, tobacco, opium, silk, rice, fruits. Chief rly. follows Vardar R.; transport is mainly by pack animals.

Maceio (*mä-sā-yo'*), tn., Brazil, S. America, 130 m. S. of Pernambuco; exports sugar, cotton, rum, skins, hides; good harbour; cotton and sugar mills. Pop. 74,000.

Macerata (*mä-chā-rä'tā*), tn., episc. see, the Marches, Italy, 22 m. S. of Ancona; univ.; glass, pottery, chemicals. Pop. 24,000.

Macgillycuddy's Reeks (*mäk'li-kud-i*), group of mts., Kerry, I.F.S., 6 m. S.W. of Killarney; chief peak,

Carrantuohill (3,414 ft.), is highest mt. in Ireland.

Machynlleth (*ma-hun'tleth*), mkt. tn., Montgomeryshire, Wales, on R. Dovey; salmon-fishing centre. Pop. 1,900.

Mackay (*mak-ī'*), port, Queensland, Australia; sugar mills; bananas and pineapples; exp. sugar. Pop. 8,800.

McKees'port, city, Pennsylvania, U.S.A., 15 m. S.E. of Pittsburgh; bituminous coal; steel and iron works, blast furnaces. Pop. 55,000.

McKees Rocks, bor., Allegheny, Pennsylvania, U.S.A., on Ohio R., opposite Pittsburgh; coal and natural gas are plentiful; manufactures iron, steel, tin, and enamelled ware; large railway workshops. Pop. 17,000.

Macken'zie. (1) Riv., Canada; rises as R. Athabasca near Mt. Brown, in Rocky Mts.; flows for 680 m. to Lake Athabasca, which it leaves as Great Slave R.; enters Great Slave Lake, then as Mackenzie R. flows N. for *c.* 1,000 m. into Mackenzie Bay. Total length, 2,300 m.; mouth closed by ice (Oct. to June). (2) Provisional Dist., N.W. Terrs., Canada; N. of 60° N. lat., and between Yukon Terr. and Keewatin; includes Great Bear and Great Slave lakes; drained by Mackenzie R.; forested; very sparsely populated. Area, 527,490 sq. m.

McKin'ley, MOUNT, highest known peak in N. America; in Alaska; alt. 20,464 ft.

Mâcon (*mă-kon*), cap., Saône-et-Loire, France, on R. Saône; agricultural implements, ropes, mats; copper foundries; celebrated for wines. Pop. 16,000.

Macon (*mā'kon*), city, Georgia, U.S.A., on Ocmulgee R.; important rly. jn.; iron foundries; large trade in fruits, vegetables, and bricks; manufactures cottons; Mercer Univ. Pop. 54,000.

Macquar'ie. (1) Island, S. Pacific, 700 m. S.S.E. of New Zealand; visited by sailors when hunting seals. Area, 170 sq. m. (2) Riv., New South Wales, Australia; formed by junction of Fish and Campbell rivs.; joins R. Darling. Length, *c.* 350 m.

Macroom', urb. dist., Cork, I.F.S., 25 m. W. of Cork; trade in grain and butter; trout and salmon fishing centre. Pop. 2,400.

Madagas'car, large isl. off S.E. coast of Africa; separated from Africa by Mozambique Channel; Fr. colony. Interior rugged, with mountains rising to 3,000–5,000 ft; highest part of island is near centre, where Ankaratra, an extinct volcano, reaches height of 9,000 ft.; drained by many streams. Climate hot and unhealthy on coasts, more temperate and healthy in interior. Thunderstorms and hurricanes are frequent. Fauna includes lemur and aye-aye. Luxuriant vegetation; bananas, coconuts, orange and mulberry trees, areca palms, pandanus, acacias, ebony; medicinal plants abound; also rubber, cotton, hemp, rice, manioc, coffee, cacao, vanilla, cloves, tobacco, sugar-cane; cattle reared. Minerals include gold, precious stones, mica, graphite, phosphates, copper, iron, lead. Manufactures: silk and cotton, Panama and straw hats; meat preserving. Cap. Antananarivo; other tns., Majunga, Antsirabe, Tamatave. Area, 241,094 sq. m.; pop. 3,621,000.

Madang', formerly FRIEDRICH-WILHELMSHAFEN, port, N.E. Mandated Terr. of New Guinea, Australia, on Astrolabe Bay; oil and coal in hinderland; cocoa, coffee, rubber, and other plantations being laid out; mission station; chief export, copra.

Madeira Islands (*mă-dā'rā*), or THE MADEIRAS, islands, Atlantic Ocean, about 400 m. W. of coast of Morocco. Rank as div. of Portugal. Group comprises Madeira (area, *c.* 270 sq. m.), Porto Santo, and three uninhabited Desertas. Surface mountainous, rising to over 6,000 ft. in Pico Ruivo; coasts steep and rocky; favourite health resort. Exports fruits, wines, vegetables, sugar, tobacco; Madeira wine is well known, and is made from mixed white and black grapes. Porto Santo is a hilly island, with practically no products; it was visited by Columbus. Fisheries are valuable. Whole group is part of submarine range of volcanic mountains. Chief tn., Funchal. Area, 314 sq. m.; pop. 180,000.

Madeley (*măd'li*), par. in bor. of Wenlock, Shropshire, England; coal and ironstone mines; large beds of potters' clay. Pop. 7,300.

Mad'ison, cap. of Wisconsin, U.S.A.; in 'four-lake' region between Lake Michigan and R. Mississippi; manufactures agricultural implements, machinery, boots and shoes, electric appliances; univ. Pop. 58,000.

Mad'iun, residency, E. Java, Dutch E. Indies; fertile plains with hills in S.; chief crops rice, sugar-cane, maize, coffee, coconuts, teak. Cap. Madiun. Area, 2,354 sq. m.; pop. 1,700,000.

Madras'. (1) Presidency, India; occupies whole width of Indian peninsula S. of R. Kistna and its tributary Tungabhadra, and extends N. along E. coast as far as Lake Chilka; low coastal strip on each side rises by E. and W. Ghats to great central tableland, sloping up from 1,000 to 3,000 ft. Coast-line on E. *c.* 1,200 m., on W. *c.* 450 m. No natural harbour of importance. Drained by rivs. Godavari, Kistna, Cauvery, and other streams. Climate very varied. Produces large crops of cotton and tobacco; also rice, millet, wheat, barley, pulse, ground-nuts, oil-seeds, sugar-cane, spices, indigo, coconuts, areca nuts, dates; on hills, tea, coffee, cinchona, cardamoms are grown; valuable forests of teak, ebony, rosewood, sandalwood, and redwood. Exports raw cotton, seeds, rice, tea, spices, indigo, oil. Chief tns., Madras (cap.), Madura, and Trichinopoly. Area, excluding Indian states, 142,260 sq. m.; pop. 42,300,000. (2) Cap. and chief port of above; grew up round Fort St. George, founded 1639; handicapped by surf, but great breakwaters render harbour more secure. Commercial part, George Town, is on shore; Europeans live farther inland; univ. Chief industries, cotton spinning, engineering, and cigar making; exports tea, coffee, cotton, sugar, dyestuffs, grain, hides, indigo. Pop. 527,000.

Madre de Dios (*mä'drā dā dē'os*), dep., E. Peru, S. America; mountainous; immense forests; gold and silver. Cap. Maldonada, 200 m. N.E. of Cuzco. Area, 58,827 sq. m.; pop. *c.* 5,000.

Madrid'. (1) Prov., New Castile, Spain, in R. Tagus basin; climate arid; agriculture; granite, lime, gypsum, and freestone quarried. Area, 3,084 sq. m.; pop. 1,160,000. (2) Cap. of Spain and of above prov., on R. Manzanares, in centre of great sandy plateau over 2,100 ft. above sea-level, subject to extremes of heat and cold. Univ., with observatory and magnificent library. Contains royal palace, royal picture gallery with paintings by Velazquez, Rubens, Titian, and other masters. Manufactures leather goods, tobacco, furniture, tapestry, glass, chemicals, soap, porcelain, gold and silver work. Pop. 817,000.

Madura (*mä-doo'rä*). (1) Mountainous isl., Dutch E. Indies, N.E. of Java, from which it is separated by the Strait of Madura; mostly plain; considerable areas wooded; rice, maize, coconuts, fruit, vegetables; fishing and cattle rearing; salt largely produced. Area, 2,189 sq. m.; pop. 1,800,000. (2) Dist., S. Madras, India; mountainous in N. and W.; elsewhere level and fertile; coffee, rice, cotton, tobacco. Area, 4,907 sq. m.; pop. 2,007,000. (3) Cap. of above dist., on R. Vaigai; contains remarkable temple; coffee industries, brass working, wood carving, and weaving of muslin. Pop. 139,000.

Maesteg (*mīs'teg*), urb. dist., Glamorganshire, Wales, 14 m. S.W. of Merthyr Tydfil; coal mining and ironworks. Pop. 25,600.

Maf'eking, tn., Brit. Bechuanaland, S. Africa, 150 m. W. of Pretoria; noted for its defence (1899–1900) by Baden-Powell in the Boer War; stock fairs; important rly. depot. Pop. *c.* 5,200 (1,800 whites).

Magallanes (*ma-gal-yä'nes*). (1) Terr., s. Chile, S. America; stretches to Cape Horn and includes a multitude of islands and w. half of Tierra del Fuego; mountainous and forest-clad; coal and gold found; sheep rearing; great expt. chilled mutton and wool. Area, 46,430 sq. m.; pop. 36,000. (2) Formerly PUNTA ARENAS, cap. of above, on Strait of Magellan; most s. town of S. America; formerly a convict station; exp. chilled mutton and wool. Pop. 27,000.

Magdala (*mag'dala*), tn. and hill fort, central Abyssinia; stormed by British under Napier (1868). Pop. over 3,000.

Magdale'na. (1) Riv., Colombia, rises in Andes Mts., flows N. between Eastern and Central Cordilleras, and enters Caribbean Sea. Navigable for 900 m.; length, 1,000. (2) Dep., Colombia, S. America; plain with hills to s., watered by R. Magdalena. Produces coffee, cotton, ivory nut palms, and rubber trees. Cap. Santa Marta. Area, 19,080 sq. m.; pop. 277,000.

Magdeburg (*mag'de-boorg*), cap., Saxony, Prussia, on R. Elbe; was prominent member of Hanseatic League. Great railway centre; iron-works; enormous trade in sugar and chicory; also deals in grain, chemicals, chocolate, pottery, cotton and silk goods; distilling and brewing. Pop. 294,000.

Magellan, STRAIT OF (*mä-jel'an*), sea-passage between S. America and Tierra del Fuego; discovered by Magellan (1520); navigation difficult for sailing vessels; chief port, Punta Arenas. Length, 360 m.; breadth, 2½ to 17 m.

Magenta (*ma-jen'tä*), tn., Lombardy, Italy, 16 m. w. of Milan; silk and matches. Pop. 9,900.

Maggiore (*mä-jō'rä*), LAKE, N. Italy and Swiss canton of Ticino; traversed by Ticino R.; has beautiful group of Borromean Islands; well stocked with fish. Length, 40 m.; breadth, 5½ m.; area, 83 sq. m.

Magh'era, mkt. tn. and par., co. Londonderry, N. Ireland, 20 m. s. of Coleraine; linens and sewed muslins. Pop. (par.) 6,600.

Magherafelt', par. and mkt. tn., co. Londonderry, N. Ireland, 26 m s. of Coleraine; manufactures linen. Pop. (par.) 4,000.

Magwe'. (1) Dist., Upper Burma; plain in w., forested upland in E.; rice, maize, cotton; petroleum wells. Area, 3,687 sq. m.; pop. 423,000. (2) Chief tn. of above, on R. Irrawaddy. Pop. 8,000.

Mahabaleshwar (*mä-hä-bul-esh-wur'*), hill station, W. Ghats, Bombay, India; sacred as source of Kistna R. Pop. 5,000.

Mahanad'i ('great river'), river, India; rises in Bastar Mts. and flows generally E. to Bay of Bengal; useful for irrigation. Length, 520 m.

Mahanoy' City, tn., Pennsylvania, U.S.A., 56 m. N.E. of Harrisburg; anthracite mining; foundry products, shirts. Pop. 16,000.

Mahé (*mä-ā'*). (1) Port and Fr. settlement, w. Madras, India; coaling station; fishing; vanilla. Pop. 11,000. (2) Largest of Seychelle Islands, Indian Ocean. Chief tn., Victoria, cap. of Seychelles. Area, 56 sq. m.

Mahedia (*mä-he-dē'a*), port, Tunisia, Africa; manufactures olive oil. Pop. 8,000.

Maid'enhead, mkt. tn. and munic. bor., on R. Thames, Berks, England; grain mills, breweries; riverside resort. Pop. 17,500.

Maid'stone, co. tn., Kent, on R. Medway, England; hops and fruit dist.; breweries, paper and oil mills; cement and lime works. Pop. 42,300.

Main (*mīn*), riv., Germany, joins R. Rhine opposite Mainz; navigable to junction with R. Regnitz. Connected with R. Danube by Ludwig's Canal. Length, 310 m. Chief tns. on banks, Würzburg, Frankfurt.

Maine, extreme N.E. state of U.S.A. and of New England states, bounded N. and E. by New Brunswick, s. by the Atlantic Ocean, w. by New Hampshire and Quebec; coast much indented, giving coast-line of 2,500 m.;

surface generally undulating, rising, towards centre of state, to 5,300 ft.; drained by Saco, Androscoggin, Kennebec, Penobscot, St. Croix, St. John, and other streams; contains great number of large lakes, including Moosehead. Climate is severe in winter and cool in summer. Northern districts forested, producing timber, bark, maple sugar; agriculture important industry, oats, maize, buckwheat, potatoes, and hay; horses, cattle, sheep, and pigs. Excellent fisheries; fish canning important. Manufactures cottons, woollens, paper, flour, clothing, boots, leather. Largest tn., Portland; cap. Augusta. Area, 33,040 sq. m.; pop. 768,000.

Maine-et-Loire (*mān-ā-lwär'*), dep., N.W. France; formed part of anc. Anjou; surface hilly; traversed by R. Loire and its trib. R. Maine; soil generally fertile—produces grain, flax, hemp, wine, fruits; linen, cotton, and woollen manufactures. Cap. Angers. Area, 2,811 sq. m.; pop. 478,000.

Mainland. (1) Or POMONA, largest isl., Orkney, Scotland; Kirkwall Bay and Scapa Flow, 2 m. apart, divide it into two unequal portions, w. part being larger; moorland with fertile tracts and good trout lochs; Kirkwall and Stromness are chief tns.; Standing Stones at Stenness. Area, 190 sq. m.; pop. 14,000. (2) Largest of Shetland Islands. Chief tn., Lerwick. Area, over 400 sq. m.; pop. 18,300.

Mainz, or MAYENCE (*mints*), tn., Hesse, Germany, on R. Rhine, below influx of R. Main; busy river port; preserves, machinery, furniture, leather, chemicals; headquarters of Rhenish wine trade; printing industries; birthplace of Gutenberg, who invented movable type. Pop. 109,000.

Mait'land, EAST AND WEST, two adjoining towns, New South Wales, 20 m. N.W. of Newcastle; centre of fertile agricultural dist.; coal in vicinity. Pop. 13,000.

Major'ca, largest of Balearic Islands, Spain, in Mediterranean Sea; climate relaxing; mountainous in N.W.; soil very fertile; grain, oil, wine, fruits in abundance; cattle rearing; marble and slate quarried. Cap. Palma. Area, 1,430 sq. m.; pop. 270,000.

Maju'ba, hill, Drakensberg range, N.W. Natal, S. Africa; alt. 2,000 ft. above surrounding land; scene of Brit. defeat by Boers (Feb. 27, 1881).

Mako (*mo'ko*), tn., Hungary, 19 m. E. Szeged; chiefly agricultural; onions largely grown; flour. Pop. 37,000.

Mak'ran, prov., Baluchistan, bordering sea; mountainous with narrow valleys; agriculture in fertile valleys; dates. Area, 26,000 sq. m.; pop. 78,000.

Mak'war, site of dam, The Gezira, Anglo-Egyptian Sudan, Africa, on R. Blue Nile, above Sennar and 170 m. S. of Khartoum; by means of dam (1914–26) *c.* 1,000 sq. m. of Gezira will ultimately be irrigated for cotton and other crops.

Malabar', mar. dist., Madras, India; slopes from W. Ghats to Indian Ocean and stretches 145 m. along W. coast; diversified surface; monsoon rainfall unfailing; extensive forests; rice, coconuts, coffee, pepper; fisheries. Cap. Calicut. Area, 5,792 sq. m.; pop. 3,099,000.

Malabon', tn., Luzon, Philippines, 3 m. N. of Manila; sugar refining; cigars and perfume. Pop. 22,000.

Malac'ca. (1) Colony, Malay Peninsula; largest of Straits Settlements; undulating surface; tropical products. Area, 780 sq. m.; pop. 153,000. (2) Cap. of above; free port; exports rice, tapioca, spices, rubber. Pop. 20,000. (3) STRAIT OF, separating Malay Peninsula from Sumatra and adjacent islands; 550 m. long; width, 35 to 185 m.

Mal'aga. (1) Prov., S. Spain, forming part of anc. kingdom of Granada; mountainous in S.; plain in N.; watered by R. Guadalquivir; very fertile; mining, agriculture, wine; fisheries. Area, 2,812 sq. m.; pop. 564,000. (2) Port, cap. of above, on Mediterranean; manufactures flour, cotton, sugar, leather, chemicals; exp. fruit, wine, lead. Pop. 160,000.

Mälar (*mä'lar*), lake, Sweden; discharges into Baltic Sea, through Stockholm, and by Södertelge Canal; numerous islands; surface 1 to 2 ft. above sea-level; 80 m. long. Area, 650 sq. m.

Malatia (*mä-lä-tē'ä*), tn., E. Asia Minor, 110 m. N.W. of Diarbekr; fruit culture, opium; suffered from earthquake (1893). Pop. 75,000.

Malay Archipelago. See EAST INDIES.

Malay Peninsula, a long narrow peninsula extending from Indo-China southward towards Sumatra, and forming extreme S. of mainland of Asia. Properly it extends from head of Gulf of Siam, with length of *c.* 900 m.; width, 45 to 210 m. See further under MALAY STATES and SIAM.

Malay States, under Brit. protection and comprising a large portion of the Malay Peninsula, include the Federated States of Pahang, Perak, Selangor and Negri Sembilan, and the Non-federated States of Kedah, Kelantan, Perlis, and Trengganu; while Johore, in extreme S. of the peninsula, has its foreign relations controlled by Britain. Surface generally flat along coast, hilly inland, as the mountain range that traverses whole peninsula passes down to W. of centre. Federal cap. Kuala Lumpur, in Selangor. Federated States: total area, 27,500 sq. m.; pop. 1,325,000. Non-federated States: total area, 22,855 sq. m.; pop. 1,162,000. See articles on each state.

Mal'da, dist., Bengal, India, lying along l. bk. of R. Ganges; cereals, oil-seeds, indigo, mangoes; silk and indigo industries. Area, 1,833 sq. m.; pop. 986,000.

Mal'den, tn., Massachusetts, U.S.A.; residential suburb of Boston; manufactures rubber goods, furniture, and hosiery. Pop. 58,000.

Mal'dive Islands, chain of thirteen coral islands in Indian Ocean, 450 m. W. of Ceylon, of which they are a dependency; chief products, coir, cowries, coconuts, fruit, and nuts. Pop. over 70,000.

Mal'don, mkt. tn., river port, Essex, England, on R. Blackwater; iron foundries; agricultural implements; oyster fisheries. Pop. 6,600.

Malines (*ma-lēn'*), or MECHLIN, city, Antwerp, Belgium; manufactures furniture, linen, woollen goods, oil; formerly famous for lace; important rly. jn.; extensive railway works. Pop. 60,000.

Mal'laig, vil., S.W. Inverness-shire, Scotland, on Sound of Sleat; terminus of W. Highland Rly.; trade in fish.

Mal'low, wat.-pl., co. Cork, I.F.S., on R. Blackwater; warm mineral springs; salmon fishing; condensed milk; flour mills, tanneries. Pop. 4,600.

Malmédy (*mäl'mä-de*), tn., Liége, Belgium; tanning, dyeing, paper-making; ceded to Belgium after Great War. Pop. 4,700.

Malmesbury (*mämz'bury*), mkt. tn. and munic. bor., Wilts, England, on R. Avon; fine market cross; lace and silk manufactures. Pop. 2,300.

Mal'mö, port, Sweden, on Sound; ironworks, cotton and woollen mills, breweries; gloves; tobacco; ferry connection with Copenhagen. Exp. dairy produce, live-stock, matches, timber products. Pop. 119,000.

Mal'ta, isl. in Mediterranean Sea, S. of Sicily; about 58 m. from Sicily; E. and N.E. coasts are broken, with good inlets; along S., cliffs are *c.* 400 ft. high, and highest point of island is *c.* 800 ft. Brit. crown colony (including islands of Gozo and Comino) and principal Brit. naval station in Mediterranean; strongly fortified. Great coaling station and port of call. During Great War was base for troops engaged in the East, and had extensive hospital accommodation. About half island is under cultivation; produces cotton, potatoes, fruits, onions, cereals, honey; cattle, sheep, and goats reared; fishing. Manufactures lace, filigree, pottery. Has 8 m. of rly. Cap. Valetta. Area, 95 sq. m.; with Gozo and Comino, 122 sq. m.; pop. 231,000.

Mal'ton, tn., N. Riding, Yorks, England, on R. Derwent, 17 m. N.E. of York; comprises New Malton, Old Malton, and Norton; corn mills, breweries, foundries, implement works. Pop. 4,400.

Malvern (*mawl'vern*), or GREAT MALVERN, wat.-pl., on slope of Malvern Hills, Worcestershire, England; comprises town of Great Malvern and several villages; has a priory church, a college, and several hydropathic establishments; mineral springs. Pop. (dist.) 15,600.

Man, ISLE OF, isl. in Irish Sea, 10 m. from Wigtownshire, 28 from Cumberland, 38 from Ireland; surface undulating, sloping up from rocky coast to central ridge, which reaches 2,024 ft. in Snaefell; popular holiday resort. Administration is carried out by lieut.-gov., council, and House of Keys. Chief industries are fishing, agriculture, mining; live-stock is raised, and oats and turnips are important crops. There is considerable mineral wealth, salt, lead, zinc, copper, and silver being mined. Chief tns. are Douglas (cap.), Ramsey, Castletown, and Peel. Area, 236 sq. m.; pop. 49,300.

Manaar' (or MANNAR), GULF OF, inlet between Ceylon and India; pearl fisheries.

Manabi (*mä-nä-bē'*), coast prov., Ecuador, S. America; flat in W., hilly in E.; produces cacao, sugar. Cap. Puertoviejo. Area, 7,892 sq. m.; pop. 100,000.

Manacor (*ma-na-kōr'*), tn., isl. of Majorca, Balearic Islands, Spain; stalactite caves; summer resort; wine. Pop. 13,000.

Managua (*mä-nä'gwa*). (1) Cap., Nicaragua, Central America, on Lake Managua; exports coffee; trade centre; univ. Severe earthquake, 1931. Pop. 33,000. (2) Lake in Nicaragua; 38 m. long, 16 m. wide; area, 438 sq. m.

Manaos (*ma-nä'os*), city and port, Brazil, on R. Negro, near its junction with R. Amazon; important centre of river trade; exports rubber, Brazil nuts, fish, hides. Pop. 76,000.

Manche (*monsh*), mar. dep., N.W. France, on English Channel; surface hilly; cereals, flax, hemp, cider apples, pears cultivated; horses reared; cider manufactured; fisheries, dairy produce. Cap. Saint-Lô; on N. coast is Cherbourg. Area, 2,475 sq. m.; pop. 431,000.

Man'chester. (1) City, co. bor., S.E. Lancs, England; centre of great manufacturing district; great staple is cotton—spinning, weaving, bleaching, printing—Manchester being central market for cotton trade; there are also works that deal with silk and almost every description of fibre; engineering, and chemical and dye works; rubber and paper industries. Manchester Ship Canal, opened in 1894, converted city into fourth port in British Isles. Modern buildings include town hall, Victoria Univ., Royal Exchange, Rylands Library, new Royal Infirmary. The art gallery has a number of pre-Raphaelite paintings. Pop. 766,300. (2) Largest city in New Hampshire, U.S.A., on R. Merrimac; extensive manufactures of cotton and woollen goods, boots, shoes, cigars, machinery, locomotives. Pop. 77,000. (3) Tn., Connecticut, U.S.A., 8 m. E. of Hartford; silk goods. Pop. 18,000.

Manchuria (*man-choo're-a*), large terr. of N.E. China; almost entirely in basin of R. Sungari, trib. of Amur R., which forms N. and N.E. frontier; surface generally mountainous; chief industries, agriculture (soya beans, millet, wheat, rice) and cattle rearing; rich in minerals, including gold, iron, coal; valuable forests. Cap. Mukden. Area, 363,610 sq. m.; pop. 24,521,000.

Man'dalay, tn., Upper Burma, formerly cap., on R. Irrawaddy; contains the royal palace; silk weaving. Pop. 149,000.

Man'di, Indian hill state, Punjab, India, in R. Beas basin; hilly with fertile valleys; salt, rice, maize, sugar-cane. Area, 1,200 sq. m.; pop. 185,000.

Manfredo'nia, tn., S.E. Italy, on Gulf of Manfredonia; cathedral;

trade in grain, almonds, figs. Pop. 15,000.

Mangalore (*mang-ga-lōr'*), port, Malabar coast, Madras, India; rly. terminus; exports coffee, timber, tiles, salted fish, spices. Pop. 54,000.

Mangotsfield, urb. dist., Glos, England, 5 m. N.E. of Bristol; coal mining. Pop. 11,300.

Manhat'tan Island, island, 13 m. long, and from ⅛ to 2¼ m. broad, at mouth of R. Hudson, U.S.A.; it constitutes the borough of Manhattan in city of New York. Area, 22 sq. m.; pop. 1,945,000.

Manihiki (*ma-nē-hē'kē*), group of coral islands, Pacific Ocean, N.E. of Samoa; dependency of New Zealand; copra, guano. Pop. over 1,000.

Manil'a, port and cap., Philippine Islands, on S.W. coast of Luzon; cathedral and archbishop's palace, univ., and mint. Fine harbour; important commercial centre; exports Manila hemp (much used for cordage), rice, cigars, sugar, copra, coffee, indigo, dyewoods, mother-of-pearl, tortoise-shell. Pop. 285,000.

Manipur'. (1) Indian state, N.E. India, bordering on Assam and Burma; mountainous, extensive valley in centre; forested; produces rice, fruits, cotton; famous breed of ponies. Area, 8,456 sq. m.; pop. 384,000. (2) Or IMPHAL, cap. of above, 240 m. N.N.W. of Mandalay. Pop. 80,000.

Manis'a, tn., Asia Minor, 20 m. N.E. of Smyrna; commercial centre; cotton and silk manufactures. Pop. 92,000.

Manistee', city, summer resort, Michigan, U.S.A., on L. Michigan; lumber and salt manufactures; fruit culture. Pop. 12,000.

Manito'ba, prov., Canada, bounded E. by Hudson Bay, Ontario, S. by U.S.A., W. by Saskatchewan, N. by Keewatin; surface is generally undulating; many large lakes, including Winnipeg, Winnipegosis, Manitoba, Island, South Indian, and Etawney; drained by Rs. Churchill, Nelson, Winnipeg, Red, Saskatchewan, and other rivs. Great wheat-growing province; other cereals produced; live-stock raised, dairy farming carried on; coal in south; gypsum deposits; valuable fisheries. Cap. Winnipeg. Area, 251,832 sq. m.; pop. 639,000.

Manitowoc' ('spirit land'), city, Wisconsin, U.S.A., on Lake Michigan at mouth of R. Manitowoc; shipbuilding yards; iron and aluminium manufactures; canned goods, flour. Pop. 18,000.

Manizal'es, city, Colombia, S. America, 100 m. N.W. of Bogota; exports coffee and cocoa. Pop. 85,000.

Mankat'o, city, S. Minnesota, U.S.A., on R. Minnesota; agricultural implements; numerous mills, breweries, foundries. Pop. 12,000.

Mannar. See MANAAR.

Mannheim (*man'hīm*), tn., Baden, Germany, at confluence of Rs. Rhine and Neckar; at head of regular Rhine navigation and principal commercial centre of Baden; manufactures machinery, electrical plant, motor-cars, glass, chemicals, carpets. Pop. 247,000.

Manresa (*man-rā'sā*), city, N.E. Spain, 30 m. N.W. of Barcelona; manufactures cotton, linen, woollen yarns, paper, chemicals; iron foundries. Pop. 27,000.

Mans, LE (*mān*), tn., cap. Sarthe, France, 50 m. N.W. of Tours; manufactures linen goods, chemicals, tobacco, and ironmongery. Pop. 73,000.

Mans'field. (1) Tn., Notts, England, on R. Maun; ironfounding and coal mining; manufactures hosiery, lace, thread, boots. Pop. 46,100. (2) City, Ohio, U.S.A., 67 m. S.W. of Cleveland; agricultural implements, machinery, paper, rubber goods. Pop. 33,000.

Mansfield Woodhouse, urb. dist., Notts, England, 1½ m. N. of Mansfield; Roman remains; stone quarries. Pop. 13,700.

Mansur'a, tn., cap. Daqahlia, Nile Delta, Egypt; centre of cotton industry; linen and sailcloth factories. Pop. 64,000.

Mantes (*mānt*), tn., Seine-et-Oise, France, on R. Seine; trade in agricultural produce; musical instruments, baskets, brushes, hosiery. Pop. 10,000.

Mantua (*man'tū-a*). (1) Prov., Lombardy, Italy; low, level, and fertile; produces cereals, rice, vines, and mulberry trees; cattle breeding carried on. Area, 903 sq. m.; pop. 381,000. (2) Cap. of above, on R. Mincio, 22 m. S.S.W. of Verona; engine shops, tanneries, breweries; manufactures cellulose for paper and artificial manures. Birthplace of Virgil. Pop. 44,000.

Manzanares (*mān-thā-nā'res*). (1) Tn., central Spain, 20 m. E. of Ciudad Real; manufactures soap, pottery, and bricks; saffron, wine, and wheat produced. Pop. 16,000. (2) Riv., New Castile, Spain; affluent of R. Jarama; Madrid on its banks; length, 40 m.

Manzanillo (*mān-sā-nēl'yo*), port, S. Cuba, W. Indies; exports sugar, tobacco, hides, cedar, mahogany. Pop. 25,000.

Maracaibo (*mā-rā-kī'bo*). (1) City, Venezuela, S. America; important commercial centre; in centre of great oil-producing region; exports petroleum, coffee, cocoa, sugar, and rubber; shipbuilding yards. Pop. 75,000. (2) Lake, Venezuela, communicating with Gulf of Venezuela; entrance obstructed by shoals. Length, 130 m.; breadth, 60 m.

Maranhão (*mā-rān-yown'*), maritime state, Brazil, on Atlantic Ocean; mountainous in the S.; well-watered and fertile, yielding rice, cotton, sugar, coffee, tobacco, vanilla; live-stock reared; much of it occupied by forests; minerals include copper and gold. São Luiz is cap. Area, 177,515 sq. m.; pop. 1,109,000.

Marash', tn., Asia Minor, 90 m. N.E. of Alexandretta; trade in Kurd carpets, embroideries. Pop. 50,000.

Mar'athon, plain (5 m. long, 2 m. wide), N.E. Attica, Greece, between Mount Pentelicus and the sea; celebrated as scene of victory of Miltiades over Persians (490 B.C.).

Marazi'on, mkt. tn. and wat.-pl., Cornwall, England, on Mount's Bay; market gardening and pilchard fisheries. Pop. 1,100.

Mar'burg. (1) Tn., Hesse-Nassau, Prussia, on R. Lahn, 48 m. N. of Frankfurt; univ.; pottery, surgical instruments, iron goods. Pop. 23,000. (2) See MARIBOR.

March. (1) Mkt. tn., Isle of Ely, Cambridgeshire, England, on R. Nen, 7 m. S.S.W. of Wisbech; engineering; agricultural implements. Pop. 11,300. (2) See MORAVA (2).

Marches, dep. E. Italy, including provs. of Ancona, Ascoli, Piceno, Macerata, and Pesaro e Urbino. In W. are Apennine Mts. Chief products, maize, wine, tobacco; chief manufactures, silk, straw plait, paper. Largest tn., Ancona. Area, 3,702 sq. m.; pop. 1,219,000.

Marcianise (*mar-chā-nē'zā*), tn., Italy, 13 m. N. by E. of Naples; trades in fruit and grain. Pop. 13,000.

Marcinelle (*mar-sē-nel'*), tn., Hainaut, Belgium, 23 m. E. by S. of Mons; coal mines; steel works. Pop. 16,000.

Mardin (*mar-dēn'*), tn., Asia Minor, 50 m. S.S.E. of Diarbekr; centre of fruitful agricultural region; weaving of woollens and cottons. Pop. 22,000.

Maree', LOCH, lake, W. Ross and Cromarty, Scotland; length, 12½ m.; breadth, ½ m. to 2¼ m.; has several islands; fishing.

Mareo'tis, LAKE, or BIRKET-EL-MARIUT, lagoon, Lower Egypt, separated from Mediterranean Sea by narrow ridge of sand on which is Alexandria.

Margarita (*mar-ga-rē'ta*), isl., Caribbean Sea, off Venezuela, to which it belongs; mountainous (Macanao, 4,490 ft.); pearl fishing and salt making; deposits of magnesite. Area, 400 sq. m.; pop. 69,000.

Mar'gate, munic. bor., wat.-pl., Isle of Thanet, Kent, England; popular holiday resort. Pop. 31,300.

Marghera. See under VENICE.

Margilan, tn., Ferghana, Central Asia, U.S.S.R., 150 m. S.E. of Tashkent; camel's-hair, woollen, and silk stuffs. Pop. 43,000. Nine miles S. is New Margilan. See FERGHANA.

Marian'as Islands, or LADRONES, archipelago, w. Pacific Ocean; comprise ten volcanic islands, four inhabited, also four inhabited coral islands, including Guam (U.S.A. dependency). Chief export, copra. Mandated to Japan, 1919. Total area (excluding Guam) is *c.* 250 sq. m.; pop. *c.* 10,000.

Maria-Theresiopel. See SUBOTICA.

Mar'ibor, formerly MARBURG, tn., Slovenia, Yugoslavia, on R. Drave; leather goods, wine; large rly. workshops. Pop. 31,000.

Marie Galante (*ma-rē ga-lont'*), isl., French W. Indies, dependency of Guadeloupe; rocky plateau with fertile soil; coffee, sugar, and cotton. Chief town, Grand Bourg. Area, 55 sq. m.; pop. 23,000.

Marienbad (*mä-rē-en-bät'*), wat.-pl., w. Bohemia, Czechoslovakia; saline springs. Pop. 6,900.

Marienburg (*mä-rē'en-boorg*), tn., E. Prussia, 27 m. S.E. of Danzig; sawmilling; sugar, agricultural implements. Pop. 21,000.

Marienwerder (*ma-rē'en-ver-der*), tn., E. Prussia, Germany, near R. Vistula; iron foundries, sawmills, sugar refineries. Pop. 14,000.

Mariet'ta, city, Ohio, U.S.A., at junction of Rs. Muskingum and Ohio; dist. rich in coal, iron, petroleum, and natural gas; foundry products, leather. Pop. 15,000.

Marinette, city, Wisconsin, U.S.A., on inlet of Lake Michigan, 220 m. N.E. of Chicago; paper, pulp, lumber, and sawmills; good harbour. Pop. 14,000.

Mar'ion. (1) City, Indiana, U.S.A., 60 m. N.E. of Indianapolis, on R. Mississinewa; glass, iron, pulp, paper; large trade in grain. Pop. 24,000. (2) City, Ohio, U.S.A., 43 m. N.W. of Columbus; an agricultural centre; machinery; agricultural implements. Pop. 31,000.

Maritime Alps. See ALPS.

Maritime Provinces, general name for Canadian provinces on Atlantic coast—Nova Scotia, New Brunswick, and Prince Edward Island.

Marit'sa, riv. of Balkan Peninsula, rises in Rhodope Mts., flows past Philippopolis to Adrianople, from which to its mouth it forms boundary between Turkey and Greece. Length, 300 m.

Mariupol (*ma-re-oo'pol*), port, Ukraine, U.S.S.R., on Sea of Azov; exports cereals, linseed, coal, and iron. Pop. 41,000.

Mar'ket Dray'ton, or DRAYTON-IN-HALES, tn., Shropshire, England, 18 m. N.E. of Shrewsbury; grammar school (1554); beer, agricultural machinery. Pop. 4,700.

Mar'ket Har'borough, tn., Leicestershire, England, 16 m. S.E. of Leicester; hunting centre; textiles, boots and shoes. Pop. 9,300.

Mark'inch, par. and burgh, Fife, Scotland, 4 m. S. of Ladybank; paper mills and bleachfields, distillery. Pop. (burgh) 2,000.

Marl'boro, city, Massachusetts, U.S.A., 28 m. W. of Boston; boots and shoes and shoemaking machinery. Pop. 15,000.

Marlborough (*mawl'boro*). (1) Tn., Wilts, England, on R. Kennet; rope making and brewing; public school. Pop. 3,500. (2) Provincial dist., S. Island, New Zealand; in N.E. of isl.; sheltered; mainly pastoral. Chief tn., Blenheim. Area, 4,225 sq. m.; pop. 18,500.

Mar'low, tn., Bucks, England, on R. Thames; river resort; paper mills, brewing, lace, chairs. Pop. 5,100.

Marmande (*mar-mand'*), tn., Lot-et-Garonne, on R. Garonne; woollens, brandy; iron foundries. Pop. 6,500.

Mar'mara, SEA OF, separates Asia Minor from Europe; communicates by Bosporus with Black Sea and by Dardanelles with Ægean; 117 m. long, 50 m. broad; area, 4,500 sq. m.; maximum depth, 4,250 ft.; no good harbours; largest isl. Marmara, 50 sq. m., famous for marble and alabaster.

Marne (*marn*). (1) Riv., N. France, rising on plateau of Langres (Haute-Marne), flows N.W. and W. past Châlons, Epernay, and Meaux to join Seine, 2 m. S.E. of Paris. Navigable to St. Dizier. Scene of critical battle of Great War (1914). Length, 326 m. (2) Dep., France, bisected by R. Marne; centre, gently-rolling country; the rest, flat and monotonous; well suited for cereals and champagne; wine matured in cellars of Reims, Epernay, and Châlons (chief tn. of dep.); tanneries, iron and copper foundries, breweries, potteries, and textile mills. Area, 3,167 sq. m.; pop. 398,000.

Marne, HAUTE-. See HAUTE-MARNE.

Maros-Vásárhely. See TARGUL-MURES.

Mar'ple, par. and urb. dist., Cheshire, England, 9 m. S.E. of Manchester; cotton factories. Pop. 7,400.

Marquesas Islands (*mar-kă'sas*), archipelago of volcanic islands, S. Pacific Ocean; annexed to France (1842); mountainous, fertile; bananas, bread-fruit, sugar-cane, copra, yams. Area, 480 sq. m.; pop. 2,500.

Marquette (*mar-ket'*), city, Michigan, U.S.A., on S. shore of Lake Superior; exports iron ore; iron smelting and manufacture of lumber; large railway works. Pop. 13,000.

Marra'kesh, or MOROCCO CITY, one of the capitals, and largest tn. of Morocco, Africa; beautiful situation; manufactures leather; centre for produce of S. Morocco. Pop. 149,000.

Marsala (*-să'la*), port, W. Sicily; gives its name to a wine of the sherry type; brandy. Pop. 31,000.

Mars'den, par. and tn., W. Riding, Yorks, England, 7 m. W.S.W. of Huddersfield; woollen, cotton, and silk factories. Pop. 5,700.

Marseilles, or MARSEILLE (*mar-sālz'*; French *mār-sī*), chief tn., Bouches-du-Rhône, France, on Mediterranean Sea; second city and chief commercial port of France; built on four hills with background of mountains; spacious modern docks; called at by Brit. liners to India and Australia; leading articles of trade: coal, oil-seeds, grain, soap, petroleum, wine; manufactures sugar, soda, glass, tiles, tobacco, matches, soap and candles; refines oil and has ore-smelting works. Pop. 652,000.

Mar'shall, city, Texas, U.S.A., 145 m. E. of Dallas; large railway shops; canning; foundries; bricks, baskets, cotton-seed oil. Pop. 14,000.

Mar'shall Islands, archipelago, Pacific Ocean; two groups—Radak (thirteen islands) in E., and Ralik (eleven islands) in W.; mandated to Japan; sugar-cane and cotton; exports copra. Total area, 150 sq. m.; pop. 10,000.

Mar'shalltown, city, Iowa, U.S.A., 48 m. N.E. of Des Moines; iron and steel; tinned foods; machinery and engines. Pop. 16,000.

Martigny (*mar-tēn-yē'*), three connected villages, Valais, Switzerland, 24 m. S.E. of L. Geneva; tourist resort; starting point for Chamonix. Pop. 5,700.

Martinique (*mar-tin-ēk'*), isl., French W. Indies, one of the Lesser Antilles; culminates in Mont Pelée (4,430 ft.); sugar, cocoa, rum, coffee, tobacco, pineapples, bananas. Chief tn. and commercial cap. Fort-de-France; St. Pierre totally destroyed by eruption of Mont Pelée in 1902. Area, 385 sq. m.; pop. 235,000.

Mar'tinsburg, town, W. Virginia, U.S.A., 65 m. N.W. of Washington; cider and cider vinegar; hosiery and worsteds; slate and limestone; railway repair shops. Pop. 13,000.

Mar'tin's Ferry, tn., Ohio, U.S.A., on R. Ohio; coal mining; iron and steel products. Pop. 12,000.

Mar'tock, par. and vil., Somerset, England, 7 m. N.W. of Yeovil; glove and jute-matting factories. Pop. (par.) 2,100.

Mar'tos, tn., Andalusia, S. Spain, 12 m. W.S.W. of Jaen; grain, wine; and oil. Pop. (comm.) 20,000.

Maryborough. (1) Co. tn., co. Leix, I.F.S.; market town with flour mills. Pop. 3,300. (2) Munic. tn., Victoria, Australia, 112 m. N.W. of Melbourne; railway centre; gold mining. Pop. 6,000. (3) Tn., Queensland, Australia, 180 m. N. of Brisbane; centre of Gympie gold field; coal, timber, and sugar; engineering works. Pop. 12,000.

Maryland, South Atlantic State, U.S.A.; bounded N. by Pennsylvania, E. by Delaware and Atlantic, S. and S.W. by Virginia, W. by W. Virginia; has only about 35 m. of coast on Atlantic, but Chesapeake Bay, the Susquehanna, Patapsco, and Potomac rivs. provide harbours; surface rises to Blue Ridge dist. of Appalachians; coal mined in extreme W.; iron, chrome, copper, brick-clay, marble, soap-stone also worked; pine, chestnut, oak, hickory, and walnut trees; lumbering important. Produces tobacco, fruits, vegetables, cereals; large trade in tinned fruit and vegetables. Live-stock raised, and dairy farming carried on. Valuable fisheries, especially oysters. Manufactures cottons, woollens, iron and steel, tin wares, flour, artificial manures. Cap. Annapolis; largest tn., Baltimore. Area, 12,327 sq. m.; pop. 1,616,000.

Marylebone, St. (*măr'i-bŭn*), metropolitan bor. of N.W. London; residential dist.; contains Regent's Park, also Lord's Cricket Ground, headquarters of Marylebone Cricket Club (M.C.C.). Pop. 97,600.

Maryport, port, Cumberland, England, on Irish Sea; coal mining; ironworks, sawmills, shipbuilding; good harbour and docks. Pop. 10,200.

Masaya (*ma-sī'a*), tn., Nicaragua, Central America, on Lake Masaya; tobacco, beans, sugar, coffee, and maize grown in vicinity. Pop. 14,000.

Mascar'a, tn., Oran, Algeria, N. Africa, 60 m. E. of Oran; white wine; trade in oil and cereals. Pop. 28,000.

Masham (*măs'am*), urb. dist., N. Riding, Yorks, England, on R. Ure, 8 m. N.W. of Ripon; sheep fair. Pop. 2,000.

Masho'naland, region, S. Rhodesia, S. Africa, between Matabeleland and R. Zambezi; plateau (alt. 3,000–5,000 ft.); gold, silver, and copper mines; maize, tobacco, citrous fruits; traversed by rly. from Salisbury to Beira. Chief tn., Salisbury. Mashonas are branch of Bantu peoples.

Ma'son City, N. Iowa, U.S.A.; cement, lime, bricks, tiles; beet sugar. Pop. 20,000.

Mas'sa, city, Tuscany, Italy, 26 m. N.W. of Pisa; centre of Carrara marble industry; paper, olive oil, tobacco. Pop. 39,000.

Massachu'setts, New England State, U.S.A., bounded N. by Vermont and New Hampshire, E. by Atlantic Ocean, S. by Atlantic Ocean, Rhode Island, Connecticut, W. by New York State; off coast are Martha's Vineyard and Nantucket islands; surface undulating, reaching height of over 3,500 ft. in W., which is occupied by Berkshire Hills, part of Appalachians; highest peak is Mt. Greylock (3,530 ft.). Drained by Rs. Housatonic, Connecticut, Millers, Merrimac, and Chicopee. Considerable area wooded, and valleys fertile; maize, potatoes, tobacco, and small fruits grown; centre of U.S.A. whale, deep-sea, and coast fishing; important centre also of commerce and export. Manufactures boots and shoes, cottons, woollens, iron and steel goods; mining is unimportant. Cap. Boston; other large tns., Worcester, Springfield, Fall River, Cambridge. Area, 8,266 sq. m.; pop. 4,290,000.

Massaw'a, fort. port, Eritrea, on coral isl. in Red Sea; pearl fishing; chief port for Abyssinia and Anglo-Egyptian Sudan; exports hides, coffee, ivory, wax. Pop. 12,000.

Mas'sillon, city, Ohio, U.S.A., 50 m. S.E. of Cleveland; coal mines; machinery, glass, enamel ware. Pop. 26,000.

Masulipatam', port, cap. of Kistna, Madras, India, on Coromandel coast; cotton manufactures; rice mills. Pop. 44,000.

Matabe'leland, or Matabililand, dist., S. Rhodesia, S. Africa, on plateau sloping S. to R. Limpopo; contains Matopo Hills; fertile; cereals, sugar, cotton; forested; some gold; traversed by rly. from Bulawayo (chief tn.) to Victoria; Matabele are Zulu warriors of Bantu stock and number *c.* 250,000.

Matad'i, riv. port, Belgian Congo,

near mouth of R. Congo; has railway communication with Stanley Pool. Pop. 15,000.

Matamo'ros, frontier tn., Mexico, near mouth of Rio Grande; trade with U.S.A. in horses, cattle, hides. Pop. 18,000.

Matan'zas. (1) Prov., Cuba; sugar, rice, tobacco. Area, 3,256 sq. m.; pop. 348,000. (2) Port, cap. of above, 58 m. E. of Havana; exports sugar, molasses, cigars. Pop. 63,000.

Mataro', port, Barcelona, Spain, on Mediterranean Sea; textiles, chemicals, paper, soap; fisheries. Pop. 24,000.

Matera (*mä-tä'rä*), tn., S. Italy, 34 m. N.W. of Taranto; leather, oil-pressing; cave habitations. Pop. 18,000.

Mat'lock, wat.-pl., on R. Derwent, Derbyshire, England; hot springs; manufactures cotton and paper; urb. dist. includes Matlock Bath. Pop. 10,600.

Matopo Hills, culmination of Matabele tableland, S. Rhodesia, S. Africa, between Limpopo and Zambezi rivs.; burial-place of Cecil Rhodes and Sir Starr Jameson is called 'World's View,' 27 m. S. of Bulawayo. Length, 100 m.; breadth, 25 m.

Matsumai. See FUKUYAMA.

Matsumo'to, tn., Honshu, Japan, 140 m. N.W. of Tokyo; trade in cocoons and silkworm eggs. Pop. 63,000.

Mat'terhorn, peak of the Alps, on border between Valais, Switzerland, and Piedmont, Italy; height, 14,780 ft.; an immense rock pinnacle; first ascended (1865) by Whymper.

Mat'to Gros'so, a western state of Brazil, bordering on Bolivia; forms part of Brazilian plateau; traversed by several low mountain chains; much dense forest; rich in minerals; diamonds; chief industry, cattle raising. Cap. Cuyaba. Area, 532,210 sq. m.; pop. 337,000.

Mattoon', city, Illinois, U.S.A., 50 m. W. of Terre Haute; foundries, machine shops; flour, brooms, bricks, tiles. Pop. 14,000.

Maubeuge', tn., Nord, France, on R. Sambre; metal goods; machine tools; rly. jn. Pop. 22,000.

Mauchline (*mawch'lin*), tn. and par., on R. Ayr, Ayrshire, Scotland; curling stones; associated with poet Burns. Pop. (par.) 2,300.

Mauna Lo'a (*mow'na*), active volcano (13,650 ft.), Hawaii; largest in world; on E. slope is crater of Kilauea.

Maurita'nia, colony, French W. Africa, bounded on W. by Atlantic; mostly in Sahara; produces gum and salt; live-stock reared. Area, 154,400 sq. m.; pop. 289,000.

Mauritius (*maw-rish'us*), Brit. isl., in Indian Ocean, 500 m. E. of Madagascar; volcanic, surrounded by coral reefs; surface consists of tableland, with mountains some 2,000 ft. high. Several volcanic lakes, of which Grand Bassin is largest; hurricanes frequently occur between Dec. and April. Produces sugar, spice, vanilla, fibres, rice, coconut oil, ebony, ironwood, bamboo, aloes, benzoin. Cap. Port Louis. Area, 720 sq. m.; pop. 385,000.

Max'welltown, tn., Dumfriesshire, Scotland, on R. Nith; woollens, hosiery; dyeworks, sawmills. Now part of Dumfries.

May, ISLE OF, isl. at entrance to Firth of Forth; 1 m. long; sheep grazing; abounds in sea-fowl.

Mayaguez (*mī-ä-gwez'*), port, Porto Rico, on W. coast; exports sugar, tobacco, coffee. Pop. 19,000.

Mayavaram', tn., on R. Cauvery, Tanjore, Madras, India; fine cloth manufactures. Pop. 24,000.

Maybole (*mā'bōl*), tn., Ayrshire, Scotland, 9 m. S. of Ayr; boots and shoes, agricultural implements. Pop. 4,200.

Mayence. See MAINZ.

Mayenne (*mä-yen'*). (1) Dep., France; surface varied and well wooded; drained by R. Mayenne, trib. of R. Loire; principal industries, agriculture, stone quarrying, cattle and horse raising; manufacture of coarse textiles. Cap. Laval. Area, 1,986 sq. m.; pop. 260,000. (2) Tn., in above, on R. Mayenne; cloth manufactures. Pop. 6,000.

May'field, par. and tn., Sussex, England, 17 m. N. of Eastbourne; roof tiles; ruins of palace formerly country seat of Archbishops of Canterbury. Pop. (par.) 3,500.

Maynooth', tn., Kildare, I.F.S., 12 m. W. of Dublin; seat of R.C. college for priests (founded 1795). Pop. 800.

May'o, mar. co. of Connaught, I.F.S., bounded by Sligo, Roscommon, Galway, Atlantic Ocean; mountainous in W., flat in E.; coast much indented; drained by R. Moy; contains Lough Conn and other lakes; cattle rearing, salmon and other fisheries, linen weaving. Chief tns., Castlebar (co. tn.), Ballina. Area, 2,084 sq. m.; pop. 173,000.

Mayotte', one of Comoro Islands, in Mozambique Channel, Africa; a French possession; vanilla, sugar, cacao. Area, 140 sq. m.; pop. 12,600.

May'wood, tn., Illinois, U.S.A., on R. Desplaines, adjoining Chicago; largely residential; manufactures include tin cans, ginger ale, and locomotive supplies. Pop. 26,000.

Mazagan', port, Atlantic coast, Morocco, Africa; exports agricultural produce and eggs. Pop. 19,000.

Mazamet (*mä-zä-ma'*), tn., Tarn, France, 50 m. E. of Toulouse; wool, tanning; stronghold of French Protestantism. Pop. 11,000.

Mazanderan', prov., N. Persia, between Caspian Sea on N. and Elburz Mts. on S.; mostly level; partly under cultivation; yields rice, cotton, sugar, fruits, iron ore. Area, 10,460 sq. m.; pop. 200,000.

Mazar'i-Sharif', tn., Afghanistan, 11 m. S.E. of Balkh; military centre, fortress of Takhtapul. Pop. 46,000.

Mazarron', tn., Murcia, S. Spain, 18 m. W. of Cartagena; iron and lead mines; flour mills, soap works. Pop. 18,000.

Mazatlan', port, Mexico, on Pacific Ocean; exp. hides, gold, silver, copper, fruit, gums. Pop. 28,000.

Mazzara del Vallo (*mät-sä'rä*), walled city, W. Sicily; oil, linseed, corn; sulphur springs. Pop. 22,000.

Mazzarino (*mät-sä-rē'no*), tn., central Sicily; sulphur springs; wine; agricultural produce. Pop. 20,000.

Mead'ville, city, Pennsylvania, U.S.A., 40 m. S. of Erie; railway and boiler shops. Pop. 15,000.

Meath, mar. co., Leinster, I.F.S.; surface level and undulating; traversed by R. Boyne; almost entirely under pasture; coarse linens and woollen goods. Cap. Trim. Area, 903 sq. m.; pop. 63,000.

Meaux (*mō*), tn., Seine-et-Marne, France, 25 m. E.N.E. of Paris; has 12th cent. cathedral; trade in cheese, corn, eggs, and poultry. Pop. 12,000.

Mec'ca, cap. of Hejaz and Nejd, Arabia; sacred city of Mohammedans; Mohammed was born here about 571. Principal building is Great Mosque, in which is the Kaaba, a small oblong building containing the sacred black stone, towards which all Moslems turn in worship. Pop. 85,000.

Mechlin. See MALINES.

Meck'lenburg, region, N. Germany, consisting of two republics, Mecklenburg-Schwerin and Mecklenburg-Strelitz, at W. end of Baltic Sea, along which there is coast-line of *c.* 66 m.; surface flat, with low ridge in centre; numerous lakes; produces cereals, amber; manufactures beet sugar, beer, spirits, leather; is famous for sheep, cattle, pigs, horses. Mecklenburg-Schwerin, cap. Wismar. Area, 5,066 sq. m.; pop. 674,000. Mecklenburg-Strelitz, cap. Neu-Strelitz. Area, 1,131 sq. m.; pop. 110,000.

Medellin (*mā-del-yēn'*), tn., Colombia, S. America, 150 m. N.W. of Bogota; univ.; commercial centre; manufactures cotton and woollen goods, cigars and cigarettes, hats, crockery, matches. Pop. 120,000.

Med'ford, tn., Massachusetts, U.S.A., residential suburb of Boston; manufactures chemicals, bricks, machinery, woollens. Pop. 60,000.

Med'icine Hat, tn., S.E. Alberta, Canada, on S. Saskatchewan R.; rly. jn.; coal mines, natural gas supplies; flour mills. Pop. 10,000.

Medina (*me-dē'na*), tn., Hejaz, Arabia; second great holy city of the

Mohammedans; contains tomb of Mohammed; strongly fortified; principal building is mosque; railway opened to Damascus in 1908. Pop. 30,000.

Medinet. See FAIYUM.

Mediterra'nean Sea, great inland sea, with Europe on N., Asia on E., Africa on S.; communicating with Atlantic by Strait of Gibraltar, with Black Sea by Dardanelles, Sea of Marmara, and Bosporus; with Red Sea by Suez Canal; uninfluenced by oceanic tidal wave; three basins of great depth revealed by soundings—viz., western basin, W. of Corsica and Sardinia, greatest depth, 10,322 ft., W. of Sardinia; Tyrrhenian depression, between Corsica and Sardinia, Sicily and Italy; eastern basin, between S. Italy and coast of Palestine; greatest depth, the Pola Deep (14,436 ft.), lying between Malta and Crete. Submerged mountains, known as the Adventure Bank, connect Sicily with Tunis. Owing to great evaporation, salinity of Mediterranean is slightly greater than that of the Atlantic, and the deep blue colour of its waters is well known. There is a constant surface current from Atlantic into Mediterranean, and also one from Black Sea. Chief islands are Balearic, Sardinia, Corsica, Sicily, Crete, Cyprus. Many species of fish inhabit the waters, and the sponge, tunny, and sardine fisheries are important. Greatest length, 2,330 m.; greatest breadth, 495 m. Area, 1,145,000 sq. m.

Medoc, dist., Gironde, France, along R. Gironde; famous wines.

Med'way, riv., Kent, England; headstreams rise in Sussex and in Surrey; at Sheerness enters R. Thames by estuary 12 m. long. Tns. on banks: Tonbridge, Maidstone, Rochester, Chatham. Length, 60 m.

Meerane (*mā-rä'nä*), tn., Saxony, Germany, 27 m. N.W. of Chemnitz; centre of cloth and woollen trade; dyeing and tanning. Pop. 24,000.

Mee'rut. (1) Dist., United Provinces, India; between Rs. Ganges and Jumna; well forested; maize, wheat, sugar-cane, pulses. Area, 2,354 sq. m.; pop. 150,000. (2) Cap. of above; scene of outbreak of Indian Mutiny (1857). Pop. 123,000.

Meiderich. See DUISBURG.

Meiktil'a, dist., Mandalay, Burma; rolling plain with low rainfall; rice, cotton, ground-nuts, peas, maize. Area, 2,287 sq. m.; pop. 290,000.

Meiningen (*mī'ning-en*), tn., S.W. Thuringia, Germany, on R. Werra; breweries, foundries; pottery, paper, chemicals. Pop. 18,000.

Meissen (*mī'sen*), tn., Saxony, Germany, on R. Elbe; noted for manufacture of 'Dresden china'; foundries, textile mills, earthenware, glass, explosives, matches. Gothic cathedral. Pop. 45,000.

Mek'nes, or MEQUINEZ, one of the caps. of Morocco, 36 m. W. by S. of Fez; centre of fertile dist. with olive plantations. Pop. 25,000.

Mekong (*mā-kong'*), riv., Indo-China; rises in Tibet; separates Annam and Siam; enters China Sea by two great arms; length, 2,800 m.

Melane'sia ('islands of the blacks'), collective name for chain of island groups in Pacific Ocean, curving round from New Guinea, comprising New Britain, Solomon, Santa Cruz, New Hebrides, New Caledonia, Loyalty, and other archipelagos. Inhabited by distinct Negro race known as Melanesians.

Melbourne (*mel'burn*). (1) Cap., Victoria, Australia; observatory, mint, univ.; fine parks and public gardens; great gold, wool, and farm-produce centre; fine harbour; exports frozen meat, wool, dairy produce, fruit, wine, grain. Pop. 1,000,000. (2) Tn. and par., Derbyshire, England, 7½ m. S.E. of Derby; market gardens; thread, silk, boots. Pop. (par.) 3,600.

Melilla (*mā-lēl'yä*), fort. port, and Spanish convict settlement, N. coast of Morocco; exports hæmatite, lead, zinc. Pop. 61,000.

Melks'ham, mkt. tn. and urb. dist., Wilts, England, on R. Bristol Avon; dairy-farming dist.; manufactures woollen goods, cordage, horsehair cloth; has engineering and rubber works. Pop. 3,900.

Melos. See MILO.

Mel'rose. (1) Mkt. tn., Roxburghshire, Scotland, on R. Tweed; dist. associated with Sir Walter Scott; ruins of Cistercian abbey (1136); holiday resort. Pop. 2,100. (2) City, Massachusetts, U.S.A.; suburb of Boston; manufactures rubber shoes, silver goods. Pop. 20,000.

Mel'tham, urb. dist., W. Riding, Yorks, England, 5 m. S.W. of Huddersfield; woollen, cotton, thread mills. Pop. 5,100.

Melton Mowbray (*mō'brā*), tn., N.E. Leicestershire, England; a hunting centre; pork pies, Stilton cheese. Pop. 10,400.

Melun (*mā-lun'*), chief tn., Seine-et-Marne, France, on R. Seine; agricultural implements, leather; mkt. for farm produce. Pop. 14,000.

Memel. See KLAIPEDA and NIEMEN.

Mem'mingen, tn., S.W. Bavaria, Germany; machinery, emery cloth, ropes, textiles. Pop. 14,000.

Mem'phis. (1) Anc. tn. of Egypt, 12 m. S. of Cairo; once cap., now in ruins. (2) Tn., Tennessee, U.S.A., on R. Mississippi; great export of cotton; rly. centre; lumber, oil, cotton seed and cake, foundry products. Pop. 252,000.

Menai Strait (*men'ī*), channel between Anglesey and Carnarvonshire, Wales, from ⅛ to 2 m. wide; 14 m. long; crossed by road suspension bridge and Britannia Tubular Bridge (railway).

Menam (*mā-näm'*), or MENAM CHAO BHRAYA, riv., Siam, flows by several mouths into Gulf of Siam; length, *c.* 900 m.; great highway of trade; Bangkok stands near mouth.

Mende (*mond*), chief tn., Lozère, France, on R. Lot; manufactures serges and shalloons. Pop. 6,000.

Men'dip Hills, range of hills, Somersetshire, England; highest point, Blackdown (1,067 ft.); numerous caverns and 'swallow-holes.'

Mendoza (*men-dō'thä*). (1) Prov., Argentina, S. America; mountainous in W.; drained by R. Mendoza and other rivs.; coal, petroleum; cereals, alfalfa, tobacco, wine. Area, 56,502 sq. m.; pop. 397,000. (2) Cap. of above; produces wine, fruit; on railway from Buenos Aires to Valparaiso. Pop. 59,000.

Menin, tn., W. Flanders, Belgium, on R. Lys; textiles, rubber goods, soap; flax and tobacco cultivated in neighbourhood. Pop. 19,000.

Menom'inee ('wild rice'), city, Michigan, U.S.A., on Green Bay; ships lumber, paper, pulp, beet sugar, electrical machinery. Pop. 11,000.

Men'ston, par., vil., Yorks, England, 12 m. N.W. of Leeds; bleach-works, stone quarries. Pop. (par.) 3,800.

Mentä'wei, group of islands off W. coast of Sumatra, Dutch E. Indies; thickly forested; tobacco, sugar-cane, coconuts. Pop. 8,000.

Menteith (*men-tēth'*), LAKE OF, lake, S.W. Perthshire, Scotland; contains three islets, to one of which, Inchmahome, Mary Queen of Scots was sent after battle of Pinkie (1547).

Mento'ne (French, *Menton*), tn., Alpes-Maritimes, France; popular winter resort of Riviera; trade in olive oil, wine, and perfumes. Pop. 20,000.

Menzies (*men'zēs*), tn., W. Australia; trade centre of the N. Coolgardie and Mount Magnet goldfields. Pop. 2,500.

Mep'pel, tn., Drente, Holland; important trade in butter, eggs, cattle; dyeing; shipbuilding. Pop. 12,000.

Mequinez. See MEKNES.

Merano (*mā-rä'no*), tn., Tyrol, N. Italy, 42 m. N. of Trent; health resort. Pop. 19,000.

Mergui (*mer-gē'*). (1) District, Tenasserim, Lower Burma; rich in timber, especially teak; tin found, but little worked. Area, 9,790 sq. m.; pop. 135,000. (2) Port, cap. of above; pearl fishing of Mergui Archipelago centred here; exports salted fish, rubber, tin. Pop. 17,000.

Mergui Archipelago, group of islands, Bay of Bengal, Lower Burma; mountainous; covered with teak trees; rice and other crops; great pearl-fishing area.

Merida (*mer'e-da*). (1) City, Badajoz, Spain, on R. Guadiana; Roman antiquities; rly. jn. Pop. 16,000. (2) Tn., Venezuela, near L. Maracaibo; manufactures woollen and cotton goods. Pop. 16,000. (3) City, cap., Yucatan, Mexico; univ.; centre of sisal-hemp industry; manufactures ropes, soap, cigars, and brandy. Pop. 79,000.

Mer'iden, city, Connecticut, U.S.A., 18 m. N. of New Haven; silver and silver-plate, hardware, cut glass. Pop. 38,000.

Merid'ian, city, E. Mississippi, U.S.A.; has machine shops, lumber and grist mills, foundries, cotton and oil mills; important rly. jn. Pop. 33,000.

Merion'eth, coast co., N. Wales; surface rugged, reaching over 2,900 ft.; among highest peaks is Cader Idris; drained by rivs. Dee, Dovey, and other streams. Has excellent breed of ponies; sheep reared; slate and limestone quarries; manufactures woollens. Cap. Dolgelly. Area, 660 sq. m.; pop. 43,200.

Mer'sea, island, Essex, England, between estuaries of Rs. Colne and Blackwater; noted for oysters; protected by strong sea-wall.

Mer'seburg, tn., Saxony, Prussia, on R. Saale, 9 m. S. of Halle; cathedral; one of oldest towns in Germany; tanning, brewing, metal founding; market gardening. Pop. 26,000.

Mer'sey, riv., England; rises in Derbyshire; flows W.; joined by Irwell; enters Irish Sea by estuary 18 m. long; ranks next to Thames in commercial importance. Chief port, Liverpool. Length, 70 m.

Mersina (*mer-sē'na*), port, Adana, S. Asia Minor; exports cotton, wool, cereals, fruit, timber. Pop. 46,000.

Merst'ham, par. and vil., Surrey, England, 2 m. N. of Redhill; lime-works; firestone quarries. Pop. (par.) 3,650.

Mer'thyr Tyd'fil ('Tydfil the Martyr'), co. bor., Glamorganshire, Wales, on R. Taff; rich in coal and iron; ironworks; brick and tile making. Pop. 71,100.

Mer'ton and Mor'den, urb. dist., Surrey, England, 3½ m. S. of Clapham Junction, London; part of Greater London; remains of priory. Pop. 41,300.

Merv, tn. and oasis, Turkmen Rep., Asia, U.S.S.R.; produces cereals, fruit; live-stock; woollen carpets; in cotton dist. Pop. of oasis, 253,000; of tn., 19,000.

Mesh'ed, tn., Khurasan, N.E. Persia; silks, carpets, rugs, shawls, sword-blades manufactured. Pop. 85,000.

Mesopotamia. See IRAQ.

Messina (*mes-sē'nä*). (1) Prov., Sicily, Italy; traversed by mountain chains (highest point, 6,055 ft.); produces corn, flax, fruit, sulphur, copper, oil. Area, 1,254 sq. m.; pop. 645,000. (2) Cap. of above, on Strait of Messina; manufactures silks, muslin, chemicals, coral ornaments; suffers from earthquakes; city devastated in 1908 and over 80,000 lives lost. Pop. 204,000. (3) STRAIT OF, separates Sicily from Italy; deep channel, strong current; 'races' in strait are the Scylla and Charybdis of *Odyssey*. Length, 19 m.

Meth'il, tn., Fife, Scotland, on Firth of Forth; forms burgh with Buckhaven and Innerleven; exports coal.

Methu'en, town, Massachusetts, U.S.A., 10 m. N.E. of Lowell; hats, shoes, cottons, woollens manufactured. Pop. 15,000.

Metz, fort. tn., Moselle, France, on R. Moselle; fine Gothic cathedral; leather goods, preserved fruit, poultry, wine, tobacco. Pop. 70,000.

Meudon (*moo-don'*), tn., France, suburb of Paris; glassworks; ammunition, linen, buttons; observatory. Forest a holiday resort of Parisians. Pop. 18,000.

Meurthe-et-Moselle (*moort-ā-mō-zel'*), frontier dep., N.E. France; hilly; drained by R. Moselle and affluents; forests, vines, fruits, sugar-beet, hops, tobacco. Chief tn. Nancy. Area, 2,036 sq. m.; pop. 552,000.

Meuse. (1) Or MAAS, river, rises in Haute-Marne, France; flows through Belgium and Holland; joins the Waal, left branch of R. Rhine; length, 570 m., 400 navigable. (2) Dep., N.E. France; surface undulating; in W., Forest of Argonne; in E., plateau of Woëvre; drained by R. Meuse; forests; horse breeding; cereals, beetroot, hemp, wine. Chief tn., Bar-le-Duc. Area, 2,408 sq. m.; pop. 218,000.

Mevagis'sey, par., vil., Cornwall, England, 5 m. S. of St. Austell; summer resort; fishing. Pop. 1,750.

Mex'borough, urb. dist., W. Riding, Yorks, England, 11 m. N.E. of Sheffield; ironworks, potteries; glass bottles, grindstones. Pop. 15,900.

Mex'ico. (1) Rep. in S. of N. America; bounded on N. by U.S.A., E. by Gulf of Mexico and Caribbean Sea, S. by Brit. Honduras and Guatemala, and W. by the Pacific. The Rio Grande forms N. boundary for over 1,100 m. Peninsula of Yucatan lies to E. of Bay of Campeachy; on W. is peninsula of Lower California; coastal strip is bordered by mt. ranges—Sierra Madre (9,000 ft.) on W., and on E. line of heights (16,000 ft.), sometimes called Sierra Madre Oriental. Low ground extends along peninsula of Yucatan. Between Sierra Madre ranges stretches great central plateau, with height varying from 7,000 to 8,000 ft. Many dormant and extinct volcanoes (Orizaba, 18,200 ft.), and in S. a few still in action. Coastal strips and low ground (*Tierra caliente*) are hot and unhealthy, with rainfall ranging up to 130 in. On the plateau (*Tierra fria*) maximum temperature in summer is about 88°, and in winter minimum may fall to 30°; between these is *Tierra templada*, or intermediate zone (3,300–6,500 ft.). Soil is fertile, and where irrigation is good two crops can be grown in one year. In N. great herds of horses, cattle, sheep, and pigs are reared, largely for U.S.A. market. Mahogany and dyewoods, wheat, maize, rice, beans, sugar, coffee, cotton, and sisal-hemp are obtained. One of richest mineral countries in world, and takes a foremost place in world's production of silver, gold, lead, copper, and zinc; ranks fourth in world's production of petroleum. Country is very unsettled politically, and this has retarded industrial development. Cap. Mexico. Vera Cruz and Tampico, on Gulf of Mexico, are chief ports. Area, 767,198 sq. m.; pop. 14,335,000. (2) Or MEXICO CITY, cap. of above; alt. 7,415 ft.; stands *c.* 3 m. from shores of Lake Texcuco; railway transit and distributing centre; foundries, and iron working; manufactures include textiles, clothing, tobacco, paper, chemicals; univ. Pop. 906,000. (3) GULF OF, inlet of Atlantic Ocean, S. of N. America, bordered by U.S.A. and Mexico; few islands; low tides; branch of N. Equatorial Current enters from Caribbean Sea, and leaves by Strait of Florida as Gulf Stream. Area, 716,000 sq. m.

Mézières (*mā-ze-ār'*), tn., Ardennes, France, on R. Meuse; nails, hardware; type-founding. Pop. 8,000.

Mezőtur (*mā'zo-toor*), tn., Hungary, 80 m. S.E. of Budapest; market for agricultural produce; flour mills and potteries. Pop. 26,000.

Miami (*mi-äm'i*), city, Florida, U.S.A., on Biscayne Bay; favourite winter resort; fruits and vegetables; fishing. Destroyed by tornado (1926). Pop. 111,000.

Michigan (*mish'e-gan*). (1) N. Central State, U.S.A., consists of two detached portions, one a peninsula between L. Superior and N. end of L. Michigan, the other a larger peninsula between L. Michigan on W. and Lakes Huron and Erie on E.; surface of northern peninsula hilly; of the other, hilly in N. and flat in S.; drained by Rs. Muskegon, Grand, Kalamazoo, and Saginaw. Extensive forests, lumbering important. Agriculture also important; cereals, fruits, vegetables; sheep and cattle raised; fresh-water fishing and large shipping trade on lakes. Minerals include iron, copper, coal, salt, gypsum. Manufactures motor-cars, furniture, flour, leather, paper; slaughtering and meat packing important. Cap. Lansing; largest tns., Detroit, Grand Rapids. Area, 57,980 sq. m.; pop. 4,600,000. (2) LAKE, one of Great Lakes of N. America, entirely included in U.S.A., bounded N. and E. by Michigan, S. by Indiana, W. by Illinois, Wisconsin; connects with Lake Huron by Strait of Mackinac. Chief port, Chicago. Fisheries are important. Length, *c.* 320 m.; breadth, 65 m.; area, 22,400 sq. m.

Michigan City, city, Indiana, U.S.A., on Lake Michigan; railway carriages, furniture, hosiery, knitted goods; trade in lumber. Pop. 27,000.

Micronesia (*mī-krō-nēzh'ya*), a number of groups of small islands, W. Pacific Ocean; includes the Caroline, Gilbert, Marianas, Marshall, and Pelew Islands.

Mid Calder. See CALDER.

Mid'delburg, chief tn., Zeeland Holland, in centre of Walcheren I., 4 m. by rail N.E. of Flushing; important member of Hanseatic League in Middle Ages; cotton mills; mkt. tn.; holiday resort. Pop. 18,000.

Mid'dlesbrough, co. bor. and port, N. Riding, Yorks, England, on estuary of R. Tees; great iron and steel manufactures, chemical works, salt. Pop. 138,500.

Mid'dlesex, metropolitan co., England, N. of R. Thames; included in Greater London; surface flat or undulating, nowhere above 450 ft.; dairy produce, market gardens, orchards; manufactures explosives, small arms, beer, soap, chemicals. Area, 232 sq. m.; pop. 1,638,500.

Mid'dleton, tn., Lancs, England, on R. Irk, 6 m. N.E. of Manchester; textiles, chemicals, soap, machinery; coal mines. Pop. 29,200.

Mid'dleton-in-Tees'dale, mkt. tn. and par., Durham, England; ironstone, spar, and building stone. Pop. (par.) 2,000.

Mid'dletown. (1) City, Connecticut, U.S.A., on R. Connecticut; Wesleyan Univ.; trades in rubber, cotton, silk, condensed milk. Pop. 23,000. (2) City, Ohio, U.S.A., on R. Miami, 30 m. N. of Cincinnati; tobacco, agricultural implements, bicycles, gas engines, paper. Pop. 30,000. (3) City, New York, U.S.A., 55 m. N.W. of New York; ironworks, railway workshops. Pop. 20,000.

Mid'dlewich, mkt. tn., Cheshire, England, 7 m. N. of Crewe; salt works, chemicals, condensed milk. Pop. 5,500.

Mid'hurst, mkt. tn., W. Sussex, England; favourite resort; sanatorium. Pop. (dist.) 15,000.

Mid'land, tn., Ontario, Canada, on S.E. branch of Georgian Bay, 80 m. N.N.W. of Toronto; lake port. Pop. 7,800.

Midleton, mkt. tn., Cork, I.F.S., 12 m. E. of Cork; whisky distilleries. Pop. 2,700.

Midlothian, co., Scotland, bordering S. shore of Firth of Forth; towards S. rise Moorfoot (2,136 ft.) and Pentland Hills (1,898 ft.); chief streams, R. Esk and Water of Leith. Extensive coalfields in E., rich oil-shale beds in W., plentiful building stone, excellent limestone; other industries, paper making, brewing and distilling, flour milling, fisheries, shipping, carpets, tweeds, gunpowder, potteries, rubber goods, rope making. Important agricultural co.; soil is fertile; much good pasture land. Cap. Edinburgh. Area, 366 sq. m.; pop. 526,300.

Midnapore'. (1) Dist., Bengal, India; mainly well-watered plain; rice, indigo. Area, 5,055 sq. m.; pop. 2,667,000. (2) Cap. of above, 68 m. W. of Calcutta; copper and brass manufactures, silk. Pop. 29,000.

Mid'somer Norton, urb. dist., Somersetshire, England, 10 m. S.W. of Bath; coal mining; textiles and leather goods. Pop. 7,500.

Mieres (*myā'rās*), tn., N. Spain, 9 m. S.E. of Oviedo; coal, iron, copper, and cinnabar mines; steel, chemicals. Pop. 41,000.

Mil'an. (1) Prov., Lombardy, N.

Italy; mostly fertile plain highly canalized; corn, rice, flax, silk, wine, dairy produce. Area, 1,078 sq. m.; pop. 1,892,000. (2) Cap. of above, on R. Olona, in fertile plain; important industrial, commercial, and railway centre, and chief financial city of Italy; partly enclosed by walls and entered by several gates. Magnificent Gothic cathedral of white marble (founded 1386; completed 1805–13); San Lorenzo, the oldest church; La Scala (famous opera-house). Centre of silk industry and of Italian book trade; velvets, woollens, cotton goods, ironware, carriages, motor-cars, electric cables, furniture, jewellery, glass, paper, porcelain, chemicals. Pop. 962,000.

Milazzo (*mē-lat'so*), port, Messina, Sicily; wine, fruit, olive oil, sulphur. Pop. 16,000.

Mil'denhall, mkt. tn., Suffolk, England, on R. Lark, 12 m. N.W. of Bury St. Edmunds; relics of Stone Age; flour milling. Pop. (dist.) 7,800.

Mildu'ra, tn., N. Victoria, Australia; an irrigation settlement adjoining Wentworth in New South Wales; fruit-growing centre. Pop. 6,000.

Milford. (1) Or MILFORD HAVEN, port, Pembrokeshire, Wales, on Milford Haven; excellent harbour; oyster beds, fish trade. Pop. 10,100. (2) Eccles. dist. and vil., Surrey, England, 1½ m. S.S.W. of Godalming; nurseries. Pop. (dist.) 2,250.

Mil'ford-on-Sea, par. and vil., Hants, England, 3½ m. S.W. of Lymington; summer resort. Pop. (par.) 2,000.

Mill'brook, par. and vil., Cornwall, England, on inlet of R. Tamar; fishing. Pop. (par.) 2,000.

Mill Hill, eccles. dist., Middlesex, England, in Hendon urban dist.; Botanical Garden; public school; residential dist. Pop. 9,100.

Mill'om, tn., Cumberland, England, 48 m. S.S.W. of Carlisle; has iron mines and works. Pop. 7,400.

Mill'port, tn., Great Cumbrae Island, Buteshire, Scotland, on Millport Bay; wat.-pl.; white freestone quarries, marine biological station. Pop. 2,100.

Mill'ville, city, New Jersey, U.S.A., on R. Maurice, 38 m. S.S.E. of Philadelphia; glass and textiles; sand mining. Pop. 15,000.

Mil'nathort, mkt. tn., Kinross-shire, Scotland, near Loch Leven; live-stock market; wool and linen industries. Pop. 1,200.

Milngavie (*mil-gī'*), tn., Dumbartonshire, Scotland, 6 m. N. of Glasgow; bleaching, calico printing, dyeing. Pop. 5,100.

Milo (*mē'lō*), anc. MELOS, one of Cyclades Islands, Ægean Sea; volcanic in origin; earthquakes frequent; mountainous in S.W.; flat and fertile in N.E.; fruits, vines, cotton, barley cultivated; exports gypsum, sulphur, china clay. Famous statue of Venus found here. Area, *c.* 52 sq. m.; pop. 5,000.

Mil'ton Re'gis, par. and tn., Kent, England, adjoining Sittingbourne; brickworks. Pop. (par.) 7,100.

Milwau'kee, tn., Wisconsin, U.S.A., on W. shore of Lake Michigan; great centre of railways and lake shipping; exports oats and other cereals, flour; manufactures machinery, brass and iron ware, agricultural implements; flour mills, meat-packing and sausage establishments, railway works; univ. Pop. 573,000.

Minas Geraes (*mē'nās zhā-rā'es*), ('mines everywhere'), state, E. Brazil, S. America; surface consists of plateau in W., elsewhere mountainous with fertile valleys; watered by R. São Francisco, Grande Parana. State has valuable mineral deposits, including gold, diamonds, iron, manganese, lead. Coffee, tobacco, cotton, rice, vines, and sugar-cane are cultivated, and cattle raised. Cap. Bello Horizonte. Area, 221,894 sq. m.; pop. 7,258,000.

Minbu'. (1) Div., Upper Burma; plain, rising to hilly country in W.; well watered. Area, 17,172 sq. m.; pop. 1,076,300. (2) Dist. of above; rice, cotton, valuable timber. Area, 3,299 sq. m.; pop. 274,000. (3) Cap. of above, on R. Irrawaddy; centre of river traffic and fishing. Pop. 5,400.

Minch, strait of Atlantic Ocean, separating N.W. mainland of Scotland from N. part of Outer Hebrides, S. portion continued as Little Minch, between Skye and Outer Hebrides.

Minchinhamp'ton, tn., Gloucestershire, England, 3½ m. S.E. of Stroud; woollens, brewing. Pop. 3,700.

Mindanā'o, second largest island of Philippines; surface mountainous, with many volcanoes; drained by the Rio Grande; numerous lakes; densely forested; copper, coal, platinum; cattle and horse raising; rice, coffee, hemp, sugar-cane, tobacco. Area, 36,906 sq. m.; pop. *c.* 560,000.

Min'den, tn., Westphalia, Prussia, on R. Weser; famous cathedral; chemicals, glass, tobacco, soap. Pop. 27,000.

Minehead (*mīn'hed*), mkt. tn. and wat.-pl., Somersetshire, England, on S. shore of Bristol Channel; beach shows at low tide remains of submerged forest; leather. Pop. 6,300.

Minho (*mēn'yō*), riv., N.W. Spain; flows W. from Cantabrian Mts. to Atlantic Ocean; estuary divides Spain from Portugal; navigable for 25 m. Length, 175 m.

Minneap'olis, city, Minnesota, U.S.A., on R. Mississippi, immediately above 'twin city' of St. Paul; on Falls of St. Anthony, water-power of which has enabled town to become centre of immense trade in flour and lumber; has great number of flour mills; manufactures of machinery, motors, iron goods, furniture, linseed oil; univ. Pop. 465,000.

Minneso'ta, North Central State, U.S.A.; bounded on N. by Manitoba, Ontario; E. by Lake Superior, Wisconsin; S. by Iowa; W. by S. and N. Dakota; surface flat or undulating; drained by Rs. Mississippi, Minnesota, Red R.; many large lakes, including Mille Lacs, Red Lake, Lake Winnibigoshish. Agriculture is chief industry; large quantities of maize, wheat, and other cereals; great pine forests in N.; maple, oak, ash farther S.; lumbering important; large quantities of iron produced; manufactures flour, leather, boots, clothing, farm machinery. Cap. St. Paul; large tns., Minneapolis, Duluth. Area, 84,682 sq. m.; pop. 2,387,000.

Minor'ca, one of Balearic Islands, Spain, in Mediterranean Sea; hilly; cattle and horses; cereals, oil, wine, fruits, flax. Area, 293 sq. m.; pop. 42,000.

Minsk, cap. of White Russia, U.S.S.R., on R. Svisloch; machinery and leather manufactures, flour mills; pigs' bristles. Pop. 132,000.

Min'ster-in-Shep'pey, par. and vil., Kent, England; rising seaside wat.-pl.; oyster beds. Pop. (par.) 3,000.

Min'ster-in-Tha'net, par. and vil., Kent, England; fruit growing. Pop. (par.) 3,000.

Minusinsk', tn., Siberian Area, U.S.S.R., on R. Yenisei; coal and copper mines; sawmills and sugar factory. Pop. 20,000.

Miquelon (*mēk'lon*), GREAT and LITTLE, isl. off S.W. coast of Newfoundland, consisting of two portions connected by a sandy isthmus; with St. Pierre forms sole colony of France in N. America; cod fishing. Area, 83 sq. m.; pop. 4,000.

Miramichi (*mir-a-mish-ē*), riv., New Brunswick, Canada; flows into Miramichi Bay, Gulf of St. Lawrence; salmon and trout fishing. Length, 230 m.

Mir'field, urb. dist., W. Riding, Yorks, England, 5 m. N.E. of Huddersfield, on R. Calder; cotton and woollen goods, carpets, blankets; collieries. Pop. 12,100.

Mirzapur'. (1) Dist., United Provinces, India; crossed by mountain ranges; much forest. Area, 4,368 sq. m.; pop. 724,000. (2) Tn. in above, on R. Ganges, between Allahabad and Benares; carpets, brassware. Pop. 55,000.

Mishawā'ka, tn., Indiana, U.S.A., 90 m. S.E. of Chicago; manufactures machinery, rubber and woollen goods, shoes. Pop. 29,000.

Mision'es, terr., N.E. Argentina, between rivs. Paraná and Uruguay, S. America; surface uneven and forest-covered; chief productions, Paraguay tea, tobacco, oranges. Cap. Posadas. Area, 11,511 sq. m.; pop. 54,000.

Miskolcz (*mish'kolts*), tn., Hungary, 85 m. N.E. of Budapest; flour, leather, boots, porcelain. Pop. 59,000.

Mississip'pi ('great river'). (1) Important river of N. America; second largest in world; rises in Lake Itasca, in Minnesota, some 1,560 ft. above sea-level, and flows southward to Gulf of Mexico. Drainage basin, nearly 1,257,000 sq. m., is over 40 per cent. of whole area of U.S.A. The Missouri, a w. affluent, is a much larger stream than the Mississippi itself when they unite at St. Louis; other w. affluents are Minnesota, Des Moines, Francis, White, Arkansas, and Red Rivers. E. tribs. are Wisconsin, Illinois, Ohio (with affluents Cumberland and Tennessee), Yazoo. On other side of the river are rich alluvial 'bottoms' of large extent, at many points below level of stream, which is prevented from overflowing by strong embankments known as levees; at mouth is large delta with many passages; river valley suffers from frequent floods; river navigable to Minneapolis; great river traffic carried on by specially constructed steamers. Length, over 4,000 m. (2) South Central State, U.S.A., bounded N. by Tennessee, E. by Alabama, s. by Mississippi Sound, Louisiana, w. by Gulf of Mexico and Louisiana; surface flat along coast, rising to low hills drained by R. Mississippi and tribs. and other streams. Soil fertile; chief industry agriculture; great quantities of cotton, also rice, maize, wheat, oats, potatoes; cattle, horses, sheep, and pigs raised. Largely forested; lumbering important. The manufactures include cottons, cotton-seed oil, turpentine, railway cars. Cap. Jackson. Area, 46,865 sq. m.; pop. 1,791,000.

Missolong'hi, fort. tn., Greece, on Gulf of Patras; Byron died here (1824); currants, valonia. Pop. 9,000.

Missoula (*miz-oo'lä*), city, w. Montana, U.S.A., on R. Clark; univ.; agricultural and fruit-growing region; railway workshops; oil refining. Pop. 13,000.

Missouri (*mis-oor'i*). (1) River, U.S.A.; chief trib. of R. Mississippi; rises in Rockies; formed by union of 'Three Forks'—Jefferson, Gallatin, Madison; receives Dakota from N., Yellowstone, Little Missouri, Cheyenne, White, Platte, Kansas, Osage from s.; navigation difficult; joins Mississippi near St. Louis. Length, over 2,500 m. (2) E. Central State, U.S.A., bounded N. by Iowa, E. by Illinois, Kentucky, Tennessee, s. by Arkansas, w. by Oklahoma, Kansas, Nebraska; surface flat or undulating in N., with wide stretches of prairie in N.W.; to s. of Missouri R. the Ozark Mts. reach height of *c.* 3,000 ft. Rivers are Mississippi, Missouri, and tribs. Principal industry agriculture; heavy crops of maize, wheat, oats, hemp, flax, cotton, tobacco, fruit; cattle, pigs, and sheep reared; minerals include coal, zinc, lead, cement, copper. Important industries are slaughtering and meat packing, flour milling, motor building, boot making, printing, and ironfounding. Cap. Jefferson. Area, 69,420 sq. m.; pop. 3,404,000.

Misurä'ta, tn., Tripolitania, Italian Libya, on Mediterranean Sea; reed mats and carpets. Pop. 14,000.

Mitau. See JELGAVA.

Mitch'am, urb. dist., Surrey, England, 7¾ m. s. of London; centre of growing of medicinal herbs (lavender, liquorice, etc.). Pop. 56,900.

Mitch'ell, tn., S. Dakota, U.S.A., on James or Dakota R.; agricultural centre; Wesleyan univ. Pop. 10,000.

Mitch'elstown, mkt. tn., N. co. Cork, I.F.S.; near by are limestone caverns with fine stalactites. Pop. 2,100.

Mitrovica (*mit-ro-vit'sa*), tn., Yugoslavia, on R. Sava, 43 m. W.N.W. of Belgrade; pig and sheep market; river trade. Pop. 12,000.

Mittweida (*mit'vī-da*), tn., Saxony, Germany, 12 m. N.E. of Chemnitz; textiles, cigars, agricultural implements. Pop. 19,000.

Mlad'a Bol'eslav, formerly JUNG-

BUNZLAU, tn., N. Bohemia, Czechoslovakia, on R. Jizera; rly. jn.; sugar, soap, candles. Pop. 17,000.

Mlawa (*mwä'vä*), tn., Poland, 60 m. N.W. of Warsaw; flour mills, vinegar, soap, oil manufactures; tanneries, brick works, and agricultural machine works. Pop. 14,000.

Mo'berly, city, Missouri, U.S.A., 135 m. N.W. of St. Louis; foundries, railway repair shops; hosiery, shoes, cheese. Pop. 21,000.

Mobile (*mo-bēl'*), seapt., Alabama, U.S.A., on Gulf of Mexico; exports cotton, lumber, timber, meat, and iron and steel products, vegetables; shipbuilding. Pop. 68,000.

Mocha (*mok'a*), port, Yemen, Arabia, on Red Sea; decaying since its former coffee trade was shipped through Hodeida. Pop. 5,000.

Mod'der, riv., Orange Free State, S. Africa, trib. of R. Vaal; length, 175 m.

Modena (*mō'dā-nä*), tn., Italy, 25 m. W.N.W. of Bologna; has 12th cent. Romanesque cathedral; univ.; observatory; manufactures leather, silk, metal ware, vinegar. Pop. 91,000.

Modes'to, tn., California, U.S.A., 85 m. S.E. of San Francisco; centre of irrigated tract; fruit and vegetables; fruit canning, creamery. Pop. 10,000.

Modica (*mō'dē-cä*), tn., Syracuse, Sicily; grain, oil, wine. Pop. 56,000.

Möd'ling, tn., Austria, 10 m. S.W. of Vienna; summer resort, with iron and sulphur springs; iron foundries; shoes. Pop. 19,000.

Moff'at, wat.-pl., Dumfriesshire, Scotland, on R. Annan; mineral springs; holiday resort. Pop. 2,000.

Mogador', port, Morocco, Africa, on Atlantic coast; exports wheat, barley, eggs, wool, gum-arabic. Pop. 18,000.

Mogilev (*mo-hēl'yōf*). (1) ON-DNIEPER, tn., White Russia, U.S.S.R.; tanning; tobacco, flour, beer. Pop. 47,000. (2) ON-DNIESTER, tn., Ukraine, U.S.S.R; distilling, brewing, sugar refining. Pop. 22,000.

Mohács (*mo'hatch*), tn., Hungary, on R. Danube, on frontier of Yugoslavia; river port; milling and brewing. Pop. 16,000.

Moham'merah, tn., port, Persia, on the Shatt-al-Arab; exports dates. Pop. 10,000.

Moji (*mō'jē*), port, Kyushu, Japan, on Shimonoseki Strait; exports coal, cotton thread, sugar, timber, cement. Pop. 95,000.

Mo'la di Bar'i, port, Apulia, S. Italy, on Adriatic Sea; exports grain, wine, olives, live-stock. Pop. 15,000.

Mold, co. tn., Flintshire, Wales, on R. Alyn; mkt. tn., collieries, lead-smelting works. Pop. 5,100.

Moldau. See VLTAVA.

Molda'via. (1) N. prov., Romania; forested in N.W.; red wine; hogs. Area, 14,668 sq. m.; pop. 2,145,400. (2) Autonomous republic, Ukraine, U.S.S.R., l. bk. of R. Dniester; upland plain with numerous streams; maize, wheat, rye, sunflower seed, tobacco, fruits. Cap. Birzulav. Area, 3,315 sq. m.; pop. 572,000.

Molesey, EAST AND WEST, urb. dist., Surrey, England, on R. Thames. E. Molesey stands at confluence of Rs. Mole and Thames, opposite Hampton Court. Residential dist.; part of Greater London. Pop. 8,500.

Molfet'ta, port, Bari, S. Italy, on Adriatic Sea; exports wine, almonds, olive oil. Pop. 46,000.

Moline (*mo-lēn'*), city, N. Illinois, U.S.A., on R. Mississippi; flour and saw mills, iron foundries; agricultural machinery. Pop. 32,000.

Molokai (*mo-lo-kī'*). See under HAWAIIAN ISLANDS.

Moluccas (*mo-luk'as*), or SPICE ISLANDS, archipelago, Dutch East Indies; volcanic; spices, copra, rice, sago, timber, pearls. Cap. Amboina. Area, 190,860 sq. m.; pop. 623,000.

Mombä'sa, chief port, Kenya Colony, E. Africa; terminus of Uganda rly.; chief harbour, Kilindini; exports ivory, copra, gum, grain, rubber, and hides. Pop. *c.* 42,000.

Mon'aco, small independent state, Europe, on French Mediterranean coast; ruled by hereditary prince under French protection; mild climate; picturesque scenery; favourite tourist resort; olive oil, oranges, citrons, perfumes, liqueurs. Tns. are Monaco, Condamine, and Monte Carlo. Area, 8 sq. m.; pop. 25,000.

Monadhliath Mts. (*mō-nă-lē′ă*), part of Grampian highlands, E. Inverness-shire, Scotland; between the upper Findhorn and Spey rivs.; highest peak, Carn Mairg, 3,087 ft.

Mon′aghan. (1) Co., Ulster, I.F.S.; surface hilly; crossed by Slievebeagh Mts.; bogs and lakes frequent; turnips, potatoes, and oats grown; trade in linen and agricultural produce. Area, 498 sq. m.; pop. 65,000. (2) Cap. of above; agricultural produce; cathedral. Pop. 4,600.

Monastir (*mo-näs-tēr′*). See BITOLJ.

Monc′ton, tn., New Brunswick, Canada, on R. Petitcodiac; E. centre of Canadian National Rlys.; rly. workshops; textiles. Pop. 17,000.

Mondovi (*mon-do-vē′*), tn., Piedmont, Italy, 50 m. S. of Turin; porcelain, paper, silk. Pop. 20,000.

Mones′sen, town, Pennsylvania, U.S.A., 40 m. S. of Pittsburgh; steel, wire, tinplate. Pop. 18,000.

Monfalco′ne, fort. tn., Trieste, Italy; sea-bathing; mineral waters; shipbuilding; oil refining; chemicals. Pop. 10,000.

Monfor′te de Lémos, tn., Galicia, Spain, 75 m. S.E. of Corunna; linen, soap. Pop. 14,000.

Monghyr (*mon-gēr′*). (1) Dist., Bengal, India; flat in N., undulating in S.; many marshes; drained by R. Ganges; mainly agricultural. Area, 3,927 sq. m.; pop. 2,069,000. (2) Cap. of above; on R. Ganges, 80 m. below Patna; manufactures cigarettes. Pop. 47,000.

Mongo′lia, vast region, Central Asia; bounded N. by Siberia, E. by Manchuria, S.E. and S.W. by China proper, N.W. by Kazak, U.S.S.R.; three physical divisions: (1) Central Mongolia, composed of stony and sandy desert passing into steppes, commonly called Gobi; (2) N.W. Mongolia, which includes various mountain ranges, including Tannu, Khanghai, and Great Altai Mts.; (3) S.E. or Inner Mongolia, including the Great Khingan and Inshan chains. Principal rivs. are Black Irtish, Yenisei, Selenga, Orkhon, Kerulen, all in northern half; Hwang-ho drains a corner of S. Climate extreme. Livestock raised; minerals include gold, copper, silver, iron, tin. Divided into two political regions, Inner Mongolia (chief tn. Kalgan), a broad belt lying adjacent to, and really constituting a part of, China; and Outer Mongolia (chief tn. Urga), an independent republic, still nominally Chinese, though with leanings towards becoming a member of the U.S.S.R. Area, *c.* 1,875,000 sq. m.; pop. *c.* 750,000.

Monifieth′, par. and burgh, Angus, Scotland, on Firth of Tay; jute and machinery. Pop. (burgh) 3,000.

Monk Bret′ton, urb. dist., Yorks, England, 1½ m. N.E. of Barnsley; collieries. Pop. 5,100.

Monk′land, NEW and OLD, adjoining pars., Lanarkshire, Scotland, containing tns. of Airdrie and Coatbridge; both rich in iron and coal. Pop., New Monkland, 38,500; Old Monkland, 62,900.

Monks′town, par. and vil., co. Cork, I.F.S., on Cork Harbour; sea-bathing. Pop. (par.) 2,000.

Mon′mouth, co. tn., Monmouthshire, England, at junction of Rs. Monnow and Wye; smelting and tinplate works, sawmills. Pop. 4,700.

Monmouthshire, mar. co., England, on Welsh border, and for certain purposes treated as part of Wales; surface flat along coast, elsewhere hilly; drained by Rs. Usk, Wye, and other streams; coal and iron found about Newport, Tredegar, and Ebbw Vale; grazing, wheat, orchards; important river fisheries. Co. tn., Monmouth. Area, 546 sq. m.; pop. 434,800.

Monop′oli, port, Apulia, S. Italy, on Adriatic Sea; exports oil, fruit, flour, soap, wine. Pop. 23,000.

Monreale (*mon-rā-ä′lā*), tn., Palermo, Sicily; oranges, olives, almonds. Pop. 24,000.

Monroe′, city, N. Louisiana, U.S.A., on R. Ouacheta; manufactures of paper, printers' ink, lumber products, bricks; centre of extensive natural gas field. Pop. 26,000.

Monro'via, port and cap. of Liberia, W. Africa, at mouth of St. Paul R.; exports dye-woods, rubber, palm oil and kernels. Pop. (including Krutown), 10,000.

Mons, cap., Hainaut, Belgium, 35 m. S.S.W. of Brussels; centre of chief coal-mining dist. of Belgium; railway, road, and canal junction; cathedral. Industries include engineering, cotton spinning, iron founding, and glass making. Famous Brit. retreat from Mons (1914). Pop. 28,000.

Montan'a, N.W. state, U.S.A., bounded N. by Canada, E. by N. and S. Dakota, S. by Wyoming, W. by Idaho; surface generally consists of undulating prairie, rising W. to Rocky Mts., drained by R. Columbia and tribs. in W. Missouri and affluents, most important of which are Milk and Yellowstone, in E. Agriculture is rendered possible by irrigation; livestock raised; cereals grown, fruit widely cultivated; important deposits of copper; also coal, gold, silver, lead, petroleum. Slopes of Rockies yield timber. Chief industries, flour milling, lumbering, copper smelting. Cap. Helena. Area, 147,182 sq. m.; pop. 540,000.

Montargis (*mon-tär-zhē'*), tn., Loiret, France, 40 m. E. of Orleans; chemicals, rubber, tar, hosiery. Pop. 12,000.

Montauban (*mōn-tō-bon'*), chief tn., Tarn-et-Garonne, France, on R. Tarn; trades in wine, oil, fruit, agricultural produce; horse fair; textiles, furniture, straw hats. Pop. 18,000.

Montbéliard (*mon-bā-le-ar'*), town, Doubs, France, 10 m. S. of Belfort; clocks, watches, files, knitting looms, textiles; trades in wine, cheese, cattle. Pop. 10,000.

Mont Blanc. See BLANC, MONT.

Montbrison (*mon-brē-zōn*), tn., Loire, France, 21 m. N.W. of St. Etienne; liqueurs, ribbons, flour. Pop. 7,000.

Montceau-les-Mines (*mōn-sō-lā-mēn'*), tn., Saône-et-Loire, France, 10 m. S. of Le Creusot; centre of Blanzy coalfield; textiles; foundries. Pop. 8,000.

Mont Cenis. See CENIS, MONT.

Montclair', tn., New Jersey, U.S.A., 15 m. from New York; summer resort; paper goods. Pop. 42,000.

Mont-de-Marsan (*mōn-de-mar-son'*), chief tn., Landes, S.W. France; resin, oil, straw envelopes for bottles. Pop. 9,000.

Mon'te Car'lo, tn., principality of Monaco, overlooking the Mediterranean Sea; has exquisite climate and beautiful gardens. Noted for its casino. Pop. 11,000.

Montefrio (*mon-tā-frē'o*), tn., S. Spain, 25 m. N.W. of Granada; remains of Moorish castle; manufactures alcohol and soap. Pop. 11,000.

Montélimar (*mon-tā-lē-mar'*), tn., Drôme, France, near R. Rhône; brick and tile works, tanneries, sawmills; coal and lignite; famed for 'nougat.' Pop. 8,000.

Montenegro (*mon-tā-nē'gro*), ('Black Mountain'), state, Yugoslavia, almost entirely cut off from Adriatic by Dalmatia. Surface is mountainous, rising to barren stony plateau, 5,000 ft. above sea-level; narrow coastal strip (28 m.) with valleys opening off it; drained by Rs. Boyana, Zeta, and Moratcha; in S. is Lake Scutari (134 sq. m.). Climate varies with elevation—warm on coast, cold in mountainous districts; roads are snow-blocked in winter. In E. are extensive forests of beech, oak, pine, undeveloped owing to lack of roads; principal crops, tobacco, maize, apples, grapes, olives, figs, mulberries; sheep, goats, cattle, swine, and horses are raised. Cap. Cetinje. Area, 3,738 sq. m.; pop. 200,000.

Montereau (*mon-te-rō'*), tn., Seine-et-Marne, France, at junction of Rs. Yonne and Seine; porcelain, bricks, boots, shoes, agricultural implements. Pop. 9,000.

Monterey (*mon-te-rā'*). (1) Tn., California, U.S.A., on Monterey Bay; fishing; sardine canneries. Pop. 4,000. (2) Or MONTERREY, cap. of Nuevo Léon, Mexico, 190 m. W. of mouth of Rio Grande; smelting works, iron foundries, cotton factories; silver, lead, zinc, copper mining. Pop. 88,000.

Mon'te Ro'sa, peak, Pennine Alps, on frontier between Switzerland and Italy; snow-clad; glaciers; observatory at 15,000 ft.; has four summits. The highest point, Dufour- or Höchste-Spitse (15,217 ft.), is in Swiss terr.

Monte Sant' Angelo (*mon'tā sänt än'je-lo*), tn., Apulia, s. Italy, 27 m. N.W. of Foggia; castle; pilgrim resort. Pop. 22,000.

Montevid'eo, cap. and chief port, Uruguay, S. America, on N. shore of Rio de la Plata; univ.; coaling station; exports live-stock, beef, wool, skins, grease, horns, cereals; beef salting an important industry. Pop. 459,000.

Montgom'ery. (1) Co. tn., Montgomeryshire, Wales; cattle market. Pop. 900. (2) Cap. of Alabama, U.S.A., on R. Alabama; important commercial centre; trade in cotton, timber; railway workshops; manufactures fertilizers. Pop. 66,000.

Montgom'eryshire, inland co., Wales; surface mountainous with fertile valleys; well wooded; chief riv., Severn, with tribs., Vyrnwy, Tanat, Dovey; sheep pasturing; lead and blende mined; slate and limestone quarries; flannel manufactures. Co. tn., Montgomery. Area, 797 sq. m.; pop. 48,500.

Montilla (*mon-tēl'yä*), city, s. Spain, 23 m. s. of Cordoba; manufactures coarse linen and pottery. Amontillado wine. Pop. 15,000.

Montluçon (*mōn-loo-son'*), tn., Allier, central France, on R. Cher; agricultural centre; trade in grain; ironworks, engineering shops; chemicals; sewing machines; mirrors. Pop. 35,000.

Montmorency (*mōn-mo-ron-sē'*), tn., near R. Seine, 10 m. N. of Paris; bleaching, dyeing; bricks, tiles. Pop. 10,000.

Monto'ro, city, Cordoba, s. Spain, on R. Guadalquivir; olive oil production; medicinal springs; agricultural products and wood. Pop. 18,000.

Montpellier (*mōn-pel-yā'*), cap. Hérault, France, near Gulf of Lions; wine, brandy, fruit, silk culture, agriculture; manufactures soap, candles, and chemicals; famous univ.; has oldest botanic garden in Europe. Pop. 83,000.

Montreal (*mont-re-ol'*), tn., Quebec, Canada; situated on E. of Montreal island, at junction of Rs. Ottawa and St. Lawrence; majority of population French; has many old French buildings; seat of M'Gill Univ.; great Victoria Railway Bridge across R. St. Lawrence; head of ocean navigation on R. St. Lawrence; chief port and largest tn. in Canada; harbour ice-free from May to November; 7 m. of wharfage; extensive canal communication with principal towns of Great Lakes; headquarters of railways; railway works; manufactures almost every article of commerce. Pop. 990,000.

Montreuil-sous-Bois (*mōn-troo-yē'-soo-bwa*), tn., France; E. suburb of Paris; famous for peaches; manufactures oils, chemicals, glass. Pop. 59,000.

Montreux (*mōn-troo'*), tn., Vaud, Switzerland, on N.E. shore of L. Geneva; holiday resort. Pop. 19,000.

Montrose', royal burgh and port, Angus, Scotland; flax spinning, timber trade, fishing, jam making, brewing; popular resort. Pop. 10,200.

Mont St. Michel (*mōn san mē-shel'*), granite islet off coast of Normandy, France, in Bay of St. Michel; rises 240 ft. above surrounding sands, and is reached by causeway; surrounded by 15th cent. walls; old town and Benedictine monastery, now restored as historical monument. Pop. 200.

Montserrat', one of Leeward Islands, Brit. W. Indies; volcanic origin; highest summit, 3,000 ft.; limes, sugar, cotton, onions. Cap. Plymouth. Area, 32 sq. m.; pop. 12,000.

Mon'za, tn., Lombardy, Italy, 10 m. N. of Milan; manufactures coarse cottons, leather, silk; dyeworks; cathedral contains famous iron crown of Lombardy. Pop. 43,000.

Moose Jaw, city, Saskatchewan, Canada, 40 m. w. of Regina; flour mills; farming machinery; general agricultural trade; rly. jn., Canadian Pacific and Canadian National Rlys. Pop. 20,000.

Moquegua (*mo-kā'gwā*), prov., s. Peru, S. America; mainly mountainous, with barren coastal strip; valleys produce cotton, maize, fruits, vegetables. Cap. Moquegua. Area, 5,549 sq. m.; pop. 43,000.

Moradabad'. (1) Dist., United Provinces, India; soil alluvial; climate healthy; wheat, rice, sugar-cane grown; sugar refining. Area, 2,285 sq. m.; pop. 1,200,000. (2) Cap. of above, 80 m. E. of Delhi; cotton weaving, calico printing; ornamental brassware. Pop. 83,000.

Mo'rar, dist., s.w. Inverness-shire, between L. Nevis, Sound of Sleat, and Sound of Arisaig; holiday resort. L. Morar deepest loch in Scotland. Chief tn. of dist., Mallaig.

Moratal'la, tn., S.E. Spain, 40 m. N.W. of Murcia; cloth, soap, alcohol; excellent wine. Pop. 13,000.

Morā'va. (1) Riv., Serbia, flows N. into R. Danube, 30 m. E.S.E. of Belgrade; main stream is formed by confluence of the S. Morava (formerly Bulgarian), and W. Morava. Length, 250 m. The Morava valley forms part of the great line of communication from w. Europe to Constantinople and Salonika. (2) Or MARCH, l. bk. trib. of R. Danube, Moravia, Czechoslovakia; flows from Sudetes Mts.; lower course forms boundary between Austria and Czechoslovakia; enters R. Danube near Bratislava. Length, 210 m., of which 50 m. is navigable.

Mora'via, prov., Czechoslovakia; surface generally mountainous, intersected by spurs of Sudetes and Carpathian Mts. drained by R. Morava and tribs.; extensive forests; produces cereals, beet sugar, hops, beer, cigars; chief minerals are coal, iron, graphite; manufactures textiles. Cap. Brno. Area, 8,616 sq. m.; pop. 2,663,000.

Mora'vian Gate, natural depression between Sudetes Mts. and Carpathian Mts., Czechoslovakia, Europe; links upper valley of Morava trib. of R. Danube with that of R. Oder; important rly. route.

Mor'avska Os'trava, formerly OSTRAU, tn., Moravia, Czechoslovakia, on R. Ostravice; in Silesian coalfield; collieries and ironworks; chemicals, soap, oil, bricks. Pop. 114,000.

Moray, formerly ELGINSHIRE, co. on s. shore of Moray Firth, Scotland; drained by Rs. Spey, Lossie, and Findhorn. Mountainous and generally well wooded towards the s.; coastal strip known as 'Laigh o' Moray' is one of most fertile parts of Scotland, producing barley, oats, potatoes, and turnips. Cattle-rearing important. Fishing and distilling are also of great importance. Culbin Sands now cover the former 'Granary of Moray.' Chief tn., Elgin. Area, 477 sq. m.; pop. 40,800.

Mor'ay Firth, part of North Sea, N.E. Scotland; consists of wide outlet of Cromarty and Beauly Firths as far as line joining Tarbat Ness and Lossiemouth; sometimes regarded as area of water w. of line joining Duncansby Head and Kinnairds Point; rich fisheries centred on Banff, Buckie, Findhorn, Cromarty, Helmsdale, and Lybster.

Morbihan (*mor-bē-on'*), maritime dep., Brittany, France; includes Belle Isle; coast much indented; extensive heaths, many stagnant pools; wheat, rye, mangels, potatoes, flax, hemp; cattle-breeding, bee-keeping; important fisheries, especially of sardines; oyster culture. Cap. Vannes. Area, 2,738 sq. m.; pop. 543,000.

Morea. See GREECE.

Morecambe and Heysham (*mŏr'-kam*), munic. bor., Lancs, England, on Morecambe Bay; wat.-pl. Pop. 24,600.

Morelia (*mo-rā'le-a*), city, Mexico, 125 m. w. of Mexico; cotton, linen, and woollen factories; sugar, sweetmeats; cathedral. Pop. 31,000.

Mor'gantown, tn., in N. of W. Virginia, U.S.A.; univ.; coal mining; manufactures glass. Pop. 12,000.

Morlaix (*mor-lā'*), tn., port, Finistère, France, 35 m. E.N.E. of Brest; manufactures paper, tobacco, beer, casks, candles; exports agricultural produce; anc. town, with old wooden houses. Pop. 11,000.

Mor'ley, munic. bor., W. Riding, Yorks, England, 4 m. S.S.W. of Leeds; woollen goods and machinery manufactured; coal mines. Pop. 23,400.

Moroc'co. (1) French protectorate and Spanish zone (*er Rif*), N.W. Africa, bordering on Atlantic Ocean and Mediterranean Sea, and separated from Europe by Strait of Gibraltar (9 m.). Country traversed by Atlas Mts., which reach an extreme height of 15,000 ft.; surface hilly almost everywhere, but especially so in N. Climate N.W. of Atlas healthy and pleasant; to S. of Atlas there is little rain and sometimes long-continued drought. Between Atlas Mts. and Mediterranean Sea, and extending westward to Atlantic Ocean, is the fertile Tell region, covering one-third of whole area, and producing heavy crops of wheat, barley, linseed, beans, hemp, olives, dates, and Mediterranean fruits. Pasture land covers about one-eighth of whole area, where numbers of cattle, sheep, goats, horses, and mules are raised. Minerals include lead, manganese, phosphates. Important coast fisheries. Sericulture is being developed. Chief exports are cereals, eggs, wool, fruit, olive oil, esparto, hides. There are no railways except the military narrow-gauge lines. Roads are being improved by the French.

Morocco has four capitals—Fez, Marrakesh, Meknes, and Rabat. Coast tns. open to foreign trade are Casablanca, Laraish, Mazagan, Mogador, Rabat, Saffi, Tangier, Tetuan. Area, 218,525 sq. m.; pop. (est.) 5,300,000. (2) See MARRAKESH.

Moron' de la Fronte'ra, tn., S. Spain, 35 m. S.E. of Seville; marble and chalk. Pop. 19,000.

Mor'peth, mkt. tn., munic. bor., Northumberland, England, on R. Wansbeck; metal founding, brewing, brick making, woollen manufactures; agricultural machinery; coal mines in vicinity. Pop. 7,400.

Mor'ristown, tn., New Jersey, U.S.A., 22 m. W. of Newark; fruit growing; summer resort; agricultural produce. Pop. 12,500.

Morshansk', tn., Tambov, central Russia, 58 m. N. of Tambov; centre of grain trade; soap, tallow, glass, tobacco. Pop. 28,000.

Mor'tier Bay, harbour, Newfoundland, 80 m. W. of Cape Race; free port in course of development.

Mort'lake, vil. and par., Greater London, on R. Thames; tapestry works; pottery; malting and brewing; terminus of Oxford and Cambridge boat-race course. Pop. 19,000.

Morvi (*mor-vē'*), Indian state, Kathiawar, Bombay, India; surface generally flat; grain, sugar, cotton grown. Cap. Morvi. Area, 822 sq. m.; pop. 91,000.

Moscow (*mos'kō*). (1) Prov. of Russia; in basin of R. Volga; surface undulating; chief manufacturing prov. of Russia; centre of Muscovite coalfield; famous limestone quarries; large forest area. Area, 17,992 sq. m.; pop. 4,534,000. (2) Cap. and largest city of Russia and U.S.S.R., on R. Moskva, a sub-trib. of R. Volga. *Kremlin,* or citadel, surrounded by a wall, contains imperial palaces, monasteries; famous Tsar Kolokol bell, and Cathedral of the Assumption (built 1474–9), where Tsars were crowned; univ. and observatory. City has great transit trade and is important industrial centre; manufactures cotton, woollens, silks, leather, machinery, and tobacco; printing trade. Pop. 2,412,000.

Moselle (*mo-zel'*). (1) Riv., rises in Vosges Mts., France, flows northward through France, Luxembourg, and Prussian Rhineland, and joins R. Rhine at Coblenz; valley noted for wines; chief tribs. Meurthe and Saar; length, 314 m. (2) Dept., N.E. France, consisting of low plateau drained by R. Moselle and its tribs.; noted for vineyards and salt deposits; important coal and iron mines giving rise to hardware and other manufactures. Chief tn., Metz. Area, 2,403 sq. m.; pop. 633,000.

Moss, port, wat.-pl., Norway, on Oslo Fiord; sawmills; shipbuilding, and waterproofing. Pop. 8,000.

Mossamedes (*mos-sä-mā'des*), port, Portuguese W. Africa; fish curing; guano and nitrate of soda. Pop. 5,000.

Mos'sel Bay, port, Cape Province, S. Africa; sea-bathing; oysters; whaling industry. Pop. 6,000.

Moss'end, tn., Lanarkshire, Scotland, 2 m. N.E. of Motherwell; iron and steel works. Pop. 3,500.

Moss'ley, munic. bor., mkt. tn., Lancs, England, 10 m. N.E. of Manchester; foundries, cotton and woollen mills. Pop. 12,000.

Most (German *Brüx*), tn., N.W. Bohemia, Czechoslovakia; sugar, brewing, chemicals; lignite mines. Pop. 27,000.

Mostaganem', port, Oran, Algeria; flour milling, tanning; trade in grain, wool, hides. Pop. 26,000.

Mos'tar, tn., Hercegovina, Yugoslavia, on R. Naretva; grapes, wine, tobacco, vegetables. Pop. 18,000.

Mosul (*mo-sool'*). (1) Vilayet, Iraq, mostly to E. of R. Tigris; great oilfield; important agricultural region. Area, 35,130 sq. m.; pop. 703,000. (2) Cap. of above, on R. Tigris; encircled by partly ruined walls; contains great mosque; flour milling; market for grain, fruit, cattle, sheep. Pop. *c.* 80,000.

Moth'erwell and Wish'aw, tn., Lanarkshire, Scotland; coal mining; iron and steel works; brick, tile, and fireclay works. Pop. 64,700.

Motril (*mo-trēl'*), tn., Granada, Spain, on Mediterranean Sea; cotton, sugar-cane, sugar-beet, and various fruits grown; zinc, lead, copper mined. Pop. 17,000.

Moukden (*mook'den*), cap. of Manchuria, China, on R. Hun-ho; important trade route centre; flour, oil, leather, paper, soap; iron industry developing; univ. Pop. 250,000.

Moulins (*moo-lan'*), cap., Allier, central France, on R. Allier; sawmills; cabinetmaking works; breweries; oil and vinegar. Pop. 20,000.

Moulmein', second seapt. of Burma, at mouth of R. Salween; exports teak, rice, cotton. Pop. 61,000.

Mounds'ville, tn., W. Virginia, U.S.A., on R. Ohio; coal mining; glass, zinc, aeroplanes. Pop. 11,000.

Moun'tain Ash, urb. dist., Glamorganshire, Wales, 18 m. N.E. of Cardiff; coal mining. Pop. 38,400.

Mount Car'mel, bor., Pennsylvania, U.S.A., 45 m. N.E. of Harrisburg; coal mining; shirts and hosiery. Pop. 18,000.

Mountmel'lick, mkt. tn., Leix co., I.F.S.; malting, tanning. Pop. 2,300.

Mount Mor'gan, tn., Queensland, Australia, 22 m. S.S.W. of Rockhampton; famous gold mine. Pop. 6,000.

Mount Ver'non. (1) City, New York, U.S.A., on R. Bronx, adjoining New York city; favourite residential place. Pop. 61,000. (2) Tn., Illinois, U.S.A., 75 m. E. by S. of St. Louis; lumber, flour, woollen industries; coal in neighbourhood. Pop. 10,000.

Moville', wat.-pl., Donegal, I.F.S., on Lough Foyle, 18 m. N.E. of Londonderry; calling place for American liners. Pop. 1,000.

Mozambique (*mo-zam-bēk'*). (1) See PORTUGUESE EAST AFRICA. (2) Prov., Portuguese E. Africa; surface rises gradually from coast, and is thickly forested; sugar, maize, cotton. Area, 293,436 sq. m.; pop. 3,652,000. (3) Port, formerly cap. of above, on island in Mossuril Bay; exports ivory, rubber, ground-nuts, oil-seeds. Pop. 7,500.

Mozdok', tn., N. Caucasian Area, U.S.S.R., on R. Terek; manufactures soap, candles; brick and tile works, distilleries. Pop. 14,000.

Mühlhausen (*mool'how-zen*), town, Saxony, Prussia, 30 m. N.W. of Erfurt; imperial free city and of great commercial importance in 14th cent.; woollens, cotton, hosiery, furniture, soap, and chemicals. Pop. 36,000.

Mukacevo (*mook'ä-chä-vo*), formerly

MUNKACS, tn., Ruthenia, E. Czechoslovakia; iron mines; alum. Pop. 21,000.

Mülheim-am-Rhein (*mool'hīm*), tn., Rhine prov., Prussia, on R. Rhine; velvet, silk, chemicals, tobacco, brewing, tanning. Pop. 53,000.

Mülheim-an-der-Ruhr (*-roor*), tn., Rhine prov., Prussia, on R. Ruhr; ironworks; leather, tobacco, paper, beer; trade in coal. Pop. 127,000.

Mulhouse (*moo-looz'*), formerly MÜLHAUSEN, tn., Haut-Rhin, France, on R. Ill; industrial centre; manufactures woollens, cottons, chemicals, machinery, railway materials. Pop. 100,000.

Mull, isl., Hebrides, Argyllshire, w. Scotland; irregular coast-line of *c.* 300 m. in length; mountainous (Ben More, 3,185 ft.); numerous freshwater lochs; cattle and sheep; tn., Tobermory. Area, 408 sq. m.; pop. 5,000.

Mullingar', mkt. tn., Westmeath, I.F.S.; brewing, tanning; farming centre; angling resort. Pop. 5,300.

Multan'. (1) Dist., Punjab, India; alluvial soil; irrigation necessary; wheat, pulses, indigo, cotton. Area, 5,939 sq. m.; pop. 890,000. (2) Tn. in above, on R. Chenab; great trading centre; carpets, pottery, enamel work. Pop. 85,000.

Mumbles, THE. See OYSTERMOUTH.

Muncie (*mun'sē*), city, Indiana, U.S.A., on R. White, 50 m. N.E. of Indianapolis; iron and glass manufactures. Pop. 47,000.

Mün'den, tn., Hanover, Germany, 21 m. N.E. of Cassel; rubber, leather; trade in timber; lignite mined. Pop. 12,000.

Mu'nich (German *München*), cap. of Bavaria, Germany, on R. Isar; one of finest and most interesting cities in Europe. Royal Palace, Old Rathaus, Ruhmeshalle (with busts of celebrities), statue of Bavaria, libraries, univ.; art centre; school of painting. Noted breweries; scientific instruments, lithographs, stained glass, leather, paper, rubber goods, furniture, machinery. Pop. 681,000.

Muni River Settlement. See SPANISH GUINEA.

Munkacs. See MUKACEVO.

Mün'ster, cap. of Westphalia, Prussia; cathedral; univ.; cotton, linen, machinery, leather, furniture, pianos; distilling, brewing; wood carving, printing. Pop. 106,000.

Mun'ster, prov., s.w. I.F.S., containing counties Tipperary, Clare, Limerick, Kerry, Cork, and Waterford; mountainous in great part; drained by Rs. Shannon, Lee, Bandon, Blackwater, Suir. Area, 9,317 sq. m.; pop. 970,000.

Muran'o, tn., on isl., Venice, Italy; noted for Venetian glass; fine cathedral. Pop. 5,000.

Murcia (*mur'she-a*). (1) S.E. prov. and former kingdom, Spain; mountainous; esparto grass, mulberry trees, cereals, fruit; lead, zinc, coal, sulphur, copper. Area, 4,453 sq. m.; pop. 671,000. (2) Cap. of above, on R. Segura; has cathedral, univ.; manufactures silk, hats, gloves, saltpetre, glass. Pop. 155,000.

Mur'mansk, prov., Russia, along Arctic coast between Norway and White Sea; shores generally lofty and rocky. Fishing industry is valuable. Chief tn. Murmansk, an ice-free port, connected with Leningrad by rly. built during Great War. Area, 51,200 sq. m.; pop. 23,000.

Murom (*moo'rom*), tn., Vladimir, central Russia, on R. Oka; flour mills, distilleries, cotton and leather factories; iron smelting. Pop. 23,000.

Mur'ray, largest riv., Australia, rises in Australian Alps; forms boundary between Victoria and New South Wales; flows into Encounter Bay by Lake Alexandrina; chief tribs., Rs. Darling and Lachlan; unimportant for navigation; water used for irrigation; length, 1,300 miles.

Murree', hill station, Punjab, India; on s. slopes of Himalaya Mts., *c.* 20 m. N.E. of Rawalpindi, from which it is reached by motor.

Mür'ren, vil., Switzerland, on N. slope of Bernese Alps, near the

Jungfrau, 10 m. s. of Interlaken; holiday resort (alt. 5,363 ft.).

Murshidabad'. (1) Dist., Bengal, India; largely well-watered plain; rice, oil-seeds, mustard, sugar-cane, indigo. Area, 2,121 sq. m.; pop. 1,488,000. (2) Chief tn. of above, on R. Hooghly; silk weaving, ivory carving, gold and silver embroidery. Pop. 11,000.

Murzuq, tn., Italian Libya, N. Africa; caravan station. Pop. 6,500.

Mus'cat, port, Oman, Arabia; centre of trade with India, Persia, and Africa; surrounded by wall; exports dates, pearls, mother-of-pearl, fish, pomegranates. Pop. (with Matrah), 20,000.

Mus'catine, city, Iowa, U.S.A., on R. Mississippi; pearl buttons; lumber manufactures; pork packing and making of preserves. Pop. 16,000.

Muskegon (*mus-kē'gon*), ('grassy bog'), city, Michigan, U.S.A., near L. Michigan; lumber trade and metal manufactures; fruit culture and dairy farming in dist. Pop. 41,000.

Muskogee (*mus-kō'gē*), city, Oklahoma, U.S.A., 125 m. E. of Oklahoma City; cotton gins; railway shops, oil refineries, flour mills. Pop. 32,000.

Mus'selburgh, tn., Midlothian, Scotland, at mouth of R. Esk; adjoins Edinburgh; wire, rope, and net works; paper, tiles. Pop. 17,000.

Mussoo'rie, hill station, United Provinces, India, 70 m. S.E. of Simla; convalescent station for European troops. Pop. 8,000.

Mustagh Range. See KARAKORAM.

Mut'tra. (1) Dist., United Provinces, India; mainly plain, watered by R. Jumna; cereals, sugar-cane, and some cotton. Area, 1,450 sq. m.; pop. 619,000. (2) Cap. of above, on R. Jumna, 30 m. N.W. of Agra; Hindu religious centre; birthplace of Krishna; has many mosques and temples; paper, brass idols. Pop. 53,000.

Muzaffargarh', dist., Punjab, India, between rivs. Indus and Chenab; cereals, pulses. Chief tn. Muzaffargarh. Area, 6,052 sq. m.; pop. 568,000.

Muzaffarnag'ar. (1) Dist., United Provinces, India; cereals, sugar-cane, rice. Area, 1,666 sq. m.; pop. 877,000. (2) Chief tn. of above, 35 m. N. of Meerut; blankets. Pop. 24,000.

Muzaffarpur'. (1) Dist., Bihar, India; fertile plain, well irrigated by numerous streams; rice, cereals, pulses, sugar-cane; saltpetre. Area 3,036 sq. m.; pop. 2,755,000. (2) Chief tn. of above, 40 m. N. of Patna; carpets, matting, castor oil. Pop. 33,000.

Mweru (*mwä'roo*), lake, Central Africa, between Belgian Congo and N. Rhodesia, traversed by R. Luapula; length, 68 m.; breadth, 24 m.; reached by Livingstone (1867).

Mymensingh'. (1) Dist., Bengal, India; mostly alluvial plain; rice, jute, pulses. Area, 6,338 sq. m.; pop. 4,838,000. (2) See NASIRABAD (1).

Mynyddislwyn (*mŭn'ŭth-ēs-loo-ŭn*), urb. dist., Mon, England, 10 m. N.W. of Newport; collieries; ironworks. Pop. 16,200.

Myslowice (*mis-wov-it'se*), tn., Silesia, Poland, 110 m. S.E. of Breslau; collieries; rly. jn.; flax mills; bricks. Pop. 17,800.

Mysore (*mī'sōr'*). (1) Indian state in S. India; almost entirely enclosed by Madras Presidency; region consists of tableland broken by hill ranges and valleys; chief rivs., Kistna and Cauvery; productions include coffee, sugar-cane, cotton, rice, silk, cinchona, sandalwood, and ivory; gold is mined at Kolar. Area, 29,607 sq. m.; pop. 5,860,000. (2) Cap. of above, 240 m. S.W. of Madras; univ. (1916); carpet weaving. Pop. 84,000.

Mytholmroyd (*mī'thom-roid*), urb. dist., W. Riding, Yorks, England, 5 m. W. of Halifax; worsted; cotton. Pop. 4,500.

Mytilene. See LESBOS.

N

Naas (*nās* or *nä'as*), mkt. tn., co. Kildare, I.F.S.; once residence of kings of Leinster. Pop. 3,400.

Nabha (*nä'bä*). (1) Indian state, Punjab, India; large portion irrigated by Sirhind Canal; cereals, pulses, cotton, sugar-cane; manufactures gold and silver ware, brass vessels, cotton carpets. Area, *c.* 1,000 sq. m.; pop. 263,000. (2) Tn., cap. of above, 130 m. N.N.W. of Delhi; surrounded by mud wall. Pop. 15,000.

Nablus (*nä-bloos'*), (anc. *Shechem*), tn., Palestine, 30 m. N. of Jerusalem; in valley between Mts. Ebal and Gerizim; manufactures soap. Pop. 16,000.

Nabua (*näb'wä*), tn., Luzon, Philippines, 20 m. S.E. of Nueva Caceres; rice and sugar. Pop. 19,000.

Nä'ga Hills, dist., extreme E. of Assam, India; hilly; densely forested; abounds in game; coal, iron, and petroleum are found but little worked. Area, 3,115 sq. m.; pop. 160,000.

Nagasak'i, seapt., S.W. Kyushu, Japan; fine natural harbour; shipbuilding and engineering important; coaling station; manufactures enamelled pottery, lacquer, and tortoiseshell ware; exports fish, coal, textiles. Pop. 190,000.

Nagina (*nä-gē'na*), tn., United Provinces, India, 52 m. N.E. of Meerut; carved ebony wares, glass, and lacquered goods. Pop. 19,000.

Nagoya (*nä'gō-ya*), tn., Honshu, Japan, 94 m. N.E. of Kyoto; pottery, cloisonné enamels, lacquer wares, straw plait, textiles. Pop. 768,000.

Nagpur'. (1) Div., Central Provs., India; large plain S. of Satpura ranges. Area, 23,521 sq. m.; pop. *c.* 3,000,000. (2) Dist. of above; cereals, cotton, rice; manganese. Area, 3,834 sq. m.; pop. 792,000. (3) Cap. of Central Provinces, 440 m. by rail E.N.E. of Bombay; trade in grain, salt; cotton weaving. Pop. 145,000.

Nagy Becskerek. See BECKEREK, VELIKI.

Nagykanizsa (*noj-kan-it'sa*), town, Hungary, 20 m. S. of L. Balaton; brick works, flour mills, distilleries, and breweries; formerly important fortress. Pop. 30,000.

Nagykaroly. See CAREI.

Nagy-Kikinda. See KIKINDA, VELIKA.

Nagy-Körös (*noj'koo-roosh*), mkt. tn., Hungary, *c.* 50 m. S.E. of Budapest; vineyards; melons. Pop. 27,000.

Nagy-Szalonta. See SALONTA.

Nagy-Szombat. See TRNAVA.

Nagy-Varad. See ORADEA.

Nails'worth, par. and tn., Gloucestershire, England, 4 m. S. of Stroud; paper, textiles. Pop. 3,100.

Naini Tal (*nī'ni täl*). (1) Dist., United Provinces; hilly and largely forest-clad; rice, wheat, tea, and fruit. Area, 2,721 sq. m.; pop. 277,000. (2) Hill station in above, in Himalayas, 120 m. E.N.E. of Meerut; summer residence of lieut.-governor of United Provinces. Pop. 10,000.

Nairn, royal burgh, seaport and co. tn., Nairnshire, Scotland; dry and bracing climate; summer resort; fishing. Pop. 4,200.

Nairn'shire, mar. co., Scotland, bounded by Moray Firth, Moray and Inverness-shire; near coast is fertile and well-wooded, other parts principally moorland; largest rivers, Findhorn and Nairn; agriculture, grazing, and fishing; sandstone and granite quarries. Chief tn., Nairn. Area, 163 sq. m.; pop. 8,300.

Nairobi (*nī-rō'bi*), cap., Kenya Colony, Brit. East Africa; 5,452 ft. high; fine climate; on Uganda Rly.; important trade centre; well-built town with many fine buildings. Pop. 33,000.

Nakhichevan (*na-chē-shev-än'*). (1) Rep., Transcaucasia, U.S.S.R.; is bounded on S. and W. by Persia, and on N. and E. by Armenia; centre for trade between Russia and Persia; chief products, silk, cotton, wine, and salt. Area, 2,488 sq. m.; pop. 103,000. (2) Cap. of above, near R. Aras; flour-milling and leather manufacture. Pop. 9,000.

Nakhichevan-on-the-Don, tn., N. Caucasian Area, U.S.S.R., on R. Don; Armenian cathedral; smelting, rope-making, cotton and silk manufactures. Pop. 71,000.

Naks'kov, seaport, Denmark, on W. coast of Laaland Island; has fine harbour; shipbuilding and sugar refining. Pop. 14,000.

Namangan', tn., Uzbek, U.S.S.R.; in valley of Sir Darya R.; market for sheep and cotton; coal and petroleum. Pop. 74,000.

Namaqualand (*na-mä'kwä-land*), region in s.w. of Africa, stretching along the coast from the neighbourhood of Walvis Bay to 31° s.; divided by the Orange R. into LITTLE NAMAQUALAND, part of the province of Cape of Good Hope, and GREAT NAMAQUALAND, part of S.W. Africa.

Namur'. (1) Hilly and fertile prov., Belgium; drained Rs. Maas and Sambre; one-third of surface forested; rich in iron, coal. Area, 1,414 sq. m.; pop. 353,000. (2) Cap. of above, at junction of Rs. Maas and Sambre; strongly fortified; has 18th cent. cathedral; iron and steel, cutlery, glass, and firearms. Pop. 31,000.

Nanaimo (*na-ni'mō*), city, E. coast of Vancouver Island, Brit. Columbia; exports coal; timber cutting, brewing, and fruit canning. Pop. 9,000.

Nanchang, cap. of province of Kiangsi, China, on R. Kan; trade in tea, rice, and cotton. Pop. *c.* 400,000.

Nancy (*nan-sē'*), cap., Meurthe-et-Moselle, France, on R. Meurthe; fine churches, old gateways, ducal palace, picture gallery, univ.; chief manufactures, cottons, woollens, paper, iron, chemicals, artificial flowers; famed for embroidery; important railway centre. Pop. 108,000.

Nan'der, tn., Hyderabad, India, on R. Godaveri; muslin, gold-broidered scarves. Pop. *c.* 14,000.

Nandgä'on, Indian state, Central Provinces, India; w. part hilly and forested; E., fertile plain; rice, wheat, linseed. Cap. Raj-Nandgaon, 120 m. E. of Nagpur. Area, *c.* 900 sq. m.; pop. *c.* 127,000.

Nanking', cap. of China, since 1928; on Yangtze Kiang; once famous for great walls and magnificent buildings, destroyed by Taiping rebels (1853–64); treaty port since 1899; silk manufactures; exports silk, hides, and frozen meat; connected with Shanghai by railway. Pop. (est.) 497,000.

Nanning', treaty port, Kwangsi, China, on Yu-Kiang; exports aniseed, beans, rice, leather, antimony. Pop. (est.) 74,000.

Nanterre (*non-ter'*), town, Seine, France, 7 m. N.W. of Paris; chemicals, aluminium, tallow. Pop. 31,000.

Nantes (*nont*), cap., Loire-Inférieure, France; on R. Loire, which permits of ships drawing 20 ft. to reach the town; exports include machinery and iron ore. Chief industries, sugar refining and manufacture of oil, soap, chemicals, leather, machinery, and textiles. Pop. 166,000.

Nan'ticoke, town, Pennsylvania, U.S.A., on R. Susquehanna, 8 m. s.w. of Wilkes-Barre; anthracite coal; hosiery, canned goods. Pop. 26,000.

Nantucket Island, isl., Massachusetts, U.S.A.; sandy, rolling, and treeless; has several summer resorts; Nantucket tn. on N. shore. Formerly chief whaling centre. Length, 15 m.

Nant'wich, tn., Cheshire, England, 4 m. s.w. of Crewe; boot and shoe manufactures; cheese; brine baths; cruciform church and old grammar school. Pop. 7,100.

Nantyglo. See BLAINA.

Napier (*nā'pi-er*), seapt., North Island, New Zealand, on Hawke Bay; exports tinned and frozen meat. Severe earthquake, 1931. Pop. 19,000.

Na'ples. (1) Prov., Campania, Italy; smallest and most densely populated prov. in Italy; contains Mt. Vesuvius in s., rich volcanic soil in N., vineyards; oil, corn, hemp, cotton, chestnuts. Area, 1,204 sq. m.; pop. 2,180,000. (2) Cap. of above; beautifully situated on Bay of Naples, at base of Vesuvius; consists of old and new town; numerous churches and palaces with paintings and sculptures. Surroundings include Pompeii, Herculaneum, Sorrento, and the islands of Capri and Ischia. Second seaport of Italy and great trading centre; manufactures macaroni and vermicelli, wine, olive oil, chemicals, textiles, lace, leather, paper, furniture, majolica wares, musical instruments, and perfumery. Shipbuilding is also carried on. Pop. (est.) 966,000.

Nä'ra, tn., Honshu, Japan, 25 m. E. of Osaka; has beautiful temples, a huge bell (37 tons), and statue of Buddha; cap. of Japan from 709 till 784; fans, toys. Pop. 54,000.

Narayanganj (*nä-rä-yan-gunj'*), tn., Bengal, India, 10 m. S. of Dacca; entrepôt for jute distributing centre. Pop. *c.* 25,000.

Narbã'da, sacred river, India; flows into Gulf of Cambay; upper course much broken by rapids; seagoing vessels ascend 50 m.; length, *c.* 800 m.

Narbonne (*nar-bon'*), tn., Aude, France, near Gulf of Lions; cathedral, and archbishop's palace, now partly used as a museum; honey, red wine, sulphur, tiles. Pop. 25,000.

Narni (*nar'nē*), tn., Perugia, Italy, 65 m. N. of Rome; mineral springs; manufactures linoleum and calcium carbide. Pop. 14,000.

Nar'va, seaport tn., Estonia; manufactures cotton goods; exports textiles and timber. Pop. 27,000.

Nar'vik, or VICTORIAHAVN, ice-free port, on Ofoten Fjord, N.W. Norway; exports iron ore from Swedish districts served by Lapland railway. Pop. 7,000.

Naseby (*naz'bi*), vil., Northamptonshire, England, 10 m. N.N.W. of Northampton; scene of Royalist defeat by Roundheads (1645). Pop. 400.

Nash'ua, city, New Hampshire, U.S.A., 30 m. S. of Concord; manufactures cotton, carpets, refrigerators, steam engines. Pop. 31,000.

Nash'ville, cap. of Tennessee, U.S.A., on Cumberland R.; important educational centre; extensive trade; manufactures flour, cotton, saddlery, fertilizers, soap, agricultural implements, furniture, and timber produce. Pop. 153,000.

Nä'sik. (1) Dist., Bombay, India; western part hilly, eastern fertile and well cultivated; wheat, millet, pulses, rice, oil-seeds, cotton. Area, 5,877 sq. m.; pop. 832,000. (2) Cap. of above, on R. Godavari; resort of Hindu pilgrims; cotton weaving, brass and copper work. Pop. 38,000.

Nasirabad (*na-zēr-a-bäd'*). (1) Formerly MYMENSINGH, cap. of Mymensingh dist., tn., Bengal, India, 70 m. N. of Dacca; oil pressing, carpet-weaving; cane chairs. Pop. 15,000. (2) Tn., Rajputana, India, 12 m. S.E. of Ajmer; military station. Pop. 22,000.

Nassau. (1) (*nä'sou*) Dist., Hesse-Nassau, Prussia, bounded S. and W. by Rs. Rhine and Main, N. by Westphalia, E. by Hesse; surface mountainous; mineral springs; wines. Cap. Wiesbaden. Area, 1,830 sq. m. (2) (*nä-sō'*) Seapt., cap. of Bahama Islands, on New Providence I.; winter resort; trades in sponges, pearls, sisal fibre, fruit. Pop. 13,000.

Natal'. (1) Prov., Union of S. Africa, on S.E. coast; bounded on S.W. by Cape Prov., W. by Basutoland and Orange Free State, N. by Transvaal and Port. E. Africa; coast-line, *c.* 370 m. Surface rises over 5,000 ft. in series of terraces with many hills and valleys to Drakensberg Mts. on W.; numerous rivers and streams (chief Tugela), but none navigable. Climate healthy; coast districts semi-tropical, but practically fever-free; more bracing farther N.; heavy summer rains, Sept. to March; frequent thunderstorms; dry, sunny winter. Most important industry is sheep farming, in midland and upland districts. Cattle are reared everywhere. Angora goats and horses thrive in higher regions. On coastal belt sugar-cane, coffee, tea, and cotton are grown, plantations being worked by Indian coolies; wheat is limited to Upper Tugela districts; wattle bark in midlands; maize is chief grain crop; orchards are mostly in the coastal belt; bananas, pineapples, citrus fruits exported; other products include kaffir corn, tobacco, lucerne, sweet potatoes, and vegetables. Irrigation is easy. Chief mineral, coal, at Newcastle and Dundee. Copper, gold, silver, iron, nickel, manganese, tin, asbestos, gypsum, limestone, and oil shale also found. Manufactures are few and small. Fish abound in coastal waters. Chief tns., Pietermaritzburg (cap.), and Durban. Area (including Zululand), 35,284 sq. m.; pop. (white) 137,000, (coloured) 1,292,000. (2) Cap. of Rio Grande do Norte, Brazil; seapt.; exports cottons, sugar. Pop. 30,000.

Natchez (*nach'ez*), tn., Mississippi, U.S.A., on Mississippi R.; active river trade in cotton, cotton products, and cattle; sawmills. Pop. 12,000.

Na'tron Lakes, or SODA LAKES, group of lakes, Libyan Desert, Lower Egypt, 60 m. N.W. of Cairo; waters charged with salt, sodium carbonate, and sodium sulphate.

Naugatuck (*naw'ga-tuk*), tn., Connecticut, U.S.A., 25 m. N.W. of New Haven; rubber goods, safety pins, aeroplanes, and iron castings. Pop. 15,000.

Nauheim (*nou'hīm*), or BAD NAUHEIM, wat.-pl., N. Hesse, Germany, on N.E. slopes of Taunus Mts.; saline springs, used in rheumatic and heart affections. Pop. 9,000.

Naumburg (*noum'boorg*), tn., Saxony, Prussia, on R. Saale, 22 m. S.S.W. of Halle; 13th cent. cathedral; leather goods, woollens, combs. Pop. 29,000.

Naur'u (*na-oor'oo*), isl. in Pacific Ocean, 400 m. S. of Marshall Islands. Under mandate of Brit. Empire. Has largest reserves of high-grade phosphates in world. Area, *c.* 8 sq. m.; pop. 2,600.

Naushahra (*nou-shă-rä'*), tn. and cantonment, N.W. Frontier Province, India, 25 m. E. of Peshawar. Pop. *c.* 10,000.

Nav'an, mkt. tn., co. Meath, I.F.S.; woollen, flour, and bacon industries. Pop. 3,700.

Navanagar (*na-wan-ug'ur*), or JAMNAGAR. (1) Indian state, Bombay, India; flat surface; grain, cotton, and oil-seeds. Area, 3,791 sq. m.; pop. 345,000. (2) Cap. of above, on Gulf of Cutch; silk and gold embroidery; locomotive works. Pop. 42,000.

Navarre (*na-vär'*), or NAVARRA, prov., N. Spain; traversed by Pyrenees and Cantabrian Mts.; chief rivers, Ebro, Aragon, Bidassoa. Chief products, grain, olives, fruits, red wine; cattle rearing; silver-lead and copper mines; iron ore and salt found. Chief town, Pamplona. Area, 4,055 sq. m.; pop. 330,000.

Navigators' Islands. See SAMOA.

Navsari', tn., Baroda, India; *c.* 150 m. N. of Bombay; metal work; boots and shoes; cotton weaving. Large Parsee colony. Pop. 19,000.

Naxos, isl., Ægean Sea; largest and most fertile of the Cyclades; wine, fruits, emery. Pop. *c.* 17,000.

Naz'areth, tn., Galilee, Palestine; 1,600 ft. above sea-level; in fertile dist. Here Jesus lived till He commenced His public ministry. Pop. 7,000.

Naze, THE (*nāz*). (1) Headland in Essex, England, 5 m. S. of Harwich. (2) Cape, most S. point of Norway.

Neagh, LOUGH (*nā*), lake, N. Ireland; largest lake in Brit. Isles; has a few small islands; receives Upper Bann R.; drained by Lower Bann R.; abounds in fish; 17 by 11 m.; area, 153 sq. m.

Neath (*nēth*), port, Glamorganshire, Wales; has copper, tinplate, engineering, chemical, and ironfounding works; exports local mineral products; site of ruined abbey and castle; near by is an anc. stone circle. Pop. 33,300.

Nebras'ka, N. Central State, U.S.A., bounded N. by South Dakota, W. by Wyoming, S.W. by Colorado, S. by

Kansas, E. by Missouri and Iowa. Surface an undulating plain. Mountains in w. belong to Rocky Mountain system; large stretch of sand-hills in N. covering *c.* 20,000 sq. m.; extensive prairies in E. and S.; swamps in S.E. Principal rivers are Missouri (on eastern border), Platte and Niobrara. Climate healthy, with dry fine atmosphere; average annual rainfall *c.* 23 in; agriculture important; chief products, maize, wheat, oats, hay, potatoes, apples, sugar-beet, livestock, and wool; large quantities of potash are obtained from Alkali Lakes of the state. Chief industries are slaughtering and meat packing. Extensive irrigation. Principal towns are Omaha, Lincoln (cap.), South Omaha. Area, 77,510 sq. m.; pop. 1,296,000.

Neckar, riv. of S. Germany; joins the Rhine at Mannheim; canalized in parts; steam navigation to Cannstatt; length, 247 m.

Needles, THE, three chalk pinnacles at W. point of Isle of Wight, England; denudation reducing them gradually; lighthouse on most westerly.

Negapatam′, seaport, Madras, India, on R. Cauvery delta; trades with Rangoon and Straits Settlements; exports ground-nuts, cotton, and tobacco. Pop. 54,000.

Negri Sembilan ('nine states'), state, Malay Peninsula, on Strait of Malacca; under British protection; produces tin, coffee, tapioca, rice. Cap. Seremban. Area, 2,550 sq. m.; pop. 179,000.

Neilston (*nēls′ton*), town, Renfrewshire, Scotland, 4 m. S. of Paisley; print works, bleachfields, cotton spinning. Pop. 3,500.

Neisse (*nī′sa*), tn., Silesia, Prussia, 50 m. S.E. of Breslau; 12th cent. Gothic church; linen and chemicals. Pop. 32,000.

Nejd (*nezhd*), kingdom (including HEJAZ), Arabia, bounded by Trans-Jordan, Iraq, Persian Gulf, Aden, Yemen, and Red Sea; surface mostly sandy desert, with occasional oases where soil is fertile; chief riv. basins are Wadi Rumma and Wadi Dawasir; horses, camels, and sheep reared; chief products are dates, wheat, barley, and fruits; chief towns, Hufuf and Riyadh. Area, *c.* 200,000 sq. m.; pop. *c.* 3,000,000.

Nellore′. (1) Dist., Madras, India; rice, pulses, millet; mica and iron occur. Area, 7,973 sq. m.; pop. *c.* 1,500,000. (2) Cap. of above, 110 m. N. of Madras; dyeing and rice-husking industries. Pop. 36,000.

Nel′son. (1) Munic. bor., Lancashire, England, 3 m. N.E. of Burnley; cotton and other textiles; coal mining. Pop. 38,300. (2) Provincial dist., South Island, New Zealand; mountainous; well timbered; fruit, hops; coal, gold, iron, lead, silver, copper ores. Area, 10,875 sq. m.; pop. 51,000. (3) Cap. of above, on N. coast; jam making. Pop. 12,000. (4) Tn., Brit. Columbia, Canada, on Kootenay Lake; silver mining, lumbering; fruit, vegetables. Pop. 5,000. (5) Riv., Canada; issues from Lake Winnipeg and discharges into Hudson Bay at Port Nelson. Length, *c.* 500 m. Navigable for *c.* 100 m.

Nemi (*nā′mē*), lake, Alban Hills, Italy, 20 m. S. of Rome; occupies volcanic crater (alt. 1,060 ft.); in surrounding woods Diana was worshipped; anc. Roman galley of Emperor Caligula was recovered from lake in 1930.

Nenagh (*nē′na*), mkt. tn., co. Tipperary, I.F.S.; has agricultural trade; remains of anc. castle. Pop. 4,500.

Nepal, NEPAUL, or NIPAL (*ne-pawl′*), independent state in N.E. of India, bounded N. by Tibet, W. by United Provs., S. by United Provs. and Bihar and Orissa, and E. by Bengal and Sikkim. Lofty and mountainous region in N., containing part of Himalayas with some of highest summits in world (Mount Everest, Kinchinjunga, and Dhaulagiri). In S. fertile and cultivated country, called *Tarai.* State is watered principally by Rs. Gogra, Gandak, Sun Kosi, and their tributaries. Great variety of flora and fauna; cotton, rice, maize, wheat, barley, oats, pulse, hemp, sugar-cane, tobacco, dyes, drugs, vegetables, fruits, and flowers are cultivated; forests produce fine timber. Among wild animals are tiger, leopard, wolf, hyena, rhinoceros, and elephant. Chief occupation is agriculture. Communication is in a backward state. State is inhabited by several different tribes, most important being warlike Gurkhas. Cap. Katmandu. Area, *c.* 54,000 sq. m.; pop. *c.* 5,600,000.

Nerbudda. See NARBADA.

Ness, LOCH, lake, Inverness, Scotland; length, 22 m.; depth, 106 to 130 fathoms; forms part of Caledonian Canal route through Glenmore.

Neston. See PARKGATE.

Netherlands. See HOLLAND.

Net'ley, par. and vil., Hampshire, England, on Southampton Water; military hospital, leading centre of military ambulance training; ruined abbey. Pop. 1,400.

Neu-Brandenburg (*noi-brand'en-boorg*), tn., Mecklenburg-Strelitz, N. Germany, on Lake Tollense; machinery and chemical products. Pop. 14,000.

Neuchâtel (*noo-shat-el'*). (1) Canton, w. Switzerland. Surface chiefly mountainous, Jura range crossing canton; chief rivers, Doubs and Thièle. Cattle are reared. Manufactures watches; cheese, cotton, hosiery, cutlery, electrical appliances, wine, and chocolate. Chief tns., Neuchâtel, La Chaux de Fonds, and Le Locle. Area, 305 sq. m.; pop. 131,000. (2) Cap. of above, on L. Neuchâtel; anc. castle and cathedral; educational establishments; watches, jewellery; condensed milk. Pop. 23,000. (3) LAKE OF, Switzerland; largest lake entirely in Swiss territory; depth, 505 ft.; area, 92 sq. m.

Neuilly-sur-Seine (*noo-ē'yē-soor-sān*), w. suburb, Paris, France; embossed leather, carpets, automobiles, perfumes, and chocolate. Pop. 50,000.

Neu-Mecklenburg. See NEW IRELAND.

Neumünster (*noi-moon'ster*), town, Schleswig-Holstein, Prussia, 20 m. s. by w. of Kiel; important tanning industry. Pop. 40,000.

Neunkirchen (*noin-kēr'chen*), tn., Rhine prov., Prussia, 38 m. s.w. of Trier; ironworks and collieries. Pop. 35,000.

Neu-Pommern. See NEW BRITAIN.

Neuquen (*nā-oo-ken'*), terr., Argentina, S. America, on Chilean frontier; mountainous; cattle, horses, sheep raised. Cap. Neuquen, *c.* 300 m. w. of Bahia Blanca. Area, 40,530 sq. m.; pop. 29,000.

Neusalz (*noi'zalts*), tn., N. Silesia, Prussia, on R. Oder; flax mills, breweries, shipyards, and ironworks. Pop. 14,000.

Neuss (*nois*), tn., Rhineland, Prussia, 7 m. s.w. of Düsseldorf; iron goods, flour, textiles. Pop. 45,000.

Neustadt (*noi'stat*), tn., s. Silesia, Prussia; tanneries; carpets, textiles, shoes, and dyes. Pop. 17,000.

Neustadt-an-der-Haardt (*noi'stat-an-der-hart*), tn., Bavarian Palatinate, Germany, 17 m. s.w. of Mannheim; wine, cloth, paper; school of viticulture. Pop. 21,000.

Neu-Stettin (*noi-stet-ēn'*), tn., Pomerania, Prussia; iron foundries; dyeworks, sawmills; trade in cattle, agricultural produce. Pop. 15,000.

Neu-Strelitz (*noi-strā'lēts*), cap. Mecklenburg-Strelitz, N. Germany; iron manufactures, distilleries, furniture factories. Pop. 12,000.

Neuwied (*noi'vēt*), tn., Rhineland, Prussia, on R. Rhine, 9 m. N.W. of Coblenz; tobacco, sugar, chicory, and buttons; ironfounding; famous Moravian schools. Pop. 20,000.

Ne'va, riv., N.W. Russia, flows from Lake Ladoga into Gulf of Finland; ice-free for seven months; lower course navigable by large vessels; length, 40 m.; Leningrad at mouth.

Nevä'da, Western State, U.S.A., bounded N. by Idaho and Oregon, W. and S. by California, E. by Arizona and Utah. Except in N.E. and S.E., lies wholly in Great Basin, which consists of elevated plateau; principal ranges are E. Humboldt Mts., Washoe Mts. (branch from Sierra Nevada), Toyabe

Mts., Humboldt Mts., and White Pine Mts. Lakes are numerous and generally salt; hot and cold springs are frequent; valleys generally desert. In S.E. are Virgin and Colorado rivers; rivers belonging to Great Basin lose themselves in lakes or sink, to reappear farther on; longest and most important river is Humboldt, flowing into Humboldt Lake. On account of dry climate agriculture depends much on irrigation; grain, hay, butter, vegetables, and fruits are produced; stock raising is a rising industry. Nevada is one of richest states in mineral wealth; gold and silver; also copper, lead, zinc, quicksilver, antimony, sulphur, gypsum, borax. Chief towns, Carson (cap.), Reno, and Virginia. Area, 110,690 sq. m.; pop. 77,000.

Nevers (*ne-văr'*), chief tn., Nièvre, France, on R. Loire; cathedral dating from 11th cent.; iron goods, agricultural implements, majolica pottery. Pop. 27,000.

Nev'in, wat.-pl., Carnarvonshire, N. Wales; fishing. Pop. 1,900.

Nevis (*nē'vis*), isl., Leeward group, Brit. W. Indies; mountainous; subject to hurricanes; exports cotton, coconuts, sugar. Cap. Charlestown. Area, 50 sq. m.; pop. 13,000.

Nevis, BEN. See BEN NEVIS.

New Abbey, vil., Kirkcudbrightshire, Scotland, 10 m. S. of Dumfries; ruins of Sweetheart Abbey. Pop. 730.

New Albany, city, Indiana, U.S.A., on Ohio R.; manufactures leather, furniture, foundry and machine-shop products. Pop. 26,000.

New'ark. (1) Munic. bor., Notts, England, on R. Trent; trade in corn and malt; agricultural implements, beer, plaster of Paris; gypsum and limestone quarries. Pop. 18,100. (2) City, New Jersey, U.S.A.; largest city in state; educational centre; manufactures foundry and machine-shop goods, chemicals, leather, jewellery. Pop. 443,000. (3) City, Ohio, U.S.A., 33 m. E. of Columbus; manufactures steel rails, locomotives, glassware, motor-cars. Pop. 30,000.

New Bed'ford, port, Massachusetts, U.S.A., on Acushnet estuary; extensive trade; formerly chief port of whale fisheries; manufactures cotton, lubricating oils, cordage, shoes, glass, paints. Pop. 113,000.

Newbiggin, urb. dist., Northumberland, England, 9 m. E. of Morpeth; wat.-pl.; fishing; coal mines in neighbourhood. Pop. 6,900.

New Bright'on, tn., Cheshire, England, on Wirral peninsula; favourite wat.-pl.; ferry to Liverpool. Part of Wallasey.

New Britain. (1) Formerly NEU POMMERN, largest island in Bismarck Archipelago, N.E. of New Guinea in W. Pacific, and includes, in addition to New Britain, New Ireland, Lavongai, and various subsidiary groups. New Britain is very mountainous; dense vegetation; interior almost unknown; climate unhealthy; Gazelle Peninsula, in N., well developed; coconuts, cocoa, and coffee are produced. Administered by Australia under mandate. Chief town, Rabaul. Area, 10,000 sq. m.; pop. *c.* 82,000. (2) City, Connecticut, U.S.A., 9 m. S.W. of Hartford; hardware; foundry and machine-shop goods. Pop. 68,000.

New Brunswick. (1) Mar. Prov., Canada, bounded by Quebec, Gulf of St. Lawrence (N.), Quebec and Maine (W.), Bay of Fundy (S.), Nova Scotia, Gulf of St. Lawrence (E.); connected with Nova Scotia by isthmus of Chignecto; seaboard, about 600 m., has excellent harbours; extensive forests; chief rivers are St. John, Miramichi, and Restigouche; surface undulating; numerous small lakes. Chief industries, agriculture, lumbering, and fishing. Coal is mined, and gypsum quarried; oil and natural gas are found. Chief towns, Fredericton (cap.), Saint John, and Moncton. Area, 27,985 sq. m.; pop. 388,000. (2) Tn., New Jersey, U.S.A., 23 m. S.W. of Newark; R.C. cathedral; rubber goods, hardware, hosiery. Pop. 34,000.

New'burgh. (1) Royal burgh, Fife, Scotland, on Firth of Tay; manufactures linen and floorcloth; important salmon fisheries; fruit dist. Pop. 2,200. (2) City, New York, U.S.A., on Hudson R.; manufactures chemicals, cotton and woollen goods, flour, machinery. Pop. 31,000.

New'burn, urban dist., Northumberland, England, on R. Tyne; coal mines, ironworks. Pop. 19,500.

New'bury, munic. bor., mkt. tn., Berkshire, England, on R. Kennet; Jacobean Cloth Hall is a relic of trade in malt and wool; fossils and antiquarian objects obtained from peat bed. Pop. 13,300.

New'buryport, city, Massachusetts, U.S.A., 40 m. N. of Boston; textiles, boots and shoes. Pop. 16,000.

New Caledonia, French isl. in South Pacific, 700 m. E. of Queensland; mountainous and forested; has penal settlement at Nou I., but no convicts sent there since 1896. Dependencies of New Caledonia are Isle of Pines, Wallis Archipelago, Loyalty Islands, Huon Islands, Futuna, and Alofi. Chief exports, coffee, copra, cotton, maize, tobacco, fruits; much mineral wealth, chrome, cobalt, nickel, iron, and manganese being particularly abundant. Cap. Numea. Area, 8,548 sq. m.; pop. 47,000.

New'castle. (1) Seaport, co. Down, N. Ireland; holiday resort; fishing. Pop. 2,100. (2) Tn., New South Wales, Australia; at mouth of Hunter R.; exports coal, wool, frozen meat; chief coal port of Australia; smelting works, iron foundries; engineering and shipbuilding. Pop. 103,000. (3) Tn., New Brunswick, Canada, on R. Miramichi; trade in lumber and fish; centre of big game district; wireless station. Pop. 3,000.

New Castle, city, Pennsylvania, U.S.A., 50 m. N.W. of Pittsburgh; iron and coal; manufactures tinplate, iron, glass, steel wire; agricultural produce. Pop. 49,000.

Newcastle-under-Lyme, munic. bor., Staffordshire, England; manufactures cotton goods, clothing, and paper; close to the Potteries. Pop. 23,200.

Newcastle-upon-Tyne, co. tn., Northumberland, England, on R. Tyne; anc. town, now one of chief commercial centres in England, owing to mineral products in vicinity; connected by bridges with Gateshead, on opposite bank of river. Castle, erected 12th cent.; many fine churches. Shipbuilding is main industry; chief export, coal; manufactures include iron, steel, machinery, glass, earthenware, chemicals. Pop. 283,100.

New'chwang, seapt., Manchuria, China; on Gulf of Liaotung; a treaty port, trading in beans, maize, cotton seed, and coal; manufactures cotton goods, hosiery, soap, and glass; important fisheries. Pop. 65,000.

New Don'gola, tn., Anglo-Egyptian Sudan, Africa, on R. Nile, 750 m. S. of Cairo; important trading station and military depot.

New England, name given to six states in N.E. of U.S.A., Maine, New Hampshire, Vermont, Massachusetts, Rhode Island, and Connecticut. Named New England by Captain Smith (1614); first successful settlement by Puritans from England was made at Plymouth (1620). Area, 61,976 sq. m.

New Forest, dist., Hampshire, England, W. of Southampton Water; well wooded, with beautiful scenery; greater part (100 sq. m.) is crown property; in S.E. are ruins of Beaulieu Abbey, founded by King John; chief village is Lyndhurst, near centre.

New'foundland, isl., N. America; Britain's oldest colony; off mouth of R. St. Lawrence; separated from Labrador by Strait of Belle Isle (11 m. wide), and from Cape Breton I. by Cabot Strait (65 m. wide). Shape roughly triangular. Coast-line much broken and surface rugged; interior a low plateau. There are innumerable lakes, about one-third of surface being water; largest lakes, Grand and Red Indian. Climate milder than that of Canada; fogs frequent. Spruce and pine forests in various parts; over 90 per cent. of adult pop. engaged in fishing, cod fisheries being staple resource; also seal, salmon, and herring fishing; considerable lumber trade; important pulp and paper mills. Minerals include iron (Bell I.), copper, asbestos, lead, coal, silver, gold. Railway mileage, 905. Chief towns are St. John's (cap.), Harbour Grace, and Bonavista. Area, 42,734 sq. m.; pop. 258,000. Colony now includes E. part of peninsula of Labrador (110,000 sq. m.).

New Glas'gow, city, Nova Scotia, Canada, 10 m. S.E. of Pictou; in Pictou coalfield area; iron and steel works. Pop. 10,000.

New Guinea, second largest isl. in the world, N. of Australia, in W. Pacific; separated from Australia by Torres Strait and Arafura Sea; length about 1,500 m.; breadth, 480 m.; area, *c.* 312,000 sq. m. Northern part is almost separated from remainder by MacCluer Inlet; western half and interior still mostly unexplored. Coast-line much indented with many fine harbours. High mountain ranges form a more or less well-defined chain running through centre of island. Chief rivers are Mamberamo, Sepik, Fly, and Digue. Rainfall heavy; temperature high; climate unhealthy for Europeans. Vegetation abundant; type varies according to height. Island is inhabited by Papuans mixed with Malays and Polynesians, and is notorious for head hunting and savage tribes. Politically New Guinea is divided into three territories—British New Guinea or Territory of Papua in S.E.; Mandated Territory of New Guinea, administered by the Commonwealth Government of Australia, in N.E.; and Dutch New Guinea in W.

Territory of Papua includes D'Entrecasteaux and Louisiade groups; Commonwealth of Australia assumed control (1901). Gold mining is important; petroleum wells discovered (1919); chief exports, rubber, osmiridium, gold, copra, and various tropical products. Cap. Port Moresby. Area, *c.* 90,540 sq. m.; pop. 276,000.

Mandated Territory of New Guinea, formerly *German New Guinea*, includes Kaiser Wilhelm's Land (area, 68,500 sq. m.), Bismarck Archipelago, Solomon Islands, and Nauru. Chief products are copra, gold, timber, mother-of-pearl, coffee, cocoa, sandalwood, and tortoise-shell. Cap. Rabaul, in New Britain. Total area, 76,000 sq. m.; pop. 747,000.

Dutch New Guinea has never been wholly explored, and is practically undeveloped. There are a few trading and mission stations, the chief being at Merauke. Area, 160,692 sq. m.; pop. 195,000.

New Hamp'shire, New England State, U.S.A.; bounded N. by Quebec, W. by Vermont, S. by Massachusetts, E. by Atlantic Ocean and Maine. Surface mountainous, except in S.E.; White Mts. in N. consist of several ranges—Presidential, with Mt. Washington (6,293 ft.); Franconia range; Carter Moriah range. Principal rivers are Connecticut, Piscataqua, Merrimac, Androscoggin; numerous lakes with fine scenery. Climate healthy, with severe winters. Extensive forests of beech, oak, yellow birch, sugar-maple. Principal products are hay, corn, potatoes, oats, fruit (especially apples), tobacco, timber; manufactures cotton and woollen goods, boots and shoes, lumber, machinery, flour, paper; granite and mica are quarried. The principal towns are Manchester, Nashua, Concord (cap.). Area, 9,341 sq. m.; pop. 443,000.

New Haven, seaport, Connecticut, U.S.A., on New Haven Bay; one of finest cities in America; seat of Yale Univ.; chief manufacturing city of state, and has extensive trade; firearms, tools, clocks, carriages, paper; meat packing an important industry. Pop. 163,000.

Newhaven. (1) Seaport, Sussex, England, at mouth of R. Ouse; large import trade carried on with Fr. ports; packet station for Dieppe. Pop. 6,800. (2) Fishing vil., Scotland, on Firth of Forth; part of city of Edinburgh; large fish market.

New Hebrides, chain of islands, Pacific Ocean, *c.* 500 m. W. of Fiji, largest being Espiritu Santo, Mallicolo, Erromango, Efaté or Sandwich, Ambrym, Tanna, and Aneityum; mostly lofty and volcanic, with luxuriant vegetation; sago-palm, sugar-cane, arrowroot, coffee grown; sulphur, copper, nickel found; leading exports are coffee, copra, maize, bananas, and cotton. Jointly administered (since 1906) by Brit. and French High Commissioners; seat of government at Port Vila in Efaté I.; inhabited by native Melanesians, British, and French. Area, *c.* 5,700 sq. m.; pop. *c.* 60,000.

New Ireland, formerly NEU-MECKLENBURG, second largest island in Bismarck Archipelago, W. Pacific; mountainous; fertile soil; coconuts, bananas. Chief town, Kavieng. Area, 3,000 sq. m.

New Jer'sey, Atlantic State, U.S.A.; bounded N. by New York, W. by Pennsylvania, S. by Delaware Bay, and E. by Atlantic. Coast-line is about 120 m., fringed with sand-bars; numerous large inlets. Surface hilly in N. where Blue or Kittatinny Mts. in High Point attain a height of 1,805 ft.; S.E. of Blue Mts. is large plateau with average elevation *c.* 1,000 ft. Coastal region is marshy. Among rivers are Hudson, Delaware, Passaic, and Raritan, many navigable; in N. are numerous lakes situated amid fine scenery. Climate healthy, esp. in highlands, where there are many summer resorts. Extensive forests (chiefly pine) in S.; oak and chestnut in N. Chief agricultural products, maize, wheat, oats, hay, potatoes, fruit. New Jersey is an important manufacturing and commercial state; minerals, zinc, cement, and iron; main industries textiles, machinery, iron and steel, leather, petroleum refining, chemicals. Valuable fisheries. Chief towns, Newark, Jersey City, Paterson, Trenton (cap.), Camden, Elizabeth, Hoboken, Bayonne, and Passaic. Area, 8,224 sq. m.; pop. 3,156,000.

New Lon'don, tn., Connecticut, U.S.A., on R. Thames, 3 m. from Long I. Sound; good harbour; agricultural machinery, hardware, silk thread, cotton and woollen goods; fruit canning; fishing; naval arsenal. Pop. 30,000.

New'lyn, seaport vil., Cornwall, England, on Mount's Bay; fishing is chief industry; formerly tin much worked and smelted. Pop. 3,900.

New'mains, tn., Lanarkshire, Scotland, 2 m. N.E. of Wishaw; coal mines and ironworks. Pop. 4,000.

Newmar'ket. (1) Mkt. tn., Suffolk, England, 12 m. E. of Cambridge; noted for horse races held on Heath; Jockey Club has extensive premises here. Pop. 9,800. (2) Tn., North Island, New Zealand, 3 m. S. of Auckland, of which it forms a suburb; large railway workshops. Pop. 3,000.

New Mex'ico, S.W. state, U.S.A.; bounded N. by Colorado, W. by Arizona, S. by Mexico and Texas, E. by Texas and Oklahoma. Region consists of high tablelands broken by lofty mountain ranges; highest peaks (some over 12,000 ft.) belong to main chain of Rocky Mt. system. Characteristic feature is flat-topped mountain or *Mesa.* In E. is vast extent of waste land known as Staked Plains or Llano Estacado. Most important rivers: Rio Grande, which crosses state from N. to S.; Canadian R. and Pecos in E. Climate is healthy. Rainfall insufficient for agriculture, valleys productive, and other regions rendered fertile by irrigation; chief crops are wheat, maize, oats; cotton, vegetables, and fruits also cultivated; leading industry stock-raising. New Mexico is rich in minerals; gold, silver, copper, coal, lead, and zinc worked; marble and sandstone quarried; turquoises and other precious stones found; mineral springs numerous. Leading industries are flour and grist milling, manufacture of cars, lumber and timber products, and blankets. Chief towns are Santa Fé (cap.) and Albuquerque (with univ.). Area, 122,634 sq. m.; pop. 360,000.

New Milford. See NEYLAND.

New Mills, urban dist., Derbyshire, England, 8 m. S.E. of Stockport; has calico-printing works, foundries, collieries. Pop. 8,600.

Newmilns' and Green'holm, tn., Ayrshire, Scotland; on riv. Irvine; muslins, laces; ruins of old castle. Pop. 4,000.

New Or'leans, port, Louisiana, U.S.A., on Mississippi R. Dykes or embankments (levees), wide enough to form promenades, have been constructed along river banks to prevent inundation. River lined with docks and piers; modern part of city wide and spacious; old French and Spanish quarters afford striking contrast; among prominent structures are city hall, custom house, cotton exchange, St. Louis Cathedral (1723), Cabilda (old Spanish city hall), and archiepiscopal palace (1730). One of chief cotton markets of world, with extensive export trade in cotton, tobacco, lumber, sugar, rice, grain, and hides; manufactures include molasses, rice, cotton goods, and machinery; one of largest sugar refineries in America. Pop. 456,000.

New Pitsli'go, vil., N. Aberdeenshire, Scotland; has extensive granite quarries. Pop. 1,400.

New'port. (1) Seapt., Monmouthshire, England, on R. Usk; important iron and chemical manufactures, agricultural implements, pottery, glass; exports large quantities of coal and iron; has ruined castle (12th cent.) and fine old church; Roman remains found. Pop. 89,200. (2) Munic. bor., Isle of Wight, England; in neighbourhood are remains of Carisbrooke Castle, where Charles I. was imprisoned. Pop. 11,300. (3) Mkt. tn. and urb. dist., Shropshire, England, 11 m. W. of Stafford; ruins of Lilleshall Abbey; agricultural college; manufactures agricultural implements and machinery. Pop. 3,400. (4) Burgh, Fife, Scotland, on Firth of Tay; residential suburb of Dundee. Pop. 3,300. (5) Port, Rhode Island, U.S.A., on Narragansett Bay; excellent harbour, well protected by forts and torpedo station; naval station; fashionable wat.-pl.; fishing is chief industry. Pop. 27,000. (6) City, Kentucky, U.S.A., on Ohio R., opposite Cincinnati; iron and steel goods. Pop. 30,000.

Newport News, port, Virginia, U.S.A.; fine harbour; large shipbuilding centre; exports coal, tobacco, and motor-cars. Pop. 34,000.

New'port Pag'nell, mkt. tn., Bucks, England, at junction of rivs. Ouse and Ousel; brewery, carriage and motor-building works; parish church (14th cent.); Queen Anne's Hospital (13th cent.). Pop. 4,000.

Newquay, urb. dist., Cornwall, England, 11 m. N. of Truro; popular summer resort; pilchard fisheries. Pop. 6,000.

New River, artificial channel, England, conveying water from springs of Chadwell and Amwell, Hertfordshire, and from R. Lea to reservoirs at Hornsey and Stoke Newington, London.

New Rochelle (*rō-shel'*), city, New York, U.S.A.; residential suburb of New York; printing. Pop. 54,000.

New Ross, tn., river port, Wexford, I.F.S., on R. Barrow; tanning, brewing, salmon fishing; agricultural trade. Pop. 5,000.

New'ry, mkt. tn., seaport, co. Down, N. Ireland, near head of Carlingford Lough; flax spinning, breweries, tanneries, and rope making; granite is quarried. Pop. 12,200.

New Siberian Islands, group of islands in Arctic Ocean, N. of Siberia, consisting of Kotelni, Byelkovski, Thaddaeus, Novaya Sibir, and Lyakhov Islands; highly interesting fossil flora and fauna (mammoth, rhinoceros, etc.); climate severe; uninhabited.

New South Wales, oldest state of Australian Commonwealth; bounded N. by Queensland, W. by South Australia, S. by Victoria, E. by Pacific Ocean; coast-line from Cape Howe to Point Danger, *c.* 700 m., contains many excellent harbours. Traversed from N. to S. by Great Dividing Range, including New England and Liverpool ranges, Blue Mts., Australian Alps, Mt. Kosciusko, highest peak in Australia (7,328 ft.). W. part consists of extensive plains with fine pasture lands; E. of Dividing Range lies a narrow coastal plain. Chief rivers are Murray, Murrumbidgee, Darling, Lachlan. Climate healthy; northern coastal districts dry and subtropical; interior and western plains hotter and drier than coast. Chief industry is sheep rearing, particularly for wool; also large numbers of cattle and horses. Mining is next in importance; chief minerals, gold, silver, copper, tin, lead, and coal. Principal agricultural products, grain, potatoes, hay, tobacco, and dairy produce. There are valuable fisheries and timber. Manufacture is rapidly increasing. Chief towns, Sydney (cap.), Newcastle, Broken Hill, Auburn, and Bankstown. Contains Canberra, the Commonwealth cap., in enclave of Federal Territory. Area, 309,432 sq. m.; pop. 2,102,000.

Lord Howe Island, *c.* 400 m. E. of Port Macquarie, is a dependency of New South Wales.

New'ton. (1) City, Massachusetts, U.S.A.; residential suburb of Boston; manufactures machinery, silk, worsted, and rubber products. Pop. 65,000. (2) Tn., Lanarkshire, Scotland, 5 m. S.E. of Glasgow; nail-making industry. Pop. 5,100.

New'ton Ab'bot, mkt. tn., S. Devonshire, England, on Teign estuary; rly. jn. Pop. 15,000.

Newtongrange, vil., Midlothian, Scotland, 2½ m. S. of Dalkeith; collieries, brick and tile works. Pop. 4,800.

Newton Heath, tn., Lancashire, England; suburb of Manchester; cotton mills, chemical and dye works. Pop. 34,700.

New'ton-in-Mak'erfield, urban dist., Lancashire, England, 15½ m. W. of Manchester; includes Newton-le-Willows and Earlestown; rly. jn.; collieries; paper, cotton, and sugar mills; glassworks, locomotive and engineering works. Pop. 20,200.

New'ton Stew'art, mkt. tn., Wigtownshire, Scotland, on R. Cree, 50 m. W.S.W. of Dumfries; woollen goods, agricultural implements. Pop. 1,800.

New'town, tn., Montgomeryshire, Wales, on R. Severn; flannel; birthplace of Robert Owen. Pop. 5,200.

Newtownards', seaport, co. Down, N. Ireland, on Strangford Lough; muslin embroidery; linens, hosiery; nurseries. Pop. 10,100.

New'town St. Bos'wells, vil., Roxburghshire, Scotland, 3½ m. S.E. of Melrose; important railway jn. (St. Boswells). Pop. 600.

New'town Stew'art, mkt. tn., co. Tyrone, N. Ireland, 10 m. N. by W. of Omagh; burned by James II. after siege of Londonderry. Pop. 1,900.

New Wash'ington, tn., Panay I., Philippine Islands; rice, sugar, cattle, and horses. Pop. 24,000.

New Wat'erford, tn., Nova Scotia, Canada, on Cape Breton I., 8 m. N.E. of Sydney. Pop. 7,500.

New West'minster, tn., former cap., Brit. Columbia, Canada, near mouth of Fraser R.; exports lumber, canned salmon, fish oil. Pop. 14,000.

New York. (1) N.E. state of U.S.A.; bounded N. by Quebec, N.W. and W. by Ontario, L. Ontario and L. Erie; S. by Pennsylvania, New Jersey, and Atlantic; E. by Connecticut, Massachusetts, and Vermont. Includes Long I. and Staten I. on Atlantic coast. Coast-line *c.* 275 m. on Lakes Erie and Ontario, with several good harbours; ocean seaboard is small but important, containing harbour of New York city. Surface mountainous in E.; Adirondack Mts. in N.E.; Catskill Mts. in S.E.; extensive tableland in central and W. regions; coastal districts level. Principal river is Hudson, which, with its tributary the Mohawk, is chief route to interior plains. Many fine falls and rapids, esp. Niagara. Climate healthy, with hot summers and severe winters. Immense forests in Adirondack, Catskill Mts.; much pasture and arable land in plateau regions. Principal products, hay, potatoes, maize, oats, wheat, dairy products, timber. Important industries are manufacturing of clothing, machinery, printing and publishing, sugar and molasses refining, slaughtering and meat packing; flour, paper, petroleum refining, silk and silk goods, cement. Minerals include magnetic iron ore, natural gas, petroleum; salt, gypsum, marble, limestone are quarried; valuable fisheries (oysters), etc. Chief tns., New York, Buffalo, Rochester, Syracuse, Albany (cap.), Schenectady, Yonkers, Utica, Troy, Binghamton. Area, 49,204 sq. m.; pop. 11,162,000. (2) City, New York state, largest in U.S.A., and second largest in world; on Hudson R. Includes Manhattan I., Long I., Staten I. It is divided into five boroughs—Manhattan, Richmond, Brooklyn, Queens, and Bronx. Harbour, one of finest in world, consists of outer harbour or Lower Bay (area, *c.* 120 sq. m.); separated from Atlantic Ocean by Sandy Hook bar, and inner harbour or Upper Bay (14 sq. m.), connected with former by the Narrows, between Long I. and Staten I. Statue of Liberty stands in Upper Bay. Larger part of city laid out very regularly. Principal business thoroughfares are Broadway, Wall and New Streets; residential streets are Fifth Avenue, Madison Avenue, Park Row. A striking feature of the city are the 'skyscrapers,' such as the Woolworth building, 750 ft. high, with 40 floors. Several fine parks. Various divisions of city linked by bridges, ferries, tunnels, and electric tramways, elevated roads, and subway lines. The suspension bridges, Williamsburg, Brooklyn, and Manhattan, are specially noteworthy. New York is first seaport of the world, and greatest manufacturing centre of U.S.A.; its foreign trade is about half that of whole country. Chief industries are manufacturing of clothing, textiles, printing and publishing, machinery, iron and steel goods, scientific and musical instruments, sugar and molasses refining, packing and preserving of meat. Pop. 6,982,000.

New Zea'land, British Dominion, S. Pacific Ocean; comprises three islands, North, South, and Stewart. Coast-line is generally broken. Plains along E. coast; largest is Canterbury in South I. In North I. volcanic mountain ranges run throughout (highest peaks, Ruapehu, 9,175 ft.; Egmont, 8,260 ft.); drained by Rs. Waikato (from Lake Taupo), Thames, Wairoa, North, Wanganui. South I. is traversed by Southern Alps and other ranges (highest peak, Mt. Cook, 12,350 ft.); drained by Rs. Clutha, Buller, Grey, and other streams. Stewart I. is mountainous; North I. subject to earthquakes and volcanic eruptions, and noted for its geysers and hot springs. Climate temperate and healthy, with moderate rainfall except on W. slopes of Southern Alps.

The flora and fauna are in general unlike those of the rest of the world. Native plants include New Zealand flax, kauri pine, and tree ferns. Mammals are almost entirely absent except those introduced by man. Native birds include several almost entirely wingless, such as the kiwi or apteryx. Colonization was begun in 1840, when Wellington was founded. The early colonists found the country already occupied by a native race called Maoris. Vast numbers of sheep and cattle raised. Horses and pigs are also bred, and wheat, oats, and other crops widely cultivated. Oranges, lemons, peaches, olives, and other fruits abound. Minerals include gold, coal, copper, silver, iron. Wool, frozen meat, and dairy produce exported; exports also include cereals, hides, kauri gum, fibre, tallow. Chief towns, Auckland, Wellington (cap.), Christchurch, Dunedin, Wanganui. Area, including Outlying Islands, 103,569 sq. m. (North I., 44,131 sq. m.; South I., 58,120 sq. m.; Stewart I., 662 sq. m.); pop. 1,474,000 (including 66,000 Maoris).

The Outlying Islands are Kermadec, Chatham, Auckland, Cook, and other S. Pacific islands. The Ross Dependency in Antarctica and the Union or Tokelau Is. are under the jurisdiction of New Zealand, which also holds mandate over W. Samoa.

Neyland (*nā'land*), or NEW MILFORD, urb. dist., Pembrokeshire, Wales, on Milford Haven; calling place for Irish steamers. Pop. 2,700.

Niag'ara, riv., N. America; forms boundary between Ontario and New York; flows from L. Erie, and flows into L. Ontario (*c.* 35 m.). *Niagara Falls*, about 20 m. below L. Erie, are divided by Goat Island into two parts; American Fall, *c.* 1,400 ft. wide, falls 167 ft.; Canadian (Horse-shoe) Fall forms curve of 2,600 ft., and falls 158 ft.; below falls, river rushes through gorge for 7 m.; total descent from L. Erie to L. Ontario is 315 ft.; part of water-power utilized to develop electric energy.

Niagara Falls. (1) Tn., New York, U.S.A., on R. Niagara; R.C. univ.; manufacturing centre deriving electrical power from falls; flour, paper, aluminium, carborundum, calcium carbide, bleaching powder. Pop. 75,000. (2) Port, Ontario, on R. Niagara, Canada; has large electrical power plants; carborundum, clothing, wire, canned goods, silver ware. Pop. 15,000.

Nias (*nē-äs'*), isl., Dutch E. Indies, 65 m. w. of Sumatra; surface mountainous and partly volcanic; chief products, coconuts, pepper, rice, sugar, tobacco. Area, *c.* 2,000 sq. m.; pop. *c.* 160,000.

Nicaragua (*nik-a-räg'wa*), republic, Central America; bounded N. by Honduras, E. by Caribbean Sea, S. by Costa Rica, W. by Pacific; Cordillera runs along S.W., 15 to 30 m. from coast; between mountains and sea is depression containing Lakes Managua and Nicaragua; to E. between base of hills and sea is extensive plain. Land is drained by Rs. Coco, Grande de Matagalpa, San Juan. Country subject to earthquakes (severe earthquake 1931, when Managua was destroyed). Climate varies with elevation; hot and damp near coast. Produces mahogany and other valuable timbers, coffee and bananas; also cacao, sugar-cane, fruit, gold, silver; stock raising and dairying important. Railway mileage, 159. Inhabitants include Europeans (very few), Indians, half-breeds. An inter-oceanic canal has been proposed by way of San Juan R. and L. Nicaragua. U.S.A. purchased (1916) exclusive right to construct and operate such a canal. Chief tns., Managua (cap.), Leon, Granada, Masaya. Area, 51,660 sq. m.; pop. 638,000.

Nicastro (*nē-cäst'rō*), tn., Calabria, S. Italy; bishop's see; ruins of a castle; wine and oil. Pop. 21,000.

Nice (*nēs*), chief tn., Alpes-Maritimes, France, on Mediterranean. Fashionable Riviera winter resort, with fine climate. Birthplace of Garibaldi; has cathedral, observatory, fort, and harbour; exports flowers, perfumes, fruits, olive oil, pottery, and carved olive-wood. Pop. 184,000.

Nicobar Islands. See ANDAMAN AND NICOBAR ISLANDS.

Nico'sia. (1) (Greek *Levkosia*) Cap. of Cyprus; seat of Gr. archbishop; manufactures leather, textiles; fruits and wine. Pop. 18,000. (2) Tn., Catania, Sicily; a salt mine and sulphur springs. Pop. 14,000.

Nictheroy (*nik-tä-rō'ē*), tn., Brazil, S. America, 4 m. E. of city of Rio de Janeiro; manufactures textiles, soap, and tobacco. Pop. 86,000.

Nidaros, formerly TRONDHJEM, port, Norway, on Trondhjem Fjord; exports lumber, copper, wood pulp, fish; shipbuilding; cathedral (11th cent.) is place of coronation of kings of Norway; former cap. of Norway. Pop. 55,000.

Niemen (*nye'men*), (German *Memel*), riv., Europe; rises near Minsk (White Russia); flows through Poland and Lithuania, and falls by several mouths into Kurisches Haff. Length, 500 m.; forms boundary between Memel Terr., Lithuania, and E. Prussia.

Nieu'port, tn., on R. Yser, W. Flanders, Belgium; shipbuilding and fisheries. Nieuport Bains, 2 m. away, is a seaside resort. Pop. 3,000.

Nièvre (*nē-ā'vr*), central dep., France;

mountainous in E.; drained by Rs. Allier, Loire, Yonne; large forest area; sheep and horses raised; coal, iron and steel manufactures; china, white wine; state ironworks at Guérigny. Chief tn., Nevers. Area, 2,658 sq. m.; pop. 260,000.

Nigde (*nēg'de*), chief tn. of vilayet, Asia Minor, 80 m. N.N.W. of Adana; fine buildings of Seljuk period. Pop. 59,000.

Niger (*nī'jĕr*). (1) Large riv. of W. Africa; rises in plateau of Fouta Jalon in French Guinea; flows N.E. through French Sudan, turns S.E., passes through Nigeria, and enters Gulf of Guinea by numerous mouths, Rio Nun at Akassa being chief, though the Forcados is main channel of communication with interior. Swampy delta extends about 120 m. along coast, and covers an area of 14,000 sq. m. Most important tributary is R. Benue, or 'Mother of Waters.' Niger is known locally under various names (Joliba, Isa, Quorra, etc.). Total length, 2,600 m., of which over 1,050 are navigable; area of basin, *c.* 1,000,000 sq. m. (2) Colony, French W. Africa, between Nigeria and Italian Libya; Sahara desert in N., forests and cattle pastures in S.; millets, manioc, dates, beans, groundnuts; cap. Niamey, on R. Niger. Area, *c.* 405,000 sq. m.; pop. 1,450,000.

Nigeria (*nī-jĕr'i-a*), Brit. colony and protectorate, W. Africa; bounded on N. by French W. Africa, E. by Lake Chad and Cameroons, S. by Gulf of Guinea, and W. by Dahomey. Coast region flat and swampy, with hot and unhealthy climate, malaria being prevalent; N. fertile, with healthier climate; interior traversed by mts.; highest ranges, 6,000 to 7,000 ft.; immense valuable forests. Chief rivers are Niger, Benue, Sokoto, Kaduna. Protectorate is divided for administrative purposes into N. Provinces and S. Provinces. Brit. mandated terr. of Cameroons is administered by Nigeria. Agriculture (with cattle rearing in N.) is principal occupation. Products are palm oil, kernels, timber, cotton, cocoa, livestock, hides and skins. Tin and coal are important minerals. Rivers and roads are chief means of communication, but railways (mileage in 1929 *c.* 1,900) are being extended. Chief tn. Lagos (cap. and chief port); inland native tns., Kano, Ilorin, and Kaduna; ports Brass, Bonny, Port Harcourt, and Calabar. Area, *c.* 335,700 sq. m.; pop. 18,966,000 (including *c.* 5,000 Europeans).

Niigata (*nē-ē-gä'tä*), seaport, Honshu, Japan, on W. coast; harbour improved by dredging; lacquerware; coal and petroleum in neighbourhood. Pop. 109,000.

Niihau. See under HAWAIIAN ISLANDS.

Nijar (*nē-har'*), tn., S.E. Spain, 16 m. N.N.E. of Almeria; iron ore, lead, and manganese mined; textiles and porcelain manufactured. Pop. 11,000.

Nijmegen, NYMWEGEN, or NIMEGUEN (*nim-ā'gen*), city, Gelderland, Holland, on R. Waal; contains church of St. Stephen (1272), Renaissance town hall, and ruined Carolingian palace; tobacco, metal-work, leather, beer. Pop. 76,000.

Nijni-Novgorod (*nizh'nē-nov'gō-rod*). (1) Prov., central Russia; watered by R. Volga and other rivs.; richly forested; produces timber, fruit, cereals; manufactures iron goods, leather; shipbuilding, sawmilling, and distilling are carried on. Area, 21,853 sq. m.; pop. 2,737,000. (2) Cap. of above; at junction of Oka and Volga rivs.; consists of Upper Town, with *Kremlin* or citadel, situated on hills; Lower Town, along banks of Oka and Volga; and Fair Town, between the two rivs. Owes its importance to traffic along the rivers and to fairs which attract merchants from all parts. Chief industries: flour-milling, distilling, manufacture of pottery and machinery, and shipbuilding. Pop. 181,000.

Nik'ko, tourist resort, Honshu, Japan, 90 m. N.W. of Tokyo; an important religious centre; many

Shinto and Buddhist shrines and temples.

Nikolaev (*nē-ko-lä'äv*), seaport, Ukraine, U.S.S.R., at head of estuary of R. Bug; naval station; has Greek cathedral, observatory, naval arsenal; manufactures flour, iron goods, glass, tobacco; exports grain, timber, iron ore, linseed, and sugar. Pop. 101,000.

Nikolaevsk. See PUGACHEV.

Nikolaistad. See VAASA.

Nile (*nīl*), river of Africa; has its farthest source in head-streams of R. Kagera, which rises between 2° and 3° S., and enters L. Victoria. Flows N. to Gondokoro (5° N.), the usual limit of navigation, and about 10° N. is joined by the Bahr-el-Ghazal and the Sobat; from this point to Khartoum it is called the White Nile (Bahr-el-Abyad). Here joined by Blue Nile (Bahr-el-Azroq), and flows in long, narrow valley to Cairo, and thence through delta to Mediterranean Sea. Below Khartoum it receives only one trib., the Atbara (Black Nile), which drains N. Abyssinia. The Nile is second longest riv. in world, being *c.* 4,000 m. long, and but for two great interruptions, is navigable for its entire course. Sudd (floating vegetation) hinders navigation on Upper Nile. Basin is *c.* 1,100,000 sq. m. Between Wadi Halfa and Khartoum there are five cataracts. At Aswan a great reservoir and dam have been constructed, affording irrigation to over 650 sq. m. of land. A dam has also been constructed across the Blue Nile at Sennar for irrigation.

The Nile enters the Mediterranean Sea by two principal distributaries, the Rosetta and Damietta branches. Once every year the Nile overflows its banks, and deposits upon the land a black and very fertilizing mud, upon which all the crops in Egypt depend. About the end of April the rise is perceived at Khartoum, but it is not until towards end of June that its effects are felt at Cairo. The overflow reaches its maximum in Sept., remains practically stationary until end of Oct., after this slowly subsides. The Nile floods depend on rainfall of Abyssinian highlands. Formerly cultivation could only be after annual floods, but with the aid of regulating dams at Asyut, near Cairo, and at Zifta and Esna, perennial irrigation is provided.

Nilgiri Hills or NILGIRIS (*nēl'gi-riz*), plateau, s. Deccan, India; highest point, Mt. Dodabetta, 8,760 ft.; coffee, tea, cinchona; mica, gold-bearing quartz. Area, 982 sq. m.; pop. 126,000.

Nimach (*nē-much'*), tn., Central India, 130 m. s. of Ajmer; British cantonment. Pop. 10,000.

Nîmes (*nēm*), chief tn., Gard, s. France; silk, cotton, shawls, hosiery, machinery, carpets, wine and brandy trade; has magnificent Roman remains; Maison Carrée, finest extant example of Greco-Roman architecture; huge amphitheatre, Tour Magne, Temple of Diana. Pop. 74,000.

Ning-po', walled tn., Chekiang, China; a treaty port; famous for wood-carving; exp. rice, cotton, tea, silk, beans, and wheat; fisheries; manufactures grass mats, lace, and hardware; many monasteries and temples. Pop. 212,000.

Niort (*nē-or'*), cap., Deux-Sèvres, w. France, on R. Sèvre-Niortaise, 35 m. N.E. of La Rochelle; market gardens; leather, gloves; beautiful Gothic church. Pop. 23,000.

Nip'igon, lake, Ontario, Canada; discharges by Nipigon R. into Lake Superior; over 1,000 islands; length, 70 m.; breadth, 50 m.

Ni'pissing, lake, Ontario, Canada; discharges into Lake Huron by French R.; length, 50 m.; breadth, 20 m.

Nippon. See JAPAN.

Niriz. See BAKHTIGAN.

Nish, tn., Yugoslavia, on the Nisava, trib. of R. Morava, 130 m. S.E. of Belgrade; important rly. jn.; rly. workshops; birthplace of Constantine the Great. Pop. 37,000.

Nith, riv., s. Scotland; rises in Ayrshire, flows N.E. to enter Dumfriesshire; flows S.E. to estuary on Solway Firth; in lower course divides Dumfriesshire from Kirkcudbrightshire;

navigable to Dumfries. Length, 79 miles.

Nivelles (*nē-vel'*), tn., Belgium, 19 m. S. of Brussels; carriages, paper, railway workshops; 11th cent. church of St. Gertrude. Pop. 13,000.

Nizhne-Tagilsk (*nyizh'ni-tag-ilsk'*), tn., Ural Area, U.S.S.R.; on rly. from Perm to Sverdlovsk; steel and iron works; wooden boxes; copper, gold, platinum. Pop. 39,000.

Nome (*nōm*), tn., w. Alaska, N. America, on s. of Seward peninsula, Bering Strait; scene of gold rush 1900, when pop. was 12,500; it is now 850.

Nord (*nor*), dep., N.E. France, on Belgian frontier; chief rivers, Schelde, Scarpe, Oise, Sambre, Lys; soil fertile, producing flax, sugar-beet, tobacco, hops, cereals, and potatoes; extensive coal mines; manufactures iron, steel, sugar, glass, chemicals, machinery. Scene of much fighting during Great War. Cap. Lille. Area, 2,228 sq. m.; pop. 1,969,000.

Nor'den, tn., Lancashire, England; woollens, cottons; suburb of Rochdale. Pop. 4,300.

Norderney (*nor'der-nā*), small isl., North Sea, off coast of E. Friesland, belongs to Hanover, Prussia; sea-bathing; length, 8 m.; breadth, 1¼ m. Area, 8 sq. m.; pop. 5,000.

Nordhausen (*nort'hou-zen*), tn., Saxony, Prussia, 32 m. E. of Göttingen; has R.C. cathedral; manufactures chiefly beer and spirits. Pop. 35,000.

Nord'kyn, CAPE, promontory, Lapland, Norway; most northerly point of mainland of Europe.

Nördlingen (*noord'ling-en*), tn., Bavaria, Germany, 50 m. S.W. of Nuremberg; manufactures carpets and soap. Scene of two battles during Thirty Years' War. Pop. 8,000.

Nore, THE, sandbank, Thames estuary, England, marked by lightship.

Nor'folk. (1) Mar. co., E. England; bounded on N. and E. by North Sea, S. by Suffolk, W. by Cambridge and Lincoln. Coast mostly low and flat, with few indentations; sea steadily encroaching; submerged forests at several places off coast. Inland are undulating plains, valleys, and woods. In W. is Fen district. The Broads lie in E. Principal streams are Great and Little Ouse, Yare, Bure, Wensum, Waveney. Soil is fertile; wheat, barley, oats, turnips, mangolds; cattle rearing, fruit growing, malting, brewing, tanning, and brick making. Manufactures include boots, shoes, mustard, starch, and agricultural implements. Fisheries are of great importance, Yarmouth being headquarters. Chief towns are Norwich (co. tn.), Yarmouth, Lynn, Cromer, Wells, and Thetford. Area, 2,044 sq. m.; pop. 504,800. (2) Port, Virginia, U.S.A.; important railway and canal centre; naval station; fine public buildings; chief exports, coal, lumber, tobacco, flour, cotton, vegetables. Pop. 129,000.

Norfolk Broads. See BROADS.

Norfolk Island, isl., S. Pacific, midway between New Zealand and New Caledonia; fertile soil, producing oranges, figs, grapes, and other fruits; live-stock; terr. of Australian Commonwealth; formerly a penal settlement; colonized by Pitcairn islanders (1856); Australian holiday resort. Area, 13 sq. m.; pop. 900.

Norham (*nor'am*), par. and vil., Northumberland, England, on R. Tweed; castle immortalized in Scott's *Marmion*. Pop. (par.) 700.

Nor'mandy, old prov. of France, between Brittany and French Flanders; N. and W. coasts washed by English Channel; now comprises the five departments, Seine-Inférieure, Eure, Calvados, Manche, and Orne.

Nor'manton, tn., on R. Calder, Yorkshire, England, 3 m. N.E. of Wakefield; coal mines, iron and chemical works. Pop. 15,700.

Nor'ristown, tn., on R. Schuylkill, Pennsylvania, U.S.A.; a residential suburb of Philadelphia; cottons, woollens, oilcloths, carpets. Pop. 36,000.

Norrköping (*nor'chip-ing*), seaport, Sweden, on R. Motala, 80 m. S.W. of Stockholm; cotton goods, sugar, paper, tobacco; shipbuilding. Pop. 61,000.

North Adams, city, on R. Hoosac, N.W. Massachusetts, U.S.A.; boots and shoes, machinery and textiles. Pop. 22,000.

Northal'lerton, mkt. tn., Yorkshire, England, 18 m. S. of Middlesbrough; near by was fought battle of the Standard (1138); agricultural produce; motor engineering. Pop. 4,800.

North'am, urb. dist., N. Devon, England, 1⅓ m. N. of Bideford; rly. station for Westward Ho! Pop. 5,800.

North America. See AMERICA.

Northamp'ton. (1) Co. tn., Northamptonshire, England, on R. Nene; of great historic interest; leather manufactures; also tanning, brewing, paper making, iron founding, bricks, tiles. Pop. 92,300. (2) Tn., Massachusetts, U.S.A., 16 m. N. of Springfield; manufactures paper, silks, cottons, woollens. Pop. 22,000.

Northamptonshire, midland co., England; bounded by Lincoln, Rutland, Leicester, Warwick, Oxford, Buckingham, Bedford, Huntingdon, and Cambridge. Surface undulating; some parts richly wooded and well cultivated. N.E. forms part of Fen district. For administrative purposes the Soke of Peterborough in the N.E. ranks as separate county. Chief rivs., Nen, Welland, Avon, Cherwell, Leam, and Ouse. Wheat and barley are principal crops; stock raising. Iron is found; main industry, manufacture of boots and shoes; others are brewing, bookbinding, brush, paper, and lace making. Several interesting churches and remains of several castles, including those of Fotheringhay and Barnwell. Chief tns. are Northampton (co. tn.), Peterborough, Kettering, and Wellingborough Area, 998 sq. m.; pop. 361,300.

North Australia. See NORTHERN TERRITORY.

North Bat'tleford, tn., Saskatchewan, Canada, on N. Saskatchewan riv., opposite Battleford; centre of agriculture. Pop. 5,000.

North Bay, city, Ontario, Canada, on N.E. shore of L. Nipissing; rly. jn. Pop. 15,500.

North Berwick (*ber'ik*), royal burgh and wat.-pl., Haddingtonshire, Scotland, on Firth of Forth; well-known golf links; near are North Berwick Law (612 ft.), Tantallon Castle, and Bass Rock. Pop. 3,500.

North Bierley. See BIERLEY, NORTH.

North Bromsgrove. See BROMSGROVE.

North Cape, promontory, Norway, on Magerö I.; generally accepted as most northerly point of Europe, though Knivskjærodde I., to the W., reaches about 1,000 ft. farther N.

North Carolina, South Atlantic State of U.S.A., bounded N. by Virginia, W. by Tennessee, S. and S.W. by S. Carolina and Georgia, E. and S.E. by Atlantic. Coast is fringed with sand reefs with three outstanding capes—Hatteras, Fear, and Lookout. Surface is mountainous in W. and S.E.; Great Smoky Mts., Black Mts., Bald Mts., Blue Ridge, etc.; highest peak Black Dome or Mt. Mitchell (6,711 ft.). Coastal plain region is level and swampy; piedmont plateau in centre is undulating. Chief rivers are: Broad, Cape Fear, Roanoke, Neuse, Chowan, Tar, Yadkin, Pamlico, Hiawassee, Catawba (many navigable); shallow lakes and swamps in coastal districts. Climate of mountain region is exceptionally fine, central part healthy; fever near swamps in coastal region. Extensive forests, esp. pine, in E.; trees include elm, cypress, cedar, oak, birch, beech, hemlock. Agriculture is the main occupation; principal prod., cereals, cotton, tobacco, cotton-seed oil, potatoes, timber; manufactures of cotton, furniture, flour, lumber; minerals unimportant; valuable fisheries (shad, oyster, etc.). Principal towns, Raleigh (cap.), Wilmington (principal port), Charlotte, Ashville, Durham, Winston-Salem. Area, 52,426 sq. m.; pop. 2,560,000 (including *c.* 760,000 Negroes).

North Caucasian Area, prov., Russia, N. of Caucasus Mts.; plain except in S.; wheat and other cereals; sunflower seeds; grapes, tobacco, live-stock. Chief export, naphtha. Largest tn., Rostov-on-Don. Area, 115,000 sq. m.; pop. 8,325,000.

North Dako'ta, N. Central State, U.S.A., bounded on N. by Canada, E. by Minnesota, S. by S. Dakota, W. by Montana; surface mainly plateau, undulating plain, and grassy prairie; no trees unless along river banks, round shores of lakes, and in sheltered spots; chief rivers, Red R. of the North, which forms E. boundary, and its tribs.; Missouri and tribs.; in N.E. is sheet of salt water, Devil's Lake. High plateau called Coteau du Missouri extends from N.W. to S.E. Climate extreme but healthy; rainfall, coming in spring and summer, is of maximum benefit for agriculture, which is the chief industry. Especially in valley of Red R. soil is rich, fertile, and highly cultivated, principal crops being wheat, barley, rye, flax, hay, potatoes, and maize; ranching in W. Manufactures include flour and grist milling. Principal towns are Bismarck (cap.), Fargo, Grand Forks. Area, 70,837 sq. m.; pop. 647,000 (including 10,000 Indians).

North Darley. See DARLEY.

North'enden, or NORTHEN, par. and vil., Cheshire, England, on R. Mersey, 4¼ m. by rail W. of Stockport; residential area for Manchester. Pop. (par.) 3,500.

Northern Ireland. See IRELAND.

Northern Territory, terr. of Commonwealth of Australia; bounded W. by W. Australia, S. by S. Australia, E. by Queensland, and N. by Arafura Sea; divided into N. Australia (cap. Darwin) and Central Australia (cap. Alice Springs), for administrative purposes. N. Australia consists of rolling country, with tableland of Arnhem Land in N.; Central Australia is similar in structure, with plateau in centre. Rising from this plateau are Macdonnell Mts. Plateau region contains much excellent pasturage, but S. mainly desert. Climate tropical, in N. equable and in S. extreme. Stock raising and mining are chief occupations. Chief minerals, gold, tin, silver, lead, and mica. Railway runs S. from Darwin to Emungalan, and N. from Oodnadatta in S. Australia to Alice Springs. Darwin is chief port. Area, 523,620 sq. m.; pop. *c.* 4,000.

Northfleet, suburb of Gravesend, Kent, England; paper mills, chemical works, shipbuilding, bricks, Portland cement. Pop. 16,400.

North Foreland. See FORELAND, NORTH AND SOUTH.

North Holland, prov. of Holland, between North Sea and Zuider Zee; it includes the islands of Texel, Vlieland, Terschelling, Marken, Wieringen, and Urk; cattle rearing, cheese making, flower bulbs, potatoes; fishing, shipping, shipbuilding. Chief towns, Amsterdam and Haarlem. Area, 1,066 sq. m.; pop. 1,463,000.

North Island. See NEW ZEALAND.

North Sea, shallow sea, part of Atlantic between Great Britain and Continent of Europe; greatest depth off Norwegian coast (440 fathoms); most of area less than 100 fathoms; bed crossed by large banks (Dogger, Jutland, etc.); communicates with Baltic through Skaggerrak and Kattegat; with English Channel through Strait of Dover; few islands except near coasts of surrounding countries; extensive fisheries; length, 600 m.; breadth, 400 m.; area, *c.* 200,000 sq. m.

North Shields, seapt., Northumberland, England, on R. Tyne; ironworks; shipbuilding; fish market; incorporated with Tynemouth.

North Tonawan'da, city, on Niagara R., New York state, U.S.A., 14 m. N. of Buffalo; lumber mills; iron and steel industries. Pop. 15,000.

Northumberland, northernmost co., England, bounded on N. by Scotland, W. by Cumberland, S. by Durham, and E. by North Sea. Shores generally low; off coast lie Holy Isle, Farne Islands, and Coquet Island. Inland mostly rugged and broken, with undulating hills and moors, rising to grass-covered Cheviot Hills (highest point Cheviot, 2,676 ft.). Well watered by rivs. Tweed, Till, Aln,

Coquet, Wansbeck, Blyth, and Tyne; valleys fertile and well wooded. Greatest sheep-rearing county in England; cattle also raised (famous herd of wild white cattle maintained at Chillingham); chief crops, barley and oats; important coast and river fisheries; county of great industrial importance, coal being chief product. R. Tyne is centre of manufactures, and has enormous shipping trade, also shipbuilding, ironworks, alkali works, manufacture of machines, tools, glass, and pottery; in other parts of county are brick and tile works, potteries, and cloth mills. Chief tns., Newcastle, Tynemouth, Wallsend, Blyth, Berwick-on-Tweed, and Morpeth. Area, 2,018 sq. m.; pop. 756,700.

North Wal'sham, mkt. tn., Norfolk, England, 16 m. N. of Norwich; agricultural implements. Pop. 4,100.

North-West Frontier Province, prov., India, originally part of Punjab prov.; formed in 1901 for protection of India against invasion. About one-third of territory is British. Mostly mountainous, Hindu Kush forming N. boundary; highest summit is Tirach Mir (25,426 ft.); climatic conditions extremely diversified. Principal rivs. are Indus, Kabul, Kurram, and Kunhar. River valleys and dist. of Peshawar are only fertile and cultivated parts. Leading occupation agriculture. Cap. Peshawar. Area, 38,665 sq. m.; pop. (mostly Pathans) *c.* 3,000,000.

Northwest Territories, unorganized area, N. Canada; lies N. of 60° N. lat. and E. of Yukon Terr.; divided into provisional dists. of Mackenzie, Keewatin, and Franklin; largely unexplored and uninhabited; forests and furs. Area, 1,309,682 sq. m.; pop. 8,000.

North'wich, mkt. tn., Cheshire, England, on R. Weaver; brine deposits, rock-salt mines, chemicals, brewing, tanning, brick making. Suffers from subsidence. Pop. 18,700.

Norton, urb. dist., E. Riding, Yorks, England, on R. Derwent, opposite Malton; breeding and training of racehorses. Pop. 3,900.

Nor'ton Canes, or NORTON-UNDER-CANNOCK, par. and vil., Staffordshire, England, 5½ m. N. of Walsall; collieries. Pop. (par.) 5,800.

Nor'ton-in-the-Moors, par. and vil., Staffordshire, England, 2 m. N.E. of Burslem; collieries, ironworks. Pop. (par.) 5,900.

Nor'walk, city, Connecticut, U.S.A., on Long I. Sound; important oyster fisheries; iron foundries; manufactures hats and clothing. Pop. 36,000.

Nor'way, kingdom, N. Europe, forming W. portion of Scandinavia; bounded N. by Arctic Ocean, E. by Finland and Sweden, S. by Skagerrak and W. by Atlantic and Arctic Oceans; extreme length, *c.* 1,150 m.; width varies from 20 to 260 m. Coast protected by fringe of islands (the Skärgård). Everywhere indented by long, narrow, winding fjords (varying in depth from 220 to 660 fathoms), which furnish many convenient harbours. The islands (largest group the Lofotens) contain about 7 per cent. of the total area. Except in S. and S.E., coast rises steeply from sea; Kjolen Mts. in N. (mean height from 4,000 to 6,000 ft.), Dovrefjeld Mts. in S. (mean height from 2,000 to 4,000 ft.); highest peak *c.* 8,200 ft. Numerous lakes, and short, rapid rivers, the longest being R. Glommen and R. Tana Elf. Climate modified by Gulf Stream Drift; cold is severe in interior; fjords allow damp winds of Atlantic to reach plateau, and snowfall there is greater than it would otherwise be. Temp. ranges from a winter mean of about 2° in the extreme N. to a summer mean of 63° in the S. Coast always ice-free; N. part is 'land of the midnight sun.' Only 3 per cent. of country fit for cultivation. Principal crops, oats, barley, wheat, rye, and potatoes. Timber and fisheries constitute the wealth of Norway. Of the forest trees nearly three-fourths are pines. Chief fish, cod, ling, and herring; whales, walrus, seals, and sharks are taken in N. Cod-liver oil exported in large quantities. The minerals—chiefly copper, silver, pyrites, felspar—are increasing in value. Norway is one of the great carrying countries of Europe—the mercantile marine has a net tonnage of 1,829,794. Principal exports are animal produce, timber and wooden goods, minerals and metals, skins, etc. Cap. Oslo; other tns. are Bergen, Nidaros, Stavanger, and Drammen. Area, *c.* 124,964 sq. m.; pop. 2,650,000.

Norwich (*nor'ich*). (1) Co. tn., Norfolk, England, on Wensum R.; fine Norman cathedral, founded in 1096; castle has Norman keep, now used as museum. Oldest town library in England; great cattle market; chief industries, engineering works, breweries, tanneries, and brickworks; manufactures include chemicals, starch, mustard, silk fabrics, vinegar. Pop. 126,200. (2) City, Connecticut, U.S.A., on Thames R., 17 m. from its mouth, at head of navigation. Manufactures machinery, firearms, textiles, cutlery. Pop. 22,000.

Nor'wood. (1) Suburb of London, Surrey, England, 5½ m. s. of St. Paul's; residential. Pop. 56,000. (2) City, Ohio, U.S.A., 7 m. N.E. of Cincinnati; pianos, furniture, electrical and railway machinery; printing. Pop. 33,000. (3) Town, Massachusetts, U.S.A., 14 m. s.w. of Boston; printing and publishing. Pop. 13,000.

Not'o, tn., Syracuse, E. Sicily; trade in oil, wine, almonds. Pop. 32,000.

Not'tingham, co. tn., Nottinghamshire, England, on R. Trent; well-built town, with large market-place; most notable buildings, St. Mary's and St. Peter's churches, R.C. cathedral, Univ. Coll., town hall, and exchange; castle now art museum; manufactures hosiery, lace, cotton, wool, bicycles, machinery, and chemicals; brassfounding, tanning, and brewing. Nottingham played a prominent part in Civil War. Pop. 268,800.

Not'tinghamshire, or NOTTS, midland co., England, in R. Trent basin; surface level along R. Trent, elsewhere undulating, rising to *c.* 600 ft.; contains Sherwood Forest, traditionally associated with Robin Hood (region now occupied by palatial residences, and locally known as 'The Dukeries'). Nearly half the area is arable; chief crops, wheat, oats, and barley; cattle reared; cheese-making important. County produces coal, gypsum, limestone; manufactures lace, hosiery. Co. tn., Nottingham. Area, 843 sq. m.; pop. 712,700.

Nova'ra, tn., Piedmont, Italy, 28 m. w. of Milan; cathedral dating in part from 5th cent.; textiles. Pop. 56,000.

No'va Sco'tia, Maritime Prov., Canada; most easterly of Dominion; connected with New Brunswick by isthmus of Chignecto, at head of Bay of Fundy; consists of Nova Scotia proper and Cape Breton Island, separated by Strait of Canso. Numerous harbours; coasts subject to fogs; many rivers and lakes. Surface is hilly and soil in lower parts fertile. Cereals, apples, pears, plums, and potatoes grow well, and there is excellent pasturage; extensive coal mines in N.; iron smelted; gypsum, gold, salt; fisheries are valuable and forests are important; timber, fruit, agricultural produce exported. Facilities for transport excellent. Chief towns, Halifax (cap.), Sydney, Glace Bay, Dartmouth, Amherst, and New Glasgow. Area, 21,428 sq. m.; pop. 524,000.

Novaya Zemlya (*nō'vĭ-a zăm'li-a*), two Russian islands in Arctic Ocean; divided by the narrow channel Matochkin Shar, and separated from Vaigach I. by Kara Strait; surface mountainous; coast-line broken by fjords; furs of arctic fox and polar bear; whale, walrus, and seal fisheries. Length, *c.* 600 m.; greatest breadth, *c.* 90 m.; area, *c.* 30,000 sq. m.

Nov'gorod. (1) Prov., Russia, is drained by Upper R. Volga; crossed by several canals; mountainous in S.; fishing, shipbuilding, lumbering; glass, matches. Area, 19,583 sq. m.; pop. 1,045,000. (2) Cap. of above, on

Volkhov R., near Lake Ilmen; saw-mills; manufactures beer, spirits, boots and shoes, and bricks. Pop. 31,000.

No'vi Sad, formerly NEUBATZ, tn., Yugoslavia, 50 m. N.W. of Belgrade; pottery and cotton goods. Pop. 51,000.

Nov'ocherkassk, tn., N. Caucasian Area, Russia, on R. Don; cereals, wine, timber, bricks. Pop. 56,000.

Nov'omoskovsk, town, Ukraine, U.S.S.R., 16 m. N.E. of Dnepropetrovsk; brick making; trades in cattle, horses, tallow, skins. Pop. 11,000.

Novo-Radomsk. See RADOMSKO.

Nov'orossiysk, seapt., N. Caucasian Area, Russia, on Black Sea; exports cement, naphtha, and tobacco. Pop. 66,000.

Nov'o Sibirsk', cap. of Siberian Area, U.S.S.R., on R. Ob; trade in grain, flour, and agricultural machinery. Pop. 121,000.

Nowawes (*nō'vă-ves*), tn., Brandenburg, Germany, 2 m. E. of Potsdam; jute and silk. Pop. 27,000.

Nowgong'. (1) Dist., Assam, India, in R. Brahmaputra valley; rice, tea. Area, 3,699 sq. m.; pop. 398,000. (2) Cantonment, Bundelkhand, Central India, 115 m. S.E. of Gwalior; trade connected with supplies for troops. Pop. 7,000.

Nowy Sacz (*no'vi sonch*), tn., Poland, 45 m. S.E. of Cracow; old castle; railway repair shops. Pop. 26,000.

Noyon (*nwă-yon*), anc. tn., Oise, France, on R. Oise, 67 m. N.N.E. of Paris; agricultural produce; iron foundries. Pop. 6,000.

Nu'bia, region N.E. Africa, stretching from Red Sea to R. Nile, and S. from Egypt to about Khartoum, but has no definite limits. In early times known as Ethiopia. Greater part of surface consists of sandy deserts and steppes; productive districts lie mostly in valley of R. Nile. Inhabitants are Hamitic peoples and Arabs.

Nuble (*noo'blā*), inland prov., Chile, S. America, bordering Argentine Republic; extends up Andean slopes; plain produces wheat, timber; stock raising. Cap. Chillan. Area, 6,098 sq. m.; pop. 229,000.

Nue'va San Salva'dor, tn., Salvador, Central America; two colleges; port La Libertad. Pop. 28,000.

Nuevo Leon (*noo-ā'vo lā'on*), state, N.E. Mexico, on slopes of Sierra Madre Oriental; sugar, agriculture, cattle raising; some mining. Cap. Monterey. Area, 25,032 sq. m.; pop. 336,000.

Nukha (*noo'ka*), town, Azerbaijan, Transcaucasia, U.S.S.R.; silk. Pop. 23,000.

Numea. See NEW CALEDONIA.

Nunea'ton, mkt. tn., N.E. Warwickshire, England, on R. Anker; ribbons, cotton, worsted and elastic goods, hats, bricks, tiles; ironworks. Pop. 46,300.

Nürn'berg, or NUREMBERG, city, Bavaria, Germany, on R. Regnitz; mediæval town with turreted walls, moat, gateways, gabled houses. Manufactures toys, carved wood and ivory, machinery, motor-cars, chemicals, lead pencils, paints; trading centre and large hop market. Pop. 392,000.

Nuwara Eliya (*nū-rāl'ya*), hill station, Ceylon, 25 m. S.S.E. of Kandy; alt. 6,200 ft.; sanatorium.

Nyasa (*ne-as'a*), LAKE, S.E. Africa, occupies S. end of great African rift valley; numerous streams flow into L. Nyasa which drains by Shire R. into R. Zambezi; first explored by Livingstone (1859); navigated by steamers and sailing vessels. Length, 350 m.; breadth, 40 m.; area, *c.* 11,000 sq. m.

Nyasaland, British Protectorate, Africa, on W. and S. shore of L. Nyasa. Surface mostly lofty plateau (over 3,000 ft.). Exports tobacco, cotton, tea, coffee. Chief tns., Zomba (cap.), Blantyre, and Port Herald. Area, 37,890 sq. m.; pop. 1,307,000.

Nyezhin (*nē-ez-hin'*), tn., Ukraine, U.S.S.R., 75 m. N.E. of Kiev; tobacco grown and manufactured. Pop. *c.* 50,000.

Nyiregyhaza (*nyē'rej-hā-zo*), tn., N.E. Hungary, 17 m. S.E. of Tokay; extensive vineyards; soda, and agricultural machinery. Pop. 47,000.

O

Oad'by, urb. dist., Leicestershire, England, 3½ m. S.E. of Leicester; boots and shoes. Pop. 4,700.

Oa'hu. See under HAWAIIAN ISLANDS.

Oajaca. See OAXACA.

Oak'engates, urb. dist., Shropshire, England, 13 m. E. of Shrewsbury; coal and iron industries. Pop. 11,200.

Oak'ham, co. tn., Rutland, England; remains of anc. castle; mkt. tn.; trade in cattle. Pop. 3,200.

Oak'land, port, California, U.S.A., on San Francisco Bay; motor vehicles; shipbuilding; electrical machinery; canneries; saw mills. Pop. 284,000.

Oak Park, tn., Illinois, U.S.A., 9 m. w. of Chicago, of which it is a residential suburb. Pop. 64,000.

Oak'worth, urb. dist., W. Riding, Yorks, England, 3 m. s.w. of Keighley; cotton and worsted goods. Pop. 4,000.

Oamaru (*ō-äm-ä-roo'*), port, South Island, New Zealand, 78 m. N. of Dunedin; fine harbour; exports wool and frozen meat; seaside resort. Pop. 7,500.

Oaxaca (*wä-hä'ka*), or OAJACA. (1) State, s. Mexico; mountainous and well-watered; produces cereals, rubber, coffee, sugar, cotton, tobacco, indigo, dyewoods, cochineal. Area, 35,689 sq. m.; pop. 976,000. (2) Cap. of above; alt. 5,085 ft.; breweries, sugar mills, fibre factories. Pop. 28,000.

Ob, or OBI (*ōp*), riv., w. Siberia, Asia; rises in Altai Mts. and flows N.W., reaching Arctic Ocean through Gulf of Ob; frozen Nov. to June; with its tribs. (Irtish, Tobol, Tavda, Tura) it provides over 15,000 m. of navigable waterways. Length, 2,500 miles.

O'ban, tn., Argyllshire, Scotland, on Firth of Lorne; summer resort and yachting centre; fish market and port for trawlers. Pop. 5,800.

O Becse. See STARI BECEJ.

O'beram'mergau (*-gou*), vil., Bavaria, Germany, 40 m. s.w. of Munich; wood and ivory carving. Passion Play performed here every ten years since passing of plague (1634); last representation, 1930. Pop. 1,600.

Oberhausen (*ō-ber-hou'zen*), town, Rhine prov., Prussia, 6 m. w. of Essen; ironworks, coal mining; glass, soap, porcelain, chemical products. Pop. 105,000.

O'berland. See BERNESE OBERLAND.

Oberschöneweide (*ō-bĕr-shoon-ĕ-vī'-dĕ*), tn., Brandenburg, Prussia; supplies Berlin with electric power. Pop. 21,000.

Ocean'ia comprises islands in Pacific Ocean; divided into various groups—viz., Melanesia (with Australasia), Polynesia, and Micronesia.

Ochil Hills (*ō'kil*), hill range, Scotland, in cos. of Clackmannan, Kinross, Fife, and Perth; of volcanic origin; highest point Bencleuch (2,363 ft.).

Ochrida (*ok'rē-da*), tn., s.w. Serbia, Yugoslavia, on L. Ochrida; numerous mosques; trade in hides. Pop. 10,000. Lake is 18 m. long, with extreme breadth of 8 m.

Od'de, tourist centre, Norway; at head of branch of Hardanger Fiord; amid beautiful scenery; carbide of calcium and cyanamide.

Ödenburg. See SOPRON.

Odenkirchen (*ō'den-kĕrch-en*), tn., Rhineland, Prussia, 21 m. s.w. of Düsseldorf; cottons, silks, leather. Pop. 20,000.

Odense (*ō'den-zä*), city, isl. of Fünen, Denmark; tanneries, breweries, cotton factories; exports butter, cheese, bacon, hides; birthplace of Hans Andersen. Pop. 52,500.

O'der, riv., Germany; rises in Sudetes Mts.; flows N.W. through Germany and enters Baltic by three arms; chief tribs., Bartsch, Neisse, Warthe; connected with Rs. Havel, Spree, and Vistula by canals; principal tns., Breslau, Stettin, Frankfurt; length, 560 m.; navigable to Ratibor.

Odes'sa, tn. and port, Ukraine, U.S.S.R.; on bay at N.W. extremity of Black Sea; large artificial harbour; freezes for a few days only; tn. undermined by catacombs, which are inhabited by casual dock labourers. Chief exports, flour, wheat, barley, rye, maize, oats, oilcake, sugar, pease, beans, alcohol, caviare, fish, and wood. Pop. 421,000.

Odiham (*ō'dē-am*), mkt. tn., Hants, England, 7½ m. E. of Basingstoke; formerly a residence of kings of Wessex. Town declined when rlys. passed it by, but is prospering again with motor traffic. Pop. 2,700.

Oels (*ools*), tn., Silesia, Prussia, 20 m. N.E. by rail of Breslau; agricultural implements, carriages, bells, shoes; trade in flax and cereals. Pop. 14,500.

Oesel, or OSEL. See SAARE MAA.

Offaly County, formerly KING'S Co., inland co., Leinster, I.F.S.; surface generally level, with Bog of Allen in centre; Slieve Bloom Mts. in S.; drained by rivs. Shannon, Brosna, Barrow, Boyne; crossed by Grand Canal; cereals, dairy farming, livestock. Co. tn., Tullamore. Area, 772 sq. m.; pop. 52,600.

Of'fenbach, tn., Hesse, Germany, on R. Main; great industrial centre; machinery, sewing machines, aniline and chemical products, leather goods, soap, varnish, perfumery, printing materials. Pop. 80,000.

Of'fenburg, tn., Baden, Germany, 27 m. S.W. of Baden; textiles, glass, cement, agricultural machinery, malt, tobacco. Pop. 17,000.

Ogasawara Jima. See BONIN ISLANDS.

Og'den, city, Utah, U.S.A.; 35 m. N. of Salt Lake City; beet sugar, flour milling, canned goods, oil refining. Pop. 40,000.

Og'densburg, city and port, New York State, U.S.A., on R. St. Lawrence; lumber manufactures; silk, flour, brassware. Pop. 15,000.

Og'more and Garw (*gar'oo*), urb. dist., Glamorganshire, S. Wales, 7 m. N. of Bridgend; coal mining. Pop. 30,200.

Og'owé, or OGOWAI, riv., Gabon, French Equatorial Africa; rises in Crystal Hill and enters Atlantic by delta; falls and rapids render main channel unnavigable; length, *c.* 750 m.

Ohi'o. (1) Riv., U.S.A., trib. of Mississippi; formed by junction of Monongahela and Allegheny rivs. at Pittsburgh; separates states of Ohio, Indiana, and Illinois from W. Virginia and Kentucky; chief tribs., Muskingum, Scioto, Wabash, Kanawha, Kentucky, Green, Cumberland, and Tennessee; most important tns. on banks, Pittsburgh, Cincinnati, Louisville, and Evansville; a great highway of commerce; navigable from Cairo to Pittsburgh; subject to floods; length, 965 m. (2) Inland state, U.S.A.; bounded on N. by Michigan and Lake Erie, E. by Pennsylvania and W. Virginia, S. by Kentucky, and W. by Indiana; surface a vast undulating high plain (average elevation, *c.* 850 ft.); drained by R. Ohio and tribs.; chief crops are maize, wheat, oats, hay; horses and cattle are raised; dairy farming important; minerals include coal, petroleum, and natural gas; industries include iron and steel working; manufacture of carriages and wagons; boots and shoes; clothing; lumber and timber working; rubber goods; flour and grist working; and slaughtering; Portland cement manufactured. Most important cities are Cleveland, Cincinnati, Toledo, Columbus (cap.), Akron, Dayton, Youngstown. Area, 41,049 sq. m.; pop. 5,760,000.

Oh'ligs, tn., Rhine Prov., Prussia, 17 m. N. of Cologne; cutlery; flour mills. Pop. 30,000.

Oil City, city, N.W. Pennsylvania, U.S.A., at junction of Oil Creek and Allegheny R.; oil, machinery for oil wells. Pop. 21,500.

Oi'rat, autonomous area, U.S.S.R.; bounded on N. by Siberian Area, S. by Kazak Rep., E. by Mongolia; traversed by Altai Mts.; drained by upper Ob R.; forests; fur-bearing animals. Cap. Ulala. Area, *c.* 36,000 sq. m.; pop. *c.* 100,000.

Oise (*wäz*). (1) Riv., France; trib. of R. Seine; rises in Belgium; canalized; navigable to Chauny; length, 186 m. (2) Dep., N. France; undulating surface with fine forests; chief rivs., Oise, Aisne, and Lerain; principal products, cereals, flax, vegetables, beetroot, fruits; manufactures iron, textiles, leather, lace, chemicals, cider, sugar. Cap. Beauvais. Area, 2,272 sq. m.; pop. 406,000.

O'ka, riv., central Russia, Europe, r. bk. trib. of R. Volga; navigable for barges from Orel, below which river winds to R. Volga at Nijni-Novgorod; connected by canal with R. Don; basin rich and fertile. Length, *c.* 950 m.

Okayam'a, city, Honshu, Japan, 90 m. by rail W. of Kobe; old castle and superb gardens; orphanage. Pop. 124,500.

Okehampton (*ōk-häm'tun*), town, Devonshire, England; 20 m. W. of Exeter; remains of Roman road; large markets for cattle and farm produce. Pop. 3,400.

Okhotsk (*ō-kotsk'*), SEA OF, arm of N. Pacific Ocean, with Kamchatka on E., isl. of Sakhalin and Siberia on W.; almost enclosed by Kuril Islands; icebound from Nov. to April; storms and fogs common.

Oklaho'ma, S. Central State, U.S.A., bounded N. by Colorado and Kansas, E. by Missouri and Arkansas, S. by Texas, W. by Texas and New Mexico; surface chiefly prairies and rolling plains rising in N.W. to elevated tableland, which forms part of Great Plains; Ozark Mts. in E. and Chautauqua Mts. in W. are principal elevations; most important riv. is Arkansas; Red R. forms S. boundary. Plains are treeless; valleys and certain upland dists. fertile and well cultivated; chief crops are maize, wheat, and oats vegetables, fruits, and cotton also produced; stock raising important in W. Chief state for production of petroleum, natural gas, and zinc; coal and lead also worked; other industries unimportant, except flour and grist milling and cotton-seed oil. Chief tns., Oklahoma City (cap.), Tulsa, and Muskogee. Area, 70,057 sq. m.; pop. 2,028,000.

Oklaho'ma City, cap. of Oklahoma, U.S.A.; cotton industries; flour, lumber, foundry and machine-shop products; univ. Pop. 185,000.

Okmul'gee, city, Oklahoma, U.S.A.; 80 m. E. of Oklahoma City; centre of great petroleum dist.; coal mining; glass. Pop. 17,500.

Ö'land (*oo'land*), Swedish isl. in Baltic Sea; interior barren, coast borders fertile; cereals, cattle rearing, cement; tn. Borgholm (pop. *c.* 10,000). Area, 519 sq. m.

Old'bury, urb. dist., Worcestershire, England, 5 m. N.W. of Birmingham; iron and steel goods, boilers, rly. carriages, chemicals, lighthouse lenses. Pop. 35,900.

Ol'denburg. (1) Rep., Germany; composed of (*a*) prov. of Oldenburg, bounded N. by North Sea, W., S., and E. by Hanover; (*b*) prov. of Lübeck, on Baltic Sea; (*c*) prov. of Birkenfeld, between Moselle and Rhine rivs. Surface flat; coast dist. marshy, with rich agricultural and pasture land; inland chiefly moorland; principal riv., Weser; several lakes. Industries include brick making, brewing, gem cutting (agates), fisheries; extensive agriculture and fine live-stock (especially horses). Total area, 2,480 sq. m.; total pop. 545,000. (2) Cap. of above; leather goods, soap, machinery, musical instruments. Pop. 53,000.

Old Flet'ton, urb. dist., Hunts, England, 1 m. S. of Peterborough; brick-fields. Pop. 7,500.

Old'ham, tn., Lancs, England, 6 m. N.E. of Manchester; one of leading cotton tns.; also manufactures silks, machinery, leather, sewing machines, gas meters; important collieries in vicinity. Pop. 140,300.

Old Mel'drum, vil., Aberdeenshire, Scotland, 16 m. N.N.W. of Aberdeen; distilling, turnip seed. Pop. 1,000.

Olean', city, New York, U.S.A., on

Allegheny R., 60 m. S.E. of Buffalo; oil refineries, natural gas, bottles, leather, oil-well supplies. Pop. 21,000.

Oléron (*ō-lā-rōn*), isl., Bay of Biscay, France, at mouth of R. Charente; surface flat and fertile; grain, wine, fruit, fisheries. Pop. 15,500.

Ol'ifants River. (1) Riv., s. Cape Prov., S. Africa; flows w. through Oudtshoorn to join Gouritz R., which falls into sea w. of Mossel Bay. Length, 157 m. (2) Riv., Cape Prov., S. Africa; enters Atlantic Ocean *c.* 75 m. N. of St. Helena Bay; chief trib., Doorn. Length, *c.* 150 m. (3) Riv., Transvaal, S. Africa; rises in Drakensbergs; flows N. and E. to join R. Limpopo in Portuguese E. Africa.

Ol'lerton, tn., Notts, England, 9 m. N.E. of Mansfield; near N. border of Sherwood Forest, and convenient centre for 'the Dukeries.' Pop. 2,000.

Ol'mütz. See OLOMOUC.

Ol'ney, tn., Bucks, England, on R. Ouse; boot and shoe making; poet Cowper resided here for many years. Pop. 2,700.

Olomouc (*ol'omōts*), formerly OLMÜTZ, tn., Moravia, Czechoslovakia, on R. Morava; cereals and cattle; manufactures malt, beer, sugar, starch. Pop. 57,500.

Ölsnitz (*ools'nĕts*). (1) Tn., Saxony, Germany, 26 m. s.w. of Zwickau; carpets, curtains, agricultural implements. Pop. 14,000. (2) Tn., Saxony, Germany, 16 m. w. by s. of Chemnitz; rich coal mines, textiles. Pop. 16,000.

Ol'ten, tn., Solothurn, Switzerland, on R. Aar; important rly. jn. Pop. 13,000.

Olympia, cap. Washington, U.S.A.; at head of Puget Sound; machinery; trades in agricultural products, wool, and timber. Pop. 8,000.

Olym'pus. Mountain range, Greece, separating Macedonia and Thessaly; greatest height, *c.* 9,800 ft.; snow-clad; legendary home of the gods.

Omagh (*ō-mä'*), cap. Tyrone, N. Ireland; mkt. tn.; linen industry; agricultural trade. Pop. 5,100.

Omaha (*ō'mä-haw*), riv. port and chief city, Nebraska, U.S.A., on the Missouri R.; important rly. centre; chief industries: ore and metal refining and smelting works, railway repair shops; flour and grist mills. South Omaha is centre of the largest meat-packing industry in the world after Chicago and Kansas City; Fort Omaha is signal service, balloon and wireless experimental station of the U.S.A. army. Pop. 214,000.

Oman', state, S.E. Arabia; between Persian Gulf, Gulf of Oman, and Indian Ocean; under supervision of govt. of India; surface mountainous (Jebel Akhdar, *c.* 10,000 ft.); climate hot and dry; irrigation necessary; produces dates, vegetables, cereals; pearls. Cap. Muscat. Area, 82,000 sq. m.; pop. (est.) 500,000.

Omdurman', tn., Anglo-Egyptian Sudan, on l. bk. of R. Nile, opposite Khartoum; Arab trade centre for ivory, ostrich feathers, gum arabic, cattle, and camels; here Dervishes were defeated by Kitchener (1898). Pop. 79,000.

Omis (*ō'mish*), port, Dalmatia, Yugoslavia, 12 m. S.E. of Split (Spalato); muscatel wine. Pop. 15,000.

Omsk, important tn. and riv. port, Siberia, at junction of Rs. Om and Irtish, on Trans-Siberian Rly.; caravan centre; brick and pottery works, breweries, distilleries, agricultural machinery; cloth; dairy produce exported. Pop. 162,000.

Onega (*o-nā'ga*). (1) Port, Archangel, Russia, at mouth of Onega R.; sawmills, boat building, fisheries, and large timber trade. Pop. 5,500. (2) Lake, Karelia Rep., N.W. Russia; connected with Volga R. by canals; ice-bound Dec. to May; fisheries. Area, 3,765 sq. m. (3) Riv., Russia; rises s. of L. Onega, but not connected with it; flows into White Sea; salmon and lamprey fisheries. Length, 240 m.

Oneida (*ō-nī'da*), city, New York, U.S.A., on Erie Canal; makes silver-plated wares. Pop. 11,000.

Onomichi (*ō-nom-ē'chē*), port, Honshu, Japan, on Inland Sea; manufactures fancy mats; two fine old temples. Pop. 31,000.

Onta'rio. (1) Province, Canada; bounded S. by St. Lawrence R., Great Lakes, and U.S.A.; stretches N. to Hudson Bay, W. to Manitoba, and E. to Quebec; crossed by Laurentian plateau; N. of plateau is Clay Belt, with fertile soil; principal rivs. are St. Lawrence and its trib. Ottawa; lakes are Nipigon, Nipissing, etc.; rainfall varies between 30 and 40 in.; great extremes of heat and cold in N., but air generally dry and bracing. Very fertile. Immense mineral wealth; gold and silver mined in increasing quantities to N. of L. Superior; nickel, copper, cobalt, arsenic, and bismuth; petroleum. Settled and agricultural portion of prov. lies S. of Laurentian plateau; 240,000 sq. m. of forests; agriculture is the great industry; maize, grapes, apples, tomatoes, peaches, and tobacco grow freely; dairy farming supplies numerous butter and cheese factories. Industries are important; the chief articles produced are farm machinery, carriages, railway rolling stock, cottons and woollens, leather goods, and furniture; pork packing; lumbering trade. Electrical energy from Niagara Falls supplies a large area; settled portion of prov. covered with a network of railways; during open season water traffic is very great; excellent canal system. Chief tns., Toronto (cap.), Ottawa (cap. of Dominion), Hamilton, London. Area, 407,262 sq. m.; pop. 3,229,000. (2) LAKE, most easterly and smallest of Great Lakes of N. America; connected with L. Erie by Niagara R. and drained by St. Lawrence. Canadian ports, Hamilton, Toronto, and Kingston; U.S. port, Oswego. Area, 7,540 sq. m.; maximum depth, 740 ft.

Onteniente (*on-tā-nē-en'tā*), tn., E. Spain, 45 m. S. of Valencia; manufactures paper, furniture, brandy, linen, woollen goods. Pop. 12,500.

Oodnadat'ta, tn., S. Australia; N.W. of L. Eyre; on rly. from Port Augusta to Alice Springs.

Ookiep (*ō-kēp'*), mining tn., Namaqualand, Cape Prov., S. Africa, 92 m. E.S.E. of Port Nolloth; copper ores in dist. Pop. 2,000 (75 whites).

Oonalashka, or UNALASKA. See ALEUTIAN ISLANDS.

Oot'acamund, tn., Nilgiri Hills dist., Madras, India; summer headquarters of Madras govt.; chief sanatorium in S. India; alt. 7,500 ft. Pop. 19,500.

Op'ava, formerly TROPPAU, cap., Silesia, Czechoslovakia, on Opava trib. of R. Oder; textiles, machinery, brewing; beet sugar. Pop. 33,500.

Opon', tn., Cebu, Philippines, on Mactan I., opposite Cebu city; scene of death of Magellan (1421); coconuts. Pop. 21,000.

Opor'to, city, Portugal, at mouth of R. Douro; important seaport and commercial centre; centre of port wine trade; sardine fisheries; cotton, wool, and silk; hats, soap, tobacco, iron and steel goods, leather; distilling, sugar refining, tanning. Pop. 216,000.

Op'peln, tn., Silesia, Prussia, on R. Oder; leather goods, cement, wood, cattle, and minerals exported. Pop. 41,000.

Oradea (*ō-räd'yä*), formerly NAGY-VARAD, tn., W. Romania; rly. jn.; agricultural market; manufactures pottery. Pop. 49,000.

Oran', port, Algeria, on Mediterranean Sea; French military centre and naval station; exports wool, cereals, wine, esparto grass, cattle, sheep, hides, tomatoes, potatoes. Pop. 150,000.

Orange (1) (*ō-ronzh'*). Tn., Vaucluse, S. France, 18 m. N. of Avignon; numerous Roman remains; silks, brooms, beet sugar, fruit. Pop. 7,000. (2) Tn., New South Wales, Australia, 30 m. N.W. of Bathurst; bracing climate; sanatorium; gold, copper, silver mines; breweries, tanneries. Pop. 8,000. (3) City, New Jersey, U.S.A., 11 m. W. of New York; electrical goods, hats, boxes.

Pop. 36,000. (4) Largest S. African riv.; rises in Drakensberg Mts., E. Basutoland; flows to Atlantic Ocean; forms S. boundary of Orange Free State; receives Caledon and Vaal on r. bk.; navigation impeded by bar at mouth and rapids 20 m. farther up. Length, *c.* 1,300 m.

Orange Free State, inland prov., Union of S. Africa; bounded N. and N.W. by Transvaal, W. and S. by Cape Prov., E. by Basutoland and Natal; surface a plateau from 3,000 to 5,000 ft. above sea-level, with a few low ridges and numerous isolated hills, known as kopjes, not exceeding 7,000 or 8,000 ft.; on borders of Natal are Drakensberg Mts. Rivers are Vaal (N. boundary), Orange (S. boundary), Modder, Caledon, Klip; none navigable; no lakes. Climate healthy, but dry and hot; ann. rainfall, *c.* 20 to 30 in. in N., *c.* 14 in. in W. and S.W., where droughts are common and severe; hottest in W., where temperatures of 105° F. are not unusual. Flora scanty; plains covered with grass after rains, but for many months dry and barren; large tracts of pasture and arable land; small area under cultivation (mainly N. and E.). Fauna includes hyena, lynx, baboon, monkey, ant-bear, wild-cat, jackal, springbok; numerous snakes, tarantulas, scorpions; destructive locust plagues. Principal products: wheat, maize, Kaffir-corn, fruit, tobacco; important stock rearing (sheep, cattle, horses, ostriches); coal mines in N.; diamond mine in W.; other products, wool, skins, ostrich feathers, hides, mohair, mealies, wheat, and dairy produce. Majority of pop. is Dutch-speaking. Cap. is Bloemfontein. Area, 49,647 sq. m.; pop. 629,000 (including 202,000 whites).

Örebro (*oo'rā-brō*). (1) Prov., central Sweden. Area, 3,561 sq. m.; pop. 221,500. (2) Cap. of above, 100 m. W. of Stockholm; trade in iron-mining products and timber; machine shops, chemical works; shoe and match factories. Pop. 37,000.

Or'egon, Pacific State, U.S.A., is bounded N. by Washington, W. by Pacific Ocean, S. by California and Nevada, and E. by Idaho; coast-line, *c.* 300 m., steep and rocky, with numerous indentations; state traversed by volcanic and snow-capped mts.—Cascade Mts. parallel with coast; Steens Mts. in S.E.; Blue Mts. in E.; extensive plains and large valleys, with fine arable and pasture land; principal rivs. are Columbia, and tribs. Willamette, Rogue; numerous lakes in S. Climate mild on coast, with heavy rainfall in winter; dry and hot E. of Cascade Mts., with severe winters; irrigation necessary in some parts; extensive forests. Principal products: wheat, oats, hay, sugar-beet, potatoes, fruits, timber, live-stock, wool, dairy produce; gold, silver, copper, coal are mined; lead, gypsum, quicksilver, nickel, opals found. Chief industries are lumbering, flour milling, fish canning, paper making, slaughtering and packing, machinery; valuable fisheries. Principal tns. are Portland and Salem (cap.). Area, 96,699 sq. m.; pop. 1,065,000.

Orel', or ORLOV. (1) Prov., European Russia; surface undulating and well-cultivated; principal rivs., Oka and Sosna; agriculture on black earth soils; rye, oats, potatoes; horses and cattle reared; manufactures machinery, manures, wagons, leather, and glass; tobacco, oil, hemp produced. Area, *c.* 12,000 sq. m.; pop. 1,883,500. (2) Cap. of above, 100 m. S.W. of Tula; produces candles, ropes, oil, flour; distilleries, breweries, tobacco factories; univ. (1919). Pop. 76,000.

O'renburg. (1) Prov., European Russia; surface hilly; desert and steppe land; 'black earth' near Ural Mts. very fertile; stock raising; coal, salt; leather; goats'-wool shawls. Area, *c.* 23,000 sq. m.; pop. 674,500. (2) Cap. of above, on Ural R.; saw-milling; textiles, metal goods, sugar are chief articles of commerce; caravan centre for central Asia. Pop. 122,000.

Oren'se. (1) Prov., N.W. Spain;

mountainous; watered by Minho R.; climate humid; black cattle and other stock. Area, 2,694 sq. m.; pop. 418,500. (2) Cap. of above, on Minho R.; manufactures flour, leather, iron, chocolate; hot springs known to Romans. Pop. 18,000.

Or'ford, fishing vil. and par., Suffolk, England, 16 m. N.E. of Ipswich; oyster and other fisheries; former importance ruined by encroachments of the sea. Pop. (par.) 850.

Oriente (*ō-rē-en'tā*), prov., E. Cuba; mountainous, with fertile valleys and plains; sugar, tobacco, coffee, cocoa, bananas produced; copper, iron, manganese, mercury, petroleum, marble, slate found. Area, 14,211 sq. m.; pop. 886,000.

Orihuela (*ō-rē-wā'lā*), tn., Alicante, S.E. Spain, 13 m. N.E. of Murcia; in fertile plain; leather; silk and other textiles; wine, cereals, fruit, oil; remains of Moorish stronghold. Pop. 37,500.

Oril'lia, tn., Ontario, Canada, on W. of L. Couchiching, 65 m. N. of Toronto. Pop. 7,900.

Orino'co, riv., S. America; rises in Sierra Parima, flows through Venezuela, and forms delta *c.* 120 m. before its entrance into Atlantic Ocean; basin densely wooded and hilly; chief port, Bolivar. The Cassiquiare, which leaves the Orinoco *c.* 150 m. below its source, establishes water communication with the Amazon by joining the Rio Negro. As the Orinoco and its tribs. are navigable for hundreds of miles, the river system is of great commercial importance. Length, *c.* 1,500 m.

Oris'sa. See BIHAR AND ORISSA.

Orizaba (*ō-rē-thā'ba*). (1) Tn., Vera Cruz, Mexico; cotton mills; coffee, cotton, sugar, maize, tobacco; first locality visited by Cortez. Pop. 42,000. (2) Volcanic mountain, between Puebla and Vera Cruz, Mexico; highest peak in Mexico (*c.* 18,300 ft.).

Ork'ney Islands, group of islands off N. coast of Scotland; separated from mainland by Pentland Firth; comprise twenty-nine inhabited islands and thirty-nine smaller islands; principal isl., Mainland or Pomona, containing more than half pop.; surface low except in Hoy; numerous lakes, principal being Stenness and Harray, in Mainland; coast-line irregular, with deep bays; navigation rendered difficult by rapid currents. Antiquities include cairns, brochs, stone circles (Standing Stones of Stennis), Picts' houses, castles, and churches. Islands were under Norse rule (875–1231); pledged to Scot. crown (1468); now form a Scottish co. Agriculture and fishing are leading industries. Chief tns., Kirkwall (cap.) and Stromness on Mainland. Area, 376 sq. m.; pop. 22,100.

Orlan'do, tn., Florida, U.S.A., 70 m. N.E. of Tampa; tourist resort, and centre of citrus fruit-growing district. Pop. 27,000.

Orleans, cap. Loiret, France, on R. Loire; commercial centre; manufactures blankets, cottons, machinery, agricultural implements, tobacco; wine, grain, wool, oil, live-stock; house and statue of Joan of Arc (Maid of Orleans). Pop. 63,000.

Orlov. See OREL.

Orme's Head, GREAT, headland, Carnarvonshire, Wales; immediately N.W. of Llandudno. To the E. is a smaller promontory known as Little Orme's Head.

Or'miston, vil. and par., E. Lothian, Scotland, 3 m. S.S.E. of Tranent; coal mines. Pop. (par.) 1,850.

Or'mond, winter resort, Florida, U.S.A., on E. coast; Ormond-Daytona beach (20 m. long) is favourite course for motor races. Pop. 1,850.

Orms'kirk, urb. dist., mkt. tn., Lancs, England, 12 m. N.E. of Liverpool; centre of potato-growing dist.; ironfounding, brewing, rope making. Pop. 17,100.

Ormuz. See HORMUZ.

Orne (*orn*), dep., N.W. France; forests in W.; chief riv., Orne; wheat, oats, barley cultivated; apples for cider extensively grown; its horses are famous; manufactures ironware, lace, linen; has iron mines, mineral springs. Chief tn., Alençon. Area, 2,371 sq. m.; pop. 278,000.

Orontes (*ō-ron'tēz*), riv., N. Syria; rises in Anti-Lebanon Mts.; flows N. to Antioch, then W.S.W. to enter Mediterranean Sea. Length, 200 m.

Or'pington, tn., Kent, England, 13 m. S.E. of London; fruit and hops grown; gives name to a well-known breed of poultry. Pop. 7,000.

Or'rell, urb. dist., Lancs, England, 3 m. W.S.W. of Wigan; cotton, nails; coal mining. Pop. 7,000.

Or'sha, tn., White Russia, U.S.S.R., on R. Dnieper; has tanneries and ironworks; river port at head of navigation on R. Dnieper. Pop. 21,500.

Orsova (*ōr'shova*), tn., Romania, on R. Danube, above the 'Iron Gates.' Pop. 5,000. On an isl. 3 m. down the riv. is New Orsova, formerly a Turkish fortress. Pop. 3,000.

Orthez (*or-tāz*), tn., Basses-Pyrénées, France, 25 m. N.W. of Pau; leather, hams, chocolate; scene of Wellington's victory over Soult (1814). Pop. 40,000.

Ortigueira (*or-tē-gā'ē-rā*), port, Corunna, N.W. Spain, S. of Cape Ortegal; sea-bathing resort. Pop. 19,000.

Ort'ler Spit'ze, mt., Tirol, Italy; highest peak in E. Alps (12,800 ft.).

Oruro (*ō-roo'rō*). (1) Dep., Bolivia; part of L. Titicaca basin; much of it is arid; tin, silver, copper. Area, 20,657 sq. m.; pop. 140,000. (2) Cap. of above; alt. 12,158 ft.; gold, silver, and tin mines; rly. centre. Pop. 33,000.

Orvieto (*or-vē-ā'tō*), city, Perugia, Italy, 60 m. N. of Rome; situated on isolated rock, 1,000 ft. high; has numerous interesting houses, palaces, and churches; wines. Pop. 19,400.

Osaka (*ō-sä'kä*), port, Honshu, Japan, on Osaka Bay; largest city in Japan; a network of canals; cotton mills, iron and glass works, sugar refining, shipbuilding. Pop. 2,115,000.

Os'borne, former royal residence near Cowes, Isle of Wight, England; now convalescent home for naval and military officers.

Oschersleben (*osh'ers-lā-ben*), tn., Saxony, Prussia, 24 m. by rail W.S.W. of Magdeburg; sugar, chocolate, bricks, tiles, agricultural implements, and artificial manures. Pop. 13,500.

Osh, town, Ferghana, Kirghiz, U.S.S.R., 100 m. E. of Khoqand; cotton, grain, fruit; trades with China; near it is 'Throne of Solomon' rock, a place of Moslem pilgrimage. Pop. 29,000.

Osh'awa, city, Ontario, Canada, on L. Ontario, 30 m. E. of Toronto; manufacturing tn. Pop. 25,600.

Osh'kosh, city, Wisconsin, U.S.A., on W. shore of L. Winnebago; lumber and allied industries; meat packing and dairy farming; flour, boilers, motors. Pop. 40,000.

Osijek (*ō'sē-yek*), formerly ESSEG, tn., Slavonia, Yugoslavia, on R. Drava; cotton, silk, leather, beet-sugar, and glass. Pop. 34,500.

Osimo (*ō-sē'mō*), tn., Marches, Italy, 8 m. S. of Ancona; silk, ribbons, and hosiery. Pop. 20,000.

Os'lo, formerly CHRISTIANIA, cap. of Norway, at head of fiord of same name; founded 1048; manufactures woollens, cotton yarns, tobacco, condensed milk, paper, oil; well-built city; has fine harbour, ice-bound in winter; exports timber, fish, matches, ice. Pop. 251,000.

Osnabrück (*oz'nä-brook*), tn., Hanover, Prussia, 28 m. N.N.E. of Münster; cigars, chemicals, nails, machinery, musical instruments. Pop. 89,000.

Os'sa, mountain, Thessaly, Greece; modern Kissavo (6,398 ft.); joins on to Pelion.

Os'sett, tn., W. Riding, Yorks, England, 2½ m. W. of Wakefield; woollen mills; collieries; centre of shoddy trade; mineral springs. Pop. 14,800.

Ostend', wat.-pl., W. Flanders, Belgium; second port of Belgium; on important passenger route between London and Continent; headquarters of Belgian fishing fleet; fashionable holiday resort; fisheries, oyster-beds; occupied by Germans 1914–18. Pop. 44,000.

Osterode (*os'tā-rō-dē*), tn., E.

Prussia, Germany, on L. Drewenz; machinery, sawmills, agricultural produce. Russians defeated here (1914). Pop. 16,000.

Os'tia, harbour of anc. Rome, Italy, at mouth of R. Tiber; place attained great commercial importance, but declined after construction of safer harbours. Modern vil. near anc. site, contains cathedral.

Ostrau. See MORAVSKA OSTRAVA.

Osuna (*ō-soo'na*), town, s. Spain, 52 m. E.S.E. of Seville; grain, fruit, mats, esparto ropes, bricks, pottery. Pop. 16,000.

Os'waldtwistle, urb. dist., Lancs, England, 3 m. E.S.E. of Blackburn; cotton mills, paper works, chemical works, potteries. Pop. 14,200.

Oswe'go, port, New York, U.S.A., on L. Ontario; falls of Oswego R. supply water-power; match factories; textiles; hosiery; engines. Deep Rock mineral springs are located here. Pop. 24,000.

Os'westry, tn., Shropshire, England, 15 m. N.W. of Shrewsbury; manufactures iron goods, leather, agricultural machinery. In neighbourhood is old British camp. Pop. 9,800.

Otago (*ot-ā'go*), provincial dist., in s. of S. Island, New Zealand; rugged mountains and forests in w.; agricultural land in E.; contains Sutherland waterfall (1,904 ft.); agriculture, sheep farming, fruit culture, gold mining. Cap. Dunedin, on Otago Harbour. Area, 25,312 sq. m.; pop. 220,000.

Otaheite. See TAHITI.

Otaru (*ō-tä'roo*), port, Hokkaido, Japan, 100 m. N. of Hakodate; centre of herring fisheries. Pop. 134,500.

Ot'ley, urb. dist., mkt. tn., W. Riding, Yorks, England, on R. Wharfe, 8 m. N. of Bradford; worsteds, leather, paper, and printing machines. Pop. 11,000.

Otran'to. (1) Port, Apulia, S.E. Italy, on Strait of Otranto, 29 m. by rail S.E. of Lecce; castle and cathedral; destroyed by Turks (1480). Pop. 3,000. (2) STRAIT OF, strait between Italy and Albania, leading to Adriatic Sea; width *c.* 40 m.

Ot'tawa. (1) Cap. of Dominion of Canada, in Ontario, on R. Ottawa; centre of lumber trade; manufactures leather, ironware, machinery, matches, furniture, electric cars; flour mills. New Parliament buildings, to replace those burnt in 1916, erected 1916–20. Pop. 125,000. (2) Riv., Canada; principal trib. of St. Lawrence, which it enters opposite Montreal I.; very large lumber trade; Chaudière and other falls furnish water-power; navigable for small craft to Ottawa, whence Rideau Canal is cut to L. Ontario. Length, 685 m.

Ot'terburn, vil., Redesdale, Northumberland, England, 18 m. N. of Hexham; scene of Douglas's defeat of Hotspur in 1388, celebrated in ballads *Chevy Chase* and *The Battle of Otterburn.*

Ot'tery St Mary, mkt. tn., Devonshire, England, 12 m. N.E. of Exeter; birthplace of Coleridge. Pop. 3,700.

Ottum'wa, city, Iowa, U.S.A., on Des Moines R.; coal mines, iron and steel works; starch, flour, canned goods. Pop. 28,000.

Oudenarde (*oo-dĕn-ärd'*), tn., E. Flanders, Belgium, on R. Schelde; textile industries, leather. Marlborough defeated French under Vendôme (1708). Pop. 7,000.

Oudh (*oud*). See UNITED PROVINCES OF AGRA AND OUDH.

Oudtshoorn (*outs'hōrn*), tn., Cape Prov., S. Africa, on Olifants R., 78 m. N. of Mossel Bay; ostrich farms; tobacco, lucerne, and fruit. Pop. 11,000 (5,650 whites).

Oullins (*ool-ăn'*), tn., Rhône, France, near Lyons; textiles, machinery, glass, leather; nursery gardens. Pop. 12,000.

Oulton Broad (*ōl'ton*), w. ward of Lowestoft bor., Suffolk, England; yachting centre for Broads. Pop. 4,650.

Oulu (*ō'lu*), formerly ULEÅBORG. (1) Dep. Finland; includes part of Lapland; forests; numerous lakes. Area, 65,263 sq. m.; pop. 414,500.

(2) Cap. of above, on Gulf of Bothnia; shipbuilding; salmon fisheries; exports timber, hides, leather, pitch, tar, butter. Pop. 23,000.

Oun'dle, tn., on R. Nen, Northants, England; public school; brewing. Pop. 2,000.

Ouro Preto (*ō'rō prā'to*), city, Minas Geraes, Brazil, 170 m. N. of Rio de Janeiro; alt. 3,750 ft.; once famous gold-mining centre, but mines now almost exhausted; iron, manganese, asbestos found in vicinity. Pop. *c.* 5,000.

Ouse (*ooz*). (1) Riv., Yorks, England; formed by junction of Rs. Swale and Ure, enters Humber; navigable to York; length, 60 m. (2) GREAT OUSE, riv., Northants, England, flows through S. Fenland into Wash; navigable to Bedford; length, 160 m. (3) LITTLE OUSE, trib. of Great Ouse. (4) Riv., Sussex, England; flows through S. Downs into English Channel.

Ovar', tn., Beira, Portugal, 20 m. S. of Oporto; fishing centre; wine, wheat, onions. Pop. 11,500.

O'ver, par. and tn., Cheshire, England, 4½ m. W. of Middlewich; salt and chemical trade; cattle and sheep fairs. Pop. (par.) 7,500.

Overyssel (*ō-ver-is'sel*), prov., Holland; between Zuyder Zee and Prussian provs. of Hanover and Westphalia; W. is generally under cultivation; rich pasture in E. Dairying, fishing, cotton manufacture, and brick making. Cap. Zwolle. Area, 1,295 sq. m.; pop. 504,000.

Oviedo (*ō-vē-ā'dō*). (1) Prov., N. Spain; former principality of Asturia; coal largely mined; forests; industries include agriculture, stock raising, and fishing. Area, 4,205 sq. m.; pop. 798,500. (2) Cap. of above, 16 m. from Gijon, Bay of Biscay; manufactures textiles, leather, matches, hardware, and has national arms factory. Pop. 72,500.

Owensboro, city, Kentucky, U.S.A., on Ohio R.; centre of oilfield; tobacco, lumber; centre of farming and stock raising region. Pop. 21,000.

Owen Sound, port, Ontario, Canada, on Georgian Bay; shipbuilding; large grain elevators. Pop. 12,500.

Ox'ford, co. tn., Oxfordshire, England; at junction of Rs. Cherwell and Thames; famous univ. is believed to date from 12th cent., and now comprises 21 colleges and one hall; univ. opened for first time to women (1920). Industries include printing and publishing; motor works. Pop. 80,500.

Ox'fordshire, or OXON, co., England; bounded N. by Warwick and Northants, E. by Bucks, S. by Berks, W. by Gloucester; surface generally level; N. is mostly bare, but in S. are finely wooded hills and valleys; S.E. crossed by Chiltern Hills; well watered by numerous rivs., including Thames and its tribs., Windrush, Evenlode, Cherwell, and Thame; one of most productive cos. in England; chief crops are barley, oats, and wheat; stock raised; paper made at Shiplake and elsewhere, gloves at Woodstock, blankets at Witney, agricultural implements at Banbury; manufactures of bricks, tweeds, and lace also carried on. Chief tns. are Oxford (co. tn.), Banbury, Henley, Chipping Norton, and Woodstock. Area, 749 sq. m.; pop. 209,600.

Ox'us, or AMU DARYA, important riv., S.W. Central Asia; rises in Pamir plateau, forms for some distance boundary between Afghanistan and Tadzhik and Uzbek reps., U.S.S.R.; flows into S. extremity of Sea of Aral; many tribs. in upper course, but few after it enters deserts of Turkmen, where streams often disappear in sand; forms a delta *c.* 90 m. from Sea of Aral; banks in some parts fertile, and irrigation canals are made; in some seasons Oxus floods large tracts; navigable to Charjui, where it is crossed by rly. from Nerv to Samarqand; regular steamer service. Length, 1,450 m.

Oys'ter Bay, summer resort, New York, U.S.A., on N. coast of Long I.; oyster fisheries. Pop. (par.) 9,200.

Oys'termouth, better known as 'The Mumbles,' coast par. and vil., Glamorganshire, Wales; a favourite wat.-pl.; oyster dredging extensively carried on. Pop. 9,000.

Ozark' Mountains, area of highlands in Missouri, Arkansas, Oklahoma, Kansas, and Illinois, U.S.A.; summer resort.

Ozorkow (*ōz-or'kuf*), tn., Lodz, Poland, 15 m. N.W. of Lodz; cloth manufactures. Pop. 11,000.

P

Paarl, tn., Cape Prov., S. Africa, 40 m. N.E. of Capetown; wines; fruit farming and tobacco growing; wool washing and carriage building. Pop. 13,500 (6,700 whites).

Pabjanice (*păb-yă-nĕt'se*), tn., Poland, 10 m. S.S.W. of Lodz; textiles; paper; agricultural machinery. Pop. 30,000.

Pabna. (1) Dist., Bengal, India; low-lying; rice, jute. Area, 1,678 sq. m.; pop. *c.* 1,500,000. (2) Cap. of above, 75 m. W.N.W. of Dacca; oil, bricks, carpets. Pop. *c.* 20,000.

Pachuca (*pă-choo'ka*), cap. of Hidalgo, Mexico, 55 m. N.N.E. of Mexico City; *gat*, *c.* 8,000 ft.; silver mines; meteorological observatory. Pop. 41,000.

Pacif'ic Ocean, largest ocean of world, occupying about half water surface of the globe; extends from Bering Strait to Antarctica, and lies between America (on E.) and Australia and Asia (on W.); total length from N. to S., *c.* 8,500 m.; greatest breadth (near equator), *c.* 9,500 m. Area, 63,785,000 sq. m. Salinity is less than that of Atlantic. Mean depth is *c.* 2,500 fathoms; greatest depth on Asiatic side, E. of Mindanao (Philippines), 35,433 ft. (greatest recorded ocean depth). Has innumerable continental and oceanic islands, mainly in centre and W., either of volcanic or coral formation. Principal prevailing winds are N.E. and S.E. trade-winds, with broad belt of equatorial calms between them, and W. belts to N. and S.; monsoons also blow regularly, and violent storms occur in China Sea, etc. Pacific Ocean was discovered by Balboa (1513); first traversed by Magellan (1520–1), and named Pacific on account of calm weather encountered there. Chief steamship routes are from Vancouver and San Francisco to New Zealand, Australia, and Japan; route from these lands to E. U.S.A. and Europe passes round Cape Horn or through Panama Canal.

Padang', port, Sumatra, Dutch E. Indies, on W. coast; exports coffee, spices, rubber, tobacco, copra, coal. Pop. 41,500.

Pad'dington, N.W. metropolitan bor., London co., England; contains terminus of Great Western Rly. Pop. 145,000.

Pad'erborn, tn., Westphalia, Prussia, 63 m. N.E. of Dortmund; glass, soap; trade in cattle and grain. Pop. 33,500.

Pad'iham, urb. dist., Lancs, England, on R. Calder, 3 m. W. of Burnley; cotton mills, coal mines, stone quarries. Pop. 11,600.

Pad'stow, mkt. tn. and port, N. Cornwall, England; harbour of refuge; fisheries; agricultural trade. Pop. 1,900.

Pad'ua. (1) Prov., S. Venetia, Italy; fertile plain; wheat, rice, wine, silk. Area, 826 sq. m.; pop. 634,000. (2) Cap. of above, on R. Bacchiglione; has arcaded streets and ancient bridges; centre of learning and art in Middle Ages and Renaissance; chief industries: machine works, chemicals, silk, distilleries. Pop. 125,500.

Padu'cah, city, Kentucky, U.S.A., at junction of Tennessee and Ohio rivs.; sawmills; rly. workshops; trade in tobacco. Pop. 34,000.

Pahang′, Federated Malay State, on E. of Malay Peninsula. Drained by Pahang and other rivs. Large stretches of forest. Tin, gold, lead; fish. Cap. Kuala Lipis. Area, 14,000 sq. m.; pop. 146,000.

Pahlevi (*pä-lā-vē′*), formerly ENZELI, port, N. Persia, on Caspian Sea, 18 m. N.W. of Resht; exports rice, hides and skins, raisins, cotton, fruit. Pop. *c.* 20,000.

Paignton (*pān′ton*), seaside resort, Devonshire, England, 2 m. S. of Torquay; cider. Pop. 18,400.

Paisley (*pāz′le*), riv. port, Renfrewshire, Scotland, on White Cart R. near its junction with R. Clyde; old abbey, founded *c.* 1163; staple industry manufacture of cotton thread; other industries include dyeing, bleaching, weaving, engineering, founding, brewing, distilling, tanning; manufactures of starch, soap, corn-flour, and preserves. Pop. 86,400.

Pakhoi′, port, Kwangtung, China, on Gulf of Tongking; exports sugar, indigo, ground-nuts. Pop. 35,000.

Pakokku (*pă-kok′oo*), cap., Pakokku dist., Upper Burma, on R. Irrawaddy; commercial centre; shipbuilding yards; millet, sugar-palms, rice, tobacco cultivated in dist.; oilfields; teak. Pop. 19,500.

Palamau′, dist., Chota-Nagpur, Bihar and Orissa, India; *c.* three-fourths jungle-covered; coal mines; silk and lace exported. Chief tn., Daltonganj, 120 m. S.E. of Benares. Area, 4,916 sq. m.; pop. 733,500.

Palamcottah′, tn., Tinnevelly, S. Madras, India; headquarters of dist. Pop. 47,000.

Palanpur′, Indian state, Gujarat, Bombay, India; mountainous and well forested in N.; wheat, rice, sugar-cane cultivated. Chief tn., Palanpur, 75 m. N. of Ahmadabad. Area, 1,766 sq. m.; pop. 237,000.

Palat′inate. See BAVARIA.

Palau, or PELEW, W. group, Caroline Islands, Pacific Ocean; mountainous; surrounded by coral reefs; bread-fruit, bananas, sugar-cane, tortoise-shell, mother-of-pearl, timber; mandated to Japan. Area, *c.* 200 sq. m.; pop. *c.* 10,000.

Palawan (*pä-lä′wan*), isl., Philippines; mountainous, forest-covered; exports rattans, resin, timber. Area, 4,500 sq. m.

Palazzolo Acreide (*pä-lät-sō′lō äk-rā-ē′dā*), tn., Syracuse, Sicily; ruins of fine Greek theatre; magnificent tombs and primitive sculptures. Pop. 15,000.

Palembang′, cap. of Palembang Residency, S. Sumatra, Dutch E. Indies; exports cotton, pepper, rubber, copra, coffee; health station for troops. Pop. 62,500.

Palencia (*pä-len′thē-ä*). (1) Prov., Old Castile, Spain; Cantabrian Mts. in N.; produces grain, wine; manufactures woollen rugs and mantles. Area, 3,256 sq. m.; pop. 192,000. (2) Cap. of above, on R. Carrion, 25 m. N. of Valladolid; centre of ironfounding, cloth, blanket, and flannel weaving. Pop. 20,000.

Paler′mo, cap. of Sicily, Italy; on N. coast; important seaport in sheltered bay; situated in fertile valley (Conca d'Oro) partly surrounded by mts.; chief products are machinery, chemicals, sumach, essences, sulphur, tartar, wine, oranges and lemons, tobacco; fine cathedral (1169–85). Pop. 394,000.

Pal′estine, country, W. Asia, on Mediterranean Sea; bounded N. by Syria, E. by Transjordan, S. by Hejaz and Egypt; length, 145 m.; average breadth W. of Jordan, 40 m. Because of its history is the "Holy Land" for Jews and Christians, and is again a national home for Jewish people. Country divided into (1) coastal plain of Philistia, Sharon, etc. (broken only by Mount Carmel), bordering Levant; (2) mountain and hill country of Judæa, Samaria, and Galilee; (3) Jordan rift-valley, El Ghor, containing the Dead Sea; principal riv., Jordan; lakes are Merom, Sea of Galilee, and

Dead Sea. Climate extremely hot in summer and wet in winter; olive, cedar, and sycamore trees; wheat, wine, olives, and many fruits; sheep and goats reared; rlys. running inland from Acre and Haifa, and from Jaffa to Jerusalem, are connected with line from Egyptian frontier; exports oranges, soap, water melons, wines, durra, barley, sesame, and almonds; trade mainly with Syria, U.K., and Egypt. During Great War Turkish sovereignty was overthrown by British under Allenby. Country now administered by Great Britain under mandate of League of Nations. Cap. Jerusalem. Area, *c.* 9,000 sq. m.; pop. 816,000 (including 572,500 Moslems, 154,500 Jews, and 80,500 Christians).

Palghat′, tn., Malabar, Madras, India; important commercially and strategically owing to position in Palghat pass S. of Nilgiri Hills; key to W. coast. Pop. 46,000.

Palk Strait, strait separating India from Ceylon; passage difficult owing to shoals and coral reefs on either side; separated from Gulf of Manaar by Rameswaram I., Adam's Bridge, and Manaar I.

Pal′ma. (1) Port, Majorca, cap. of Balearic Isles; cathedral and palaces; trade in wine, cereals, fruit, and silk. Pop. 81,000. (2) Or SAN MIGUEL DE LA PALMA, one of Canary Islands, in Atlantic Ocean off African coast; mountainous; wines, silk, fruits, wax produced. Chief tn. Santa Cruz. Area, 280 sq. m.; pop. 53,000.

Palm Beach, vil., Florida, U.S.A., 66 m. N.E. of Miami; shore washed by Gulf Stream; fashionable winter resort. Pop. 1,000.

Palmerston. See DARWIN.

Palmerston North, tn., N. Island, New Zealand, 87 m. N. of Wellington; rly. jn.; dairy farming, sheep raising. Pop. 21,000.

Palmy′ra, anc. city, Syria, *c.* 130 m. N.E. of Damascus; once important centre of caravan trade; under Zenobia extended its sway far and wide, till captured by Romans; now inhabited by wandering Arabs; ruins of city are extensive and magnificent.

Palwal′, tn., Punjab, India, *c.* 40 m. S. of Delhi; of great antiquity; depot for cotton of dist. Pop. 9,500.

Pamiers (*pä-mē-ā′*), tn., Ariège, France, 34 m. S.E. of Toulouse; wine, woollen goods, leather, chains and carriage springs. Pop. 10,000.

Pamirs (*pä-mērs′*), known as the 'Roof of the World,' lofty plateau region, Central Asia; where Hindu Kush, Himalayas, Kunlun, and Tien Shan Mts. converge; average height, *c.* 13,000 ft.; ranges are separated by broad valleys or *pamirs*; almost destitute of vegetation, except along banks of rivs. and lakes, where there is fine pasturage during summer months for great-horned sheep, etc.; climate severe and storms sudden and violent; inhabited by Kirghiz tribes.

Pam′pa, terr., Argentina, S. America, W. of Buenos Aires; belongs almost entirely to pampas region; cereals cultivated; large sheep and cattle ranches. Cap. Santa Rosa. Area, 56,320 sq. m.; pop. *c.* 105,000.

Pamplo′na. (1) City, cap. of Navarre, Spain; strong fortress on spur of Pyrenees; agricultural trade. Pop. 33,500. (2) Tn., N.E. Colombia, S. America, 220 m. N.N.E. of Bogota; breweries, match factories; in vicinity are abandoned gold and silver mines. Pop. 20,000.

Panama′. (1) Rep., Central America; dep. of Colombia till 1903; traversed by Sierra de Chiriqui and Cordillera de Veragua; chief riv., Chagres; crossed by Panama Canal; climate tropical; soil very fertile, but greater portion unoccupied; industries are cattle raising, agriculture, and pearl fishing; important products are bananas, cocoa, coconuts, mother-of-pearl, rubber, sugar, coffee, and hides. Rep. is divided into nine provs.; chief ports, Panama and Colon. Area, 32,380 sq. m.; pop. 442,500. See also PANAMA CANAL and CANAL ZONE. (2) Cap. of above rep., on Panama Gulf, at Pacific terminus of Panama Canal;

cathedral; city (founded 1519) and harbour under jurisdiction of U.S.A. in all that relates to sanitation and quarantine. Pop. 59,500.

Panama' Canal, ship canal crossing Isthmus of Panama. A French attempt to construct a canal began in 1882 but failed. The task was resumed by U.S.A., which purchased Canal Zone from Panama in 1904 (see CANAL ZONE), and the canal was formally opened on Aug. 15, 1914. The canal begins on Atlantic side at Cristobal, a dredged channel leading to the Gatun locks, where a lift of 85 ft. brings a ship into the artificial L. Gatun. The construction of Gatun dam, 1½ m. long, 100 ft. high, ½ m. wide at the bottom, was the outstanding engineering feature. After crossing lake (24 m.), canal enters Gaillard or Culebra Cut, 9 m. long, leaves it by Pedro Miguel lock, passes through Miraflores lock to sea-level, and then for 8 m. to Balboa on the Pacific. Length of canal proper is *c.* 42 m., ranging in width from 300 to 1,000 ft.; minimum depth, 41 ft. Time of transit from 7 to 8 hours. A rly. (47 m.) follows course of canal, connecting Colon and Panama; it belongs to U.S.A. Canal is open to world's shipping on equal terms. Opening of canal has changed routes between many countries; sea distances between European ports and Pacific coast of N. and S. America shortened by about 6,000 m. During 1930 6,185 vessels sailed through the Canal, of which 1,536 were British and 2,885 were U.S.A.

Panay (*pä-nī'*), isl., Philippines; mountainous, well watered; cotton, rice, sugar-cane, coffee; port, Iloilo. Area, 4,448 sq. m.; pop. 750,000.

Panch Mahals', dist., Gujarat, Bombay, India; large forests; manganese and mica found in hills; timber exported. Chief tn. Godhra, 40 m. N.E. of Baroda. Area, 1,606 sq. m.; pop. 375,000.

Pandharpur', tn., Bombay, India, on R. Bhima, trib. of R. Kistna; temple; resort of pilgrims. Pop. 25,500.

Pangan'i, port, Tanganyika Terr., E. Africa, at mouth of R. Ruvu (Pangani); grows coconuts, sisal, maize, and sugar; dist. (6,000 sq. m.) not suitable for European settlement. Pop. 3,000.

Pang'bourne, par. and vil., Berks, England, on R. Thames, 5½ m. N.W. of Reading; nautical college. Pop. 1,950.

Pang'o-Pang'o, or PAGO-PAGO, port, Tutuila, Samoan Islands, Pacific Ocean, on S.E. coast; U.S.A. naval and coaling station. Has the only good harbour in group; high-powered radio station.

Panipat', tn., Punjab, India, 53 m. N. of Delhi; manufactures brass vessels, silver and glass ornaments, cotton goods, blankets. Pop. 27,500.

Panteg (*pan-tāg'*), urb. dist., Monmouthshire, England, 2 m. S.E. of Pontypool; coal mines, stone quarries, and foundries. Pop. 11,500.

Pantin (*pon-tăn'*), tn., Seine, France; N.E. suburb of Paris; glass works, sugar refineries, rly. shops, tobacco and chemicals, distilleries. Pop. 39,000.

Papeete (*pä-pē-ā'tē*), cap. Tahiti, Society Islands, S. Pacific Ocean; fine harbour; copra, phosphates, mother-of-pearl. Pop. 5,000.

Papua (*pă'poo-a*). See NEW GUINEA.

Par, seaport tn., Cornwall, England, 8 m. S. of Bodmin; large pilchard fishery. Pop. 2,000.

Pará (*pä-rä'*). (1) State, Brazil, S. America; bounded on N. by three Guianas; thickly wooded and well-watered region; communication carried on by rivs., especially Amazon; rubber is chief product; fruits and cacao cultivated; rubber, gutta-percha, tonka beans, sarsaparilla, gums, and Brazil nuts exported. Cap. Pará. Area, 443,789 sq. m.; pop. 1,376,000. (2) Or BELEM, or BELEM DO PARÁ, cap. of above, on Pará R.; founded (1615) by Portuguese. Chief export, rubber; entrepôt for Amazon river trade; naval arsenal. Pop. 236,500.

Paraguay (*pä-rä-gwī'*), inland rep., S. America; bounded by Bolivia, Brazil, and Argentina; divided from N. to S. by Paraguay R., E. portion being larger and more important; large tract to w. of riv. unexplored. Surface consists of undulating plains, low hills, swamps, and dense forests; highest ground in N. and E.; chief rivs., Paraguay, Pilcomayo, and Paraná; soil fertile, vegetation luxuriant; leading industries are stock raising and cultivation of yerba maté (Paraguay tea), oranges, sugar, tobacco, maize, and cotton; forests produce fine timber, gums, dyes, and oils; iron, manganese, and copper abound; hides, timber, maté, tobacco, quebracho extract, cattle, and meat products exported. Inhabitants are chiefly Spaniards and Indians. Principal tns., Asuncion (cap.) and Villa Rica. Area, *c.* 161,647 sq. m., of which *c.* 100,000 claimed by Bolivia; pop *c.* 836,500.

Parahyba (*pä-rä-ē'ba*). (1) N.E. state, Brazil, S. America; surface elevated; chief products are cotton, coffee, cocoa, sugar, rubber, tobacco. Area, 28,846 sq. m.; pop. 1,278,000. (2) Cap. of above; exports sugar and cotton. Pop. 53,000.

Paramar'ibo, cap. Dutch Guiana, S. America, on Surinam R.; coffee, cocoa, rubber, sugar, rum exported. Pop. 47,000.

Paraná (*pä-rä-nä'*). (1) River, S. America; formed by junction of Rio Grande and Paranahyba; flows w. between Paraguay and Argentina; chief trib., Paraguay; enters Rio de la Plata; navigable by steamers to Brazilian frontier near Iguassu Falls. Length, 2,000 m. (2) S. state, Brazil, S. America; drained by Paraná R.; extensive forests; exports Paraguay tea. Area, 93,269 sq. m.; pop. *c.* 938,500. (3) Cap. Entre Rios, Argentina, S. America, on Paraná R.; centre of fertile dist.; former cap. of Argentina. Pop. 36,000.

Paranagua (*pä-rä-nä-gwä'*), seapt, Paraná, s. Brazil; exports Paraguay tea. Pop. 19,000.

Pardubice (*pär'doo-bit-se*), tn., Bohemia, Czechoslovakia, on R. Elbe; breweries, distilleries, sawmills, iron foundries; horse fairs. Pop. 25,000.

Paren'zo, port, Pola, Italy, 30 m. s. by w. of Trieste; fishing, shipbuilding; cathedral; Roman remains. Pop. 12,500.

Par'is. (1) Cap. of France; largest city of continental Europe, on R. Seine; important rly., riv., road, and canal centre; Seine divides the city into two regions, and is crossed by many bridges; heart of Paris is the Ile de la Cité, in midstream, with famous Gothic cathedral, Notre-Dame (13th cent.); city is comparatively flat, with exception of Montmartre, Buttes-Chaumont, and Montagne Ste. Geneviève. On r. bk. of R. Seine are Place de la Concorde; Place du Carrousel; Place Vendôme; Place de l'Etoile, with Arc de Triomphe, from which radiate twelve avenues, including the Champs Elysées, the most fashionable promenade; Place de la Bastille; Palais du Louvre, extending about ½ m. along the river, with world-famous art collections; Jardin des Tuileries; Palais Royal, built by Richelieu; many famous churches, including La Madeleine; Hôtel de Ville (munic. headquarters); Bourse; Bibliothèque Nationale; Grand Opera (1861, largest in world); Trocadéro (1867, in Oriental style), with museums of sculpture and ethnography. On l. bk. is large Champ de Mars, with Eiffel Tower (984 ft.); opposite Ile de la Cité is Latin quarter, with Sorbonne (univ., founded 1253); Musée de Cluny; Panthéon; Luxembourg (1612–20), which includes fine modern art gallery; Hôtel des Invalides, with tomb of Napoleon I. Round Paris lie suburbs of Versailles, Saint-Cloud, Meudon, Sèvres, Saint-Denis, Montreuil, etc.; the famous Bois de Boulogne, with Longchamps (racecourse), and Bois de Vincennes. Principal industries: ladies' clothes, hats, boots, shoes, perfume, jewellery, bronzes, mirrors, clocks, watches, decorative articles, scientific instruments, book publishing, objets d'art. City was the scene of the Peace Conference in 1919. Pop. 2,871,500. (2) City, Texas, U.S.A., 98 m. N.E.

of Dallas; ships cotton, vegetables, and fruit; makes flour, canned goods, and cotton-seed oil. Pop. 15,500.

Par'kersburg, city, W. Virginia, U.S.A., on Ohio R.; petroleum dist.; oil refining, iron and steel works, lumber mills, furniture factories. Pop. 30,000.

Park'gate, vil., Cheshire, England, on estuary of R. Dee, 13 m. N.W. of Chester; part of urb. dist. of Neston and Parkgate; fishing; seaside resort. Pop. 5,700.

Par'ma. (1) Prov., Emilia, N. Italy; traversed by Apennines in S.; N. is fertile plain watered by tributaries of R. Po; produces corn, wine, fruit, cheese, and silk; several mineral springs. Area, 1,334 sq. m.; pop. 374,000. (2) Cap. of above; rose to great importance during Middle Ages; Parmesan cheese, silks, ironware, pianos, tobacco. Pop. 72,000.

Parnahyba (*pär-nä-ē'bä*). (1) Riv., N.E. Brazil; rises in Serra da Tabatinga; flows N.E. and enters Atlantic by a delta. Length, 800 m. (2) Port, Brazil, on above riv.; exports cattle, hides, cotton, tobacco. Pop. 24,500.

Parnas'sus (modern *Liakoura*), mt., Greece, to N. of Gulf of Corinth; sacred to Apollo and the Muses; alt. 8,070 ft.

Pär'nu, or PERNAU, port, wat.-pl., Estonia, close to Gulf of Riga; exports flax, timber, wood pulp. Pop. 21,000.

Parramat'ta, tn., New South Wales, Australia, 14 m. W. of Sydney; fruit growing, esp. oranges; tweed manufactured; racecourse. Pop. 16,000.

Par'ry Sound, tn., Ontario, Canada, on E. of Georgian Bay; lake port. Pop. 5,500.

Par'sons, city, S.E. Kansas, U.S.A.; gas and coal in vicinity; rly. workshops, foundry and machine shops, flour mills. Pop. 16,000.

Par'sonstown. See BIRR.

Par'tick, part of Glasgow, Lanarkshire, Scotland, on R. Clyde; shipbuilding, brass foundries, cotton factories, flour mills. Pop. (par.) 14,500.

Partinico (*pär-tē-nē'kō*), tn., Sicily, 15 m. W.S.W. of Palermo; silk and woollen goods. Pop. 24,000.

Pasade'na, city, California, U.S.A., 10 m. N.N.E. of Los Angeles; fruit packing and canning; Mt. Wilson with solar observatory (alt. 5,900 ft.), and Echo Mt. with Lowe Observatory. Pop. 76,000.

Pasco. See CERRO DE PASCO.

Pas-de-Calais (*pä-dē-kä-lā'*), maritime dep., N. France; surface generally flat; very fertile; extensive coalfields and iron mines; large agricultural production; live-stock, poultry, and fishing; beet-sugar refining, distilling; glass, paper, pottery, leather manufactures. In Great War dep. suffered severely. Cap. Arras. Area, 2,606 sq. m. Pop. 1,172,000.

Pas'sage West, port, Cork, I.F.S., 7 m. S.E. of Cork, on Cork Harbour. Pop. 2,000.

Passaic (*pä-sā'ik*). (1) City, New Jersey, U.S.A., 5 m. N. of Newark; manufactures worsteds, cotton, silk, and rubber goods; submarine cables. Pop. 63,000. (2) Riv., New Jersey, U.S.A.; rises near Morristown, and flows N.E. and S. to Newark Bay; abundant water-power afforded by falls (70 ft.) at Paterson. Length, *c.* 100 m.

Passau (*pä'sou*), frontier tn., Bavaria, Germany, at junction of Inn and Danube rivs.; tobacco, leather, china, paper, and graphite industries; breweries; tourist centre. Pop. 24,500.

Pas'to, tn., Colombia, S. America, near boundary of Ecuador; at foot of volcano of same name (14,000 ft.); woollen goods; gold mines in vicinity. Pop. 30,000.

Pasuruan', chief tn., residency of same name, Java, Dutch E. Indies; 30 m. S.S.E. of Surabaya; sugar. Pop. 25,000.

Patago'nia, extensive region, S. Argentine and Chile, S. America; stretches from Rio Negro on N. to Straits of Magellan on S., and divided by Andes. Discovered by Magellan in 1520; Patagonians (now almost extinct) are very tall and uncivilized. Portion E. of Andes, belonging to Argentina, consists of vast plateau region; in hollows lakes are frequent; chief rivs. are Rio Negro, Chubut, Chico, and Santa Cruz; most fertile and productive country is at base of Andes; gold, silver, copper, lead, coal found, but not worked; large tracts devoted to rearing of sheep, horses, and cattle. Area, *c.* 330,000 sq. m.; pop. *c.* 150,000. To W. of Andes is Chilean Patagonia, strip of rugged mountainous country with luxuriant forests; cattle in N. Area, *c.* 128,000 sq. m.; pop. *c.* 800,000.

Patan'. (1) Tn., Nepal, India, 4 m. S. of Katmandu; has several fine old temples. Pop. *c.* 30,000. (2) Walled tn., Baroda, Bombay, India, 64 m. N.W. of Ahmadabad; manufactures swords and spears; trades in silk and cotton goods. Pop. 32,000.

Pate'ley Bridge, mkt. tn., W. Riding, Yorks, England, on R. Nidd, 10 m. N.W. of Harrogate; lead mines, stone quarries; cattle and sheep fairs; stalactite caverns in vicinity. Pop. (rural dist.) 7,100.

Pater'no, tn., Sicily, on S.W. slope of Mt. Etna; mineral springs; olive oil and wine produced. Pop. 34,000.

Pat'erson, city, New Jersey, U.S.A., at falls of Passaic R.; chief centre of silk manufacture in U.S.A.; foundry and machine-shop products. Pop. 138,000.

Patial'a. (1) Indian state, Punjab, India; valuable forests of pine, oak, bamboo; slate, limestone, sandstone quarried; copper and lead mined; cotton, tobacco. Area, 5,932 sq. m.; pop. 1,500,000. (2) Cap. of above, 120 m. N.W. of Meerut; centre of local trade. Pop. 47,500.

Pat'mos, isl., Sporades group, Ægean Sea, belongs to Italy; here, according to tradition, St. John wrote the Apocalypse. Area, 12 sq. m.; pop. 4,500.

Pat'na. (1) Cap., Bihar and Orissa, India, on R. Ganges; univ.; rice, opium, indigo, cotton, salt, oil-seeds. Pop. 120,000. (2) Indian state, Bihar and Orissa, India; flat; watered by R. Mahanadi; wheat, tobacco. Cap. Bolangir. Area, 2,399 sq. m.; pop. 495,000.

Patras', port, Greece, on N. coast of Morea; exports currants, wine, olive oil. Pop. 61,500.

Pat'ricroft, tn., Lancs, England, 5 m. W. of Manchester; ironworks, cotton mills. Pop. 18,000.

Pat'terdale, vil., Westmorland, England, at S. end of Ullswater; tourist resort. Pop. 1,000.

Pâturages (*pä-too-räzh'*), tn., Belgium, 4 m. S.W. of Mons; coal mines; steam engines. Pop. 10,000.

Pau (*pō*), tn., Basses-Pyrénées, France, on Gave-de-Pau, trib. of R. Adour; fine castle (14th cent.); winter health resort; linen, chocolate, hams, wine. Pop. 34,000.

Paul, par. and tn., Cornwall, England, 2 m. S. of Penzance; fisheries. Pop. (par.) 5,800.

Paumotu Islands. See TUAMOTU.

Pavia (*pä-vē'a*), tn., Lombardy, Italy, on R. Ticino, 20 m. S. of Milan; univ. (1361), and 5 m. N. is Certosa di Pavia (Carthusian monastery); Francis I. of France defeated here and captured by Charles V. (1525); iron foundries, chemicals. Pop. (comm.) 42,000.

Pav'lovo, town, Nijni-Novgorod, Russia, on R. Oka; iron and steel foundries; cutlery. Pop. 16,500.

Pawtuck'et, city, Rhode I., U.S.A.; manufactures cotton and silk fabrics, machinery, chemicals; first cotton-spinning works in U.S.A. established here (1790). Pop. 77,000.

Paysandu (*pī-sän-doo'*). (1) W. dep., Uruguay, S. America; traversed by Uruguay R.; stock raising. Area, 5,115 sq. m.; pop. 67,500. (2) Cap. of above, on Uruguay R.; important riv. port; exports preserved meat, cattle, sheep, hides, wool. Pop. *c.* 26,000.

Pea'body, city, Massachusetts, U.S.A., 2 m. W. of Salem; manufactures leather, machinery, and electrical supplies. Pop. 21,000.

Peace, riv., W. Canada; rises in

British Columbia; breaks through Rocky Mts.; flows N.E. to join Slave R. near Lake Athabasca; large area of basin well suited for grain growing; dist. linked by rail to Edmonton.

Peaceha'ven, seaside garden city, Sussex, England, 6½ m. E. of Brighton. Pop. 5,000.

Peak, THE, hill dist., Derbyshire, England; S. extremity of Pennine Chain; highest point, Kinder Scout (2,088 ft.); ruins of Peveril Castle in vicinity.

Pearl Harbour, port, Oahu, Hawaiian Islands, 6 m. W. of Honolulu; landlocked harbour, with narrow entrance guarded by coral reef; U.S.A. coaling and naval station.

Pearl River. See CANTON (3).

Pec (*pech*), formerly IPEK, tn., Montenegro, Yugoslavia, 90 m. S.W. of Nish; fruit, tobacco; silk. Centre for Serbian refugees during Great War. Pop. 15,000.

Pechili. See HOPEH.

Pechili, GULF OF. See POHAI.

Pechora (*pye-cho'rä*), riv., N.E. Russia; rises in Ural Mts.; flows N., S.W., and N. to enter Gulf of Pechora by a delta; length, 1,000 m., 700 m. navigable; basin forested.

Pécs (*pāch*), formerly FÜNFKIRCHEN, tn., Hungary, 110 m. S.W. of Budapest; univ.; leather, paper, cloth, and pottery. Pop. 47,500.

Pee'bles, co. tn., Peeblesshire, Scotland, on R. Tweed; tweeds and woollens; tourist resort. Pop. 5,900.

Pee'blesshire, or TWEEDDALE, inland co., Scotland; bordered N. by Midlothian, W. by Lanarkshire, S. by Dumfriesshire, E. by Selkirkshire; drained by R. Tweed; country rough and hilly, rising to 2,754 ft. (Broad Law); sheep farming; manufacture of woollen goods. Co. tn., Peebles. Area, 348 sq. m.; pop. 15,100.

Peeks'kill, tn., New York, U.S.A., on Hudson R.; ironworks; boilers, stoves, bricks. Pop. 17,500.

Peel, wat.-pl., Isle of Man; fishing; bathing resort; ruins of castle. Pop. 3,000.

Pegs'wood, par. and vil., Northumberland, England, 2 m. N.E. of Morpeth; coal mines. Pop. (par.) 3,000.

Pegu (*pe-goo'*), cap. Pegu dist., Lower Burma, India, on Pegu R.; rice is chief product; large pagoda (320 ft. high); captured by British (1852). Pop. 19,000.

Pei-ho (*pā-hō'*), riv., Hopeh, China; rises on slopes of Mongolian Mts., near Great Wall, flows S.E. to enter Gulf of Pohai, near Taku forts; navigable by steamer to Tientsin, and by boat to Tungchau. Length, 285 m.; connected by canal with Hwang Ho and Yangtze Kiang.

Peine (*pī'nĕ*), tn., Hanover, Prussia, Germany, 20 m. E.S.E. of Hanover; iron industries; manufactures sugar and jute. Pop. 17,000.

Peiping. See PEKING.

Peipus (*pī-poos*), lake between N.W. Russia, and Estonia; S. part known as Pskov L.; drains to Gulf of Finland by R. Narova; important fisheries. Area, 1,356 sq. m.

Peking, or PEIPING, former cap. China; between Pei-ho and Hun-ho rivs., Hopeh prov.; consists of two cities, each surrounded by high walls; Tatar or Manchu city in N. includes old Imperial City and Forbidden City, with palaces and parks; Chinese city on S. has Temple of Heaven with Altar of Agriculture. Cap. transferred to Nanking in 1928, when Peking became Peiping. Pop. 1,298,000.

Pelée (*pe-lā'*), MONT, active volcano, Martinique, French W. Indies; in 1902 tn. of St. Pierre was destroyed; alt. *c.* 4,400 ft.

Pelew Islands. See PALAU.

Pe'lion, mountain, Magnesia, E. Thessaly, Greece; celebrated in Greek mythology; modern Plessidi is chief summit (5,308 ft.).

Peloponne'sus, ancient name of peninsula forming S. part of Greece; the modern Morea.

Pelo'tas, city, Rio Grande do Sul, S. Brazil; trade in cattle; meat-preserving works. Pop. 40,000.

Pem'ba, isl. off E. coast of Africa; N. of Zanzibar and part of Zanzibar

Protectorate; coral formation; very fertile; produces cloves, coconuts, rubber; wireless station. Area, 380 sq. m.; pop. 88,000.

Pem'broke. (1) Chief tn., Pembrokeshire, Wales; mediæval castle; remains of Monkton Priory; Pembroke Dock, 2 m. distant, is naval dockyard. Pop. 12,000. (2) Tn., Ontario, Canada, on R. Ottawa, 75 m. N.W. of Ottawa. Pop. 9,300.

Pem'brokeshire, most westerly co., Wales; bounded N., W., and S. by sea, E. by Cardigan and Carmarthen. Coast is wild and rugged; chief inlets, Milford Haven and St. Bride's Bay: includes several coastal islands; chief riv., Teifi; inland are fertile hills and valleys; chief industry, stock raising; deep-sea fishing; coal, lead, iron, zinc, and slate worked. Owing to settlement of Flemings (12th cent.), who adopted Eng. language, pop. is mostly English-speaking. Chief tns., Pembroke (co. tn.), Haverfordwest, and Tenby. Area, 614 sq. m.; pop. 87,200.

Penang', isl., N. of Straits of Malacca, off W. coast of Malay Pen.; with prov. of Wellesley and the Dindings (on mainland) it forms one of Brit. Straits Settlements; surface generally flat; coconuts and rice grown; exports pepper and other spices, betel nuts, sugar, rattans. Cap. Georgetown. Area, 108 sq. m.; pop. 304,500.

Penarth', port, wat.-pl., Glamorganshire, Wales, on Bristol Channel; exports iron and coal. Pop. 17,700.

Pen'dleton, suburb of Salford, Lancs, England; manufactures silk and cotton. Pop. 32,000.

Penge (*penj*), urb. dist., Kent, England; part of Greater London; contains Crystal Palace. Pop. 27,800.

Penicuik (*pen'e-kook*), tn., Midlothian, Scotland, 10 m. S. of Edinburgh; paper mills. Pop. 2,800.

Pen'istone, urb. dist., mkt. tn., W. Riding, Yorks, England, on R. Don, 12½ m. N.W. of Sheffield; steel works and coal mines. Pop. 3,300.

Penk'ridge, par. and tn., Staffs, England, 6 m. S. of Stafford; coal mines. Pop. (par.) 2,600.

Penmaenmawr (*pen-mä'en-mawr*), wat.-pl., N. coast, Carnarvonshire, Wales, 4½ m. S.W. of Conway; to W. rises Penmaenmawr, with quarries and prehistoric remains. Pop. 4,000.

Penn, UPPER and LOWER, two pars. and vil., Staffs, England, 2 m. S.W. of Wolverhampton; hardware. Pop. (Upper) 5,500, (Lower) 400.

Pen'nine Alps. See ALPS.

Pen'nine Chain, range of mts., England, extending N. and S. from R. Tyne in Northumberland to Derbyshire and Staffs.; called the 'backbone of England'; summits include Cross Fell (2,930 ft.), Mickle Fell (2,591 ft.), Whernside (2,414 ft.), Ingleborough (2,373 ft.), Penyghent (2,273 ft.), and Kinder Scout (2,088 ft.).

Pennsylva'nia, Atlantic State, U.S.A., one of the thirteen colonies, and an original state; surface rolling in S.E.; drained mainly by the Delaware and Susquehanna rivs.; farther N. and W. rise Appalachian Mts.; Alleghany plateau slopes N.W.; W. contains Allegheny and Monongahela rivs., which unite at Pittsburgh to form R. Ohio. The most important mineral-producing state in U.S.A.; contains much bituminous coal, and almost the only deposits of anthracite in the country; in W. petroleum and natural gas are abundant and iron ore is found. Principal crops: maize, oats, wheat, rye, buck-wheat, and tobacco. Most important state for manufacture of iron and steel; other industries: manufacture of textiles, foundry and machine-shop products, cars, leather, flour, sugar and molasses refining, lumber, petroleum refining, and tobacco. Iron smelting is carried on mainly in and around Pittsburgh. Chief tns., Philadelphia, Pittsburgh, Scranton, Reading, Erie, and Harrisburg (cap.). Area, 45,126 sq. m.; pop. 9,854,000.

Pen'rhyn (*-rin*). (1) Dist. near Bangor, Carnarvonshire, Wales; slate quarries, largest in Wales (5 m.

S.S.E. of Bethesda); on coast is Port Penrhyn, shipping point for slates. (2) Or TONGAREVA, isl., S. Pacific Ocean; *c.* 1,650 m. E.N.E. of Fiji group; annexed to New Zealand (1901). Pop. 400.

Pen'rith. (1) Tn., Cumberland, England; agricultural centre, on borders of Lake District. Pop. 9,100. (2) Munic. township, New South Wales, Australia, 34 m. W. of Sydney. Pop. 3,500.

Penryn (*pen-rin'*), mkt. tn., port, Cornwall, England, 3½ m. N.W. of Falmouth; granite; chemicals. Pop. 3,400.

Pensaco'la, city and port, N.W. Florida, U.S.A., on Pensacola Bay, near boundary of Alabama; fine land-locked harbour; naval air station; trade in timber, fish, naval stores, tallow, hides, wool, cotton, and fertilizers; paper, cotton-seed oil, and lumber mills. Pop. 32,000.

Pens'hurst, vil., Kent, England, 4 m. S.W. of Tonbridge; Sir Philip Sidney born at Penshurst Place (1554). Pop. 1,500.

Pens'nett, tn., Staffs, England, 2 m. S.W. of Dudley; coal mines, ironworks; glass. Pop. 6,000.

Pent'land Firth, strait between Orkney Islands and Caithness, Scotland; 14 m. long, 6 m. to 8 m. broad; has rapid tidal currents and dangerous whirlpools. Pentland Skerries, 4 m. N.E. of Duncansby Head, comprise several islets or rocks.

Pent'land Hills, range running S.W. through cos. of Midlothian, Peebles, and Lanark, Scotland; length, 16 m.; breadth, 4 m. to 6 m.; summits, Scald Law (1,898 ft.) and Carnethy (1,890 ft.); contain several reservoirs of Edinburgh water supply. At Rullion Green, on N.E. side, Covenanters were routed (1666).

Pen'tyrch, par. and vil., Glamorganshire, Wales, 7 m. N.W. of Cardiff; coal mines and ironworks. Pop. (par.) 2,500.

Penygroes', vil., Carnarvon, Wales, 7 m. S. of Carnarvon; slate trade. Pop. 2,700.

Pen'za. (1) Prov., central Russia; watered by tribs. of Rs. Don and Volga; produces grain; sawmills; manufactures leather and woollens. Area, 18,500 sq. m.; pop. 2,210,000. (2) Chief tn. of above, *c.* 350 m. S.E. of Moscow; at junction of Sura and Penza rivs.; paper and timber mills; soap, candles, cloth. Pop. 91,500.

Penzance', port, Cornwall, England, on Mount's Bay; mild climate; health resort and bathing place; exports fish, early vegetables and flowers; near town are tin-smelting works. Pop. 11,300.

Peoria (*pē-ō'rē-a*), city, Illinois, U.S.A., 130 m. S.W. of Chicago; riv. port; manufactures agricultural implements, starch, and glucose; stockyards; trades in grain. Pop. 105,000.

Perak (*pā'rä*), Federated Malay State, in N.W. Malay Peninsula, drained by Perak R. and other streams; much dense forest; produces tin, sugar, rice, rubber, copper, ramie. Cap. Taiping. Area, 7,800 sq. m.; pop. 600,000.

Pergamos. See BERGAMA.

Périgueux (*pā-rē-goo'*), chief tn., Dordogne, France, 80 m. E.N.E. of Bordeaux; Roman remains; famous for its *pâtés de foie gras* and truffled partridge; china ware, iron, and woollens. Pop. 30,500.

Perim (*pā-rēm'*), isl., Strait of Bab-el-Mandeb, S. end of Red Sea; Brit. coaling and cable station. Area, 5 sq. m.; pop. *c.* 200.

Perlis', Unfederated Malay State, in N.W. of Malay Peninsula; drained by R. Perlis; produces rice, tin, coconuts, guano. Cap. Kangar. Area, 316 sq. m.; pop. 40,000.

Perm. (1) Dist., Ural Area, U.S.S.R.; consists of hilly central zone (Urals), E. plain, and W. region of rolling downs; drained by R. Kama; forests; agriculture backward; rich in minerals (gold, silver, copper, iron, lead, platinum, nickel, manganese, coal, salt, etc.); many and varied industries. (2) Chief tn. of above; port on Kama R.; sawmills, tanneries, brick fields, machinery; centre of transit trade across Urals. Pop. 85,000.

Pernambuco (*per-năm-boo'kō*). (1) State, Brazil, on Atlantic coast; mountainous interior; coast lands produce sugar-cane and fruits; cotton, coffee, tobacco grown on slopes. Cap. Recife. Area, 38,312 sq. m.; pop. 2,155,000. (2) See RECIFE.

Pernau. See PÄRNU.

Péronne (*pā-ron'*), tn., Somme, France, 22 m. S.S.W. of Cambrai. Changed hands several times during Great War. Pop. 4,000.

Perpignan (*per-pēn-yan*), cap. Pyrénées-Orientales, France, 34 m. S. of Narbonne; trades in wine, brandy, silk, and wool. Pop. 57,500.

Perranporth', vil., Cornwall, England, 7½ m. N.W. of Truro; pilchard fishing; seaside resort. Pop. 2,380.

Per'shore, tn., Worcestershire, England, 8 m. S.E. of Worcester; orchards; jam factories; agricultural implements. Pop. 4,000.

Persia, kingdom, S.W. Asia; bounded N. by Azerbaijan, Caspian Sea, Armenia, and Turkmen rep., E. by Afghanistan and Baluchistan, S. by Gulf of Oman and Persian Gulf, and W. by Mesopotamia and Asia Minor. In N. are Elburz Mts. (Demavend, 18,600 ft.); along S.W. are Zagros Mts.; in centre and W. is dry, barren plateau of Iran (6,000 to 8,500 ft.); dist. S.E. of Tehran includes Dasht-i-Kavir or Great Salt Desert and Dasht-i-Lut, covered with thin deposits of salt; more than half the entire area is drained towards interior to salt marshes or lakes, more than one-fourth to inland seas and lakes (Caspian, Aral, etc.), less than a quarter to the open sea; chief riv. of S. is the Karun, flowing to the Shatt-al-Arab. Climate on plateaus is continental; in S.E., winter and spring are temperate, summer warm, autumn oppressively hot; rainfall is 5 to 10 in. on the plateaus, and occurs mostly in winter; snow of hills provides summer supply of water, used for irrigation; vegetation luxuriant on coast, where roses grow in great profusion; date palm widely spread; forest dist. mainly confined to N. slope of Elburz; Mediterranean fruits, rice, cotton, tobacco, opium poppy, and cereals are found; oil is worked by Anglo-Persian Oil Co. Hand manufacture of carpets, shawls, silk, cotton, leather, copper, brassware, enamelled work, pottery, glazed tiles, and attar of roses; trade in pearls and pearl-shell. Of the inhabitants *c.* one-third are nomads, the chief nomadic tribes being Turks, Kurds, Leks, Arabs, Lurs, Baluchis, and gipsies. Chief tns., Tehran (cap.), Tabriz, Isfahan, Meshed, Resht, Kerman, and Shiraz; principal ports are Bandar Abbas, Bushire, and Mohammerah on Persian Gulf, Barfrush, Pahlevi, and Meshed-i-Sar on Caspian Sea. Area, 628,000 sq. m.; pop. *c.* 10,000,000.

Persian Gulf, inlet of Arabian Sea, running N.W. from Strait of Ormuz between Persia and Arabia; shores sterile; Shatt-al-Arab and Karun R. enter head of gulf; Bahrein, Qishm, and Ormuz are chief islands; Bushire chief port; Gulf is in Brit. sphere of influence. Area, *c.* 95,000 sq. m.

Perth. (1) Royal burgh, co. tn., Perthshire, Scotland, on R. Tay; the 'Fair City'; till assassination of James I. (1437) the cap. of Scotland; Scone Palace 2 m. distant; 13th cent. church of St. John (restored as War Memorial, 1928); dye works, cattle markets; industries also include linen, iron, carpets, glass, and ink; salmon fisheries in Tay. Pop. 34,800. (2) Tn., cap. W. Australia, on Swan R., 12 m. above its port Fremantle; observatory; univ. (1913); racecourses. Pop. (with suburbs), 185,000.

Perth Amboy, city, New Jersey, U.S.A., on Raritan Bay, 20 m. S.W. of New York; shipyards and dry docks; terra-cotta, lead, copper, steel, emery, and chemicals; coal is shipped. Pop. 44,000.

Perthshire, co., Scotland; bounded by Inverness, Aberdeen, Angus, Fife, Kinross, Clackmannan, Stirling, Dumbarton, and Argyll; famed for mountain and loch scenery; in W. and N.

is Grampian plateau (peaks: Ben More, Ben Lawers, Schiehallion, Ben-y-Gloe); to S.E. and S. are Sidlaw and Ochil Hills; Trossachs and Pass of Killiecrankie are in co.; R. Tay (tribs. Garry, Tummel, Earn, etc.) drains almost whole co.; S. watered by Forth and Teith; lochs are Tay, Earn, Rannoch, Katrine, Vennachar, and Achray. Roman camps and standing stones; cathedrals at Dunblane and Dunkeld; palace at Scone. Agriculture, sheep farming, fruit growing; deer forests; coal and iron in the Ochils; distilling; woollen, cotton, and linen industries. Chief tns., Perth, Crieff, Blairgowrie, and Dunblane. Area, 2,494 sq. m.; pop. 120,800.

Peru (*pe-roo'*). (1) Rep., S. America; bounded N. by Ecuador and Colombia, E. by Brazil and Bolivia, S. by Chile, W. by Pacific Ocean; a narrow coastal strip rises sharply to the Andes (width *c.* 250 m.) running parallel with coast and having great fertile valleys and tablelands; many volcanic peaks over 19,000 ft.; plateaus attain alt. of 12,000 to 13,000 ft. above sea-level. To E. is region of forest and savanna sloping to Amazon basin and drained by headwaters of Amazon (Marañon and Ucayali); in extreme S.E. is L. Titicaca, largest lake in S. America (alt. 12,466 ft.). Climate varies with elevation; average annual temperature on coast, 65° to 75° F.; on tablelands, 40° to 60° F.; in E. dists., 70° to 80° F.; rainfall heaviest in E., coastal strip on W. practically rainless. Mineral resources enormous, but difficulty of transport has arrested development; silver occurs in vast quantities, and copper, lead, petroleum, and silver are worked; guano from the coastal islands is important; forests of E. slopes produce valuable timber, in addition to cinchona, coca, cacao, and balata; chief agricultural products are sugar, cotton, coffee, wool, hides and skins; tobacco, wheat, rice, maize, olives, and fruits are grown; llamas and cattle are raised. Exports include petroleum, sugar, silver, cotton, wool, copper. Majority of pop. are Indians; whites, chiefly Spanish, form *c.* one-seventh. Cap. Lima; chief port, Callao. Area, 532,047 sq. m.; pop. *c.* 6,150,000. (2) City, Indiana, U.S.A., on Wabash R., 70 m. N. of Indianapolis; furniture, basket-ware, electrical appliances; rly. workshops; grain. Pop. 12,500. (3) City, Illinois, U.S.A., 85 m. S.W. of Chicago; coal mining; zinc. Pop. 10,000.

Perugia (*pa-roo'jä*), tn., Umbria, Italy, on R. Tiber, 126 m. by rail N. of Rome; univ. (founded 1308); observatory; woollens, silks, liqueurs. Pop. 73,000.

Pesaro (*pez'ä-rō*), tn., Italy, on Adriatic Sea, 37 m. N.W. of Ancona; wat.-pl.; exports figs, wine, oil, silk, soap, wax, lead, and iron. Pop. 30,000.

Pescado'res, or BOKOTO, group of islands W. of Formosa, China Sea; belong to Japan; fish, ground-nuts, rice, millet. Pop. *c.* 70,000.

Pescia (*pesh'ä*), tn., Tuscany, Italy, 30 m. N.W. of Florence; silk, olive oil, paper, leather. Pop. 18,000.

Peshaw'ar, cap., N.W. Frontier prov., India; on Khyber Pass rly.; commands caravan route between Afghanistan and India; military station. Pop. 104,500.

Petchora. See PECHORA.

Pe'terborough. (1) City, Northants, England, on R. Nen; rly. centre; cathedral; agricultural produce, bricks; rly. workshops. Pop. 43,600. (2) Tn., Ontario, Canada, 69 m. N.E. of Toronto; rly. jn.; electrical machinery, flour, lumber; woollen mills. Pop. 21,000. (3) SOKE OF, administrative county, N.E. Northants, England. Area, 84 sq. m.; pop. 51,800.

Peterhead', port, Aberdeenshire, Scotland, 44 m. N.E. of Aberdeen; herring and other fisheries; red granite quarries and polishing works; convict station. Pop. 12,500.

Peterhof, tn., Russia, on Gulf of Finland, 19 m. S.W. of Leningrad; gem cutting; agricultural implements; great palace of Peter I. (1720). Pop. 9,000.

Pe'tersburg, city, Virginia, U.S.A., 22 m. S. of Richmond, at head of navigation of Appomattox R.; accessible to coastwise steamers; manufactures tobacco and trunks; exports peanuts, tobacco, and cotton. Pop. 28,000.

Petersfield, mkt. tn., Hants, England, 19 m. N.E. of Portsmouth; church of St. Peter. Pop. 4,400.

Pe'tra, anc. tn., Trans-Jordan, W. Asia, in rift valley midway between Dead Sea and Gulf of Aqaba; formerly important caravan centre; temples and rock tombs; Roman ruins.

Petrograd. See LENINGRAD.

Petropavlovsk'. (1) Tn., Kazak rep., U.S.S.R., on Trans-Siberian Rly. and R. Ishim; caravan trade in steppe products (cattle, wool, etc.). Pop. 44,500. (2) Port, S.E. Kamchatka Peninsula, Siberia; exports furs. Pop. 2,000.

Petrop'olis, city, health resort, Brazil, 28 m. N. of Rio de Janeiro; alt. 2,600 ft.; cotton goods, beer, cheese, cigars. Pop. 68,000.

Petrovarä'din, fortified town, E. Slavonia, Yugoslavia, on R. Danube, opposite Novi Sad; Peter the Hermit assembled first crusade here in 1096. Pop. 5,000.

Petrovsk', town, Saratov prov., Russia, 60 m. N.N.W. of Saratov city; tanneries, distilleries, flour mills, oil works. Pop. 19,500.

Petrozavodsk', chief tn. and lake port, Karelia, N.W. Russia, on W. shore of L. Onega; cannon foundry; gunpowder; tanneries, brick works; iron and copper ware. Pop. 26,500.

Pet'worth, par. and mkt. tn., W. Sussex, England, 17 m. S. of Guildford; building-stone quarries near. Pop. (par.) 8,400.

Pev'ensey, vil. and par., Sussex, England, 4 m. N.E. of Eastbourne; one of Cinque ports; landing-place of William the Conqueror. Pop. (par.) 770.

Pforzheim (*pforts'hīm*), tn., Baden, Germany, 16 m. S.E. of Karlsruhe; gold and silver ornaments, chemicals, paper, leather, and machinery. Pop. 79,000.

Philadel'phia, cap. of Pennsylvania, U.S.A.; between Delaware R. and its trib. the Schuylkill; univ.; 10 m. W.N.W. is Women's Coll. of Bryn Mawr; foundry and machine-shop products; shipbuilding; locomotives; carpets, rugs, and clothing; refining of sugar, molasses, and petroleum; exports: petroleum, maize, coal, meat, cattle, wheat, and flour; port extends along 20 m. of Delaware front. City founded by William Penn in 1682; Declaration of Independence adopted here (1776); cap. of Union (1790–1800). Pop. 1,964,000.

Philæ (*fē'lā*), isl. in R. Nile, Egypt, above Aswan Dam; has interesting temples and other buildings, of which most notable are great columned hall known as 'Pharaoh's bed,' and temple of Isis; buildings usually submerged by waters of the Dam.

Philippeville (*fē-lēp-vēl'*), port, N. Algeria, Africa, 50 m. N.N.E. of Constantine; exports wine, sheep, cattle, cereals, esparto grass, minerals, and cork. Pop. 29,500.

Phil'ippine Islands, group of over 7,000 islands, Pacific Ocean, off S.E. Asia; bounded N. and W. by China Sea, E. by Pacific, S. by Celebes Sea; connected by submarine ridge with Borneo and Celebes; largest islands, Luzon in N., Mindañao in S., Mindoro, Samar, Leyte, Cebú, Negros, Panay in centre, and Palawan in W.; coral reefs, especially on E.; traversed by high mt. ranges (mostly volcanic); highest peak, Mt. Apo (10,312 ft.) on Mindañao; twelve active and several extinct volcanoes; subject to frequent earthquakes, heavy rains, and typhoons; climate fairly healthy. Vegetation luxuriant; immense forests of valuable timber; fauna includes buffalo, boar, deer, antelope, water-buffalo (caraboa); numerous birds, bats, reptiles, sea and land turtles; fish abound; chief exports: sugar, hemp, rice, tobacco, copra, coconut oil, cigars, timber, edible birds' nests; gold mined; pearl fisheries; trade mainly with U.S.A., Japan, Britain, and China; rlys. (789 m.) on Luzon, Panay, and Cebú. Islands were discovered by Magellan (1521); named (1543) in honour of Philip II.; ceded by Spain to U.S.A. (1898). Natives are mostly of Malayan origin. Principal tns., Manila (cap.), Cebú, and Iloilo. Area, 114,400 sq. m.; pop. 10,314,500.

Philippop'olis, tn., Bulgaria, 97 m. W.N.W. of Adrianople, on R. Maritsa; on fertile plain producing wheat, grapes, mulberries; silks, woollens, leather, and tobacco. Pop. 85,000.

Phill'ack, urban dist., Cornwall, England, on St. Ives Bay, 8 m. N.E. of Penzance; ironworks. Pop. 3,200.

Phil'lipsburg, tn., New Jersey, U.S.A., on Delaware R., 53 m. N. of Philadelphia; water power; foundry and machine-shop products, mining machinery and tools; rly. workshops; silk and pulp mills. Pop. 19,500.

Phœnicia (*fe-nish'i-a*), anc. country bordering E. shores of Levant; most important cities, Tyre and Sidon.

Phœnix (*fē'niks*), cap. Arizona, U.S.A., 100 m. N.E. of Tucson; winter resort; cotton, lucerne, fruits, and vegetables; trade in fruit, live-stock, and minerals. Pop. 48,000.

Phœnix Group (*fē'niks*), eight small Brit. islands in W. Pacific Ocean, *c.* 1,200 m. N.E. of Fiji. Area, 16 sq. m.; pop. 60.

Phœnixville (*fē'niks-*), tn., Pennsylvania, U.S.A., at mouth of French Creek, 28 m. N.W. of Philadelphia; iron mills, blast furnaces, bridge and boiler works; graphite and plumbago in vicinity. Pop. 12,000.

Phrygia (*frij'i-ä*), anc. country, Asia Minor; celebrated for marble, vines, and wool; now comprised in vilayets of Brusa, Konia, and Aidin.

Piacenza (*pē-ä-chen'zä*), tn., Italy, near R. Po, 92 m. N.W. of Bologna; cathedral; Palazzo Farnese and other palaces; agricultural mkt.; motor cars. Pop. 62,000.

Piatra (*pyä'trä*), tn., Moldavia, Romania, near E. foot of Carpathians; summer resort; textiles; timber trade. Pop. 26,000.

Piauhy (*pē-ou-ē'*), state, N.E. Brazil; R. Parnahyba forms W. boundary; cattle grazing; cotton, sugar, tobacco, rubber, wax, and dyewoods; silver, iron, lead. Cap. Therezina. Area, 116,494 sq. m.; pop. 785,500.

Piave (*pē-ä've*), riv. rising in Carnic Alps, Treviso, N. Italy; below Belluno it runs S.W., then bends eastward, and flows to Porto di Cortellazzo on Adriatic Sea through marshy meadows intersected by canals. Length, 135 m. Scene of much fighting between Italians and Austrians during Great War.

Piazza Armerina (*pē-ät'sä är-mä-rē'nä*), tn., central Sicily, Italy; trades in oil, wine, and nuts; manufactures woollens. Pop. 38,500.

Pic'ardy, old prov., N. France; now comprised in dep. of Somme and portions of Pas-de-Calais, Aisne, and Oise. Within it are mediæval battlefields of Agincourt and Crécy, and Great War added those of the Aisne, Oise, Somme, Amiens, and St. Quentin.

Pick'ering, mkt. tn., N. Riding, Yorks, England, 22 m. N.E. of York; ruins of castle in which Richard II. was imprisoned (1399); agricultural implements. Pop. 3,700.

Pico (*pē'kō*), isl., Azores, Atlantic Ocean; fruit growing; has volcanic peak 7,600 ft. high. Chief tn. Lagens. Area, 175 sq. m.; pop. 25,000.

Pictou (*pik'too*), port, Nova Scotia, Canada, on N. side of Pictou Bay, 80 m. N.E. of Halifax; exports coal. Pop. 3,000.

Piedmont (*pēd'mont*), dep., Italy, between Alps and Apennines; rice, wheat, maize, vines, fruits; silk, cotton, woollens. Area, 11,331 sq. m.; pop. 3,554,500.

Piedras Negras (*pē-ä'dräs nä'gräs*), formerly CIUDAD PORFIRIO DIAZ, tn., N. Mexico, on Rio Grande del Norte; frontier terminus of rly. that connects with U.S. line; stock raising, agriculture. Pop. 14,500.

Pietermar'itzburg, or MARITZBURG,

cap. of Natal, S. Africa, 46 m. N.W. of Durban; founded by Boers (1839); govt. and educational buildings; agricultural show in June. Alt. 2,220 ft. Pop. 38,000 (Europeans, 20,000).

Pietersburg (*pē'ters-*), tn., N. Transvaal, S. Africa, 150 m. N. of Pretoria; alt. 4,269 ft.; gold, asbestos, tin, corundum; cereals, tobacco, groundnuts, and cotton cultivated; oranges and lemons. Pop. 6,500 (2,500 whites).

Pike's Peak, mt., Rocky Mts., Colorado, U.S.A., 12 m. W. of Colorado Springs; cogwheel railway (8¾ m.) to summit; meteorological station; alt. 14,108 ft.

Pilat'us, MOUNT, peak, central Switzerland, at S.W. extremity of L. Lucerne; rack rly. to summit; alt. 6,998 ft.

Pilibhit (*pēl-lē-bēt'*), tn., United Prov., India, 31 m. N.E. of Bareilly; metal vessels; exports rice, borax, pepper, and sugar. Pop. 34,000.

Pillau (*pē'lou*), port and wat.-pl., E. Prussia, Germany; navigable channel to Königsberg (29 m.); shipbuilding; fishing. Pop. 7,000.

Pil'sen, or PLZEN, tn., Bohemia, Czechoslovakia, 70 m. S.W. of Prague; famous for its beer (*Pilsener*); sugar, clothing, pottery, machinery, alum, furniture, hardware, spirits, leather, and paper. Pop. 88,500.

Pinar del Rio (*pē-när' del rē'ō*). (1) Prov., W. Cuba; tobacco, rice, coffee, cotton, and fine woods. Area, 5,206 sq. m.; pop. 301,000. (2) Cap. of above; tobacco. Pop. 16,000.

Pin'dus, mt. chain, Greece; divides Thessaly from Epirus; greatest alt. 7,665 ft.

Pine Bluff, city, Arkansas, U.S.A., on Arkansas R.; cotton; vehicles. Pop. 20,000.

Pinerolo (*pē-nā-rō'lō*), city, Italy, 25 m. S.W. of Turin; cathedral; place of imprisonment of Man in the Iron Mask (1679–81); silk, cotton, woollens. Pop. 19,000.

Pin'ner, par. and vil., Middlesex, England, 2½ m. N.W. of Harrow; residential resort. Pop. (par.) 16,000.

Pinsk, tn., Poland, on trib. of R. Pripet, 100 m. E. of Brest-Litovsk; extensive marshes in neighbourhood; potteries, tanneries, breweries, oil and soap works. Ceded to Poland (1920). Pop. 36,500.

Pinx'ton, par. and vil., Derbyshire, England, 3 m. E. of Alfreton; coal mines. Pop. (par.) 5,350.

Piombino (*pē-om-bē'nō*), port, Tuscany, Italy; port for Elba; iron and tinplate. Pop. 24,000.

Piotrków (*pyo'tr-kuf*), tn., Poland, 25 m. S. of Lodz; flour mills, timber, leather, agricultural machinery. Pop. 41,500.

Piqua (*pik'wä*), city, Ohio, U.S.A., 28 m. N. of Dayton; iron and furniture works; woollen goods, linseed oil, flour. Pop. 15,000.

Piræus (*pī-rē'us*), port, Greece, 5 m. S.W. of Athens; port of Athens and chief port of Greece; arsenal; exports wines, brandy, currants, marble, vinegar; flour and cotton mills, machinery, soap. Pop. 133,500.

Pirano (*pē-rä'no*), port, Istria, Italy, 12 m. S.W. of Trieste; salt works; wines and olives. Pop. 14,500.

Pir'masens, tn., Bavarian Palatinate, Germany, 43 m. S.W. of Mannheim; boots, shoes, leather goods, musical instruments. Pop. 43,000.

Pir'na, tn., Saxony, Germany, on R. Elbe; glass-blowing, tanning, and brewing; porcelain and enamelled ware. Pop. 30,500.

Pirot (*pē-rot'*), tn., Serbia, Yugoslavia, 36 m. S.E. of Nish; cloth and carpets. Pop. 11,000.

Pisa (*pē'zä*). (1) Prov., Tuscany, Italy; produces wheat, oil, and wine; manufactures silk, cotton, linen goods, pottery, glass, soap, and candles; marble quarries; copper and coal mines. Area, 942 sq. m.; pop. 334,500. (2) Cap. of above, on R. Arno; 11th cent. Gothic cathedral of white marble; campanile, known as Leaning Tower (1174–1350), built entirely of marble, 178½ ft. high and over 16 ft. out of perpendicular; univ. founded in 14th cent.; birthplace of Galileo; silk, cotton, linen, coral, and alabaster work. Pop. 77,000.

Pisek (*pēs'ek*), tn., Bohemia, Czechoslovakia, 45 m. S.E. of Pilsen; breweries; iron and brass foundries. Pop. 16,000.

Pistoia, or PISTOJA (*pēs-tō'yä*), tn., Tuscany, Italy, 20 m. N.W. of Florence; was noted for pistols, which are said to have derived their name from tn.; iron and steel ware, glass, silk, paper, macaroni. Pop. 70,000.

Pitcairn', isl., centre of S. Pacific Ocean; produces sweet potatoes, bananas, sugar-cane, oranges, coconuts, coffee, and arrowroot; colonized by mutineers of the *Bounty* (1790); annexed by Great Britain (1839). Area, 2 sq. m.; pop. 175.

Pitesti (*pē-tesh'ti*), tn., Romania, on R. Argas, 65 m. W.N.W. of Bucharest; petroleum, salt; fruit, grain. Pop. 25,000.

Pitloch'ry, vil., Perthshire, Scotland, on R. Tummel, 25 m. N. of Perth; near Pass of Killiecrankie; tourist resort. Pop. 2,250.

Pittenweem', port and royal burgh, Fife, Scotland, on Firth of Forth; fishing and fish curing. Pop. 1,600.

Pitts'burg, city, S.E. Kansas, U.S.A.; in coal, lead, and zinc region; rly. works; bricks, tiles, sewer pipes, glass, meat packing. Pop. 18,000.

Pitts'burgh, city, Pennsylvania, U.S.A.; on Allegheny, Monongahela, and Ohio rivs.; headquarters of the U.S. Steel Corporation; in centre of richest coalfields in America, and largest distributing point for coal in U.S.A.; region also produces natural gas and petroleum; centre of extensive rly. system; great river traffic; iron and steel products of all kinds; glass, rolled brass and copper, foundry and machine-shop products, silver and nickel-plated ware, earthenware, tinplate, electrical machinery, bricks, carriages, and furniture; slaughtering and meat packing. Built by French (1754) and known as Fort Duquesne; afterwards called Fort Pitt. Pop. 645,000.

Pitts'field, city, Massachusetts, U.S.A., 150 m. W. of Boston; electrical goods, motor-cars, cotton and woollen goods, boots and paper; winter resort and tourist centre. Pop. 50,000.

Pitts'ton, city, Pennsylvania, U.S.A., 11 m. S.W. of Scranton; coal mining; machinery, vulcanized iron, terracotta, paper, silk. Pop. 18,500.

Piura (*pē-oo'rä*). (1) Coast dep., N.W. Peru; partly desert and almost rainless; chief petroleum-producing dist. of Peru; cotton-seed and castor oil; valley lands irrigated. Area, 15,190 sq. m.; pop. *c.* 300,000. (2) Cap. of above; was first Spanish colony in country; petroleum and cotton. Pop. 15,000.

Plain'field, city, New Jersey, U.S.A.; residential suburb of New York. Pop. 34,000.

Plaistow (*plas'tō*), part of co. bor. of W. Ham, Essex, England; industrial area. Pop. 58,500.

Plas'sey, vil., Bengal, India, 80 m. N. of Calcutta; scene of Clive's victory over Suraj-ud-Dowlah (1757).

Plata (*plä'tä*), RIO DE LA, or RIVER PLATE, E. inlet, S. America, between Argentina and Uruguay, forming estuary of Paraná and Uruguay rivs.; width at mouth, *c.* 130 m.; length, *c.* 170 m.; of great commercial importance, but navigation hampered by shallowness.

Platts'burg, city, New York, U.S.A., on W. of Lake Champlain; tourist centre; wood-pulp, paper, typewriters. Pop. 13,500.

Plauen (*plou'en*), tn., S.W. Saxony, Germany; lace making and embroidery. Pop. 111,500.

Plenty, BAY OF, wide bend or bight, N.E. coast, North Island, New Zealand, contains several islands. Width, 130 miles.

Plev'na (Bulgarian *Pleven*), tn., Bulgaria, 57 m. N.W. of Trnovo; woollens, silks, wines, live-stock; captured by Russians from Turks after famous siege (1877). Pop. 29,000.

Plinlim'mon, or PLYNLIMMON, mt. on border of Cardiganshire and Montgomeryshire, Wales; centre of great mt. group containing source of riv. Severn; alt. 2,468 ft.

Plock, or PLOTSK (*pwot'sk*), tn., Warsaw, Poland, on R. Vistula, 56 m. N. of Warsaw; exports grain, beet sugar, wool. Pop. 26,000.

Ploesti (*plō-yesht'i*), tn., Romania, 36 m. N. of Bucharest; rly. jn.; on oilfield; tanneries and petroleum refineries. Pop. 57,500.

Plymouth (*plim'ŭth*). (1) Port and co. bor., Devon, England; at head of Plymouth Sound, between estuaries of Rs. Plym and Tamar; includes Stonehouse and Devonport, and constitutes with them the 'Three Towns'; citadel; on Hoe (esplanade overlooking Sound) is statue of Drake, Armada memorial, and tower of Smeaton's lighthouse. At Stonehouse are marine barracks, naval victualling yard, and naval hospital; Devonport contains important dockyards; fortified; important naval station; shipbuilding yards, foundries, starch works, flour and flax mills; manufactures include sailcloth, rope, and brushes; fishing. Among famous men connected with tn. are Drake, Raleigh, Hawkins, and Grenville. Pop. 208,200. (2) Tn., Massachusetts, U.S.A.; landing-place of Pilgrim Fathers (1620); cordage, hardware, cotton and woollen goods, and machinery. Pop. 13,000. (3) Tn., Pennsylvania, U.S.A., on R. Susquehanna; coal mines; silk. Pop. 17,000.

Plym'pton, tn., Devon, England, 4½ m. E. of Plymouth; consists of Plympton St. Mary and Plympton Erle; ruined castle; birthplace of Sir Joshua Reynolds. Pop. 5,000.

Plzen. See PILSEN.

Pnom-Penh (*pnom-pen*), cap. of Cambodia, French Indo-China, on R. Mekong; rice, cotton, pepper, fish, tobacco. Pop. 83,000.

Po, riv., Italy; rises in Monte Viso (Cottian Alps), flows N.E. and E., through Piedmont and Lombardy, and enters Adriatic Sea by delta; length, 400 m.; navigable to Turin; chief tribs., Dora Riparia, Dora Baltea, Ticino, Adda, Mincio; enclosed by embankments from Piacenza to the sea.

Pocatel'lo, city, S.E. Idaho, U.S.A.; alt. 4,460 ft.; rly. shops; cheese; irrigation farms. Pop. 16,000.

Pock'lington, urb. dist. and mkt. tn., E. Riding, Yorks, England, 12 m. S.E. of York; corn mills; agricultural implements; brewing; important fairs. Pop. 2,600.

Podgorica, or PODGORITSA (*pod'gor-it-sä*), tn., Montenegro, Yugoslavia, 19 m. N.E. of Cettinje; tobacco; sawmills. Pop. 9,000.

Pod'mokly (German *Bodenbach*), tn., Bohemia, Czechoslovakia, on R. Elbe; rly. jn.; textiles, chemicals, porcelain. Pop. 15,000.

Podol'sk, tn., Moscow province, Russia, 25 m. S. of Moscow; silks, cement. Pop. 19,500.

Pohai', formerly CHIHLI, Gulf of, N. arm of Yellow Sea, China; entered by STRAIT OF POHAI between Shantung and Liaotung peninsulas; receives waters of Hwang-Ho and Peiho; shallow.

Poitiers (*pwä-tē-ā'*), chief tn., Vienne, France, 60 m. S. of Tours; cathedral founded 1161 by Eleanor, queen of Henry II. of England; brewing; manufactures hosiery and cloth. Here Black Prince defeated French (1356). Pop. 41,000.

Poitou (*pwä-too'*), old prov., W. France; comprises roughly modern deps. of Vienne, Deux-Sèvres, and La Vendée; appanage of Eng. crown at different periods from 12th to 14th cent.; chief tn., Poitiers.

Po'la, fortified port, Istria, Italy, on Adriatic Sea; former Austrian naval station; during Great War major portion of Austrian fleet was shut up in Pola; occupied by Italians (Nov. 1918). Pop. 54,500.

Po'land, rep., E. Europe; bounded N. by Baltic Sea, Danzig, E. Prussia, and Lithuania, E. by Russia, S. by Romania and Czechoslovakia, W. by Germany; surface is plain, only highland being Tatra and Carpathian Mts. in S.; R. Vistula flows through rep.; climate is extreme; over 20 per cent. of surface forested; *c.* one half arable land; rye, oats, wheat, and barley are chief cereals; potatoes, rye, and beetroot yield largest crops; cattle, sheep, swine, and horses reared. Among minerals are coal, iron, zinc, salt, petroleum, natural gas; industries include textiles, paper, chemicals, timber, oil, and sugar. Country was divided by successive partitions among Russia, Austria, and Prussia (1772, 1793, 1795), but reconstituted as a nation after the Great War. Chief tns., Warsaw (cap.), Lodz, Lwow, Poznan, Cracow, and Wilnau. Area, 149,958 sq. m.; pop. 27,177,000.

Polar Regions. See ARCTIC OCEAN and ANTARCTIC OCEAN.

Poldhu (*pol-dū'*), wireless station, Cornwall, England, on Mount's Bay, 5 m. S. of Helston.

Polesworth (*pōlz'worth*), par. and vil., Warwickshire, England, 8 m. N.W. of Nuneaton; collieries, quarries, and clay works. Pop. (par.) 6,300.

Pollokshaws', tn., incorporated in S.W. Glasgow, Scotland, on White Cart R.; cotton factories and iron foundries. Pop. 17,500.

Po'lotsk, tn., White Russia, U.S.S.R., at jn. of Polota and Dvina rivs.; cathedral; timber; flour. Pop. 21,500.

Poltav'a, tn., Ukraine, U.S.S.R., *c.* 88 m. W. of Kharkov; horses, cattle, and grain; flour mills, tobacco factories, and tanneries. Pop. 89,000.

Polynesia (*pol-i-nēzh'ya*) ('many islands'), term generally applied to S. Pacific islands eastward of a line drawn from New Zealand through Samoa to Hawaii and extending from *c.* 120° to 180° W.

Pomera'nia, prov., Prussia, Germany; stretches along Baltic E. and W. of mouth of R. Oder; includes Rügen, Usedom, and Wollin islands; numerous small lakes; agriculture; fishing; shipbuilding. Cap. Stettin. Area, 11,664 sq. m.; pop. 1,879,000.

Pomfret. See PONTEFRACT.

Pomo'na. (1) City, California, U.S.A., 32 m. E. of Los Angeles; residential and health resort; fruit and vegetables; fruit canning. Pop. 21,000. (2) See MAINLAND.

Pompeii (*pom-pā'ē*), ancient tn., Campania, Italy, at foot of Mt. Vesuvius, on Bay of Naples; for *c.* 160 years a prosperous Roman tn. and favourite seaside resort of upper classes; in A.D. 79 overwhelmed by volcanic ashes during eruption of Mt. Vesuvius; excavation begun in 1748, and steadily carried on since 1860; much of tn. now exposed to view.

Ponce (*pon'thā*), tn., Porto Rico, W. Indies; on S. coast; coffee, sugar, rum, molasses, and tobacco. Pop. 47,000.

Pondicherry (*pon-di-sher'ri*), cap. French possessions, India, on E. coast, 100 m. S. of Madras; no harbour; rice and ground-nuts. First settled by French (1674); frequently taken by British, but finally restored to French (1816). Area (terr.), 115 sq. m.; pop. (tn.) 48,000, (terr.) 284,500.

Pon'doland, coastal dist., part of Transkeian Terrs., Cape Prov., S. Africa, bordering on Natal; progressive native reserve; forests; fine scenery. Area, *c.* 4,000 sq. m.; pop. 250,000.

Pon'ta Delgad'a, largest tn., Azores, on São Miguel; exports grain and fruit. Pop. 16,000.

Pont-à-Mousson (*pōn-tā-moo-sōn'*), tn., Meurthe-et-Moselle, France, on R. Moselle, 16 m. N.N.W. of Nancy; ironworks; paper; velvet. Pop. 11,000.

Pontarlier (*pōn-tär-lē-ā'*), tn., Doubs, France, on R. Doubs, 36 m. S.E. of Besançon; on main rly. route through Jura Mts. into Switzerland; liqueurs; watches and clocks. Pop. 11,000.

Pon'tefract, or POMFRET, tn., W. Riding, Yorks, England, 14 m. S.E. of Leeds; ruined castle (*c.* 1080) where Richard II. was killed (1400); market gardens; grain; iron industries, tanning; makes 'Pomfret cakes' from liquorice. Pop. 19,100.

Pontevedra (*pon-tā-vā'drā*), city, cap. prov. Pontevedra, N.W. Spain, 30 m. S.W. of Santiago, at head of deep bay; fishing, food preserving; leather and pottery. Pop. 27,000.

Pontiac (*pon'ti-ak*), city, Michigan,

U.S.A., 26 m. N.W. of Detroit; summer resort; exports wool and agricultural produce; motor-car industries. Named after famous Indian chief (*c.* 1712–69) who assisted French against British. Pop. 65,000.

Pontresina (*pon-trā-zē'nā*), vil., Grisons, Switzerland, in Upper Engadine, 3 m. E. of St. Moritz; tourist resort; alt. 5,916 ft. Pop. 950.

Pon'typool, urb. dist., Monmouthshire, England, 9¼ m. N. of Newport; great centre of coal and iron trade; tin and iron works. Pop. 6,800.

Pontypridd (*pon'ti-prith*), urb. dist., Glamorganshire, Wales, at confluence of Rs. Rhondda and Taff, 12 m. N.W. of Cardiff; iron and coal mines, foundries, chain and cable works. Pop. 42,700.

Poole, port, Dorsetshire, England, on Poole Harbour (7 m. long), 30 m. E. of Dorchester; yacht building; fishing. During Great War shipbuilding yards were established and large cordite works were erected. On Branksea I., at mouth of harbour, is Branksea Castle; potter's clay quarried. Pop. 57,300.

Poo'na, tn., Bombay, India, in W. Ghats, 80 m. S.E. of Bombay; headquarters of Bombay army; seat of govt. of Bombay during wet season; alt. 1,850 ft.; cotton, paper, sugar, and rice mills. Pop. 215,000.

Popayan', chief tn., dep. Popayan, s. Colombia, S. America, on R. Cauca; at foot of volcano Purace, 245 m. S.W. of Bogota; cathedral; univ. Pop. 20,000.

Poperinghe (*pō-per-äng'*), tn., W. Flanders, Belgium, 8 m. W. of Ypres; woollen and linen goods; hops. During Great War important military railhead. Pop. 12,500.

Pop'lar, bor., London, England, 3 m. E. of St. Paul's; contains E. and W. India and Milwall Docks; shipbuilding, chain cable works, tank works, and wire-rope factories. Pop. 155,100.

Popocatepet'l ('smoking mt.'), dormant volcano, Mexico, 45 m. S.E. of Mexico City; sulphur obtained from crater; alt. 17,876 ft.

Porban'dar, port, Bombay, India, on Kathiawar peninsula; cement; silk and cotton. Pop. 29,500.

Pordenone (*pōr-dā-nō'nā*), tn., Udine prov., Venetia, Italy, 38 m. N.N.E. of Venice; cotton, silk, pottery. Pop. 20,000.

Po'ri, formerly BJÖRNEBORG, port, Finland, at mouth of R. Kumo, on Gulf of Bothnia; timber products, textiles. Pop. 17,500.

Port Ad'elaide, port of Adelaide, S. Australia, on Gulf of St. Vincent; silver and copper smelting works.

Portadown', mkt. tn., Armagh, N. Ireland, 25 m. S.W. of Belfast, on Upper Bann; linen. Pop. 12,000.

Port'age la Prai'rie, tn., Manitoba, Canada, on Assiniboine R., 56 m. W. of Winnipeg; agricultural market; grain elevators; flour mills; railway workshops. Pop. 6,500.

Portalegre (*pōr-tä-lā'grā*), tn., Alemtejo, Portugal, 37 m. N.W. of Badajoz; cathedral; cloth. Pop. 11,500.

Portar'lington, mkt. tn., Leix and Offaly cos., I.F.S., on R. Barrow, 42 m. S.W. of Dublin. Pop. 2,000.

Port Ar'thur. (1) Port, Ontario, Canada, on L. Superior; great grain port, lumbering and mining centre; bricks. Pop. 16,500. (2) (Chinese *Lushunkau*), harbour, Manchuria, China, on S.E. side of Liaotung peninsula; in Japanese terr. of Kwantung; formerly leased by China to Russia, who fortified it and made it terminus of Siberian Railway; capitulated to Japanese (Jan. 1905), after a siege of eleven months. Pop. 24,500. (3) Port, Texas, U.S.A., on Lake Sabine, on Louisiana border; oil refining; petroleum and oil products. Pop. 50,000.

Port Augus'ta, port, S. Australia; at head of Spencer Gulf, on transcontinental rly.; exports flour, copper, tallow, and hides. Pop. 1,500.

Port-au-Prince (*pōr-tō-präns'*), cap., Haiti Rep., W. Indies, on W. coast; exports coffee; also logwood and cacao; good harbour. Pop. *c.* 125,000.

Port Blair, tn. and harbour, S.

Andaman I., Bay of Bengal; Indian convict settlement. Pop. 13,500.

Port Chalmers, tn., South Island, New Zealand; port of Dunedin. Pop. 2,600.

Port'chester, par. and vil., Hants, England, 4 m. N.W. of Portsmouth; has ruins of Roman fort and of Norman castle; superseded by Portsmouth as naval port. Pop. 2,000.

Port Ches'ter, vil., New York, U.S.A., on Long Island Sound, 26 m. N.E. of New York; summer resort; cotton and woollen goods, carriages, and ironware. Pop. 17,000.

Port Col'borne, tn., Ontario, Canada, on N.E. shore of L. Erie; S. entrance to Welland Canal. Pop. 5,500.

Port Darwin. See DARWIN.

Port Eliz'abeth, port, Cape Prov., S. Africa, on Algoa Bay, 436 m. by sea E. of Cape Town; open harbour but safe roadstead; exports wool, mohair, ostrich feathers, fruit. Pop. 53,000.

Port Er'in, wat.-pl., Isle of Man, 4½ m. W. of Castletown; marine biological laboratory and fish hatchery.

Port Florence. See KISUMU.

Port Fu'ad, tn., at Mediterranean entrance to Suez Canal, opposite Port Said; engineering and repair shops; garden city for workpeople of Port Said. Pop. 30,000.

Port-Glasgow, port, Renfrewshire, Scotland, on R. Clyde, 2½ m. S.E. of Greenock; graving dock, shipbuilding yards; sails, tents, ropes, brass and iron founding. Founded in 1668 as a port for Glasgow. Pop. 19,600.

Portglenone (*pōrt-glen-ōn'*), par. and mkt. tn., Antrim, N. Ireland, on R. Bann, 9 m. W. of Ballymena; linen and salmon fishing. Pop. (par.) 3,400.

Port Har'court, port, Nigeria, W. Africa, on Bonny R.; outlet for Udi coalfield; palm oil.

Porth'cawl, urb. dist., Glamorganshire, Wales, on Bristol Channel; bathing resort; exports coal and iron. Pop. 6,400.

Port Her'ald, vil., Nyasaland, Africa, on Shiré riv.; depot of Brit. Cotton-growing Association; on rly. from Chindio to Blantyre.

Porthle'ven, port, Cornwall, England, on Mount's Bay; fishing. Pop. (eccles. dist.) 1,600.

Port Hu'ron, city, Michigan, U.S.A., on L. Huron, at mouth of St. Clair R.; opposite Sarnia, Ontario; summer resort; mineral springs; port of entry on Great Lakes; dry docks, shipyards, grain elevators. Pop. 31,000.

Portici (*pōr'tē-chē*), port, Campania, Italy, on Bay of Naples; fishing; silk; built over part of site of Herculaneum. Pop. 21,500.

Portishead (locally POSSET), urb. dist., Somerset, England, on Severn estuary, 11½ m. W. of Bristol; port with grain warehouses; naval college; wat.-pl. Pop. 3,900.

Port Jack'son. See SYDNEY.

Port'land. (1) City, Oregon, U.S.A., at head of navigation of Willamette trib. of Colombia riv.; lumber and wheat exports; timber manufactures, meat packing. Pop. 302,000. (2) Port, Maine, U.S.A.; winter port for several transatlantic lines; deep and spacious harbour; fishing; shipbuilding; foundries, machine shops. Birthplace of Longfellow. Pop. 71,000.

Port'land, ISLE OF, peninsula, with urb. dist., S. Dorsetshire, England; connected with mainland by Chesil Bank; breakwater on N.E. forms harbour of refuge; convict prison on isl.; extensive quarries of fine building stone; fishing. Pop. of urb. dist., 12,000.

Port Louis, cap. and port, Mauritius, Indian Ocean, on N.W. coast; cathedrals, observatory; exports sugar. Pop. 54,500.

Port Lyttelton. See LYTTELTON.

Portmad'oc, urb. dist., Carnarvonshire, Wales, on Tremadoc Bay, 11 m. E. of Pwllheli; exports slates from Festiniog quarries. Pop. 4,000.

Port Mahon' (or *mä'ōn*), cap. of Minorca, Balearic Islands, Spain, on S.E. coast; exports live-stock, cheese, boots and shoes; strongly fortified; safe port. Pop. 18,000.

Port Natal'. See DURBAN.

Port Nelson, port, Manitoba, Canada,

at mouth of Nelson R., Hudson Bay; old Hudson's Bay Company's fort.

Port Nol'loth, port, N.W. Cape Prov., S. Africa, 50 m. S.E. of mouth of Orange R.; rly. to Ookiep copper dist.; exports copper; diamonds found. Pop. 1,000.

Por'to Alegre (*ä-lä'grä*), cap., Rio Grande do Sul, Brazil; extensive harbour; cathedral; cottons, boots and shoes; jerked beef, hides, beans, and cereals exported. Pop. 180,000.

Portobel'lo, wat.-pl., Scotland, on Firth of Forth, within city of Edinburgh; bottles, bricks, and pottery.

Porto Bello, or PUERTO BELLO, seaport, Panama, 20 m. N.E. of Colon; port from which Spanish treasure fleet used to sail; captured by British (1739) during war with Spain.

Por'to Ferrajo (*fer-ä'yō*), cap., isl. of Elba, w. Italy; exports iron ore. Pop. 12,000.

Port of Spain, chief tn. and port, Trinidad, Brit. W. Indies; on shallow but sheltered harbour; place of call for ocean steamers; exports petroleum, cocoa, sugar. Pop. 67,000.

Por'to No'vo. (1) Port, Madras, India, on Coromandel coast; here Haidar Ali was defeated by Sir Eyre Coote (1781). Pop. 13,000. (2) Cap. Dahomey, French W. Africa; on a lagoon in Gulf of Guinea; exports palm kernels and oil. Pop. 27,000.

Por'to Rico (*rē'kō*), isl., W. Indies; most easterly and smallest of Greater Antilles, 75 m. E. of Haiti; interior rugged and mountainous; low coastal plain; no navigable rivs.; climate equable and comparatively healthy; cane-sugar, coffee, tobacco, and fruits produced. Discovered by Columbus (1493); ceded to U.S.A. (1898) after Spanish-American War. Chief tn., San Juan. Area, 3,435 sq. m.; pop. 1,300,000.

Portpat'rick, fishing vil. and seaside resort, in w. of Rhinns of Galloway, Wigtownshire, Scotland, 7½ m. s.w. of Stranraer, 21½ m. N.E. of Donaghadee. Pop. 1,500.

Port Phil'lip, landlocked bay, Victoria, Australia, on s. coast; with Melbourne on N. and Geelong on w.

Port Pir'ie, port, S. Australia, on Spencer Gulf, 130 m. N. of Adelaide; smelting and refining of Broken Hill ores; exports wheat and minerals. Pop. 10,000.

Portree', port and vil., on E. of Isle of Skye, Inverness-shire, Scotland; tourist resort. Pop. (par.) 2,120.

Portrush', summer resort, N. Antrim, N. Ireland; electric tramway to Giant's Causeway, 8 m. E.; excellent golf links. Pop. 2,100.

Port Said (*sä-ēd'*), tn. at entrance to Suez Canal, Egypt; one of largest coaling stations in world; rly. communication with Cairo and Suez; exports cotton; statue of Lesseps on breakwater. Pop. 101,000.

Port'slade-by-Sea, urb. dist., Sussex, England, 4 m. w. of Brighton; seaside resort. Pop. 9,500.

Ports'mouth. (1) Co. bor., Hants, England, 27 m. S.E. of Southampton, on Portsea I.; includes Portsmouth proper, Portsea (naval dockyard), Southsea, and Landport; greatest arsenal, chief naval station, and most strongly fortified place in U.K. Whale I. is school of gunnery. Pop. 249,300. (2) City, New Hampshire, U.S.A., 58 m. N.E. of Boston; only seaport of state; large navy yard; builds submarines; summer resort. Treaty of Portsmouth (1905) ended war between Japan and Russia. Pop. 14,000. (3) Tn., Norfolk, S.E. Virginia, on R. Elizabeth; naval yard; exports oysters, vegetables, farm produce, lumber, and cotton. Pop. 45,000. (4) Tn., Ohio, U.S.A., on R. Ohio; manufactures aeroplanes, iron and steel goods, shoes, bricks, stoves and ranges. Pop. 43,000.

Port'soy, port, Banffshire, Scotland, 8½ m. w. of Banff; fish curing; oatmeal mills; holiday resort. Pop. 1,700.

Port Sudan', port, Anglo-Egyptian Sudan, on Red Sea; gum, ivory, cotton, sesame, durra; rly. to Berber on R. Nile. Pop. 21,500.

Port Sun'light, model industrial vil.,

Cheshire, England, 3 m. S.E. of Birkenhead; built (1890) by Lever Brothers, Ltd., in connection with their soap works.

Port Tal'bot, port, Glamorganshire, Wales, on E. of Swansea Bay, 10¾ m. S.E. of Swansea; Cwm Avon copper works. Pop. 40,700.

Port Tew'fik, tn., Egypt, at Red Sea entrance to Suez Canal, opposite Suez.

Por'tugal, rep., forming W. part of Iberian Peninsula, Europe; bounded on N. and E. by Spain, W. and S. by Atlantic Ocean; consists of six provs.—Entre Minho-e-Douro, Beira, Tras-os-Montes, Alemtejo, Estremadura, Algarve; Azores and Madeira Islands regarded integral parts of Portugal; length, N. to S., *c.* 360 m.; average breadth, 100 m.; coast-line, *c.* 460 m., with two large indentations—Bay of Setubal and estuary of R. Tagus. Surface is generally mountainous, especially N. of Douro, where Cantabrian Mts. terminate; between Douro and Tagus rivs. is Serra da Estrella (6,532 ft.), which reaches ocean at Cape Roca, the most westerly point of Europe; the Serra de Monchique (2,963 ft.) runs into Atlantic at Cape St. Vincent; plains stretch S. of R. Tagus; coastal dists. generally flat (except near Lisbon and in S.) and marshy; principal rivs., Minho, Douro, Tagus, and Guadiana. Climate is generally equable; marshy dists. unhealthy; country subject to heavy rainfalls (greatest in N. and Serra da Estrella); extensive forests of cork oak, pine, cypress, mainly in S.; large tracts of pastureland; principal products are wheat, maize, oats, barley, rice, potatoes; figs, olives, grapes and other fruits; timber; wine-making important; famous port-wine dist. is Alto Douro; cattle rearing in N.; sheep and goats in mts., and pigs in S.; valuable fisheries (sardine, tunny, oyster, whiting); mineral wealth considerable but undeveloped; industries are cotton spinning, weaving of woollens, silks, linen, cork-cutting, tanning, porcelain tiles; chief exports: wine, fish, cork, cottons, fruits, timber. Cap. Lisbon. Area (including Azores and Madeira), 35,490 sq. m.; pop. 6,000,000.

Dependencies and colonies: Cape Verde Islands, Portuguese Guinea, Angola, São Thomé and Principe (islands), and Mozambique, in Africa; Goa, Daman, Diu (India), Macao (China), and part of Timor in E. Indian Archipelago. Total area, 945,575 sq. m.; pop. 10,500,000.

Portuguese East Africa, or MOZAMBIQUE, Portuguese colony, between Tanganyika Terr. on N. and Natal on S., with other Brit. terrs. on W. and Indian Ocean on E. N. of R. Zambezi surface mountainous; S. of Zambezi occupied by scattered mountain groups; rivs. S. of Zambezi include Pungwe, Sabi, and Limpopo. Rainy season Nov. to March; mean temp. at Tete is 84° F., July (coldest month) 72° F.; marshy coasts unhealthy; highlands temperate and salubrious; products include sugar, maize, cotton, gold, silver; highlands yield timber; chief exports: sisal, vegetable oils, sugar. Rlys. from Beira to S. Rhodesia and Murraça on R. Zambezi (for Nyasaland); from Delagoa Bay to Swaziland and Transvaal. Cap. Lourenço Marques. Area, *c.* 300,000 sq. m.; pop. *c.* 3,500,000 (18,000 whites).

Portuguese Guinea, Portuguese colony, Senegambia, W. Africa; along Atlantic Ocean and enclosed landward by French terr.; consists of low coast and Bissagos Archipelago; rubber, palm nuts, ground nuts, hides, wax. Cap. Bolama; chief port, Bissau. Area, 22,000 sq. m.; pop. 344,000.

Portuguese India. See INDIA, PORTUGUESE.

Portuguese West Africa. See ANGOLA.

Por'voo, formerly BORGÅ, port, Finland, on Gulf of Finland, *c.* 30 m. N.E. of Helsinki; sailcloth, tobacco. Pop. 5,500.

Posen. See POZNAN.

Postu'mia-Grot'te, formerly ADELS-

BERG, tn., Italy, in Karst country, 23 m. N.E. of Trieste; stalactite caves and subterranean riv. Pop. 4,500.

Potchefstroom (*pō'chef-strōm*), tn., Transvaal, S. Africa, on Mooi R., 88 m. S.W. of Johannesburg; govt. experimental farm; oldest tn. in prov. (founded 1839). Pop. 15,000 (9,500 whites).

Poten'za, tn., Italy, 70 m. W. by N. of Taranto; cathedral; almost wholly destroyed by earthquake (1857). Pop. 18,500.

Poti (*pō'tē*), port, Georgia, U.S.S.R., on Black Sea, at mouth of R. Rion; rly. to Baku oilfields; sawmills. Pop. 14,000.

Poto'mac, riv., U.S.A.; rises in Alleghany Mts., forms boundary between Maryland on N., and W. Virginia and Virginia on S.; flows into Chesapeake Bay; navigable below Washington; chief trib. Shenandoah. Length, *c.* 450 m. Has many associations with American Civil War.

Poto'si, tn., Bolivia; cap. of dep. of same name, 50 m. S.W. of Sucre, on flank of Cerro de Potosi (15,381 ft.); founded 1547; formerly celebrated for silver mines; tin mines; cathedral (1810); alt. 13,600 ft. Pop. 30,000.

Pototan', tn., Panay, Philippine Islands, *c.* 17 m. N.E. of Iloilo; sugar, rice, tobacco; cattle. Pop. 26,000.

Pots'dam, chief tn., Brandenburg, Prussia, Germany, on R. Havel, 16 m. S.W. of Berlin; former royal palaces with luxurious gardens; Brandenburg gate is noteworthy; furniture, chemicals, tobacco, and sugar; flower gardens. Pop. 64,000.

Pot'teries, THE, dist., N. Staffs, England; coalfields; chief seat of Eng. porcelain industries; principal tn., Stoke-on-Trent.

Potts'town, bor., Pennsylvania, U.S.A., on Schuylkill R., 35 m. N.W. of Philadelphia; iron and steel; agricultural implements, silk, and hosiery. Pop. 17,500.

Potts'ville, city, Pennsylvania, U.S.A., on Schuylkill R., 90 m. N.W. of Philadelphia; steel, iron, lumber; rly. repair shops; large coal shipments; anthracite. Pop. 22,000.

Poughkeepsie (*pō-kip'sē*), city, New York, U.S.A., on Hudson R., 70 m. N. of New York city; educational institutions; agricultural implements. Pop. 40,000.

Poul'ton-le-Fylde, urban dist. and mkt. tn., Lancs, England, 3 m. N.E. of Blackpool; agricultural centre. Pop. 3,400.

Poyn'ton, eccles. dist. and vil., Cheshire, England, 6½ m. N. of Macclesfield; coal mines. Pop. (dist.) 3,500.

Pozar'evac, or PASSAR'OWITZ, tn., Serbia, Yugoslavia, 12 m. S.E. of Smederevo (Semendria); agricultural market. Pop. 11,000.

Po'znan, formerly POSEN, tn., Poland, on R. Warta, 90 m. N. of Breslau; rly. jn.; agricultural machinery, locomotives; trade in grain, cattle, timber, wool; one of oldest tns. in Poland. Pop. 185,000.

Pozoblan'co, tn., S. Spain, 37 m. N. of Cordoba; cloth and woollen weaving; zinc and silver-lead mines in vicinity. Pop. 18,000.

Pozsony. See BRATISLAVA.

Pozzuoli (*pot-soo-ō'lē*), formerly PUTE'OLI, port, Campania, Italy, 7½ m. by rail W. of Naples; iron industries; ordnance works; Roman remains. Pop. 24,000.

Prague, or PRAHA, cap. Czechoslovakia, on R. Vltava. Notable features include fortress of Hradcany (Hradschin), Gothic cathedral (begun 1344), palaces, monasteries, and gardens, Parliament House and Wallenstein's palace. Chief financial and industrial centre; engineering and iron works; sugar and flour mills; chemicals, vehicles, cement. Pop. 677,000.

Prat'o, tn., Italy, 11 m. N.W. of Florence; 12th cent. cathedral; straw, woollen and cotton goods; quarries of serpentine in vicinity. Pop. 61,000.

Prenzlau (*prents'lou*), or PRENZLOW, tn., Brandenburg, Prussia, 30 m. W. by S. of Stettin; sugar, beer, tobacco, cigars, margarine, woollen goods, machinery. Pop. 22,000.

Prerov (*przher'of*), tn., Moravia, Czechoslovakia, 12 m. S.E. of Olomouc; old castle; textiles, hardware, machinery, sugar. Pop. 21,500.

Pres'cot, urb. dist., Lancs, England, 7 m. E. of Liverpool; reservoirs for Liverpool water supply; watches; electric cables; coal mines. Pop. 9,400.

Presov (*presh'of*), formerly EPERIES, tn., E. Slovakia, Czechoslovakia; rly. jn.; administrative centre. Pop. 16,500.

Pressburg. See BRATISLAVA.

Prestat'yn, mkt. tn., Flintshire, Wales, 4 m. E. of Rhyl; wat.-pl. and health resort; Offa's Dyke begins in vicinity; remains of submerged forest. Pop. 4,500.

Presteigne (*pres-tēn'*), co. tn., Radnorshire, Wales, on R. Lugg, 6½ m. N.E. of New Radnor; wool manufactures; limestone quarries. Pop. 1,100.

Pres'ton. (1) Tn., Lancs, England, near mouth of R. Ribble; rly. jn.; cotton spinning; iron and brass foundries; electrical engineering; shipbuilding; docks; exports coal. Pop. 118,800. (2) Tn., Ontario, Canada, 25 m. N.W. of Hamilton. Pop. 5,900.

Prestonpans', tn., E. Lothian, Scotland, on Firth of Forth, 9 m. E. of Edinburgh; soap, breweries, pottery; coal mines. Scene of defeat of Sir John Cope by Prince Charles Edward (Sept. 21, 1745). Pop. 2,400.

Prest'wich, urb. dist., Lancs, England, 4½ m. by rail N.W. of Manchester, of which it is a residential suburb; cotton industry. Pop. 23,900.

Prest'wick, tn., Ayrshire, Scotland, 2½ m. N. of Ayr; golf links. Pop. 8,500.

Preto'ria, cap. Transvaal, S. Africa; administrative cap. of Union of S. Africa; Parliament House and other govt. buildings; alt. 4,471 ft. Pop. 83,500 (54,500 whites).

Pribilof' Islands, in Bering Sea, Alaska, U.S.A.; of volcanic origin; centre of fur-seal fishing. Pop. 500.

Prib'ram, tn., Bohemia, Czechoslovakia, 12½ m. S. of Pilsen; silver, lead, zinc, antimony, bismuth mines; Heiliger Berg, place of pilgrimage, in vicinity. Pop. 12,000.

Priego de Cor'doba (*prē-ā'gō*), tn., S. Spain, 45 m. S.E. of Cordoba; anc. stronghold of Moors; oil, silk, and wine. Pop. 17,000.

Prince Al'bert, tn., Saskatchewan, Canada, on N. Saskatchewan riv., 85 m. N.E. of Saskatoon; lumbering centre; fur trade; rly. jn. Pop. 7,850.

Prince Edward Island, smallest prov., Canada, in Gulf of St. Lawrence; surface flat; temperature, Jan., 16° F., July, 65° F.; oats, potatoes; livestock; dairy produce; fox farms. Discovered by Sebastian Cabot (1497). Cap. Charlottetown. Area, 2,184 sq. m.; pop. 89,000.

Prince Rupert, port, Brit. Columbia, Canada, on isl. N. of mouth of Skeena R.; terminus of Canadian National Rly.; fishing, lumbering, mining. Pop. 7,500.

Prince's Island. See PRINCIPE.

Princes Islands, group of nine islets in E. of Sea of Marmara, Turkey, 15 m. S.E. of Constantinople; frequented for their beauty and mild climate.

Prin'ces Ris'borough, mkt. tn., Bucks, England, 7½ m. S. of Aylesbury; in gap of Chiltern Hills; chair-making; bead and sequin work. Pop. 2,440.

Princeton, bor., New Jersey, U.S.A., 10 m. N.E. of Trenton; univ. Pop. 6,000.

Prince'town, or PRINCE TOWN, eccles. dist. and vil., Devon, England, 15 m. N.N.E. of Plymouth; Dartmoor convict prison and granite quarries in vicinity. Pop. (dist.) 2,070.

Principe (or PRINCE'S) **Island** (*prēn'-sē-pā*), Portuguese isl., Gulf of Guinea, Africa; volcanic origin; cocoa. Area, 42 sq. m.; pop. 5,000.

Pripet', riv., one of chief tribs. of R. Dnieper; rises in Poland, flows through White Russia into Ukraine to join Dnieper 50 m. N. of Kiev; flows sluggishly through Pripet Marshes (30,000 sq. m., of which over 20,000 sq. m. have been reclaimed). During the Great War the Germans in 1915 drove Russian armies back as far as Pripet Marshes.

Priz'ren, tn., s. Serbia, Yugoslavia, near N.E. boundary of Albania; weapons, steel, glass, pottery, leather; seat of Serbian government after outbreak of Great War; captured by Bulgars (Dec. 1915). Pop. 16,500.

Procida (*prō'chē-dä*). (1) Volcanic isl., Italy, in w. of Gulf of Naples, 2 m. from mainland; wine, fruit, fishing. Pop. 11,000. (2) Tn., on E. coast of isl.; castle. Pop. 3,500.

Prome, tn., Lower Burma, India, on R. Irrawaddy, 160 m. N. of Rangoon by rail; silk, cotton, rice, tobacco; teak; ornamental woodwork. Pop. 26,000.

Prostejov (*pros'tye-yof*), tn., Moravia, Czechoslovakia, 12 m. s.w. of Olomouc; clothing, shoes, agricultural implements, beer; geese largely reared. Pop. 31,000.

Provence (*prō-vons'*), anc. prov., S.E. France; now forms deps. Bouches-du-Rhône, Var, Basses-Alpes, and E. part of Vaucluse; formerly the *Provincia Romana* of the Romans; joined to France in 1486. Dist. remarkably rich in Roman and mediæval remains.

Prov'idence, cap. Rhode I., U.S.A., 44 m. s.w. of Boston; many educational institutions; important port; industrial centre; foundry and machine-shop products; woollen and worsted goods; jewellery. Pop. 252,000.

Prud'hoe (or *proo'dō*), urb. dist., Northumberland, England, on R. Tyne, 11 m. w. of Newcastle; collieries; anc. castle. Pop. 9,300.

Prussia, rep., Germany; mainly situated in great N. German Plain; contains fifteen provs.: East Prussia, Brandenburg, Berlin, Pomerania, Border Prov. (Grenzmark), Lower Silesia, Upper Silesia, Saxony, Schleswig-Holstein, Hanover, Westphalia, Hesse-Nassau, Rhine, Hohenzollern, Waldeck; E. Prussia is separated from other provs. by Poland and Free City of Danzig. Seaboard *c.* 900 m. —750 on Baltic, rest on North Sea. Large stretches of moorland, sandy plains, and marshland along coast; mts. lie in s. and s.w.; Riesengebirge, in Silesia; Harz Mts., in Saxony; Hunsrück, Taunus, Eifel, Westerwald, in Rhine Prov.; principal rivs.: Rhine, Weser, Elbe, Oder, Ems; many navigable and linked by canals; Kiel Canal zone is under control of League of Nations; many lakes, especially in Pomerania, Border Prov., and E. Prussia; lagoons on coast—Kurisches Haff, Frische Haff, and Stettiner Haff. Climate generally healthy; E. more extreme than w.; average ann. rainfall is *c.* 21 in.; forests of fir, spruce, larch, beech, birch, oak; important agricultural, mining, and manufacturing industries; principal products are cereals, beet, hemp, flax, potatoes, hops, oil-seed, live-stock, timber; famous wines made in Nassau and Rhine Prov.; horses bred in E. Prussia; rich in minerals —coal, iron, zinc, copper, lead, cobalt, arsenic, sulphur, nickel; important mining centres are Westphalia, Silesia, Rhine Prov., Harz Mts., Saxony, Brandenburg, Nassau; manufactures include textiles, iron and steel goods, leather, glass, china, earthenware, chemicals, musical instruments, paper; breweries and distilleries; salmon, herring, cod, oyster fisheries; many mineral springs. The principal towns are: Berlin (cap.), Cologne, Breslau, Frankfurt-on-Main, Essen, Dortmund, Düsseldorf, Hanover, Gelsenkirchen-Buer, Magdeburg, Königsberg, Duisburg; Altona, Stettin, Kiel important seaports. Area, 113,038 sq. m.; pop. 38,176,000.

Prut (*proot*), riv., Romania; rises on N. of Carpathians and flows s. to join R. Danube below Galatz. Length, *c.* 500 m.

Przemysl (*pzhem'ishl*), tn., Poland, on R. San, trib. of R. Vistula, 60 m. w. of Lwow; two cathedrals; wood, leather, corn, and linen; before Great

War the strongest fortress in Galicia; important rly. jn.; scene of heavy fighting during Great War. Pop. 48,000.

Pskov, tn., Leningrad area, Russia, *c.* 10 m. s. of L. Pskov and near Estonian boundary; rly. jn.; educational centre; flax; timber; leather. Pop. 40,000.

Pud'sey, munic. bor., W. Riding, Yorks, England, 3 m. E. of Bradford; woollen and worsted goods; leather; iron and brass founding, electro-plating, and engineering. Pop. 14,800.

Pueb'la, tn., Mexico, 75 m. S.E. of Mexico City; one of oldest cities in rep.; alt. *c.* 7,000 ft.; cathedral; cotton and woollen mills. Pop. 96,000.

Pueb'lo, city, Colorado, U.S.A., on Arkansas R., 120 m. s. of Denver; alt. 4,680 ft.; fine climate; mineral springs in irrigated area; oilfields, deposits of coal and other minerals near city; steel and iron works; large smelting centre for gold, silver, copper, zinc, and lead. Pop. 50,000.

Puente Genil (*pwen'tā hā-nēl*), tn., Cordoba, s. Spain, on Genil trib. of R. Guadalquivir; olive oil. Pop. 18,000.

Puerto Cabello (*pwer'tō kā-bel'yo*), port, Venezuela, on Caribbean Sea, *c.* 90 m. w. of La Guayra; rly. to Caracas; exports coffee, cacao, hides, tobacco, dyewoods, timber, copper ore. Pop. 23,000.

Puerto de Santa Maria (*pwer'tō dā sän'tä mär-ē'ä*), port, Spain, on Bay of Cadiz, opposite Cadiz; exports sherry; important fisheries; leather, glass, and soap. Pop. 19,000.

Puer'to Montt, port, cap. Chiloe, s. Chile; coasting trade; rly. terminus; serves sheep-farming dist. Pop. *c.* 10,000.

Puerto Principe. See CAMAGÜEY.

Puerto Rico. See PORTO RICO.

Pug'achev, formerly NIKOLAEVSK, tn., S.E. Russia, 100 m. s. of Samara; agricultural market. Pop. 17,500.

Puget Sound (*pū'jĕt*), land-locked arm of Pacific Ocean, Washington, U.S.A.; extends s. from Vancouver I.; navigable throughout; shores wooded; fisheries. Chief ports are Seattle and Tacoma. Length, 125 m.

Puket (*poo-ket'*), or TONGKAH, port and chief tn. of Junk Ceylon; Siamese isl. N.W. of Malay Peninsula; tin mines; edible birds' nests. Pop. *c.* 30,000.

Pul'borough, par. and mkt. tn., Sussex, England, on R. Arun, 11 m. S.W. of Horsham. Pop. (par.) 2,100.

Pulkovo (*pool'kō-vō*), or PULKOWA, vil., Russia, 10 m. s. of Leningrad; on adjacent hill (248 ft.) is famous meteorological observatory; univ.

Pultusk (*pool'toosk*), tn., Poland, on R. Narew, 32 m. N. of Warsaw; woollens, linens, hosiery, copper wares, and pottery. Pop. 16,000.

Punjab' ('land of the five rivs.'—*i.e.*, Jhelum, Chenab, Ravi, Beas, Sutlej), prov., N.W. India; bounded on N. by Kashmir, E. by United Provs., s. by Rajputana and Sind, and w. by Baluchistan and N.W. Frontier Prov.; vast alluvial plain of R. Indus; Himalayas in N.; includes irrigation areas on Lower Chenab and Lower Jhelum canals—fertile, wealthy, and populous; agriculture is staple industry; wheat most important crop; other crops barley, rice, millet, maize, oilseeds, cotton, and sugar-cane; livestock; mineral wealth small; cotton factories; govt. college at Lahore; art colleges and professional schools; chief tns.: Lahore (cap.), Amritsar, Multan, and Rawalpindi; over half pop. Mohammedan, one-third Hindu, and one-tenth Sikh. Area, 99,846 sq. m.; pop. 20,685,000 (including Indian States, 37,059 sq. m.; pop. 4,416,000).

Punta Arenas. See MAGALLANES (2).

Pur'beck, ISLE OF, peninsula, S.E. Dorset, England, s. of Poole Harbour; traversed by chalk hills; quarries; contains Corfe Castle and town of Swanage. Length, 12 m.

Pur'fleet, urb. dist., Essex, England, on R. Thames, 16 m. E. of London; small harbour. Pop. 8,500.

Puri (*poo'rē*), JAGANNATH, or JUGGERNAUT, chief tn., Orissa, India, on

Bay of Bengal; temple of Vishnu containing idol of Jagannath; great car festival (held annually) formerly associated with cruel rites. Pop. 39,000.

Puteaux (*poo-tō'*), tn., Seine, France, on R. Seine, 7 m. w. of Paris, of which it is a suburb; woollens; dyes. Pop. 40,000.

Puteoli. See POZZUOLI.

Put'ney, metropolitan dist., Wandsworth, London, on river Thames; bridge is starting-place for Oxford and Cambridge boat race. Pop. 29,000.

Puy-de-Dôme (*pwē-dē-dōm'*). (1) Dep., central France, on N.E. edge of Auvergne plateau; surface generally mountainous; watered by rivs. Allier, Cher, Dordogne; rich plain of Limagne produces vine, fruits, and sugar-beet; coal and silver lead; mineral springs (Mont Dore). Cap. Clermont-Ferrand. Area, 3,090 sq. m.; pop. 515,000. (2) Mt., in above dep.; chief peak of Auvergne volcanic group; meteorological observatory; alt. 4,806 ft.

Pwllheli (*pool-hel'ē*), port, Carnarvonshire, Wales, on Cardigan Bay; harbour of refuge; fishing centre; exports slates. Pop. 3,600.

Pyat'igorsk ('five mountains'), tn., North Caucasian Area, Russia, 80 m. S.E. of Stavropol; surrounded by five peaks; alt. 1,500 ft.; wat.-pl. with sulphur springs. Pop. 53,500.

Pyrenees (*pir'en-ēz*), mt. chain, Europe; stretches from S.E. Bay of Biscay to Mediterranean Sea; boundary between France and Spain; total length, *c.* 250 m.; width varies from 90 m. to *c.* 25 m. at Mediterranean end; chief summits: Aneto or Pic de Néthou (11,168 ft.), Pic de Poseto (11,047 ft.), and Mont Perdu (10,998 ft.); limit of perpetual snow, 9,000 ft. on N. and 10,000 ft. on S.; characteristic features are gullies enclosed on all sides by towering crags (*cirques*); poor in minerals; iron mines at Biscay end; slopes wooded with box, fir, and pine; five passes practicable for motor transport; crossed by three rlys.

Pyrénées-Orientales (*pē-rā-nāz-or-ē-on-täl'*), dep., S. France; consists of slopes of main chain of E. Pyrenees; climate cool on mts., dry on plain along Mediterranean Sea; wine; oranges and other sub-tropical fruits; iron mined; coast lagoons produce salt. Amélie-les-Bains has sulphur springs. Cap. Perpignan. Area, 1,598 sq. m.; pop. 230,000.

Pyr'gos, tn., Achæa and Elis, Morea, Greece, 42 m. S.W. of Patras; devastated by Turks (1825); fishing and vines. Pop. 14,000.

Pytchley (*pich'li*), par. and vil., Northants, England, 3 m. S. of Kettering; Pytchley Hunt established in 18th cent.; kennels at Brixworth, near Northampton. Pop. (par.) 500.

Q

Qabes, or GABES (*kä'bez*), oasis tn., Tunisia, N. Africa, on gulf of same name; dates and other fruits; henna, wool, esparto grass. Pop. 20,000.

Qairwan, or KAIRWAN (*kīr-wan'*), anc. walled tn., Tunisia, N. Africa; sacred to Mohammedans; has citadel and many beautiful mosques; leather goods and carpets. Pop. 19,000.

Qais (*kīs*), island, Persian Gulf; measures 10 m. by 5 m.; pearl fishing. Pop. *c.* 2,000.

Qantara, EL. See SUEZ CANAL.

Qara Qum (*kä'ra koom*). (1) Flat, sandy desert, Central Asia; between R. Oxus on N.E. and Persia on S.W.; surrounds oasis of Merv. Area, *c.* 110,000 sq. m. (2) Desert region in the N. of the province of Sir Darya, Kazak, U.S.S.R.

Qena (*kēn'a*), cap. of province of same name in Upper Egypt, *c.* 380 m. S.S.E. of Cairo; famous for earthenware. Pop. 23,000.

Qishm (*kishm*), largest isl., Persian Gulf; length, *c.* 70 m.; breadth, 2 to 15 m.; produces grain, fruits, and salt. Chief town, Qishm. Pop. (isl.) *c.* 15,000. (tn.) *c.* 3,000.

Qizil Qum (*kiz'il koom*), desert tract of w. Asia; is dried-up bed of anc. sea of which Aral Sea is remnant. Length (N. to S.), 200 m.; breadth, 380 m.

Qoseir, El (*ko-sēr*), seapt., w. coast of Red Sea, Egypt; terminus for caravan route from R. Nile.

Quantock Hills, hills, Somerset, England, stretch 10 m. S.E. from Bristol Channel; reach 1,262 ft. in Will's Neck.

Quarry Bank, urb. dist., Staffs, England, in extreme s. of co.; in Black Country. Pop. 8,100.

Quebec (*kwe-bek'*). (1) Eastern prov., Dominion of Canada, lies along lower course of St. Lawrence R., and extends N. to Hudson Strait; bounded on w. by Hudson Bay and Ontario, on E. by Labrador, s. by New Brunswick and U.S.A.; surface generally undulating; drained by R. St. Lawrence and tribs. (Ottawa, St. Maurice, and Saguenay). Much of surface forested, and Quebec has more than half Canadian production of pulpwood; cereals, flax, fruits, potatoes, and maple products; fur farming is important; yields most of world's supply of asbestos; other minerals include gold, copper, lead, silver, platinum; fisheries are extensive; manufactures include cement, textiles, leather, hardware, paper. Inhabitants are mainly of French extraction. Settled parts mostly on both sides of R. St. Lawrence, Eastern Townships lying between R. St. Lawrence and U.S.A. Chief towns are Montreal and Quebec (cap.). Area, 594,434 sq. m.; pop. 2,361,000. (2) Cap. of above, on St. Lawrence R., at mouth of St. Charles R.; founded (1608) by Champlain; taken by British under Wolfe (1759); battlefield now a national park, with monument to Wolfe and Montcalm. Consists of Upper and Lower Town, former residential, latter devoted to commerce. Among principal buildings are Prot. and R.C. cathedrals, Parliament House, and archiepiscopal palace. There is an excellent harbour and large dry dock; important rly. centre. Quebec bridge crosses R. St. Lawrence 7 m. above city; exports include timber, grain, cattle, and cheese; manufactures woollens, hardware, and machinery. Pop. 131,000.

Quedlinburg (*kwed'lin-boorg*), town, Saxony, Prussia, 13 m. S.W. of Magdeburg; flower and vegetable seeds, cloth, wire goods, starch, aniline dyes. Pop. 27,000.

Queen'borough, munic. bor., Isle of Sheppey, Kent, England; packet station for Flushing; chemical manure and cement. Pop. 2,900.

Queen Charlotte Islands, off coast of Brit. Columbia, Canada; important fisheries; rich in timber; gold, copper, iron, and anthracite coal exist, but are not worked. Pop. *c.* 2,000.

Queens'bury, urb. dist., W. Riding, Yorks, England, 4 m. N. of Halifax; makes alpaca, mohair, worsted, and dress goods. Pop. 5,800.

Queen's County. See Leix.

Queens'ferry. (1) Vil., Flintshire, England, on R. Dee, 5½ m. S.E. of Flint; shipbuilding; ferry over Dee. Pop. (dist.) 10,000. (2) North, vil., Fife, Scotland, at N. end of Forth Bridge; ferry to S. Queensferry. Pop. 1,650. (3) South, seapt. and royal burgh, West Lothian, Scotland, at s. end of Forth Bridge; of historic interest. Pop. 1,800.

Queensland, second largest state of Australia, bounded N. by Gulf of Carpentaria and Torres Strait, E. by S. Pacific, s. by New South Wales, and w. by S., Central, and N. Australia. Divided into two areas by Great Dividing Range, which follows coastline at distance of from 100 to 300 m.; country between range and coast consists of alluvial areas and rich river valleys. The Brisbane, Mary, Burnett, Fitzroy, Burdekin, and Johnstone rivers are the most important of E. watershed, while w. watershed has rivers flowing N. to Gulf of Carpentaria, s. to Murray-Darling system, and w. to S. Australian lakes. Climate varies with latitude and height, N. being tropical and sub-tropical, S. having mean temp. of 70° F. Rainfall is generally adequate, being heavy in tropical regions of N., and averaging 60 in. in S.E., but inland parts suffer from drought. Thus artesian wells have been of great service. Chief agricultural products are cereals, sugar-cane, wine, cotton, tea, fruits, timber. Sheep, cattle, and horses are extensively reared, and form one of chief sources of wealth; and dairy farming is a rapidly expanding industry. Minerals are of great importance, including gold, silver, copper, tin, coal. Industries include manufactures of sugar, tobacco, leather, boots, spirits, flour, machinery, textiles, soap. Meat preserving is largely carried on. Chief exports are copper, tin, coal, meat, hides, skins, tallow, wool, and sugar. The population is more mixed than in any other part of Australia, and includes English, Chinese, Japanese, and Polynesians. Chief towns are Brisbane (cap.), Rockhampton, Townsville, Maryborough, Ipswich, and Toowoomba. Area, *c.* 670,500 sq. m.; pop. 756,000.

Queenstown. (1) See COBH. (2) Tn., w. Tasmania, Australia; smelting works. Pop. 2,600. (3) Tn., Cape Prov., S. Africa, on railway, midway between E. London and Aliwal N.; wheat and wool. Pop. 13,000 (5,000 whites).

Quelimane (*kel-i-mān'e*), seaport, Portuguese E. Africa; exports copra, ground-nuts, sugar, sisal, and cotton. Pop. *c.* 4,000.

Quelpart (*kwel'part*), Japanese isl. off s.w. of Korea; was long used as Korean convict station. Chief industries are agriculture, manufacture of bamboo hats and mats, and pearl fishing. Length, 40 m.; breadth, 10 to 20 m. Pop. *c.* 115,000.

Queretaro (*kā-rā-tā'rō*). (1) Central state of Mexico; produces maize, wheat, and fruits, and has silver, gold, copper, lead, tin, and antimony mines. Area, 4,493 sq. m.; pop. 220,000. (2) Cap. of above, 115 m. N.W. of Mexico City; cotton and woollen goods; pottery. Pop. 30,000.

Quetta (*kwet'a*), cap. of Brit. Baluchistan, N.W. of Bolan Pass. Has great strategical position commanding w. gate to India; strongly fortified and connected with railway system of India; seat of Indian Staff Coll. Pop. 49,000.

Quezaltenango (*kā-zal-ten-an'gō*), tn., Guatemala, 70 m. w. of Guatemala city; trade in coffee, sugar, rubber, and hides; manufactures textiles. Pop. 20,000.

Quilon (*kwē-lon'*), seapt., Travancore, Madras, India; timber, coconuts, pepper, cardamoms. Pop. 25,000.

Quimper (*kan-pār'*), tn., Finistère, France, *c.* 70 m. S.E. of Brest; 13th cent. cathedral; manufactures pottery; sardine fisheries. Pop. 15,000.

Quincy (*kwin'si*). (1) City, Illinois, U.S.A., 95 m. w. of Springfield; machinery, vehicles, stoves, ironware, bricks, flour, and tobacco. Pop. 40,000. (2) City, Massachusetts, U.S.A.; residential suburb of Boston; granite quarrying and shipbuilding; foundry products. Pop. 72,000.

Quito (*kē'to*), cap. of Ecuador, S. America; on plateau of Andes (alt. 9,350 ft.); one of oldest cities in S. America and at one time Inca cap.; suffers from earthquakes; cathedral and univ.; carpets, blankets, shoes, saddles, woollen and cotton goods, rubber and hides. Pop. 82,000.

Qum (*koom*), tn., Persia, 90 m. s. of Tehran; place of pilgrimage; glass, pottery, and shoes. Pop. *c.* 25,000.

Quorn'don, urb. dist., Leicestershire, England, 2½ m. S.E. of Loughborough; has kennels of Quorn Hunt; hosiery. Pop. 2,600.

R

Raab. See GYÖR.

Raasay (*räz'ä*), isl., Inner Hebrides, Inverness-shire, Scotland, separated from I. of Skye by Sound of Raasay, from mainland by Inner Sound; iron ore. Area, 24 sq. m.; pop. 370.

Rabat', seaport, Morocco, 110 m. W. of Fez; has sultan's palace; carpets and mats. Pop. 38,000.

Rabaul (*ra-ba'ool*), tn., Bismarck Archipelago, on New Britain Island; seat of government for mandated terr. of New Guinea. Pop. (white) 1,350.

Racine (*rä-sēn'*), city, Wisconsin, U.S.A., on L. Michigan, 60 m. N. of Chicago; agricultural machinery and motors; shipping trade in lumber and coal. Pop. 68,000.

Radauti (*rä'dä-oots'*), tn., Bukovina, Romania, 32 m. S. of Cernauti; glass and paper works. Pop. 17,000.

Rad'cliffe, urb. dist., Lancashire, England, on R. Irwell, 8 m. N.W. of Manchester; cotton spinning, weaving, dyeing and bleaching, iron foundries and collieries. Pop. 24,700.

Radeberg (*rä'de-berg*), tn., Saxony, Germany, 10 m. N.E. of Dresden; glass, enamels, beer, paper; cattle markets. Mineral springs. Pop. 16,000.

Rad'norshire, inland co., S. Wales, between Cardigan on W. and Hereford on E.; drained by Rs. Wye and Teme; surface hilly, except in the vale of Radnor, Radnor Forest reaching 2,186 ft.; mineral springs at Llandrindod and elsewhere; oats and wheat grown, but three-fourths of land under permanent pasture; sheep rearing and breeding of Welsh ponies very successful, also butter making; sandstone and limestone are quarried. Co. tn., Presteigne. Area, 470 sq. m.; pop. 21,300.

Rad'om, tn., Poland, 60 m. S. of Warsaw; coal, leather, machine shops. Pop. 62,000.

Radom'sko, tn., Poland, 50 m. S. of Lodz, on R. Warta; textiles, furniture, tanneries, and sawmills. Pop. *c.* 20,000.

Rad'stock, urb. dist., Somerset, England, 16 m. by rail S.E. of Bristol; coal mines. Pop. 3,600.

Ragusa. (1) See DUBROVNIK. (2) Tn., Sicily, 35 m. S.W. of Syracuse; oil and paving stone. Pop. 48,000.

Raichur (*rī-choor'*), tn., Hyderabad, India, 80 m. N. of Bellary; cotton presses; famed for glazed pottery. Pop. 26,000.

Raigarh (*rī-gur'*), Indian state, Central Provinces, India; grows rice and pulses; has 1,800 irrigation tanks; manufactures silk. Cap. Raigarh, 360 m. W. of Calcutta. Area, 1,486 sq. m.; pop. 242,000.

Rain'ford, urb. dist., Lancs, England, 4 m. N.W. of St. Helens; coal mines. Pop. 3,500.

Rain'ham. (1) Par. and vil., Essex, England, 12½ m. E. of London; brick and tile making. Pop. (par.) 2,850. (2) Par. and vil., Kent, England, 4 m. S.E. of Chatham; bricks and cement made. Pop. (par.) 5,600.

Rainhill, par. and vil., Lancs, England, 9 m. E. of Liverpool; brass-founding; small tools made. Pop. (par.) 2,850.

Rainier (*rä'nēr*), MOUNT, volcanic cone, Cascade Range, Washington, U.S.A., in Mt. Rainier National Park, *c.* 50 m. S.E. of Tacoma; above forests are many glaciers; steam and sulphurous fumes still come from crater; discovered by Vancouver (1792). Alt. 14,408 ft.

Raipur (*rī-poor'*), chief tn., Raipur dist., Central Provinces, India, 160 m. E. of Nagpur; exports grain and cotton; has a leper asylum; fort dates from 1460. Pop. 30,000.

Rajahmun'dry, tn., Madras, Brit. India, on R. Godavari, at head of delta; of growing importance. Pop. 54,000.

Rajkot′, chief town, Rajkot state, Kathiawar, Bombay, India; has a coll. for the sons of Indian chiefs; headquarters of political agent for Kathiawar. Pop. 36,000.

Rajputa′na ('land of the Rajputs'), largest Indian state, bounded on W. by Sind, on N.W. by Bahawalpur, on N. and N.E. by Punjab, on E. by United Provinces and Gwalior; S. boundary runs across central region of India in zigzag line. The region includes nineteen Indian states, one chiefship, and Brit. prov. of Ajmer-Merwara. Aravalli Hills intersect country almost from S.W. to N.E. Tract to N.W. of hills is generally sandy and unproductive, but relatively fertile in N.E. To S.E. of hills lie higher and more fertile regions traversed by considerable rivers (Banas and Chambal, tribs. of Jumna). Majority of people engaged in agriculture. The manufactures include cotton, woollens, ivory, and metal goods. Chief tns., Jaipur, Udaipur, Alwar, Ajmer, Jodhpur. Area, 131,698 sq. m.; pop. 10,300,000.

Ral′eigh, cap. of N. Carolina, U.S.A.; cotton mills; wood-working; printing; railway workshops. Educational centre. Pop. 37,000.

Rames′waram, tn., Madras, India, on isl. in Palk Strait; famous Hindu shrine; on rly. to Adam's Bridge.

Ramillies (*rā-mē-yē′*), vil., Brabant, Belgium, 13 m. N.E. of Namur; scene of Marlborough's victory over French and Bavarians (1706).

Rampur′. (1) Indian state, United Provinces, India. Area, 892 sq. m.; pop. 454,000. (2) Cap. of above, 38 m. N.W. of Bareilly; damask, sugar, and pottery. Pop. 73,000.

Rams′bottom, urb. dist., Lancashire, England, on riv. Irwell, 4 m. N. of Bury; cotton and woollen factories; iron and brass foundries. Pop. 14,900.

Ram′sey. (1) Seaport and bathing resort, N.E. Isle of Man, with park, Albert Memorial Tower, and House of Keys building. Pop. 4,700. (2) Mkt. tn., Hunts, England, 10 m. N.E. of Huntingdon. Ramsey Mere, 2 m. N.E., has been drained, and produces fine crops of wheat. Pop. 5,200.

Rams′gate, munic. bor., Cinque port, wat.-pl., Isle of Thanet, Kent, England. Pop. 33,600.

Ranchi (*ran-chē′*), tn., Chota Nagpur div., Bihar and Orissa, India; rice, tea, shellac; missionary centre; seat of provincial government in hot season. Pop. (tn.) 40,000.

Rand. See WITWATERSRAND.

Randazzo (*ran-dăt′sō*), tn., Sicily; alt. 2,500 ft., at N. foot of Mt. Etna; fine palaces and picturesque churches; wine, oil, cheese. Pop. 17,000.

Ran′ders, tn., Jutland, Denmark, on Guden Aa, 23 m. N. by W. of Aarhus; has a 14th cent. church; iron foundries, machine and railway carriage shops, glove and watchmaking factories. Pop. 27,000.

Rangoon′, cap. and chief port, Burma, India, on Rangoon R. (E. delta stream of R. Irrawaddy), 20 m. from sea; largest trade of any Indian port except Calcutta and Bombay; many pagodas, including Shwe Dagon (6th cent.), height 370 ft., covered with gold leaf and plates of gold. Rice mills, sawmills, wood and ivory carving, petroleum refineries (pipe line to oilfields). Chief exports: rice, petroleum, teak, hides, and skins. Pop. 342,000.

Rannoch (*ran′och*), dist., N.W. Perthshire and N.E. Argyllshire, Scotland; elevated desolate moorland. Rannoch station is 5 m. W. of head of Loch Rannoch (9 m. long by 1 m. wide; alt. 668 ft.); fed by R. Ericht and other streams; drains by R. Tummel into R. Tay. A hydro-electric station for the Grampians area on Loch Rannoch-side uses the fall of water brought by tunnel from Loch Ericht.

Rapal′lo, seaport and winter resort, Italy, on Gulf of Genoa, 16 m. E.S.E. of Genoa; lace, olive oil. Pop. 14,000.

Raphoe (*ra-fō′*), par. and mkt. tn., co. Donegal, I.F.S., 5 m. W.N.W. of Lifford; cathedral; episc. palace; tweeds and other woollens. Pop. (par.) 2,600.

Rarotong'a, isl., Cook Islands, S. Pacific Ocean; volcanic (peak, 2,900 ft.); exports oranges, copra, bananas, tomatoes; wireless station; Polynesian inhabitants are Christians; isl. *c.* 20 m. in circumference. Pop. 4,000.

Ras'tatt, tn., Baden, Germany, 14 m. S.S.W. of Karlsruhe; lace, beer, stoves, and cigars. Pop. 14,000.

Ras'tenburg, tn., E. Prussia, Germany, 65 m. S.E. of Königsberg; manufactures machinery, beer, flour, and sugar. Pop. 14,000.

Rastrick. See BRIGHOUSE.

Rathenow (*rä'te-nō*), tn., Brandenburg, Prussia, on R. Havel, 45 m. W. by N. of Berlin; spectacles, optical instruments, bricks. Pop. 28,000.

Rathfarn'ham, par. and vil., co. Dublin, I.F.S., 3 m. S. of Dublin; residential centre. Pop. (par.) 11,100.

Rathkeale (*rath-kēl'*), par. and mkt. tn., co. Limerick, I.F.S., 18 m. S.W. of Limerick. Pop. (par.) 2,900.

Rath'lin, isl., co. Antrim, N. Ireland, 6 m. N. of Ballycastle (5 m. by 1 m.); at N.E. end are ruins of castle in which Robert Bruce took refuge (1306), according to tradition. Pop. 350.

Rath'o, par. and vil., Midlothian, Scotland, 8 m. W. of Edinburgh; market gardening and quarrying. Pop. (par.) 1,700.

Rat'ibor, tn., Silesia, Prussia, on R. Oder, 90 m. S.E. of Breslau; railway workshops and iron foundries. Pop. 41,000.

Ratisbon. See REGENSBURG.

Rat'lam, chief tn., Ratlam state, Central India, 65 m. N.W. of Indore; grain trade. Pop. *c.* 36,000.

Rat'tray, burgh, Perthshire, Scotland, on R. Ericht, opposite to and part of Blairgowrie; flax and jute spinning.

Raunds, urb. dist., Northants, England, 16½ m. N.E. of Northampton; makes boots and shoes, especially for army. Pop. 3,700.

Raven'na. (1) Prov., Italy, bounded E. by Adriatic and W. by Bologna; fertile but marshy plain; drained by R. Po di Primaro and intersected by canals; produces wheat, rice, hemp, chestnuts, and olive oil; manufactures of faience, glass, paper, silk, linen, and leather. Area, 715 sq. m.; pop. 267,000. (2) Cap. of above, 45 m. E. of Bologna; many fine churches, including the Basilica Ursiana (4th cent.), San Giovanni Evangelista (founded 425), and San Francesco (near which is tomb of Dante); mausoleum of Theodoric outside walls. Manufactures include silk and lace, paper and glass, agricultural implements and wine. Pop. 79,000.

Rav'ensburg, tn., Württemberg, Germany, on R. Schussen, 46 m. S.W. of Ulm; flax, cotton and linen goods, leather, machinery. Pop. 17,000.

Ravi. See INDUS.

Rawalpin'di, tn., military station, Punjab, India, 90 m. E.S.E. of Peshawar; largest military station in India; protected by forts; arsenal and locomotive works; ironfounding, oil refining, and brewing. Pop. 102,000.

Raw'don, urb. dist., W. Riding, Yorks, England, 5 m. N.E. of Bradford; many country mansions in vicinity. Pop. 4,600.

Rawicz (*rä'vich*), Poland, 55 m. S.W. of Poznan; snuff, cigars, carpets, agricultural implements. Pop. *c.* 12,000.

Raw'marsh, tn., W. Riding, Yorkshire, England, 2 m. N. of Rotherham; steel and iron works, brickfields, potteries, collieries. Pop. 18,600.

Raw'tenstall, munic. bor., Lancashire, England, 8 m. N. of Bury; cotton, woollen, slipper and carpet-felt factories; coal mines and stone quarries. Pop. 28,600.

Ray'leigh, urb. dist., Essex, England, 7 m. W.N.W. of Southend; moated mound near village is site of Sweyn's castle. Pop. 6,300.

Ré, ILE DE (*ēl de rā'*), isl., Charente-Inférieure, France, 2 m. off W. coast, opposite Rochelle; 15 m. long, 2 m. broad; area, *c.* 33 sq. m.; oyster culture and salt production. Chief town, St. Martin. Pop. 10,000.

Reading (*red'ing*). (1) Co. tn., Berks, England, 36 m. W. of London, at junction of Rs. Kennet and Thames; agricultural produce; seeds; biscuit works, engine works, breweries. Pop. 97,200. (2) City, Pennsylvania, U.S.A., on Schuylkill R., 50 m. N.W. of Philadelphia; important industrial centre; railway workshops, brick-works; manufactures include iron and steel, paper, cotton, hosiery. Pop. 110,000.

Recife (*rā-sē'fā*), or PERNAMBUCO, seapt., cap. of state of Pernambuco, Brazil, on Atlantic; partly on island connected with mainland by bridges. Railway terminus; palaces of governor and bishop; cottons, machinery, and glass; large export trade in cotton, sugar, rum, dyewoods, rubber, and cacao; improved harbour. Pop. 239,000.

Recklinghausen (*rek'ling-hou-zen*), town, Westphalia, Prussia, 15 m. N.N.E. of Essen; linen, beer, cement, and soap; coal mines and iron foundries. Pop. 84,000.

Recul'ver, vil., Kent, England, 8 m. W. of Margate; former Roman port; Roman remains; Reculver cliff is a noted sea-mark.

Redbourn, par. and vil., Herts, England, 4½ m. N.W. of St. Albans; on Roman Watling Street. Pop. (par.) 2,000.

Red'car, seaside resort, N. Riding, Yorks, England, 8 m. N.E. of Middlesbrough; fine stretch of sands. Racecourse. Pop. 20,200.

Red'dish, par., Lancs, England, 5 m. S.E. of Manchester. Pop. 15,400.

Red'ditch, urb. dist., Worcestershire, England, 15 m. S. of Birmingham; needles, fishing tackle, pins, and motor engineering. Pop. 19,300.

Redesdale (*rēds'dāl*), the valley of R. Rede, a l. bk. trib. of N. Tyne, Northumberland, England, near S. end of which is the battlefield of Otterburn or Chevy Chase (1388).

Redhill. See REIGATE.

Red'lands, tn., California, U.S.A., 70 m. E. of Los Angeles; centre of important orange-growing dist.; citrus fruits; beautiful mountain scenery. Pop. 14,000.

Red River. (1) R. bk. trib. of R. Mississippi, U.S.A.; rises in N.W. Texas, flows between Texas and Oklahoma, and enters Mississippi 340 m. above Gulf of Mexico; middle basin fertile; lower course meandering and subject to floods; navigable, but sometimes obstructed by fallen trees. Length, *c.* 1,500 m. (2) Or RED R. OF THE NORTH, rises in Minnesota, U.S.A.; flows N. between Minnesota and N. Dakota into Manitoba (Canada) and enters L. Winnipeg; basin formerly a great lake (L. Agassiz), now a rich wheat region; chief tn., Winnipeg, at confluence of Assiniboine trib.; Red R. Settlement of Scots founded by Lord Selkirk (1811). Length, *c.* 700 m.

Redruth', mkt. tn., Cornwall, England, 9 m. W.S.W. of Truro; tin sales are held; breweries and railway works. Pop. 9,900.

Red Sea, inland sea separating N.E. Africa from Arabia. Gulfs of Aqaba and Suez in N. enclose peninsula of Sinai; in S. Strait of Bab-el-Mandeb connects with Indian Ocean; greatest depth is *c.* 1,200 fathoms, and average depth is 250 fathoms; islands and coral reefs are numerous; heavy gales, variable winds, and intense heat make navigation difficult. Seaports (Arabian coast): Mocha, Hodeida, Jidda; (African coast): Suez, El Qoseir, Suakin, and Massawa. Length, *c.* 1,200 m.; maximum breadth, *c.* 250 m.

Re'gensburg, or RATISBON, city, Bavaria, Germany, on R. Danube; exceptionally rich in mediæval remains and works of art; Gothic cathedral (1275); tobacco, furniture, musical instruments, pottery, boats, pencils, and soap. Pop. 77,000.

Reggio di Calabria (*rej'ō dē ka-lab'-rē-a*), tn., Italy, on Strait of Messina; seat of archbishop; fine cathedral; perfumes, silks, and terra-cotta; exports olive oil, dried fruits, and essences. Enormous damage by earthquakes in 1783, 1894, and Dec. 1908. Pop. 59,000.

Reggio nell' Emilia (*rej'ō nel em-ē'-lē-a*), city, Italy, 35 m. N.W. of Bologna; seat of bishop; cathedral and numerous churches; manufactures include locomotives, tramcars, and cheese. Pop. 83,000.

Regina (*re-jī'na*), cap., Saskatchewan, Canada, 357 m. w. of Winnipeg; provincial legislative buildings, city hall, and various educational establishments. Western headquarters of Royal Canadian Mounted Police; wholesale distributing centre; foundries and machine shops, oil works, timber mills. Pop. 37,000.

Reichenbach (*rīch'en-bäch*). (1) Tn., Saxony, Germany, 11 m. s.w. of Zwickau; wool spinning, carding, and dyeing; school of weaving. Pop. 31,000. (2) Tn., Silesia, Prussia, 30 m. s.w. of Breslau; dyeing, brewing, chemicals. Pop. 16,000.

Reichenberg. See LIBEREC.

Reigate (*rī'gāt*), mkt. tn., Surrey, England, 23 m. s. of London; Church of St. Mary, partly Norman, with tomb of Lord Howard of Effingham; Redhill, a modern town, on E., is continuous with and included in borough. Pop. 30,800.

Reims, or RHEIMS (*rēmz* or *rans*), tn., Marne, France, 85 m. E.N.E. of Paris. Was prosperous town when Cæsar invaded Gaul. French kings crowned here; associated with Joan of Arc. Cathedral of Notre Dame (begun 1212), one of finest Gothic edifices in Europe, suffered severely in Great War, but afterwards restored. Important woollen and wool-and-silk manufactures; also glass, linoleum, chemicals, machinery, paper manufactured; headquarters of champagne industry. Important rly. jn. Pop. 98,000.

Remiremont (*rā-mēr-mon'*), town, Vosges, France, on R. Moselle; cotton spinning and weaving; manufactures hosiery, iron and copper goods, and brushes. Pop. 8,000.

Remscheid (*rem'shīt*), tn., Rhine prov., Prussia, 6 m. s. of Barmen; centre of cutlery trade; enormous export of locks, saws, scythes, skates, tools. Pop. 77,000.

Renaix (*re-nā'*), tn., E. Flanders, Belgium, 8 m. s. of Oudenarde; woollen and linen goods. Pop. 23,000.

Rends'burg, tn., Schleswig-Holstein, Prussia, on Kiel Canal, 20 m. w. of Kiel; breweries, tanneries, and dyeworks; textiles and manures. Pop. 17,000.

Ren'frew. (1) Royal burgh and co. tn., Renfrewshire, Scotland, on R. Clyde; shipbuilding yards, largest boiler works in Britain; engineering, weaving, and manufacture of soap. Pop. 15,000. (2) Tn., Ontario, Canada, 50 m. w. of Ottawa. Pop. 5,250.

Ren'frewshire, co., s.w. Scotland, lying along R. Clyde; surface flat in N.E., rising to high moorland in w. and s.; agriculture, dairy farming, and stock raising carried on; produces coal, iron, and shale; manufactures thread, cotton, and chemicals; has shipbuilding, engineering, sugar refining, print and bleach works; chief towns, Renfrew, Paisley, Greenock, Gourock, and Port-Glasgow. Area, 237 sq. m.; pop. 288,600.

Rennes (*ren*), chief tn., Ille-et-Vilaine, France, at junction of Rs. Ille and Vilaine; anc. cap. of Brittany; archiepisc. see; univ.; dairy produce; manufactures sailcloth, table linen, leather, and agricultural implements. Pop. 74,000.

Re'no, tn., Nevada, U.S.A., 30 m. N. of Carson City; agricultural and mining centre; univ.; machinery and flour. Pop. 11,000.

Rensselaer (*rens'ler*), tn., New York, U.S.A., on Hudson R. opposite Albany; manufacturing and railway centre; chief manufactures, felt, shoddy, blankets, and chemicals. Pop. 11,000.

Ren'ton, tn., Dumbartonshire, Scotland, on R. Leven, 2 m. N. of Dumbarton; calico printing, bleaching, dyeing. Pop. 5,000.

Rep'ton, par. and vil., Derbyshire, England, 4 m. N.E. of Burton-on-Trent; famous school; anc. cap. of Mercia; church has Saxon crypt. Pop. (par.) 1,900.

Requena (*rā-kān'ya*), tn., E. Spain, 40 m. w. of Valencia; wine and fruits; manufactures taffetas and velvets. Pop. 20,000.

Resht, tn., Gilan, Persia; Pahlevi, its port, is 18 m. N.W. on the Caspian Sea; centre of important trade routes; trades chiefly in rice and silk. Pop. 80,000.

Restigouche (*rest'i-goosh*), riv., between New Brunswick and Quebec, Canada; flows into Bay of Chaleur; lumbering; salmon fishing.

Ret'ford, EAST, mkt. tn., Notts, England, on R. Idle and Chesterfield Canal, 22 m. E.S.E. of Sheffield; iron foundries, paper and corn mills, india-rubber works. Pop. 14,200.

Rethel (*rā-tel'*), tn., Ardennes, France, on R. Aisne; fine woollen cloth. Pop. 5,000.

Réunion (*rā-ūn'yon*) (or BOURBON), French isl., Indian Ocean, *c.* 400 m. E. of Madagascar; divided by chain of volcanic mts. into two distinct E. and W. parts; drained by many short streams; chief products are rum, sugar, coffee, manioc, tapioca, vanilla, and spices. Chief tns., St. Denis (cap.) and Pointe des Galets (chief port). Area, 970 sq. m.; pop. 187,000.

Reus (*rā-oos'*), tn., E. Spain, 10 m. N.W. of Tarragona; silk, calico, soap, and leather; exports fruit and wines. Pop. 30,000.

Reutlingen (*roit-ling'en*), tn., Württemberg, Germany, 20 m. S. of Stuttgart; centre of hop, wine, and fruit dist.; leather, woollen and cotton goods, machinery. Pop. 30,000.

Revel. See TALLINN.

Rev'elstoke, tn., S.E. Brit. Columbia, Canada, on Columbia R. and C.P.R.; mining industries, railway workshops. Pop. 3,000.

Revere (*re-vēr'*), tn., Massachusetts, U.S.A., N.E. and adjoining Boston; popular seaside resort. Pop. 36,000.

Rewah (*rē'wa*). (1) Indian state, Baghelkhand, Central India; well watered and very fertile, producing rice, wheat, millet, and timber; rich in minerals, particularly coal. Area, 13,000 sq. m.; pop. 1,401,000. (2) Chief tn. of above, 72 m. S.W. of Allahabad. Pop. 21,000.

Re'wa Kan'tha, political agency, Bombay, India; comprises about sixty separate states in Gujarat. Area, 4,946 sq. m.; pop. 665,000.

Reykjavik (*rīk'yă-vik*), cap. of Iceland; contains cathedral and government buildings; exports are salt cod and other fish, wool, and skins. Pop. 25,000.

Rez'ekne, tn., Latvia, on Leningrad-Warsaw railway; agricultural centre. Pop. *c.* 20,000.

Rhætian Alps (*rā'ti-an* or *rēsh'i-an*), or BERNINA ALPS, central chain of Middle Alps, between Rs. Inn, Adda, and Upper Adige. Highest peaks: Piz Bernina (13,300 ft.), Piz Roseg (12,936 ft.), and Ortler Spitze (12,800 ft.). Chief pass is the Splügen (6,945 ft.).

Rhayader, mkt. tn., Radnorshire, Wales, on upper course of R. Wye; centre for tourists and anglers; tanyards; sheep and cattle fairs. Pop. 5,000.

Rhé, ILE DE. See RÉ.

Rheims. See REIMS.

Rhenish Prussia. See under RHINE PROVINCE.

Rheydt (*rīt*), tn., Rhineland, Prussia, 19 m. W. of Düsseldorf; textiles, machinery, shoes, soap, and tobacco. Pop. 45,000.

Rhine (*rīn*) (Ger. *Rhein*), riv., W. Europe; rises in Switzerland, where two streams, the Hinter Rhein and the Vorder Rhein, unite at Reichenau to form the main stream; after passing through L. Constance forms falls at Schaffhausen; forms boundary between Switzerland and Austria, between Switzerland and Germany, and between France and Germany. Chief tribs. are Aar, Ill, Neckar, Main, Lahn, Moselle, Ruhr, Lippe; total length, 760 m., over 500 navigable to Basle; connected by canals with Rs. Danube, Rhone, and Marne, and also with Zuider Zee; most picturesque part is between Bingen and Coblenz, with many anc. castles, most famous being Ehrenbreitstein, immediately opposite the confluence of R. Moselle. From Cologne to its mouth the river passes through flat country, and on its way through Holland divides into several arms; the left or s. arm, which falls into the North Sea at the Hook of Holland, is known as the Waal, which farther on receives the Maas; the right or N. arm splits up into the Ijssel and the Rijn. For commercial purposes the most important arms of the delta are the Waal and the Lek. The Rhine has always played an important part in history, romance, literature, and commerce. By Treaty of Versailles (1919) river navigation was placed under control of the International Rhine Commission.

Rhine Province, RHINELAND, or RHENISH PRUSSIA, the most w. province of Prussia; drained by R. Rhine and tribs.; wine extensively produced in the valleys of Rs. Rhine, Moselle, and Saar; sugar, hops, and flax grown; fruit abundant; most important occupations are mining and manufacturing; chief minerals, coal, iron, and lead; manufactures include iron, brass, and steel goods, cutlery, textiles, chemicals; chief tns. are Coblenz (cap.), Essen, Duisburg, Düsseldorf, Cologne, Elberfeld-Barmen, Crefeld. Area, 9,478 sq. m.; pop. 7,257,000.

Rhinns (*rinz*) (Gaelic 'point' or 'promontory'). (1) RHINNS, or RINNS OF GALLOWAY, low-lying dist., w. Wigtownshire, Scotland; extends from Corsewall Point to Mull of Galloway. Area, 120 sq. m. (2) RHINNS, or RHYNNS OF KELLS, range of mts., N.W. Kirkcudbrightshire, Scotland; highest peak Corserine (2,668 ft.). (3) THE RHINNS, peninsula, S.W. Islay, Argyllshire, Scotland.

Rhio-Lingga (*rē'o-ling'ga*), archipelago, Dutch E. Indies; consists of five groups of islands, of which Lingga group lies on the equator; others are Karimon, Batam, Bintang, and Singkep groups; products include rubber, pepper, and rice. Area, 12,506 sq. m.; pop. 223,000.

Rhode Island, New England state, U.S.A., bounded N. and E. by Massachusetts, on S. by Atlantic Ocean, on w. by Connecticut. Surface generally hilly; divided into two unequal portions by Narragansett Bay, with islands including Rhode I. (summer resort); numerous lakes; watered by Blackstone, Pawtuxet, and Pawcatuck rivs. Climate fairly equable. Mean ann. rainfall is 45 to 50 in. Fisheries (oysters) very important; agriculture is relatively unimportant. Pre-eminently a manufacturing state; chief industries: woollen, worsted, and felt goods, cotton goods, jewellery, foundry and machine-shop products, electrical machinery, silverware and plated goods, gold and silver refining. Chief towns, Providence (cap.), Pawtucket, Woonsocket, Newport. Area, 1,300 sq. m. (smallest state in the Union); pop. 679,000.

Rhodes (*rōdz*), island; most E. of Ægean Islands; crossed by mountains from N. to S.; highest point, 4,560 ft.; fine climate and fertile soil; produces figs, pomegranates, oranges, and grapes. Cap. Rhodes. Area, 540 sq. m.; pop. 45,000.

Rhodesia (*rō-dēzh'i-a*), Brit. terr., S. Africa; bounded N. by Belgian Congo and Tanganyika Terr., E. by Nyasaland and Portuguese E. Africa, S. by Transvaal, W. by Bechuanaland, Angola, and Belgian Congo; divided into Northern and Southern Rhodesia by R. Zambezi. Originally governed by British South Africa Co., founded by Cecil Rhodes (1889); in 1922 declined an offer to join the Union of S. Africa; S. Rhodesia was granted responsible govt. in 1923, and N. Rhodesia passed under the direct control of the British Crown in 1924.

SOUTHERN RHODESIA, Brit. Dominion; mainly an elevated plateau (alt. 3,000 to 5,000 ft.); drained to R. Zambezi in N., to R. Limpopo in S.; climate sub-tropical; tableland healthy, riv. valleys and lowlands unhealthy; rainy season between Oct. and April; chief crops, tobacco and maize; citrus fruit orchards; numerous cattle and dairy products; minerals include gold, asbestos, chrome iron, coal; rly. from Union divides at

Bulawayo, one line N. to Zambezi and N. Rhodesia, other by Salisbury (cap.) to Beira in Portuguese E. Africa. Includes Matabeleland and Mashonaland. Area, 150,344 sq. m.; pop. *c.* 1,000,000 (45,000 Europeans).

NORTHERN RHODESIA, Brit. Protectorate; plateau surface (alt. 3,000 to 4,500 ft.) rising to over 5,000 ft. in N.E., with climate suited to Europeans; drained by R. Zambezi and R. Congo; includes L. Bangweulu and part of Ls. Tanganyika and Mweru; timber; principal crops, maize, tobacco, cotton, sisal, oil-seeds, millet, wheat; citrus fruits on irrigated lands; cattle; much mineral wealth, coal, copper, zinc, lead, and vanadium; traversed by rly. to Belgian Congo; rivs. navigable for considerable distances. Cap. Livingstone. Area, 287,950 sq. m.; pop. 1,270,000 (7,600 Europeans).

Rhodope Mountains (*rō'dō-pā*), part of Balkan Mts., dividing Macedonia from Thrace. Muss Alla (9,615 ft.), culminating point in W. portion.

Rhondda (*ron'tha*), urb. dist., Glamorganshire, Wales, watered by Rhondda R., trib. of Taff; valley densely populated and rich in coal. Pop. 141,300.

Rhone (*rōn*), riv., swiftest and second longest of France, rises in Switzerland on W. slopes of Mt. St. Gothard, flows into and through L. Geneva, enters France 12 m. S. of Geneva, and flows W. to Lyons, where it is joined by the Saône, then S. to Mediterranean, discharging by La Camargue delta into Gulf of Lions; chief tribs., Ain, Saône, Arve, Isère, Drôme, Durance; strong current prevents navigation above Lyons; canals connect Rhone with Loire, Seine, Rhine, and Moselle; length, 500 m., of which 45 are in Lake Geneva.

Rhône (*rōn*), dep., S.E. France, along r. bk. of Middle Rhone and Lower Saône; soil moderately fertile; wheat, oats, rye, potatoes, and wine are chief agricultural products; silk and textile industries are important; copper, coal, manganese, and iron are worked. Chief tn., Lyons. Area, 1,104 sq. m.; pop. 994,000.

Rhu, or Row (*roo*), vil., Dumbartonshire, Scotland, on S.E. shore of Gareloch; summer resort. Pop. 1,200.

Rhyl (*ril*), wat.-pl., Flintshire, Wales, near mouth of R. Clwyd. Pop. 13,500.

Rhymney (*rŭm'ni*), urb. dist., Monmouthshire, England, 2½ m. W. of Tredegar; ironworks, collieries. Pop. 10,500.

Rib'ble, riv., England; rises in Pennine chain; flows W. through Yorkshire and Lancashire to Irish Sea; estuary 5½ m. wide between Southport and Lytham. Chief tn. on banks, Preston. Length, 75 m.

Rib'chester, par. and town, Lancashire, England, on R. Ribble; anc. Roman station. Pop. (par.) 1,400.

Ribeira (*rē-bā-ē'rā*), tn., Spain, 64 m. S.S.W. of Corunna; its port is Santa Eugenia de Ribeira. Pop. 16,000.

Ric'carton, par. and vil., Ayrshire, Scotland; par. contains greater part of tn. of Hurlford; vil. adjoins Kilmarnock; coal mining. Pop. (par.) 8,000.

Rich'borough, port, Sandwich, Kent, England; important Roman remains; used during Great War as base for cross-Channel train-ferry service to Calais and Dunkirk. Port and equipment bought (1925) for development of Kent coalfields.

Rich'mond. (1) Mkt. tn., N. Riding, Yorks, England, on R. Swale; ruined castle (1071); agricultural produce. Pop. 4,800. (2) Munic. bor., Surrey, England, part of Greater London, on R. Thames and Richmond Hill; residential town and favourite resort; Richmond Park contains red deer; bor. includes Kew. Pop. 37,800. (3) Cap., Virginia, U.S.A., on James R.; many fine public buildings; leading industry tobacco production; lumber products, foundry and machine-shop products, carriages, and wagons. Cap. of Southern Confederacy and scene of much fighting during American Civil War. Pop. 183,000. (4) Cap., Wayne co., Indiana, U.S.A., 69 m. N.E. of Indianapolis; 'Quaker City of the

West'; agricultural machinery. Pop. 33,000.

Rick'mansworth, urb. dist., s.w. Herts, England, on R. Colne; paper mills, breweries. Pop. 10,800.

Rideau Canal (*rē'dō'*), canal, Ontario, Canada, connecting Kingston, L. Ontario, with Ottawa by way of Rideau R. and L. Rideau, thence N. to Ottawa R. Constructed as alternative route to that part of R. St. Lawrence which is shared with U.S.A.; length, 126½ m.

Riesa (*rē'za*), tn., Saxony, Germany, on R. Elbe; large harbour, sawmills, ironworks. Pop. 24,000.

Riesengebirge (*rē'zen-ge-bir'ga*), or GIANT MOUNTAINS, highest portion of Sudetic Mts., partly in Czechoslovakia and partly in Germany; 23 m. long and 13 to 15 m. wide; highest summit, Schneekoppe (5,258 ft.).

Rif. See under MOROCCO (1).

Riga (*rē'ga*), seapt., cap., Latvia, near mouth of R. Dvina; old castle; was member of Hanseatic League; harbour frozen for four months every year, but kept open by ice-breakers; exports corn, flax, hemp, timber, skins, linseed, eggs; manufactures include cottons, machinery, glass, paper; old town preserves mediæval aspect; new town has fine boulevards and buildings. Pop. 338,000.

Rigi (*rē'gē*), or RIGHI, mountain mass rising E. of Lucerne, Switzerland, between Lakes Lucerne and Zug; highest point, Rigi Kulm (5,906 ft.), crowned by a hotel; mountain railways from E. and S.

Rimini (*rē'mē-nē*), tn., Italy, on Adriatic, 70 m. S.E. of Bologna; Roman remains and fine cathedral; manufactures silk, rope, and sailcloth; bathing resort. Pop. 58,000.

Rimouski (*re-moos'kē*), port and wat.-pl., Quebec, Canada, on S. bank of Gulf of St. Lawrence, 180 m. N.E. of Quebec; port of call for ocean mails. Pop. 3,600.

Ring'wood, mkt. tn., W. Hants, England, on R. Avon; agricultural trade, gloves, milling machinery. Pop. 5,100.

Riobamba (*rē'ō-bam'ba*), cap., Chimborazo prov., Ecuador, 85 m. N.E. of Guayaquil; alt. 9,000 ft.; cathedral; national college. Pop. *c.* 12,000.

Rio Cuarto (*rē'ō kwar'tō*), tn., Cordoba prov., Argentina, S. America, on Andine Rly.; of great strategical importance; has arsenal. Pop. 18,000.

Rio de Janeiro (*rē'ō dā zhan-ā'rō*). (1) Maritime state, Brazil; interior mountainous; drained by R. Parahyba; coffee, sugar, tobacco, cotton, manioc, and fruits grown. Cap. Nictheroy. Area, 26,627 sq. m.; pop. 1,560,000. (2) Cap. of Brazil, second largest city of S. America, on bay of same name; important seapt.; beautifully situated; defended by forts at harbour entrance; regular steamship connections with European and American ports. Botanical and zoological gardens; aerial railway to top of Sugar Loaf hill (1,260 ft.); many notable buildings and educational institutions. Flour mills, foundries, breweries, sugar refineries; railway workshops and rubber factory. Harbour continuously improved since 1904. Exports include coffee, sugar, hides, ores, and diamonds. Pop. 1,158,000.

Ri'o de O'ro and Ad'rar, Span. possession, W. Africa, extending from Cape Bojador along Atlantic Ocean to Cape Blanco (400 m.); occupies strip of W. Sahara (average breadth, 170 m.); fishing. Area, 109,200 sq. m.; pop. *c.* 100,000 (including 500 Europeans).

Rio Grande del Norte (*rē'ō gran'dā del nor'tā*), riv., N. America; rises in mountains of southern Colorado, flows S. and S.E. through New Mexico, and thence south-eastward between Texas and Mexico to Gulf of Mexico; owing to silting in lower part of its course it is of little use for navigation; is much used for irrigation.

Rio Grande do Norte (*rē'ō grän'dā dō nor'tā*), state, N.E. Brazil, S. America; lies behind Cape San Roque; interior mountainous; cattle raising; sugar, cotton, cereals, salt; rly. to Pernambuco from Natal (cap.). Area, 20,231 sq. m.; pop. (est.) 667,000.

Rio Grande do Sul (*rē'ō gran'dā dō sool*). (1) Most southerly state, Brazil, lying between Atlantic and Uruguay R.; plateau in N., grass-covered plains in S. Soil is fertile; pastures of S. and S.W. given up to rearing of cattle, horses, and sheep, the principal exports being hides, horse-hair, bones, tallow, and preserved meat. Cereals, vegetables, fruit, coffee, and sugar-cane are grown. Minerals include copper, iron, and gold. Chief tns., Porto Alegre and Rio Grande do Sul. Area, 91,310 sq. m.; pop. 2,183,000. (2) Or RIO GRANDE, seapt. in above, Brazil, at entrance to Lagos do Patos; wireless station; extensive harbour works; cloth, rugs, leather, and beer; exports hides, dried beef, wool, and hair. Pop. 53,000.

Rio Muni. See SPANISH GUINEA.

Rio Negro (*rē'ō nā'grō*). (1) Terr. of Argentine Republic, forming part of Patagonia; bounded on N. by Rio Colorado, E. by Atlantic Ocean, S. by Chubut, W. by Chile; soil is generally fertile; leading industry is stock raising. Cap. Viedma. Area, 79,805 sq. m.; pop. 42,000. (2) L. bk. trib. of R. Amazon, S. America; rises as R. Guainia in S.E. Colombia, between which and Venezuela it forms boundary before flowing S. into Brazil; enters R. Amazon 12 m. below Manaos; in upper course Cassiquiare trib. links Rio Negro with Orinoco R.; navigable for steamers to Santa Isabel, 420 m. above Manaos. Length, *c.* 1,350 m.

Rio Tin'to, tn., S. Spain, 50 m. N.N.E. of its port, Huelva; in rich copper-mining dist. worked since Phœnician and Roman times. Pop. 10,000.

Rip'ley, mkt. tn., Derbyshire, England, 10 m. N. of Derby; agricultural machinery; ironworks and collieries. Pop. 13,400.

Rip'on, munic. bor., W. Riding, Yorks, England, on R. Ure, 30 m. N. of Leeds; cathedral (12th and 13th centuries); leather goods. Pop. 8,600.

Ris'ca, urb. dist., Monmouthshire, England, on R. Ebbw, 6½ m. N.W. of Newport; collieries. Pop. 16,600.

Rish'ton, urb. dist., Lancs, England, 3 m. N.E. of Blackburn, on Leeds and Liverpool Canal; cotton and paper mills. Pop. 6,600.

Rive-de-Gier (*rēv-de-zhē-ār'*), tn., Loire, France, 13 m. N.E. of St. Etienne; coal-mining centre; iron, steel, and glass works; steam-engines and silk. Pop. 16,000.

Riverin'a, tract of pastoral country, New South Wales, between rivers Lachlan-Murrumbidgee and Murray; important sheep-farming area; soil is fertile, producing much wheat and fruit; agriculture is being steadily developed by irrigation; minerals include gold and coal. Chief towns are Albury and Wagga Wagga. Area, *c.* 26,600 sq. m.; pop. *c.* 71,000.

Riv'erside, city, California, U.S.A., 50 m. E. by S. of Los Angeles; residential city; grain, dairy produce, and poultry; state horticultural experiment station; oranges and lemons. Pop. 31,000.

Riviera (*rē-vē-ā'ra*), narrow strip of coast on Gulf of Genoa, between Nice and Spezia; mild winters and fine scenery make it celebrated holiday resort. Towns include Pegli, San Remo, Ospedaletti, Bordighera, Mentone, Monte Carlo, Monaco, and Nice. Vegetation luxuriant and even subtropical.

Riyadh (*rē-ād'*), city, Nejd, Arabia; situated on oasis of same name; cap. of Nejd. Pop. *c.* 30,000.

Roanne (*rō-ān'*), tn., Loire, France, at head of navigation on R. Loire, 54 m. N.W. of Lyons; transit trade; cotton, woollen, and silk manufactures. Pop. 36,000.

Roanoke (*rō-an-ōk'*), city, Virginia, U.S.A., 175 m. W.S.W. of Richmond; in valley between Blue Mts. and Alleghanies; railway repair shops, bridge and structural ironworks, smelters. Pop. 69,000.

Robin Hood's Bay, fishing tn. and seaside resort, N. Riding, Yorks, on lofty cliffs encircling fine bay, 5 m. S.E. of Whitby.

Roch'dale, co. bor., Lancs, England, 11 m. N.E. of Manchester; woollens, cottons, plush velvet; ironworks and machine factories. Pop. 90,300.

Rochefort (*rōsh-fōr'*), tn., Charente-Inférieure, France, on R. Charente, 20 m. S.S.E. of La Rochelle; shipbuilding and cannon founding, manufacture of bricks and tiles; trade in salt, timber, oysters, and colonial wares. Pop. 24,000.

Rochelle, LA. See LA ROCHELLE.

Roch'ester. (1) Seapt., Kent, England, on R. Medway; continuous with Chatham on E., and opposite Strood; agricultural implements; brick and cement works, oil mills, and oyster fisheries. Cathedral founded by Ethelbert *c.* 604. Many associations with Dickens. Pop. 31,200. (2) City, New York, U.S.A., 6 m. S. of Lake Ontario, on Genesee R. River cuts gorge through centre of city; three falls within city limits. Imposing city buildings; univ.; water-power and flour-milling centre; electrical machinery and tools, photographic materials; nursery centre for fruit and ornamental trees. Pop. 325,000.

Roch'ford, tn., Essex, England, 3 m. N. of Southend; agricultural trade. Pop. 2,100.

Rock'ford, city, Illinois, U.S.A., 82 m. N.W. of Chicago, on both sides of Rock R.; furniture, milling tools, lathes, farm machinery, bolts and locks, watches, woollens. Pop. 86,000.

Rockhamp'ton, seapt., Queensland, Australia, on Fitzroy R., 42 m. from mouth. Gold, silver, copper, coal, iron, and precious stones are mined; meat preserving. Pop. 30,000.

Rock Island, city, Illinois, U.S.A., 180 m. S.W. of Chicago, on Mississippi R. Arsenal with extensive workshops and armoury. Lumber products, agricultural implements. Coal mined in vicinity. Pop. 39,000.

Rocky Mountains, great complex system of parallel mountain ranges in N. America; extends from Alaska to Mexico; name strictly applies only to most easterly of Cordilleran ranges, other ranges being known as Selkirk Mts. and Coast Range in British Columbia, Cascade Range and Sierra Nevada in U.S.A.; highest peaks are in Alaska—Mt. M'Kinley (20,300 ft.), Mt. St. Elias (18,100 ft.); many peaks exceed 14,000 ft.; system is source of almost all the large rivers of N. America; great cañons cut across outer barriers by the main rivers, most notable is Grand Cañon of the Colorado; numerous glaciers, chiefly in Canada and Alaska; best known passes (Yellowhead, Kicking Horse, Crow's Nest, Lewis and Clark's, Hagerman, Marshall) are traversed by the great transcontinental railway lines. Chief mineral resources are gold, silver, lead, copper, coal; as a rule, agriculture is profitable only in the valleys capable of irrigation; higher valleys and mountain slopes are grazing lands of great value; western ranges are heavily timbered. First formal exploration was by Lewis and Clark in 1804, and since 1840 numerous expeditions have been organized.

Rodez (*rō-dā'*), chief tn., Aveyron, S. France, on R. Aveyron, 85 m. N.W. of Montpellier; on high river bluff crowned by a Gothic cathedral (1274–1535); 15th and 16th cent. houses; woollens, serge, and straw hats; Roman aqueduct. Pop. 11,000.

Rodos'to, tn., Turkey, on European side of Sea of Marmara, 80 m. W. of Constantinople; excellent roadstead; canary seed, grain, silkworms, vegetables, and grapes. Pop. 35,000.

Rodriguez (*rō-drē'gāz*), Brit. isl., Indian Ocean, 370 m. E. of Mauritius, of which it is a dependency. Very fertile; grain, sugar, rice, cotton, coffee, tobacco, fruits, and woods. Station of 'All-British' cable between S. Africa and Australia. Area, 42 sq. m.; pop. 7.000.

Roermond (*roor'mont*), tn., Holland, on R. Maas, 29 m. N.N.E. of Maastricht; 13th cent. church; woollens, cottons, silks, paper, beer. Pop. 17,000.

Roeskilde. See ROSKILDE.

Rohilkhand', div. of United Provinces, India, having Ganges on W. and S., and Himalayas on N. and N.E.

Chief tn., Bareilly. Area, 10,828 sq. m.; pop. 5,200,000.

Roh'tak, tn., Punjab, India, 42 m. N.W. of Delhi; cotton turbans. Pop. 25,000.

Român, tn., Romania, 35 m. S.W. of Jassy; famous cathedral (1541); fine bridge; seat of Gr. bishop. Pop. 25,000.

Roman'ia, kingdom, S.E. Europe; bounded N. by Czechoslovakia, Poland, and Ukraine, E. by Black Sea, S. by Bulgaria, W. by Yugoslavia and Hungary; surface rises from plain of R. Danube to Carpathian Mts.; includes Moldavian valley, highlands of Bukovina, Dobruja steppe, the low-lying dist. of Bessarabia, between the Dniester and Prut rivers, and Transylvania W. of Carpathian Mts. Drainage is to R. Danube, which forms S. frontier for part of its course; chief tribs. are Muresul (Maros), Oltul, Siret (Sereth), and Prut; R. Danube is navigable, the Sulina distributary being dredged to the Black Sea; navigation impeded by ice in winter, and by low water in summer. Climate extreme; mean annual rainfall is *c.* 25 in. Agriculture is very important; chief grain crops are wheat, maize, barley, oats, rye, and millet; other products are sugar, tobacco, flax, hemp, fruit (including grapes). Pastoral occupations are also largely followed. Forests cover *c.* 17,000,000 acres, resinous woods and beech predominating. Carpathians and Transylvania are rich in minerals; petroleum, coal, iron, copper, and salt are worked, and the mining industry is being rapidly developed. Chief industries are petroleum refining, flour milling, brewing, and distilling. Chief tns., Bucharest (cap.), Chisinau, Cernauti, Ismail, Jassy, Galatz, and Timisoara. Area, 122,282 sq. m.; pop. 17,400,000.

Romans (*ro-mon'*), tn., Drome, S. France, on R. Isère; bootmaking, distilling, oil refining. Pop. 15,000.

Rome. (1) Famous city, seat of the papal court, cap. of Italy, on R. Tiber, 15 m. from its mouth; noted for its vast ruins and glorious monuments. R. Tiber is spanned by twelve bridges, most of them of anc. origin. Rome was not only the cap. of the vast Roman Empire, but was also for centuries the great religious centre of the world, and is still the headquarters of the Roman Catholic Church. The cathedral of St. Peter's is the largest church in the world. Other interesting churches are San Giovanni, San Paolo, San Lorenzo, Santa Maria Maggiore (one of the oldest churches in Rome, containing magnificent frescoes), Santa Maria del Popolo (with chapel by Raphael), the Gesù or Jesuit Church, containing the tomb of Ignatius Loyola, and Santa Maria del Rotonda (the anc. Pantheon). Among the great palaces are the Vatican (residence of the Pope), and the Quirinal (residence of the king). Others are the Lateran (also belonging to the Pope), with a large sculpture gallery, a picture gallery, and museum of Christian antiquities; Palazzo di Venezia, Palazzo Borghese, and the villas Medici and Borghese. Among noteworthy modern buildings are the famous national library, the Biblioteca Nazionale Centrale Vittorio Emanuele (founded 1875; 850,000 vols.). Many remains of anc. Rome—the Pantheon; Roman forum; temples of Concord, Vespasian, and Saturn; Carcer Mamertinus, said to have been the prison of St. Peter; Cloaca Maxima; temples of Castor and Pollux and of Vesta; Arch of Titus, with sculptures illustrating the capture of Jerusalem and showing the seven-branched golden candlestick; and the Colosseum, a circus built A.D. 80 by Titus, capable of seating 50,000 spectators, and with a circuit of 573 yds. No manufactures of importance are carried on in Rome. Since 1929 the Pope has been recognized as full and independent sovereign of the Holy See in the City of the Vatican, that part of Rome comprising the Vatican and Lateran palaces with their grounds, and the villa of Castel Gandolfo. Pop. *c.* 900,000. (2) City, New York, U.S.A., on Mohawk R.; manufacturing centre; brass and copper works. Pop. 32,000. (3) City, Georgia, U.S.A., 60 m. N.W. of Atlanta, at head of Coosa R.; cotton mills and presses, mining machinery. Pop. 13,000.

Romford (*rum'furd*), mkt. tn., Essex, England, 12 m. N.E. of London; iron-works and electrical engineering. Pop. 35,900.

Romiley, par. in urb. dist. of Bredbury and Romiley, Cheshire, England, 3 m. N.E. of Stockport; cotton industries; hat making. Pop. (par.) 3,810; (urb. dist.) 9,200.

Romney (*rum'ni*), NEW, tn., s. Kent, England; was one of Cinque ports; now more than a mile from the sea; charters, etc., of Cinque ports kept here; sheep fairs. Pop. 1,600. Old Romney lies 2 m. w. by N.

Roms'dal, valley of R. Rauma, Norway; celebrated for its scenery; notable peaks, Romsdalshorn (5,100 ft.), Troldtinder (6,010 ft.); Virmafos waterfall nearly 1,000 ft. high; Romsdal Fjord on w. coast.

Romsey (*rum'zi*), mkt. tn., Hants, England, 10 m. N.W. of Southampton; fine Norman church; manufactures paper and leather. Pop. 4,900.

Ronaldsay (*ron'al-sā*). (1) NORTH, most northerly of Orkney Islands, Scotland, separated from Sanday by the dangerous N. Ronaldsay Firth; N. Ronaldsay lighthouse 140 ft. high; surface low and flat. Area, 4 sq. m.; pop. 350. (2) SOUTH, most southerly of Orkney Islands, Scotland, 6 m. N.N.E. of Dunscansby Head; well cultivated. Area (with small adjacent islands), 18 sq. m.; pop. 1,500.

Roncesvalles (*ron-thes-val'yez*; French *rōns-väl*), vil. in Pyrenees, Navarre, Spain; abbey and 13th cent. church; near is the famous pass where rearguard of Charlemagne's army was defeated, and Roland was killed (778).

Ron'da, tn., s. Spain, on R. Guadiaro, 44 m. w. of Malaga; old tn. separated from new by deep gorge; Roman and Moorish remains; famous bull-fights; soap, hats, leather, wines. Pop. 30,000.

Roor'kee, tn., United Provinces, India, 55 m. N. of Meerut; has Thomason Engineering Coll. Pop. 17,000.

Ror'schach, wat.-pl., St. Gall, Switzerland, on Lake Constance; grain, lace. Pop. 11,000.

Ro'sa, MONTE, mt. mass between Switzerland and Italy, S.E. of Zermatt; has ten peaks, highest Dufourspitze (15,217 ft.).

Rosar'io, tn., Santa Fé, Argentina, S. America, on R. Paraná; terminus of four railways; commercial centre; exports grain and hides; sugar refineries, flour mills, and breweries. Pop. 265,000.

Roscom'mon. (1) Inland co., Connaught, I.F.S., on central limestone plain; surface level or undulating; hills on N. (Mt. Cashel, 1,377 ft.); chief rivs.: Shannon (with loughs Allen, Boderg, and Ree) and Suck; agriculture; extensive grazing on 'Plain of Boyle'; some coal, iron, and marble; interesting antiquities. Area, 950 sq. m.; pop. 83,600. (2) Co. tn. of above; cattle trade; mediæval castle. Pop. 1,800.

Roscrea (*ros-crā'*), mkt. tn., N. Tipperary, I.F.S.; church part of 11th cent. abbey; flour mills, agricultural centre. Pop. 2,800.

Roseneath', vil. and par., Dumbartonshire, Scotland, on Gareloch; has Princess Louise Home for Invalid Soldiers; castle a seat of Duke of Argyll. Pop. (par.) 2,700.

Ros'enheim, wat.-pl., Bavaria, Germany, on R. Inn, 40 m. S.E. of Munich; saline and sulphur baths; cement and salt works. Pop. 18,000.

Roset'ta, tn., Egypt, at one of the mouths of R. Nile; formerly a seaport, but now of little importance; rice market. The Rosetta stone, discovered in 1799, furnished key to interpretation of Egyptian hieroglyphics. Pop. 27,000.

Roskilde (*ros'kēl-de*), or ROESKILDE, tn., isl. of Zealand, Denmark, on Roskilde Fjord, 20 m. w. of Copenhagen;

cap. of Denmark before 1443; has 11th cent. cathedral. Pop. 13,000.

Ros'lin, or ROSSLYN, vil. and par., Midlothian, Scotland, on riv. N. Esk, 6 m. s. of Edinburgh; has ruined castle and highly decorated 15th cent. chapel with famous ''Prentice Pillar'; bleach fields, gunpowder factory. Pop. 1,100.

Ross, mkt. tn., Herefordshire, England, on R. Wye; corn mills, agricultural implement works. Pop. 4,700.

Ross and Crom'arty, co., Scotland, stretching across Scotland from Moray Firth on E. and including Lewis in Outer Hebrides; two counties united (1889); surface wild and mountainous, dotted with lakes, of which largest is Loch Maree (13 m. long, with thirty islands); chief mountain peaks, Carn Eige (3,877 ft.), Mam Soul, Ben Attow (near which are Falls of Glomach, 370 ft.), Ben Wyvis. Coasts much indented, having Dornoch Firth, Cromarty Firth, and Beauly Firth on E., and Lochs Broom, Ewe, Gair, Torridon, Carron, and Alsh on W.; industries: agriculture (mainly in Black Isle dist. between Dornoch and Cromarty Firths), sheep farming, salmon and sea fishing, and distilling. Co. tn., Dingwall. Area, 3,089 sq. m.; pop. 62,800.

Rossan'o, city, Italy, on S. coast of Gulf of Taranto; archiepisc. see; cathedral and castle; olive oil and silk manufactures; marble and alabaster quarries. Pop. 16,000.

Rosslare (*ros-lār'*), vil. and par., Wexford, I.F.S., 6 m. S.E. of Wexford; packet station for steamers from Fishguard, Wales (55 m.). Pop. (par.) 670.

Rosstre'vor, seaport and wat.-pl., co. Down, N. Ireland, in lee of Mourne Mts. Pop. 750.

Ros'tock, tn., Mecklenburg-Schwerin, Germany, on R. Warnow; important Baltic port; univ. (1419), 12th cent. church (St. Peter's), and palace; commercial centre; fisheries; manufactures machinery, sugar, chemicals; exports grain. Pop. 70,000.

Rostov', tn., Yaroslav prov., Russia, 120 m. N.E. of Moscow; church (1230); fisheries, market gardens; manufactures textiles, tallow products, flour. Pop. 20,000.

Rostov-on-Don, tn. and port, N. Caucasian Area, U.S.S.R., at head of delta of R. Don; exports wheat, linen, and wool; manufactures include flour, ropes, tobacco, boots and shoes; important fisheries. Pop. 233,000.

Rosyth (*rō-sith'*), suburb of Dunfermline, Fife, Scotland; naval base of great importance during Great War; dockyard was closed in 1925.

Roth'erham, co. bor. and mkt. tn., W. Riding, Yorks, England, on R. Don; iron, steel, brass, railway wagon and glass works; sawmills, breweries, coal. Pop. 69,700.

Roth'erhithe, dist., S.E. London, England, on R. Thames; contains Surrey commercial docks; Thames Tunnel between Rotherhithe and Ratcliff (opened 1908) is 4,865 ft. long, of which 1,400 ft. are under the river.

Rothesay (*roth'sā*), royal burgh and wat.-pl., Isle of Bute, Scotland; headquarters of Royal Northern Yacht Club; gives title of duke to heir-apparent to the throne. Pop. 9,300.

Roth'well. (1) Urb. dist., W. Riding, Yorks, England, 4 m. S.E. of Leeds; extensive collieries; manufactures ropes, matches. Pop. 15,600. (2) Or ROWELL, urb. dist., Northants, England, 4 m. N.W. of Kettering; makes boots and shoes, and clothing. Pop. 4,500.

Rotorua (*rō-tō-roo'a*), tn., North Island, New Zealand, on S.W. shore of lake of same name; hot springs; great summer resort. Pop. 4,000.

Rot'terdam, chief seaport and commercial tn. of Holland, on R. Maas, 20 m. from North Sea; about 70 per cent. of trade of Netherlands and about 80 per cent. of R. Rhine traffic passes through the town; transit trade in grain, timber, metals, hardware, petroleum, drugs and chemicals, rice, coffee, tobacco, and palm kernels; industries include shipbuilding, making of furniture, clocks, chocolate, chemical products, distilling and brewing; great emigration port. Pop. 563,000.

Roubaix (*roo-bā'*), tn., Nord, France, 6 m. N.E. of Lille; woollen, cotton, and silk goods; connected with the Schelde by canal. Pop. 114,000.

Rouen (*rwan*), tn., cap. of Seine-Inférieure, France, on R. Seine, which is navigable up to that point; important railway centre and chief cotton port of France; industries include spinning and weaving of cottons, velvets, woollens, linens, mixed silk, machinery, shipbuilding, refining of petroleum, chemicals. Streets of old town are narrow and picturesque; contains some of finest churches in France. Was anc. cap. of Normandy. Pop. 116,000.

Roulers (*roo-lār'*), tn., W. Flanders, Belgium, 13 m. N.W. of Courtrai; linen and cotton goods, lace, and silk ribbons. Pop. 27,000.

Roumania. See ROMANIA.

Rou'yn, mining camp, N.W. Quebec, Canada, *c.* 35 m. S. of E. end of L. Abitibi; on branch of Canadian National Rly.; copper, zinc, gold; copper smelted at Noranda mine by hydro-electric power.

Rovereto (*rō-ver-ā'tō*), or ROVEREDO, tn., N. Italy, on R. Adige, 13 m. S.W. of Trent; paper, leather, silks, cottons. Pop. 14,000.

Rovigno (*rō-vēn'yō*), seaport, Istria, Italy, on E. of Gulf of Venice; wine, olives, and hazel nuts; tobacco; tunny and sardine fisheries. Pop. 11,000.

Rovigo (*rō-vē'gō*), tn., Italy, 28 m. S. of Padua; has remains of 10th cent. walls; beer, leather, wool, silk, linen, candles. Pop. 16,000.

Rov'no. See ROWNE.

Row. See RHU.

Row'ley Re'gis, urb. dist., Staffs, England, 5 m. W. of Birmingham; nails and chains; collieries, potteries. Pop. 41,200.

Rowne (*ruv'ne*), formerly ROVNO, tn., Poland, 150 m. S.E. of Brest-Litovsk; rly. jn.; agricultural centre; horses and cattle. Pop. 30,000.

Roxburghshire, border co., Scotland, including Teviotdale and parts of Tweeddale and Liddesdale; hilly in S.; highest points: Auchopecairn (2,382 ft.), Ruberslaw, Blacklaw, and the three Eildons, near Melrose; drained by R. Tweed, with tributaries Gala and Teviot and their tribs., and by R. Liddel; industries: farming, sheep rearing, woollen and tweed manufacture; monastic remains at Jedburgh, Kelso, and Melrose; noted border keeps, including Branxholm, Harden, and Hermitage; 'Watling Street' runs through county. Chief tns.: Jedburgh (co. town), Hawick, Kelso, and Melrose. Area, 666 sq. m.; pop. 45,800.

Roy'ston, urb. dist. and mkt. tn., Herts, England, 12½ m. N.E. of Hitchin, on Roman Icknield Way; church belonged to 12th cent. Augustinian priory. Pop. 3,800. (2) Urb. dist., W. Riding, Yorks, England, 4 m. N. of Barnsley; collieries. Pop. 7,200.

Roy'ton, tn., Lancashire, England, 2 m. N. of Oldham; cotton factories. Pop. 16,700.

R.S.F.S.R. See under RUSSIA.

Ruabon (*roo-ă'bon*), tn., Denbighshire, Wales, on R. Dee; coal mines, iron, chemicals, bricks. Pop. 3,300.

Rüdesheim (*roo'des-hīm*), tn., Hesse-Nassau, Prussia, on R. Rhine opposite Bingen; wines. Pop. 4,000.

Ru'dolf, or BASSO-NAROK, lake, Africa, in Anglo-Egyptian Sudan, Abyssinia, Uganda, and Kenya, 185 m. long (N. to S.) and over 35 m. wide; in African Rift Valley. Alt. 1,200 ft.

Ru'dolstadt, tn., Thuringia, Germany, 18 m. S. of Weimar, on R. Sale; machinery, leather, porcelain, chemicals; tourist resort. Pop. 16,000.

Rueil (*roo-āl'*), tn., Seine-et-Oise, France, 6 m. W. of Paris, at foot of Mont Valérien; photographic materials; château of Malmaison near by. Pop. 15,000.

Rufiji (*roo-fē'jē*), riv., Tanganyika, E. Africa, rises in Livingstone Mts., breaks through Tundusi Mts., forming

Pangani rapids, below which it is navigable for small craft; enters Indian Ocean, forming delta 50 m. wide.

Rug'by, tn., Warwickshire, England, on the R. Avon; famous public school; rly. centre; cattle markets, electrical and engineering works; hunting centre; important wireless transmitting station. Pop. 23,800.

Rugeley (*rooj'li*), urb. dist., Staffs, England, on R. Trent, 8 m. S.E. of Stafford; coal mines, iron foundries, tanneries, corn mills. Pop. 5,300.

Rü'gen, isl. and summer resort, Pomerania, Prussia, in Baltic Sea; separated from mainland by Strela Sund; well-wooded, fertile; chief industry, herring fishing. Cap. Bergen. Area, 373 sq. m.; pop. *c.* 40,000.

Ruhr (*roor*), riv., W. Prussia, flows N. and W. to R. Rhine, 14 m. N. of Düsseldorf; length, 145 m. Flows through one of richest coal, iron, and steel districts in the world. Occupied by French (1923–25) as guarantee for payment of reparations by Germany after Great War. Chief tns. in dist.: Düsseldorf, Elberfeld, Barmen, Essen, Dortmund, Bochum, Mühlheim.

Ruislip Northwood (*rī'slip*), urb. dist., Middlesex, England, 4 m. W. of Harrow; part of Greater London. Pop. 16,000.

Rum, or RHUM, isl., Inner Hebrides, Inverness-shire, Scotland; separated from Skye by Cuillin Sound; deer forest; mountainous; highest point, 2,667 ft. Area, 42 sq. m.; pop. 150.

Rumania. See ROMANIA.

Run'corn, canal port on the Manchester Ship Canal and R. Mersey, Cheshire, England; Bridgewater Canal here descends to Mersey by locks; iron foundries, tanneries, roperies, and chemical works. Pop. 18,200.

Run'nymede, meadow, with racecourse, W. Surrey, England, on r. bk. of Thames, 2 m. W. of Staines; here King John is reputed to have sealed Magna Charta.

Ruschuk (*roos-chook*), tn., Bulgaria, on R. Danube; manufactures sugar, tobacco, soap, beer, bricks, and pottery. Pop. 46,000.

Rush'den, urb. dist., Northants, England, 1¼ m. S. of Higham Ferrers; shoemaking industry. Pop. 14,200.

Russia (*rush'ya*), popular name for certain European terr. of U.S.S.R.; bounded N. by Arctic Ocean, E. by Ural Mts., S. by Caspian Sea, Transcaucasia, Black Sea, and Ukraine, W. by White Russia, Latvia, Estonia, and Finland. This area represents the European territory of the Russian Socialist Federal Soviet Republic (R.S.F.S.R.). Surface is an undulating plain; highest point (1,100 ft.) in Valdai Hills, the source of many rivers; plain rises to Ural Mts. in E., Caucasus Mts. in S.; drained to Caspian Sea by Ural and Volga river systems; to Black Sea by Rs. Don and Dnieper; to Baltic by S. Dvina, Neva, etc.; to Arctic by Rs. Onega, N. Dvina, and Pechora. Climate continental, with hot summers and severe winters. In N. rivers are frozen for over 6 months, in centre for 3½ to 4½, and in S. for 2½ to 4. Rainfall varies from 25 in. along Baltic to 6 in. at N. end of Caspian; rain falls chiefly in summer.

Tundras border the Arctic Ocean; S. of this belt and extending round the Baltic Sea are great forests; flax is grown round the Baltic. S. of the forest comes the region of 'black earth,' one of the richest soils in the world, which stretches from the R. Dniester to the Ural Mts. The Black Sea is surrounded by pasture, arable land, and vineyards; the dist. round the Caspian, known as the Steppes, is chiefly pastoral, with horse breeding and sheep and cattle rearing. Probably *c.* 70 per cent. of the population is engaged in agriculture. The chief agricultural products are cereals—wheat, rye, barley, oats—sugar-beet, flax, tobacco, potatoes, and maize. Russia is exceedingly rich in minerals; gold, platinum, silver, lead, zinc, copper, iron, coal, naphtha, and salt are increasingly mined. Wood is exported largely, chiefly fir, pine, oak, larch, elm, and silver birch. There are sawmills, manufactures of furniture, textiles, iron and steel, paper, leather, etc. The rivers are frozen in winter and low in summer, but excellent highways in spring and autumn. The Volga is connected with the Neva, and also with the N. Dvina, by a system of canals; the Dnieper is connected with the S. Dvina, and with the Niemen and the Vistula. Cap. of R.S.F.S.R. is Moscow. Area of European part of R.S.F.S.R., 1,541,530 sq. m.; pop. *c.* 89,000,000. See also UNION OF SOCIALIST SOVIET REPUBLICS.

Ruthe'nia, or CARPATHIAN RUTHENIA, prov., E. Czechoslovakia, on S. slopes of Carpathian Mts.; bounded N. by Poland, S. by Hungary and Romania; chief riv., Tisza; maize, oats, wheat; tobacco; vineyards; Ruthenians mainly illiterate peasants. Chief tns., Mukacevo, Uzhorod. Area, 4,886 sq. m.; pop. 683,500.

Ruth'erglen (locally *rug'len*), royal and munic. burgh, Lanarkshire, Scotland, adjoining Glasgow; collieries, ironworks, chemical works, paper mills. Pop. 25,200.

Ruthin (*roo'thin*), mkt. tn., Denbighshire, Wales, on R. Clwyd; mineral water works; small trade in agricultural produce and building materials. Pop. 2,900.

Rut'land. (1) Smallest co. of England; borders on Leicestershire, Lincolnshire, and Northamptonshire; drained by R. Welland; surface diversified by hills; considerable tracts of woodland; main industry agriculture; live-stock raised and cheese manufactured; stone quarries and iron mines. Co. town, Oakham. Area, 152 sq. m.; pop. 17,400. (2) City, Vermont, U.S.A., 85 m. N.E. of Albany; marble quarries; ironworks. Pop. 15,000.

Ruvo di Puglia (*roo'vo de pool'ya*), tn., S. Italy, 20 m. W. of Bari; 12th cent. cathedral; potteries. Pop. 24,000.

Ruwenzo'ri, or RUNSORO, nonvolcanic mountain mass, Central Africa between Ls. Edward and Albert. Discovered by Stanley (1888). Over twenty peaks are between 15,000 and 17,000 ft. in height, and snow-clad.

Ry'an, LOCH, sea loch, Wigtownshire, Scotland; forms a safe anchorage, 8 m. long, 1½ to 2 m. wide. At head of loch is Stranraer.

Ryazan (*rē-ä-zan'*), tn. and archiepisc. see, Russia, 150 m. S.E. of Moscow; distilleries; candles, malt, cotton stuffs, leather goods, and machinery. Pop. 49,000.

Rybinsk (*rib'insk*), tn. and episc. see, Yaroslav prov., central Russia; at head of steamer navigation on R. Volga; great agricultural trade; breweries, distilleries, rope works, flour mills, and shipyards. Pop. 54,000.

Ry'dal, par. and vil., in Lake District, Westmorland, England; contains Rydal Water, with Rydal Mount, the home of Wordsworth. Pop. (par.) 500.

Ryde (*rīd*), tn., Isle of Wight, England; wat.-pl.; overlooking Spithead; yachting centre. Pop. 10,500.

Rye (*rī*), tn., E. Sussex, England; one of the Cinque Ports; has a fine Norman and Early Eng. church; fishing and shipbuilding. Pop. 3,900.

Ry'hope, par. and vil., Durham, England, 3 m. S. of Sunderland; seabathing resort; coal mines in vicinity. Pop. (par.) 11,700.

Ry'ton, urb. dist., Durham, England, 6 m. W. of Newcastle; iron and steel; limestone quarries. Pop. 14,200.

Ryukyu Archipelago, formerly LIUKIU or LOOCHOO ISLANDS, group of Jap. islands stretching from Japan to Formosa; partly volcanic, partly coralline; mainly mountainous; sugar-cane is staple article of trade. Area, 935 sq. m.; pop. *c.* 455,000.

Rzeszów (*zhesh'uf*), tn., Poland, 90 m. W. of Lwow; horse fairs; agricultural centre. Pop. 25,000.

Rzhev, or RZHOV, tn., Russia, on R. Volga, 130 m. W. of Moscow; shipbuilding, breweries, and tanneries; silk and leather. Pop. 32,000.

S

Saale (*zä'la*), riv., Germany; trib. of R. Elbe; rises in Fichtelgebirge; navigable for 100 m. Chief tns. on banks, Jena and Halle. Length, 226 m.

Saalfeld (*zäl'felt*), tn., Thuringia, Germany, on R. Saale, 22 m. S. of Weimar; machinery, lithographs, cigars, beer; ochre and iron mines. Pop. 18,000.

Saar, or SARRE (*zär*), trib. of R. Moselle, France and Germany, rises in Vosges Mts., flows roughly N., joining R. Moselle above Trier; connected by Saar Canal with Marne-Rhone Canal. The valley has extensive coal and iron fields, and many manufactures; noted for its wines. See also SAAR TERRITORY.

Saarbrücken (*zär'brook-en*), chief tn., Saar Terr., on R. Saar; centre of important coal-mining dist.; ironworks; manufactures include glass, chemicals, tobacco, textiles, and leather. Pop. 125,000.

Saarburg. See SARREBOURG.

Saa're Maa, formerly OESEL, isl., Estonia, in Gulf of Riga, Baltic Sea; agricultural and forest industries; exports ponies, grain, potatoes, fish, spirits. Chief tn., Arensburg. Area, 1,010 sq. m.; pop. 60,000.

Saargemünd. See SARREGUEMINES.

Saarlouis (*zär'loo-ē*), tn., Saar Terr.; manufactures leather, porcelain, glass; coal mines in vicinity. Pop. 16,000.

Saar Territory, tract of country on Franco-German frontier, N. of Lorraine, in valley of R. Saar. By the Treaty of Versailles France secured the output of its coal mines as compensation for the destruction of her N.E. coalfields. Administered till 1935 by Commission responsible to League of Nations. Chief tn., Saarbrücken. Area, 726 sq. m.; pop. 790,000.

Saaz. See ZATEC.

Sabac (*shä'bats*), or SHABATZ, tn., Serbia, Yugoslavia, on R. Sava, 40 m. W. of Belgrade; exports grain, livestock, and prunes. Pop. 9,000.

Sabadell', Spain, on R. Ripoll, 10 m. N. of Barcelona; manufactures textiles, paper, flour; iron foundries and distilleries. Pop. 38,000.

Sabak'i, river, Kenya Colony, E. Africa; rises N. of Nairobi and enters Indian Ocean. Length, 400 m.

Sables d'Olonne (*säb-l dōl-on'*), LES, fishing port, Vendée, France, on Bay of Biscay; favourite wat.-pl.; sardine fishing and canning. Pop. 14,000.

Sacramen'to, cap., California, U.S.A., on Sacramento R.; two cathedrals; has Southern Pacific Rly. workshops; manufactures furniture, pottery, boxes; flour milling, ore smelting, meat packing, fruit canning. Pop. 94,000.

Sac'riston, eccles. par. and vil., Durham, England, 3½ m. N.W. of Durham; large coal mines. Pop. (par.) 8,400.

Sad'dleback, mt., Cumberland, England; near Skiddaw; alt. 2,847 ft.

Sad'dleworth, urb. dist., Yorks, England, on R. Tame, 12 m. S.W. of Huddersfield; manufactures woollen and cotton goods. Pop. 12,600.

Sad'o, isl., Sea of Japan, off W. coast of Honshu; hilly; gold and silver. Area, 336 sq. m.; pop. 115,000.

Sadowa. See HRADEC KRÁLOVÉ.

Safed' Koh, mt. range, on N.W. frontier of India, running parallel to and S. of R. Kabul. Sikaram (15,620 ft.) is highest point.

Saf'fron Wal'den, munic. bor., Essex, England, near R. Cam; anc. castle and church; grammar school (1623), training coll.; iron foundries, malting, brewing. Pop. 5,900.

Saf'i, port, Morocco, on Atlantic coast; exports grain, wool, hair. Pop. 27,000.

Sagaing (*sa-ga-ēng'*). (1) Dist., Burma, drained by R. Irrawaddy; wheat, rice, peas, and cotton are grown. Area, 1,825 sq. m.; pop. 327,000. (2) Cap. of above, 10 m. S.W. of Mandalay; anc. cap. of Burma. Pop. 12,000.

Sagan (*zä'gan*), tn., Silesia, Prussia, on Bober R., trib. of R. Oder, 45 m. N.W. of Leibnitz; manufactures cloth, woollen and cotton goods, porcelain, glass and bricks. Pop. 18,000.

Sag'inaw, city, Michigan, U.S.A., on R. Saginaw, 90 m. N.W. of Detroit; railway workshops, machinery, sawmills, beet sugar, furniture. Pop. 81,000.

Saguenay (*sag'ĕn-ā*), riv., Quebec, Canada, enters R. St. Lawrence at Tadoussac; majestic scenery; harnessed for power; length, 120 m.

Sahara (*sa-hä'ra*, or *sä'ha-ra*), great belt of desert, N. Africa, stretching E. from Atlantic Ocean to R. Nile, and S. from Atlas Mts. toward R. Niger and L. Chad. Practically whole region is in Fr. sphere of influence. In the centre are important plateaus, with Mts. Ahaggar, Tibesti, Tummo, and Air (Asben), covered with snow three months of the year, and reaching a height of 6,500–8,000 ft. In the valleys water is found below the surface. The Sahara is crossed by many caravan routes, which connect the oases; routes from Murzuk in Italian Libya to L. Chad, and from Morocco to Cairo via Tafilelt, are of particular importance. Motor-cars are being used on these routes. Vegetation scarce except in oases, where fig trees and date palms are principal trees. The camel is the chief animal used by the nomads; horses, cattle, and sheep are raised in many of the valleys. The inhabitants are chiefly Berbers, Tuaregs, Arabs, and Tibbus; all profess Mohammedanism. Trade in gold dust, dates, salt, soda, saltpetre, and ostrich feathers. Area (est.), 3,000,000 sq. m.; pop. (est.) 2,000,000.

Saharanpur', tn., United Provinces, India, 70 m. N. of Meerut; has botanical gardens; railway workshops and wood-carving establishments. Pop. 62,000.

Saida. See SIDON.

Saigon (*sī-gon'*), cap., Cochin-China, French Indo-China, on R. Saigon; important seapt.; rice, spices. Pop. 143,000.

Saima (*sī'mä*), LAKE, largest lake of Finland. Area, 502 sq. m.

St. Ag'nes, port, Cornwall, England, 8½ m. N.W. of Truro; mkt. tn. Pop. 4,000.

St. Al'bans, city, Herts, England; famous cathedral; manufacture of straw hats, brushes, silk; printing, brewing. Pop. 28,600.

St. Amand-les-Eaux (*san-tam-an'-lāz-ō'*), tn., Nord, France, at junction of Rs. Elnon and Scarpe, 8 m. N.W. of Valenciennes; ironfounding, porcelain, hosiery; sulphur and mud baths. Pop. 11,000.

St. And'rews, royal burgh and wat.-pl., Fife, Scotland, on North Sea; the 'Mecca' of golf. Industries include fishing and manufacture of golf balls and clubs. Univ. is oldest in Scotland (founded 1411). Ruined cathedral, and remains of church of St. Regulus. Pop. 8,300.

St. Anne's on the Sea, wt.-pl., Lancs, England. Now part of Lytham St. Anne's.

St. As'aph, city, Flintshire, Wales, in Vale of Clwyd; cathedral (13th cent.). Pop. 1,800.

St. Aus'tell, mkt. tn., Cornwall, England, near St. Austell Bay; china-clay works, pilchard fisheries; tin and copper mines in vicinity. Pop. 8,300.

St. Bernard Pass. See GREAT ST. BERNARD PASS and LITTLE ST. BERNARD PASS.

St. Bla'zey, par. and small tn., Cornwall, England, 4 m. N.E. of St. Austell; active trade connected with surrounding tin-mining dist. Pop. (par.) 3,000.

St. Bon'iface, city, Manitoba, Canada, on Red R., opposite Winnipeg, of which it is a suburb; French-speaking; one of oldest settlements in prov. Pop. 15,500.

St. Bos'wells, or LESSUDDEN, vil.

and summer resort, Roxburghshire, Scotland, 3 m. S.E. of Melrose; Dryburgh Abbey. Pop. 580.

St. Brieuc (*san brē-oo'*), tn., Côtes-du-Nord, France, 35 m. W. of St. Malo; industries include wool, timber, iron, steel, agricultural implements. Pop. 24,000.

St. Cath'erines, city, Ontario, Canada, on Welland Canal; in fruit region; mineral springs; iron manufactures. Pop. 20,000.

St. Chamond (*san shä-mon'*), tn., Loire, France, on R. Gier, 6 m. N.E. of St. Etienne; coal mines; silk ribbon manufacture. Pop. 15,000.

St. Christopher. See ST. KITTS.

St. Clair, LAKE, part of system of Great Lakes, Canada, receiving St. Clair R. from L. Huron and discharging by Detroit R. into L. Erie; on international boundary; several islands; alt. 576 ft. Area, 460 sq. m.

St. Claude (*san klōd'*), tn., Jura, E. France, on R. Bienne; cathedral; briar pipes, chessmen, and other hardwood articles. Pop. 12,000.

St. Cloud. (1) (*san kloo'*) Tn., Seine-et-Oise, France, on R. Seine, 10 m. W. of Paris; in park is famous Sèvres porcelain factory. Pop. 13,000. (2) Tn., Minnesota, U.S.A., on R. Mississippi, 60 m. N.W. of Minneapolis; butter and grain produced in vicinity. Pop. 16,000.

St. Columb Major (*cul'lum*), mkt. tn., Cornwall, England, 14½ m. N.E. of Truro; anc. stone circle of the Nine Maidens. Pop. 2,500.

St. Columb Minor, par. and vil., Cornwall, England, 5 m. W. of above; annual stock fair. Pop. (par.) 1,400.

St. Cyr (*san sēr*), tn., France, 2½ m. W. of Versailles; famous military school. Pop. 4,000.

St. Denis (*san de-nē'*). (1) Tn., Seine, France, on R. Seine, 4 m. N. of Paris; its abbey church (7th century) was burial-place of kings of France; chemicals, machinery, spirits, soap, etc. Pop. 80,000. (2) Cap. of French isl. of Réunion, Indian Ocean; cathedral. Pop. 24,000.

St. Dié (*san dē-ā'*), tn., Vosges, France, 25 m. E. of Epinal; cathedral; iron and copper founding, machinery, woodwork, hosiery, bleaching. Pop. 15,000.

St. Dizier (*san de-zē-ā'*), tn., Haute-Marne, France, on R. Marne; ironworks, boat building. Pop. 15,000.

St. Domingo. See HAITI; SANTO DOMINGO.

Sainte-Croix (*krwa*), or SANTA CRUZ, isl., W. Indies, belonging to U.S.A.; one of Virgin Islands; sugar, rum. Cap. Christiansted. Area, 84 sq. m.; pop. 20,000.

St. Eli'as, MOUNT, volcanic mt., N. America, part of range between Alaska and Canada; perpetually snow-covered; at foot is Malaspina Glacier; alt. 18,017 ft.

Saintes (*sant*), tn., Charente-Inférieure, France, on R. Charente; agricultural machinery and earthenware; cathedral. Pop. 16,000.

St. Etienne (*san-tā-tē-en'*), cap., Loire, France, on R. Furens; on coal and iron field; firearms, machinery, ribbons, velvets, dyeing, distilling; school of mining. Pop. 194,000.

St. Fil'lans, vil., Perthshire, Scotland, at E. end of Loch Earn; a summer resort. Pop. 300.

St. Gallen (French *St. Gall*). (1) Canton, Switzerland, bordering R. Rhine and L. Constance; mountainous, with several glaciers; some small low-lying plains; chief industries, cattle rearing, cotton spinning, embroidery and lace manufacture. Area, 785 sq. m.; pop. 301,000. (2) Cap. of above, in valley of R. Steinach, 6 m. from L. Constance; manufactures embroidery and cotton goods; cathedral; large library. Pop. 65,000.

Saint-Germain-en-Laye (*san-zher-man-on-lā'*), tn., Seine-et-Oise, France, 13 m. W. of Paris, on R. Seine; summer resort; fine forest; historic castle; manufactures cottons and woollens. Pop. 19,000.

St. Ger'mans, small tn., Cornwall, England, 7 m. W. of Plymouth, on an arm of Plymouth Sound; exports coal; fisheries. Pop. 2,000.

St. Gotthard Pass (*san go-tär'*), pass, Alps, Switzerland, between upper valleys of Rs. Reuss and Ticino; alt. 6,936 ft.; motor and railway route across Alps to Italy; rly. tunnel over 9 m. long.

St. Hele'na, British isl., S. Atlantic, 1,200 m. off w. coast of Africa; of volcanic origin; mountainous and rocky; highest point, 2,700 ft.; healthy climate; coaling and cable station; cattle, fruit, vegetables, flax, lace; scene of Napoleon's exile at Longwood (1815–21). Cap. and port, Jamestown. Area, 47 sq. m.; pop. 3,700.

St. Hel'ens. (1) Co. bor., Lancs, England, 12 m. N.E. of Liverpool; important glass manufacture; foundries, chemical works, copper-smelting works, pottery. Pop. 106,800. (2) Urb. dist., Isle of Wight, England, 4 m. S.E. of Ryde; wat.-pl. Pop. 5,500.

St. Helier (*hĕl'yer*), cap., Jersey, Channel Islands, on St. Aubin's Bay; seapt., wat.-pl. Pop. 26,000.

St. Hyacinthe (*sant ē-ä-sant*), tn., Quebec, Canada, on R. Yamaska, 32 m. N.E. of Montreal; agricultural machinery, woollens, leather, organs. Pop. 11,000.

St. Ing'bert, tn., Saar Terr., 6 m. N.E. of Saarbrücken; coal mines, iron and steel works; manufactures glass, machinery, leather, soap. Pop. 17,000.

St. Ives (*īvz*). (1) Munic. bor. and winter resort, Cornwall, England, on St. Ives Bay; boat building; pilchard, herring, and mackerel fisheries. Pop. 6,700. (2) Munic. bor., Hunts, England, on R. Ouse; cattle market; agricultural produce. Pop. 2,700.

Saint John, largest city and port, New Brunswick, Canada, on Bay of Fundy, at mouth of R. St. John; manufactures cottons, woollens, tools, machinery, paper; lumber trade; grain elevators for winter shipment of wheat; sugar refinery; valuable fisheries; harbour ice-free all year. Pop. 47,000.

St. John, riv., New Brunswick, Canada, rising in two branches, one in Maine, U.S.A., and one in Quebec; notable reversing falls at mouth; enters Bay of Fundy; navigable for 86 m. Length, 450 m.

St. John's. (1) Cap. Newfoundland; fine harbour, two cathedrals; shipping and fisheries; exports fish, esp. cod; manufactures seal oil; foundries, tanneries. Pop. 41,000. (2) Tn., Quebec, Canada, on R. Richelieu, 21 m. S.E. of Montreal; manufactures flour, pottery, silk, sewing machines. Pop. 7,700. (3) Cap. of Antigua, Brit. W. Indies. Pop. 8,000.

St. Joseph. (1) City, Missouri, U.S.A., on Missouri R., 50 m. N.N.W. of Kansas City; important railway centre; in rich agricultural region; manufactures blankets, clothing, patent foods, agricultural implements; meat packing. Pop. 81,000. (2) Tn., s.w. Michigan, U.S.A., on L. Michigan; health resort, with mineral springs; fruit farms. Pop. 10,000.

St. Julien, vil., France, on R. Gironde, 35 m. N. of Bordeaux; noted for its claret.

St. Junien (*san zhoo-nē-än'*), tn., Haute-Vienne, France, 18 m. N.W. of Limoges; gloves and leather goods. Pop. 11,000.

St. Just, mkt. tn. and urb. dist., Cornwall, England, 7 m. w. of Penzance; tin and copper mine region. Pop. 4,400.

St. Kil'da. (1) Rocky isl., largest of small group, Outer Hebrides, Scotland, 40 m. w. of North Uist; population transferred to mainland of Scotland (1930). (2) Wat.-pl., Victoria, Australia, 3 m. S.E. of Melbourne; longest pier in Australia. Pop. 25,000.

St. Kitts, or ST. CHRISTOPHER, isl., Leeward Group, Brit. W. Indies; mountainous; soil fertile and highly cultivated; sugar, rum, cotton. Cap. Basseterre. Area, 65 sq. m.; pop. 27,000.

St. Lambert (*sän lon-ber'*), tn., Quebec, Canada, on R. St. Lawrence, opposite Montreal. Pop. 6,000.

St. Law'rence, great riv. of Canada, carries off surplus waters of Great Lakes; length from Lake Ontario to opening into Gulf of St. Lawrence *c.* 750 m.; expands during course into several lakes, as those of the Thousand Isles, St. Francis, and St. Peter, and in other places contracts and forms rapids, as Long Sault and Lachine; canals have been constructed to avoid the rapids; gives access to navigation of some 2,200 m. to head of the Great Lakes. Chief tribs. from N. are Ottawa, St. Maurice, Saguenay, Portneuf, Betsiamites, Bustard, and Manicouagan; and from S., Richelieu and Chaudière. Except in winter, when river is ice-bound, seagoing vessels can ascend to Montreal.

St. Leonards. See HASTINGS.

St. Lo (*san lō*), cap., La Manche, France, 16 m. S.E. of Cherbourg; manufactures paper, drugget; tanning and bleaching industries. Pop. 10,000.

St. Louis. (1) (*loo'is*, or *loo'ē*) City, Missouri, U.S.A., on R. Mississippi a few miles below its junction with R. Missouri; has frontage of 19 m. along river, which is here crossed by two magnificent bridges, connecting the city with East St. Louis. Seat of Washington Univ. and St. Louis R.C. Univ. Great trading centre both by railway and river, and leading raw fur market of the world; important shoe manufactures; grain and cotton market; has meat-packing establishments, printing works; manufactures include machinery, hardware, motor-cars, chemicals, flour. Pop. 822,000. (2) (*san loo-e*) Cap., Senegal, French W. Africa; cathedral, governor's palace; educational centre. Pop. 20,000.

St. Lucia (*loo-sē'a*), largest and most northerly of Windward Islands, British W. Indies; surface hilly and forested; famed for beautiful scenery; produces sugar, cocoa, lime-juice, coconuts; chief coaling station and base for fleet in W. Indies. Cap. Castries. Area, 233 sq. m.; pop. 57,000.

St. Malo (*san mä-lō'*), fortified port, Ille-et-Vilaine, France, on English Channel; built on rocky islet communicating with mainland by causeway; favourite bathing resort; cathedral; shipbuilding and iron-founding; exports cereals, early potatoes and vegetables, fruit, eggs, wine, meat. Pop. 12,000.

St. Martin, isl., Leeward Islands, W. Indies, N. part French, S. part Dutch; salt manufacture. Area, 38 sq. m.

St. Mary's Loch, fresh-water loch, Selkirkshire, Scotland, joined to smaller Loch of the Lowes; 814 ft. above sea-level; river Yarrow issues from it.

Saint Michaels, or SÃO MIGUEL, volcanic isl., largest of the Azores; hot springs; hemp, wine, fruit. Cap. Porta Delgada. Area, 299 sq. m.; pop. 125,000.

St. Michael's Mount, rocky islet, Cornwall, England, in Mount's Bay; mansion and chapel on summit; at low tide joined to mainland by natural causeway.

St. Michel, MONT. See MONT ST. MICHEL.

St. Mihiel (*san mē-yel'*), tn., Meuse, France, 20 m. S. by E. of Verdun, on R. Meuse; noted Benedictine abbey; embroidery and lace manufactures. Pop. 4,300.

St. Mor'itz, tourist resort, Upper Engadine, Grisons canton, Switzerland; winter sports; mineral springs. Pop. 2,600.

St. Nazaire (*san nä-zär'*), port, Loire-Inférieure, France, on R. Loire estuary; considerable trade, chiefly with England; iron shipbuilding, blast furnaces, and steel works. Pop. 35,000.

St. Neots (*nēts*, or *nē'ots*), mkt. tn., Hunts, England, on R. Ouse; paper and flour mills, and engineering works. Pop. 4,300.

St. Nicolas (*san nē-ko-lä'*), tn., E. Flanders, Belgium; cottons, linen, woollens, and lace. Pop. 37,000.

St. Nin'ians, or ST. RINGANS, par., Stirlingshire, Scotland, suburb of Stirling; woollens, nails, screw-bolts, tanneries; close to battlefield of Bannockburn. Pop. 14,800.

St. Omer (*san-tō-mār'*), tn., Pas-de-Calais, France, 26 m. by rail S.E. of Calais; breweries, distilleries, soap-works, and linen manufactures; cathedral; ruins of Benedictine abbey. Pop. 17,000.

St. Pancras, metropolitan bor., N. London, England; contains part of Regent's Park. King's Cross, Euston, and St. Pancras rly. stations are in bor. Pop. 198,100.

St. Paul, tn., Minnesota, U.S.A., on R. Mississippi, close to Minneapolis, its 'twin city'; railway centre; furs, lumber products, meat packing, flour milling, boots and shoes, clothing; motor-car workshops; univ.; cathedral. Pop. 271,000.

St. Paul de Loanda. See LOANDA.

St. Peter Port, tn., cap., Guernsey, Channel Islands; fine harbour; exports fruit, vegetables, and flowers. Pop. 16,000.

St. Petersburg. (1) See LENINGRAD. (2) Tn., Florida, U.S.A., on W. coast, 20 m. S.W. of Tampa; holiday resort; winter vegetables, fruit, and fish exported. Pop. 40,000.

St. Pierre (*san pē-ār'*). (1) Tn., Martinique, French W. Indies; utterly destroyed, with its 26,000 inhabitants, by eruption of Mont Pelée (May 8, 1902). (2) Tn., Réunion, Indian Ocean; sugar. Pop. 20,000. (3) Rocky isl. in Atlantic, S. of Newfoundland, forming with Miquelon Islands the French colony of St. Pierre and Miquelon; cod fishing. Total area, 93 sq. m.; pop. 4,000.

St. Pölten', tn., Lower Austria, Austria, on R. Traisen, 30 m. W. of Vienna; iron and hardware goods; cotton. Pop. 32,000.

St. Quentin (*san kon-tan'*), tn., Aisne, France, 80 m. N.N.E. of Paris; connected by canal with Rs. Schelde, Somme, Oise, and Seine; manufactures of cotton, wool, silk, sugar, machinery, chemicals. Pop. 49,000.

St. Servan (*san ser-von'*), port and wat.-pl., Ille-et-Vilaine, France, adjoining St. Malo; boat building, rope making, manufacture of ship biscuits. Pop. 11,000.

St. Thomas. (1) Tn., Ontario, Canada, 15 m. S. of London; railway centre and workshops; flax, flour, and planing mills. Pop. 16,000. (2) Or SÃO THOMÉ, volcanic isl., Portuguese W. Africa, in Gulf of Guinea; highest summit, Pico de São Thomé (7,020 ft.); cocoa, coconuts, coffee, rubber, cinchona; fruit; more than half of isl. is forested. Cap. St. Thomas. Area (with San Principe I.), 320 sq. m.; pop. 52,000. (3) Volcanic isl., U.S.A. Virgin Islands, W. Indies; sugar, cotton. Cap. St. Thomas. Area, 27 sq. m.; pop. 9,000.

St. Trond (*san trōn'*), tn., Limburg, Belgium, 18 m. N.W. of Liége; beer, spirits, sugar, tobacco. Pop. 16,000.

St. Vin'cent, volcanic isl., Windward Islands, Brit. W. Indies; well wooded; arrowroot, cotton, sugar, rum, peanuts. Cap. Kingstown. Area, 150 sq. m.; pop. 51,000.

Sakai, seapt., Honshu, Japan, on Osaka Bay; manufactures cotton goods, cutlery, bricks, and saké. Pop. 105,000.

Sakhalin (*sa-ka-lēn'*), long, narrow isl. in N. Pacific, N.E. Asia; the N. half belongs to Russia and the S., known as Karafuto, to Japan; traversed N. to S. by forest-clad mountain ranges; climate severe; large areas fit for agriculture and grazing; coal and naphtha are worked; salmon fishery. Total area, 24,560 sq. m.; total pop. 216,000.

Salamanca (*sa-la-mang'ka*). (1) Prov., Spain; mountainous in S.; watered by R. Douro; timber plentiful on mountain slopes, and grain on plains; much live-stock raised; gold, iron, coal, copper, and other minerals are found. Area, 4,829 sq. m.; pop. 332,000. (2) Cap. of above; anc. city with many beautiful old buildings and cathedral; univ.; great railway centre. Pop. 37,000.

Sal'as, tn., N. Spain, 21 m. W. of Oviedo; coal-mining dist. Pop. 18,000.

Salayar (*sa-lī'ar*), isl. group, Dutch

E. Indies; maize, coconuts, tortoise-shell, indigo. Pop. 63,000.

Sal'combe, urb. dist., Devon, England, 26½ m. S.E. of Plymouth; wat.-pl. and port. Pop. 2,400.

Sale (*sāl*), urb. dist., Cheshire, England, on R. Mersey, suburb of Manchester; market gardening. Pop. 28,100.

Salé, or SALLEE (*să-lā*), port, Morocco, W. Africa, on Atlantic coast; exports carpets and wool. Pop. 21,000.

Salem (*sā'lem*). (1) Dist., Madras, India; hilly, with broad plains; well-watered; rice, millet, pulses, oil-seeds, coffee. Area, 6,912 sq. m.; pop. 2,112,000. (2) Cap. of above, 75 m. N.W. of Trichinopoly; weaving and carpet manufacture; agricultural centre. Pop. 52,000. (3) Tn., Massachusetts, U.S.A., on Massachusetts Bay; has good harbour; manufactures cotton goods, lumber products, machinery, boots, shoes, and leather. Pop. 43,000. (4) Cap. of Oregon, U.S.A., on R. Willamette; flour mills, fruit packing, canneries, and lumbering. Pop. 26,000.

Saler'no, port, S.W. Italy, on Gulf of Salerno; cathedral; manufactures cotton and silk goods. Pop. 63,000.

Sal'ford, co. bor., Lancs, England, on R. Irwell; adjoins Manchester; engineering; electrical instruments, furniture, rubber articles; chief industries are cotton and chemical manufactures. Pop. 223,400.

Salina (*sa-lē'na*), tn., central Kansas, U.S.A., on R. Smoky Hill; univ.; flour milling is most important industry. Pop. 16,000.

Salisbury (*sawlz'ber-e*). (1) Tn., Wilts, England, on R. Avon; famous Early Eng. cathedral; the spire (404 ft.) is the loftiest, and the cloisters are the most perfect in England. Several old churches and other interesting buildings. Pop. 26,500. (2) Cap. of S. Rhodesia, S. Africa; centre of goldfields; has an agricultural laboratory. Pop. 22,000 (8,000 whites).

Salisbury Plain, tract of rolling downs, Wilts, England, about 20 m. by 16 m. Many barrows and other ancient remains, including Stonehenge. Important military camp.

Sallee. See SALÉ.

Salon (*să-lon'*), tn., Bouches-du-Rhône, France, 40 m. N.W. of Marseilles; olive oil, silk, soap, trade in almonds and early produce. Pop. 9,000.

Salonika (*să-lon-ē'ka*), tn., Macedonia, Greece, on gulf of same name; notable for its antiquities, including Roman triumphal arch and old church of St. Sophia; anc. citadel; cotton and woollen mills, soap works, breweries, flour mills; safe and roomy harbour. As Thessalonica, visited by St. Paul. Allied base during Great War. Pop. 237,000.

Salon'ta, formerly NAGY SZALONTA, tn., Romania, on border of Hungary; pig rearing; trade in timber and cereals. Pop. 14,000.

Salop. See SHROPSHIRE.

Salsette (*sal-set'*) ('sixty-six villages'), isl., N. of Bombay, India; connected with Bombay by two bridges and Sion causeway; rice fields. Chief tn., Thana. Area, 246 sq. m.; pop. 150,000.

Sal'ta. (1) Prov., N.W. Argentina, S. America; plains in E., slopes of Andes Mts. in W.; part of prov. well timbered; soil very fertile, but irrigation necessary; agriculture is chief occupation; some stock rearing; sugar, wine, maize, wheat, tobacco. Area, 48,302 sq. m.; pop. 166,000. (2) Cap. of above, on R. Arias; contains college and cathedral; has large trade with Bolivia. Pop. 28,000.

Salt'aire, model vil., W. Riding, Yorks, England, on R. Aire, 3 m. N.W. of Bradford; founded in 1853 by Sir Titus Salt; alpaca and mohair. Pop. 4,800.

Salt'ash, tn. and port, Cornwall, England, on R. Tamar, 5 m. N.W. of Plymouth; coasting trade. Pop. 3,600.

Salt'burn-by-the-Sea, wat.-pl., N. Riding, Yorks, England; fine sandy beach, cliffs, and pleasure grounds. Pop. 3,900.

Salt'coats, port and wat.-pl., Ayrshire, Scotland; salt formerly manufactured; its shipbuilding has been transferred to Ardrossan. Pop. 10,200.

Saltillo (*sal-tēl'yo*), cap. of Coahuila, Mexico, 37 m. s.w. of Monterey; cottons, woollens, flour; cereals are produced. Pop. 40,000.

Salt Lake, GREAT. See GREAT SALT LAKE.

Salt Lake City, cap. of Utah, U.S.A., on R. Jordan; settled by Mormons (1847); contains Mormon temple, tabernacle, and administration building and univ.; commercial centre; chief industries are meat packing, smelting, manufacture of cars, printing and publishing, lumber products, leather goods, copper, tin, and sheet-iron products, and wireless equipment. Pop. 140,000.

Salt'ney, par. and vil., Flintshire, Wales, on R. Dee; anchors, chain cables, and railway carriage works; large docks. Pop. (par.) 6,000.

Sal'to, port, Uruguay, S. America, on Uruguay R.; trade in leather and salted meats; wine. Pop. 30,000.

Salut, ILES DU (*säl-oo, ēl doo*) ('isles of safety'), group of three islands (Isles Joseph, Royale, and du Diable), French Guiana, S. America, 31 m. N.W. of Cayenne; convict settlements. Pop. *c.* 15,000.

Saluzzo (*sa-loot'so*), tn., Cuneo, Italy, 40 m. s. of Turin; cathedral and old castle; silk, leather, hats are manufactured. Pop. 16,000.

Salvador', republic, Central America; smallest but most densely populated state; surface generally high tableland, with hills rising above it to 12,000 ft.; earthquakes frequent; produces large quantities of coffee; rubber, sugar, tobacco, hemp, cacao, and balsam are also produced; minerals include gold, silver, iron, and mercury. Chief tn., San Salvador. Area, 13,176 sq. m.; pop. 1,723,000.

Salween'. (1) River, Burma; rises in Tibet; enters Upper Burma on E., traverses the Shan states, and flowing s. enters the Gulf of Martaban; length estimated at 1,800 m. (2) Dist., Tenasserim, Lower Burma; extremely mountainous, with many rivers. Area, 2,666 sq. m.; pop. 50,000.

Salzbrunn (*zalts'broon*), tn., Silesia, Prussia, 30 m. s.w. of Breslau; manufactures porcelain and glass; mineral springs; health resort. Pop. 15,000.

Salzburg (*zalts'boorg*). (1) Prov., Austria, N. and E. of Tirol; mountainous; forests and pasture land; numerous lakes; watered by R. Salzach; rich in minerals, especially salt; chief industries are cattle raising, dairy farming, and the timber trade. Area, 2,762 sq. m.; pop. 223,000. (2) Cap. of above; beautifully situated on R. Salzach; fine castle; cathedral; manufactures musical instruments and marble ornaments; brewing. Pop. 38,000.

Salzkammergut (*zalts-kam'er-goot*), lake district in Austrian Alps; contains over forty lakes, including Attersee or Kammersee, the largest lake in Austria (16 sq. m.); salt mines. Area, 240 sq. m.

Salzwedel (*zalts'vā-del*), tn., Saxony, Prussia, 70 m. S.E. of Hamburg; cloth, linen, leather, needles, chemicals, sugar, and alcohol. Pop. 14,000.

Samar'a. (1) Province of S.E. Russia, in basin of R. Volga; slopes of Ural Mts. in N., steppe land in S.; soil mostly fertile, especially in R. Samara valley; produces cereals, vegetables, tobacco, honey; dairy farming is increasing in importance. Area, 41,358 sq. m.; pop. 2,410,000. (2) Cap. of above, at junction of Rs. Samara and Volga; river port and rly. jn.; trade in grain; flour mills and breweries; machinery, matches. Pop. 176,000.

Samarang', port, Java, Dutch E. Indies, on N. coast, *c.* 200 m. w. Surabaya by rail; important commercial centre; exports sugar, coffee, tobacco, indigo. Pop. 158,000.

Sama'ria, city and prov. of anc. Palestine. The city lay N.W. of Shechem, 35 m. N. of Jerusalem.

Samarqand', formerly SAMARKAND,

cap. of Uzbek, U.S.S.R.; connected by rly. with Caspian Sea; many beautiful architectural remains, including finest mosque in Central Asia; manufactures cloth, leather, flour, bricks; distilleries. Pop. 105,000.

Samarra′, tn., Iraq, on R. Tigris, 65 m. N.N.W. of Baghdad; former residence of the caliphs; station on Baghdad Rly. Pop. *c.* 3,000.

Samä′wa, tn., Iraq, on R. Euphrates, and on Baghdad Rly.; trades in vegetables and cereals; manufactures carpets. Pop. 10,000.

Sambalpur′. (1) Dist., Bihar and Orissa, India; mostly plain, with hilly portions; chief riv., Mahanadi; large area under forest. Area, 3,824 sq. m.; pop. 789,000. (2) Tn. in above, on R. Mahanadi; manufactures tussore silk and cotton cloth. Pop. 14,000.

Sambre (*san-br*), riv. of France and Belgium, rises in Aisne dep., France, flows E.N.E. and joins R. Meuse at Namur; navigable for barges; united by canals with Rs. Senne, Schelde, and Oise. Length, 118 m.

Samoa (*sam-ō′a*), or NAVIGATORS' ISLANDS, group of fourteen volcanic islands surrounded by coral reefs in S. Pacific; generally mountainous and fertile. The islands are subject to hurricanes. Chief products, coconuts, oranges, pineapples, bananas, and other fruits; exports copra, cocoa beans. The Territory of Western Samoa (islands of Savaii, Upolu, Apolima, and Manona), formerly German, now under mandate, governed by New Zealand; Tutuila and the other islands belong to U.S.A. R. L. Stevenson is buried on top of Vaea mountain near his home of Vailima in Upolu. Chief ports, Apia in Upolu, Pago-Pago in Tutuila. Western Samoa: area, *c.* 1,250 sq. m.; pop. 44,000. American Samoa: area, 75 sq. m.; pop. 8,000.

Sa′mos, isl., Greece, Ægean Sea; surface mountainous, with fertile valleys; many vineyards; cotton, tobacco, and silk are produced; exports wine, oil, tobacco, leather, hides. Area, 180 sq. m.; pop. 70,000.

Sam′othrace, isl., Greece, in Ægean Sea; sponge fisheries; hot sulphur springs. Area, 30 sq. m.; pop. 3,500.

Samsun, port, Asiatic Turkey, on Black Sea; exports copper, timber, tobacco, wool, agricultural produce. Pop. 76,000.

San, riv., Galicia, Poland; rises in Beskid Mts., flows past Przemysl, and joins R. Vistula below Sandomir; length, *c.* 280 m.

Sana, cap. of Yemen, S.W. Arabia; celebrated for its fruit; trades in coffee. Pop. 20,000.

San Anto′nio, tn., Texas, U.S.A., on R. San Antonio; rly. jn.; manufactures iron and steel goods, textiles, leather, soap, cigars; oilfields in vicinity; large trade in cattle, cotton, wool, and hides; winter health resort. Pop. 255,000.

San Bernardino (*ber-nar-dē′no*), city, California, U.S.A., 50 m. E. of Los Angeles; important fruit-growing centre — oranges, lemons, citrons; manufactures lumber and meat products. Pop. 37,000.

San Catal′do, tn., central Sicily, 4 m. W. of Caltanisetta; has a picturesque cathedral; sulphur is mined. Pop. 18,000.

San Cristo′bal, tn., Mexico, in isthmus of Tehuantepec; cathedral; textiles and earthenware. Pop. 13,000.

Sancti Spiritus (*sangk′tē spē′rē-toos*), city, Santa Clara, central Cuba, on R. Yayabo; centre of extensive agricultural and grazing dist. Pop. 26,000.

Sand′ay, isl., Orkney group, Scotland; surface flat, except in W.; herring fishing. Area, 26 sq. m.; pop. 1,400.

Sand′bach, mkt. tn., Cheshire, England, 4½ m. N.E. of Crewe; manufactures boots and shoes, chemicals, and fustian. Pop. 6,400.

Sand′gate, wat.-pl., Kent, England, 1½ m. S.W. of Folkestone. Pop. 3,000.

Sand′hurst, par. and vil., Berks, England, 9 m. N. of Aldershot; about 2 m. S.E. is Royal Military Coll. for the training of officers. Wellington College is near by. Pop. 3,800

San Diego (*dē-ā'go*), city, California, U.S.A., on Pacific Ocean; health resort; good harbour; exports fruit; manufactures aeroplanes, furniture; fish canning. Pop. 148,000.

Sandoway'. (1) Dist., Arakan, Lower Burma; mountainous and well wooded; small patches produce rice and tobacco. Area, 3,784 sq. m.; pop. 112,000. (2) Tn. in above, on Bay of Bengal; small coasting trade. Pop. 4,000.

San'down, wat.-pl., Isle of Wight, England, 6 m. s. of Ryde; picturesque situation and fine beach. Pop. 6,200.

Sand'ringham, par. and vil., Norfolk, England, 6 m. E. of the Wash; church of St. Mary Magdalene contains numerous memorials of the royal family. Sandringham House is a royal residence. Pop. 100.

Sandus'ky, city and port, Ohio, U.S.A., on Sandusky Bay, Lake Erie; chief products are paper goods, agricultural implements, and chemicals; fresh-water fisheries. Pop. 26,000.

Sand'wich. (1) Tn., Kent, England, on R. Stour; one of the Cinque Ports; now two miles from the sea. Pop. 3,300. (2) City, Ontario, Canada, on Detroit R., 4 m. s.w. of Windsor. Pop. 10,300.

Sandwich Islands. See HAWAIIAN ISLANDS.

San'dy, par. and vil., Beds, England, 8½ m. E. of Bedford; mkt. gardens; sand pits. Pop. (par.) 3,600.

Sandy Hook, peninsula, New Jersey, U.S.A., 6 m. long; America Cup yacht races take place in vicinity.

San Fernan'do, port, Spain, on Cadiz Bay; one of chief naval ports; naval academy, observatory; manufactures beer, leather, soap, rope, and sails; iron foundry and distilleries. Pop. 27,000.

San Francis'co, second largest city, California, U.S.A., and greatest commercial town on w. coast of America; at point of a peninsula separating San Francisco Bay from Pacific, and on strait known as Golden Gate giving access to the Pacific; seat of several departments of California Univ. and of various educational establishments; fine parks; terminus of three trans-continental lines of railway; steamer services to China, Japan, Australia, and Hawaiian Islands; manufactures chemicals, motor-cars, agricultural and mining machinery; sugar and oil refineries, canneries, lumber mills; printing and publishing; exports precious metals, wheat, flour, tinned fruits and vegetables, timber, wine. San Francisco's prosperity dates from discovery of gold in California (*c.* 1849). In 1906 a terrible earthquake and fire caused great loss of life and destruction of property; town rapidly rebuilt. Pop. 637,000.

Sangerhausen (*zang'er-hou-zen*), tn., Saxony, Prussia, on R. Gonna, 30 m. w. of Halle; manufactures sugar and agricultural machinery. Pop. 12,000.

San José (*sän ho-sā'*). (1) Cap., Costa Rica, Central America; large coffee trade; cathedral. Pop. 63,000. (2) City, health resort, California, U.S.A., 40 m. S.E. of San Francisco; industries include canning of fruits and vegetables, lumber and planing mills, manufacture of woollen goods, leather, wine. Pop. 58,000.

San Juan (*sän hoo-än'*). (1) Prov., Argentina, S. America, bordering on Chile; mountainous, with plains to E.; drained by several streams; agriculture; wine; cattle rearing; gold, silver, copper; coal and iron found. Area, 37,865 sq. m.; pop. 162,000. (2) Cap. of above, on R. San Juan; exports wine; trade with Chile in cattle and dried fruit. Pop. 17,000. (3) Cap., Porto Rico, W. Indies; excellent harbour; naval station; cathedral; exports sugar, tobacco, coffee, fruits. Pop. 71,000.

San Juan del Norte. See GREYTOWN.

Sanlúcar de Barrameda (*sän-loo'kar dā bar-ra-mā'da*), tn., port, and wat.-pl., Cadiz, Spain, at mouth of R. Guadalquivir; trade in wine and cereals; fisheries. Pop. 27,000.

San Luis (*sän loo-ēs'*). (1) Prov., central Argentina, S. America; mountainous in N., pampas in S.; grazing important; some wheat, maize, alfalfa, fruit grown, under irrigation; gold mines. Area, 29,035 sq. m.; pop. 154,000. (2) Cap. of above, on Transandine Railway; grapes, oranges largely cultivated; horses, hides, and wool exported. Pop. 18,000.

San Luis Potosi (*sän loo-ēs' po-to'sē*). (1) Inland state, Mexico; chiefly plateau land; soil fertile; cereals, sugar, pepper; excellent grazing; large mineral resources, but little developed. Area, 24,004 sq. m.; pop. 446,000. (2) Cap. of above; rly. jn.; clothing and cotton factories, railway workshops; large trade in wool, cattle, hides, and tallow. Pop. 57,000.

San Marino (*mä-rē'no*), small independent republic, N.E. Italy, 14 m. from Rimini, on Adriatic Sea; agriculture, cattle raising; wine, building stone, cattle exported. It claims to be oldest state in Europe. Area, 38 sq. m.; pop. 13,000.

San Miguel (*mē-gel'*), tn., S.E. Salvador, Central America; rubber, indigo, grain; famous annual fair. Pop. 39,000.

San Miniat'o, tn., Italy, on R. Arno, 28 m. W.S.W. of Florence; cathedral; glass, leather, hats, olive oil. Pop. 8,000.

San Nicolas' de los Arro'yos, port, Argentina, S. America, on R. Paraná, 35 m. S.E. of Rosario; wheat, maize, wool, frozen mutton exported; extensive meat-preserving industry. Pop. *c.* 30,000.

San Pab'lo, tn., Luzon I., Philippines, 35 m. S.S.E. of Manila; rice and copra. Pop. 31,000.

Sanquhar (*sank'ar*), royal burgh, Dumfriesshire, Scotland, on R. Nith; coal mines, iron forges, brick and tile works. Pop. 1,800.

San Remo (*rā'mo*), port, Italian Riviera, on Gulf of Genoa, 28 m. E. of Nice; winter resort; produces olive oil, lemons, wine, and flowers. Pop. 21,000.

San Salvador', cap., Salvador, Central America, 25 m. from its port La Libertad; univ.; silk goods, cotton cloth, cigars, soap. Pop. 89,000.

San Sebastian (*sä-bäs-tē-än'*), port, Spain, on Bay of Biscay, near French frontier; exports wine, wool, skins, fruit; manufactures sailcloth, paper, cotton, glass, soap, candles; valuable fisheries. Pop. 76,000.

San Severo (*sä-vä'ro*), tn., Apulia, S. Italy, 20 m. N.W. of Foggia; wine and olive oil. Pop. 35,000.

San'ta An'a. (1) Tn., Salvador, Central America, 40 m. N.W. of San Salvador; centre of a coffee and sugar growing dist.; sugar, cigars, textiles, and pottery manufactured. Pop. 76,000. (2) Tn., S. California, U.S.A., 30 m. S.E. of Los Angeles; trade centre of rich fruit-growing valley, and of neighbouring oilfields; manufactures aeroplanes, farm implements, glass, preserved fruits, perfumes; fruit packing, canneries. Pop. 30,000.

Santa Barbara, coast tn., California, U.S.A.; wat.-pl.; fruit-growing centre; oilfield in neighbourhood. Pop. 34,000.

Santa Catharina (*kä-ta-rē'nä*), state, S. Brazil; with a low coastal zone bordering Atlantic Ocean, and a plateau to the W.; densely forested and drained by numerous streams; coffee and sugar are grown, also cotton, tobacco, wheat; Paraguay tea is exported, and coal is mined. Cap. Florianopolis. Area, 20,785 sq. m.; pop. 914,000.

Santa Clara. (1) Prov., central Cuba; fertile soil; sugar, coffee, fruits, wax, honey, timber, cattle, asphalt, gold, silver, and copper are produced. Area, 8,257 sq. m.; pop. 755,000. (2) Cap. of above; trade in sugar and cattle. Pop. 22,000.

Santa Cruz (*krooz*). (1) Wat.-pl., California, U.S.A., on Monterey Bay; fruit and vegetable canning; fisheries. Pop. 11,000. (2) Dep., central Bolivia, S. America; surface mostly flat; grazing; products include sugar, coffee, cacao, rice in W. portion. Area, 144,941 sq. m.; pop. 341,000. (3) Or SANTA CRUZ DE LA SIERRA, tn., cap. of Santa Cruz, Bolivia, on R. Piray; flour, sugar, leather; distilling. Pop.

30,000. (4) Or SANTA CRUZ DE TENERIFE, port and cap. of Canary Islands; good coaling station; exports wine; brandy, grain, silk, cochineal, sugar, and bananas. Pop. 53,000. (5) See SAINTE-CROIX.

Santa Fé. (1) Prov., Argentina, S. America; plain, drained by R. Paraná; agriculture and stock raising. Area, 50,713 sq. m.; pop. 1,251,000. (2) Cap. of above, on Salado R.; cathedral and provincial univ.; shipbuilding. Pop. 60,000.

San'tal Parganas', dist., Bhagalpur, Bihar and Orissa, India; undulating country with alluvial plains; cereals; coal is mined. Chief commercial tn., Sahibganj, on R. Ganges, 35 m. E. of Bhagalpur. Area, 5,462 sq. m.; pop. 1,799,000.

San'ta Mar'ta, port and cap. of Magdalena, Colombia, S. America; important trade centre. Pop. 18,000.

San'ta Maura (*mou'ra*), isl. in Ionian Is., Greece; mountainous; produces much olive oil; wine, currants. Area, 110 sq. m.; pop. 30,000.

San'ta Mon'ica, tn., Los Angeles, California, U.S.A., on Pacific Ocean; popular seaside resort. Pop. 37,000.

Santander'. (1) Prov., N. Spain, on Bay of Biscay; traversed by Cantabrian Mts. (Picos de Europa, 8,600 ft.); well wooded; rich pasture land; has iron and zinc mines; good harbours and maritime trade. Area, 2,108 sq. m.; pop. 353,000. (2) Cap. of above, on Santander Bay; large trade, chiefly in iron and zinc ore; fishing; cathedral; fashionable summer resort. Pop. 83,000.

Santarem', tn., Para, Brazil, on R. Tapajos, near confluence with R. Amazon; cacao, rubber, brazil nuts, tobacco, sugar, cattle. Pop. 42,000.

San'ta Ro'sa, tn., California, U.S.A., 50 m. N.W. of San Francisco; dairy produce, fruit, hops. Pop. 16,000.

Santiago, or SANTIAGO DE CHILE (*sant-yä-gō*), cap. of Chile, S. America; finely situated on W. slopes of Andes; cathedral, univ., national library; commercial centre; manufactures leather, soap, beer, and foundry products. Pop. 507,000.

Santiago de Composte'la, tn., Galicia, N.W. Spain; cathedral, univ.; has ruins of many religious houses; produces spirits, beer, chocolate, paper, and linen. Pop. 26,000.

Santiago de Cuba, port, S.E. coast, Cuba, W. Indies; cathedral; centre of mineral dist.; iron foundries, machine shops, tobacco factories, tanneries; chief exports are sugar, tobacco, timber, fruit, cacao, coffee, rum, iron ore. Pop. 49,000.

Santia'go del Estero (*es-tā'ro*). (1) N. central prov., Argentina, S. America; mostly level plains with saltpans; alfalfa is chief crop; sugar, tobacco, cotton. Area, 55,385 sq. m.; pop. 361,000. (2) Cap. of above, on R. Dulce. Pop. 23,000.

San'to Domin'go. (1) Republic, eastern portion of island of Haiti, W. Indies; surface generally mountainous, with fertile valleys between ranges; climate is hot in low districts, cooler in higher lands; large deposits of rock salt in S.W.; rich in minerals, but little worked; sugar is the chief crop; much forest; exports are coffee, cocoa, sugar, tobacco, logwood, mahogany. Area, 19,332 sq. m.; pop. 897,000. (2) Cap. of above, at mouth of R. Ozama; exports tobacco, sugar. Cathedral claims to contain tomb of Columbus. Pop. 31,000.

Santos (*sän-tosh'*), tn., chief port, São Paulo, Brazil, S. America. Chief coffee port of the world; also exports bananas, rubber, hides. Pop. 103,000.

San Vicente (*vē-sen'tā*). (1) Central dep. of Salvador; mountainous; has extinct volcanoes, active geysers, and hot springs. Pop. 93,000. (2) Cap. of above; indigo and tobacco plantations; cloth, silks, shoes, hats, and cigars. Pop. 35,000.

São Francisco (*soun fran-sēs'ko*), riv., E. Brazil, S. America; rises in S.W. Minas Geraes and flows N. and E. in a great curve to enter Atlantic Ocean; navigation impeded by falls. Length, 1,800 m.

São Leopol'do, tn., Rio Grande do

Sul, Brazil, on R. Sinos; hats, leather goods, earthenware. Pop. 47,000.

São Luiz de Maranhão (*mä-rän-youn'*), port, cap. of Maranhão state, N.E. Brazil, S. America, on island of São Luiz; exports cotton and sugar. Pop. 53,000.

Saône (*sōn*), riv., France; rises in plateau of Langres; joined by R. Doubs at Verdun, then flows S. to join R. Rhone at Lyons; connected by canals with Rs. Meuse and Moselle, Marne, Rhine, Seine, Loire. Length, 301 m.

Saône-et-Loire (*sōn-ā-lwär*), dep., France; mountainous; watered by Rs. Saône, Loire, and Arroux; produces wine, coal, cattle, and cereals; flourishing manufactures of iron, steel, copper, bronze, and porcelain; distilleries, oil works, and chemical works. Cap. Macon. Area, 3,330 sq. m.; pop. 549,000.

São Paulo (*soun pou'lo*). (1) Coast state, S. Brazil, S. America. Surface consists of plateau in interior, crossed by several ranges, and low-lying coastal strip; much of surface forested; drained by affluents of R. Paraná. Chiefly an agricultural state; large cultivation of coffee, considerable crops of sugar-cane, cotton, tobacco, cereals, grapes, bananas. Manufactures cottons, wine, tobacco. Cap. São Paulo; chief port, Santos. Area, 112,278 sq. m.; pop. 6,176,000. (2) Cap. of above, on R. Tieté; cathedral, several monasteries, convents; great manufacturing centre; cotton, woollen, jute, glass, and furniture factories. Pop. 579,000.

São Salvador. See BAHIA (2).

Sapporo (*sap-ō'ro*), tn., cap. of Hokkaido, Japan; saw and flour mills, hemp and flax factories, breweries. Pop. 145,000.

Saragos'sa. (1) Prov., Aragon, Spain; mountainous in N. and W.; drained by R. Ebro. Area, 6,726 sq. m.; pop. 520,000. (2) Cap. of above, on R. Ebro; two cathedrals, univ.; rly. jn.; manufactures include beer, spirits, porcelain, woollens, silk, leather, iron goods. Pop. 156,000.

Sarajevo (*sär-ā-yĕv'ō*), cap., Bosnia, Yugoslavia; manufactures pottery, silk, flour, sugar; carpet factories and hand-loom weaving; became famous as the scene of the murder of the Austrian heir-apparent and his wife (June 28, 1914), the event which precipitated the Great War. Pop. 65,000.

Saran', dist., Bihar and Orissa, India; alluvial plain watered by Rs. Ganges, Gandak, and Gogra; large crops of cereals, rice, sugar-cane, oil-seeds. Chief tn., Chapra, on R. Ganges, 35 m. above Patna. Area, 2,683 sq. m.; pop. 2,340,000.

Sarapul', tn. and river port, Ural Area, Russia, on Kama R., 130 m. S.W. of Perm; important centre for manufacture of boots, shoes, and gloves; rope factories, flax mills. Pop. 25,000.

Sarato'ga Springs, health resort, New York, U.S.A., 38 m. N. of Albany; famous mineral springs. Pop. 14,000.

Sarat'ov. (1) Province, Russia; steppe lands in S., hilly in N.; has large forests; drained by affluents of Rs. Don and Volga; soil fertile, producing cereals, flax, linseed, sunflowers, mustard. Area, 35,676 sq. m.; pop. 2,891,000. (2) Cap. of above, on R. Volga; commercial centre; distilleries, flour mills, tobacco factories, and ironworks; trade in corn; univ. Pop. 215,000.

Sarawak (*sä-rä-wa*), state, Brit. N. Borneo; surface generally mountainous, and very well watered; produces timber, rubber, sago, pepper, rattans; minerals include coal, gold, silver, mercury; diamonds and sapphires found; large oilfield. Chief tn., Kuching. Area, *c.* 50,000 sq. m.; pop. *c.* 600,000.

Sardin'ia, large island in E. Mediterranean, forming a dep. of Italy; immediately S. of Corsica, from which it is separated by Strait of Bonifacio; surface mountainous; almost equally divided between forest, arable land, and pasture; drained by Rs. Tirso, Samassi, and Flumendosa. Climate hot and unhealthy in lower districts.

Produces lead, zinc, silver, lignite, and blende. Forest products, oak, olive, and other timber; cork, tanning bark, charcoal. Principal industry is agriculture; wheat, barley, and other crops grown; fruit largely cultivated; horses, cattle, sheep, and goats reared. Wine largely produced; tunny, sardine, and anchovy fisheries. Chief tn., Cagliari. Area, 9,299 sq. m.; pop. 864,000.

Sargas'so Sea, part of Atlantic Ocean; first discovered by Columbus; in belt of calms between Gulf Stream and North Equatorial Current, extending from W. Indies to 40° w. longitude; remarkable for its floating gulf-weed, but surface not continuously covered; s. edge of this sea is spawning ground of the fresh-water eel.

Sarisbury (*sărs'* or *sărs'*), par. and vil., Hants, England, 6½ m. s.e. of Southampton; early strawberries cultivated. Pop. (par.) 4,000.

Sark, one of Channel Islands, English Channel; consists of Great and Little Sark, connected by Coupée isthmus; scenery wild and beautiful; fishing and farming. Chief landing-place, Creux; length, 3½ m. Pop. 600.

Sar'nia, tn., Ontario, Canada, on R. St. Clair; oil refineries; manufactures castings, machinery, woollens. Pop. 15,000.

Sar'no, tn., Salerno, Italy, 20 m. e. of Naples; wine, paper, leather goods; mineral springs; cathedral. Pop. 15,000.

Sarps'borg, port, Norway, on R. Glommen, 10 m. from Oslo Fjord; manufactures chemicals, wood pulp, paper, aluminium; textiles. Pop. 11,000.

Sarrebourg (*sär-boor'*) (German *Saarburg*), tn., s. Moselle, France, on R. Saar, 44 m. by rail n.w. of Strasbourg; watch springs, gloves, lace; belonged to Germany (1871–1918). Pop. 9,000.

Sarreguemines (*sar-ge-mēn'*) (German *Saargemünd*), tn., Lorraine, France, on R. Saar; manufactures porcelain, leather, matches, papier-mâche boxes. Pop. 13,000.

Sarthe (*sart*). (1) Riv., France; at Angers joins R. Mayenne, trib. of R. Loire. Length, 165 m. (2) Dep., France; traversed by R. Sarthe; generally flat or undulating; well wooded; fertile; barley, hemp, and apples extensively grown; horses and cattle reared; minerals include coal, marble, freestone; manufactures hemp, linen; potteries, iron foundries, distilleries, flour mills. Cap. Le Mans. Area, 2,410 sq. m.; pop. 387,000.

Sarzana (*sard-zä'nä*), tn., Genoa, Italy, 7 m. e. of Spezia; wine, olives, and silk are exported. Pop. 11,000.

Saskat'chewan ('rapid river'). (1) Riv., Canada; rises in two branches (N. Saskatchewan and S. Saskatchewan) in Rocky Mts.; flows e. through Cedar Lake into Lake Winnipeg, and thence by Nelson R. to Hudson Bay. Total length, *c.* 1,200 m. (2) Prairie prov., Canada; bounded n. by Mackenzie dist., e. by Manitoba, s. by U.S.A., w. by Alberta. Crossed in s. by Saskatchewan R.; considerable area forested; many lakes; several Indian reserves; largest wheat-growing prov.; also produces oats, barley, flax; excellent fisheries; live-stock raised and large butter output; trades in furs; coal is mined; enormous quantities of wheat are exported annually. Cap. Regina. Area, 251,700 sq. m.; pop. 821,000.

Saskatoon', town, Saskatchewan, Canada, on S. Saskatchewan R., 150 m. n.w. of Regina; univ.; agricultural coll.; wood-working factories, flour mills; cement. Pop. 31,000.

Sas'sari. (1) Prov., Italy, forming n. part of Sardinia; mountainous; produces corn, tobacco, wine, olives. Area, 2,903 sq. m.; pop. 283,000. (2) Cap. of above; cathedral; univ.; trade in oil, grain. Pop. 51,000.

Satara. (1) Dist., Bombay, India, in W. Ghats; watered by Rs. Bhima and Kistna and their tribs.; sugar-cane, pulses, and millet grown; much timber. Area, 4,916 sq. m.; pop. 1,026,000. (2) Cap. of above, 60 m. s. of Poona; manufactures brass ware. Pop. 22,000.

Satpu'ra, mt. range, Central Provs., India, stretching 600 m. E. to W., greatest breadth 100 m.; densely wooded; highest point, 4,500 ft.

Satsuma (*sät-soo'mä*), former prov., S.W. Kyushu, Japan; in prefecture of Kagoshima; noted for fine porcelain (Satsuma ware).

Sat'ul-Mar'e, formerly SZATMAR-NEMETI, tn., Romania, on Hungarian border; on R. Somesul; pottery; textile weaving. Pop. 35,000.

Sau'gor. (1) Dist., Central Provs., India; plain, with hilly undulations, watered by many streams; cereals grown; sandstone quarries. Area, 3,962 sq. m.; pop. 528,000. (2) Cap. of above, 100 m. N.W. of Jubbulpore; built round lake (alt. 1,940 ft.); railway station; exports salt, sugar, cloth. Pop. 39,000. (3) Isl. at mouth of R. Hugli, Bengal, India; Hindu pilgrim resort.

Sault Sainte-Marie (*soo sint-mä'ri*). (1) Or THE SOO, rapids in the St. Mary's R., which connects L. Superior and L. Huron and forms part of the boundary between Ontario, Canada, and Michigan, U.S.A. Passage for shipping is provided by two great canals on the Canadian and U.S.A. sides respectively, which carry more shipping than any other canal in the world, though ice-bound for over four months every year. (2) Tn., Ontario, Canada, on St. Mary's R., at the Canal; copper, iron, cobalt, and silver mines in vicinity. Pop. 21,000. (3) Tn., Michigan, U.S.A., on St. Mary's R., connected with preceding by rly. bridge over river; important lumber, paper, flour, and woollen mills; manufactures dredges, engines, boats. Pop. 14,000.

Saumur (*sō-moor'*), tn., Maine-et-Loire, France, on R. Loire, 27 m. S.E. of Angers; noted for white wine; manufactures brandy, liqueurs, enamels, rosaries. Pop. 14,000.

Sauternes (*sō-tern'*), vil., Gironde, France, *c.* 35 m. S. of Bordeaux; gives name to white wines of dist. Pop. 1,000.

Sav'a, river, Yugoslavia; rises in Alps in Carniola, and falls into R. Danube at Belgrade. Length, 442 m.

Savan'nah, port, Georgia, U.S.A., on R. Savannah; exports cotton, timber, rice, flour, and tobacco; manufactures manure, turpentine, soap, and sugar. Pop. 85,000.

Savantwad'i, Indian state, Bombay, India, bounded on S. by Goa; hilly and thickly wooded; coconuts and betel nuts. Area, 926 sq. m.; pop. 206,000.

Saverne (*sä-vern'*) (German *Zabern*), tn., Bas-Rhin, France, 27 m. by rail N.W. of Strasbourg; at entrance to pass through Vosges Mts.; tanneries. Pop. 7,000.

Savoie (*sä-vwä'*), dep., S.E. France; mountainous; watered by R. Isère; chiefly under pasture; cheese and dairy products are important; mineral springs. Cap. Chambéry. Area, 2,388 sq. m.; pop. 231,000.

Savo'na, port, Genoa, Italy; cathedral; centre of Italian iron industry; shipbuilding yards, railway workshops; manufactures tinplate and glass. Pop. 66,000.

Saw'bridgeworth (or *säts'worth*), urb. dist., Herts, England, 4 m. S. of Bishop's Stortford; plant nurseries; malt trade. Pop. 2,600.

Saw'ley and Wils'thorpe, par. and vil., Derbyshire, England, on R. Trent, 8 m. E.S.E. of Derby; lace making. Pop. (par.) 3,500.

Sax'e-Al'tenburg, Sax'e-Co'burg-Got'ha, Sax'e-Mein'ingen, Sax'e-Wei'mar-Ei'senach, states of the former German Empire, all of which except Gotha merged (1919) in the rep. of Thuringia; Gotha merged with Bavaria (1920).

Sax'ony. (1) Rep., Germany; bounded W., N., and E. by Prussia, S. by Czechoslovakia, W. by Bavaria and Thuringia; length, 130 m.; breadth, 93 m. Flat in N.W.; mt. ranges mainly in S. and S.E.; Erzgebirge on Bohemian border, and the picturesque Saxon Switzerland on both sides of R. Elbe. Chief rivs. are Elbe, Mulde, Schwarze Elster. Climate healthy. Extensive forests (mainly fir and pine), and fine arable and pasture land. Saxony is a great industrial centre, and an important agricultural and mining country. Chief products are rye, wheat, barley, potatoes, oats, beet, hay, vegetables, fruit, timber. Cattle, swine, geese, and poultry are reared. Principal manufactures, textiles, machinery, porcelain, glass, chemicals, musical instruments, watches, printing, typefounding, lace, paper, toys, tobacco, beer, spirits. Coal, iron, cobalt, tin are mined; numerous mineral springs. Chief tns., Leipzig, Dresden (cap.), Chemnitz. Area, 5,786 sq. m.; pop. 4,994,000. (2) Prov., Prussia; watered by R. Elbe; includes parts of Harz Mts. and Thuringian Forest; parts of soil very fertile; produces cereals and sugar-beets; goats reared; has salt, coal, and copper mines; mineral springs; extensive manufactures. Cap. Magdeburg. Area, 9,759 sq. m.; pop. 3,277,000.

Sayan' Mountains, E. continuation of Altai Mts., Asia, forming boundary between Siberia and N.W. Mongolia; some parts well wooded; highest peak, Munko Sardyk (11,450 ft.).

Scafell (*skaw'fel*), mt., Lake District, Cumberland, England; 15-in. gauge railway has been constructed to the summit. Scafell Pike, separated from Scafell by a ravine, is highest peak in England (3,210 ft.) and belongs to the nation.

Scalby, urb. dist., N. Riding, Yorks, England, 3 m. N.W. of Scarborough; residential dist. Pop. 2,800.

Scal'loway, port, Shetland, Scotland, on W. coast of Mainland, 6 m. W. of Lerwick; fishing; anc. cap. of Shetland. Pop. 700.

Scandina'via, peninsula, N. Europe; includes Norway and Sweden; name also loosely applied to lands of Scandinavian peoples, *i.e.* Norway, Sweden, and Denmark. See articles on separate countries.

Scapa Flow, large expanse of sheltered waters in S. Orkney, Scotland, with an area of *c.* 100 sq. m. Surrounded by Mainland Burray S. Ronaldsay, and Hoy. Entrances by Hoy Sound (W.), Hoxa Sound (S.), and Holm Sound (E.). Chief naval base during Great War. After surrender of German fleet, vessels were interned in the Flow, but scuttled by order of Rear-admiral von Reuter. The hulls of many of the ships have been raised and broken up.

Scar'borough, munic. bor., port, and fashionable wat.-pl., N. Riding, Yorks, England, on North Sea; mineral springs; fisheries. Pop. 41,800.

Scarpe, river, France, deps. Pas-de-Calais and Nord; rises on plateau of Artois, 7½ m. E. of Saint Pol; flows E.S.E. past Arras, then N.E. past Douai, and finally unites with R. Schelde near Belgian frontier. Length, 62 m.

Schaffhausen (*shäf'how-zen*). (1) Canton, Switzerland, N. of R. Rhine; undulating, fertile; chief occupations, agriculture and vine culture; forest products are important. Area, 114 sq. m.; pop. 53,000. (2) Cap. of above, on R. Rhine near famous falls; manufactures iron, steel, and aluminium ware; cotton goods, soap; breweries and distilleries. Pop. 22,000.

Schaumburg-Lippe (*shoum'boorg-lip'a*), republic, Germany, between Westphalia and Hanover; part of N. German plain, hilly towards S.; agriculture and coal mining. Cap. Bückeburg. Area, 131 sq. m.; pop. 49,000.

Schelde, or SCHELDT (*skel'de*), river, France, Belgium, and Holland; rises in Aisne dep., and enters North Sea; passes Valenciennes, Tournai, Oudenarde, Ghent, Termonde, Antwerp; navigable to Cambrai, where a network of canals connects it with basins of Rs. Oise and Somme; principal tribs., Lys and Dendre. Length, 250 miles.

Schenectady (*sken-ek'ta-de*), city, New York, U.S.A., on R. Mohawk; electrical works, foundries, and locomotive works; knitted goods, agricultural implements. Pop. 96,000.

Scheveningen (*skā'ven-ing-en*), fashionable seaside resort, Holland, 2 m. N.W. of The Hague; imposing

Kurhaus; important fisheries. Pop. 23,000.

Schiedam (*skē-dam′*), tn., Holland, 3 m. w. of Rotterdam, on R. Schie; noted for gin and other liquors; candles and yeast; cork-cutting. Pop. 45,000.

Schiehallion (*shē-hal′yun*), isolated mountain, Perthshire, Scotland, 11 m. N.W. of Aberfeldy; alt. 3,547 ft.; owing to regularity of outline was scene of experiments (1774) by Dr. Nevil Maskelyne to ascertain the mean density of the earth.

Schleswig (*shlāz′vig*), port, E. Schleswig-Holstein, Prussia, on Schlei inlet; tanneries, flour mills; fishing. Pop. 20,000.

Schleswig-Holstein (*shlāz′vig-hol′-shtīn*), province, N.W. Prussia, S. of Denmark; surface generally plains and moors; agriculture important; live-stock raised; manufactures textiles, tobacco, beer; fishing carried on. Cap. Schleswig. Area, 5,815 sq. m.; pop. 1,519,000.

Schmalkalden (*shmal-kal′den*), tn., summer resort, Hesse-Nassau, Prussia, 30 m. s.w. of Erfurt; manufactures iron and steel goods, toys, beer, soap. Pop. 10,000.

Schneeberg (*shnā′berg*), tn., Saxony, Germany, 20 m. s.w. of Chemnitz; lace, embroidery, shoes. Pop. 9,000.

Schneidemühl (*shnī′da-mool*), cap., Grenzmark, Prussia, on R. Cüddow, 50 m. N. of Posen; manufactures iron goods, lumber, bricks, starch. Pop. 38,000.

Schönebeck (*shoo′na-bek*), tn., Saxony, Prussia, Germany, on R. Elbe, 9 m. s. of Magdeburg; salt is chief product; manufactures chemicals, machinery, explosives. Pop. 21,000.

Schwabach (*shvä′bach*), tn., Bavaria, Germany, 9 m. s.w. of Nuremberg; manufactures needles, wire, silver, brass, and steel goods. Pop. 11,000.

Schwarzwald. See BLACK FOREST.

Schweidnitz (*shvīd′nits*), tn., Silesia, Prussia, on R. Weistritz, 28 m. s.w. of Breslau; manufactures textiles, leather, paper, agricultural implements, machinery; beer. Pop. 31,000.

Schweinfurt (*shvīn′foort*), tn., N. Bavaria, Germany, on R. Main; manufactures machinery, bicycles, soap, tobacco, paint. Pop. 36,000.

Schwelm (*shvelm*), tn., Westphalia, Prussia, 3 m. E. by N. of Barmen; manufactures iron and steel goods, textiles; in vicinity are the Harkort iron and sulphur mines. Pop. 20,000.

Schwerin (*shvā-rēn*) ('game preserve'), cap., Mecklenburg-Schwerin, N. Germany, on Lake Schwerin; chief buildings are the former ducal palace and 15th cent. cathedral; manufactures furniture, pianos, varnish, soap, bricks. Pop. 48,000.

Schwyz (*shvits*). (1) Canton, Switzerland; extends along N.E. shore of Lake of Lucerne; agricultural and pastoral; highest point, Böser Faulen (9,199 ft.). Gives its name to Switzerland. Area, 348 sq. m.; pop. 62,000. (2) Tn., cap. of above, 18 m. E. of Lucerne. Pop. 8,000.

Sciacca (*shä′ka*), port, Girgenti, Sicily, on S. coast; cathedral; trade in sardines, olives, coral; hot mineral springs are near by. Pop. 20,000.

Scilly Isles (*sil′i*), group of islands lying 25 m. s.w. of Land's End, England; largest is St. Mary's, next in importance being Tresco and St. Martin's; mild climate; most of inhabitants employed in cultivating early vegetables and flowers for London market; fisheries. St. Mary's contains the only town, Hugh Town. Area, over 6 sq. m.; pop. 1,700.

Scone (*skoon*), vil. and par., Perthshire, Scotland, on R. Tay, 2 m. N. of Perth; royal residence and place of coronation for Scottish kings from 1153 to 1488. Pop. (par.) 2,900.

Scotch Corner, meeting-place of roads, N. Riding, Yorks, England, 4 m. N.E. of Richmond; here Scottish traffic from S. along Watling Street divided, part passing N.W. to Carlisle, remainder continuing N. to Carter Bar, or to Berwick; now important motor road junction.

Scotland, N. part of Great Britain; bounded by England and Solway Firth on S., Atlantic Ocean on W. and

N., North Sea on E.; greatest breadth, 146 m.; greatest length, 274 m.; coastline (2,300 m.) is exceedingly irregular, esp. in W. Chief island groups are Outer and Inner Hebrides in W., and Orkney and Shetland Islands in N. Scotland is divided into three regions by two lines of faulting. One series of faults, stretching from Stonehaven in E. to Arran in W., separates the Highlands from the Midland Valley or Central Lowlands; the other, from Dunbar to Girvan, separates the Central Lowlands from the Southern Uplands. The Highlands are divided into two parts by Glenmore; loftiest heights occur in Grampian plateau S.E. of Glenmore, where several summits rise above 4,000 ft. (Ben Nevis, 4,406 ft., is the highest peak in the British Isles). In the Highland region are low-lying and fertile areas along E. coast. The Central Lowlands are crossed by parallel ranges of low hills. The more important stretches of low ground are Strathmore, between the Sidlaws and the Grampians; Carse of Gowrie, between the Sidlaws and the Firth of Tay; the valleys of Rs. Forth and Clyde; and the Ayrshire coastal plain. No part of the Southern Uplands reaches 3,000 ft. (highest peak, Merrick, 2,764 ft.); and the Merse, in the lower basin of R. Tweed, is the largest continuous area of low ground in Scotland. Chief rivs. flowing E. are Tweed, Forth, Tay, S. Esk, Dee, Don, Deveron, and Spey. On W. and S. chief rivers are Clyde and Nith. In the Highland area are numerous lochs or lakes, the largest being Loch Lomond.

Climate is equable; agriculture is pursued in the drier E. and grazing in the W. About 22 per cent. of the surface is uncultivatable. Much of the Highlands is covered with peat and heather, and used as grouse moors and deer forests. The Central Lowlands contain much fine arable and pasture land. The Southern Uplands afford excellent sheep pasture, while the plain land that borders them in the W. is the dairy region of Scotland. The Merse is one of the richest agricultural districts in the country. Oats is the chief cereal. Wheat is produced in the Lothians, Fife, and the Merse, where the average number of bushels to the acre is the largest in Great Britain. Barley, potatoes, and roots are other E. coast crops. Important fruit-growing districts are the Carse of Gowrie, and round Blairgowrie, and in Lanarkshire. Notable breeds of cattle are Ayrshire (dairy), black-polled Aberdeen-Angus (beef), West Highlanders or kylos, and black-polled Galloways. Clydesdale gives its name to a famous breed of horses. The sea-fisheries, esp. herring, are very important.

In the Midland Valley are extensive coalfields, with iron ore, now nearly exhausted, near the coal. Other minerals are oil shale, granite, slate, and lead. The most important manufactures are those of textiles, metals and machinery, and shipbuilding. The cotton industry centres chiefly in Glasgow and Paisley, the latter noted for its thread. Woollen cloth (tweed) is manufactured in the towns of the R. Tweed valley; linen is manufactured in several Angus towns and in Dunfermline, jute in Dundee, and linoleum in Kirkcaldy. Glasgow is the centre of a region noted for its machinery and iron-smelting. The Clyde area is the largest shipbuilding district in the world. Aluminium works, dependent on water power, exist at Kinlochleven, the Falls of Foyers, and Fort William. Paper is manufactured in Midlothian; Edinburgh, next to London, is the greatest printing centre in the U.K.; whisky is distilled in the Highland districts, and sugar refining is carried on at Greenock.

The railways are grouped into two systems—the London and North Eastern Railway, and the London, Midland, and Scottish Railway—the main lines of which connect Edinburgh and Glasgow with London and the S., and also with all the principal towns in Scotland. The W. ports trade chiefly with America, the W. of England, and Ireland; the E. ports chiefly with the countries bordering the North Sea and the Baltic.

Scotland is exceedingly popular as a holiday resort, and the Highlands afford splendid shooting, deer-stalking, and fishing. There are univs. at St. Andrews, Glasgow, Aberdeen, and Edinburgh. Scotland is divided into 33 counties. Edinburgh is the cap., and Glasgow the largest tn. Area, 29,796 sq. m.; pop. 4,843,000.

Scran'ton, city, N.E. Pennsylvania, U.S.A., on R. Lackawanna; in great anthracite coal region, and coal mining is chief industry; rolling mills, steel works, machinery, locomotives, silk goods. Pop. 143,000.

Scun'thorpe and Frodingham, urb. dist., Lincolnshire, England, 12 m. S.E. of Goole; blast furnaces and steel works. Pop. 33,800.

Scu'tari. (1) Tn., Asia Minor, on Bosporus opposite Constantinople, of which it is a suburb; manufactures silk, cotton, and muslin. Pop. 125,000. (2) Tn., Albania, on Lake Scutari; castle, cathedral; manufactures small-arms, textiles, and exports grain, wool, tobacco, hides. Pop. 24,000.

Sea'ford, urb. dist. and wat.-pl., Sussex, England; formerly one of Cinque Ports; fishing. Pop. 6,600.

Sea'ham Harbour, urb. dist. and port, Durham, England, 5½ m. S. of Sunderland; coal port; bottles, chemicals; imports timber. Pop. 19,400.

Sea'thwaite. (1) Par., N. Lancs, England, 5 m. W. of L. Coniston; fine scenery of Duddon valley. (2) Vil., Cumberland, England, at head of Borrowdale, 8 m. S. of Keswick; heaviest rainfall in England (mean ann. 130 in.).

Seaton, urb. dist., S.E. Devon, England, near mouth of R. Axe; wat.-pl. Pop. 2,400.

Sea'ton, NORTH, coast par. and vil., Northumberland, England, 3 m. N. of Blyth; collieries. Pop. (par.) 2,000.

Seaton Carew (*sē'ton kă-roo'*), wat.-pl., Durham, England, 2 m. S. of and in co. bor. of W. Hartlepool; residential dist. Pop. 2,170.

Sea'ton Del'aval, urb. dist., Northumberland, England, 3 m. S.W. of Blyth; collieries; manufactures chemicals. Pop. 7,400.

Seattle (*sē-at'l*), principal port, Washington, U.S.A., on Puget Sound; State univ.; fine cathedral; ship-building, fish canning, glass making, and lumber trade; whaling and fishing centre; coal found in district; great trading centre. Pop. 366,000.

Sebastopol. See SEVASTOPOL.

Seben'ico. See SIBENIK.

Sebu (*se-boo'*). (1) Isl. and prov., Philippine Is.; mountainous; forested; coal. Area, 1,695 sq. m.; pop. 855,000. (2) Port, cap. of above; exports copra, tobacco, sugar. Pop. 66,000.

Secunderabad', tn., Hyderabad, India, 6 m. N.E. of Hyderabad, of which it forms a suburb; one of largest military stations in India. Pop. 9,500.

Seda'lia, city, Missouri, U.S.A., 80 m. E.S.E. of Kansas City; in agricultural, coal mining, and limestone region; manufactures machinery, locomotives, textiles, flour; meat-packing industry. Pop. 21,000.

Sedan', tn., frontier fortress, Ardennes, France, on R. Meuse; chief industries are machinery, metal ware, woollens, flour; battle of Sedan in Franco-German war (1870) resulted in total defeat of French. Pop. 16,000.

Sed'bergh, mkt. tn. and par., Yorks, England, 10 m. E. of Kendal; manufactures woollens; public school. Pop. (par.) 2,600.

Sedge'moor, marshy tract, Somersetshire, England, 5 m. S.E. of Bridgwater; largely reclaimed for pasture; Monmouth's rebellion quelled here (1685).

Sedg'ley, urb. dist., Staffs, England, 4 m. S.W. of Wolverhampton; manufactures nails, gas retorts, hardware; coal, limestone, ironstone, and fire-clay are worked. Pop. 19,300.

Seeland. See ZEALAND.

Seghill, urb. dist., Northumberland, England, 6 m. N.W. of North Shields; coal mining. Pop. 2,600.

Sego'via. (1) Prov., Spain; table-land producing flax, wheat, rye, barley; live-stock raised. Area, 2,635 sq. m.; pop. 174,000. (2) Cap. of above, 42 m. N.N.W. of Madrid; cathedral; formerly cloth centre of Spain; iron goods, earthenware, paper, porcelain, flour. Pop. 16,000.

Seine (*sān*). (1) Riv., France, rises in Côte-d'Or Mts., flows with a winding course to N.W.; enters Eng. Channel at Havre; receives as tribs. the Aube, Marne (which joins it above Paris), Oise, Yonne, Loing, Essonne; length, 482 m.; connected by elaborate system of canals with Rs. Loire, Rhone, Rhine, Somme, Schelde. Navigable for ocean vessels as far as Rouen, and for vessels of 1,000 tons up to Paris. (2) Dep., France; traversed by R. Seine; low hills; market gardening is chief industry; gypsum and free-stone quarries; includes all Paris and part of suburbs; most densely populated dep. of France. Area, 185 sq. m.; pop. 4,629,000.

Seine-et-Marne (*sān-ā-mārn*), dep., France; low plateau drained by Rs. Seine and Marne; fertile region of La Brie between the two rivers; produces grain and 'Brie' cheese. Viticulture; flagstone and gypsum quarries; manufactures beet sugar, paper, porcelain. Cap. Melun. Area, 2,275 sq. m.; pop. 380,000.

Seine-et-Oise (*sān-ā-wāz*), dep., France; drained by Rs. Seine and Oise; surface in parts hilly and forest-covered; vineyards and good pastures; wheat, fruit, vegetables grown; manufactures machinery, chemicals, gunpowder, sugar, paper, porcelain; building stone and gypsum quarried. Cap. Versailles. Area, 2,184 sq. m.; pop. 1,138,000.

Seine-Inférieure (*sān-an-fā-re-oor'*), maritime dep., France; drained by R. Seine; undulating and generally fertile; wheat, oats; dairy farming; large quantities of butter and cheese; important textile, iron, and shipbuilding industries; manufactures flax, chemicals, tobacco, dyes, cider; productive fisheries; contains ports of Havre and Dieppe. Cap. Rouen. Area, 2,448 sq. m.; pop. 885,000.

Seistan (*sī-stan'*), region in S.W. Asia, between S.W. Afghanistan and E. Persia, deriving its name from Lake Seistan, a large swamp in W. of Afghanistan; considerably more than half belongs to Afghanistan, the remainder to Persia; surface is chiefly steppe land, but large area is rendered fertile by periodic floodings of Lake Seistan; produces cereals, pulse, cotton, wool, fruits. Some of native tribes are nomadic. Area, 7,000 sq. m.; pop. 205,000.

Sekondi', port, Gold Coast, British W. Africa; an old trading station and important business centre; rail connection with Takoradi harbour. Pop. 10,000.

Selangor', Federated Malay State, on W. coast of Malay Peninsula; drained by R. Selangor and other rivs.; produces tin, coffee, rice, pepper, rubber. Cap. Kuala Lumpur. Area, 3,150 sq. m.; pop. 401,000.

Sel'borne, par. and vil., Hants, England, 16 m. W.N.W. of Winchester; birthplace of Gilbert White, the naturalist. Pop. (par.) 2,000.

Sel'by, urb. dist., W. Riding, Yorks, England, on R. Ouse, 15 m. S. of York; Benedictine abbey; manufactures rope, twine, mustard; malting and shipbuilding. Pop. 10,100.

Selen'ga-Ork'hon, riv., Central Asia; rises in N.W. Mongolia in two streams (Selenga and Orkhon); falls into Lake Baikal. Length, 750 m.

Sel'kirk, royal burgh and co. tn., Selkirkshire, Scotland, on R. Ettrick; tweed and hosiery mills; formerly noted for manufacture of brogue shoes, hence the name 'souters (shoemakers) of Selkirk.' Pop. 5,700.

Sel'kirk Mountains, mt. range, British Columbia, Canada; W. of Rocky Mts., and bounded E., N., and W. by Columbia R. Alpine in character, with snowfields and glaciers; highest peak, Sir Donald (10,645 ft.). Canadian Pacific Rly. crosses the range by Roger's Pass (4,300 ft.).

Sel'kirkshire, inland co., S.E. Scotland; surface generally mountainous; highest point, Broad Law; contains St. Mary's Loch; beautiful pastoral scenery; drained by Rs. Tweed, Ettrick, Yarrow; has extensive sheep farming and manufactures of woollen cloth; tanning. Co. tn., Selkirk. Area, 267 sq. m.; pop. 22,600.

Sel'ma, city, Alabama, U.S.A., on Alabama R.; centre for dairy and lumber products; cotton factories, structural iron and bridge works; manufactures cotton-seed oil, fertilizers. Pop. 16,000.

Selmeczbanya (*sel-mets-ban'ya*), tn., Czechoslovakia, 65 m. N. of Budapest; famous silver mines; potteries. Pop. 13,000.

Sel'sey, or SELSEA, par. and vil., Sussex, England, 7 m. S. of Chichester; beside cape known as Selsea Bill; fisheries; cathedral now beneath the sea. Pop. (par.) 3,600.

Semarang'. (1) Residency, Java, Dutch E. Indies; coastal plain backed by hills and mountains; well watered; sugar and coffee in W.; petroleum and teak in E. Area, 11,300 sq. m.; pop. 2,787,000. (2) Cap. and port of above, on N. coast; exports sugar and kapok. Pop. 147,000.

Semipalatinsk', tn., Kazak, U.S.S.R., on island in R. Irtish, 470 m. S.E. of Omsk; distilleries, breweries, leather factories, and flour mills. Pop. 57,000.

Semlin. See ZEMUN.

Sem'mering Pass, pass in Austrian Alps between Vienna and Graz; lowest of the great passes across Alps; summit, 3,225 ft.

Semnan', tn., Persia, 110 m. E. of Tehran; in centre of tobacco-growing region; very anc. tn.; noted for cotton goods and almond paste. Pop. 20,000.

Sendai (*sen-dī'*), tn., Honshu, Japan, on E. coast; trade in fish and salt. Pop. 143,000.

Senegal'. (1) River, French W. Africa; flows through the colony of Senegal, to which it gives its name, and flows into Atlantic near St. Louis; has large number of tributaries from the S. Sudan; navigation interrupted by Kayes rapids; length, 1,000 m. (2) Colony, French W. Africa; bounded N. by Mauritania, E. by R. Faleme, trib. of R. Senegal, S. by French Guinea and Portuguese Guinea, and W. by Atlantic Ocean. Surface mountainous in E., flat in W.; watered by Rs. Senegal and Gambia; sheep, goats, cattle, asses, and horses reared; produces ground-nuts, rubber, oil-seeds, millet, maize, rice; salt industry; weaving and pottery. Chief exports, ground-nuts, cotton, gum. Cap. St. Louis. Area, 74,112 sq. m.; pop. 1,318,000.

Senigal'lia, tn., Italy, on Adriatic Sea, 15 m. N.W. of Ancona; famous fair held annually till 1869. Pop. 12,000.

Senj (*sen'yi*), tn., Croatia-Slavonia, Yugoslavia, on Adriatic Sea; trades in fish, salt, and tobacco. Pop. 3,000.

Sen'lac, heath between Hastings and Battle, Sussex, England; site of battle of Hastings (1066).

Sennar', dist., Anglo-Egyptian Sudan, Africa, lying between Rs. Blue Nile and White Nile; produces durra, wheat, sesame, and other cereals, cotton, tobacco, vegetables; Sennar Dam at Makwar irrigates region known as El Gezira. Cap. Sennar.

Sens (*son*), tn., Yonne, France, on R. Yonne, 63 m. S.E. of Paris; walled tn.; 12th cent. Gothic cathedral; manufactures boots and shoes, agricultural implements, chemicals. cutlery; flour mills and tanneries. Pop. 15,000.

Sensée (*son-sā'*), river, deps. Pas-de-Calais and Nord, France, rises S.E. of Arras and flows through Haucourt to Arleux, where it is canalized to its junction with the Schelde at Bouchain; length, 40 m.

Sen'ta, tn., Yugoslavia, on R. Tisa, 30 m. S. of Szeged; centre of trade in live-stock and agricultural produce. Pop. 31,000.

Seoul (*sē-ool'*), cap., Korea; city walls, 20 to 30 ft. high; an open port and important railway centre; manufactures brass ware, pottery, fans, and silk. Pop. 315,000.

Seraing (*se-rang'*), tn., Liége, Belgium, on R. Meuse; large engineering and machinery works. Pop. 44,000.

Serajevo. See SARAJEVO.

Serampore', tn., Bengal, India, on R. Hooghly; hand weaving of cotton and silk; bricks, pottery, mats. Pop. 33,000.

Ser'bia, former Balkan kingdom, now principal state of Yugoslavia. Cap. Belgrade. See YUGOSLAVIA.

Serena (*sā-rā'nā*), tn., cap. of Coquimbo, Chile, on R. Coquimbo, 220 m. N. of Valparaiso; brewing and fruit preserving. Pop. 15,000.

Ser'es, tn. on Lake Takhino, Macedonia, Greece, 45 m. N.E. of Salonika; cottons, woollens; trades in wool, cereals, rice, tobacco, hides. Pop. 30,000.

Sereth. See SIRET.

Serginsk', UPPER AND LOWER, two tns., Ural Area, U.S.S.R., 58 m. S.E. of Sverdlovsk; ironworks; mineral waters in dist. Pop. (united) *c.* 30,000.

Sergipe (*ser-zhē'pā*), state, N.E. Brazil, S. America; forested coast lands with hilly country behind; much of it fertile; tobacco, cotton, sugar, maize. Cap. Aracaju. Area, 15,089 sq. m.; pop. 540,000.

Seringapatam', tn., Mysore, India, on isl. in R. Cauvery, 10 m. N.E. of Mysore; fort stormed by Brit. (1799). Pop. 7,500.

Ser'pukhov, riv. port, central Russia, on R. Nara, 57 m. S. of Moscow; manufactures paper, textiles, chintz, leather, chemicals; copper and iron works. Pop. 56,000.

Ses'sa Aurunca (*ou-roon'ka*), tn., Italy, 32 m. N.N.W. of Naples; old cathedral, Roman remains; wine-growing centre. Pop. 21,000.

Ses'tri Ponen'te, tn., Italy, 3 m. W. of Genoa; summer resort; shipbuilding yards, machinery workshops, alabaster quarries. Pop. 26,000.

Set'tle, mkt. tn. and par., Yorks, England, on R. Ribble, 13 m. N.W. of Skipton; manufactures cotton; tannery. Pop. (par.) 2,400.

Setu'bal, port, Estremadura, Portugal, 20 m. S.E. of Lisbon; important sardine fisheries; exports salt, wine, cork, oranges, grapes; manufactures lace and fish fertiliser. Pop. 37,000.

Sevast'opol, or SEBASTOPOL, port, seaside resort, Crimea, on Black Sea; before Great War was important naval station for Black Sea fleet; zoological marine station; has extensive dockyards, naval arsenals; manufactures tiles, leather, soap, machinery; famous for its siege (1854–55). Pop. 75,000.

Sevenoaks, mkt. tn., Kent, England, 20 m. S.E. of London; anc. church; grammar school. Pop. 10,500.

Sev'ern, river, England and Wales, rises on Plinlimmon, Montgomeryshire, and traverses Shropshire, Worcestershire, and Gloucestershire; forms estuary opening into Bristol Channel; chief tribs., Vyrnwy, Terne, Upper and Lower Avon, Teme, Wye, and Usk; connected with Rs. Thames and Trent by canal; navigable to Welshpool; railway tunnel (4½ m.) passes under estuary; noted for its eagre or bore. Length, 180 m.

Seville (*se-vil'*). (1) Prov., S. Spain; flat and fertile in E., hilly in W.; watered by Rs. Guadalquivir and Genil; agriculture, cattle rearing, mining; wool, silk, oranges, oil, cork, wine produced; copper, iron, coal, marble mined. Area, 5,428 sq. m.; pop. 746,000. (2) Cap. of above, on R. Guadalquivir; has many beautiful Moorish buildings, the finest of which is the Alcazar or palace; fine cathedral, largest in Spain; univ.; centre of sport of bull-fighting; exports lead, quicksilver, oranges, lemons, olives, olive oil, cork, wine; manufactures iron goods, machinery, pottery, silk, cotton, cigars. Pop. 217,000.

Sèvres (*sāvr*), tn., Seine-et-Oise, France, on R. Seine, 6 m. S.W. of Paris; noted for porcelain; painted glass, mosaic work. Pop. 14,000.

Seychelles (*sā-shel'*), British crown colony, comprising over 100 islands in the Indian Ocean, N. of Mauritius; volcanic, and surrounded by coral reefs; principal isl. Mahé; surface generally mountainous; climate tropical but healthy; produces maize, manioc, coconuts, vanilla, cloves, fruit, rubber. Cap. Victoria. Area, 156 sq. m.; pop. 27,000.

Seyne-sur-Mer (*sān*), tn., Var, s. France, opposite Toulon; extensive shipbuilding yards; maritime workshops; oyster beds. Pop. 18,000.

Sfax, port, Tunisia, N. Africa, on Gulf of Qabes; manufactures textiles; exports fruits, sponges, oil, phosphates, esparto grass. Pop. 28,000.

Shabin Kara-Hissar. See KARA-HISSAR SHARKI.

Shaftesbury, mun. bor., Dorset, England, 18 m. s.s.w. of Salisbury; agricultural implements. Pop. 2,400.

Shahabad′, dist., Patna div., Bengal, India; fertile plain in N.; densely wooded Kaimur Hills in s.; chief rivs., Ganges and Son; rice, wheat; oil-seeds, poppy, sugar, millet grown. Cap. Arrah, 36 m. w. of Patna. Area, 4,373 sq. m.; pop. 1,817,000.

Shahjahanpur′, tn., United Provinces, India, on R. Deoha, 95 m. N.W. of Lucknow; manufactures sugar. Pop. 73,000.

Shamo′kin, town, Pennsylvania, U.S.A., 40 m. N.N.E. of Harrisburg; in anthracite coal region; iron and steel industries. Pop. 21,000.

Shanghai (*shang-hī′*), tn., Kiangsu, China, near mouth of Yangtze Kiang; chief commercial city and greatest foreign market of China; central and walled parts of town consist of narrow and dirty streets; well-built suburbs outside the walls. Situated in midst of great plain, producing rice, cotton, and fruits. Shipbuilding and engineering extensively carried on; cotton, leather, paper, cigarettes, and many other articles are manufactured. Pop. 2,677,000.

Shanhai-kwan′ ('gate between mountain and sea'), frontier tn., Hopeh prov., China; important strategic point at terminus of Great Wall, 3 m. from sea. Pop. 30,000.

Shank′lin, wat.-pl., E. Isle of Wight, England; chalybeate springs. Pop. 5,100.

Shan′non, riv., I.F.S.; rises in co. Cavan; winds s. and s.w. through Loughs Allen, Boderg, Ree, and Derg to Limerick, then widens into estuary entering Atlantic Ocean; navigable to Lough Allen. A large power plant to supply electricity to the greater part of the I.F.S. is being constructed near Limerick. Length, 224 m.

Shansi, prov., N. China; mountainous; rich in coal, iron ore, salt, petroleum. Cap. Tai-yuan. Area, 81,940 sq. m.; pop. 12,153,000.

Shan States, in N. and E. of Burma, in R. Salween basin; two groups—Northern (six states) and Southern (thirty-five states). Mainly plateau; largely undeveloped. Total area, 56,313 sq. m.; pop. 1,433,000.

Shantung′, maritime prov., China, bordering on Yellow Sea and Gulf of Pohai; w. is fertile plain traversed by the Grand Canal; mountainous in E.; R. Hwang-Ho flows s.w. to N.E. through prov.; extensive deposits of coal, iron, lead, copper, and gold; produces grain, fruit, indigo, silk. Cap. Tsinan. Area, 55,970 sq. m.; pop. 30,803,000.

Shap, urb. dist., Westmorland, England, 12 m. S.S.E. of Penrith. To south Shap Fell, a well-known granitic mt., and Shap Summit, the most important pass in the county, traversed by L.M.S. Rly. Pop. of urb. dist. 1,200.

Shari (*shä′rē*), river, N. Central Africa; rises N. of equator and flows N.W. into Lake Chad; length, 1,400 m.

Sharle′ston, vil. and par., Yorks, England, 4 m. S.E. of Wakefield; brick making; large colliery. Pop. (par.) 2,800.

Sharon (*shār′on*), tn., Pennsylvania, U.S.A., on border of Ohio, 50 m. s. of L. Erie; iron manufactures, bricks, electrical articles. Pop. 22,000.

Shas′i, port, Hupeh, China, on R. Yangtze; manufactures cotton cloth; exports seeds, vegetable tallow, wood oil. Pop. 190,000.

Shatt-al-Arab′, riv. formed by jn. of Rs. Euphrates and Tigris, Iraq, Asia; extends from Qurna to Persian Gulf; enters sea by several mouths;

carries much silt. Chief ports, Basra, Mohammerah, and Fao. Length, 123 m.

Shawinigan Falls (*shä'in-i-gan*), falls and tn., Quebec, Canada, on St. Maurice R., 21 m. N. of Three Rivers; alt. of falls, 150 ft.; supply power for wood-pulp and paper mills. Pop. (tn.) 11,000.

Shawnee', city, Oklahoma, U.S.A., on North Canadian R., 40 m. S.E. of Oklahoma City; cotton manufactures; meat preserving; railway workshops. Pop. 15,000.

Sheboy'gan, city, Wisconsin, U.S.A., on Lake Michigan; furniture, leather goods, enamelled ware, pianos, gloves; mineral waters; exports coal; fisheries. Pop. 39,000.

Sheer'ness, fort. port, dockyard, naval arsenal, at junction of Rs. Medway and Thames, on Isle of Sheppey, Kent, England; dockyard extends to 60 ac.; industries chiefly connected with government works. Pop. 16,700.

Shef'field, co. bor., W. Riding, Yorks, England, on R. Don; chief seat of English cutlery trade, manufacturing every kind of cutting tool; other industries include steel manufacture and the production of armour-plates, guns, rails, bicycles, optical and mathematical instruments, britannia metal, and electro-plated goods, gramophones and needles; coal is mined in vicinity. Has fine public buildings and univ. Pop. 511,700.

Shenando'ah. (1) City, Pennsylvania, U.S.A., 33 m. S.W. of Wilkes-Barre; coal-mining centre. Pop. 25,000. (2) Largest trib. of Potomac R., Virginia and W. Virginia, U.S.A.; valley fertile, with orchards and poultry farming. Valley was scene of much fighting in American Civil War. Length, 200 m.

Shen'di, tn., Anglo-Egyptian Sudan, on R. Nile, between Khartoum and Berber; railway works; manufactures cotton and leather. Pop. 11,000.

Shengking. See LIAONING.

Shensi', inland prov., China; mountainous; watered by R. Wei, trib. of Hwang-Ho; coal, petroleum; produces wheat, cotton. Cap. Sian. Area, 75,270 sq. m.; pop. 9,466,000.

Shep'shed, urb. dist., Leicestershire, England, 4 m. W. of Loughborough; on edge of Charnwood Forest. Pop. 5,800.

Shep'ton-Mallet, mkt. tn., Somersetshire, England, 5 m. S.E. of Wells; breweries, roperies, pottery industries. Pop. 4,100.

Sher'borne, mkt. tn., Dorsetshire, England, 5 m. E. of Yeovil; 12th cent. abbey church, grammar school; gloves. Pop. 6,500.

Sher'brooke, city, S. Quebec, Canada, on R. St. Francis, 80 m. E. of Montreal; woollens and worsteds, carpets, machinery, sawmills. Pop. 26,000.

Sher'ingham, urb. dist., N. Norfolk, England; seaside resort; seat of Norfolk crab-fishery. Pop. 4,100.

Sher'man, city, Texas, U.S.A., 62 m. N. of Dallas; manufactures cotton-seed oil, flour, iron goods. Pop. 15,000.

's Herto'genbosch (French *Bois-le-Duc*), tn., cap. of N. Brabant, Holland, at junction of Rs. Aa and Dommel; manufactures cloth, hats, needles, cutlery; cathedral. Pop. 41,000.

Sherwood Forest, anc. royal forest, Notts, England, extending into Derby and Yorks; traditional retreat of Robin Hood; includes the district of the 'Dukeries.'

Shet'land, or ZETLAND, group of nearly 100 islands lying N.N.E. of mainland of Scotland, constituting a county of Scotland; 27 islands are inhabited, of which largest are Mainland, Yell, and Unst; surface hilly, reaching extreme height of 1,475 ft. in Ronas Hill in Mainland; principal industry is fishing, esp. herring; sheep, cattle, and breed of small ponies reared; much of soil is peaty; oats, barley, potatoes, turnips cultivated; knitted woollen goods an important household industry. Chief tn., Lerwick. Area, 550 sq. m.; pop. 21,400.

Shet'tleston, tn., Lanarkshire, Scotland; now forming part of Glasgow; collieries. Pop. 14,000.

Shif'nal, mkt. tn., Shropshire, England, 17 m. E. of Shrewsbury; ironworks, coal and iron mines. Pop. 3,300.

Shigat'se, tn., Tibet, Asia, on upper R. Brahmaputra or Tsang-po; important religious and trading centre. Pop. 9,000.

Shikarpur', tn., Sind, India, on railway to Quetta; great bazaar; important trading centre; trade in gems and silk. Pop. 56,000.

Shikoku (*shē-kō'koo*), isl., s. Japan; separated from Honshu and Kyushu by Inland Sea; mountainous; valleys fertile; forests; rice, fruits, sugar-cane; copper. Area, 6,856 sq. m.; pop. *c.* 3,500,000.

Shil'don, tn., Durham, England, 3 m. S.E. of Bishop Auckland; railway workshops, foundries, coal mines, quarries. Pop. 12,700.

Shillong', cap. of Assam, India, on R. Brahmaputra; health and holiday resort. Pop. 17,000.

Shimonosek'i, port, Honshu, Japan, on w. entrance of Inland Sea; peace treaty between China and Japan signed here (1895); open to foreign trade since 1890. Pop. 92,000.

Ship'ley, par. and tn., W. Riding, Yorks, England, on R. Aire, 3 m. N.W. of Bradford; manufactures worsted. Pop. 30,200.

Shiraz', cap., Fars prov., s. Persia; fine mosques and good bazaars; manufactures mosaics, silks, carpets, wine; exports gums, opium, rose water, cotton, skins. Pop. 35,000.

Shiré (*shē'rā*), riv., Africa; issues from S.E. corner of Lake Nyasa, and joins R. Zambezi; navigable to Chiromo, and for smaller vessels as far as Katunga. Length, 370 m.

Shir'ley, former urb. dist., now included in Southampton. Pop. 17,400.

Sho'a, div., formerly kingdom, Abyssinia; agriculture, oranges; in 1889 Menelik II., King of Shoa, became King of Abyssinia. Chief tn., Addis Ababa, cap. of Abyssinia. Area, *c.* 26,000 sq. m.; pop. 1,500,000.

Shoeburyness', tn., Essex, England; opposite Sheerness; garrison town, with school of gunnery and Royal Artillery works. Pop. 6,700.

Sholapur', tn., Bombay, India, 147 m. S.E. of Poona; important trading centre; manufactures silk and cotton cloth. Pop. 120,000.

Shore'ditch, E. metropolitan bor., London, England; furniture, cabinet-making, boots and shoes. Pop. 97,000.

Shore'ham by Sea, urb. dist. and port, Sussex, England, at mouth of R. Adur; fine church; shipbuilding, fisheries; seaside resort. Pop. 8,800.

Shorn'cliffe Camp, military station, Kent, England, 1¾ m. w. of Folkestone; camp dates from Peninsular and Crimean Wars.

Short Heath, tn., Staffs, England, 4½ m. N.E. of Wolverhampton; coal mining. Pop. 5,000.

Shotts, par. and vil., Lanarkshire, Scotland, 18 m. S.E. of Glasgow; coal and ironstone mining; quarrying. Pop. (par.) 21,000.

Shreveport, city, Louisiana, U.S.A., on Red R.; railway centre; petroleum refineries. Pop. 77,000.

Shrews'bury, co. tn., Shropshire, England, on R. Severn. Remains of city walls and Norman castle; famous school founded by Edward VI.; great road and rail centre; glass staining and ironfounding; brewing, tanning; agricultural implements, linen yarns. Pop. 32,400.

Shrop'shire, or SALOP, co. of w. England, near centre of Welsh border; mountainous in s. and w.; crossed by Clee Hills, Caradoc Hills, and other ranges; drained by R. Severn and tribs. Agriculture is principal industry; sheep and cattle are reared. Several small coalfields, of which Coalbrookdale is most important; other minerals found include iron, lead, limestone, and small quantities of zinc and barytes; blast furnaces, iron manufactures. Cap. Shrewsbury. Area, 1,346 sq. m.; pop. 244,200.

Shu'men, tn., Bulgaria, 56 m. w. of Varna; military centre; slippers, clothing, copper and tin ware. Pop. 25,000.

Shu'shtar, tn., Persia, on R. Karun, 116 m. N.E. of Mohammerah; carpets, woollens, earthenware, saddles; brass and copper work. Pop. 20,000.

Shuya (*shoo'yă*), tn., central Russia, 63 m. N.W. of Vladimir; cotton, linen, soap, and pottery; hides and furs. Pop. 20,000.

Shwebo'. (1) Dist., Burma; mainly plain, surrounded by hills, watered by R. Mu; rice, maize, cotton, and peas. Area, 5,714 sq. m.; pop. 391,000. (2) Cap. of above, 53 m. N.E. of Mandalay; in centre of rice-growing region. Pop. 11,000.

Sialkot'. (1) Dist., N. Punjab, India; very fertile; cereals, sugar. Area, 1,796 sq. m.; pop. 1,090,000. (2) Cap. of above, near Kashmir boundary N. of Lahore; garrison town; tents, surgical instruments, boots, cotton, and paper. Pop. 71,000.

Siam, kingdom, Indo-China; lies mainly in centre of Indo-China peninsula, with Burma on N. and W., and French Indo-China on E. It has a long strip running down N. half of Malay Peninsula between Strait of Malacca and Gulf of Siam, with Malay States to the S. The W. half of main portion consists of valley of R. Menam and E. half of Korat plateau, which stretches to R. Mekong basin. N. is mountainous, rising to heights of 6,000 to 8,000 ft.; S. is an alluvial plain, drained by rivers mentioned and their tribs., chief of which is R. Meping, joining R. Menam. Bangkok is the capital. Climate is of the monsoon type, wet season lasting from May till October. Chief wealth is rice in S., teak and other timber trees in N. Forestry is almost entirely in British hands; labourers of S. largely Chinese coolies. Rice is chief export; other exports include teak, hides, pepper, silk. Mineral resources are widespread and various, including coal, tin, iron, zinc, wolfram, tungsten, antimony, and manganese. Railways connect with Federated Malay States lines. Cap. Bangkok. Area, 200,148 sq. m.; pop. 9,207,000.

Sian', formerly HSI-AN or SINGAN, city, cap. of Shensi, China, at junction of important trade routes; great trading centre in silk, tea, cotton, sugar, paper, porcelain, skins. Pop. 1,000,000.

Siangtan', formerly HSIANG-TAN, tn., Hunan, China, on Siang trib. of Yangtse Kiang, 25 m. S. of Chang-sha; general trade and transhipment of goods. Pop. 300,000.

Sibenik, or SEBENICO (*shib-en'ik*), port, Dalmatia, Yugoslavia, on Adriatic Sea, 30 m. N.W. of Split; cathedral; naval base; fishing; weaving, oil refining; woollens, chemicals; exports bauxite. Pop. 20,000.

Siberia (*sī-bē're-a*), terr., N. Asia, between Ural Mts. and Pacific Ocean, and between Arctic Ocean and Kazak, Mongolia, Manchuria, and Korea. The name, which was the former designation of Russian territory in Asia, now includes Ural Area, Siberian Area, Yakutsk Rep., Buriat Mongol Rep., and Far Eastern Area. See separate articles.

Siberian Area, one of administrative units of U.S.S.R., Asia; N. is Arctic Ocean; E. are Yakutsk Rep. and Buriat Mongol Rep.; S. are Mongolia and Kazak; W. is Ural Area. Mountainous and hilly in S. and E., plain in W., large portion of it being the basin of R. Yenisei. Crossed by Trans-Siberian Rly. Chief crops, wheat, rye, barley, potatoes, grown in vicinity of rly. Farther N. is forest, succeeded by tundra. Horses and cattle bred; reindeer important. Rich mineral deposits, esp. gold, silver, asbestos, magnetic iron ore. Chief tns., Novo-Sibirsk (cap.), Omsk, Tomsk, Irkutsk. Area, 1,611,446 sq. m.; pop. 8,668,000.

Sibiu, formerly HERMANNSTADT, tn., Transylvania, Romania, on R. Sibiu; linen, leather, ropes, soap; brewing and distilling. Pop. 33,000.

Sibon'ga, tn., Sebu I., Philippine Is., on E. coast; maize and tobacco are chief products. Pop. 27,000.

Sibsag'ar, dist., N.E. Assam, India; plain, with much jungle; watered by tribs. of R. Brahmaputra; produces large quantities of tea. Chief tn., Sibsagar. Area, 5,202 sq. m.; pop. 823,000.

Sicily (*sis'i-li*), isl., Italy; largest in Mediterranean, about 2 m. from s.w. extremity of Italian mainland, from which it is separated by the deep, narrow Strait of Messina; 80 m. from African coast; 180 m. long, 120 wide; triangular in shape. Surface is mountainous; most of island over 500 ft. above sea-level; highest point, Etna, a volcano (11,870 ft.). Good harbours on N. but not on S. coast. Rivs. unimportant. Summer hot and dry, winter mild and rainy. Sicily suffers from earthquakes, eruptions, sirocco in summer; malaria in parts. Chief crop wheat; fruit trees and olives, especially on N. and E. coasts, vines mainly in W.; soil fertile, but agricultural methods backward; trees scarce; principal exports, citrus fruits, almonds, nuts, wine (Marsala), preserved vegetables, sulphur, salt, silk, tunny, and sardines, sumach (for tanning). Deep-sea fisheries are valuable. Cap. Palermo. Area, 9,935 sq. m.; pop. 4,426,000.

Sid'cup, urb. dist., Kent, England, 12 m. S.E. of London; residential centre; part of Greater London. Pop. 12,400.

Sidi-bel-Abbès (*sē-dē'bel-ab-ās'*), tn., Oran, Algeria, N. Africa, on R. Mekerra; exports grain, tobacco, cattle; one of headquarters of French Foreign Legion. Pop. 43,000.

Sid'mouth, fashionable wat.-pl., S. Devon, England, on R. Sid and Lyme Bay, surrounded by high cliffs; encroachment of sea has destroyed harbour. Pop. 6,100.

Si'don, modern SAIDA, anc. seapt., Great Lebanon, Syria, 20 m. S. of Beirut; exports olive oil, lemons, oranges. Pop. 10,000.

Siedlce (*syedl'tse*), tn., Poland, 53 m. E. of Warsaw; famous castle; scene of massacres of Jews and others (1906). Pop. 31,000.

Siegburg (*zēg'boorg*), tn., Rhineland, Prussia, on R. Sieg, 15 m. S.E. of Cologne; manufactures fireworks, earthenware. Pop. 19,000.

Siegen (*zē'gen*), tn., Westphalia, Germany, on R. Sieg, 47 m. E. of Cologne; manufactures iron, leather, machinery. Pop. 31,000.

Siena (*sē-ā'na*). (1) Prov., N. Italy; wheat, wine, olives, silk. Area, 1,471 sq. m.; pop. 255,000. (2) Cap. of above, 31 m. S. of Florence; mediæval tn., with old walls and gateways, narrow steep streets, splendid churches and palaces; magnificent Gothic cathedral of black and white marble; univ.; ranks next to Florence, Rome, and Venice in the history of art. Chief industries are machinery, ironwork, wood carving, marzipan. Pop. 48,000.

Siero (*sē-ā'ro*), tn., N. Spain, on R. Nora, 9 m. E. of Oviedo; tanneries, saline springs. Pop. 27,000.

Sierra Leone (*sē-er'a lē-ō'nā*), British colony with inland protectorate, W. Africa, between Liberia and French Guinea, with Atlantic Ocean on W.; low and swampy near shore, N. part rises in Mt. Daro to 4,396 ft. Chief exports: palm kernels, palm oil, kola nuts, ginger, piassava, hides. Gold discovered recently. Chief tn., Freetown. Area (colony), *c.* 4,000 sq. m.; (protectorate), 27,000 sq. m. Pop. (colony), 85,000; (protectorate), 1,456,000.

Sierra Nevada (*sē-er'a nā-vā'dā*) (' snowy mountains '). (1) Highest mt. range, Spain, between valley of R. Guadalquivir and Mediterranean; highest peak, Mulhacen (11,421 ft.). (2) Mt. range, California, U.S.A.; highest summit, Mt. Whitney (14,500 ft.). In S. occur groves of giant redwoods.

Si Kiang', most important river, S. China; rises in Yunnan plateau, enters China Sea by great delta, on branch of which stands Canton; navigable to Wuchow. Length, over 1,250 m.

Sik'kim, Indian state, Himalayas, India; situated between Nepal and Bhutan; mountainous; watered by R. Tista, affluent of R. Brahmaputra; produces maize, rice, fruit; woollens; much of country is forested. Cap. Gangtok. Area, 2,818 sq. m.; pop. 82,000.

Sil'chester, vil., Hants, England, 7 m. N. of Basingstoke; site of Roman tn. (*Calleva Atrebatum*), whence five Roman roads radiated. Pop. 390.

Silesia (*si-lē'she-a*). (1) Prov., Czechoslovakia, between Moravia and Prussian Silesia; has Sudetic Mts. in N., spurs of Carpathians in E.; drained by upper waters of Rs. Oder and Vistula; in N.W. sheep are reared, and forestry and dairy farming are important; in S.E. poultry, cereals, and fruit are produced; has valuable coalfield. Area, 1,708 sq. m.; pop. 720,000. (2) Prov., S.E. Prussia, divided into Upper and Lower Silesia; hilly in S., where Sudetic Mts. reach extreme height of 5,260 ft.; elsewhere surface is flat; drained by R. Oder: large area forested; Upper and Lower Silesia have each a coalfield, that in Upper being larger and more valuable; produces also zinc, iron, silver-lead, arsenic; agriculture is carried on, and sugar-beet, cereals, fruits, and oil plants are cultivated; manufactures linens, cottons, woollens, zinc and iron goods, paper. Chief tn., Breslau. Area, 14,022 sq. m.; pop. 4,512,000.

Silis'tra, formerly SILISTRIA, tn., Romania, on R. Danube, 72 m. N.W. of Varna; important trade centre; cloth manufactures, distilleries and sawmills; tobacco and grapes grown in vicinity. Pop. 18,000.

Sil'loth, tn., Cumberland, England, on Solway Firth; wat.-pl.; steam communication with Isle of Man and Dublin; coal and grain exported. Pop. 3,500.

Sils'den, urb. dist., W. Riding, Yorks, England, 4 m. N.W. of Keighley; manufactures worsted and nails. Pop. 4,900.

Simbirsk. See ULIANOV.

Simfero'pol, tn., Crimea, U.S.S.R., 30 m. N.E. of Sevastopol; manufactures soap, candles, tobacco; noted for fruit and vineyards. Pop. 88,000.

Sim'la, tn., E. Punjab, India, on spur of the Himalayas; seat of Indian Government during hot season. Pop. (winter) 27,000.

Si'mon's Town, naval station, on False Bay, Cape Prov., S. Africa, 22 m. S. of Cape Town; residential and educational centre; large docks. Pop. 5,000.

Simplon Pass (*san-plon'*), mt. pass (6,590 ft.) between Switzerland and N. Italy, traversed by a fine carriage road. Double railway tunnel under pass (12¼ m. long).

Sinai (*sī'nī*), triangular peninsula, Egypt, between Gulf of Suez and Gulf of Aqaba; mountains in S., rest desert; length, 230 m.; breadth, 150 m.; practically waterless and barren. Pop. 15,000.

Sinalo'a, state, Mexico, bordering Gulf of California; narrow coastal plain rising to Sierra Madre Mts. in E.; cereals, sugar, coffee, tobacco, and fruit are grown; mining of silver, iron, and copper is important. Cap. Culiacan. Area, 27,557 sq. m.; pop. 341,000.

Sind, prov, Bombay, India; bounded on N. by Baluchistan and Punjab, on S. by Indian Ocean, on E. by Rajputana, on W. by Baluchistan. Chief riv. Indus; land near it is fertile and watered by irrigation. Climate very dry and hot. Chief occupation, agriculture; wheat, rice, sugar, tobacco, indigo, hemp, cotton grown. Chief tns., Karachi and Hyderabad. Area, 46,506 sq. m.; pop. 3,279,000.

Singan. See SIAN.

Singapore'. (1) Isl., Straits Settlements, S.E. Asia; S. of Malay Peninsula, to which it is joined by a causeway; surface generally rolling and forested. Area, 206 sq. m.; pop. 426,000. (2) Tn., in S.E. of above isl., cap. of Straits Settlements; seat of government and contains governor's palace, cathedrals, and Raffles Museum; free port; chief commercial emporium of S.E. Asia; coaling station; naval base being constructed; shipbuilding, engineering works; busy manufacturing town producing biscuits, shoes, rubber, leather, and tinned fruit. Pop. 350,000.

Sinkiang' ('new territory'), prov., W. China; extends from W. Mongolia to W. Tibet. Much of surface occupied by Takla Makan Desert in s., to N. of which flows R. Tarim, ending in Lob Nor Lake. Towards s. are Altyn-Tagh Mts.; in N. Tien Shan Mts. There are three passes to w. and two into India, trade with India being chiefly by way of Karakoram Pass. Climate has great extremes of heat and cold. Cereals, fruits, vegetables, cotton, wool, silk, are produced and exported; jade and gold are worked. Cap. Urumtsi. Area, 550,340 sq. m.; pop. 2,688,000.

Sinope (*sē-no'pē*), port, Asia Minor, on Black Sea; anc. tn.; good harbour. Pop. 32,000.

Sion (*sē-on'*), cap. of Valais, Switzerland, on R. Rhone; ruined castles; cathedral. Pop. 7,000.

Sioux City (*soo*), city, Iowa, U.S.A., on R. Missouri; meat-packing, foundries, potteries; electrical supplies, cement, soap. Pop. 79,000.

Sioux Falls (*soo*), city, S. Dakota, U.S.A., on R. Missouri at junction of Big Sioux R.; manufactures machinery, carriages, and agricultural implements. Pop. 33,000.

Siquijor (*sē-kē-hor'*), isl., Philippines, 20 m. s. of Sebu; produces tobacco, rice, maize, and coconuts. Area, 126 sq. m.; pop. 46,000.

Sir Dar'ya, formerly JAXARTES, river, Central Asia; rises in Tien Shan Mts., flows w. and N.W. through desert region, and enters Sea of Aral by three channels; has numerous tribs. Length, 1,500 m.

Siret (*sē-ret'*), formerly SERETH, riv., Romania; rises in Carpathian Mts. s.w. of Cernauti, and flows S.S.E. through Moldavia into R. Danube above Galatz. Length, *c.* 300 m.

Sistova. See SVISHTOV.

Sitapur', tn., United Provinces, India, 52 m. N. of Lucknow; commercial centre; exports grain; military cantonment. Pop. 22,000.

Sith'ney, par. and vil., Cornwall, England, 10 m. E. of Penzance; anc. earthworks and cromlech. Pop. (par.) 2,500.

Sit'ka, formerly NEW ARCHANGEL, tn., Baranov I., Alaska; U.S. naval coaling station; has magnetic observatory; salmon canning industry; lumbering, mining. Pop. 1,200.

Sit'tingbourne and Milton, tn., Kent, England, 9 m. E. by s. of Chatham; centre of large fruit and hops dist.; manufactures cement, bricks, and paper; oyster fishing. Pop. 20,200.

Sivas (*sē-vas'*). (1) Vilayet, N. Asiatic Turkey; wheat, barley grown on plateau, vines in lower districts; silver, lead, copper, iron, lignite, salt abundant. Area, 23,970 sq. m.; pop. 330,000. (2) Cap. of above, 170 m. s.w. of Trebizond; coarse woollen goods. Pop. 30,000.

Siv'ri-hissar' ('pointed castle'), tn., Asia Minor, 82 m. s.w. of Angora; trade in opium and mohair. Pop. 31,000.

Siwa (*sē'wä*), oasis, Libyan Desert, Egypt, 350 m. w. of Cairo; very fertile, and produces dates. Remains of Temple of Ammon. Area, 23 sq. m.; pop. 4,000.

Skag'errak, strait between Jutland and s. Norway; communicates with Baltic Sea by Kattegat; length, 150 m.; breadth, 70 to 90 m.

Skeg'ness, tn., bathing resort, Lincolnshire, England, with fine sands. Pop. 9,100.

Skel'manthorpe, urb. dist., W. Riding, Yorks, England, 7 m. E.S.E. of Huddersfield; fancy woollen goods. Pop. 3,700.

Skel'mersdale, tn., Lancs, England, 7 m. w. of Wigan; coal mining, brick making. Pop. 6,200.

Skel'morlie, vil., Ayrshire, Scotland, on the Firth of Clyde, 8 m. s.w. of Greenock; fashionable summer resort; castle in vicinity. Pop. 1,900.

Skel'ton and Brot'ton, urb. dist., Yorks, England, 10 m. E. by s. of Middlesbrough; extensive iron mines. Pop. 13,700.

Sker'ries, port and wat.-pl., co. Dublin, I.F.S., 18 m. N. of Dublin; muslin embroidery is manufactured; fishing port; four small islands, the Skerries, lie off the coast; pop. 1,800.

Skibbereen', mkt. tn. and port, co. Cork, I.F.S., 12 m. S.E. of Bantry;

trade in agricultural produce; fishing. Pop. 2,600.

Skid'daw, mt., Cumberland, England, 3 m. N. of Keswick; alt. 3,054 ft.

Skien (*shēn*), tn., Norway, on R. Skien, 60 m. s.w. of Oslo; timber, cotton, and paper factories. Pop. 17,000.

Skierniewice (*skyer-nē-ā-wēt'sā*), tn., Poland, 42 m. s.w. of Warsaw; manufactures cloth and linen; contains celebrated palace. Pop. 14,000.

Skip'ton, tn., W. Riding, Yorks, England, 18 m. N.W. of Bradford; woollen, spinning, and sewing-cotton factories. Pop. 12,400.

Skoplje (*skop'lyā*), formerly USKUB, tn., Serbia, Yugoslavia, on R. Vardar; important rly. jn.; has tanning, soap, metal, flour, wine, and sugar industries; centre of silver filigree work. Pop. 72,000.

Skye, largest isl. of Inner Hebrides, Inverness-shire, Scotland; bleak moor and rugged mts. (Coolin Hills, 3,234 ft.); deeply indented coasts; fishing, sheep farming, and distilling. Cap. Portree. Area, 670 sq. m.; pop. 11,000.

Slaith'waite, urb. dist. and mkt. tn., W. Riding, Yorks, England, on R. Colne, 4 m. s.w. of Huddersfield; cottons and woollens; mineral baths attract summer visitors. Pop. 5,200.

Slavonia. See CROATIA-SLAVONIA.

Slea'ford, tn., Lincolnshire, England, on R. Slea, 17 m. s. of Lincoln; brewing and trade in agricultural produce. Pop. 7,000.

Sles'vig, most s. part of Denmark, extending to Flensburg Fiord; plain in E. includes Alsen I.; fertile marshes in w. with off-lying Röm I.; ceded to Denmark by Germany after Great War; forms S. Jutland Provs. Area, 1,502 sq. m.; pop. 176,500.

Slez'ska Os'trava, tn., Silesia, Czechoslovakia, near Prussian Silesia; on important coalfield; coal mining. Pop. 23,000.

Sli'go. (1) Maritime co., Connaught, I.F.S., bordering on Atlantic Ocean; surface diversified, well-wooded hills being interspersed with lakes, bogs, and fertile tracts; occupation chiefly pastoral; sea and salmon fishing important. Area, 694 sq. m.; pop. 71,400. (2) Cap. of above, on Sligo Bay; cathedral; exports cattle and agricultural produce; centre of extensive fisheries; flour and saw mills. Pop. 11,400.

Sliv'en, tn., Bulgaria, 70 m. N. by w. of Adrianople; government factory for military clothing; mulberry orchards; black wine. Pop. 29,000.

Slon'im, tn., Poland, 75 m. S.E. of Grodno; distilleries, tanneries, brick-fields; factories for woollen and linen cloth. Pop. 25,000.

Slough (*slou*), mkt. tn., Bucks, England, 2 m. N.E. of Windsor; engineering; seed-testing grounds. Pop. 33,600.

Slovak'ia, prov., Czechoslovakia, between Moravia and Ruthenia; chiefly mountainous, with small plains in E. and W.; forestry and sheep rearing; iron, antimony, manganese, and silver are mined; weaving and wood carving are home crafts; in lowlands cereals, tobacco, and sugar-beet are grown. Cap. Bratislava. Area, 18,895 sq. m.; pop. 3,001,000.

Slove'nia, prov., N.W. Yugoslavia; mainly mountainous; dairying and stock raising largely carried on; vines, walnuts, chestnuts, and fruit in valleys; extensive forests. Chief tn., Ljubljana. Area, 6,253 sq. m.; pop. 1,056,000.

Sluys (*sloo'is*) (French *Ecluse* = 'sluice'), tn., Zeeland, Holland, 10 m. N.E. of Bruges; scene of Eng. naval victory over French (1340); former roadstead silted up, and town now 2 m. from the sea.

Smed'erevo, formerly SEMENDRIA, tn., Yugoslavia, on R. Danube, 20 m. S.E. of Belgrade; manufactures railway wagons; exports grain, live-stock, wine, oils. Pop. 6,000.

Smethwick (*smeth'ik*), co. bor., Staffs, England, 3 m. N.W. of Birmingham; manufactures chemicals, glass, machinery, and lighthouse fittings; iron foundries, engineering works. Pop. 84,400.

Smithfield, dist., London, N. of St. Paul's; from 12th cent. a famous cattle market; scene of fairs; in Tudor period heretics burned here; now contains Central Meat Market of London.

Smith's Falls, tn., Ontario, Canada, 50 m. N.E. of Kingston. Pop. 7,100.

Smolensk'. (1) Prov., Russia, S.W. of Moscow; hilly, or undulating plains; forest-clad; numerous lakes; principal river is the Dnieper; chief occupation, agriculture; live-stock reared; minerals are coal, phosphorite, iron. Area, 22,880 sq. m.; pop. 2,258,000. (2) Cap. of above, on R. Dnieper; important rly. jn.; manufactures soap, tallow, linen, leather; iron and copper smelting. Pop. 79,000.

Smyrna (*smir'na*) (Turkish *Izmir*), chief port, Asia Minor, at head of Gulf of Smyrna, on arm of Ægean Sea; has Turkish and European quarters; important depot for Turkey carpets; machine shops, foundries, flour mills; olive oil, perfumery, pottery; exports raisins, figs, tobacco, silk, and carpets. Occupied by Greece after Great War; recaptured by Turkey (1922), with great destruction of life and property. Pop. 154,000.

Snae Fell, highest mt. in Isle of Man; alt. 2,034 ft.; electric tramway to summit.

Sneek (*snāk*), tn., Friesland, Holland; important horse fair; butter and cheese market. Pop. 15,000.

Snod'land, par. and vil., Kent, England, on R. Medway; lime working, paper manufactured. Pop. (par.) 4,500.

Snow'don, mt. range containing five distinct peaks, Carnarvonshire, Wales; loftiest mountain in Wales (3,560 ft.); other peaks in range are Carnedd Dafydd, Carnedd Llewelyn, and Moel Siabod; railway from Llanberis to summit of Snowdon.

So'bat, riv., N.E. Africa; rises in Abyssinian highlands, flows W.N.W.; joins White Nile, and gives it its milky colour. Length, 450 m.

Society Islands, archipelago of eleven islands in Polynesia, S. Pacific; belong to France; volcanic and fertile; coconuts, copra, oranges, phosphates. Tahiti is largest isl.; its chief tn., Papeete, is cap. of group. Total area, *c.* 700 sq. m.; pop. *c.* 15,000.

Soco'tra, Brit. isl., Indian Ocean, 150 m. off Cape Gardafui, E. Africa; surface mountainous, reaching height of over 4,500 ft.; soil fertile; large numbers of cattle, sheep, and goats raised; fishing; dates, gums, and aloes produced; butter exported. Area, 1,382 sq. m.; pop. *c.* 12,000.

Söderhamn', port, on Gulf of Bothnia, Sweden; exports timber, wood pulp, iron; manufactures cellulose. Pop. 12,000.

Södertälje (*soo-der-tel'yā*), tn., Sweden, on Lake Malar; engineering, jute, and matches; holiday resort. Pop. 15,000.

Soest (*zōst*), tn., Westphalia, Prussia, 26 m. E. of Dortmund; machinery, soap, hats, cigars, sugar, bricks; formerly important member of Hanseatic League. Pop. 21,000.

Sofia (*sō-fē'a*), cap. of Bulgaria; has cathedral and several mosques; univ.; manufactures beer, flour, leather, sugar, silk, tobacco; exports hides, maize, linen, silk. Pop. 213,000.

Sogne Fjord (*son'yā*), longest fjord in Norway; on W. coast; 136 m. long; 2¼ to 4½ m. broad; over 4,000 ft. deep; surrounded by steep rocky cliffs.

So'ham, tn., Cambridgeshire, England, 5 m. S.E. of Ely; fruit growing and market gardening. Pop. 4,700.

Soignies (*swăn-yē'*), tn., Hainaut, Belgium; granite quarries, flax spinning and bleaching. Pop. 11,000.

Soissons (*swă-son'*), tn., Aisne, France, on R. Aisne, 65 m. N.E. of Paris; manufactures iron and copper goods, agricultural machinery, glass, sugar, and rubber goods. Pop. 16,000.

Soke of Peterborough. See PETERBOROUGH (3).

Soko'to, inland dist. of N. Nigeria, W. Africa; in R. Niger basin and drained by R. Sokoto; elevated plain; cotton culture increasing; dates, bananas, yams, onions; cattle rearing. Area, 38,860 sq. m.; pop. 1,667,000.

Solent', THE, strait, separating W. Isle of Wight from Hampshire, England, and extending between the Needles and Cowes; favourite yachting stretch; length, 17 m.; greatest breadth, 5 m.

Solesmes (*so-lām'*), town, Nord, France, on R. Selle, 10 m. E. of Cambrai; textiles, sugar. Pop. 6,200.

Soleure. See SOLOTHURN.

Solihull', mkt. tn., Warwickshire, England, 6½ m. S.E. of Birmingham, of which it is a residential suburb; cattle fairs. Pop. 11,600.

So'lingen, tn., Rhineland, Prussia, 13 m. S.E. of Düsseldorf; cutlery and sword blades. Pop. 52,000.

Solola', tn., Guatemala, Central America, on Lake Atitlan; cloth, cigars, soap, pottery. Pop. 17,000.

Solomon Islands, group, W. Pacific, 500 m. E. of New Guinea; partly Brit., and partly administered by Australia under mandate; mountainous and volcanic; heavy rainfall; bananas, coconuts, sweet potatoes; exports are copra, ivory, turtle-shell, pearl-shell, sandalwood, nuts. Area, 11,000 sq. m.; pop. *c.* 150,000.

Solothurn (*zō'lō-toorn*) (Fr. *Soleure*). (1) Canton, N.W. Switzerland; traversed by Jura Mts. and R. Aar; agricultural, pastoral, and industrial. German is principal language. Area, 305 sq. m.; pop. 141,600. (2) Cap. of above, on R. Aar; rly. jn.; watches, jewellery, shoes, cottons; motor industries. Pop. 13,750.

Sol'way Firth, inlet of Irish Sea, separating Cumberland, England, from Kirkcudbright and Dumfries, Scotland; length, *c.* 40 m.; valuable salmon fisheries; notorious for rapid tides.

Somal'iland, part of E. Africa, jutting into Ind. Ocean. Country is undulating plateau with much desert. Chief rivs. (both in Italian Somaliland) are Webi Shebeli, which flows S.E. from Abyssinia, turns S.W., and disappears in the sand, and R. Juba, the only riv. to reach the ocean. Political divisions are French, British, and Italian Somaliland.

French Somaliland, or *Somali Coast*, lies between Eritrea and British Somaliland; has salt mines and coastal fisheries; large inland trade, especially by railway from Jibuti to Addis Ababa; chief exports: coffee, ivory, hides, and skins. Chief tns., Jibuti (cap.) and Obok. Area, 5,790 sq. m.; pop. 86,000.

British Somaliland, or *Somaliland Protectorate*, S. of Gulf of Aden, lies between French and Italian Somaliland. Gums, ghee, cattle, sheep, hides, and skins are exported. Transport is by camels. Cap. Berbera. Area, 68,000 sq. m.; pop. *c.* 345,000.

Italian Somaliland lies between British Somaliland, Abyssinia, Kenya, and Indian Ocean. Cattle, sheep, and camels are raised. Oil, gum, hides, butter, cotton, and ivory are exported. Chief tn., Mogadishu. Area, *c.* 190,000 sq. m.; pop. *c.* 1,200,000.

Som'bor, tn., Voivodina, Yugoslavia, 94 m. N.W. of Belgrade; trading centre for corn and cattle. Pop. 33,000.

Som'ersetshire, maritime co., S.W. England; bounded N. by Bristol Channel and Gloucestershire, E. by Wilts, S. by Dorset, W. by Devon. Surface is varied; crossed by ranges of hills, including the Mendip, Polden, Quantock, and Brendon Hills; drained by Rs. Bristol, Avon, Frome, Yeo, Parret, and other streams; fine orchards; noted for cider and Cheddar cheese; agriculture is carried on and live-stock raised; chief minerals are coal, iron, and freestone; manufactures include silks and woollens, lace, gloves, pottery, beer, bath-bricks, and basket chairs. Thermal springs at Bath; valuable fisheries in Bristol Channel. Co. tn., Taunton. Area, 1,590 sq. m.; pop. 475,100.

Som'erville, city, Massachusetts,

U.S.A., on R. Mystic, adjoining Boston; meat-packing establishments; boots, shoes, and copper tubes. Pop. 104,000.

Somme (*som*). (1) Riv., France; rises in Aisne dep. and flows into English Channel; partly canalized. Scene of intense fighting during Great War; length, 140 m. (2) Dep., France; traversed by R. Somme; surface slightly undulating, fertile and well cultivated, yielding cereals, sugar-beets; textile industries and sugar refining. Cap. Amiens. Area, 2,443 sq. m.; pop. 474,000.

Som'merfeld, tn., Brandenburg, Prussia, 44 m. S.E. of Frankfurt-on-Oder; manufactures cloth and machine-shop goods. Pop. 11,900.

Son'derborg, port, seaside resort, on isl. of Alsen, Sleswig, Denmark; connected with mainland by pontoon bridge. Pop. 10,000.

Sondershausen (*zon-ders-hou'zen*), tn., Thuringia, Germany, 35 m. N.W. of Weimar; manufactures woollens and bricks; salt mining. Pop. 10,000.

Song-Do. See KAISENG.

Son'neberg, tn., Thuringia, Germany, 10 m. N.E. of Coburg; manufactures toys. Pop. 19,000.

Sono'ra, state, N.W. Mexico; mountainous in E.; valleys very fertile under irrigation; silver-mining and stock-raising industries; some grain, tobacco, cotton, and sugar-cane produced. Cap. Hermosillo. Area, 76,633 sq. m.; pop. 275,000.

Sonsonate (*son-so-nä'tā*), tn., Salvador, Central America; agricultural centre; manufactures cotton cloth. Pop. 17,000.

Soo. See SAULT STE. MARIE.

Soochow, city, Kiangsu, China, on Grand Canal, 55 m. W.N.W. of Shanghai; one of wealthiest towns in China; great silk centre; cotton mills, and trade in rice. Pop. 350,000.

Sop'ron, formerly ÖDENBURG, tn., Hungary, on Austrian frontier, commands important trade-route from Vienna; manufactures sugar, preserved fruit, agricultural implements; trade in cattle. Pop. 35,000.

So'ra, city, Campania, Italy, 60 m. E.S.E. of Rome; cathedral; manufactures paper and cloth. Pop. 18,000.

Sorau (*zo'rou*), tn., Brandenburg, Prussia, on R. Sorebach, 54 m. S.E. of Frankfurt-on-Oder; manufactures of textiles, machinery, starch, glass, pottery. Pop. 18,000.

Sorel', tn., Quebec, Canada, at junction of Rs. Richelieu and St. Lawrence; foundries, engineering works, and sawmills. Pop. 8,000.

So'ria, prov., Spain; bleak hill land drained by upper waters of R. Douro; much forest, and large tracts of pasture land. Cap. Soria. Area, 3,983 sq. m.; pop. 156,000.

Sorn, par. and vil., Ayrshire, Scotland, on R. Ayr; hæmatite found. Pop. (par.) 3,500.

Soro'ki, tn., Bessarabia, Romania, on R. Dniester; on Russian frontier; vineyards, tobacco; an important river port. Pop. 27,000.

Sorren'to, tn. and wat.-pl. on Bay of Naples, Italy; wood-inlaying industry; strawplait, lace; centre of wine region. Pop. 7,000.

Sosnowiec (*sos-nov'yets*), tn., Poland, 45 m. N.W. of Cracow; great centre of industry; coal mining, iron foundries, and textile mills. Pop. 86,000.

Soufrière (*soo-fre-ār'*), volcano, St. Vincent, Brit. W. Indies; during eruption (1902) two villages, with *c.* 1,500 inhabitants, were destroyed.

Sound, THE, strait between Sweden and Zealand I., connecting Kattegat with Baltic Sea; length, 70 m.

Sousse, formerly SUSA, tn. and port, Tunisia, N. Africa; oil mills; exports phosphates; esparto grass. Pop. 21,000.

South Africa, general name for area S. of Zambezi R., Africa; comprises Union of S. Africa, S. Rhodesia, Bechuanaland, S.W. Africa Protectorate, Basutoland and Swaziland, all Brit. possessions or under Brit. control; and some 150,000 sq. m. of Mozambique (Port. E. Africa), with a pop. of less than 3,000,000. For further information see separate articles.

South Africa, THE UNION OF, Brit. Dominion, Africa; bounded N. by Portuguese W. Africa and N. and S. Rhodesia, on N.E. by Portuguese E. Africa, and elsewhere surrounded by Indian and Atlantic Oceans; coast-line regular, few natural harbours; surface a plateau, highest in E., where Drakensbergs rise to 10,763 ft. in Mont-aux-Sources, and in S., where veld is reached by Little and Great Karroos; chief rivs., Orange, flowing W. to Atlantic Ocean, and Limpopo, entering Indian Ocean through Portuguese terr. The climate is warm and generally healthy; summer rains heaviest on E. of Drakensbergs, where S.E. Trades prevail; winter rains in S.W. form Brave W. Winds; much of W. is arid (Kalahari Desert); irrigation necessary; few forests. Principal resources are mineral—gold, diamonds, coal, copper, tin; pastoral lands support sheep, goats, cattle, and horses; many ostriches; chief crops are maize, wheat, oats, barley, Kaffir corn, tobacco and cotton, with smaller quantities of sugar-cane and tea; fruits include grapes, oranges, pears. Over half the foreign trade is carried on with Brit. Empire; principal exports, gold, wool, diamonds, hides and skins, maize, wattle-bark, and coal. Main rly. lines link Cape Town with S. Rhodesia and with Orange Free State and Transvaal, whence lines to Durban and to Lourenço Marques (Portuguese E. Africa).

Union consists of four original provs. (Cape of Good Hope, Natal, Orange Free State, and Transvaal), federated in 1910; administers mandated S.W. Africa; Basutoland and Swaziland not included in Union. Provs. have each an administrative and a provincial council to administer local affairs; English and Dutch languages are both official. There are four univs., one at Cape Town, one at Stellenbosch, the Witwatersrand Univ. at Johannesburg, and the Univ. of S. Africa with constituent colleges at Pretoria, Grahamstown, Pietermaritzburg, Bloemfontein, Wellington, and Potchefstroom. Pretoria is the seat of administration for the Union, and Cape Town the seat of legislature. Of the total pop. *c.* 1,700,000 are Europeans; of remainder, 4,700,000 are Bantus, and 170,000 are Indians. Area, 472,000 sq. m.; pop. 7,000,000. See articles on separate provs.

South'all Nor'wood, urb. dist. and mkt. tn., Middlesex, England, part of Greater London; chemical works. Pop. 38,900.

South America. See AMERICA.

Southamp'ton, port and co. bor., Hants, England, situated on Southampton Water between Rs. Itchen and Test; has remains of old fortifications, including the Bar Gate, dating from 11th cent.; Univ. Coll.; headquarters of Ordnance Survey Dept.; has splendid harbour, with advantage of double tides, due to the passage of high tide from the English Channel up the Solent and two hours later up Spithead; most important mail-packet station in England; map making; yacht building and marine engineering works. Pop. 176,000.

Southamptonshire. See HAMPSHIRE.

South Austra'lia, state of Australia; bounded E. by Queensland, New South Wales, and Victoria; S. by Indian Ocean; W. by Western Australia; N. by Central Australia. In S.E. are estuary of Murray R. at Encounter Bay, Gulf of St. Vincent (with Kangaroo I. at its mouth), and Spencer Gulf; the last runs inland for over 200 m., and from its head northward are the basins of Lake Torrens and Lake Eyre; to W. of Lake Torrens is Lake Gairdner. Interior forms part of great central plateau of continent; very largely desert, though N.E. portion can provide artesian water; crossed by various mountain ranges (Flinders, Gawler, Stuart, Musgrave). There is a considerable variation in temperature and rainfall. Agriculture is the principal industry; live-stock largely raised; wheat, oats, and barley produced; oranges, olives, and other fruits are grown. Minerals include copper, iron, gypsum, phosphate rock; manufactures wines, olive oil, flour; chief exports, wool, wheat, flour, copper, skins and hides, frozen meat, wine, fruits, butter, leather. Cap. is Adelaide. Area, 380,070 sq. m.; pop. 579,000.

South'bank in Normanby, par. and vil., Yorks, England, in Eston urb. dist.; iron and steel works. Pop. (par.) 17,000.

South Bend, city, Indiana, U.S.A., on R. St. Joseph, 75 m. E. of Chicago; carriage and wagon works, iron foundries, paper mills, flour mills; agricultural machinery. Pop. 104,000.

South'borough, urb. dist., Kent, England, 1½ m. N. of Tunbridge Wells; residential dist., with mineral springs. Pop. 7,400.

South'bridge, tn., Massachusetts, U.S.A., 18 m. S.W. of Worcester; optical instruments and cutlery. Pop. 14,000.

South Carolina, South Atlantic State, U.S.A., bounded N. and N.E. by N. Carolina, S.E. by Atlantic, W. by Georgia. Surface is level in E., where a low-lying plain extends a considerable distance inland from the coast; undulating in centre, and mountainous in W., reaching an extreme height of 3,548 ft. in Mt. Sassafras, on boundary between N. and S. Carolina; drained by Great Peedee (with Little Peedee and Lynches), Santee, and Edisto rivers. Climate is healthy and temperate, but coast regions suffer from hurricanes. Principal industry is agriculture; produces wheat, maize, oats, rice. Live-stock is extensively raised; cotton and tobacco are grown in large quantities. Minerals are relatively unimportant. Fisheries are of increasing importance, and lumbering is carried on. Manufactures include cottons, timber, and lumber products, fertilizers, cotton-seed oil. Chief towns are Columbia (cap.), Charleston (chief port), Greenville, and Spartanburg. Area, 30,989 sq. m. Pop. 1,683,000.

South Dako'ta, North Central State, U.S.A.; bounded N. by North Dakota, W. by Montana, Wyoming, S. by Nebraska, E. by Iowa, Minnesota. Surface generally undulating prairie land; drained by R. Missouri and tribs. In S.W. are the Black Hills and the Bad Lands. Principal industry is agriculture; cattle, sheep, horses, mules, and pigs are extensively raised, and wheat, maize, oats, barley, rye, and flax are grown; dairy farming is carried on, and fruits and vegetables are cultivated. Minerals include gold, silver, lead, copper. Manufactures include flour milling, butter and cheese making. Lumbering is carried on in the forest districts of the Black Hills. Chief tns., Pierre (cap.), Sioux Falls, and Aberdeen. Area, 77,615 sq. m.; pop. 681,000.

South'end-on-Sea, co. bor., Essex, England, at mouth of R. Thames; seaside resort much frequented by Londoners. Pop. 120,100.

South Foreland. See FORELAND.

South'gate, urb. dist., Middlesex, England; residential suburb of London. Pop. 55,600.

South Georgia, Brit. island, S. Atlantic; centre of whaling and sealing. Uninhabited except for whaling settlement. Area, 1,000 sq. m.

South Holl'and, prov., Holland; deltaic plain between Rs. Maas and Waal; chief occupations are agriculture and dairy farming. Chief tn., Rotterdam. Area, 1,134 sq. m.; pop. 1,900,000.

South Mol'ton, mkt. tn., N. Devon, England, on R. Mole, 10 m. S.E. of Barnstaple; corn mills; agricultural implements. Pop. 2,800.

South Ork'neys, group of small islands in S. Atlantic Ocean, *c.* 800 m. S.E. of Falkland Is., of which they are a dependency; whaling centre.

South'owram, urb. dist., W. Riding, Yorks, England; near Halifax; woollen goods; coal mines and stone quarries. Pop. 2,600.

South'port, co. bor. and wat.-pl., Lancs, England, on Irish Sea, 18 m. N. of Liverpool; extends 2 m. along the coast. Pop. 78,900.

South'sea, tn., Hants, England; forms part of Portsmouth; residential suburb and wat.-pl. Pop. 44,600.

South Shetland Islands, mountainous archipelago in S. Atlantic Ocean; whaling centre. Area, 880 sq. m.

South Shields, co. bor. and port, Durham, England, at mouth of R. Tyne; manufactures glass, chemicals; shipbuilding; printing machinery; exports coal. Pop. 113,400.

Southwark (*suth'ark*), metropolitan bor., London, on S. side of Thames, opposite the City. Contains Guy's Hospital. Glass making, brewing, tanning. Pop. 171,700.

Southwell (*suth'el*), mkt. tn., Notts, England, 6 m. W. of Newark; cathedral; silk and lace factories. Pop. 3,000.

South-West Africa, formerly GERMAN S.W. AFRICA, terr., S. Africa; bounded N. by Portuguese W. Africa, N. Rhodesia, E. by Bechuanaland and Cape Prov., S. by Cape Prov., W. by Atlantic Ocean. Administered under mandate by Union of S. Africa. Coastal belt, 30 to 40 m. broad, is desert. Surface, a series of undulating plateaus (2,000–6,000 ft.); Kalahari Desert in E.; of rivs. only Okavango, Kunene, and Orange have water all year round. Country suited for stock raising; cattle and ostriches reared on plateaus; maize, potatoes, pumpkins, Kaffir corn, and beans grown; cotton in Outjo dist.; diamonds, tin, and copper are chief minerals. Cap. Windhoek. Area, 311,820 sq. m.; pop. 259,000 (24,000 whites).

Southwick. (1) Town, Durham, England, on R. Wear; suburb of Sunderland; manufactures glass and earthenware. Pop. 13,800. (2) Urb. dist., Sussex, England, 4 m. W. of Brighton; oyster fisheries; wat.-pl. Pop. 6,100.

South'wold, mkt. tn. and port, Suffolk, England; seaside resort; fisheries. Pop. 2,800.

Sowerby Bridge (*sor'bi*), urb. dist., W. Riding, Yorks, England, on R. Calder, 2½ m. S.W. of Halifax; textiles, engineering, chemical works. Pop. 14,700.

Soy'land, urb. dist., W. Riding, Yorks, England, 4 m. S.W. of Halifax; textiles. Pop. 3,100.

Spa, wat.-pl., Belgium, 20 m. S.E. of Liége; mineral springs; wooden lacquered articles. Pop. 8,300.

Spain, rep., W. Europe; a kingdom until 1931; occupies larger part of Iberian peninsula; bounded on N. by Bay of Biscay and France, W. by Atlantic Ocean and Portugal, S. and E. by Mediterranean Sea; separated from African coast by Strait of Gibraltar (minimum width about 9 m.); coast rocky, with numerous rias in N. and N.W.; S. and E. coasts generally flat, with few indentations. Interior consists mainly of tableland known as the Meseta (average elevation 2,000–3,000 ft.), deeply dissected by rivers flowing from E. to W. Chief mts., Pyrenees in N.W. (forming boundary between France and Spain), with Maladetta (11,165 ft.); Cantabrian Mts. in N., a continuation of Pyrenees; Sierra de Guadarrama and Toledo Mts. in central region; Sierra de Gredo and Sierra de Gata, W.; Sierra Nevada, with Mulhacen (11,420 ft.), S. Principal rivs. are Douro, Tagus, Guadiana, and Guadalquivir, flowing into Atlantic Ocean, and Ebro, flowing into Mediterranean. Climate of tableland is continental, with scanty rainfall; N. and N.W. are mild, with heavy rainfall; S. districts have Mediterranean climate. Flora is varied: N. mar. provinces have central European vegetation; most of the central region contains steppe-like vegetation, chiefly esparto grass; flora of Mediterranean districts includes date-palm, sugar-cane, and other tropical plants. Agriculture is the main occupation, the principal products being wheat, barley, olives, flax, hemp, esparto grass, fruits (oranges, lemons, grapes, almonds); important wine industries—famous sherries made in S., and red wines in N.; manufactures of cotton and woollen goods, silks, machinery, paper, tobacco (a state monopoly), sugar, cork; principal industries are in

Catalonia; fine horses are bred in Andalusia, sheep and swine in Estremadura, cattle in Galicia; extensive fisheries (tunny, sardines, cod); rich in minerals—iron, copper, coal, lead, zinc, mercury, sulphur, manganese; numerous mineral springs. The Canary islands are treated as an integral part of Spain; Ceuta, on the African shore, forms a prov. with Cadiz. Chief tns., Madrid (cap.), Barcelona, Valencia, Seville, Malaga, Murcia. Area, 190,050 sq. m.; pop. 22,000,000.

Foreign possessions of Spain are: Spanish Morocco, and on W. coast of Africa Rio de Oro and Adrar; Spanish Guinea (Rio Muni Settlement); Fernando Po and other islands in Gulf of Guinea.

Spalato. See SPLIT.

Spal'ding, mkt. tn. and port, Lincolnshire, England, on R. Welland; agricultural centre; industries include bulb growing, market gardening, sawmilling, brewing. Pop. 12,600.

Span'dau, tn., Brandenburg, Prussia, at junction of Rs. Havel and Spree; suburb of Berlin; manufactures small-arms, artillery. Pop. 110,000.

Spanish Guinea, or RIO MUNI SETTLEMENT, Spanish colony, W. Africa, on E. of Gulf of Guinea between R. Campo and R. Muni; much of surface covered by marshes and forests. Produces rubber, timber, palm oil, and coffee. Chief tn., Santa Isabel. Area, 10,036 sq. m.; pop. 140,000.

Spar'ta, city of anc. Greece, cap. of Laconia in the Peloponnesus, famous for the warlike prowess of its citizens. Modern tn. is also cap. of Laconia. Pop. 6,000.

Spar'tanburg, city, S. Carolina, U.S.A., 93 m. N.W. of Columbia; cotton-growing region; cotton mills; fertilizers. Pop. 29,000.

Spen'borough, urb. dist., W. Riding, Yorks, England, 6 m. S.E. of Bradford; woollens. Pop. 31,000.

Spen'nymoor, urb. dist. and mkt. tn., Durham, England, 5 m. S. of Durham; coal is mined; great iron and steel works. Pop. 16,400.

Spey (*spā*), river, Scotland; rises in Monadhliath Mts., and flows in N.E. direction to Moray Firth; most rapid river in Scotland; salmon fisheries. Length, 107 m.

Speyer (*spī'er*), or SPIRES, tn., Bavaria, Germany, on R. Rhine; cap. of Palatinate; tobacco, beer, sugar, paper, vinegar, and musical instruments are manufactured. Pop. 26,000.

Spezia (*spā'tsi-a*), wat.-pl., Liguria, N.W. Italy, on Bay of Spezia; chief Italian arsenal and naval station; docks and shipbuilding yards; electrical machinery; exports olive oil. Pop. 110,000.

Spice Islands. See MOLUCCAS.

Spils'by, mkt. tn., Lincolnshire, England, 15 m. N. of Boston; trade in agricultural produce; birthplace of Sir John Franklin, the Arctic explorer. Pop. 1,400.

Spires. See SPEYER.

Spit'alfields, dist., Stepney, London, 1 m. N.E. of St. Paul's; former seat of silk-weaving industry. Pop. 24,200.

Spit'head, strait, English Channel, separating E. Isle of Wight from Hampshire, England; leads to Southampton Water; 12 m. long by 4 m. broad.

Spits'bergen, or SVALBARD, Norwegian archipelago of five large and several small islands in Arctic Ocean, *c.* 300 m. to N. of Norway; largest are W. Spitsbergen, North-East Land, and Edge I.; surface generally an ice-covered plateau, with highest point over 5,000 ft.; climate arctic; S.W. winds and Atlantic drift keep W. Spitsbergen free from ice in summer; considerable wealth of plant life in summer, but no trees; animals include reindeer, polar bear, ptarmigan, and eider duck; seals and whales are fast disappearing from vicinity, and fur-bearing animals need protection. Important mineral deposts have been discovered; coal is mined; iron ore, gypsum, zinc, and asbestos exist. Longyearbyen is chief camp. Area, 25,000 sq. m.; pop. *c.* 1,500.

Split, formerly SPALATO, port, Dalmatia, Yugoslavia, on Adriatic Sea;

fine harbour; exports wine and oil; numerous Roman remains. Pop. 30,000.

Splügen Pass, pass across Alps, leading from Grisons to Como; highest point, 6,946 feet.

Spokane (*spō-kan'*), city, E. Washington, U.S.A., on falls of R. Spokane; extensive trade in lumber; flour and saw mills; wheat, fruit, and live-stock extensively shipped; has immense water-power from river. Pop. 116,000.

Spoleto (*spo-lā'to*), tn., Italy, 60 m. N. of Rome; has cathedral containing frescoes by Filippo Lippi; produces truffles, preserved goods, and earthenware; tanning and spinning of cotton and wool. Pop. 28,000.

Sporades (*spor'ad-ēz*), islands of the Archipelago, s. Ægean Sea, consisting of two groups surrounding Cyclades, the northern group belonging to Greece, the southern to Italy.

Spree (*sprā*), river, Prussia; rises in Saxony, flows N.W. through Berlin, and joins R. Havel at Spandau. Length, 227 m.; navigable for 100 m.

Sprem'berg, town, Brandenburg, Prussia, on isl. of R. Spree, 14 m. s. of Kottbus; cloth, machinery, bicycles, tobacco. Pop. 13,000.

Spring'field. (1) City, Massachusetts, U.S.A., on R. Connecticut, 85 m. W.S.W. of Boston; U.S. arsenal; manufactures paper, electrical machinery, motor-cars. Pop. 150,000. (2) Tn., cap., Illinois, U.S.A., on R. Sangamon, 180 m. s.w. of Chicago; important railway centre; state capitol and arsenal; coal mining, iron industries, watches, agricultural machinery, shoes, miners' lamps; was home and burial-place of Abraham Lincoln. Pop. 72,000. (3) City, Ohio, U.S.A., on R. Lagonda, 68 m. N.E. of Cincinnati; produces machinery, hardware, agricultural implements. Pop. 68,000. (4) City, Missouri, U.S.A., 150 m. S.E. of Kansas City; manufactures machinery; surrounding country noted for fruit, poultry, and dairy products. Pop. 58,000.

Spring'head, urb. dist., W. Riding, Yorks, England, 1 m. S.E. of Oldham; large cotton manufactures. Pop. 4,800.

Springhill', tn., Nova Scotia, Canada, 75 m. N.W. of Halifax; coal mining. Pop. 5,800.

Srinag'ar, cap., Kashmir, N. India, on R. Jhelum, 115 m. N.E. of Rawalpindi; formerly shawl-weaving centre, now engaged in silver and copper working, wood carving, carpet weaving, and manufacture of paper and leather. Pop. 142,000.

Stade (*stä'da*), tn., Hanover, Germany, on R. Schwinge, 20 m. W. by N. of Hamburg; leather, cigars, alcohol. Pop. 12,000.

Staf'fa, small, uninhabited isl., Inner Hebrides, Argyllshire, Scotland, 6 m. N. of Iona, contains numerous basaltic caverns (largest, Fingal's Cave); excellent pasture. Area, 71 ac.

Staf'ford, co. tn., Staffs, England, on R. Sow, 16 m. N. of Wolverhampton; makes boots and shoes; salt made from brine spring. Pop. 29,500.

Staf'fordshire (STAFFS), midland co., W. England; bounded by Cheshire, Derbyshire, Leicestershire, Warwickshire, Worcestershire, and Shropshire. Surface is generally level in centre, with hills in N. and S.; drained by R. Trent and its affluents, of which most important is the Dove. Large coalfields in N. and S., former almost entirely covered with towns engaged in manufacture of pottery; 'Black Country,' on S. coalfield, with large iron manufactures; agriculture is carried on, oats being the chief crop; beer is largely manufactured at Burton; gypsum, zinc ore, and copper ore also occur. Co. tn., Stafford. Area, 1,158 sq. m.; pop. 1,431,200.

Staines (*stānz*), urb. dist., Middlesex, England, at confluence of Rs. Colne and Thames, 6 m. S.E. of Windsor; part of Greater London; breweries and mustard mills. Pop. 21,200.

Stain'land, urb. dist., W. Riding, Yorks, England, 3 m. s.w. of Halifax; cottons and woollens. Pop. 4,200.

Staithes (*stāthz*), fishing vil., Yorks, England, 9 m. N.W. of Whitby.

Stal'in, formerly YUZOVKA, tn., Ukraine, U.S.S.R., 150 m. S.E. of Kharkov; coal, iron, and manganese in vicinity; iron rails. Pop. 106,000.

Stal'ingrad, formerly TSARITSYN. (1) Prov., Russia; plain on both sides of lower R. Volga; chief crops are wheat, rye, sunflower, barley, oats, potatoes, maize. Area, 34,065 sq. m.; pop. 1,407,000. (2) Cap. of above, on R. Volga; metal ware, machinery, chemicals; oil refinery. Pop. 149,000.

Sta'lybridge, tn., Cheshire, England, on R. Tame, 7 m. E. of Manchester; cotton mills, foundries, engineering works. Pop. 24,800.

Stam'ford. (1) Mkt. tn., Lincolnshire, England, on R. Welland, 12 m. N.W. of Peterborough; centre of agricultural dist.; coach and wagon factories, motor and engineering works, breweries. Pop. 9,900. (2) Tn., Connecticut, U.S.A., on Long Island Sound; mainly residential; hardware and chemicals. Pop. 46,000.

Stan'derton, tn., Transvaal, S. Africa, on R. Vaal, 80 m. S.E. of Johannesburg; coal mines; agricultural centre. Pop. (white) 2,300.

Standish with Langtree, urb. dist., Lancs, England, 3 m. N.W. of Wigan; coal mines. Pop. 7,300.

Stan'hope, mkt. tn., Durham, England, 17 m. W. by S. of Durham, on R. Wear; ironstone and limestone occur in vicinity. Pop. 2,000.

Stanimak'a (German *Stanislau*), tn., Bulgaria, 13 m. S.E. of Philippopolis; large trade in wine. Pop. 17,000.

Stanislawow (*stan-is-wäv'uf*). (1) County, Poland; fertile plain in N., and rising to Carpathian Mts. in S.; watered by tribs. of R. Dniester; heavily forested; horses and dairy cattle; oilfields. Area, 7,092 sq. m.; pop. 1,339,000. (2) Chief tn. in above, 58 m. S.W. of Tarnopol; rly. centre and workshops; tanneries, flour mills, dye works; trade in agricultural produce. Pop. 28,000.

Stan'ley. (1) Urb. dist., Durham, England, 7 m. W. of Durham; coal mines. Pop. 24,500. (2) Par. and vil., Derbyshire, England, 5 m. N.E. of Derby; coal mines, ironworks, brickfield. Pop. (par.) 1,400. (3) Urb. dist., W. Riding, Yorks, England, 2 m. N.E. of Wakefield; collieries. Pop. 14,600. (4) Vil., Perthshire, Scotland, on R. Tay, 7 m. N. of Perth; cotton mills. Pop. 1,200. (5) Tn., Falkland Is.; whaling centre. Pop. 1,000.

Stanley Pool, expansion (20 m. by 15 m.) of lower R. Congo, Africa; edged by mountains (1,000–3,000 ft. on S. side); contains island of Bamu and numerous sandbanks; Brazzaville stands at W. end.

Stanleyville, station, Belgian Congo, Africa, on R. Congo, below Stanley Falls and just N. of equator; railway laid round Falls to Ponthierville.

Stan'more, GREAT, par. and vil., Middlesex, England, 3 m. N.E. of Harrow; anc. Roman station; brewing. Pop. (par.) 2,100.

Stan'ningley, eccles. dist., W. Riding, Yorks, England, 5 m. W. of Leeds; woollens. Pop. 4,500.

Stan'nington, vil., Yorks, England, 4 m. W. by N. of Sheffield; paper and corn mills, collieries. Pop. 4,000.

Stan'ton and New'hall, par., Derbyshire, England, 2 m. S.E. of Burton-on-Trent; manufactures pottery; large coal mines. Pop. 6,000.

Sta'pleford, par., mkt. tn., Notts, England, 6 m. W. of Nottingham; manufactures silk and lace. Pop. 8,500.

Staraya-Russa (*stä-rī'ä-roo'sä*), tn., N.W. Russia, 36 m. S. of Novgorod; saline baths, salt deposits; trade in cereals and flax. Pop. 22,000.

Star'a-Zag'ora, tn., Bulgaria, 50 m. N.E. of Philippopolis; copper foundries, tanneries, mineral springs; attar of roses and silk produced in vicinity. Pop. 29,000.

Star'cross, wat.-pl., Devonshire, England, on estuary of R. Exe; connected to Exmouth by ferry. Pop. 1,100.

Star'gard, tn., Pomerania, Prussia, 22 m. by rail E. of Stettin; machinery, tobacco, spirits, woollen and cotton goods; was member of Hanseatic League. Pop. 33,000.

Star'i Becej (*bech'ēy*), formerly O BECSE, tn., Yugoslavia, 60 m. N.W. of Belgrade; trade in grain and fruit. Pop. 20,000.

Stassfurt (*stass'foort*), tn., Saxony, Prussia, 19 m. S. of Magdeburg; potash and rock-salt mines; chemical works. Pop. 16,000.

Staten Island (*stă'ten*), at mouth of R. Hudson, U.S.A., included in city of New York; lumber mills and shipyards. Area, 57 sq. m.; pop. 117,000.

Stavang'er, port, S.W. Norway, on Bukken Fjord; fishing station; important fish canneries; shipbuilding; iodine. Pop. 44,000.

Staveley (*stāv'le*), tn., Derbyshire, England, 12 m. S.E. of Sheffield; collieries, ironworks, corn mills; manufactures brushes, and spades and shovels. Pop. 13,000.

Stav'ropol, tn., N. Caucasian Area, Russia; agricultural implements; textiles, oil. Pop. 59,000.

Stawell', tn., Victoria, Australia, 80 m. W.N.W. of Melbourne; gold mining. Pop. 4,400.

Stee'ton with Eastburn, par. and vil., Yorks, England, 3 m. N.W. of Keighley; worsted and ribbon mills. Pop. (par.) 2,300.

Stel'larton, tn., Nova Scotia, Canada, 75 m. N.E. of Halifax; on Pictou coalfield; iron and steel. Pop. 5,400.

Stel'lenbosch, tn., Cape Prov., S. Africa, 25 m. E. of Cape Town; important educational centre; univ.; wine and fruit-growing centre; manufactures jam. Pop. 7,000.

Sten'dal, tn., Saxony, Prussia, 33 m. N. of Magdeburg; railway workshops; manufactures machinery, tobacco, textiles, gold-leaf. Pop. 30,000.

Step'ney, metropolitan bor., London, 2 m. E. of St. Paul's; varied industries carried on. Pop. 225,200.

Stern'berg, tn., Moravia, Czechoslovakia, 47 m. N.E. of Brno; centre of cotton and linen industry; manufactures sugar, liqueurs, and bricks; flax and tobacco are grown in vicinity. Pop. 15,000.

Stettin', Free Port, Pomerania, Prussia, on R. Oder; former member of Hanseatic League; waterway connects with Berlin; shipbuilding, machinery, chemicals, oil refining, sugar, paper, porcelain, cement. Pop. 254,000.

Steubenville (*stū'ben-vil*), city, Ohio, U.S.A., on R. Ohio, 23 m. N. of Wheeling; manufactures iron, steel, paper, glass; coal, petroleum, and natural gas occur in neighbourhood. Pop. 35,000.

Stev'enage, urb. dist. and mkt. tn., Herts, England, 4 m. S.E. of Hitchin. Pop. 5,500.

Ste'venston, tn., Ayrshire, Scotland, 1½ m. N.E. of Saltcoats; coal, iron, chemicals, and explosives. Pop. 8,200.

Stew'art Island, New Zealand; separated from S. end of South Island by Foveaux Strait; mountainous and heavily wooded; tourist centre; oyster fishing. Area, 665 sq. m.; pop. 300.

Stew'arton, tn., Ayrshire, Scotland, on R. Annick, 5 m. N. of Kilmarnock; dairy produce; carding and spinning industries; manufactures Scotch 'bonnets.' Pop. 2,700.

Steyning (*sten'ing*), mkt. tn., Sussex, England, 5 m. N.W. of Shoreham; anc. place, formerly on coast; manufactures parchment and beer. Pop. 1,900.

Steyr (*stīr*), tn., Upper Austria, 20 m. S. of Linz; manufactures iron and steel, electrical plant, and bicycles. Pop. 22,000.

Still'water, city, Minnesota, U.S.A., on R. St. Croix, 20 m. N.E. of St. Paul; lumber trade; manufactures agricultural machinery. Pop. 7,000.

Stil'ton, vil., N. Hunts, England; gives name to a famous variety of cheese. Pop. 500.

Stir'ling, royal burgh and co. tn., Stirlingshire, Scotland, on R. Forth; anc. royal castle; Wallace Monument on neighbouring Abbey Craig. Stirling is surrounded by battlefields, including Bannockburn. Chief manufactures are carpets, tartans, tweeds, rubber goods, agricultural implements, furniture; railway centre. Pop. 22,600.

Stir'lingshire, midland co., Scotland, bounded by cos. of Perth, Dumbarton, Lanark, W. Lothian, and Clackmannan. Surface hilly in N.W. and centre (Ben Lomond, 3,193 ft.); in E. are wide fertile plains or carses of Stirling and Falkirk; drained mostly by R. Forth; large deposits of coal and iron; has ironworks and manufactures of textiles and chemicals. Co. tn., Stirling. Area, 451 sq. m.; pop. 166,400.

Stockholm (*stok'hōm*), cap., Sweden; beautifully situated on rocky islands and mainland at outlet of Lake Mälar to Baltic. Staden (old town) has narrow steep streets, quaint gabled houses, royal palace, Storkyrka (great church). Norrmalm, residential quarter, has fine broad streets, large squares, parks, univ., Royal Opera-house, national museum, national library and statues. Busy port and large industrial centre; chief industries are shipbuilding, iron foundries, machinery, cotton, linen, leather, sugar, breweries, chemicals. Pop. 474,000.

Stock'ingford, eccles. dist. and vil., Warwickshire, England, 1½ m. W. of Nuneaton; collieries; manufactures tiles, blue bricks, and drain pipes. Pop. (dist.) 11,000.

Stock'port, co. bor., Cheshire, England, on R. Mersey; cotton, hat making, and alkali industries; iron and brass founding, machinery, leather. Pop. 125,500.

Stocks'bridge, urb. dist., W. Riding, Yorks, England, 7½ m. N.W. of Sheffield; coal mines and steel wire works. Pop. 9,300.

Stock'ton, city, California, U.S.A., on R. San Joaquin, 75 m. E. of San Francisco; commercial centre; agricultural implements, flour, lumber, leather. Pop. 48,000.

Stock'ton Heath, par. and vil., Cheshire, England, on Bridgewater Canal, 1 m. S. of Warrington; spades are manufactured. Pop. (par.) 4,700.

Stock'ton-on-Tees, river port, Durham, England, on R. Tees; blast furnaces and rolling mills; manufactures marine engines, railway and bridge material, pottery, glass. First railway in Great Britain laid between Stockton and Darlington (1825). Pop. 67,700.

Stoke New'ington, metropolitan bor., London, England, 3 m. N. of St. Paul's; waterworks and reservoirs. Pop. 51,200.

Stoke Poges (*pō'jis*), vil. and par., Bucks, England, 2 m. N. of Slough station; old church; churchyard is scene of Gray's *Elegy*. Pop. (par.) 1,700.

Stoke Pri'or, par. and vil., Worcestershire, England, 4 m. N.E. of Droitwich; salt and alkali works. Pop. 3,000.

Stoke-upon-Trent, co. bor., Staffs, England; chief centre of porcelain and earthenware manufacture; coal mining, manufacture of machinery; important railway centre. Stoke-upon-Trent includes Burslem (the 'Mother of the Potteries'), Fenton, Hanley, Longton, and Tunstall. Pop. 276,600.

Stol'berg, tn., Rhineland, Prussia, 6 m. E. of Aachen; manufactures iron, zinc, and brass goods. Pop. 17,000.

Stolp, tn., Pomerania, Prussia, 65 m. W. of Danzig; manufactures machinery, amber goods, linen, tobacco, alcohol. Pop. 42,000.

Stone, mkt. tn. and urb. dist., Staffs, England, on R. Trent, 7 m. N. of Stafford; breweries, boot and shoe factory. Pop. 6,000.

Stone'field, tn., Lanarkshire, Scotland, 3 m. N.W. of Hamilton; coal mining. Pop. 8,000.

Stonehaven, seaside resort, Kincardineshire, Scotland, 16 m. by rail S.S.W. of Aberdeen; herring-fishing centre; tanneries, distilleries. Pop. 4,200.

Stone'henge, remarkable group of huge stone circles in Salisbury Plain, Wilts, England, 7 m. N. of Salisbury. Their erection is generally attributed to the late Stone or the Bronze Age, and their use was probably both monumental and religious. Stonehenge is now the property of the nation.

Stone'house. (1) Tn., Lanarkshire, Scotland, on Avon Water, 6 m. S.E. of Hamilton; coal mining. Pop. 3,600. (2) Par. and vil., Gloucestershire, England, 3 m. N.W. of Stroud; manufactures woollen goods. Pop. (par.) 2,400. (3) Or EAST STONEHOUSE. See under PLYMOUTH.

Sto'ny Strat'ford, mkt. tn., Bucks, England, on R. Ouse, 8 m. N.E. of Buckingham; engineering works. Pop. 2,000.

Stor'noway, port, Lewis I., Ross-shire, Scotland; chief town in Outer Hebrides; herring-fishery centre. Pop. 3,800.

Stour'bridge, tn., Worcestershire, England, on R. Stour, 10 m. W. of Birmingham; glass manufacture; iron and chain works, manufacture of parchment, fire-clay goods; coal mined in vicinity. Pop. 19,900.

Stour'port, tn., Worcestershire, England, 4 m. S.W. of Kidderminster, at confluence of Rs. Stour and Severn; ironfounding, carpet weaving, tanning, tin stamping. Pop. 5,900.

Stowmarket, mkt. tn., Suffolk, England, 12½ m. N.W. of Ipswich; agricultural implements, gun-cotton and cordite, leather. Pop. 4,300.

Stow-on-the-Wold (*stō-*), urb. dist., Glos, England, in Cotswold Hills, 13 m. E. of Cheltenham; mkt. tn. Pop. 1,300.

Strabane (*stra-ban'*), mkt. tn., co. Tyrone, N. Ireland, at head of R. Foyle; market gardens; shirt making. Pop. 5,200.

Straits Settlements, British crown colony, Malay Peninsula, Asia; comprises Singapore (including Cocos Is., Christmas I., and Labuan), Penang (including Prov. Wellesley and the Dindings), Malacca. Ports are free from customs duties; trade mainly transit; exports are rubber, tin, spices, copra, sago, tapioca. Cap. Singapore. Area, *c.* 1,600 sq. m.; pop. 884,000. See separate articles.

Stral'sund, tn., Pomerania, Prussia, on Baltic Sea, 86 m. by rail N.W. of Stettin; manufactures machinery, electric lamps, gloves, paper, soap, cement. Pop. 39,000.

Stranraer (*stran-rär'*), royal burgh and port, Wigtownshire, Scotland, on Loch Ryan; creameries; manufactures dairy implements; daily steamer service to Larne, Ireland (shortest sea passage); fisheries. Pop. 6,500.

Stras'bourg, chief tn., Bas-Rhin, France, on R. Ill; famous cathedral with remarkable astronomical clock; univ. Great German fortress (1870–1918). Chief products are machinery, jewellery, hardware, tobacco, *pâté de foie gras*; brewing, tanning, printing. Pop. 174,000.

Strat'ford. (1) Dist., Essex, England, on R. Lea; part of Greater London; chemicals, candles, paint, varnish manufactured; large railway shops. Pop. 28,000. (2) Tn., Ontario, Canada, on R. Avon, 83 m. S.W. of Toronto; manufactures woollen goods, furniture, threshing machines; sawmills, flour mills, locomotive repair shops. Pop. 16,000.

Strat'ford-on-A'von, tn., Warwickshire, England, on R. Avon, 8 m. S.W. of Warwick; birthplace of Shakespeare; contains his tomb and numerous other associations with the poet. Trade chiefly agricultural. Anne Hathaway's cottage. Pop. 11,600.

Strathaven (*strā'ven*), mkt. tn., W. Lanarkshire, Scotland, near R. Avon, 16 m. S.E. of Glasgow; manufactures silk, cotton, hosiery; trade in cattle and cheese. Pop. 4,200.

Strathmore' ('great valley'), plain, Scotland, between Grampian Mts. and Ochil and Sidlaw Hills; extremely fertile. Length, *c.* 100 m.; breadth, up to 10 m.

Strathpef'fer, health resort, Ross and Cromarty, Scotland, 5 m. W. of Dingwall; sulphurous and chalybeate mineral wells. Pop. 900.

Stratton and Bude. See BUDE.

Straubing (*strou'bing*), tn., Bavaria, Germany, on R. Danube, 25 m. by rail S.E. of Ratisbon; manufactures machinery and chemicals; breweries and tanneries. Pop. 24,000.

Streatham (*stret'am*), residential dist., S.W. London, England; Magdalen Hospital and Brit. Home for Incurables; Streatham Common covers about 60 ac. Pop. 53,000.

Streator (*strē'tor*), city, Illinois, U.S.A., on R. Vermilion, 82 m. s.w. of Chicago; manufactures bricks and tiles, glass, hardware, agricultural implements; coal. Pop. 15,000.

Street, urb. dist., Somerset, England, 2 m. s.w. of Glastonbury; boots and shoes. Pop. 4,500.

Stret'ford, urb. dist., Lancs, England, 4 m. s.w. of Manchester; textiles and machinery. Pop. 56,800.

Stromboli (*strom'bō-lē*), isl., Lipari group, N. of Sicily, Mediterranean Sea; volcano (alt. 3,090 ft.), known as 'Lighthouse of the Mediterranean,' almost constantly active.

Strom'ness, port, s.w. Mainland, Orkney, Scotland, 14 m. w. of Kirkwall; summer resort; fishing and distilling; noted harbour of refuge. Pop. 1,600.

Strood, tn., Kent, England, on R. Medway, connected by bridge with Chatham and Rochester; large seed-crushing mills. Pop. 10,000.

Stroud, mkt. tn., Gloucestershire, England, 8 m. s. of Gloucester; chief seat of w. of England fine cloth manufacture; long famous for scarlet dyes; breweries, sawmills, iron foundries. Pop. 8,400.

Struma (*stroo'ma*), river, Balkan Peninsula, Europe; rises in Bulgaria about 20 m. s. of Sofia; flows w. and s.e. through Bulgaria and Macedonia to enter Ægean Sea. Length, 150 m.

Stryj (*strē*), tn., Poland, on R. Stryj, 40 m. s.w. of Lwow; tanneries, sawmills, manufacture of matches. Pop. 27,000.

Stud'ley, par. and vil., Warwickshire, England, 13 m. w. of Warwick; manufactures needles, bodkins, and fish-hooks. Pop. (par.) 3,000.

Stuttgart (*stoot'gart*), cap., Württemberg, Germany, on R. Neckar; old churches and many fine modern buildings; great publishing centre; also textiles, pianos, chemicals, furniture, artists' colours, jewellery, cigars. Pop. 342,000.

Styria (*stir'e-a*), prov., Austria, divided into northern or Upper Styria, and southern or Lower Styria; in E. Alps; traversed by Rs. Mur, Drave, and Enns; rich mineral deposits (iron, coal, copper); extensive forests; fertile mountain valleys; prov. contains numerous mineral springs; manufactures iron and steel. Cap. Graz. Area, 6,323 sq. m.; pop. 979,000.

Suakin (*soo-ä'kin*), port, Anglo-Egyptian Sudan, on w. coast of Red Sea; occupies coral islet close to mainland; connected by rly. with Berber; exports tobacco, ivory, gums, mother-of-pearl; valuable pearl fisheries. Pop. 8,000.

Subiaco (*soo-be-ä'ko*), tn., Italy, on R. Anio; surrounded by Sabine Mts., 30 m. E. of Rome; ironworks, paper mills. Pop. 8,200.

Subotica (*sub-o-tit'sa*), formerly SZABADKA or MARIA-THERESIOPEL, tn., Voivodina, Yugoslavia, near Hungarian frontier; centre of agricultural and cattle-rearing region; boots, railway trucks, and furniture. Pop. 104,000.

Su-chow. See SOOCHOW.

Sucre (*soo'krā*), nominal cap., Bolivia, S. America, situated on watershed between basins of Rs. Amazon and La Plata; cathedral, univ. of San Xavier. Pop. 34,000.

Sudan (*soo-dän'*) ('land of the Blacks'), vast region in Africa with no strictly defined limits, but roughly bounded N. by Egypt and Sahara, W. by Atlantic Ocean, S. by Guinea Lands, Congo Basin, and Uganda, E. by Abyssinia and Red Sea. There is a great diversity of physical features, but Sudan is chiefly an elevated region, mountainous in parts, with grassy, steppe-like plains and considerable forest-land; region is watered by several great rivers, including Senegal, Niger, and Nile; in centre is Lake Chad; climate hot and unhealthy. Chief occupations are ostrich farming, sheep, goat, and camel rearing, cultivation of cotton, durra, barley, wheat, and dates;

exports include cotton, gum, rubber, ivory, ostrich feathers, and dates.

Anglo-Egyptian Sudan, situated in Upper Nile valley, is bounded on N. by Egypt, on E. by Red Sea, Eritrea, and Abyssinia, on S. by Uganda Protectorate and Belgian Congo, and on W. by French Equatorial Africa. In N. between the Red Sea and R. Nile is Nubian Desert, a bare, desolate tract with little vegetation. Sudan consists chiefly of grassy plains, and the S. is a swampy, unhealthy dist. The only fertile part is in neighbourhood of R. Nile and its tribs. and in oases. Forests yield rubber, gum, ivory, and much valuable timber; iron, gold, copper, and lignite are produced; cattle raising important; cotton successfully cultivated under irrigation, and in parts where rain is sufficient. Chief tns. are Khartoum (cap.), Omdurman, Halfa, El Obeid, Suakin, Port Sudan. Area, 1,008,100 sq. m.; pop. 5,484,000.

French Sudan, colony of French W. Africa, mainly consisting of plateau land, and including valley of Upper Senegal R. and more than half of R. Niger basin; many cattle reared, and millet, maize, rice, cotton are produced. Chief tns. are Bamako (cap.), Kayes, and Timbuktu. Area, 360,331 sq. m.; pop. 2,633,000.

Sud'bury. (1) Munic. bor., Suffolk, England, on R. Stour, 16 m. S. of Bury St. Edmunds; silks, velvets, coco-fibre matting; horsehair weaving. Pop. 7,000. (2) Tn., Ontario, Canada, *c.* 150 m. E. of Sault Ste. Marie; great mining and smelting tn. producing nickel and copper. Pop. 9,000.

Sudetes Mts. (*soo-dā'tes*), mt. system, central Europe, separating Prussian Silesia from Czechoslovakia; include Riesengebirge; at S.E. extremity is Moravian Gate; chief peak Schneekoppe (5,260 ft.).

Sueca (*soo-ā'ka*), tn., E. Spain, 19 m. S. of Valencia; trade in fruit and grain. Pop. 18,000.

Suez (*soo-ez'*), port, Egypt, on Gulf of Suez, at S. terminus of Suez Canal. Pop. 41,000.

Suez, Gulf of, W. arm of Red Sea, extends 190 m. to N.W.; width, *c.* 30 m.; connected with Mediterranean Sea by Suez Canal.

Suez Canal, ship canal between Mediterranean Sea and Red Sea, from Port Said to Suez, constructed by Ferdinand de Lesseps (1859–69); subsequently enlarged. Canal is 101 m. long; runs through Lakes Menzala, Balah, Timsah, and Bitter Lakes; depth, *c.* 32 ft.; greatest width, *c.* 350 ft.; time of passage, 15–18 hours. There is a railway swing bridge across the canal at El Qantara. The canal is of the greatest value to commerce as it provides a short route to the East. More than half the shipping passing through the canal is British.

Suf'folk, coast co., E. England; bounded N. by Norfolk, E. by North Sea, S. by Essex, W. by Cambridgeshire; surface generally level or slightly undulating, with low ridge of hills in N.W.; coasts low and much encroached on by sea; drained by Rs. Little Ouse, Waveney, Blythe, Alde, Orwell, and Stour. County is chiefly of chalk formation; principal industry is agriculture; there are important fisheries on coast; malting is carried on; manufactures include chemical manures, agricultural implements. Co. tn., Ipswich. Area, 1,482 sq. m.; pop. 401,100.

Suhl (*zool*), tn., Saxony, Prussia, on R. Lauter, on S. side of Thuringian Forest, 13 m. E.N.E. of Meiningen; long famous for manufacture of firearms; iron and machine works, potteries, tanneries. Pop. 16,000.

Sui, tn., Szechwan, China, on R. Yangtze Kiang; wax; exports cotton goods; large trade with Yunnan. Pop. 125,000.

Suir (*shoor*), riv., I.F.S.; rises in Tipperary and enters Waterford Harbour. Chief tns. on banks, Clonmel, Carrick-on-Suir, Waterford. Length, *c.* 100 m.

Suk'kur, tn., Sind, Bombay, India, on R. Indus, 25 m. S.E. of Shikarpur; trade in silk, cotton, wool, opium, piece goods. An irrigation dam is being constructed across the R. Indus here. Pop. 43,000.

Su'la Islands, chain of islands, Dutch E. Indies; E. of Celebes; mountainous and forested; rice, maize, tobacco. Pop. 16,000.

Sulaiman Mountains (*soo-lă-măn'*) extend along the N.W. frontier of India for 350 m. Khyber Pass is most important route through mts. Highest point, Takht-i-Sulaiman ('throne of Solomon'), 11,070.

Sulina (*soo-lē'na*), free port, Romania, at mouth of Sulina branch of R. Danube; grain transhipping centre. Pop. 8,000.

Sulmo'na, tn., Aquila, Italy, 80 m. E. of Rome; manufactures paper; copper factories; noted wine. Birthplace of Ovid. Pop. 19,000.

Sulu. See HOLO.

Sumatra (*soo-mä'trä*), largest isl. of Malay Archipelago, one of Dutch E. Indies; separated from Malay Peninsula by Strait of Malacca, and from Java by Sunda Strait; volcanic mts. run lengthwise along S.W. (Mt. Korinchi, 12,400 ft.); in N.E. are marshy and sandy plains; watered by Rs. Musi, Jambi, Indragiri, and other streams, all flowing E.; there are many small islands off the coasts. Climate is hot, but healthy, except in lower districts; rainfall heavy. Dense forests of teak, oak, and other timber trees; produces rice, maize, sugar, coffee, spices, sago, coconuts, tobacco, betel, gutta-percha, gums; minerals include coal, gold, silver, petroleum, iron, lead, saltpetre. Principal ports, Padang, Palembang, Benkulen, Achin. Area, 163,138 sq. m.; pop. 6,164,000.

Sumba (*soom'bä*), one of Lesser Sunda Islands, Dutch E. Indies; soil fertile; rice, maize, tobacco; sandalwood. Area, 4,600 sq. m.; pop. 124,000.

Sumbawa (*soom-bä'wä*), one of Lesser Sunda Islands, Dutch E. Indies; mountainous, volcanic, fertile; rice, cotton, coffee, tobacco, vegetables are grown; live-stock rearing. Area, 5,240 sq. m.; pop. 246,000.

Sumy (*soo'mē*), town, Ukraine, U.S.S.R., on R. Isel, 84 m. N.W. of Kharkov; sugar refineries, breweries, textile and leather factories; agricultural implements. Pop. 40,000.

Sun'bury, tn., Pennsylvania, U.S.A., on R. Susquehanna, 30 m. S. of Williamsport; manufactures textiles, flour, furniture, machinery. Pop. 16,000.

Sun'bury-on-Thames, urb. dist., Middlesex, England, part of Greater London; residential dist.; fishing resort. Pop. 13,300.

Sun'da Islands, collective name for group of islands, Malay Archipelago, divided into Greater Sunda Islands (Borneo, Sumatra, Java, Celebes) and Lesser Sunda Islands (Bali, Lombok, Sumbawa, and others).

Sundarbans', coast land of R. Ganges delta, India; largely forest and swamp intersected by numerous distributaries of Ganges–Brahmaputra; rice in N. portion; S. part is jungle, haunt of tigers and crocodiles. Area, 7,500 sq. m.

Sun'derland, co. bor. and port, Durham, England, at mouth of R. Wear; includes Bishopwearmouth and Monkwearmouth; large trade in coal; shipbuilding centre; engineering, anchor, and chain-cable works, roperies, glass and paper works; imports timber. Pop. 185,900.

Sundsvall (*soonds'väl*), port, Sweden, on Gulf of Bothnia; sawmills and shipbuilding yards; exports timber. Pop. 18,000.

Sungari (*soon-gä-rē'*), riv., Manchuria; trib. of R. Amur; navigable for light craft to Kirin; teems with sturgeon, trout, and salmon; icebound for five months. Length, 800 m.

Sun'ningdale, par. and vil., Berks, England, 6 m. S. of Windsor; golfing centre. Pop. (par.) 2,000.

Sun'ninghill, par. and vil., S.E. Berks, England; residential; popular wat.-pl. in 18th cent. Pop. (par.) 5,800.

Supe'rior. (1) LAKE, largest freshwater lake in world, and most W. of the five Great Lakes of N. America; between U.S.A. and Canada; length, 400 m.; breadth, 160 m.; area, 32,000 sq. m.; elevation above sea-level, 600 ft.; discharges by St. Mary's R. into Lake Huron. Surrounding region is extremely rich in iron and copper. (2) Port, Wisconsin, U.S.A., at W. end of L. Superior; shipbuilding yards; flour and lumber mills; manufactures railway stock, furniture, wooden articles; market for cereals. Pop. 36,000.

Suq ash Shuyukh', tn., Iraq, on R. Euphrates, 85 m. N.W. of Basra; surrounding region fertile; manufactures Arab woollen cloaks; boat building. Pop. *c.* 12,000.

Surabaya (*soo-rä-bï'ä*). (1) Residency, E. Java, Dutch E. Indies; fertile, well-watered plain; sugar, tobacco, coffee, rice, and other food crops; cattle rearing; oilfields. Area, 3,682 sq. m.; pop. 2,556,000. (2) Port in above; government dockyards and arsenals; exports coffee, rice, cotton, sugar, tobacco, tapioca. Pop. 250,000.

Surakar'ta. (1) Residency, central Java; hilly, with fertile valley of R. Solo; tobacco, coffee, sugar-cane extensively grown. Area, 2,500 sq. m.; pop. 2,257,000. (2) Cap. of above; commercial centre; pop. 130,000.

Surat'. (1) Dist., Bombay, India; alluvial plain yielding luxuriant crops; rice, cotton, wheat. Area, 1,651 sq. m.; pop. 674,000. (2) Port, cap. of above, on R. Tapti; manufactures cotton and silk, gold and silver wire, sandalwood, and exports agricultural produce and cotton. Was first English settlement in India. Pop. 117,000.

Sur'biton, residential suburb of Kingston-on-Thames, Surrey, England; part of Greater London; headquarters of rowing and sailing clubs. Pop. 29,400.

Surinam. See under GUIANA (*Dutch Guiana*).

Sur'rey, inland co., S. England; bounded by Middlesex, Kent, Sussex, Hants, Berks, and Bucks. Surface is generally undulating, with well-wooded parks and large commons; crossed by N. Downs; drained by Rs. Thames, Wey, Mole, and other streams. Agriculture is important; wheat, oats, barley, and pulse grown; hops, vegetables and medicinal herbs; market gardening; live-stock raised. Co. tn., Guildford. Area, 721 sq. m.; pop. 1,180,800.

Sus (*zoos*), prov., Morocco, bordering Atlantic Ocean; mountainous; drained by R. Sus; produces saltpetre; believed to be rich in copper. Area, *c.* 8,000 sq. m.; pop. *c.* 400,000.

Susa. See SOUSSE.

Susquehanna (*sus-kwe-han'a*), riv., E. U.S.A.; rises in two main branches which unite at Sunbury, Pennsylvania, and enters Chesapeake Bay; length, 422 m.

Sus'sex, mar. co., S. England; bounded by Hants, Surrey, and Kent; crossed by S. Downs, which terminate at Beachy Head; the Weald, formerly forested, occupies interior, and in N.E. are Forest Hills; drained by Rs. Rother, Brede, Ouse, Adur, Arun, and other streams. Chief industry is agriculture; principal crops, wheat, barley, pulse, potatoes, hops; excellent pasturage in marshland of S.E. and on Downs; great numbers of cattle, sheep, and horses reared; fruits and vegetables extensively grown for London markets. Coast fisheries are valuable. Manufactures include paper, bricks, pottery, cement, gunpowder. Co. tn., Lewes. Area, 1,457 sq. m.; pop. 770,100.

Suth'erland, mar. co., N. Scotland, extends from Atlantic Ocean to Moray Firth; bounded N.E. by Caithness, S. by Ross and Cromarty; surface mountainous with wide moorlands and some fertile valleys in E.; highest point, Ben More Assynt (3,273 ft.); drained by Rs. Oykell, Brora, Helmsdale, and other streams; has numerous lakes, including Lochs Assynt and Shin. Little agriculture; sheep are extensively reared; salmon, herring, and other fisheries; a considerable area consists of deer forests and grouse moors. Small coalfield at

Brora. Co. tn., Dornoch. Area, 2,028 sq. m.; pop. 16,100.

Sut'lej, riv., Punjab, India, trib. of R. Indus; rises in Tibet and flows generally s.w.; joins R. Indus at Mithankot; navigable for steamers to Ferozepur; supplies several systems of irrigation works; length, 900 m.

Sutton, Long, urb. dist., S.E. Lincolnshire, England, 11 m. w. of King's Lynn; mkt. tn. Pop. 2,900.

Sut'ton and Cheam, urb. dist., Surrey, England, 4 m. s.w. of Croydon; residential dist. Pop. 46,500.

Sut'ton Bridge, urb. dist., Lincs, England, on R. Nen, 7 m. N. of Wisbech; port. Pop. 2,800.

Sut'ton Cold'field, munic. bor., Warwickshire, England; residential suburb of Birmingham; hardware. Pop. 29,900.

Sut'ton-in-Ash'field, tn., Notts, England, 13 m. N. of Nottingham; manufactures hosiery and cotton thread; collieries in vicinity. Pop. 25,200.

Sut'ton-on-Sea, wat.-pl., Lincolnshire, England, united with Mablethorpe; summer resort.

Suwalki (*soo-väl'kē*). (1) Prov., s.w. Lithuania; part of former Russian prov., now divided between Lithuania and Poland. Agriculture, timber felling, and weaving of woollen and linen cloth are the chief industries. Area, 4,800 sq. m.; pop. 667,000. (2) Tn., Poland, near Lithuanian frontier; timber, grain, and woollens. Pop. 24,000.

Svalbard. See SPITSBERGEN.

Svend'borg, port, on isl. of Fünen, Denmark; exports agricultural produce; manufactures tobacco; weaving, ironfounding, and brewing. Pop. 14,000.

Sverdlovsk', formerly EKATERINBURG, tn., Ural Area, Russia, on E. slopes of Ural Mts.; univ.; centre of important mining district; coal, platinum, copper, gold; manufactures linen, machinery; jewel cutting. Pop. 136,000.

Svishtov (*shish-tov'*), formerly SISTOVA, tn., Bulgaria, on R. Danube; centre of grain trade; exports wine. Pop. 12,000.

Swabia (*swä'bē-a*), or SUABIA (Ger. *Schwaben*), anc. duchy (917–1268), s.w. Germany; devastated in Thirty Years' War (1618–48); broken up by Napoleon (1805); much of terr. now administrative dist. of Bavaria, stretching from Switzerland to beyond R. Danube. Chief tn., Augsburg.

Swad'lincote, urb. dist., Derbyshire, England, 5 m. S.E. of Burton-on-Trent; coal mines and potteries. Pop. 20,300.

Swaff'ham, tn., Norfolk, England, 15 m. S.E. of King's Lynn; ironfounding. Pop. 2,800.

Swak'opmund, port, S.W. Africa, 30 m. N. of Walvis Bay; trading and mission station; wat.-pl. Pop. 1,800.

Swal'well, vil., Durham, England, 5 m. s.w. of Newcastle; coal mines and steel works. Pop. 4,600.

Swan'age, wat.-pl. and port, Isle of Purbeck, Dorset, England; exports Purbeck stone. Pop. 6,300.

Swan'ley, vil., Kent, England, 15 m. S.E. of London; school of gardening. Pop. (dist.) 3,000.

Swans'combe, urb. dist., Kent, England, on R. Thames, 2 m. w. of Gravesend; cement. Pop. 8,500.

Swans'ea, co. bor. and port, Glamorganshire, Wales, at mouth of R. Tawe; chief seat of tinplate manufacture; one of most important copper-smelting and refining towns in world; extensive coal mines; manufacture of iron and steel, zinc, alkali, arsenic, machinery. Huge oil refineries. Extensive docks and fine harbour. Pop. 164,800.

Swat, region, N.W. Frontier Prov., India, consisting of upper valley of Swat R., which flows s. for about 400 m. to join R. Kabul. Pop. (mainly Pathans) *c.* 170,000.

Swatow', port, Kwang-tung, S. China, at mouth of R. Han; manufactures bean cake; wolfram mining; exports sugar, paper, grass-cloth, china ware, fruits, vegetable oil, tea, and tobacco. Pop. 93,000.

Swa'ziland, terr., Brit. S. Africa,

between Transvaal and Portuguese E. Africa; W. surface is a grass-covered plateau; centre is fertile rolling downs; climate healthy; low bush lands malarious; chief crops are maize, millet, tobacco, beans; fruit (especially oranges); cotton; cattle and sheep raised; minerals include gold, tin. Administered by Resident Commissioner subject to High Commissioner for S. Africa. Mbabane is administrative centre. Area, 6,704 sq. m.; pop. 113,000 (including 2,200 whites).

Swe'den, kingdom, N.W. Europe; occupies E. and larger part of Scandinavia; bounded E. by the Baltic Sea, Gulf of Bothnia, and Finland; N. and W. by Norway. On the whole forms a great plain, very slightly elevated above sea-level. Only N. part along Norwegian border is mountainous; has innumerable islands fringing the shores and affording protection against winds and waves. Land is exceedingly well watered. Principal rivs. are Tornio, Kalix, Lule, Pite, Ume, Angerman, Ljusna, and Mottala, falling into Baltic; and Göta and Klar into Kattegat. Most important canal is Göta Canal, which, by means of Göta R. and lakes Vener and Vetter, unites North Sea with Baltic. Lakes cover 8.3 per cent. of total area. Climate generally equable, but more extreme than that of Norway; Gulf of Bothnia and Baltic Sea ice-bound in winter. Coniferous forests cover the greater part of the country; in N. flora is arctic, and reindeer is nomadic. Agriculture is important; greater part of land owned by small proprietors. Barley, oats, sugar-beet, fodder roots, and hay are largely grown; potato flourishes everywhere. Large quantities of butter, hides, wool, bacon, and live-stock are exported, as are timber, wrought and unwrought, and wood pulp. Fisheries, esp. herring, are important; salmon is principal river fish. Mining is most productive industry; excellent iron ore in the central provinces, and at Gellivara in the N. Woollen and cotton goods, electrical goods, porcelain, brandy, sugar, machinery are principal manufactured products. Excellent harbours abound. Principal exports are timber, wood pulp, metals, and animal products. The population is most dense in the S., where all the largest tns. are. Cap. Stockholm. Area, 173,156 sq. m.; pop. 6,105,000.

Swilly, LOUGH ('lake of shadows'), inlet, Donegal, I.F.S.; length, about 30 m.; largest battleships can anchor in Buncrana Bay.

Swin'don, munic. bor., Wilts, England, 77 m. W. of London; has extensive locomotive and carriage works; limestone quarrying in vicinity; cloth mills. Pop. 62,400.

Swinemünde (*swē'ne-moon-da*), tn. and wat.-pl., Pomerania, Prussia, on isl. of Usedom, and on R. Swine, 35 m. N.N.W. of Stettin, fairway to which is kept open in winter by icebreakers. Pop. 18,000.

Swin'ton, tn., W. Riding, Yorks, England, 10½ m. N.E. of Sheffield; has railway works; bottles, glass, and pottery. Pop. 13,800.

Swin'ton and Pen'dlebury, urb. dist., Lancs, England, 4 m. N.W. of Manchester; has cotton mills and coal mines. Pop. 32,800.

Swit'zerland, rep., central Europe; bounded N. by Germany, E. by Austria, S. by Italy, and W. by France; S. part consists of ranges of Alps including Pennine Alps, with Monte Rosa (15,217 ft.) and the Matterhorn (14,705 ft.), both on Italian boundary, Lepontine Alps, and Rhaetian Alps; in centre are Bernese Alps (Oberland), with Finsteraarhorn, Aletschhorn, and Jungfrau, and Glarus Alps, separated by plateau from Jura Mts., which form N.W. frontier. Numerous glaciers. Principal drainage is by Rs. Rhine and Rhone; R. Aar receives Alpine streams which traverse lakes Neuchâtel, Lucerne, Zurich, etc., and joins R. Rhine, which flows through L. Constance (partly in Germany); R. Rhone leaves Switzerland through L. Geneva (partly in France); R. Ticino (trib. of R. Po) flows through L. Maggiore (mainly in Italy); and R. Inn (trib. of R. Danube) flows through Engadine. Many important passes, esp. Simplon, Lötschen, and St. Gotthard, which have been tunnelled and carry railway routes to Italy. Tourist traffic gives employment to many of the inhabitants, both in summer and for winter sports. Country known as the 'Playground of Europe.' About one quarter of the country is forested. The land is pastoral rather than agricultural; cattle, pigs, goats, and sheep are reared, esp. in plateau region. Most of the food crops are imported. Vineyards are on the decrease. Large water-power resources. Of manufactures the chief are textiles, especially silk and cotton. Watch and clock making carried on for centuries. The chief manufactured articles exported are cheese, condensed milk, chocolate, and other food products; silk and cotton goods, including embroidery; and clocks and watches, machinery, shoes, and chemicals. German is spoken by 70 per cent. of the inhabitants, but French is the chief language of the five S.W. cantons, and Italian in Ticino. Berne is the cap. Area, 15,940 sq. m.; pop. 4,018,000.

Swords, par. and tn., co. Dublin, I.F.S., 8 m. N. of Dublin; has round tower and ruins of an abbey and a castle. Pop. (par.) 1,900.

Syd'enham, residential dist., London, England, partly within the metropolitan bor. of Lewisham. Here is the Crystal Palace. Pop. 32,000.

Syd'ney. (1) Cap. of New South Wales, Australia, on S. shore of Port Jackson, one of finest natural harbours in world. Quays and wharves are over 23 m. in extent and can accommodate vessels of largest tonnage. City is laid out with wide streets and fine public buildings, including governor-general's residence, univ., mint, and two cathedrals; has fine parks and botanical gardens. Is the main commercial and industrial centre of New South Wales, and the most important port in Australia. Great wool sales. Among its many industrial establishments are foundries, engineering and electrical works, and cloth mills. *Greater Sydney* includes the cap. Sydney, and forty surrounding municipalities. Sydney Harbour Bridge connects Sydney with N. Sydney. Area, 181 sq. m.; pop. 1,239,000. (2) Port and mining tn., Cape Breton I., Nova Scotia, Canada; iron and steel works; cement, coke, chemicals. Pop. 23,000.

Syd'ney Mines, tn., Nova Scotia, Canada, on Cape Breton I., 8 m. N. of Sydney; coal mining. Pop. 7,000.

Sylhet'. (1) Dist., S. Assam, India; largely plain in lower valley of R. Surma; hilly towards S.; very well watered; most important crop is tea. Area, 5,680 sq. m.; pop. 2,541,000. (2) Chief tn. of above, on R. Surma; weaving, oil-pressing, bamboo work. Pop. 17,000.

Sylt, largest German isl., N. Frisian group, North Sea; off W. coast of Jutland; holiday resort. Length, 23 m. Area, 38 sq. m.; pop. 4,500.

Syra. See SYROS.

Syr'acuse. (1) Prov., E. Sicily; hilly, with fertile valleys; fruit. Area, 852 sq. m.; pop. 312,000. (2) Cap. of above, on Mediterranean Sea; chemicals and pottery; exports fruit, wine, oil. Anc. city, founded 733 B.C., was chief Greek city in W. Extensive and interesting ruins of anc. tn. Pop. 56,000. (3) Tn., New York, U.S.A., on Lake Onondaga, 76 m. E. of Rochester; important rly. and canal centre; univ.; brine springs, salt production formerly important; typewriters, machinery, clothing. Pop. 207,000.

Syr-Daria. See SIR DARYA.

Sy'ria, state, Asia, under French mandate; bounded N. by Asia Minor, E. by Iraq, S. by Transjordan and Palestine, W. by Mediterranean Sea. Surface elevated; Lebanon and Anti-Lebanon Mts. extend along Mediterranean coast; E. of these a plateau slopes gradually to E. desert; in S. is fertile Hauran; chief riv. is Orontes. Climate is Mediterranean. Cereals, linseed, grapes, tobacco, and olives are grown; lentils and beans; sheep and goats reared; exports silk, wool, cereals, fruit, olive oil. From Aleppo the 'Pilgrims' rly. runs s. through Damascus, with branches to the coast at Tripoli and Beirut. Cap. Damascus. Area, *c.* 60,000 sq. m.; pop. 1,700,000.

Sy'ros, isl. of Cyclades group, Greece; mountainous; exports sponges, tobacco, citrons. Chief tn., Hermoupolis. Area, 42 sq. m.; pop. 34,000.

Sys'ton, par. and vil., Leicestershire, England, 5 m. N.N.E. of Leicester; boot and shoe factories. Pop. (par.) 3,200.

Syzran (*sis-rän'*), tn., Ulianovsk prov., Russia, on R. Volga, 17 m. w. of Samara; tanneries, iron foundries, distilleries, breweries, flour mills, and sawmills. Pop. 48,000.

Szabadka. See SUBOTICA.

Szatmar-Nemeti. See SATUL-MARE.

Szechwan' ('four rivers'), largest prov. of China Proper, in centre of w.; surface mountainous, reaching extreme height of *c.* 19,000 ft.; drained by R. Yangtze and its tribs.; soil fertile; produces cereals, oil, sugar, tea, cotton, opium, tobacco, oranges, white wax, silk; minerals include coal, iron, salt, gold, silver, lead. Cap. Chengtu. Area, 218,480 sq. m.; pop. *c.* 50,000,000.

Szeged (*seg'ed*), tn., Hungary, at junction of Rs. Tisa and Maros; univ.; manufactures soap, cloth, leather; breweries, distilleries; important trade centre. Pop. 125,000.

Szek'esfehervar, tn., Hungary, 35 m. s.w. of Budapest; manufactures leather and shoes; trade in horses, wine, and fruit. Pop. 39,000.

Szentes (*sen'tesh*), tn., Hungary, on branch of R. Tisa, 30 m. N. by E. of Szeged; protected against the frequent inundations of R. Tisa by huge stone dykes. Pop. 32,000.

Szolnok (*sol'nok*), tn., w. Hungary, on R. Tisa, 58 m. E.S.E. of Budapest; linen thread and machinery; trade in timber, salt, and tobacco. Pop. 32,500.

Szom'bathely, tn., Hungary, 31 m. s. of Sopron; centre of wine-producing and agricultural country; textiles, agricultural implements, flour, and lumber. Pop. 35,000.

T

Taal (*tä-äl'*), tn., Luzon I., Philippines, 50 m. s. of Manila; rice and sugar mills; exports sulphur. Pop. 21,500.

Tabaco (*tä-bä'ko*), tn., Luzon I., Philippines, on S.E. coast; trades with Manila; hemp. Pop. 25,000.

Tabas'co, state, Mexico, on s. of Bay of Campeche; low, flat, and forested; no rlys. Cap. Villa Hermosa. Area, 10,374 sq. m.; pop. 210,500.

Ta'ble Mountain, mt., Cape Prov., S. Africa, overlooking Cape Town and Table Bay; named from flat summit; alt. 3,550 ft.

Tabor (*tä'bor*), tn., Bohemia, Czechoslovakia, 65 m. by rail s. of Prague; tobacco, beer, flour produced; partly surrounded with walls built by Hussites (1420). Pop. 13,000.

Tabo'ra, tn., Tanganyika Terr., E. Africa; junction of rlys. from Dar-es-Salaam to Ls. Tanganyika and Victoria; aerodrome; founded *c.* 1820 for trade in slaves and ivory. Pop. *c.* 25,000.

Tabriz (*tä-brēz'*), tn., cap., Azerbaijan, N.W. Persia, 40 m. E. of L. Urmia; alt. 4,400 ft.; mineral springs in vicinity; exports dried fruit, cotton, carpets; Blue Mosque, and citadel containing famous tower built by Greeks; several times devastated by earthquakes. Pop. 180,000.

Tac'na. (1) Prov., Peru, S. America, bordering Chile; transferred from Chile by treaty of 1929; largely desert; nitrate of soda, silver, copper; subject to earthquakes. Area, 12,600 sq. m.; pop. 60,000. (2) Cap. of above, on oasis; rly. to Arica. Pop. *c.* 14,500.

Taco'ma, city, Washington, U.S.A., 25 m. s. by w. of Seattle; important seaport of Pacific coast; lumber and timber manufactures, copper smelting, flour mills. Pop. 107,000.

Tad'caster, tn., W. Riding, Yorks, England, 9 m. s.w. of York; breweries, limestone quarries; Roman remains discovered; divided into E. and W. Tadcaster. Pop. (E.) 1,500, (W.) 2,000.

Tadzhik Republic (*tä-zhēk*), rep., U.S.S.R.; in central Asia, N. of Afghanistan; mountainous (Mt. Kaufmann, 23,386 ft.); chief riv., Oxus; under irrigation, wheat, barley, cotton, and fruits are raised; coal, iron; peasant industries. Cap. Diushambe. Area, 52,110 sq. m.; pop. *c.* 824,000.

Tafilelt (*tä-fĕl'elt*), oasis, Morocco, Africa, in N.W. Sahara, *c.* 200 m. s. of Fez; caravan centre; noted for dates and leather. Pop. 150,000.

Taganrog', port, N. Caucasian Area, Russia, on Sea of Azov, 35 m. w. of Rostov-on-Don; tanneries, tobacco factories, fisheries; exports grain. Pop. 86,500.

Ta'gus, longest riv., Iberian peninsula; rises in Sierra de Albarracin; flows N.W. and W. in narrow and generally deep valley across Meseta into broad lake at Lisbon; navigable by steamers to Santarem; estuary an important European harbour. Length, 265 m.

Tahiti (*tä-hē'tē*), formerly OTAHEITE, largest of Society Islands, Pacific Ocean; belongs to France; of volcanic formation; surface mountainous, reaching 7,340 ft.; surrounded by coral reefs; fertile along coast; produces bread-fruit, oranges, bananas, and other fruits, sugar, coffee, cocoa, vanilla, cotton; exports copra, pearl-shell, vanilla, coconuts, phosphates. Native inhabitants belong to Polynesian group. Chief tn., Papeete. Area, 600 sq. m.; pop. 9,000.

Tain, port and royal burgh, Ross and Cromarty, Scotland, on s. shore of Dornoch Firth, 44 m. N. of Inverness; distillery, woollen mills; church of St. Duthus (1471). Pop. 1,400.

Taiwan. See FORMOSA.

Tai-Yuan (*tī-yoo-än'*), cap., Shansi, China; coalfields in vicinity; meteorological station. Pop. *c.* 80,000.

Takamat'su, tn., Japan, N. coast of Shikoku I., 80 m. w.s.w. of Osaka; ruined castle. Pop. 72,000.

Tak'la Makan', w. section of Gobi Desert, Sinkiang, China; between Kunlun Mts. and Tarim R.; largely covered with sand dunes. Area, 115,000 sq. m.

Takorad'i, port, Gold Coast, W. Africa; w. of Sekondi; deep water harbour, opened 1928, is the only one between Sierra Leone and Nigeria; exports cocoa, gold, manganese, diamonds.

Taku (*tä-koo'*), fortified port, Hopeh, China, on Pei-ho; dockyard; taken by European Allies (1900).

Talavera, or TALAVERA DE LA REINA (*tä-lä-vä'rä*), tn., Toledo, Spain, on R. Tagus, 84 m. by rail s.w. of Madrid; cloth, leather, soap; Roman and Moorish remains; scene of battle in Peninsular War (1809). Pop. 13,500.

Tal'ca, tn., cap. of prov. of same name, Chile, 155 m. by rail s. of Santiago; trades in cereals and wine; partly destroyed by earthquake (1928). Pop. 36,000. Area (prov.) 5,622 sq. m.; pop. 228,000.

Talcahuan'o, port, Concepcion, Chile; exports grain; naval station. Pop. 22,500.

Talé-Sap. See TONLÉ-SAP.

Talgarth', mkt. tn. and par., Brecknock, Wales, 7 m. N.E. of Brecon; contains anc. Brit. relics. Pop. (par.) 1,900.

Talke (*tawk*), or TALK-O'-TH'-HILL, eccles. dist. and vil., Staffs, England, 5 m. N. of Newcastle-under-Lyme; coal mining. Pop. (dist.) 6,200.

Tallinn', formerly REVEL, port and cap., Estonia, s. Gulf of Finland; shipbuilding; textiles, cement, timber. Pop. 132,000.

Ta'mar, riv., Cornwall and Devon, England; rises in N.E. Cornwall and flows S. to Plymouth Sound; estuary called the Hamoaze; navigable to Launceston. Length, 60 m.

Tamatave (*tă-mă-tä'vă*), port, Madagascar; meat-preserving factories; *c.* half of total foreign trade passes through it; exports gold dust, hides, raffia. Pop. 15,000.

Tamaulipas (*tä-mou-lē'päs*), state, N.E. Mexico, on Gulf of Mexico; surface mountainous in interior, lagoons on coast; cereals, sugar, coffee; cattle-rearing; hides and live-stock exported; copper, asphalt, petroleum obtained. Cap. Ciudad Victoria. Area, 30,831 sq. m.; pop. 287,000.

Tambov'. (1) Prov., European Russia; surface undulating; drained by Don and Oka rivs.; cereals, hemp, flax, sugar-beet grown; horses and cattle reared; minerals include iron, coal, gypsum; chief export, grain. Area, 18,700 sq. m.; pop. 2,721,500. (2) Cap. of above, on R. Tsna, 180 m. S.E. of Tula; manufactures woollens, soap, candles, tobacco, tiles. Pop. 76,500.

Tam'merfors. See TAMPERE.

Tam'pa, city, W. Florida, U.S.A., on Tampa Bay; winter resort; exports cigars and phosphates. Pop. 101,000.

Tam'pere, formerly TAMMERFORS, tn., Finland, 100 m. N.W. of Helsinki; rly. jn.; textiles, leather, paper. Pop. 52,000.

Tampico (*täm-pē'ko*), port, E. coast of Mexico, on R. Panuco; outlet for oilfields; sugar, maize, fruits, fibres. Pop. 76,000.

Tam'worth. (1) Tn., Staffs, England, at junction of Tame and Anker rivs., 6½ m. S.E. of Lichfield; castle was residence of kings of Mercia; textile smallwares; coal and fireclay mines. Pop. 7,500. (2) Tn., New S. Wales, Australia, *c.* 150 m. N.W. of Newcastle; flour. Pop. 7,500.

Tana. (1) Or DEMBEA. Lake, Abyssinia; drained by Blue Nile riv.; alt. 5,700 ft.; area, 1,100 sq. m. (2) Riv., Kenya Colony, Africa; enters Indian Ocean *c.* 100 m. N. of Mombasa; length, 500 m.; navigable for 150 m. from sea.

Tananarivo. See ANTANANARIVO.

Tan'field, urb. dist., Durham, England, 7 m. S.W. of Gateshead; coal mining, lime quarrying; brick and tile works. Pop. 9,200.

Tan'ga, port, Tanganyika Terr., Africa; terminus of Usambara Rly.; exports sisal and coffee. Pop. 11,000.

Tanganyika (*tän-gä-nyē'ka*), fresh-water lake, central Africa, in rift-valley; length, *c.* 450 m.; breadth, 30–45 m.; 2,550 ft. above sea-level; N. and W. border on Belgian Congo, S. on Rhodesia, E. on Tanganyika Terr.; discovered by Burton and Speke (1858); explored by Livingstone; on Cape-to-Cairo route; steamer service; rlys. to Albertville on W. shore and Kigoma on E. Area, 12,700 sq. m.

Tanganyika Territory (*tän-gä-nyē'-ka*), terr., E. Africa; former German colony now administered by Britain under mandate; bounded N. by Uganda and Kenya, E. by Indian Ocean, S. by Portuguese E. Africa, Nyasaland, and N. Rhodesia, W. by L. Tanganyika and Belgian Congo; surface a plateau rising to *c.* 6,000 ft. (Mt. Kilimanjaro, 19,710 ft.); chief rivs. are Kagera, flowing to L. Victoria, Pangani and Rufiji to Indian Ocean; climate of coastal belt tropical, most of plateau unhealthy. Two rainy seasons, March to May, and Nov. to Dec.; areas suitable for Europeans are highlands in N.E. and S.W.; in coastal belt mangroves, coconut-palms, baobabs, tamarinds thrive; forests of acacia, cotton-tree, sycamore, etc., on plateau, also plantations of rubber, sugar, vanilla, cinchona; fibre plants, *e.g.* sisal, succeed; rice and coffee; cattle, sheep, and goats grazed; among minerals are mica, gold and diamonds; chief exports are grain, coffee, cotton, hides and skins, sisal, ground-nuts, ghee, beeswax, copra. Rlys. from Dar-es-Salaam to Kigoma, with line from Tabora to Mwanza, and from Tanga to Arusha. Cap. Dar-es-Salaam. Area, *c.* 374,000 sq. m. Pop.

(natives), 4,120,000; (other coloured) 15,000; (Europeans), 3,000.

Tang'ermunde, tn., Saxony, Prussia, at jn. of R. Tanger with R. Elbe, 43 m. N.E. of Magdeburg; river port; manufactures iron; shipbuilding yards and sugar refineries. Pop. 13,500.

Tangier (*tăn-jēr'*), port, Morocco, on Strait of Gibraltar, under international control; rly. to Fez; exports oxen, hides, goatskins, eggs, slippers; great mosque and sultan's palace; wireless station; trade suffers from international jealousies. Pop. 60,000.

Tanjore (*tăn-jōr*). (1) Dist., Madras, India; drained by R. Cauvery; mostly plain, largely deltaic; very fertile; rice and coconut palms. Area, 3,727 sq. m.; pop. 2,326,500. (2) Cap. of above, on R. Cauvery; literary and religious centre; palace of former rajahs; manufactures jewellery, carpets, silks, inlaid metal work. Pop. 60,000.

Tank'ersley, tn., Yorks, England, 4½ m. s. of Barnsley; ironworks, collieries, chemical works. Pop. 2,500.

Tan'ta, tn., Gharbia, in Nile delta, Egypt; rly. jn.; famous fairs. Pop. 90,000.

Taormina (*tä-or-mē'nä*), tn., Messina, Sicily; winter resort; ruins of Greek theatre. Pop. 5,000.

Tap'low, par. and vil., Bucks, England, on R. Thames; summer resort; paper making. Pop. (par.) 1,500.

Tapti, riv., w. India; rises in Central Provs., flows w., and enters Gulf of Cambay; length, 450 m.

Tara (*tä-rä*), vil., co. Meath, I.F.S., 6 m. S.E. of Navan; traditional early residence of Irish monarchs.

Tarai', dist. on s. slopes of Himalayas, United Provs., India; covered with marshes and jungle.

Tar'anto, port, Apulia, Italy, on Gulf of Taranto; castle, cathedral, and museum; naval arsenal; oyster and mussel fisheries; manufactures soap, oil, velvets, and cottons. Pop. 122,000.

Tarapaca', prov., N. Chile, in Atacama Desert; rich nitrate deposits; silver mined. Cap. Iquique. Area, 16,438 sq. m.; pop. 111,000.

Tarare (*tä-rär'*), tn., Rhône, France, on R. Turdine, 28 m. N.W. of Lyons; manufactures muslins, silks, and velvets. Pop. 11,000.

Tarascon (*tä-räs-kōn'*), tn., Bouches-du-Rhône, France, on R. Rhone; silk spinning and hat manufactures; trade in fruit. Pop. 5,000.

Tarawera (*tä-rä-wä'rä*), MOUNT, dormant volcano, Auckland, North I., New Zealand; slopes steeply to L. Tarawera; eruption destroyed Pink and White Terraces (June 10, 1886); highest peak, 3,770 ft.

Tar'bert, vil., Argyllshire, Scotland, near entrance to Loch Fyne; remains of castle built by Robert the Bruce (1326); herring fisheries. Pop. 2,000.

Tarbes (*tärb*), cap., Hautes-Pyrénées, France, on R. Adour; coarse woollen goods, machinery, leather, paper; breeds horses; race meetings. Pop. 27,000.

Tar'bet, vil., Dumbartonshire, Scotland, on w. shore of L. Lomond; holiday resort.

Tarbol'ton, vil., Ayrshire, Scotland, 7 m. N.E. of Ayr; has associations with Robert Burns. Pop. 1,000.

Târgoviste (*tŏ-ĕr-gov'ĕsh-te*), tn., Romania, 48 m. N.W. of Bucharest; petroleum and salt; military centre; former cap. of Walachia. Pop. 17,000.

Târgu Jiu (*tŏ-ĕr'goo zhyoo*), tn., Romania, in foothills of Transylvanian Alps, 60 m. N.W. of Craiova; timber, coal, petroleum; military centre. Pop. 20,000.

Târgul-Mures (*tŏ'ĕr-gool-moor'esh*), formerly MAROS-VASERHELY, tn., Transylvania, Romania, on R. Muresul; citadel and Gothic church, manufactures sugar, spirits, tobacco. Pop. 23,500.

Tarifa (*tä-rē'fä*), port, Cadiz, Spain, at extreme s.w. of peninsula, on Strait of Gibraltar; Cape Tarifa (Punta Marroqui) is most s. point of Europe; anc. castle and strong fortress on adjacent isl.; tunny and anchovy fishing; oranges, wine, and cereals. Pop. 12,000.

Tarija (*tä-rē'hä*), dep., s. Bolivia, S.

America; largely a fertile plain used for stock raising. Area, 31,567 sq. m.; pop. 140,000. Chief tn., Tarija (pop. 11,000).

Tarim (*tä-rēm*), riv., Central Asia; formed by jn. of Kashgar and Yarkand Rs.; flows between Kunlun and Tien Shan ranges; empties itself into Lop Nor; rich loess country of w. capable of cultivation; flows through Takla Makan Desert; length, *c.* 1,000 m.; remains of two anc. cities buried in westward-moving sand dunes.

Tar'lac, tn., Luzon, Philippine Islands, 70 m. N.W. of Manila; rice, sugar, tobacco, coconuts, and industries connected with these. Pop. 24,000.

Tarn. (1) Riv., s. France; rises in Cévennes, flows N.W. to join R. Garonne between Toulouse and Agen; length, 230 m. (2) Dep., s. France; hilly or mountainous; belongs chiefly to basin of R. Garonne; produces wheat, wine, coal. Cap. Albi. Area, 2,231 sq. m.; pop. 302,000.

Tarn-et-Garonne (*tärn-ā-gä-ron'*), dep., s. France; mostly tableland; watered by Rs. Garonne, Tarn, and Abeyron; cereals, fruit, and vine largely grown; coarse woollens, paper, leather, silk manufactured. Cap. Montauban. Area, 1,440 sq. m.; pop. 164,000.

Tarno'pol, tn., s. Poland, on R. Seret, 75 m. E.S.E. of Lwow; brewing, spirit refining, corn milling. Pop. 31,000.

Tarnow (*tär'nuf*), tn., Poland, 46 m. E. of Cracow; cathedral; manufactures agricultural implements and glass. Pop. 36,000.

Tar'porley, urb. dist., mkt. tn., Cheshire, England, 10 m. S.E. of Chester; manufactures stockings, leather breeches; headquarters of the Cheshire Hunt. Pop. 2,500.

Tarrago'na. (1) Prov., Catalonia, N.E. Spain; borders on Mediterranean Sea; mountainous; includes delta of R. Ebro; wine, grain, fruit, timber; lead, marble, copper, silver occur. Area, 2,505 sq. m.; pop. 356,000. (2) Cap. of above, on Mediterranean coast, 50 m. S.W. of Barcelona; cathedral; Roman remains, including aqueduct; silks, wine; large shipping trade. Pop. 28,000.

Tarras'a, tn., Barcelona, Spain, 15 m. N.W. of Barcelona; fine cloth, serges, tweeds, flannels; Roman remains. Pop. 31,000.

Tar'sus, tn., S.E. Asia Minor, on R. Cydnus; chief tn. of Cilicia in anc. times; birthplace of St. Paul. Exports hides, skins, cotton, wool. Pop. 74,000.

Tartar. See TATAR.

Tar'tu, formerly DORPAT, tn., Estonia, on R. Embach; univ.; printing works, sawmills; trades in timber and flax. Pop. 65,000.

Tashkent', tn., Uzbek, U.S.S.R., on oasis watered by tribs. of Sir Darya; on central Asia rly.; grain, fruit; univ. (1919); manufactures silk, leather, tobacco, cotton; dist. subject to earthquakes. Pop. 324,000.

Tasma'nia, island state, Australia; bounded N. by Bass Strait, E. and s. by Pacific Ocean, and w. by Indian Ocean; isl. is continuation of E. Australian highlands; plateau, with fertile valleys rising to Cradle Mountain (5,069 ft.); chief rivs., Derwent and Tamar; lakes include Great L.; coast much indented. Climate equable; flora and fauna resemble those of Australia; oats, barley, potatoes; fruit growing; sheep and cattle extensively raised; large area forested; minerals include copper, tin, lead, zinc, silver, coal; exports are wool, timber, fruits, metals. First visited in 1642 by Tasman, who named it Van Diemen's Land. Cap. Hobart. Area, 26,215 sq. m.; pop. 212,000.

Tatar-Pazardjik (*tä-tär'pä-zär-jēk'*), tn., Bulgaria, on Maritsa R., 22 m. w. of Philippopolis; dist. produces tobacco, millet, rice, silk. Pop. 22,000.

Tatar' Republic, rep., European Russia; drained by R. Volga and its trib. R. Kama; climate extreme; chief crops rye, oats, maize, potato, sugar-beet, flax, hemp; forests; leather goods, agricultural machinery.

Chief tn., Kazan. Area, 26,000 sq. m.; pop. 2,625,000.

Tat'ra Mountains, group, central Carpathians, Czechoslovakia and Poland; highest point, Gerlachovka, 8,737 ft.; many tourist resorts.

Taung-gyi, chief tn., Shan States, Burma, 90 m. S.E. of Mandalay; alt. 5,000 ft.; taken by British (1852); native bazaar. Pop. 17,000.

Taunton (*tawn'ton*). (1) Co. tn. of Somerset, England, 45 m. s.w. of Bristol; remains of Norman castle; noted for apples and cider; gloves, silk, agricultural implements; scene of Jeffreys' 'Bloody Assize.' Pop. 25,200. (2) City, Massachusetts, U.S.A., 35 m. s. of Boston; silver ware, cotton goods, machinery. Pop. 37,000.

Taunus (*tou'noos*), wooded range of mts., Germany, extending 55 m. E. to W. between Rs. Rhine and Main on S., and R. Lahn on N.; highest point, Grosser Feldburg, 2,887 ft.; vines on lower slopes; contains numerous mineral springs.

Tau'po, largest lake, New Zealand; in centre of North I.; Waikato R. feeds and drains lake; surroundings picturesque; numerous geysers, mud volcanoes, and hot springs in dist.; alt. 1,211 ft. Area, 238 sq. m.

Taurus Mountains (*tou'roos*), ALA-DAGH, or BULGHAR-DAGH, range of mts., s. Asia Minor; stretches from R. Euphrates to Ægean Sea; chief pass Cilician Gate; pierced by tunnel of Baghdad Rly.; alt. 9,000–10,000 ft. Anti-Taurus is N. extension from near E. end.

Tavira (*tă-vē'rä*), port, s. Portugal, *c.* 15 m. from Spanish boundary; fisheries; trade in white wine, fruit, locust beans. Pop. 11,000.

Tav'istock, urb. dist., Devonshire, England, on border of Dartmoor, 16 m. N. of Plymouth; remains of 10th cent. Benedictine abbey; copper, lead, and tin mines; extraction of arsenic. Pop. 4,500.

Tavoy', port, Tenasserim, Lower Burma, 30 m. above mouth of Tavoy R.; low lying and subject to floods. Exports edible birds' nests, pearl, tin, and timber. Pop. 27,500.

Taw, riv., Devonshire, England; rises on Dartmoor, flows N. to Barnstaple Bay.

Tay. (1) Longest river of Scotland; rises as Fillan, trib. of R. Dochart, in Ben Lui; traverses Loch Tay; passes Aberfeldy and Dunkeld to Perth, whence Firth of Tay stretches 24½ m. to North Sea; chief tribs. are Tummel, Earn, and Isla; length, 118 m.; navigable to Perth; salmon fisheries; Firth crossed at Dundee by Tay Bridge (1888), over 2 m. long. (2) LOCH, Perthshire, Scotland; stretches 14 m. from Killin N.E. to Kenmore; greatest depth, 508 ft. Area, over 10 sq. m.

Tay'port, or FERRYPORT-ON-CRAIG, port, Fifeshire, Scotland, on Firth of Tay; opposite Broughty Ferry; jute, linen, and sawmills. Pop. 3,200.

Tchernigov. See CHERNIGOV.

Tczew (*tchef*) (German *Dirschau*), tn., Poland, on R. Vistula, 20 m. s. of Danzig; rly. works; sugar, agricultural implements, cement; timber trade. Pop. 36,000.

Tecuci (*tă-kootch'ē*), tn., Romania, 40 m. N.W. of Galatz; cattle and horses; grain and timber. Pop. 21,000.

Ted'dington, urb. dist., Middlesex, England, on R. Thames; residential tn.; part of Greater London; near by is Bushey Park, with the National Physical Laboratory. Pop. 23,400.

Tees, riv., England; rises in Cross Fell, Cumberland, and flows mainly E., separating Durham from Yorks; forms navigable estuary below Stockton; length, 75 m.

Tegucigalpa (*tă-goo-thē-gäl'pä*), cap. of Honduras; old Aztec city; cathedral and univ.; gold, silver, and marble; bananas. Pop. 40,000.

Tehran (*tă-rän'*), cap., Persia; situated on fertile plain; alt. 3,810 ft.; contains royal palace, museum, polytechnic school, and numerous fine mosques; modern part well laid out; caravan centre; carpets and iron goods. Pop. *c.* 350,000.

Tehri (*tā-rē′*), Indian state, Himalayas, India; includes sources of rivs. Ganges and Jumna; forest produce, rice, etc. Cap. Tehri. Area, 4,180 sq. m.; pop. 318,500.

Tehuantepec (*tā-wän-tā-pek′*), isthmus, Mexico; between Gulfs of Campeche and Tehuantepec; forests; rich pasture on plateau; rly. across isthmus. (2) Tn., Oaxaca, Mexico, 13 m. from Salina Cruz; cathedral; textiles. Pop. 9,500.

Teign (*tin*), riv., Devonshire, England; rises on Dartmoor; flows 30 m. S.E. and S., falling into Lyme Bay at Teignmouth.

Teignmouth (*tin′muth*), port and seaside resort, S. Devon, England; yacht building, brewing, and fisheries. Pop. 10,000.

Tekrit. See TIKRIT.

Tell, hilly region, N.W. Africa, between Mediterranean Sea and Atlas Mts.; stretches through Morocco, Algeria, and Tunisia; fertile, well watered; wheat and barley are chief crops.

Tellicher′ry, port, Malabar, Madras, India; exp. coffee, cardamoms, coconuts, and sandalwood. Pop. 28,000.

Tembuland. See under TRANSKEIAN TERRITORY.

Temesvar. See TIMISOARA.

Templemore′, mkt. tn., urb. dist., Tipperary, I.F.S., on R. Suir; remains of church and castle of Knights Templars. Pop. 2,200.

Templenew′sam, par., Yorks, England, 4 m. E. of Leeds; Templar residence, original of 'Templestowe' in Scott's *Ivanhoe*; birthplace of Darnley, husband of Mary Queen of Scots. Pop. 3,400.

Temps′ford, vil., Beds, England, 4½ m. S.W. of St. Neots; in vicinity are earthworks believed to be Danish. Pop. 470.

Tenas′serim. (1) Div., Lower Burma, India, between Siamese mts. and Bay of Bengal. Cap. Moulmein. Area, 35,788 sq. m.; pop. 1,614,000. (2) Tn., in above div., on Tenasserim R.; rice. Pop. 5,000.

Ten′bury, mkt. tn., Worcestershire, England, on R. Teme; centre of hop-growing dist.; fruit, cider; medicinal waters. Pop. 1,950.

Ten′by, tn., wat.-pl., Pembrokeshire, Wales, on Carmarthen Bay; fisheries, meteorological station. Pop. 4,100.

Ten′edos, isl., Ægean Sea, near entrance to Dardanelles; exports wine and raisins; ceded to Greece (1920); restored to Turkey (1923).

Tenerife (*ten-er-ēf′*), largest of Canary Islands; traversed by volcanic mts. with famous Peak (highest point, El Piton, 12,200 ft.); drawn linen, maize, wheat, potatoes, wine, tropical fruit; exports fruit and early vegetables for Brit. markets; tourist and invalid resort. Cap. Santa Cruz. Area, 785 sq. m.; pop. 150,000.

Teng′yneh, tn., Yunnan, China, near Burmese frontier; exports carpets, raw silk; trades with Bhamo (Burma). Pop. *c.* 20,000.

Tenimber Islands. See TIMOR-LAUT.

Ten′nessee, south central state, U.S.A.; bounded N. by Virginia, Kentucky, W. by Missouri, Arkansas, S. by Mississippi, Alabama, Georgia, E. by N. Carolina; surface mountainous in E., where Appalachians reach 6,636 ft. in Mt. Guyot; in centre is valley of E. Tennessee R., and in W. is plateau of Cumberland Mts.; R. Ohio receives waters of Cumberland and Tennessee rivs. and their tribs., and unites with R. Mississippi, which forms W. boundary. Climate is extreme; flora includes timber and fruit trees; maize, wheat, oats, vegetables, and fruit grown; tobacco and cotton cultivated. Minerals include coal, petroleum, iron, copper, zinc, limestone; principal industries, lumbering, flour milling, manufacture of iron and steel goods, cotton-seed oil and cake, furniture, leather, textiles. Chief tns., Nashville (cap.), Memphis, Knoxville, Chattanooga. Area, 42,022 sq. m.; pop. 2,500,000.

Ten′terden, mkt. tn., Kent, England, 8¼ m. N.N.W. of Rye; formerly counted part of anc. Cinque Port of Rye; hops. Pop. 3,500.

Teplice-Sanov (*tep'litse-shän'of*), formerly TEPLITZ, tn. and wat.-pl., Bohemia, Czechoslovakia, at s. foot of Erzgebirge, 12 m. by rail w.s.w. of Usti; long famed for mineral springs; in largest and richest lignite basin in Bohemia; ironworks; porcelain, glass, textiles, and machinery. Pop. 29,000.

Terai. See TARAI.

Ter'amo, cap., Abruzzi, Italy, 80 m. s. of Ancona; silk spinning, potteries, straw hat making, tanneries; cathedral. Pop. 28,500.

Terceira (*tār-sā'ē-rä*), isl., Azores, Atlantic Ocean. Cap. Angra. Area, 224 sq. m.; pop. 50,000.

Terlizzi (*ter-lēt'sē*), tn., Apulia, s. Italy, 20 m. w. of Bari; produces wine and almonds. Pop. 24,000.

Termini Imerese (*ter'mē-nē ē-mā-rā'zā*), port, Palermo, Sicily; warm mineral springs; tunny and sardine fisheries. Pop. 20,000.

Termon'de, or DENDERMON'DE, tn., E. Flanders, Belgium, on R. Schelde, 20 m. s.w. of Antwerp; cotton yarn, lace, woollens; tn. reduced to ruins in Great War. Pop. 10,000.

Terni (*ter'nē*), tn., Umbria, Italy, 50 m. N. of Rome; iron and steel works; manufactures jute; ordnance works; Roman antiquities. Pop. 71,500.

Terrano'va, port, s. coast of Sicily; tunny and sardine fisheries; textiles; exports wine, grain, and sulphur. Pop. 27,000.

Terre Haute (*ter'e hōt*), city, Indiana, U.S.A., on R. Wabash, 70 m. s.w. of Indianapolis; coal mining; petroleum; foundry products, glass, paper, flour. Pop. 63,000.

Teruel (*tā-roo-el'*). (1) Prov., Spain, s. of lower course of R. Ebro; mountainous; grain, fruits, wine, flax, hemp, timber. Area, 5,720 sq. m.; pop. 260,000. (2) Cap. of above, on R. Guadalaviar; agriculture, forestry, coal mining, weaving; cathedral. Pop. 12,000.

Teschen (*tesh'en*). (1) Dist., S.E. Silesia, divided between Poland and Czechoslovakia; coal-mining area in Czechoslovakia. Area, 853 sq. m.; pop. 145,000. (2) Or CIESZYN, tn., Poland, in above; w. suburb is in Czechoslovakia.

Tet'bury, mkt. tn., Gloucestershire, England, 8 m. S.E. of Stroud; Elizabethan tn. hall. Pop. 2,200.

Tetschen. See DECIN.

Tet'tenhall, urb. dist., Staffs, England; suburb of Wolverhampton; hardware; contains Wolverhampton waterworks. Pop. 5,800.

Tetuan (*tet-oo'än*), fort. seapt., Morocco, on Mediterranean; exports eggs, slippers, beeswax, linseed, almonds, raisins. Pop. 24,000.

Tewkesbury (*tūks'ber-e*), mkt. tn., Gloucestershire, England, at jn. of Rs. Avon and Severn; flour mills, shirt factory; fine Norman abbey church (12th cent.); scene of battle in Wars of Roses (1471). Pop. 4,400.

Tex'as, south central state, U.S.A., on Gulf of Mexico, and separated from Mexico by Rio Grande del Norte; mountainous in w., prairie lands and forests in centre; coastal plain in the E.; drained by Grande, Colorado, and other rivs.; climate equable near coast, more extreme inland; desert in w.; flora includes many kinds of cactus and valuable timber trees. Agriculture is highly important; principal cotton-growing state; 850,000 ac. irrigated; maize, wheat, oats, rice, and potatoes cultivated; cattle, horses, mules, sheep, and pigs raised; timber, tobacco, fruits; chief petroleum-producing state in U.S.A.; other minerals include sulphur, natural gas, mercury, cement; manufactures lumber, flour, cottonseed oil and cake, hardware, and ice; meat packing; fisheries. Principal tns., San Antonio, Dallas, Houston, Fort Worth, El Paso, and Galveston; cap. Austin. Area, 265,896 sq. m.; pop. 5,487,000.

Tex'el, largest isl., W. Frisian Islands, N. Holland prov., Holland, at entrance to Zuider Zee; wool and cheese from sheep; scene of several sea-fights between 1653 and 1799. Area, 67 sq. m.

Thale (*tä'le*), tn., Saxony, Prussia, in N. Harz Mts., 36 m. S.W. of Magdeburg; health resort with mineral springs; cement, enamelled goods, machinery. Pop. 14,000.

Thame (*tām*), mkt. tn., Oxfordshire, England, 12 m. E. of Oxford. Pop. 3,000. (2) Riv., England; rises in Bucks, and flows S.W. through Oxfordshire to join R. Thames; length, 30 m.

Thames (*temz*). (1) Riv., S. England; rises in Cotswold Hills (Gloucestershire) and flows between Oxfordshire, Bucks, Middlesex, and Essex on N., and Berks, Surrey, and Kent on S.; widens to 5 m. at the Nore; tidal to Teddington, and riv. steamers can ascend to Oxford; communicates by canal with Severn, Bristol, Midland cos., and S. coast; chief N. tribs., Cherwell, Thame, Coln, Lea; from S., Kennet, Mole, Medway. During summer riv. is a favourite resort; regattas at Henley, Kingston, etc.; Oxford and Cambridge boat race rowed between Putney and Mortlake. Part between the Nore and Teddington constitutes Port of London; between Tower and Wapping Old Stairs is the Pool. Length, 210 m.; area of basin (including that of Medway), over 6,000 sq. m. (2) Port, on R. Thames, North Island, New Zealand; gold and silver mining centre. Pop. 5,000.

Thames Dit'ton, par. and vil., Surrey, England, on R. Thames, opposite Hampton Court Palace; motor-car and engineering works, bronze foundry, cinema works. Pop. 8,500.

Thana. (1) Dist., Bombay, India; includes isl. of Salsette; rice, timber, pulses, oil-seeds; fisheries. Area, 3,434 sq. m.; pop. 760,000. (2) Cap. of above, on Salsette I., practically a suburb of Bombay; striped cotton cloth; from here rly. crosses to mainland. Pop. 23,000.

Than'et, ISLE OF, dist., N.E. Kent, England, now a peninsula; many Roman and Saxon relics. Landing-place of St. Augustine, and, traditionally, of Hengist and Horsa; on coast are Margate, Ramsgate, and Broadstairs. Length E. to W., 9 m.; N. to S., 5 m.

Thas'os, mountainous isl., Ægean Sea, Greece; trades in timber, oil, and wax; anc. gold mines. Area, 168 sq. m.; pop. *c.* 8,000.

Thebes (*thēbz*). (1) Anc. cap., Upper Egypt, on R. Nile, 300 m. from Cairo; founded *c.* 2500 B.C.; site now marked by vil. of Luxor, where there are vast ruins. (2) Anc. city of Bœotia, Greece, 44 m. N.W. of Athens; destroyed by Alexander (335); modern tn. has pop. of *c.* 3,000.

Theiss. See TISA.

Theodo'sia, port, Crimea, U.S.S.R.; excellent harbour; exports grain; trade in fruit, wine, and tobacco; under name of 'Kaffa of the Genoese' was most famous mediæval port on Black Sea. Pop. 27,500.

Therap'ia, residential quarter and summer resort on Bosporus, 9 m. N.N.E. of Constantinople.

Therezina (*ter-ā-zē'nā*), city, cap. of Piauhy, Brazil, on R. Parnahyba; cotton, thread; soap works, iron foundry. Pop. 25,000.

Thermopylæ (*ther-mop'i-lē*), pass, S. Thessaly, Greece; name derived from hot springs at E. end; famous for stand of Spartans against invading Persians (480 B.C.).

Thes'saly, N.E. dist., Greece, between Ægean Sea and Epirus; generally level plain bordered by mts., which include Olympus and Pindus; horse breeding. Port is Volo.

Thet'ford, mkt. tn., S. Norfolk, England; anc. cap. of E. Anglia; brewing, tanning, chemical works, agricultural implements. Pop. 4,100.

Thiaka. See ITHACA.

Thielt (*tēlt*), cap., prov. W. Flanders, Belgium, 20 m. S.W. of Ghent; lace, wool, cotton, and linen; for a time in 1914 headquarters of German army. Pop. 12,000.

Thiers (*tē-ār'*), tn., Puy-de-Dôme, France, 24 m. E.N.E. of Clermont-Ferrand; cutlery, bank-note paper. Pop. 12,000.

Thionville (*tē-ōn-vēl'*) (Ger. *Diedenhofen*), fort. tn., Moselle, France, on

R. Moselle, 22 m. N. of Metz; important rly. jn.; brewing and tanning; vines, fruit, and vegetables. Pop. 12,000.

Thirl'mere, or LEATHES WATER, lake, Cumberland, England; chief source of Manchester water supply; length, 3½ m.; breadth, ¼ m.; depth, over 100 ft.

Thirsk, mkt. tn., Yorks, England, 22 m. N. of York; agricultural implements, leather, flour; important rly. jn. Pop. 2,800.

Thomastown, mkt. tn. and par., Kilkenny, I.F.S., on R. Nore; frieze factory and corn mills. Pop. (par.) 1,400.

Thorn. See TORUN.

Thorn'aby-on-Tees, munic. bor., Yorks, England, on R. Tees; ironworks, shipbuilding yards, flour and sawmills, potteries. Pop. 21,200.

Thorne, tn., S. Yorks, England, on R. Don, 9 m. N.E. of Doncaster; manufactures agricultural implements, ropes. Pop. 6,000.

Thornhill'. (1) Urb. dist., W. Riding, Yorks, England, 1½ m. S.W. of Dewsbury; woollens and carpets; anc. church of St. Michael. Pop. 11,700. (2) Vil., Nithsdale, Dumfriesshire, Scotland; sandstone quarries. Pop. 1,600.

Thorn'ley, par. and vil., Durham, England, 6 m. S.E. of Durham; collieries. Pop. (par.) 3,750.

Thornliebank (*thorn'lē-bank*), par., Renfrewshire, Scotland; part of Glasgow; cotton spinning, calico printing, bleaching. Pop. 2,600.

Thorn'ton. (1) Or THORNTON CLEVELEYS, urb. dist., Lancs, England, between Blackpool and Fleetwood; agricultural dist. Pop. 10,100. (2) Vil., Fife, Scotland, 4 m. N. of Kirkcaldy; rly. jn. Pop. 2,500.

Thourout (*too-roo'*), tn., W. Flanders, Belgium, 11 m. S.W. of Bruges; linen, hats, and woollen goods; horse fairs. Pop. 11,000.

Thrace, name applied in anc. times to extensive dist. N.E. of Macedonia; mountainous; drained by R. Maritsa; tobacco cultivated. Now divided among Greece, Bulgaria, and Turkey.

Thraps'ton, mkt. tn., Northants, England, on R. Nen, 21 m. N.E. of Northampton; blast furnaces. Pop. 1,700.

Three Rivers, city, Quebec, Canada, situated where the three branches of the R. St. Maurice enter the R. St. Lawrence; exports lumber, wood pulp, grain, cattle. Pop. 35,000.

Thun (*toon*). (1) Tn., Berne, Switzerland, on R. Aar, where it leaves L. Thun; pottery factories. Pop. 18,000. (2) LAKE OF, in canton of Berne; traversed by R. Aar; length, 11½ m.; maximum depth, 700 ft.

Thurgau (*toor'gou*), canton, N.E. Switzerland, on W. shore of L. Constance; surface generally undulating; drained by Thur, trib. of R. Rhine; agriculture; dairy farming; fruit and wine produced; manufactures leather, woollens, cottons, embroidery; most of inhabitants are German-speaking and Protestants. Cap. Frauenfeld. Area, 386 sq. m.; pop. 140,000.

Thurin'gia, rep., Germany; situated W. of Saxony and N. of Bavaria, with outlying portion surrounded by Prussia; drained to rivs. Weser and Elbe; forests; potatoes, oats, wheat, rye; live-stock raised; manufactures potash. Chief tns., Weimar (cap.), Jera, Jena, and Gotha. Area, 4,541 sq. m.; pop. 1,196,500.

Thurin'gian Forest, or THÜRINGERWALD, range of hills, Thuringia, Germany; highest point, Grosser Beerberg (3,225 ft.); densely wooded, with beautiful valleys; 70 m. long and from 6 to 22 m. broad.

Thur'les, mkt. tn., Tipperary, I.F.S., on R. Suir; remains of castle of Knights Templars. Pop. 4,800.

Thurl'stone, urb. dist., W. Riding, Yorks, England, 10 m. S.E. of Huddersfield; woollen cloth. Pop. 2,600.

Thurm'aston, urb. dist., Leicestershire, England, 3 m. N.N.E. of Leicester; shoemaking. Pop. 3,700.

Thurns'coe, urb. dist., W. Riding, Yorks, England, 8 m. W. of Doncaster. Pop. 10,500.

Thurs'day Island, small isl., Queensland, Australia, in Torres Strait; pearl fisheries and bêche-de-mer; coaling station at Port Kennedy. Pop. 1,700.

Thur'so, port, Caithness, Scotland, on Thurso Bay; good harbour; exports flagstones; fishing. Pop. 2,900.

Tian-Shan. See TIEN SHAN.

Ti'ber, chief riv., central Italy; rises in Tuscan Apennines; flows S. past Perugia, Rome, Ostia, and enters Mediterranean Sea; liable to floods; navigable to confluence with R. Nera; length, 250 m.

Tibe'rias (modern *Tabariya*), anc. tn., Palestine, on Sea of Galilee; 680 ft. below sea-level; medicinal springs; long a great centre of Jewish learning. Pop. 6,950.

Tibet', Outer Terr., China; stretches from Himalayas on S. to Kunlun and Altyn Tagh on N.; surface consists of high mts., plateaus, and great rolling plains; wide regions still not explored; highest peak, Mustagh (23,890 ft.); desert lands in W.; R. Tsangpo (length, 1,300 m.) traverses S. of country and enters India as R. Brahmaputra; other rivs. are head streams of Ganges, Indus, Sutlej, Yangtze Kiang, Hwang-Ho, Mekong, and Salween; numerous lakes, many of them salt; hot springs. Climate extreme; great lack of moisture; barley, wheat, vegetables, and fruits cultivated in favoured areas; sheep, yaks, pigs, camels, and buffaloes reared; minerals include salt, gold, borax; industries are weaving, knitting, pottery making, and metal working; trade chiefly with China and India; principal exports, skins, wool, precious stones, live-stock. Until 1903 Europeans were forbidden to enter the country; political mission under Younghusband reached Lhasa in 1904, and agreement was signed giving facilities for trade between Tibet and Brit. India. Tibetans are of Mongoloid stock and of good physique; chief religion is Lamaism, a corrupt form of Buddhism. Cap. Lhasa. Area, 463,200 sq. m.; pop. *c.* 2,000,000.

Ticehurst, par. and vil., Sussex, England, 10½ m. S.E. of Tunbridge Wells; cattle fair. Pop. 2,610.

Ticino (*tē-chē'nō*). (1) Riv., Switzerland and Italy; rises W. of Mt. St. Gotthard; flows through L. Maggiore; joins R. Po near Pavia; length, 150 m. (2) Canton, S.E. Switzerland; mountainous in N., sloping to plain of Lombardy in S.; watered by R. Ticino and its tribs.; contains part of Lakes Maggiore and Lugano; forests; olives, grapes, other fruits, cereals, tobacco, silk, wine; people are Italian-speaking Roman Catholics. Cap. Bellinzona. Area, 1,085 sq. m.; pop. 153,000.

Ticondero'ga, vil., New York, U.S.A., 100 m. N. of Albany; manufactures paper-pulp and paper; graphite. Important strategic point in struggle for Canada against French, and later in American War of Independence. Pop. 4,000.

Tideswell, mkt. tn., Derbyshire, England, 6½ m. E.N.E. of Buxton; lead mined in vicinity. Pop. 2,000.

Tiel (*tēl*), tn., Gelderland, Holland, on R. Waal; agricultural machinery, paper. Pop. 12,500.

Tien Shan (*tē-en shan'*), or CELESTIAL MTS., system of mts., Asia, stretching N.E. from Pamir plateau towards Gobi Desert; highest peak, Nicholas Mikailovich (22,670 ft.); source of rivs. Ili, Tarim, and Sir Darya; many glaciers; Terek Pass between Kashgar and Ferghana has alt. of over 9,000 ft.

Tientsin (*tē-en-tsēn'*), city, Hopeh, China, at jn. of Pei-ho and Hun-ho rivs.; port for N. China; centre of transit trade; exports wool, skins, beans and peas; cotton mills; univ.; rice and salt markets. Pop. *c.* 1,389,000.

Tierra del Fuego (*tē-er'ä del fwā'gō*), archipelago off S. end of S. America; belongs partly to Chile and partly to Argentina; separated from mainland by Strait of Magellan; mountainous (Mt. Sarmiento, 7,540 ft.); sheep raised; natives, now few in number, in state of barbarism. Discovered by Magellan (1520). Area, *c.* 28,000 sq. m.

Tif'fin, city, Ohio, U.S.A., 40 m. S.E. of Toledo; univ.; foundries, machine shops, flour mills, breweries. Pop. 14,500.

Tif'lis, cap. of Georgia and of Transcaucasia, U.S.S.R., on R. Kura; on rly. between Batum and Baku; univ. (1918); exports silk, carpets, cotton, tobacco, and silver ornaments in filigree and enamel work. Pop. 283,000.

Tighina. See TUGHINA.

Tighnabruaich (*tī-na-broo'a*ch), vil., Argyllshire, Scotland, on Kyles of Bute, 10 m. N.W. of Rothesay; summer resort. Pop. 1,500.

Tigré (*tē-grā'*), N. div., Abyssinia; stock raising; chief tns., Aduwa and Aksum.

Ti'gris, riv., Iraq; rises in two head streams in mts. of Kurdistan and Armenia; flows S.E. and, after a course of 1,150 m., unites with Euphrates at Kurna to form Shatt-al-Arab; chief tribs., Greater Zab, Lesser Zab, and Diyala; flows through fertile alluvial dist., the home of one of oldest civilizations of world; important tns. and ruins on banks are Diarbekr, Nineveh, Mosul, Tikrit, Baghdad, Ctesiphon, and Kut; navigable by steamers to Baghdad.

Tikrit (*tēk-rēt'*), tn., Iraq, on R. Tigris and on rly. 100 m. N. of Baghdad; birthplace of Saladin. Pop. *c.* 3,000.

Til'burg, tn., N. Brabant, Holland; woollens, tobacco, and leather. Pop. 71,500.

Til'bury, urb. dist. and port, Essex, England, on R. Thames, 22 m. E. of London; fort built by Henry VIII.; chief defence of Thames above Sheerness; docks accommodate largest vessels; packet station for Dunkirk; connected with Gravesend by steam ferry. Pop. 16,800.

Tillicoultry (*til-i-koo'tri*), tn., Clackmannanshire, Scotland, on R. Devon; woollen fabrics, tartan, shawls; coal mining. Pop. 3,000.

Til'sit, tn., E. Prussia, Germany, on R. Niemen; glass, soap, and oil; engineering and chemical works, iron foundries, tanneries, and distilleries; scene of signing of treaty between Alexander I. of Russia and Napoleon (1807). Pop. 51,000.

Timar'u, port, South I., New Zealand, on E. coast; wool, skins, tallow, flour, and frozen mutton. Pop. 18,000.

Timbuktu', tn., French Sudan, Africa, 9 m. from N. bend of R. Niger; founded by Tuaregs (11th cent.); great caravan centre, linking Niger basin with N. Africa; trade in gums, rubber, gold, salt, wax, ivory, and grain; wireless station. Pop. *c.* 7,000.

Timisoara (*tē-mēsh-wä'rä*), formerly TEMESVAR, tn., W. Romania, near Hungarian frontier; tobacco, cloth, paper, oil. Pop. 72,500.

Tim'mins, city, N. Ontario, Canada, 44 m. S.W. of Cochrane; mining. Pop. 12,000.

Timor', largest and most easterly of Lesser Sunda Islands, Malay Archipelago; coast rugged, and interior mountainous and well wooded; N.E. part is Portuguese (cap. Dilli), and S.W. belongs to Dutch (cap. Kupang); exports copra, coffee, sandalwood, and wax; fisheries. Area, *c.* 12,400 sq. m.; pop. *c.* 800,000.

Timor'-Laut, or TENIMBER ISLANDS, group of islands, Malay Archipelago; belong to Dutch; largest isl., Yemdena, hilly and well wooded; smaller islands low and of coralline formation; exports trepang, turtle, and pearl oysters. Area, 2,060 sq. m.; pop. *c.* 25,000.

Tine'o, tn., N. Spain, 28 m. W. of Oviedo, in mining, agricultural, and stock-rearing dist. Pop. 22,000.

Tinnevel'ly. (1) Dist., S. Madras, British India; rice, cotton, oil-seeds. Area, 4,325 sq. m.; pop. 2,000,000. (2) Tn. in above dist.; mission centre; fine Siva temple. Pop. 54,000.

Tintagel (*tin-taj'el*), par., Cornwall, England, 5 m. N.W. of Camelford; on Tintagel Head (300 ft.) are ruins of Tintagel Castle, traditional birthplace of King Arthur. Pop. 1,300.

Tin'tern Abbey, Monmouthshire, England, near R. Wye, 4 m. N. of Chepstow; founded by Cistercians in 1131; ruins purchased for nation in 1900.

Tippera', dist., Bengal, India, E. of Dacca; drained by R. Meghna; adjoining Tripura (Hill Tippera); jute cultivated. Cap. Comilla. Area, 2,560 sq. m.; pop. 2,743,000.

Tippera'ry. (1) Co., Munster, I.F.S.; surface generally flat, but crossed by Galtee, Knockmealdown, and other mts.; chief rivs., Shannon and Suir; Golden Vale, N. of Galtee Mts., very fertile; cereals and dairy produce; co. tn., Clonmel. Area, 1,643 sq. m.; pop. 141,000. (2) Tn. in above, 25 m. S.E. of Limerick; military barracks, condensed milk factory, and butter market. Pop. 5,600.

Tip'ton, tn., Staffs, England, 1½ m. N. of Dudley; collieries; cement and brick works; ironworks; galvanizing, cables, anchors, boilers. Pop. 35,800.

Tip'tree Heath, eccles. dist., Essex, England, *c.* 7 m. N.E. of Maldon; fruit farms and preserve works. Pop. 3,000.

Tirah', mountainous dist., Peshawar, N.W. Frontier Prov., India; pasturage in valleys in summer; inhabited by Afridi and Orakzai tribes, who rose against British in 1897–98.

Tiran'a, cap., Albania; olive groves. Pop. 17,000.

Tiras'pol, tn., Moldavian rep., U.S.S.R.; port on R. Dniester; tobacco, candles, tallow, flour. Pop. 30,000.

Tircon'aill. See DONEGAL.

Tiree. See TYREE.

Tireh (*tē-rā'*), tn., Aidin, Asia Minor, 45 m. S.E. of Smyrna; trade in raisins, tobacco, cotton. Pop. *c.* 15,000.

Tirhut', div., Bihar and Orissa, Brit. India, between R. Ganges and Nepal; rich soil; rice, maize, wheat, barley, oil-seeds. Area, 12,598 sq. m.; pop. 9,950,000.

Tirlemont (*tēr-le-mōn*), tn., Brabant, Belgium, 25 m. E. by S. of Brussels; woollen goods, leather, machinery. Pop. 20,500.

Tirnovo. See TRNOVO.

Tirol, prov., W. Austria, traversed by E. Alps; magnificent scenery; drained by Inn, trib. of R. Danube; Brenner Pass gives easy access between Italy and Austria; pastoral; forests; salt worked; textiles made by water-power; metal goods, sawmills. Chief tn., Innsbrück. Area, 4,882 sq. m.; pop. 314,000.

Tiru'pati, tn., Madras, India, 84 m. N.E. of Madras; brasswork, wood carving. Pop. 17,500.

Tisa (*tē'zä*) (Magyar *Tisza,* German *Theiss*), riv., trib. of R. Danube, Europe; rises as Black Tisa and White Tisa in N.E. Carpathian Mts., Czechoslovakia; flows S. through Hungary and Yugoslavia for 800 m.; navigable to Szolnok. Chief tn. on banks, Szeged.

Titchfield, par. and vil., Hants, England, 9½ m. S.E. of Southampton; strawberries cultivated; Charles I. sailed from here to Isle of Wight in attempt to escape from Roundheads. Pop. 2,000.

Titicac'a, lake, Bolivia and Peru, S. America; alt. 12,500 ft.; contains several islands, largest of which, Titicaca, has ruins of Inca palace; navigated by small steamers. Length, 130 m.; breath, 35 m.; area, *c.* 5,500 sq. m.

Tiv'erton, mkt. tn., Devonshire, England, 12 m. N. of Exeter; lace, flour, beer. Pop. 9,600.

Tiv'oli, tn., Italy, 18 m. N.E. of Rome; grapes and olives; electric power from falls of R. Anio; favourite resort in Roman times; remains of Hadrian's villa. Pop. 16,500.

Tlaxcala (*tläsh-kä'lä*). (1) State, Mexico, on central plateau; chief industry, agriculture. Area, 1,534 sq. m.; pop. 180,000. (2) Cap. of above, 60 m. E. of Mexico; cloth factories. Pop. 2,000.

Tlemsen', tn., Oran, Algeria; on high rock, surrounded by walls; exports cork, ostrich feathers, textiles, carpets, leather goods. Pop. 27,000.

Toba'go, isl., Brit. W. Indies, 20 m. N.E. of Trinidad; hilly; forests; chief product cocoa; also coconuts, vegetables and fruit, spices; politically and commercially connected with Trinidad. Cap. Scarborough. Area, 114 sq. m.; pop. 23,500.

Tobermo'ry, vil. and port, Mull, Argyllshire, Scotland, on Sound of Mull; distillery; *Almirante de Florencia*, treasure ship of Spanish Armada, sunk here; attempts to recover treasure unsuccessful. Pop. 800.

Tobolsk', tn., Ural Area, R.S.F.S.R., on R. Irtish, at mouth of R. Tobol; makes fishing nets; mammoth ivory carving; skins. Pop. 15,000.

Tocantins', riv., Brazil; rises in Brazilian Highlands and flows N. to Rio Para, at R. Amazon estuary; many falls and rapids; navigable for 400 m. from mouth, and 400 m. above rapids; length, 1,500 m.

Tod'dington, mkt. tn., Beds, England, 4½ m. N. of Dunstable; market gardening. Pop. 2,000.

Todi (*tō-dē'*), tn., Umbria, Italy, 28 m. S. of Perugia; cathedral; Etruscan remains; church of S. Maria della Consolazione, W. of tn., is a pilgrim resort. Pop. 18,500.

Tod'morden, tn., W. Riding, Yorks, England, on R. Calder, 12 m. W. of Halifax; rly. jn.; cotton spinning, weaving, and machinery. Pop. 22,200.

To'goland, country, W. Africa; divided between Gold Coast and Dahomey; surface rises from coast to interior (over 3,000 ft.); forests; drained by Oti, trib. of R. Volta; dyewoods, rubber, cocoa, oil-palms, maize, fruits; exports palm oil, cocoa, copra, cotton; native industries are weaving, pottery, straw plaiting. Former German colony; under mandate of League of Nations, Great Britain obtained about one-third of country (12,500 sq. m.), and France the remainder. Chief French tn., Lome. Total area, 33,700 sq. m.; pop. 747,000.

Tokat', tn., Asia Minor, 70 m. S. of Samsun, on Black Sea; copper and leather. Pop. 78,000.

Tokay', or TO'KAJ, tn., N.E. Hungary, on R. Tisa; noted for wines. Pop. 5,000.

Tokelau. See UNION.

Tokyo (*tō'kē-o*), cap., Japan, on Honshu isl.; imperial palace; univ., largely rebuilt after earthquake of 1923; beautiful parks; dockyards; manufactures machinery, silk, lacquer, earthenware, china, and enamels. Pop. 1,996,000.

Toledo (*tō-lā'dō*). (1) Prov., central Spain; mountainous; agriculture, and some weaving; gold, silver, iron, lead, and other minerals found. Area, 5,919 sq. m.; pop. 443,000. (2) Cap. of above, on R. Tagus; surrounded by old walls; anc. cathedral; Moorish architecture; long famous for manufacture of swords; other manufactures are gold and silver church ornaments, and cloth. Pop. 25,000. (3) City, Ohio, U.S.A., near L. Erie; important rly. jn.; great commercial centre; important grain and clover seed market; exports coal; manufactures include flour, lumber, bicycles, agricultural implements, engines, motors. Pop. 291,000.

Tolentino (*tol-en-tē'nō*), tn., Marches, Italy, on R. Chienti, 36 m. S.W. of Ancona; cathedral; manufactures silks, woollen goods, wine. Pop. 13,000.

Tolu'ca, tn., Mexico, 40 m. S.W. of Mexico City; cotton and flour mills, breweries. Pop. 34,000.

Tomaszow (*tom-ā'shuf*), tn., Poland, 28 m. S.E. of Lodz; silk, woollens, hardware, and flour. Pop. 28,000.

Tomsk, tn., Siberian Area, U.S.S.R., on R. Tom; educational centre; headquarters of mining dist.; tanneries; trade centre; connected by branch line with Trans-Siberian Rly. Pop. 92,000.

Ton'bridge, tn., Kent, England, on Medway, 27 m. S.E. of London; remains of castle; public school. Pop. 16,300.

Ton'ga (or FRIENDLY) **Islands,** in Pacific, midway between Fiji and Samoa; under Brit. protection; divided into Tongatabu, Haabai, and Vavau groups; of coral and volcanic formation, with active volcanoes; chief product, copra. Chief town,

Nukualofa. Area, *c.* 385 sq. m.; pop. *c.* 27,000.

Tongkah. See PUKET.

Tongking', province of French Indo-China; bounded N. by China, E. by Gulf of Tongking, S. by Annam, W. by Laos; surface consists of delta of Red R., with its great tributaries, Black R. and Clear R., in the S.E.; plateau in N., and forest region in W. Delta is very fertile; two harvests yearly. Produces great quantities of rice, coffee, tobacco, cotton, jute, and sugar; manufactures cotton, furniture, and paper. Minerals include coal, tin, limestone. Chief tns., Hanoi (cap.), and Haiphong, an important port. Area, 40,530 sq. m.; pop. 7,402,000.

Tongres (*tongr*), tn., Limburg, Belgium, on R. Geer, 12 m. N.W. of Liége; church of Notre Dame (13th–14th cent.); mineral springs. Pop. 10,000.

Tongue (*tung*), par. and vil., Sutherlandshire, Scotland, 44 m. W. of Thurso; on E. shore of Kyle of Tongue, a sea loch, 9 m. long. Pop. (par.) 1,350.

Tonlé-Sap, lake, Cambodia, Indo-China; connected with R. Mekong by Bras du Lac channel. Area (during dry season), 100 sq. m.; depth, 2–6 ft.; (during flood season of R. Mekong), 800 sq. m.; depth, 50 ft.

Töns'berg, seaport, Norway, near entrance of Oslo Fjord; headquarters of sealing and whaling fisheries. Pop. 12,000.

Toot'ing, dist., Surrey, England, 8½ m. S. of London; on beautiful common. Pop. 40,700.

Toowoom'ba, tn., Queensland, Australia, 100 m. by rail W. of Brisbane; on summit of Great Dividing Range (alt. 2,000 ft.); centre of fertile dist.; has flour mills, tanneries, and brewery; manufactures wine. Pop. 24,000.

Tope'ka, cap., Kansas, U.S.A., 70 m. W. of Kansas City; rly. workshops; manufactures flour and machinery. Pop. 64,000.

Tops'ham, tn., Devonshire, England, on R. Exe; sawmill; formerly important seaport; coasting trade. Pop. 3,300.

Tor Bay, inlet, S. Devon, England, 18 m. S. of Exeter; important haven for shipping; landing-place of William of Orange (1688).

Torgau (*tor'gou*), tn., Saxony, Prussia, on R. Elbe, 31 m. E.N.E. of Leipzig; manufactures gloves, glass, pottery; 15th cent. castle. Pop. 13,000.

Toron'to, cap., Ontario, Canada, on N.W. shore of L. Ontario; educational centre; univ.; important rly., lake shipping, manufacturing, and trading centre; deals in lumber, cattle, grain, and fruit; electrical energy generated at Niagara Falls. Pop. 570,000.

Torphichen (*tor-fich'en*), vil., W. Lothian, Scotland, 2½ m. N. of Bathgate; coal mines, ironworks. Pop. 650.

Tor'point, urb. dist., Cornwall, England, on estuary of R. Tamar, opposite Devonport; sulphuric acid and manure. Pop. 4,000.

Torquay (*tor-kē'*), port, wat.-pl., S. Devon, England, on Tor Bay; remains of Tor Abbey (12th cent.); Kent's Cavern, a noted bone cave, is near by; terra-cotta ware; marble polishing. Pop. 46,200.

Torre Annunziata (*tor'rā ä-noont-sē-ä'tä*), tn., Italy, at S. base of Mt. Vesuvius, 14 m. by rail S.E. of Naples; mineral springs; govt. factory for arms; ironworks; macaroni; silk; fishing; suffered during eruption of Vesuvius (1906). Pop. 32,500.

Torre del Greco (*tor'rā del grā'kō*), port, fishing tn., seaside resort, Italy, at S.W. base of Mt. Vesuvius, 8 m. S.E. of Naples; chiefly built of lava; suffered during eruptions of Vesuvius; coral working; tunny, sardine, and oyster fisheries. Pop. 34,000.

Tor'rens, LAKE, large salt lake, S. Australia, W. of Flinders Range, 35 m. N. of Port Augusta; extends 130 m. N. to S.; marsh in dry seasons; discovered by Eyre (1841).

Tor'res Strait, between New Guinea and York Peninsula, Queensland,

Australia; navigation rendered difficult by reefs, shoals, and islands (including Thursday I.); first navigated by Spaniard Torres (1606); breadth, 80–90 m.

Tor'res Vedras (*vä'dräs*), tn., Estremadura, Portugal, 26 m. N.W. of Lisbon; Moorish citadel; hot sulphur baths; Wellington's famous lines (1810–11) extended from near tn. to R. Tagus. Pop. 8,000.

Tor'rington, city, Connecticut, U.S.A., 23 m. W. of Hartford; brass, silver, copper, nickel, and gold-plated goods, machinery, woollen goods. Pop. 26,000.

Tor'rington, GREAT, munic. bor., mkt. tn., Devonshire, England, 6 m. S.E. of Bideford; gloves; flour milling, leather dressing. Pop. 2,900.

Tortola. See under VIRGIN ISLANDS.

Torto'na, tn., Piedmont, N. Italy, 12 m. E. of Alessandria; silk manufactures; 9th cent. cathedral. Pop. 20,000.

Torto'sa, city, Catalonia, N.E. Spain, near mouth of R. Ebro; Gothic cathedral (14th cent.), manufactures paper, leather, majolica, soap, liquorice. Pop. 33,000.

To'run (German *Thorn*), fortified tn., Poland, on R. Vistula, 92 m. S. of Danzig; machinery; trades in timber and grain; birthplace of astronomer Copernicus. Pop. 39,500.

Torzhok', tn., European Russia, 40 m. N.W. of Tver; noted for gold and silver embroidered articles. Pop. 15,000.

Totan'a, tn., Murcia, S.E. Spain, 10 m. N.E. of Lorca; exports fruit; manufactures linen, leather, earthenware jars. Pop. 14,000.

Totnes, tn., riv. port, S. Devon, England, on R. Dart, 10 m. N.W. of Dartmouth; cider; riv. fisheries; anc. buildings; Norman keep. Pop. 4,500.

Toto'nicapan, tn., Guatemala, Central America, 62 m. N.W. of Guatemala city; textiles, pottery, and musical instruments; thermal springs in vicinity. Pop. 31,000.

Tot'tenham, urb. dist., part of London, England, 6 m. N. of St. Paul's Cathedral; contains Bruce Castle, which belonged to the father of Robert the Bruce. Pop. 157,700.

Tot'tington, urb. dist., Lancs, England, 2½ m. N.W. of Bury; cotton-spinning works. Pop. 6,500.

Tot'ton, vil., Hants, England, near head of Southampton Water, 4 m. W.N.W. of Southampton; flour and saw mills. Pop. 4,000.

Toul (*tool*), tn., Meurthe-et-Moselle, France, on l. bk. of R. Moselle, 14 m. W. of Nancy; frontier fortress; manufactures earthenware, hats, embroidery, and lace; trades in wine and brandy. Pop. 10,000.

Toulon (*too-lōn*), port, first-class fortress and naval station, Var, France, 42 m. E.S.E. of Marseilles; headquarters of Mediterranean fleet; cathedral (11th to 12th cent.); naval shipbuilding yards; exports fruits, oil, wine, salt. Pop. 93,000.

Toulouse (*too-loos'*), tn., cap., Haute-Garonne, France, on R. Garonne and Canal du Midi; cathedral (11th cent. onwards), univ., art academy; iron and copper foundries, cannon making, powder factory, stained glass, leather, paper, tobacco, brandy. Pop. 152,500.

Touraine (*too-rān'*), anc. prov., France, now forms Indre-et-Loire and part of Vienne; cap. Tours; formed part of French possessions of Plantagenet kings of England.

Tourcoing (*toor-kwăn'*), tn., Nord, France, near Belgian frontier; woollens, cottons, carpets; occupied by Germans (1914–18). Pop. 79,500.

Tournai (*toor-nā'*) (Flemish *Doornik*), tn., Hainaut, Belgium, on R. Schelde; textiles, carpets, embroideries, cement; in Great War occupied by Germans (1914–18). Pop. 36,500.

Tours (*toor*), cap. of Indre-et-Loire, France, on R. Loire; cathedral (12th to 16th century); ruined Château Plessis-lès-Tours in vicinity; iron and steel industries, leather, wine, woollens, silks, printing; here Charles Martel defeated Saracens (732). Pop. 73,000.

Towcester (*tō'ster*), mkt. tn. and

par., Northants, England, 9 m. s.w. of Northampton; boots and shoes, lace; occupies site of Roman station. Pop. (par.) 2,400.

Tow Law (*tou'*), tn., Durham, England, 8 m. N.W. of Bishop Auckland; coal and clay mined. Pop. 3,600.

Towns'ville, port, Queensland, Australia, on Cleveland Bay; outlet for gold-mining and pastoral dist.; manufactures soap, ice, beer, stationery. Pop. 30,000.

Towton (*tou'ton*), par., W. Riding, Yorks, England, 2½ m. s. of Tadcaster; scene of battle (1461) in Wars of Roses. Pop. 80.

Towyn (*tou'in*), tn., Merionethshire, Wales, 3 m. N.W. of Aberdovey; seaside resort; lead mining, fishing. Pop. 3,800.

Toyam'a, tn., Honshu, Japan; on w. coast, on Toyama Bay; centre of trade and manufactures. Pop. 67,500.

Trafal'gar (Spanish *trafalgar'*), CAPE, low promontory, s. Spain, at w. entrance to Straits of Gibraltar; scene of Nelson's victory over French and Spanish fleets (1805).

Trail, tn., Brit. Columbia, Canada, near U.S. border and L. Kootenay, 6 m. N.E. of Rossland; large electric smelter for lead, zinc, and copper. Pop. 6,000.

Tralee', co. tn., port, and mkt. tn., Kerry, I.F.S., on R. Lee; connected with Tralee Bay by ship canal for 200-ton vessels; exports grain and butter. Pop. 10,500.

Tramore (*trä-mōr'*), mkt. tn., Waterford, I.F.S., on Tramore Bay; seaside resort. Pop. 1,800.

Tranent', tn., E. Lothian, Scotland, 9½ m. E. of Edinburgh; collieries. Pop. 4,500.

Trani (*trä'nē*), port, Bari, Italy, on Adriatic Sea; cathedral; trade in wine and olive oil; harbour now silted up. Pop. 35,000.

Transcauca'sia, Soviet rep., U.S.S.R., s. of Caucasus Mts.; consists of reps. of Georgia, Azerbaijan, and Armenia. See separate articles.

Transco'na, tn., Manitoba, Canada, 10 m. N.E. of Winnipeg; industrial centre. Pop. 5,000.

Trans-Jor'dan, terr., Asia, E. of Palestine; in w. contains fertile lands of Gilead, Moab, and Edom, producing grapes and wheat; stretches E. to desert; mandated to Britain by League of Nations; traversed by Hejaz Rly. Chief tn., Amman. Pop. *c.* 260,000.

Transkeian Territories, region, Cape Prov., between Kei R. and Natal, Union of S. Africa, includes Griqualand E., Tembuland, Transkei, Pondoland; surface level near coast, mountainous farther inland; watered by St. John's and other rivs.; produces timber, cereals, bananas, oranges, lemons; cattle, sheep, and horses raised; mainly a native reserve; annexed to Cape Colony between 1879 and 1894. Total area, 16,351 sq. m.; pop. *c.* 900,000 (13,700 whites).

Transvaal', inland prov., Union of S. Africa, between Vaal and Limpopo rivs.; bounded N. by S. Rhodesia, E. by Portuguese E. Africa and Swaziland, s. by Orange Free State and Natal, w. by Cape Prov. and Bechuanaland; length from N. to s., *c.* 400 m.; breadth, *c.* 470 m.; an undulating plateau from 1,000 to 7,000 ft., traversed by mountain ranges and isolated hills (kopjes); in E. are Drakensberg Mts.; Witwatersrand, *c.* 6,000 ft., N.W. of Johannesburg; large part of plateau, known as High Veld, generally covered with good pasture, but treeless; Bush Veld, in N. and on E. border, low, and fairly well wooded; principal rivs. are Limpopo and Vaal, with Olifants and other tribs.; none navigable. Climate hot and dry, and subject to dust storms; Bush Veld tropical; unhealthy during rainy season, when malaria is prevalent; summer (Oct.–March) is rainy season; average ann. rainfall *c.* 25 to 30 in., greatest in E. Mainly a stock-raising country, with large areas suited for agriculture; chief crops, maize and tobacco; rich in gold, diamonds, iron ore, coal, silver, copper, lead; largest goldfields in Witwatersrand; Premier Mine, near Pretoria, is chief diamond mine; engineering, brewing, pottery, tobacco, soap, candles, wagons; chief exports, minerals, cattle, hides, wool. Chief tns., Johannesburg, Pretoria (cap.). Area, 110,450 sq. m.; pop.—natives (1921) 1,544,000, whites (1926) 608,600.

Transylva'nia, div., w. Romania, bordering on Hungary; surface a plateau, *c.* 1,200 ft., bounded by Transylvanian Alps and Carpathian Mts.; forested; drained by Rs. Somesul and Muresul; produces cereals, pulse, tobacco, fruits; cattle, horses, sheep, and pigs raised; minerals include gold, silver, salt, coal, iron, lead, copper; belonged to Hungary (1867–1918); ceded to Romania (1920). Chief tns., Cluj and Brasov. Area, 22,312 sq. m.; pop. 2,678,500.

Transylva'nian Alps, continuation of Carpathian Mts. on s. border of Transylvania, Romania; several peaks are over 8,000 ft.

Trap'ani, port, w. Sicily; manufactures coral, alabaster, and mother-of-pearl goods; exports salt, wine, cheese, olive oil; was a Carthaginian stronghold. Pop. 84,000.

Trau. See TROGIR.

Trau'tenau. See TRUTNOV.

Travancore', Indian state, s.w. Madras, India; includes part of Cardamom Hills; fertile; rice, coconuts, pepper, tapioca, cardamoms, timber. Cap. Trivandrum. Area, 7,625 sq. m.; pop. 4,000,000.

Treb'izond (Turkish *Trabzon*), tn., Asia Minor, on s. coast of Black Sea; originally a Greek colony; captured by Turkey (1461); caravan centre; exports tobacco, carpets, hides, and skins. Pop. 61,000.

Tred'egar, urb. dist., Monmouthshire, England, 7 m. E.N.E. of Merthyr Tydfil; ironworks and collieries. Pop. 23,200.

Tremad'oc, tn., Carnarvonshire, Wales, on bay at N.E. of Cardigan Bay, 4 m. N.E. of Criccieth; built on reclaimed land; trade lost to Portmadoc. Pop. 4,200.

Trengganu', Unfederated Malay State, E. coast of Malay Peninsula; produces fish, tin, rubber, hæmatite, copra. Chief tn., Kuala Trengganu. Area, 3,500 sq. m.; pop. 154,000.

Trent. (1) Riv., England; chief riv. of Midlands; rises N. Staffs; flows through Staffs, Derbyshire, Notts, Lincolnshire; unites with Ouse to form Humber; chief tribs., Dove, Derwent, Idle, and Soar; chief tns. on its banks, Stoke, Burton, Nottingham, Newark, and Gainsborough; navigable for barges to Burton; length, 170 m. (2) (Italian *Trento*), chief tn., Trentino, Italy, on R. Adige; cathedral; silk weaving; pottery, wines; meeting-place of famous Council of Trent (1545–63). Pop. 62,500.

Trent'ham, par. and vil., Staffs, England, on R. Trent, 3 m. s. of Stoke-upon-Trent; its Hall, residence of Duke of Sutherland, was dismantled in 1911. Pop. (par.) 2,550.

Trentino (*tren-tē'nō*), area of N. Italy, on s. slope of Alps; drained by R. Adige; formerly part of Austrian Tirol; ceded to Italy after Great War; now forms dep. of Venezia Tridentina.

Tren'ton. (1) Cap., New Jersey, U.S.A.; at head of navigation of Delaware R.; manufactures earthenware and pottery, iron and steel, rubber goods, machinery, woollens. Pop. 123,000. (2) Tn., Ontario, Canada, on N. shore of L. Ontario, 55 m. w. of Kingston. Pop. 6,000.

Tréport. See LE TRÉPORT.

Trèves. See TRIER.

Treviso (*trev-ē'zō*), tn., Italy, 18 m. N. of Venice; 15th cent. cathedral; iron goods, pottery, silks, and woollens. Pop. 58,000.

Trichinop'oly. (1) Dist., Madras, India; generally an undulating plain watered by R. Cauvery; rice, groundnuts, cotton. Area, 4,319 sq. m.; pop. 1,903,000. (2) Cap. of above, on R. Cauvery; built round Rock (273 ft.); rly. jn.; temples attract pilgrims; cigars, cheroots, hardware, and gold and silver jewellery. Pop. 120,500.

Trier (*trēr*) (French *Trèves*), tn.,

Rhineland, Prussia, on R. Moselle; manufactures linen, cottons, woollens, leather, stained glass; iron foundries, machinery, dyeing; claims to be oldest town in Germany; interesting Roman remains; cathedral (11th to 13th cent.). Pop. 58,500.

Trieste (*trē-es'tā*), port, Italy, at N.E. of Adriatic Sea; formerly chief seaport of Austria; trades in grain, wine, and oil with Levant and Far East; old tn., with narrow and steep streets, has cathedral and castle; univ. (1924); shipbuilding and ironfounding; assigned to Italy (1918). Pop. 255,500.

Trik'kala, tn., Thessaly, Greece, 38 m. W. of Larissa; cotton and woollen goods, leather; trades in wheat, silk, tobacco. Pop. 19,000.

Trim, co. tn., Meath, I.F.S., on R. Boyne; mkt. tn.; ruined castle (12th cent.). Pop. 1,300.

Trimdon, par. and vil., Durham, England, 8 m. S.E. of Durham; collieries and iron foundries. Pop (par.) 5,400.

Trincomali (*tring-kō-mă-lē'*), port, N.E. Ceylon; fine natural harbour; place of pilgrimage. Pop. 10,000.

Tring, mkt. tn., Herts, England, 5 m. N.W. of Berkhampstead; Rothschild Museum. Pop. 4,400.

Trinidad'. (1) Isl., Brit. W. Indies, off N.E. coast of Venezuela, S. America; surface hilly; rises to 3,000 ft.; contains Pitch L. (104 ac.) in S.W., source of natural asphalt; oilfields; climate tropical; produces sugar and cacao; manufactures rum, angostura bitters, coconut oil; exports petroleum, asphalt, sugar, cocoa, copra, bitters. Discovered by Columbus (1498). Chief tn., Port of Spain. Area, 1,862 sq. m.; pop. 397,000. (2) Tn., S. Cuba; exports sugar, molasses, and honey. Pop. 46,000.

Trip'oli. (1) Tn., cap., Tripolitania, N. Africa, on Mediterranean Sea; caravan centre; carpets; tobacco factory. Pop. 60,000. (2) Tn., Syria, Asia, 44 m. N.E. of Beirut; exports oranges, silk, grain, sponges. Pop. 37,500.

Tripolita'nia, dist., Italian Libya, N. Africa; mainly desert; includes N. part of Sahara plateau, *c.* 2,000 ft. high; coastal oases yield tobacco, dates, olives, oranges; steppes for pasture, wheat, barley, esparto; in desert are oases of Ghadames and Ghat; sponge and tunny fisheries; trades in ostrich feathers brought by caravans. Annexed by Italy (1911). Inhabitants are Negroes, Arabs, Jews, and Europeans. Chief tns., Tripoli (cap.), Misurata, Homs. Area, *c.* 360,000 sq. m.; pop. *c.* 570,000.

Tripolit'sa, or TRIPOLIS, cap., Arcadia, Morea, Greece; manufactures tapestries and leather goods. Pop. 14,500.

Tripu'ra, formerly HILL TIPPERA, semi-independent state, Bengal, India, on boundary of Assam; hills forested; elephants, tigers, leopards; rice and tea. Area, 4,116 sq. m.; pop. 304,500.

Tris'tan da Cunha (*koon'yă*), largest of three volcanic islands in S. Atlantic Ocean, more than half-way between Rio de la Plata and Cape Town; surface mountainous; produces potatoes and apples; cattle and sheep raised; discovered by Portuguese admiral, from whom they take their name (1506); annexed by Brit. (1816). Area, 16 sq. m.; pop. 130.

Trivan'drum, cap., Travancore, Madras, India; military cantonments to N. of tn.; religious centre and place of pilgrimage; observatory. Pop. 73,000.

Trnava (*ter'nă-vă*), formerly NAGY-SZOMBAT, tn., Czechoslovakia, 26 m. N.E. of Bratislava; mkt. tn.; cloth, sugar, and chemicals. Pop. 18,000.

Trnovo (*tir'nō-vō*), city, Bulgaria, 80 m. N.E. of Philippopolis; copperware; cap. of Bulgaria from 1186 to 1393. Pop. 13,000.

Tro'gir (Italian *Trau*), port, Dalmatia, Yugoslavia, 10 m. W. of Split; cathedral (13th cent.); trades in fruit and wine. Pop. 3,500.

Tro'itsk, town, S. Ural Area, R.S.F.S.R, on l. bk. of trib. of R. Tobol; tanneries; flour mills. Pop. 30,000.

Troitsokosavsk (*trō-its-kō-sävsk'*), tn., Buriat Mongol rep., U.S.S.R., on Kiakhta, trib. of R. Selenga, 2 m. N. of frontier tn. of Kiakhta; gold, osmiridium, and salt. Pop. 9,000.

Trollhät'tan, tn., Elfsborg, Sweden, 45 m. by rail N. of Göteborg; famous falls with locks leading to Gota Canal; falls supply water-power for lumber and other industries, and for electricity to Copenhagen. Pop. 16,000.

Trom'sö, port, N. Norway, on Tromsö I.; exports furs, whale and seal oil; also fish. Pop. 11,500.

Trondhjem (*trond'yem*). See NIDAROS.

Troon, port, Ayrshire, Scotland, 6 m. N. of Ayr; shipbuilding; exports coal; golfing centre. Pop. 8,500.

Trop'pau. See OPAVA.

Trossachs (*tros'aks*), wooded glen (1 m. long), Perthshire, Scotland, between Lochs Achray and Katrine, 8 m. S.W. of Callander; immortalized in Scott's *Lady of the Lake.*

Trotsk, formerly GATCHINA, tn., Russia, 25 m. S. of Leningrad; summer resort. Pop. 15,000.

Trouville (*troo-vēl'*), seaside resort, Calvados, France, on English Channel, 9 m. S. of Le Havre; boat building, fishing; its port is shared by Deauville. Pop. 6,000.

Trowbridge (*troo'brij*), tn., Wilts, England, 11 m. S.E. of Bath; broadcloths and kerseymeres manufactured since 16th cent. Pop. 12,000.

Troy. (1) Famous city of legendary Greek history, N.W. Asia Minor, near entrance to Dardanelles; city of Homer's *Iliad*; last or ninth city on this site was ruined by Turks in 1306. (2) City, New York, U.S.A., on Hudson R., and on Erie and Champlain canals; collars, shirts. Pop. 72,000.

Troyes (*trwä'*), chief tn., Aube, France, on R. Seine, 104 m. by rail E.S.E. of Paris; hosiery, iron goods, looms; cathedral (begun 1208). Treaty between England and France signed here (1420). Pop. 58,500.

Trujillo (*troo-hēl'yō*). (1) City, Estremadura, Spain, 75 m. N.E. of Badajoz; birthplace of Pizarro; dist. produces fruit, wine, oil. Pop. 11,500. (2) Tn., Peru, S. America, near Pacific Ocean; univ.; in irrigated sugar-cane dist.; exports copper, gold, and silver. Pop. 30,000.

Tru'ro. (1) City, Cornwall, England, 11 m. N. of Falmouth; cathedral; former trade in tin and copper, now chiefly mkt. tn.; exports china clay. Pop. 11,100. (2) Tn., Nova Scotia, 51 m. N.N.E. of Halifax; hosiery; govt. college of agriculture. Pop. 8,000.

Trutnov (*trut'nof*) (German *Trautenau*), tn., Bohemia, Czechoslovakia, at base of Riesengebirge; coal mining; linens. Pop. 15,000.

Tsana. See TANA.

Tsangpo, riv., Tibet, Asia; rises near R. Sutlej at alt. of 15,958 ft.; flows E. between Himalayas and Trans-Himalayas for *c.* 900 m.; breaks through gorge of Himalayas into Assam, where it is named R. Brahmaputra.

Tsarit'syn. See STALINGRAD.

Tsarskoye Selo. See DYETSKOYE SELO.

Tsinan (*tsē-nän'*), or CHINAN, cap., Shantung, China, at base of Shantung Highlands and near Hwang-Ho; rly. jn.; flour mills, cotton factories. Pop. 300,000.

Tsingtao (*tsing-tou'*), port, Shantung, China, on Kiaochow Bay; connected by rly. with Tsinan; salt fields; exports straw braid, silk. Pop. 318,000.

Tsushima (*tsoo'shē-mä*), isl. between Korea and Japan; in centre of strait of Tsushima or Korea, where Japanese destroyed Russian fleet (1905). Area, 260 sq. m.; pop. 40,000.

Tu'am, tn., Galway, I.F.S., on R. Clare, 18 m. N.E. of Galway; cathedral; college for R.C. clergy. Pop. 3,000.

Tuamo'tu (formerly PAUMOTU), or Low ARCHIPELAGO, includes *c.* 80 low coral reefs in S. Pacific Ocean; pearl fishing; belong to France. Area, *c.* 350 sq. m.; pop. 4,500.

Tuap'se, tn., N. Caucasian Area, Russia, on Black Sea; oil refineries. Pop. 12,500.

Tuat, or Twat, Berber name applied to oases in w. Sahara, Africa; more particularly to fertile region in valley of Wadi Saura; included in Algeria; dates, barley, wheat, cotton, and tobacco. Pop. *c.* 50,000.

Tü'bingen, tn., Württemberg, Germany, on R. Neckar; univ. (1477); 16th cent. castle; printing, dyeing, chemical manufacture, making of scientific instruments. Pop. 20,500.

Tubuai (*too-boo-ä'ē*), or Austral, **Islands,** group of French islands in Pacific Ocean, s. of Society Islands. Area, 115 sq. m.; pop. 3,500.

Tucson (*too-son'*), city, s. Arizona, U.S.A., on Santa Cruz R.; seat of univ. of Arizona; rly. workshops; gold, silver, and copper smelting industries; stockyards. Pop. 32,000.

Tucuman (*too-koo-män'*). (1) Prov., N. Argentina; well wooded; mountainous towards the N.W.; sugar. Area, 10,422 sq. m.; pop. 418,000. (2) Cap. of above, 90 m. N.W. of Santiago del Estero; univ.; breweries, sawmills, flour mills, sugar factories, and tanneries; trade in oxen and mules. Pop. 91,500.

Tudela (*too-dä'lä*), city, Navarra, N. Spain, on R. Ebro; cathedral; timber industries. Pop. 10,500.

Tudhoe (*tud'o*), par., Durham, England, 5 m. N.E. of Bishop Auckland; ironworks and collieries. Pop. 7,900.

Tugela (*too-gä'la*), riv., Natal, S. Africa; rises in Drakensberg Mts., and flows E. and S.E. past Colenso and Ladysmith to Indian Ocean; scene of much fighting during S. African War (1900). Length, 300 m.

Tuggurt (*too-goort'*), terr., Algeria; comprises dists. of Biskra and Tuggurt. Tn. of Tuggurt in oasis of Sahara desert; large trade in dates. Pop. (terr.) 213,000; (dist.) 95,000; (tn.) 12,000.

Tughina (*too-gē'nä*) (Turkish *Bender*), tn., Bessarabia, Romania, on R. Dniester; timber and sawmills. Pop. 36,500.

Tuguegarao (*too-gä-gä-rä'ō*), tn., N. Luzon I., Philippines; tobacco. Pop. 19,500.

Tu'la. (1) Prov., central Russia, in R. Don basin; agriculture; coal deposits; metal wares. Area, 9,700 sq. m.; pop. 1,500,000. (2) Cap. of above; iron foundries and factories for arms, machinery, and metal articles of all kinds; tanneries; flour mills. Pop. 150,000.

Tulcea (*tool'chä*), riv. port, Dobruja, Romania, on R. Danube; grain, wool, and fish. Pop. 28,000.

Tullamore', co. tn., Offaly, I.F.S., on Grand Canal; distilling and brewing; agricultural produce. Pop. 5,000.

Tulle (*tool*), chief tn., Corrèze, central France; cathedral; small-arms factory. Pop. 10,500.

Tul'low, mkt. tn., Carlow, I.F.S., on R. Slaney; grain and butter. Pop. 1,600.

Tul'sa, city, Oklahoma, U.S.A., on Arkansas R.; oilfields; grain and live-stock region. Pop. 141,000.

Tumkur (*toom-koor*), hill station, Mysore, India, 40 m. N.W. of Bangalore. Pop. 14,500.

Tum'mel, riv., Perthshire, Scotland; rises near Glencoe, and flows E. through Lochs Rannoch and Tummel to join R. Tay at Ballinluig; trout and salmon. Length, 60 m.

Tun'bridge Wells, Royal, inland wat.-pl., Kent and Sussex, England, 4 m. s. of Tonbridge; chalybeate springs; fine promenade (the Pantiles); manufactures wooden (inlaid) ware. Pop. 35,400.

Tung-chow', city, Hopeh, China, on Pei-ho, 15 m. E. of Peking; starting-place for tea caravans to Siberia. Pop. *c.* 50,000.

Tung Keng, largest of s. Shan States, Burma; mountainous; drained to Mekong and Salween rivs.; rice, sugar-cane; teak. Chief tn., Tung Keng. Area, 12,400 sq. m.; pop. 210,000.

Tu'nis, cap., Tunisia, N. Africa; connected with Mediterranean Sea at La Goulette by canal; Mohammedan univ.; important trading centre; manufactures silk and woollen textiles, pottery, leather; exports olive oil, cereals, cattle and hides, ores, dates, gems. Founded by Carthaginians; ruins of Carthage near by. Pop. 186,000.

Tunis'ia, French protectorate, N. Africa; bounded N. by Mediterranean, W. by Algeria, S. by Sahara, E. by Libya and Mediterranean; consists of five regions: (i.) mountainous N. (Atlas Mts.) with rich Mejerda valley; (ii.) N.E. with orange and lemon groves; (iii.) Sahel, E. coast region, olives; (iv.) central tableland (average elevation *c.* 2,000 ft.), pastures; (v.) Sahara in S., containing famous dried-up salt lakes (largest, Shott Kebir); country around lakes is known as Belad-el-Geriad (land of dates). Climate hot, but healthy; ann. temp., 60° to 90° F.; winter rainfall 10 to 50 in., heaviest in N.; principal products and exports, cereals, minerals and metals, hides, olives, dates, wines, esparto grass, henna, cork, fruits, tobacco; manufactures morocco leather, pottery, carpets, rugs, and woollen fabrics; extensive fisheries (tunny, sardines, sponges); iron, lead, and zinc mined; valuable phosphates; numerous hot springs; pop. consists mainly of Bedouin Arabs, Kabyles, and Jews (54,500); European pop. 173,500 (Italians, 90,000; French civilians, 71,000; Maltese, 8,500). Cap. Tunis. Area, *c.* 50,000 sq. m.; pop. 2,160,000.

Tun'stall, tn., Staffs, England; bricks and tiles; now included in Stoke-on-Trent. Pop. 23,000.

Turcoman. See TURKMEN.

Turin (Italian *Torino*), tn., Piedmont, Italy, on R. Po; 15th cent. Gothic cathedral; univ. (founded 1404); important rly. and military centre; manufactures silk, woollen goods, paper, cotton, linen, leather, motor-cars and aeroplanes; cap. of kingdom of Savoy till 1860, and for five years thereafter of Italy. Pop. 591,000.

Tur'key, rep., Europe and Asia, consisting of E. Thrace with Constantinople, and whole of Asia Minor, S. shores of Sea of Marmara, the Bosporus, and the Dardanelles; in Europe N. boundary runs roughly E., and W. boundary roughly S. along R. Maritsa, from Adrianople. In Asia, Turkish terr. is bounded on N. by Black Sea and Georgia, on E. by Armenia and Persia, and on S. by Iraq and Syria. Chief religion of Turkey is Mohammedanism. Chief tns. in European Turkey, Constantinople, Adrianople; in Asia Minor, Angora (cap. of all Turkey), Smyrna, Scutari, Adana, Brusa, and Konia. Area, 294,416 sq. m.; pop. 13,648,500. See ASIA MINOR.

Turkistan. (1) General name for extensive region of central Asia; Chinese terr. formerly E. Turkistan is described under Sinkiang; present Turkistan includes Uzbek, Turkmen, Tajik, Kazak, and Kirghiz reps. of U.S.S.R., situated between Caspian Sea and Pamir plateau; partially overrun by Mongols in 11th cent., formed part of Tamerlane's empire in 14th cent., and later was carved into independent states; came under Russian control in 19th cent. (2) Or HAZRET, tn., Kazak rep., U.S.S.R., on R. Sir Darya; cotton industry; wool market; Mohammedan pilgrim resort. Pop. 22,000.

Turkmen, or TURCOMAN, rep., Asia, U.S.S.R., S.E. of Caspian Sea; drained by R. Atrek to Caspian Sea, R. Oxus to Aral Sea, and R. Murghab in S.; mainly desert with oases; silk and fruit; live-stock. Chief tns., Ashqabad (cap.), Merv, and Krasnovodsk. Area, 189,603 sq. m.; pop. 1,030,000.

Turks and Caicos Islands. See CAICOS AND TURKS ISLANDS.

Tur'ku, formerly ÅBO, port, Finland, on Gulf of Bothnia; shipbuilding; exports timber, dairy produce, grain. Pop. 61,000.

Turnhout (*toor-nout'*), tn., Belgium, 25 m. E.N.E. of Antwerp; textiles, paper, lace. Pop. 25,500.

Tur'nu-Severin', riv. port, Romania, on R. Danube, 10 m. E. of Orsova; exports grain, salt, petroleum; remains of bridge built by Trajan and of tn. erected by Severus; large govt. shipyards. Pop. 31,000.

Tur'riff, burgh, Aberdeenshire, Scotland, 12 m. s. of Macduff; anc. tn.; the 'Trot of Turriff' (1639) was fought between Covenanters and Royalists. Pop. 2,300.

Tur'ton, urb. dist., Lancs, England, 4 m. N. of Bolton; manufactures cotton; stone quarries. Pop. 11,800.

Tus'cany, w. central dep., Italy; comprises nine provs.—Arezzo, Florence, Leghorn, Grosseto, Lucca, Massa-Carrara, Pisa, Pistoia, and Siena; Apennines to N. and E.; chief riv. Arno; wheat, maize, wine, olive oil, chestnuts; copper, lead, iron ore, mercury, marble, salt, lignite; mineral and hot springs; industries include textiles, porcelain, and straw hats; cradle of Italian language and literature. Principal tns., Florence, Siena, Pisa, Leghorn. Area, 8,890 sq. m.; pop. 2,886,000.

Tuskegee (*tus-kē'gē*), tn., Alabama, U.S.A., on Tuskegee R., 38 m. E. of Montgomery; seat of Tuskegee Normal and Industrial Institute, founded (1881) by Booker T. Washington for education of Negroes. Pop. 2,500.

Tut'bury, tn. and par., Staffs, England, on R. Dove, 9 m. s.w. of Derby; ruins of castle; manufactures glass; alabaster found in vicinity. Pop. (par.) 2,000.

Tuticor'in, port, Madras, India, on Gulf of Manaar, 65 m. N.E. of Cape Comorin; cotton spinning, and manufacture of salt; passenger port for Ceylon; pearl fisheries. Pop. 44,500.

Tuttlingen (*toot'ling-en*), tn., Württemberg, Germany, on R. Danube, 28 m. N.W. of Konstanz; manufactures cutlery, shoes, and woollens. Pop. 16,000.

Tuy (*too'ē*), tn., Pontevedra, Spain, on R. Minho, on Portuguese frontier; cathedral; preserve manufactures; hot mineral springs. Pop. 13,000.

Tuz'la, tn., Bosnia, Yugoslavia, on R. Jala, 47 m. N. of Sarajevo; salt springs; manufactures soda; trade in timber, coal, bricks, live-stock, fruit, and grain. Pop. 13,000.

Tver. (1) Province of central Russia; level plateau containing watershed between Rs. Volga, W. Dvina, and Msta; numerous lakes and marshes; one-third of prov. covered by coniferous forest; rye, oats, and potatoes are cultivated; dairy farming is extending. Area, 24,438 sq. m.; pop. 2,239,000. (2) Cap. of above, on Upper R. Volga; cathedral; cotton, sailcloth, linen, earthenware, leather, and machinery; river port and important distributing centre. Pop. 106,000.

Tweed, principal riv., S.E. Scotland; rises in Peeblesshire (1,500 ft.); flows N.E. past Peebles, Melrose, and Kelso; forms boundary between England and Scotland, and enters North Sea at Berwick; chief tribs., Gala, Ettrick, Leader, Teviot, and Whiteadder; valuable salmon fisheries; length, 97 m.

Tweed'mouth, port, Northumberland, England, on R. Tweed, suburb of Berwick-upon-Tweed; salmon fishing, fish curing; ironfounding, engineering. Pop. 5,000.

Twenty-four Parganas', THE, dist., Bengal, India; part of Ganges Delta, including most of Sundarbans; partly forested, partly cultivated; rice, jute, pulses. Area, 4,856 sq. m.; pop. 2,628,000.

Twick'enham, residential suburb of Greater London, England, on R. Thames, 2 m. s.w. of Richmond; fashionable resort in 18th cent.; river-fishing centre. Pop. 39,900.

Twy'ford, par. and vil., Hants, England, on R. Itchen, 3 m. s. of Winchester; Alexander Pope educated here; venerable yew tree in churchyard. Pop. (par.) 2,215.

Tyldesley with Shakerley (*tildz'le*), urb. dist., Lancs, England, 10 m. w. of Manchester; cotton manufactures; foundries, collieries. Pop. 14,800.

Ty'ler, city, Texas, U.S.A., 93 m. E.S.E. of Dallas; centre for fruit, live-stock, cotton. Pop. 12,000.

Tyne (*tīn*), riv., England, formed by junction of N. and S. Tyne, 2 m. N.W. of Hexham Bridge; flows E. past Newcastle to enter North Sea at Tynemouth. Shipbuilding yards and engineering works line its banks. Length, 80 m.

Tynemouth (*tin'muth*), co. bor., port, and wat.-pl., at mouth of R. Tyne, Northumberland, England, 8 m. N.E. of Newcastle; includes North Shields; shipbuilding; harbour sheltered by two piers; fisheries; ropes and sails. Pop. 64,900.

Tyre (*tīr*) (modern *Sur*), tn., Great Lebanon, Syria, on Mediterranean Sea; ancient city of Phœnicia; one of most flourishing maritime cities of ancient times; famous for purple dyes.

Tyree (*tir-ē'*), or TIREE, isl., Inner Hebrides, Argyllshire, Scotland, 19 m. N.W. of Iona; treeless, flat; several fresh-water lakes; horses bred. Area, 30 sq. m.; pop. 1,700.

Tyrol. See TIROL.

Tyrone (*tī-rōn'*). (1) Inland co., N. Ireland; surface mostly hilly, rising into mts. in N. and S.; fertile and well-cultivated in low-lying dists.; watered by rivs. Foyle and Blackwater; agriculture and cattle rearing; coal and marble; linens and coarse woollens manufactured. Cap. Omagh. Area, 1,218 sq. m.; pop. 133,000. (2) Tn., Pennsylvania, U.S.A., 95 m. E. by N. of Pittsburgh; in agricultural and lumber region; iron deposits. Pop. 9,000.

Tyumen', tn., Ural Area, Russia, on R. Tura; on rly. between Perm and Omsk; leather, carpets. Pop. 50,500.

Tywardreath', par. and vil., Cornwall, England, 5 m. N.E. of St. Austell; Roman camp and old priory in vicinity. Pop. (par.) 2,500.

U

Ubangi, or MOBANGI, riv., Africa, formed by union of Rs. Mbomu and Uele; chief N. trib. of R. Congo; length, 1,400 m.

Ubeda (*oo-bā'da*), tn., Jaen, S. Spain, on plain between R. Guadalquivir and its trib. Guadalimar; trade in soap, oil, and agricultural produce. Pop. 20,000.

Uck'field, urb. dist., Sussex, England, 8 m. N.E. of Lewes; malting and brewing; trade in corn and timber. Pop. 3,600.

Udaipur (*oo-dī-poor'*), or MEWAR. (1) Indian state, S. Rajputana, India; maize, cotton, sugar-cane, wheat, poppy. Area, 12,756 sq. m.; pop. 1,380,000. (2) Cap. of above; very picturesque; royal palace on margin of Pichola lake; embroidery, cotton cloth, swords. Pop. 35,000.

Ud'dingston, tn., Lanarkshire, Scotland, 7 m. S.E. of Glasgow, of which it is a residential suburb; agricultural implements, machinery, jam, and confectionery. Pop. 8,400.

Udine (*oo'dē-nä*), tn., Italy, 85 m. N.E. of Venice; silks, linens, leather. Pop. 56,000.

Ufa (*oo'fa*), chief tn., Bashkir, E. Russia, on R. Ufa, *c.* 250 m. N.E. of Samara; important agricultural market; iron and copper works; sawmills, flour mills, and breweries. Pop. 97,000.

Uganda (*ū-gän'dä*), inland British protectorate, E. Africa, bounded N. by Anglo-Egyptian Sudan, E. by Kenya, S. by Tanganyika Terr., W. by Belgian Congo. Surface is plateau, over 3,000 ft., with mountains in S. and W. rising to 20,000 ft.; chief river is Nile; lakes include part of Victoria, Edward, Albert, and Rudolf, and whole of Kioga. Climate tropical; healthy in higher regions to S. and W.; malaria prevalent in lower dists.; soil in general very fertile. S. dists. abound with magnificent timber; swamps are rank with papyrus, rushes, reeds, and coarse grass. Tropical forest fringes margin of L. Victoria. Products are cotton, rubber, cocoa, coffee, oil-seeds, ivory, hides, and skins. Uganda has an excellent system of roads. Uganda Rly. runs from Mombasa to the Nile, passing through the cotton area, for which it provides an outlet. Uganda is divided into four provs.: (1) Buganda, on w. shores of Lake Victoria; (2) W. prov., on w. boundary; (3) N. prov., along w. to N. boundary; (4) E. prov., lying E. of Buganda. Chief tns., Entebbe (cap.), and Kampala. Area, 94,204 sq. m.; pop. 3,157,000, including 1,870 Europeans.

Uig (*oo'ig*), par., s.w. Lewis, Outer Hebrides, Ross and Cromarty, Scotland; contains islands of Bernera and Flannen. Pop. 4,000.

Uist (*oo'ist*), NORTH and SOUTH, two islands, Outer Hebrides, Inverness-shire, Scotland; inhabitants mainly crofter-fishermen. Pop. N. Uist, 2,600; S. Uist, 3,200.

Uitenhage (*oi-ten-hä'gä*), tn., Cape Prov., S. Africa, 21 m. N.W. of Port Elizabeth; railway works; wool-washing industry; irrigated fruit and flower nurseries; summer resort. Pop. 14,000.

Ujiji (*oo-jē'jē*), tn., on Lake Tanganyika, Tanganyika Terr.; at terminus for rly. from Dar-es-Salaam; trading centre for ivory; here Stanley found Livingstone (1871). Pop. *c.* 25,000.

Ujjain (*oo'jīn*), sacred city, Gwalior, central India, 32 m. N. of Indore; exports opium; prime meridian of Hindu geographers runs through it. Pop. *c.* 40,000.

Ukraine', rep., U.S.S.R.; bounded N. and E. by other units of U.S.S.R., S. by Crimea and the Black Sea, w. by Romania and Poland; surface marshy in N., low plateau in S.; chief rivers are Dnieper, Dniester, Bug, and Donetz, trib. of Don. Climate continental; rain mainly in summer. Very fertile soil; *c.* 80 per cent. of population engaged in agriculture; maize, wheat, barley, rye, and oats are chief crops; sugar-beet, potatoes, tobacco, also grown. Stock raising is important, particularly sheep and pigs. Among minerals found are coal from Donetz valley; iron ore, manganese, mercury, salt. Manufactures include flour milling, sugar refining, brewing, distilling, and tobacco; metal smelting, chemical industries, brick and pottery manufacture. Chief tns., Kharkov (cap.), Kiev, Dnepropetrovsk, Stalingrad, and the Black Sea ports, Odessa, Kherson, and Nikolaev. Area, 166,368 sq. m.; pop. 29,000,000.

Ulcinj (*oolt'siny*), formerly DULCIGNO, tn., Yugoslavia, on Adriatic; tobacco growing; olive oil; fishing and boat building. Pop. 3,000.

Uleåborg (*oo'lă-ō-bor*). See OULU.

U'lianov, formerly SIMBIRSK, prov., Russia, situated to w. of middle R. Volga; consists of an extensive and fertile plain, but broken and hilly in S. and S.W.; drained by Volga and tributaries; has deposits of bituminous shale, asphalt, salt, iron ore, and ochre; chief occupation is agriculture, and products include maize, rye, oats, and vegetables; chief industries: woollen manufacture, distilling, brewing, and flour milling. Chief tn., Ulianovsk. Area, 13,500 sq. m.; pop. 1,381,000.

Ulianovsk', cap. of Ulianov prov., Russia; river port on R. Volga; brewing, tanning, iron and copper foundries, flour mills. Pop. 70,000.

Ul'lapool, vil., Ross and Cromarty, Scotland, on Loch Broom; fishing; safe and spacious harbour. Pop. 600.

Ullswater. See LAKE DISTRICT.

Ulm (*oolm*), city, Württemberg, Germany, on R. Danube; magnificent Gothic cathedral with famous spire; cottons, linens, woollens, leather, tobacco, cement, machinery; flour milling, distilling. Pop. 57,000.

Ul'ster, prov. in N. of Ireland, consisting of cos. of Antrim, Armagh, Down, Fermanagh, Londonderry, Tyrone (now N. Ireland) and Cavan, Donegal, Monaghan (now in I.F.S.); a flourishing industrial region; manufactures are linen, muslin, and iron goods; shipbuilding and distilling are important; bauxite and rock salt worked in Antrim; mainly Protestant in religion. Area, 8,330 sq. m.; pop. 1,556,000.

Ul'verston, mkt. tn. and urb. dist., on Morecambe Bay, Lancs, England; ironworks, chemical works, breweries. Pop. 9,200.

Uman (*oo-mân'*), town, Ukraine, U.S.S.R., 40 m. s. of Kiev; iron foundries, flour mills, distilleries. Pop. 44,000.

Umbal'la. See AMBALA.

Um'bria, dep. of central Italy, comprising provs. of Perugia and Terni; mountainous, with fertile valleys and good pasturage; contains many objects of artistic and architectural interest. Area, 3,377 sq. m.; pop. 639,000.

Unalaska. See under ALEUTIAN ISLANDS.

Unao. (1) Dist., United Provinces, India; undulating upland; cereals, poppy, sugar-cane. Area, 1,787 sq. m.; pop. 819,000. (2) Cap. of above, 10 m. N.E. of Cawnpore; has thriving local trade. Pop. 11,000.

Ungava (*ung-gâ'va*). (1) Terr., Quebec, Canada, occupies N.W. of Labrador peninsula; treeless in N.; numerous lakes; iron, copper, gold, and nickel occur. Area, 351,780 sq. m. (2) BAY, large inlet, N. Labrador, leading into Hudson Strait; shallow; ice-free in summer, when cod-fishing takes place. Length, 150 m.; breadth, 130 m.

Union, or TOKELAU, group of Brit. islands in Pacific, N. of Samoa; administered by the Commissioner of Western Samoa. Area, 7 sq. m.; pop. 1,000.

Union City, tn., New Jersey, U.S.A., on Hudson R., opposite New York; silk goods. Pop. 59,000.

Union of Socialist Soviet Republics (U.S.S.R.), official title of the state formed out of the old Russian Empire. It comprises seven republics: Russian Socialist Federal Soviet Republic (Russia proper), Ukraine, White Russia, Transcaucasia, Uzbek, Turkmen, and Tadzhik Socialist Soviet Republics. Within these there are 15 Autonomous Republics and 14 Autonomous Areas. The most important of the Autonomous Republics are the following in the Russian Socialist Federal Soviet Republic: Bashkir, Tatar, Kirghiz, Daghestan, Crimea, Yakutsk, Karelia, Buriat-Mongolia, Kazak. Cap. Moscow. Total area, 8,242,000 sq. miles; total pop. 147,000,000. See separate articles on these states, and for the Russian Socialist Federal Soviet Republic consult articles on Russia and Siberia.

Uniontown, town, Pennsylvania, U.S.A., 40 m. s. of Pittsburgh; foundries and machine shops; lumber and flour mills. Pop. 16,000.

United Kingdom, former official title for 'United Kingdom of Great Britain and Ireland'; now sometimes used politically to mean Great Britain and N. Ireland, and geographically to mean the British Isles.

United Provinces of Agra and Oudh, prov., British India; bounded by Tibet, Nepal, Bihar and Orissa, Central India, Rajputana, and the Punjab. Surface generally plain, with Himalayas on N. boundary; watered by R. Ganges, with Jumna and other affluents. Agriculture is extensively carried on assisted by irrigation; chief food-growing prov. in India; chief crops, wheat, rice, millet, barley, maize, and pulse, while cotton, sugar-cane, opium-poppy, and oil-seeds are also cultivated. Densely populated. Chief tns., Allahabad (cap.), Lucknow, Benares, Cawnpore, Agra, Meerut. Area, 106,295 sq. m.; pop. *c.* 45,500,000.

United States of America, federal rep., N. America; bounded N. by Canada, E. by Atlantic, S. by Gulf of Mexico and Mexico, and W. by Pacific; Alaska to N.W. of Canada is a detached terr. Surface is divided into three natural regions: (1) Appalachian Mts. along E. coast, with coastal plain (200 m. wide); (2) Central Plains, which are divided into Gulf Plain extending inland from Gulf of Mexico, Prairies N. of Gulf Plain stretching to Great Lakes, and Great Plains at a higher elevation, W. of Gulf Plains and Prairies. Central Plains occupy largest area of country, and are broken by Ozark Mts. between Gulf Plain and Great Plains; (3) Rocky Mt. system in W., of great elevation (extreme height, 14,898 ft.). The N.E. is drained by streams flowing to Great Lakes and R. St. Lawrence; coastal strip by Penobscot, Connecticut, Hudson, Delaware, Susquehanna, Potomac, James, Roanoke, Savannah; Central Plain by Mississippi-Missouri system, Alabama, Sabine, Trinity, flowing direct to Gulf of Mexico; s.w. by Rio Grande del Norte (flowing into Gulf of Mexico) and Colorado into Gulf of California; N.W. by Columbia, which breaks across coast mountains.

The great rivers of Central Plain are navigable for long distances; R. Hudson is navigable, but other E. rivers are chiefly important for power and harbour purposes; w. rivers mostly flow through deep gorges (cañons), and, except R. Columbia, are of no commercial importance. E. coast as far s. as Long I. is rocky, with many good harbours; farther s. it is low and sandy, and broken only by great openings of Delaware and Chesapeake Rs.; along Gulf of Mexico it is low and swampy, while near middle R. Mississippi delta projects some 50 m. out to sea. The long line of w. cliffs is broken only in extreme N., and near centre, at Golden Gate, San Francisco.

Climate varies from winter snows and cold of central N. to mildness of Pacific slopes and sub-tropical conditions of s. and S.E. Greatest range of temperature is in interior, and is much greater on N.E. coast than on Pacific Coast. Rainfall in E. half varies from over 60 in. in s. to 20 in N.; in w. half it decreases to 15 in. at base of Rocky Mts.; along Pacific coast-strip it is abundant in N. and scanty in s.; some parts of w. hills and w. plateau are desert.

Agriculture is chief industry, but others are increasing rapidly in importance. Of country E. of 100° long., nearly two-thirds is under crop —N. districts producing crops of ordinary grains and green crops, centre maize and tobacco, s. cotton, with rice and sugar-cane in much smaller proportion on shores of Gulf of Mexico. Chief grain crops are maize, wheat, and oats; barley, flax, rye, buckwheat, and rice are also important crops. Chief wheat-growing states lie in a central strip and in N.W. Chief maize-producing states lie s. and w. of Great Lakes. Great cotton states are in S.E.; area under cotton is over 45,000,000 ac. Chief tobacco states lie roughly N. of cotton belt. Sugar-cane is grown in Louisiana, Georgia, etc.; over 1,000,000 ac. (chiefly in Louisiana and Texas) are under rice. Vines succeed best in California. Among temperate fruits are apples, peaches, plums, and pears; many tropical and sub-tropical fruits are cultivated in California and several s. states. Stock rearing is important in w. half of country (chiefly cattle, pigs, sheep, horses), the crops being produced chiefly for feeding. There are great tracts of forest land on the Atlantic side, the Pacific coast, the Rocky Mts., and W. Central States, occupying about one-fifth of whole country. Salmon fishing of w., fisheries of Grand Bank of Newfoundland and Alaska, and whale and seal fishing are exceedingly valuable.

Minerals are also of very great importance. Over two-thirds of world's petroleum is produced in U.S.A.; other important minerals include gold, silver, copper, lead, zinc, aluminium, iron, coal, and natural gas. Manufactures are very important in N.E., especially in states of New York and Pennsylvania; the cotton factories of s. are developing rapidly. Textiles and iron and steel goods of all kinds are manufactured. Leading exports in order of value are: iron and steel ore and goods, wheat and flour, raw cotton, mineral oils, cotton goods, and tobacco; meat and dairy products.

The densely populated states have a network of convenient railway communications. An enormous amount of traffic is carried on Great Lakes and on canals connected with them—Sault Ste. Marie, Erie, Hudson R., Hudson and St. Lawrence, Ohio to Susquehanna, and Lake Michigan to the Mississippi, etc. The Mississippi-

Missouri river system is navigable for nearly 14,000 m. Washington is cap.; largest tns. are New York, Chicago, Philadelphia, and Detroit. Area of the U.S.A. (excluding Alaska), 3,026,789 sq. m.; pop. 105,710,000. Indian reservations cover 47,000 sq. m., with pop. of 355,000; there are over 10,000,000 Negroes.

University City, city, Missouri, U.S.A., close to St. Louis, of which it is a residential suburb; seat of Washington University. Pop. 26,000.

Unst, most N. of Shetland Islands, Scotland; fishing and agriculture; Shetland hosiery. Pop. 1,800.

Unterwalden (*oon'ter-väl-den*), canton, Switzerland, s.w. of L. Lucerne; divided into Obwalden and Nidwalden. Surface mountainous, reaching *c.* 10,600 ft. in Mt. Titlis; drained by R. Aa, flowing into L. Lucerne. Dairy farming carried on; fruit cultivated and live-stock raised. Chief tn. of Obwalden is Sarnen; of Nidwalden, Stans. Area, 296 sq. m.; pop. 31,000.

Uper'nivik. See GREENLAND.

Up'hall, par. and vil., West Lothian, Scotland, 3 m. N.N.W. of Mid Calder; sandstone quarries, coal mines, shale mines; paraffin works. Pop. (par.) 12,500.

Uphol'land, urb. dist., Lancs, England, 4 m. w. of Wigan; coal mines, quarries. Pop. 5,500.

Up'ington, tn., Bechuanaland, S. Africa, on Orange R.; copper ore in vicinity; ostrich farming. Pop. 1,700 whites.

Upper Vol'ta, colony, French W. Africa, within bend of R. Niger, N. of Ivory Coast, Gold Coast, Togo, and Dahomey; drained by R. Volta and tribs.; cattle; ground-nuts, millet, maize, cotton, rubber. Cap. Ouagadoudou. Area, *c.* 142,000 sq. m.; pop. 3,000,000.

Up'pingham, mkt. tn., Rutlandshire, England; has famous public school (1584). Pop. (of dist.) 5,300.

Uppsala (*up'sa-la*), city, Sweden, 40 m. N. of Stockholm; seat of an archbishop (primate of Sweden) and of a univ. (1477); cathedral (1260) contains monuments of many Swedish kings and of Linnæus. Pop. 30,000.

Upton-on-Severn, mkt. tn., Worcestershire, England; has considerable river trade. Pop. 2,000.

Ur, anc. city (*Ur of the Chaldees*), Iraq, near anc. confluence of Euphrates and Tigris rivs., 110 m. w. of Basra; formerly a caravan market; supposed birthplace of Abraham; change of course of Euphrates left Ur in desert; uninhabited since 350 B.C.; scene of excavations from 1918.

Ural (*oo-räl'*), riv., European Russia, rises in s. Ural Mts.; flows s. to enter Caspian Sea through delta; navigable to Orenburg; fisheries below Uralsk. Length 1,400 m.

Ural Area (*oo-räl'*), administrative division of Russia; partly in Europe, partly in Asia; bounded on E. by Siberian Area, s. by Kazak Republic, N. by Arctic Ocean, and w. by Bashkir Republic, Votiak Terr., and Viatka Prov. Ural Mts. lie almost entirely within its borders. Its w. rivers, particularly the Kama and its tributaries, link the region with the Volga river system, and by canals with Leningrad. Eastward it drains to R. Ob and Arctic Ocean. Mining is an important industry, iron, copper, gold, platinum, salt, phosphates, and precious stones being obtained. Among chief industries are smelting; manufacture of machinery; china, glass, cement, leather, flour, and tobacco. Agriculture is relatively unimportant. Crossed in s. by railway line linking Perm, Sverdlovsk, and Tyumen. Cap. is Sverdlovsk. Area, 653,424 sq. m.; pop. 6,792,000.

Ural Mountains (*oo-räl'*), mountain system forming boundary between Europe and Asia, with a total length of *c.* 1,650 m.; average height, 1,200–1,500 ft., reaching extreme height of 5,500 ft. in N. Rich in minerals—gold, copper, iron, platinum, silver, coal, salt, malachite, precious stones. Many large forests on slopes.

Uralsk (*oo-rälsk'*), cap. of Ural Province, Kazak, U.S.S.R., on Ural R.; trade in cattle; manufactures flour, leather, iron, and woollen goods. Pop. 36,000.

Urbino (*oor-bē'nō*), tn., Marches, Italy, 45 m. N.W. of Ancona; modern cathedral; old churches; ducal palace containing fine art collections; birthplace of Raphael; cheese, silks, olive oil. Pop. 20,000.

Ur'fa, modern name for anc. city of EDESSA, S.E. Asia Minor, 90 m. S.W. of Diarbekr; interesting archæological remains; modern city is an important trade centre; cotton and grain. Pop. *c.* 100,000.

Urga (*oor'ga*), city, N. Mongolia; religious and commercial centre. Pop. *c.* 40,000.

Uri (*oor'ē*), canton, Switzerland, running S. from L. Lucerne; comprises upper valley of R. Reuss, and is traversed by St. Gotthard Rly.; stock and dairy farming. Cap. Altdorf. Area, 415 sq. m.; pop. 24,000.

Urmia (*oor'mē-a*). (1) Tn., Azerbaijan, N.W. Persia, 64 m. S.W. of Tabriz; a flourishing tn. before Great War, exporting raisins and molasses, and centre of large agricultural trade. Owing to massacre and exodus of Christians during the War its importance declined. Attempts are being made to restore its prosperity. (2) Salt lake, N.W. Persia; has no visible outlet; length, 80 m.; breadth, from 30 to 45 m.

Urms'ton, urb. dist., Lancs, England, 5½ m. W.S.W. of Manchester; residential. Pop. 9,300.

Uruguay (*oo-roo-gwī'*). (1) Republic, S. America, N. of Rio de la Plata; bounded N.E. by Brazil, S.E. by Atlantic, S. by the R. Plate, and W. by Argentina. Surface is flat grass-land, with low ridges of hills in N.; drained by Rio Negro and other tribs. of Uruguay R. Climate is healthy; mean ann. temp. 61° F.; ann. rainfall, 35 in. Principal industry is rearing of cattle and sheep; extensive exports of meat, wool, and animal products. Wheat is chief crop; grapes, olives, and tobacco are grown. Minerals include gold, copper, lead, silver, lignite, but mining is only of slight importance. Chief tns., Montevideo (cap.), Paysandu, Saeto, Mercedes. Area, 72,153 sq. m.; pop. 1,808,000. (2) Riv., S. America; rises in Sierra do Mar, S.E. Brazil; flows W. and S., divides Argentina from Brazil and then from Uruguay; flows into Rio de la Plata; navigable to cataract at Salto. Length, *c.* 1,000 m.

Uruguayana (*oo-roo-gwī-ä'nä*), tn., Rio Grande do Sul, Brazil, on R. Uruguay; centre of grazing industry. Pop. 21,000.

Urumtsi (*oo-room'tsē*), cap. of Sinkiang, China; in valley of Tien Shan Mts.; trade in furs and skins. Pop. *c.* 50,000.

Usedom (*oo'ze-dom*), isl., Pomerania, Prussia, at mouth of R. Oder; with Wollin I. separates Stettiner Haff from the Baltic; summer resort; agriculture, forestry, fishing. Area, 158 sq. miles.

Ushak (*oo-shak'*), tn., Asia Minor, 125 m. E. of Smyrna; famous for carpets. Pop. 89,000.

Ush'ant (French *Ouessant*), isl., Finistère, France; most W. part of France; marks entrance to English Channel; fishing; important wireless station. Pop. 2,500.

Usk. (1) Tn., Monmouthshire, England, on R. Usk; agricultural centre. Pop. 1,300. (2) Riv., S. Wales and Monmouthshire, England; flows into estuary of Severn; salmon fisheries; length, 60 m.

Uskub. See SKOPLJE.

Usti nad Labem (*oos'tē*), formerly AUSSIG, tn., Czechoslovakia; 45 m. N. by W. of Prague; at confluence of Rs. Bela and Elbe; chemical works and coal mines. Pop. 40,000.

Ustyug-Velikiy (*oos-te-oog'-vä-lē'kē*), tn., N. Russia, on R. Sukhona, trib. of N. Dvina; brewing, distilling, timber, leather. Pop. 19,000.

Us'worth, par., Durham, England, 4 m. S.E. of Gateshead; extensive coal mines. Pop. 8,000.

U'tah, inland mountain state, U.S.A., lies among western ridges of the Rocky Mts.; bounded by Idaho, Wyoming, Colorado, Arizona, and

Nevada; Wasatch Mts., which run roughly N. and S., reach *c.* 13,000 ft., and the Uinta range in N.E. rises to *c.* 14,000 ft.; in N.W. is Great Salt Lake; watered by Colorado R. and tribs., and by R. Sevier and other streams. Climate extreme in mountainous districts, healthy and temperate in valleys; rainfall very small and irregular. Agriculture carried on in fertile regions where water is obtainable; chief crops, wheat, oats, potatoes, hay; sugar-beet is an important product. Fruits and vegetables are grown; horses, cattle, sheep, and pigs reared. Minerals include copper, silver, lead, gold, coal. Industries of importance are copper refining, flour milling, fruit canning, and the manufacture of boots and shoes, sugar, cheese, and butter. Chief tns., Salt Lake City (cap.) and Ogden. Area, 84,990 sq. m.; pop. 449,000.

U'tica, city, New York, U.S.A., on R. Mohawk; manufactures cotton goods, hosiery, clothing, boots and shoes. Pop. 103,000.

Utrecht (*oo-trecht'*), city, Holland, in R. Rhine delta, 22 m. S.S.E. of Amsterdam; strong fortress; intersected by two canals. Many fine buildings. Treaty of Utrecht signed here (1713). Chief industries are printing, machinery, chemicals, woollens, silks, velvets, tobacco, cigars, plate glass. Pop. 151,000.

Utrera (*oo-trā'ra*), city, Spain, 16 m. S.E. of Seville; 14th cent. church; productive region, rich in grain and fruit. Pop. 21,000.

Uttox'eter, urb. dist. and mkt. tn., Staffs, England, 13 m. N.E. of Stafford; agricultural implements; quarries marble. Pop. 5,900.

Uxbridge, urb. dist. and mkt. tn., Middlesex, on R. Colne; part of Greater London. Pop. 31,900.

Uzbek, Asiatic rep., U.S.S.R.; bounded S. by Afghanistan, W. by Turkmen, N. by Kazak, and E. by Tadzhik; mainly plateau with extreme climate and scanty rainfall; watered by Sir Darya and Oxus rivers; soil fertile under irrigation; cotton and rice are chief products, also wheat, maize, barley, and fruits; live-stock reared; naphtha, coal, iron, silver, lead, and copper are found, but are little exploited. Cap., Samarqand. Area, 131,394 sq. m.; pop. 5,270,000.

Uzhorod (*oozh-hor-ot*), formerly UNGVAR, tn., Czechoslovakia, on W. border of Ruthenia; has trade in timber; manufactures pottery and wine. Pop. 21,000.

V

Vaal (*väl*), riv., S. Africa; rises in Drakensberg Mts.; flows W. and S.W. between Transvaal and Orange Free State provinces, then through Griqualand West to join Orange R.; length, 750 m.

Vaasa (*väz'a*), formerly NIKOLAISTAD, seaport, Finland, on Gulf of Bothnia; shipbuilding; exports timber and tar. Pop. 24,000.

Vacz (*voch*), tn., Hungary, on R. Danube, 20 m. N. of Budapest; exports are wine and cattle; Roman antiquities. Pop. 19,000.

Vaigach, isl., Russia, in Arctic Ocean, between mainland and Novaya Zemlya; mountainous; visited during summer for pelts and fish. Length, 68 m.; breadth, 27 m.

Valais (*vă-lā'*), border canton, S. Switzerland. Surface consists of a deep valley about 80 m. long and 2 m. broad, between Pennine and Bernese Alps; drained by R. Rhone; forests with valuable timber trees on mountain slopes; considerable area covered with excellent pasturage; cattle raised; silkworms reared; wine produced; connected with Italy by the Simplon and Great St. Bernard Passes. Chief town, Sion. Area, 2,020 sq. m.; pop. 128,000.

Valdai Hills (*văl'dī*), low, undulating plateau, European Russia, between Leningrad and Moscow; wooded; source of R. Volga. Highest point, 1,150 ft.

Valdepeñas (*val-dā-pān'yas*), town, New Castile, Spain, 30 m. S.E. of Ciudad Real; famous for wine; hot mineral springs in vicinity. Pop. 25,000.

Valdivia (*val-dē'vi-a*), cap. of Valdivia prov., Chile; breweries; its port, Corral, has one of best harbours on W. coast of S. America; wireless station. Pop. 27,000.

Valence (*val-ons*), tn., cap. Drôme, France, on R. Rhone, 58 m. S. of Lyons; manufactures glass, silk, hosiery; cathedral consecrated by Urban II. (1095). Pop. 26,000.

Valencia (*val-en'shē-a*). (1) Prov., Spain, bordering Mediterranean; fertile and well cultivated; chief rivers, Guadalaviar and Jucar; chief products, rice, wheat, maize, mulberry, wine, and oil. Area, 4,150 sq. m.; pop. 926,000. (2) Chief tn. of above, on R. Guadalaviar; archbishop's see, cathedral (12th cent.); univ.; exports olives and olive oil, various fruits; manufactures silks, tiles, linen, leather, cigars. Pop. 251,000. (3) City, N. Venezuela, S. America; important agricultural centre; manufactures cotton and tobacco. Pop. 37,000.

Valenciennes (*vă-lon-sē-en'*), tn., Nord, France, 18 m. N.E. of Cambrai; coal-mining centre; manufactures iron, sugar, glass, chemicals; formerly famous for its lace. Pop. 36,000.

Valen'tia, rocky isl., S.W. Kerry, I.F.S.; slate quarries; terminus of Atlantic cables and of cables to Europe; radio station.

Valet'ta, or VALLETTA, cap. Malta, on rocky peninsula on N.E. coast; most important Brit. naval and coaling station in Mediterranean; fortified; 16th cent. cathedral; univ., governor's palace (formerly palace of grand masters of Knights of St. John). Pop. 48,000.

Valladolid (*val-ya-dō-lēd'*). (1) Prov., Spain; traversed by R. Douro chief industry, agriculture; produces cereals, hemp, flax, and fruit. Area, 2,922 sq. m.; pop. 281,000. (2) Cap. of above, on trib. of R. Douro; univ. (1346); archbishopric; royal palace; unfinished cathedral (1585); manufactures include cloth, pottery, and flour; has agricultural trade. Pop. 77,000.

Vallejo (*val-ā'hō*), seaport, California, U.S.A., at mouth of R. Napa; good harbour; outlet to agricultural district; flour milling; U.S. navy yard. Pop. 21,000.

Valleyfield, port, Quebec, Canada, on R. St. Lawrence, 36 m. S.W. of Montreal; seat of Roman Catholic bishopric; cotton, flour, and sawmills. Pop. 9,000.

Valls, city, E. Spain, 11 m. N. of Tarragona; cotton, hemp, woollens, weaving; wine and nuts. Pop. 11,000.

Valo'na, formerly AVLONA, seaport, Albania; exports cereals, cotton, olives, live-stock; oil refining. Pop. *c.* 10,000.

Valparaiso (*val-pa-rī'sō*), seapt., Chile, on Pacific Ocean; chief commercial and manufacturing centre in Chile; industrial univ.; most important seaport on Pacific coast of S. America; wireless station; has several times been destroyed by earthquake. Pop. 182,000.

Van. (1) Tn., Asia Minor, 260 m. S.E. of Trebizond; built at S. face of high isolated rock, on which is inscription of Xerxes; is encircled by walls. Several mosques and churches; in neighbourhood are orchards and vineyards; local trade in agricultural produce. Pop. 22,000. (2) LAKE, close to above; salt; no visible outlet; extends about 80 m. E. to W., and from 20 to 40 m. N. to S.

Vancouver (*van-koo'ver*). (1) Tn., British Columbia, Canada, on Burrard Inlet; W. terminus of transcontinental rlys.; excellent harbour; lumber, shipbuilding, flour mills, foundries, sugar and oil refineries. Pop. 117,000. (2) City, Washington,

U.S.A., 7 m. N. of Portland, lumbering, fruit growing, dairying; flour mills, canneries. Pop. 13,000.

Vancouver Island, isl., Brit. Columbia, Canada; separated from mainland of Brit. Columbia by Strait of Georgia and Queen Charlotte Sound, and from U.S.A. by Strait of Juan de Fuca; mountainous and forest-clad; coasts bold and rugged; coalfields; fisheries. Cap. Victoria. Area, *c.* 20,000 sq. m.

Van Diemen's Land. See under TASMANIA.

Vannes (*van*), tn., cap. Morbihan, France, on R. Vannes, 28 m. E. of Lorient; shipbuilding, oyster fishing; manufactures ropes, leather. Chief tn., Morbihan. Pop. 16,000.

Vanua Levu. See FIJI.

Var, mar. dep., S.E. France; mountainous, with fertile valleys; coast deeply indented; produces wine, olives, tobacco; manufactures paper, silk, soap. Cap. Draguignan; chief town, Toulon. Area, 2,333 sq. m.; pop. 348,000.

Varaz'din, tn., Croatia, Yugoslavia, on R. Drava; coal mining; woollen manufacture; trade in timber, fruit, and tobacco. Pop. 14,000.

Vardar', riv., rises in Serbia, Yugoslavia; flows S.E. past Skoplje and Veles; enters Greece and discharges into the Gulf of Salonica. Length, 200 m.

Varese (*va-rā'sā*), tn., Lombardy, N. Italy, 30 m. N.W. of Milan; autumn resort; manufactures silk, leather, paper, wine. Pop. 24,000.

Var'na, fortified seapt., Bulgaria, on Black Sea; wine, leather, cloth, butter, grain. Pop. 61,000.

Vasilkov', tn., Ukraine, U.S.S.R., 24 m. S.S.W. of Kiev; breweries, brick works; manufactures tobacco, candles, soap. Pop. 21,000.

Västerås, or VESTERÅS (*ves'ter-ōs*), tn., Sweden, on Lake Malar; cathedral and castle. Pop. 29,000,

Vas'to, fortified tn., Abruzzi, Italy, on Adriatic Sea, 30 m. S.E. of Chieti; silk, wine; extensive cultivation of olives. Pop. 14,000.

Vaucluse (*vō - klooz'*), dep., S.E. France; wine, potatoes, wheat, fruit, manufactures linen, silk, pottery, paper, chemicals. Cap. Avignon. Area, 1,381 sq. m.; pop. 230,000.

Vaud (*vō*), canton, W. Switzerland, N. and E. of L. Geneva; surface mountainous (Diablerets, 10,600 ft.); extensive plain slopes down to Lakes Geneva and Neuchâtel. Produces white wines; cattle raised; tanning, condensed milk, tobacco, clocks, salt mining. Chief tn., Lausanne. Area, 1,238 sq. m.; pop. 317,000.

Veglia. See KRK.

Vejer de la Frontera (*vā'hār dā lā fron-tā'rä*), tn., Spain, 30 m. S.E. of Cadiz; oranges. Pop. 15,000.

Vel'es, formerly KOPRÜLÜ or KÖPRILI, tn., S. Serbia, Yugoslavia, on R. Vardar; silk, maize, and mulberries. Pop. *c.* 22,000.

Velez-Malaga (*vā'leth-mä'lā'-gä*), tn., Malaga, S. Spain; raisins, olive oil, and sugar. Pop. 25,000.

Velika Kikinda. See KIKINDA.

Veliki Beckarek. See BECKEREK VELIKI.

Vellet'ri, tn., Italy, 22 m. S.E. of Rome; cathedral; wine. Pop. 26,000.

Vellore (*vel-ōr*), tn., Madras, India, 80 m. S.W. of Madras; military station; trades in grain. Pop. 50,000.

Vel'sen, tn., Holland, on North Sea; connected with Amsterdam by North Sea Canal. Pop. 36,000.

Vendée (*von-dā'*), mar. dep., W. France, woodland in E., fertile plain in S., and marsh in W.; chief products, grain, wine, coal, salt. Cap. La Roche-sur-Yon. Area, 2,690 sq. m.; pop. 395,000.

Vener (*vā'ner*), largest lake, Sweden, drained by the R. Göta to the Kattegat. Area, 2,150 sq. m.

Venetia (*ven-esh'ya*), or VENETO, dep. of N.E. Italy; comprises provinces of Verona, Vicenza, Venice, Padua, Belluno, Rovigo, Treviso, Udine. Mountainous in the N.; remainder a fertile plain watered by Rs. Tagliamento, Piave, and Brenta. Chief industries include manufacture of textiles, glass, tobacco, straw-plait, paper, iron goods, and shipbuilding. Area, 9,818 sq. m.; pop. 4,252,000.

Venetia Julia, dep., N.E. Italy; comprises provinces of Gorizia, Pola, Trieste, Fiume, and Zara; Julian Alps in N., drained by Rs. Isonzo and Timavo; wine, silk, barley, and potatoes. Area, 3,355 sq. m.; pop. 1,004,000.

Venetia Tridentina (*trē-dent-ē'na*), department, N. Italy, comprises provinces of Bolzano and Trento; mountainous; marble quarries, lead and zinc; rye, barley, oats. Area, 5,371 sq. m.; pop. 684,000.

Venezuela (*ven-ez-wē'la*), republic, S. America; bounded N. by Caribbean Sea, E. by Brit. Guiana, S. by Brazil, W. by Colombia. Country falls into four divisions: low lands round L. Maracaibo, mountain land in N., plains (llanos) of R. Orinoco, and Guiana highlands. Drained by R. Orinoco and tribs. Climate tropical; temperature varies with elevation, warmest along R. Orinoco; rainy season, May to Oct. or Nov. Land is exceedingly rich in natural resources. Forests contain much valuable timber. Llanos provide pasture for large herds of cattle. Soil, extremely fertile, produces maize, cotton, cacao, indigo, rice, rubber, sugar-cane, coffee, tobacco, fruits. Petroleum is found round L. Maracaibo, and Venezuela is second petroleum-producing country in world; other minerals include gold, silver, copper, iron, coal, salt, asphalt, magnesite; pearl fisheries; few industries. Inhabitants include Spaniards, Indians, and half-breeds. Cap. Caracas; chief port, Maracaibo. Area, 393,874 sq. m.; pop. 3,027,000.

Ven'ice, or VENEZIA. (1) Prov., N. Italy; fertile plain bordering Adriatic Sea. Area, 943 sq. m.; pop. 519,000. (2) Seaport, N. Italy, cap. of above; situated on 117 islands in the lagoons at head of Adriatic; traversed by *c.* 170 canals crossed by innumerable bridges. City is divided into two main parts by Grand Canal; connected with mainland by railway viaduct 2 m. long. Lagoons are protected from sea by sandhills and masonry work; shipping enters by several channels; aqueduct carries water supply from mainland. Notable features are magnificent Cathedral of St. Mark (begun 830; destroyed by fire and rebuilt, 976 onwards); opposite is famous Campanile (322 ft. high); Giacomo di Rialto (*c.* 520), Venice's oldest church; Santi Giovanni e Paolo, with tombs of Doges; Palace of the Doges (founded *c.* 814; rebuilt after fires, 976, 1105), with magnificent court (1485); Scala dei Giganti, great Council Hall, and Bridge of Sighs connecting palace with prison; museums, with fine examples; Rialto, bridge across Grand Canal; Piazza of St. Mark; Lido (bathing resort) on neighbouring Malamocco I. Famous for glassware and mosaics; gold and silver filigree work, embroidery, lace, damasks, brocades, *objets d'art*, chemicals, leather, cotton and woollen goods, shipbuilding. Until discovery of Cape route to India, Venice was chief European port for trade with East. New port Marghera being built on mainland. Pop. 172,000.

Ven'lo, tn., Limburg, S. Holland, near German frontier; beer, leather, needles, tobacco. Pop. 22,000.

Ventimiglia (*ven-ti-mēl'yä*), seaport, Riviera, Italy, on French frontier; Roman antiquities and Gothic cathedral. Pop. 16,000.

Vent'nor, wat.-pl., S. Isle of Wight, England; Royal National Consumption Hospital. Pop. 5,100.

Vent'spils, formerly WINDAU, seaport and seaside resort, Latvia, on Baltic Sea, 110 m. W.N.W. of Riga; exports timber, butter, hemp, and grain. Pop. *c.* 17,000.

Vera Cruz (*vä'ra krooz*). (1) State, Mexico, on Gulf of Mexico; interior mountainous and fertile; coast low and sandy; produces chiefly cotton, rum, sugar, maize, wheat, tobacco, coffee; cap. Jalapa. Area, 27,880 sq. m.; pop. 1,160,000. (2) Seapt. in above, on Gulf of Mexico; exports above products; wireless station. Pop. 53,000.

Vercelli (*ver-chel'ē*), tn., Piedmont, Italy, 37 m. s.w. of Milan; cathedral contains 4th cent. MS. of the Gospels, and Vercelli Book, a collection of Old English homilies and poems; Roman antiquities. Pop. 33,000.

Verdun, tn., fortress, Meuse, France, on R. Meuse; hardware, machinery; 12th cent. cathedral; was a centre of resistance to German invasion during Great War. Pop. 29,000.

Vereeniging (*ver-ăn'ig-ing*), town, Transvaal, S. Africa, 36 m. s. of Johannesburg; coal mining; peace between Boers and British signed here (1902). Pop. 2,500 (whites).

Verkhne-Udinsk (*verch'ne-oo-dinsk'*), chief town, Buriat Mongol Rep., U.S.S.R., on Trans-Siberian Rly., E. of L. Baikal; tea, grain, hides, bristles; important annual fair. Pop. 27,000.

Vermont', New England State, U.S.A., w. of New Hampshire; surface generally undulating and hilly; among highest peaks are Mansfield (4,393 ft.) and Killington (4,241 ft.). Watered by Connecticut R. and tribs., and by Rs. Otter Creek and Missisquoi. Climate healthy, but subject to intense cold in winter. Most important industry is agriculture; hay, oats, maize, wheat, barley, potatoes, and fruit grown. Maple sugar largely produced, and tobacco cultivated. Cattle, horses, sheep, and pigs reared; dairy-farming carried on. Large forests, producing hardwood; and lumbering is important. Woollens and flour are also manufactured. Marble, granite, and limestone are quarried. Chief tns., Montpelier (cap.), Burlington, Rutland, Barre. Area, 9,564 sq. m.; pop. 352,000.

Verni. See ALMA ATA.

Vero'na. (1) Province, N.E. Italy, borders Tirol and L. Gardi. Area, 1,195 sq. m.; pop. 549,000. (2) Cap. of above, on R. Adige; fortress. Roman remains; many mediæval churches, palaces, and houses; silk, iron goods, furniture, paper. Pop. 151,000.

Versailles (*văr-să'ē*), chief tn. Seine-et-Oise, France, 12 m. s.w. of Paris; magnificent palace erected by Louis XIV.; made National Museum (1833); King of Prussia proclaimed German Emperor here (1871). Treaty of Versailles (1783) ended American War of Independence. Here was held the Peace Conference following the Great War, and Treaty signed 1919. Pop. 69,000.

Versecz. See VRSAC.

Verviers (*ver-vē-ā'*), tn., Liége, Belgium; manufactures woollen cloth, woollen yarn, and glass. Pop. 42,000.

Vesu'vius, active volcano, Italy, 7 m. S.E. of Naples, *c.* 4,000 ft. high. Eruption (A.D. 79) buried Pompeii in mud and ashes, and Herculaneum by flow of lava; more recent eruptions, 1871–72 and 1906. Wire rope railway carries visitors close to edge of crater; observatory at foot.

Vet'ter, or WETTER, lake, Sweden, drained by R. Motala to the Baltic; noted for frequent and sudden surface disturbances. Length, 80 m.; area, 740 sq. m.

Vevey (*vē-vā'*), tn., Vaud, Switzerland, on Lake Geneva; tourist resort; manufactures chocolate, watches, machinery, tobacco. Pop. 13,000.

Viareggio (*vē'a-red'jō*), seaport and wat.-pl., Italy, 13 m. N.W. of Pisa; exports marble; monument to Shelley, whose body was washed ashore here. Pop. 28,000.

Viat'ka. (1) Province, Russia; surface undulating plateau; low hills on N.E.; forested; many lakes and marshes; watered by Rs. Kama and Viatka; soils mainly unproductive; chief crops, rye, oats, and flax; chief minerals, iron and phosphorite. Area, 43,144 sq. m. Pop. 2,223,000. (2) Chief tn. of above, on R. Viatka, 260 m. N.E. of Nijni-Novgorod; rlv. jn.; matches, leather, and agricultural implements. Pop. 57,000.

Viborg (*vē'borg*). (1) Tn., Jutland, Denmark, 35 m N.W. of Aarhus; 12th cent. cathedral; iron foundries, cloth factories, distilleries. Pop. 15,000. (2) See VIIPURI.

Vicenza (*vē-chent'sa*), tn., Italy, 40 m. W. of Venice; noted for its fine buildings; manufactures silk, woollen, cotton goods, bricks, pottery. Pop. 60,000.

Vichy (*vē-shē*), wat.-pl., Allier, central France, on R. Allier; mineral springs; Vichy water exported. Pop. 17,000.

Vicks'burg, tn., Mississippi, U.S.A., on Mississippi R.; trading centre; manufactures furniture, hardware, cotton-seed oil, machinery; exports cotton, lumber. Stronghold of Confederates during Civil War; captured by General Grant (1863). Pop. 18,000.

Victo'ria. (1) State, S.E. Australia; bounded N. and N.E. by New South Wales, S.E. by Pacific, S. by Indian Ocean, W. by S. Australia. Surface mountainous, with level tract along Murray R. in N.W.; principal mts. are Great Dividing Range, crossing country from E. to W.; drained by R. Murray and tribs., and by rivs. flowing S. from Great Dividing Range. There are many lakes. Climate healthy and temperate. Agriculture important; chief crops, wheat, oats, and barley; potatoes widely grown; grapes and other fruits and tobacco extensively cultivated; horses, cattle, sheep, and pigs reared; dairy farming carried on. Large forests, producing valuable timber. Gold mines important; other minerals, coal, tin, antimony. Manufactures include machinery, hardware, textiles, wine. Chief exports are wool, meat, hides and skins, live animals, flour, and butter. Chief tns., Melbourne (cap.), Geelong, Ballarat, and Bendigo. Area, 87,884 sq. m.; pop. 1,531,000. (2) Cap. of Brit. Columbia, Canada, on Vancouver I.; residential tn.; connected with transcontinental lines by ferries; sawmills, iron working, cement and chemical factories, fish canneries; fine harbour; large dry dock. Pop. 39,000. (3) Cap. and chief port, Hong-Kong, China; sugar, cotton. Pop. *c.* 500,000. (4) Seapt., Espirito Santo, Brazil, 290 m. N.E. of Rio de Janeiro; port of call for coasting steamers; exports coffee, sugar, and rice. Pop. 22,000. (5) Cap. of Seychelles Islands, on Mahé I. (6) LAKE, largest fresh-water lake, central Africa; surrounded by Uganda, Kenya, and Tanganyika terr.; entered by the Kagera, Katonga, and other rivers; chief reservoir of R. Nile, to which it drains by Ripon Falls. There are many islands. Frequented by alligators and hippopotami. Discovered by Speke (1858). Area, *c.* 26,000 sq. m.

Victo'ria Falls, cataract of the R. Zambezi, Rhodesia, S. Africa; height, *c.* 400 ft.; width, *c.* 1 m.; discovered by Livingstone (1855); volume of water greatest in April.

Victoriahavn. See NARVIK.

Vidin (*vē-dēn'*), tn., river port, Bulgaria, on R. Danube; gold and silver filigree; exports cereals; active commerce. Pop. 19,000.

Vien'na, cap. Austria, on R. Danube; one of finest, largest, and most historical cities of Europe, renowned for art, architecture, learning, industry, music. Ringstrasse, on site of old fortifications (destroyed 1858), claims to be handsomest street in the world. Votive Church (1856–79); univ. (founded 1365); Rathaus; celebrated Burg Theater and Opera House; Parliament House; Art Gallery (one of finest in Europe); Maria Theresa, Schiller, and Goethe monuments. Schönbrunn palace and park lie near the city. Vienna is centre of Austrian trade and industry, chief manufactures being iron and steel goods, silk, ornamental leather, *objets d'art,* blouses, hats, clothing, and furniture. Pop. 1,857,000.

Vienne (*vē-en'*). (1) Riv., France; rises in dep. Corrèze, joins R. Loire; length, 220 m. (2) Dep., France, generally level; traversed by R. Vienne; produces grain, wine; manufactures cutlery, arms; cap. Poitiers. Area, 2,711 sq. m.; pop. 310,000. (3) Tn., Isère, France, on R. Rhone; has Romanesque-Gothic cathedral and Roman remains; manufactures textiles, hardware, gloves; large trade in wine. Pop. 22,000.

Viersen (*fēr′sen*), tn., Rhineland, Prussia, 11 m. s.w. of Crefeld; velvets, silks, damask. Pop. 32,000.

Vierzon (*vē-er-zon′*), tn., Cher, central France, on R. Cher, trib. of R. Loire; manufactures agricultural machinery, glass, porcelain. Pop. 11,000.

Vigevano (*vē-jā-vä′nō*), tn., Lombardy, Italy, on R. Ticino, 18 m. s.w. of Milan; cathedral; silk. Pop. 30,000.

Vigo (*vē′gō*), seaport and naval station, Pontevedra, N.W. Spain, on Ria de Vigo; fisheries; flour, sugar, petroleum, leather; wireless station. Pop. 53,000.

Viipuri (*vē′poor-ē*), formerly VIBORG, seaport, Finland, at mouth of Saima Canal, near Gulf of Finland; exports cement and farm produce. Pop. 48,000.

Villach (*vil′ach*), tn., Carinthia, s. Austria, on R. Drava; lead-mining centre; manufactures wooden articles and metallic colours. Pop. 22,000.

Villafranca di Verona (*vēl-a-frang′-ka dē ver-ō′na*), tn., Venetia, Italy, 10 m. s.w. of Verona; silk industry. Pop. 12,000.

Villalba (*vēl-yal′ba*), town, Lugo, N.W. Spain; cloth and pottery; livestock and grain trade. Pop. 15,000.

Villanueva de la Serena (*vēl-ya-nwā-va dā la sē-rā′na*), tn., Badajoz, Spain, on R. Guadiana; grain, hemp, melons, and wine. Pop. 15,000.

Villanueva y Geltru (*ē hel-trō′*), seaport, Barcelona, Spain, on Mediterranean Sea; textiles, paper, iron goods. Pop. 14,000.

Villarreal (*vēl′ya-rā′al*), tn., Castellon, E. Spain, 4 m. from Mediterranean Sea; oranges; manufactures paper and woollen goods. Pop. 17,000.

Villarrica (*vēl′la-rē′ka*) tn., Paraguay, 80 m. S.E. of Asuncion; in rich agricultural region; tobacco, yerba maté; oranges. Pop. *c.* 25,000.

Villaviciosa (*vēl′ya-vi-chōs′a*), seaport, Oviedo, N. Spain; fisheries and coasting trade. Pop. 21,000.

Villefranche-sur-Saône (*vēl-fronsh′*), tn., Rhône, France, on R. Saône; cottons, steel cables, agricultural machinery, motor-cars, wines. Pop. 16,000.

Villena (*vēl-yā′na*), tn., s. Spain, 28 m. N.W. of Alicante; soap, brandy, silk, salt. Pop. 16,000.

Villeneuve-sur-Lot (*vēl-noov-sür-lō′*), tn., Lot-et-Garonne, s.w. France, on R. Lot; boots and shoes, tin boxes; trade in agricultural produce and wine. Pop. 7,000.

Vilna. See WILNO.

Vincennes. (1) (*van-sen′*) Suburb of Paris, Seine, France; manufactures chemicals and cartridges; castle. Pop. 42,000. (2) (*vin-senz′*) City, Indiana, U.S.A., on Wabash R., between Indiana and Illinois; manufactures steel, buttons, flour, glass; railway centre. Pop. 17,000.

Vindhya (*vind′yä*), mt. range, India, forming N. boundary of the Deccan; length, *c.* 700 m.; alt. 1,500 to 4,500 ft.

Virgin′ia, S. Atlantic State, U.S.A. Surface greatly diversified, sloping being from W. to E.; in E. is low-lying coastal region known as Tidewater; in centre is Piedmont plateau; farther W. Blue Ridge extends across state from S.W. to N.E. (highest point, Roger Mt., 5,720 ft.). Between Blue Ridge and Alleghany Mts. farther W. lies Great Valley of Virginia, famed for scenery. Watered by Rs. Potomac (with trib. Shenandoah), Rappahannock, York, James. Temperate and healthy, except in the marshy districts in E. Flora includes oak, pine, cedar, and other timber trees. Agriculture is an important industry, principal crops being maize, wheat, oats, and potatoes. Tobacco is extensively cultivated, and cotton grown in considerable quantities. Horses, cattle, sheep, and pigs reared. Excellent fisheries, esp. oysters. Coal is most important mineral. Important industries are flour milling, lumbering, manufacture of textiles, tobacco, leather, hardware. Chief tns., Richmond (cap.), Norfolk, Roanoke, and Portsmouth. Area, 42,627 sq. m.; pop. 2,309,000.

Virgin Islands, group, W. Indies,

E. of Porto Rico, belonging partly to Britain and partly to U.S.A.; mountainous. Anegada, Virgin Gorda, Tortola, and a number of smaller islands belong to Great Britain. Chief products, sugar, cotton, tobacco. St. Thomas, St. John, and St. Croix belong to U.S.A.; chief product, bay rum. Total area, 190 sq. m.; total pop. 31,000 (Brit. 58 sq. m.; pop. 5,000).

Vis (Italian *Lissa*), island, Yugoslavia, in Adriatic Sea, off coast of Dalmatia; wine and sardines. Chief tn., Vis. Pop. 5,000.

Visby, or WISBY, cap., isl. Gottland, Sweden; seaport and wat.-pl.; important commercial city in anc. times; has cathedral, ruined churches, towers, walls. Pop. 10,000.

Vistula, riv., Poland; rises in Carpathian Mts., flows N. through Poland and Danzig, divides into several branches, two of which empty into Frisches Haff; main stream, turning W., enters Baltic near Danzig; length, 650 m.; navigable to Cracow.

Vitebsk′, town, White Russia, U.S.S.R., on S. Dvina R.; cathedral; manufactures include boots and shoes, glass, and agricultural machinery. Pop. 91,000.

Viter′bo, tn., Italy, 40 m. N.N.W. of Rome; surrounded by ancient Lombard fortifications; Etruscan cemeteries in neighbourhood. Pop. 25,000.

Viti Levu. See under FIJI.

Vitor′ia, or VITTORIA, tn., N. Spain, 40 m. S.S.E. of Bilbao; trade in hardware, wine, mules, and horses; 12th cent. cathedral; here Wellington defeated the French. Pop. 35,000.

Vittor′ia, tn., Sicily, 45 m. W. by S. of Syracuse; trade in wine and soda. Pop. 32,000.

Vittor′io, tn., Italy, 40 m. N. of Venice; mineral springs; silk mills; seat of bishopric. Pop. 24,000.

Vivero (*ve-vā′rō*), seaport, Spain, 43 m. N. of Lugo, on Bay of Biscay. Pop. 13,100.

Vizagapatam′, seaport, E. coast, Madras, India, 178 m. N.E. of Masulipatam; manufactures native cloth; ivory, horn, sandalwood carving; exports grain, manganese ore, and sugar. Pop. 45,000.

Vizcaya. See BISCAY.

Vizianagram′, tn., Madras, India, 30 m. N.E. of Vizagapatam; trade centre; military cantonment and residence of maharajah. Pop. 40,000.

Vlaar′dingen, fishing port, S. Holland, Holland, 6 m. W. of Rotterdam; one of headquarters of Dutch cod and herring fisheries. Pop. 27,000.

Vladikavkaz′ ('key of the Caucasus'), tn., N. Caucasian Area, Russia, on R. Terek; of great strategic importance. Pop. 74,000.

Vladimir (*vlad-yē′mēr*). (1) Prov., Russia, between Nijni-Novgorod and Moscow; surface undulating, and mostly unfertile; lakes and marshes drained by R. Oka and its trib. the Klyazma; chief minerals, alabaster and iron ore; manufactures linens, cottons; fruit culture; extensive domestic industries. Area, 12,041 sq. m.; pop. 1,320,000. (2) Cap. of above, on R. Klyazma; two anc. cathedrals; manufactures cotton, tobacco; gardening, fruit growing. Pop. 35,000.

Vladivostok (*vlä-dē-vos-tok′*), seaport and naval station, Far Eastern Area, U.S.S.R., on Gulf of Peter the Great (Sea of Japan); has naval and mechanical works; state dockyards; most important naval and commercial centre of Russian Pacific coast; terminus of Trans-Siberian Rly. Pop. 102,000.

Vlissingen. See FLUSHING.

Vltava (*vul′ta-va*) (German *Moldau*), riv., Czechoslovakia; rises in Bohemian Forest; tributary of R. Elbe. Length, 270 m.

Vode′na, tn., Greece, 40 m. E.S.E. of Monastir; see of Greek archbishop; anc. capital of Macedonia; rice, tobacco, cotton, leather. Pop. *c.* 25,000.

Voghera (*vō-gā′ra*), tn., Lombardy, Italy, 16 m. S.S.W. of Pavia; manufactures silk. Pop. 21,000.

Voiron (*vwa-ron′*), tn., Isère, S.E. France, 14 m. N.W. of Grenoble; cloth, silk, and paper. Pop. 9,000.

Voivodina, prov., N.E. Yugoslavia, N. of Danube and Drave rivs.; drained by R. Tisa; agriculture. Chief tn., Gombor. Area, 7,607 sq. m.; pop. 1,380,000.

Vol'ga, riv., Russia, longest in Europe (*c.* 2,400 m.); rises in Valdai Hills; flows E. to Kazan, then turns S., S.W., and S.E. to enter Caspian Sea by innumerable mouths near Astrakhan; chief tribs., Unzha, Sura, Oka, Sheksna, Kama. Navigation begins near source; one of chief commercial rivers of world; connected by canals with Baltic, Black, and White Seas, also with rivers Dnieper, Dniester, Don, etc. Sturgeon, pike, and other fisheries; ice-bound in winter.

Vo'lo, seapt., E. Greece, at head of Gulf of Volo, 33 m. S.E. of Larissa; archiepiscopal see. Pop. 41,000.

Volog'da. (1) Prov., Russia, separated on E. from Siberia by Ural Mts.; surface flat; forest-covered; drained by Rs. N. Dvina and Pechora; cereals cultivated; chief mineral products, salt and iron ore. Area, 44,145 sq. m.; pop. 1,053,000. (2) Cap. of above, on R. Vologda; rly. jn.; manufactures agricultural implements, beer, and leather goods; trade in flax, linseed. Pop. 57,000.

Volsk, tn., Russia, on R. Volga, 65 m. N.E. of Saratov; ironworks, tanneries, and flour mills. Pop. 36,000.

Volta, riv., W. Africa, between Rs. Comoë and Niger; flows generally S.E. and S. through Gold Coast to Gulf of Guinea, near Adda. Length, 900 m.

Volter'ra, tn., Italy, 32 m. S.E. of Pisa; manufactures alabaster goods; museum with Etruscan collection. Pop. 17,000.

Vol'tri, tn., Italy, on Gulf of Genoa, 9 m. N.W. of Genoa; paper, cotton, and woollen goods, iron; shipuilding. Pop. 16,000.

Vorarl'berg, mountainous prov., Austria, bordering Lake of Constance; cattle and goats raised; manufactures textiles. Cap. Bregenz. Area, 1,005 sq. m.; pop. 140,000.

Voronezh (*vor-on-yezh'*). (1) Prov., S. Russia; hilly; drained by R. Don; fertile, producing grain, sugar-beets; horses and cattle reared; leather and flour manufactured. Area, 26,147 sq. m.; pop. 3,300,000. (2) Cap. of above, on R. Voronezh; centre for agricultural trade; flour-mills, brick-making, and breweries. Pop. 98,000.

Vosges (*vōzh*). (1) Mts., E. France, lying to W. of R. Rhine; highest point, Ballon de Guebviller, *c.* 4,670 ft.; drained to N. by Rs. Moselle and Saar; W. slopes thickly wooded, E. slopes vine-clad; excellent pasturage; noted for cattle. (2) Dep., E. France; traversed in E. by Vosges Mts. and in W. by spurs of the Langres plateau; forests; numerous mineral springs; coal, stone quarries; textile industries. Cap. Épinal. Area, 2,303 sq. m.; pop. 382,000.

Vo'tiak, Autonomous Area, Russia; between province of Viatka on W. and Ural Area on E.; includes part of foothills of Ural Mts.; largely forested; agriculture chief occupation; rye, oats, flax, and potatoes; minerals include iron, slate, and copper. Chief tn., Izhevok. Area, 12,142 sq. m.; pop. 756,000.

Votkinsk', tn., Ural Area, Russia, 110 m. S. of Perm; manufactures agricultural machinery. Pop. 19,000.

Voznesensk', tn., riv. port, Ukraine, U.S.S.R., 80 m. N.N.E. of Odessa, on R. Bug; cathedral; distilleries, breweries. Pop. 21,000.

Vrat'tsa, tn., Bulgaria, 38 m. N.N.E. of Sofia; seat of archbishop; tanneries, wine, gold and silver filigree. Pop. 15,000.

Vrede (*vrā'da*), tn., N. Orange Free State, S. Africa, 34 m. S. of Standerton; centre of one of best stock-breeding districts in prov. Pop. (white) 2,000.

Vriesland. See FRIESLAND.

Vrsac (*ver-shats'*), tn., Voivodina, Yugoslavia, 40 m. N.E. of Belgrade; wine and brandy; flour milling and distilling. Pop. 27,000.

Vry'burg, cap., Brit. Bechuanaland, Cape Prov., S. Africa, on Cape-to-Cairo Rly., 126 m. N. of Kimberley; alt. 3,890 ft.; stock rearing. Pop. 2,500.

Vryheid (*vrī'hīt*), tn., Natal, S. Africa, 80 m. N.E. of Ladysmith; in rich mineral dist. (coal, iron, copper, gold, silver, lead). Pop. 4,000.

Vyatka. See VIATKA.

Vyaz'ma, tn., W. Russia, 90 m. E.N.E. of Smolensk; cathedral (1596), citadel; leather goods, tobacco. Pop. 17,000.

Vyernyi, or VERNI. See ALMA ATA.

Vyrnwy (*virn'wi*), riv., Wales, rises in N.W. Montgomeryshire, and joins R. Severn on Shropshire border; upper valley has been converted into a lake by a dam, and forms head reservoir for Liverpool water supply.

Vyshniy-Volochok (*vish'nē-vō-lō-chok'*), tn., Russia, 68 m. N.W. of Tver; saw-milling, textiles, glass, and beer. Pop. *c.* 20,000.

W

Waco (*wā'ko*), city, Texas, U.S.A., 95 m. N.E. of Austin; manufactures of flour, woollens, saddlery, harness; centre of cotton-growing dist. Pop. 53,000.

Wadai (*wā'dī*), dist., Chad Colony, French Equatorial Africa; W. of Lake Chad; surface generally desert; several oases and dense forests; produces rice, wheat; cattle, camels, sheep, and horses raised; cattle, horses, and coffee exported. Cap. Abeshr. Area, *c.* 170,000 sq. m.; pop. *c.* 1,000,000.

Wade'bridge, port, Cornwall, England, on R. Camel, 7 m. N.W. of Bodmin; exports granite, china clay, agricultural produce. Pop. 2,500.

Wad'hurst, par. and vil., Sussex, England, 7 m. S.E. of Tunbridge Wells; sandstone quarries. Pop. (par.) 3,850.

Wadh'wan, tn., Bombay, India, on Kathiawar Peninsula; manufactures soap and saddlery; centre of cotton and grain trade. Pop. 16,000.

Wa'di Hal'fa, tn., Anglo-Egyptian Sudan, Africa, on R. Nile, below second cataract; rly. connection with Khartoum. Pop. 3,000.

Wad Med'ani, tn., Anglo-Egyptian Sudan, Africa, on R. Blue Nile; depot for grain; oil and soap works. Pop. 19,000.

Wagga-Wagga (*wag'a*), tn., New South Wales, Australia, on R. Murrumbidgee; pastoral and gold-mining region; wine, tobacco. Pop. 8,800.

Waikato (*wī-kā'to*), riv., North I., New Zealand; rises on Mt. Ruapehu, traverses Lake Taupo, flows N.W. into Pacific; navigable for 75 m.; length, 175 m.

Wain'fleet, mkt. tn., Lincolnshire, England, 14 m. N.E. of Boston, on R. Steeping; grammar school; formerly a seaport of importance; harbour silted up. Pop. 1,400.

Wakefield. (1) Co. bor., W. Riding, Yorks, England, on R. Calder, 9 m. S. of Leeds; manufactures agricultural machinery and boilers, worsted yarn, flour, soap, chemicals, coco matting; trade in grain; coal mining in neighbourhood; cathedral; grammar school. Pop. 59,100. (2) Tn., Massachusetts, U.S.A., 10 m. N. of Boston; manufactures of rattan, boots and shoes, stoves. Pop. 13,000.

Walachia (*wal-āk'-e-a*), part of Romania between Transylvanian Mts. and R. Danube; cereals and fruits. Area, 20,267 sq. m.; pop. 3,486,000.

Walcheren (*val'ker-en*), isl., Zeeland, Holland, between mouths of Rs. E. and W. Schelde, protected against sea by dunes and dykes; agriculture; scene of disastrous expedition under Chatham (1809). Chief tns., Flushing and Middelburg (cap.). Area, 81 sq. m.

Waldeck (*val'dek*), former prov., Germany, between Westphalia and Hesse-Nassau; now part of Hesse-Nassau, Prussia; hilly; drained by Rs. Eder and Diemel, tribs. of R. Weser; poor soil; oats, rye, potatoes. Cap. Arolsen. Area, 433 sq. m.; pop. 72,000.

Waldenburg (*val'den-boorg*), town, Silesia, Prussia, 40 m. S.W. of Breslau; centre of a coal-mining district; manufactures porcelain, stone ware, fire bricks; textiles in neighbourhood. Pop. 44,000.

Wales (*wālz*), principality of Great Britain; bounded N. by Irish Sea, W. by St. George's Channel, S. by Bristol Channel, E. by Monmouthshire, Herefordshire, Shropshire, and Cheshire. In N.W., Anglesey forms an island cut off from mainland by Menai Strait. Coast-line broken in N. by opening of R. Dee and mouths of Rs. Clwyd and Conway, on W. by Carnarvon and Cardigan Bays, on S.W. by St. Bride's Bay and Milford Haven, and on S. by Carmarthen and Swansea Bays. Drainage in N. is by upper waters of Rs. Severn and Dee, and by Clwyd, Conway, and other streams; in W. by Rs. Dovey, Teifi; and in S. by upper waters of Wye and Usk, and by Taff, Tawe, and Towy. Anglesey is low and undulating, and there is a stretch of low ground in S.W. peninsula; but elsewhere the country is uniformly hilly, rising to many peaks of from 2,000 to over 3,000 ft., and reaching extreme height of 3,560 ft. in Snowdon, the highest peak in Great Britain outside of Scotland. Climate resembles that of England, except that rainfall is greater. Chief crops, hay, oats, barley, turnips, potatoes; horses, cattle, and sheep reared. Great wealth lies in minerals and connected industries, especially in coal; S. Wales coalfield is one of most important in Britain; smaller coalfield in N. Large production of slate in N.; extensive smelting of iron, copper, and tin in S.; flannel manufactured at Newtown and Montgomery. Largest tns. are Cardiff, Swansea, Rhondda, and Merthyr-Tydfil. Area, 7,466 sq. m.; pop. 2,158,000.

Walfish Bay. See WALVIS BAY.

Walk'erburn, vil., Peeblesshire, Scotland, on R. Tweed; manufactures woollen goods. Pop. 1,200.

Walk'erville, city, Ontario, Canada, on Detroit R.; suburb of Windsor. Pop. 11,000.

Wallachia. See WALACHIA.

Wallaroo', port, S. Australia; copper-mining centre. Pop. 3,000.

Wall'asey, co. bor., Cheshire, England; suburb of Birkenhead; residential dist. Pop. 97,500.

Wall'a Wall'a, tn., S.E. Washington, U.S.A., on Oregon boundary; centre of wheat and fruit region; poultry rearing; agricultural machinery; flour, leather. Pop. 16,000.

Wall'ingford. (1) Mkt. tn., Berks, England, on R. Thames; has ruined Norman castle; trade in agricultural produce. Pop. 2,800. (2) Tn., Connecticut, U.S.A., 11 m. N.E. of New Haven; manufactures silver and plated goods, rubber goods, firearms. Pop. 10,000.

Wall'ington, vil., Surrey, England, in urb. dist. of BEDDINGTON AND WALLINGTON.

Walls'end, tn., Northumberland, England, on R. Tyne, at E. end of Hadrian's Wall; collieries; shipbuilding, engineering, lead and copper smelting; bricks, tiles, cement. Pop. 44,600.

Wal'mer, wat.-pl., Kent, England, adjoining Deal; castle is official residence of Warden of Cinque Ports. Pop. 5,300.

Wal'sall, co. bor., S. Staffs, England, in Black Country; manufactures iron and brass ware, saddlery, gloves, motor fittings; in neighbourhood of coal, lime, and iron mines. Pop. 103,100.

Wal'sham, NORTH, urb. dist. and mkt. tn., Norfolk, England, 16 m. N. of Norwich; agricultural implements; old market cross. Pop. 4,000.

Wal'soken, urb. dist., Norfolk, England, suburb of Wisbech; agricultural produce. Pop. 4,100.

Wal'tham, city, Massachusetts, U.S.A., on Charles R., 10 m. W. of Boston; watchmaking, textiles, motors, bicycles. Pop. 39,000.

Wal'tham Abbey, or WALTHAM HOLY CROSS, tn., Essex, England, on R. Lea, 12 m. N. of London; brewing and market gardening; manufactures of explosives. Pop. 7,100.

Wal'thamstow, industrial suburb of London, in Essex, England, 7 m. N.E. of St. Paul's, near Epping Forest; breweries. Pop. 133,000.

Wal'ton-le-Dale, urb. dist., Lancs, England, on R. Ribble, 2 m. S.E. of Preston; cotton mills; market gardening. Pop. 12,700.

Wal'ton-on-Thames, mkt. tn., Surrey, England; angling and tourist resort. Pop. 18,000.

Wal'ton-on-the-Hill, par., Lancs, England; suburban dist. of Liverpool. Pop. 83,000.

Wal'ton-on-the-Naze, wat.-pl., Essex, England; iron foundries and brick works. Pop. 3,100.

Wal'vis Bay, formerly WALFISH, Brit. bay and port, S.W. Africa, on Atlantic Ocean; only good harbour between Angola and R. Orange; fishing and whaling; exports chilled meat. Pop. 1,900.

Wandsbeck (*vands'bek*), tn., Holstein, Prussia; suburb of Hamburg; beer, leather, tobacco. Pop. 40,000.

Wands'worth, suburb of London, England, on R. Thames, 5½ m. S.W. of St. Paul's; oil mills, dyeworks, paper works, calico printing, brewing. Pop. 353,100.

Wanganui (*wan-ga-noo'ē*), port, S.W. coast, North I., New Zealand, on R. Wanganui; exports wool, grain, meat, dairy produce; freezing works. Pop. 28,000.

Wanlockhead', vil., N. Dumfriesshire, Scotland, on Wanlock Water; lead mining. Pop. 600.

Wan'stead, urb. dist. and par., Essex, England, N.W. suburb of London. Pop. 19,200.

Wan'tage, urb. dist., mkt. tn., and par., Berks, England, 9 m. S.W. of Abingdon; ironworks; trade in agricultural produce; birthplace of Alfred the Great. Pop. 3,400.

Wap'ping, dist., E. London, England, on N. bank of R. Thames; contains London Dock. Pop. 3,200.

Warasdin. See VARAZDIN.

Ward'le, urb. dist., S.E. Lancs, England, adjoining Rochdale; cotton and woollen manufactures. Pop. 4,800.

Ware (*wār*), urb. dist., Herts, England, on R. Lea, 2 m. N.E. of Hertford; trade in malt; brickfields. Pop. 6,200.

Ware'ham, munic. bor. and mkt. tn., Dorsetshire, England, near Poole Harbour; old earth wall nearly surrounds the town; lime, clay, cement; cordite factory near by. Pop. 2,100.

War'minster, urb. dist. and mkt. tn., Wilts, England, 20 m. N.W. of Salisbury; silk, and agricultural implements. Pop. 5,200.

Warnsdorf (*varnz'dorf*), frontier tn., N.E. Bohemia, Czechoslovakia; silk and cotton. Pop. 20,000.

War'gla, tn., Algerian Sahara, Africa, 350 m. S. of Algiers; on oasis; surrounded by a wall; dates. Pop. 3,000.

War'ren. (1) City, Ohio, U.S.A., on R. Mahoning, 50 m. S.E. of Cleveland; manufactures iron and steel, electrical apparatus; coal and iron mining. Pop. 41,000. (2) Tn., Pennsylvania, U.S.A., on R. Alleghany, 70 m. S.S.E. of Buffalo; natural gas and oil region; oil refineries; engines, boilers, pianos. Pop. 14,000.

War'renpoint, port, co. Down, N. Ireland, on Carlingford Lough; wat.-pl. Pop. 2,200.

War'rington, co. bor., Lancs, England, on R. Mersey; manufactures leather, cotton, ironware, glass, chemicals; rly. jn. Pop. 79,300.

Warrnambool', port, Victoria, Australia, on Warrnambool Bay; marketing centre for agricultural and dairy products. Pop. 8,000.

War'saw. (1) Co., Poland; surface low and flat; drained by R. Vistula; stretches of forest; rye, oats, barley, potatoes are cultivated. Area, 11,316 sq. m.; pop. 2,115,000. (2) Cap., Poland, on R. Vistula; railway centre; iron and steel works; manufactures boots and shoes, hosiery, wooden wares, sugar, tobacco; agricultural market; wool and hop fairs; cathedral, univ. Pop. 1,000,000.

War'sop, tn., Notts, England, 5 m. N.E. of Mansfield; limestone quarries and gravel pits. Pop. 10,700.

Warta (*var'ta*), or WARTHE, riv., Poland and Prussia; rises in Carpathian Mts. and flows generally N.W. with many windings to join R. Oder at Küstrin; length, 445 m.

Warwick (*wor'ik*). (1) Co. tn., Warwickshire, England, on R. Avon; manufactures agricultural implements, gelatine, and bricks; famous castle. Pop. 13,500. (2) Tn., Rhode I., U.S.A., on Narragansett Bay; manufactures cotton, silk, and woollen goods. Pop. 18,000.

War'wickshire, W. midland co. of England; surrounded by cos. of Leicester, Northants, Oxford, Glos, Worcester, and Staffs. Surface flat or slightly rolling, with low hills in S.; drained by Rs. Avon, Tame, and Leam; has canal communication with Rs. Severn, Mersey, Trent, Thames; in N. was Forest of Arden. Fireclay, limestone, ironstone; orchards; agriculture; cattle and sheep raised; important industrial dist. in N., with coalfield and manufactures of heavy iron goods, hardware, firearms, jewellery, ribbons, watches, bicycles, motor-cars. Cap. Warwick; largest tns., Birmingham and Coventry. Area, 946 sq. m.; pop. 1,534,800.

Wash, THE, arm of North Sea, between Norfolk and Lincoln, England; numerous sandbanks; very shallow. Length, 22 m.; breadth, 15 m.

Wash'ington. (1) Pacific State, U.S.A., bounded N. by Canada, E. by Idaho, S. by Oregon, W. by Pacific Ocean. Surface crossed from N. to S. by Cascade Mts., to E. of which is high plateau, while in W. country is mountainous and heavily wooded, with fertile prairies and valleys; watered by R. Columbia and tribs. The climate temperate in W., extreme in E. Chief crops: wheat, barley, oats; horses, cattle, and sheep raised; dairy farming; fruit largely grown; lumbering important. Excellent salmon, oyster, and other fisheries. Minerals include coal, gold, copper, lead, granite, marble. Meat packing, flour milling, and fish canning important. Chief tns., Olympia (cap.), Seattle, Spokane, Tacoma. Area, 69,127 sq. m.; pop. 1,357,000. (2) Cap. of U.S.A., in District of Columbia, with which it is co-extensive, on R. Potomac, on W. border of Maryland; many splendid public buildings. Almost in the centre stands the Capitol, where Congress meets, and the Supreme Court sits. Other important buildings are White House, official residence of president of the U.S.A.; Library of Congress, and National Observatory, George Washington Univ., Howard Univ. for Negroes, Catholic Univ. White marble obelisk to memory of George Washington. Fine parks and botanic gardens. Engraving and plate printing. Pop. 487,000. (3) City, Pennsylvania, U.S.A., 23 m. S.W. of Pittsburgh; coal and oil region; manufactures iron, tinplate, glass, carriages, flour. Pop. 21,500. (4) Urb. dist., Durham, England, 5 m. W. of Sunderland; coal mining; chemical manufactures. Pop. 17,000.

Watch'et, port, Somerset, England, on Bristol Channel; ironfounding and paper making. Pop. 1,900.

Wa'terbury, city, Connecticut, U.S.A., on R. Naugatuck, 18 m. N.W. of New Haven; manufactures brass, watches, rolling mill and foundry products, photographic materials, electrical supplies, chemicals. Pop. 101,000.

Wa'terford. (1) Maritime co., Munster, I.F.S. bounded by Cork, Tipperary, Kilkenny; surface mountainous except in E., which is flat and in parts marshy; chief rivs., Blackwater and Suir; cattle breeding and dairying; large amounts of bacon and butter exported; minerals include copper and marble; valuable coast and river fisheries. Area, 710 sq. m.; pop. 79,000. (2) Co. tn. of above, on R. Suir; two cathedrals; exports agricultural produce; breweries, fisheries. Pop. 26,600.

Waterloo'. (1) Vil., Brabant, Belgium, 11 m. S. of Brussels; Wellington defeated Napoleon here in 1815. (2) City, Iowa, U.S.A., on R. Cedar; agricultural region; canning and packing industries; tractors, motor-cars, gas engines, agricultural and dairying machinery. Pop. 46,000. (3) Tn., Ontario, Canada, 35 m. N.W. of Hamilton; fruit growing. Pop. 7,500.

Waterloo′-with-Sea′forth, wat.-pl., Lancs, England, 4 m. N.W. of Liverpool; residential. Pop. 31,200.

Wa′terside, vil., Ayrshire, Scotland, on R. Doon; ironworks. Pop. 1,400.

Wa′tertown. (1) City, New York, U.S.A., 65 m. N.E. of Syracuse, on Black R.; carriage and wagon works; manufactures steam engines, paper, silk, clothing, farm implements, air brakes, thermometers. Pop. 32,000. (2) Tn., Massachusetts, U.S.A., on R. Charles, 6 m. W. of Boston; govt. arsenal; rubber and woollen goods, paper, motor-cars. Pop. 21,000. (3) Tn., S. Dakota, U.S.A., on R. Big Sioux; machinery; flour mills; meat-packing. Pop. 10,000.

Wa′terville, city, Maine, U.S.A., on R. Kennebec, 20 m. N.E. of Augusta; manufactures cottons, woollens, and has railway workshops. Pop. 13,000.

Watervliet (*-vlēt*), city, New York, U.S.A., on R. Hudson, 5 m. N.E. of Albany; U.S. arsenal; bells, ironware, woollens, asbestos products. Pop. 16,000.

Wat′ford, tn., S. Herts, England, on R. Colne; brewing and malting industries, and corn mills. Pop. 56,800.

Wath-upon-Dearne (*dŭrn*), urb. dist., Yorks, England, 8 m. S.E. of Barnsley; coal mines, ironworks, quarries; oil, soap, and bottle works. Pop. 13,700.

Wat′ling Island, isl., Bahamas, W. Indies; supposed landing-place of Columbus (1492). Pop. 700.

Wattrelos (*vatr-lō′*), tn., Nord, France, near Belgian frontier; textiles, incense boxes, chicory, and sabots. Pop. 33,000.

Wauke′gan, city, Illinois, U.S.A., on Lake Michigan; mineral springs; manufactures iron goods, brass wire, leather, sugar. Pop. 19,000.

Wau′sau, city, Wisconsin, U.S.A., on R. Wisconsin, 140 m. N. of Madison; silver fox farms; centre of dairying industry. Pop. 19,000.

Wavre (*wävr*), tn., Brabant, Belgium, 16 m. S.E. of Brussels; tanning, brewing; manufactures lace and paper. Pop. 8,600.

Way′cross, city, Georgia, U.S.A., 95 m. S.W. of Savannah; railway shops; manufactures lumber, naval stores, machinery; vegetable and fruit canneries. Pop. 18,000.

Wazirabad (*wa-zēr-a-bad′*), tn., Punjab, India, near r. bk. of R. Chenab; manufactures steel and iron; trade in timber, grain, sugar. Pop. 19,000.

Waziristan (*wa-zēr-ē-stan′*), dist., N.W. Frontier Province, India, in Sulaiman Mts.; mountainous, with numerous streams; some parts well wooded, but most of country barren. Area, *c.* 5,000 sq. m.; pop. uncertain.

Waz′zan, sacred tn., Morocco, Africa, 60 m. N.W. of Fez; coarse woollen cloth produced. Pop. 13,000.

Weald (*wēld*), THE, dist. between N. and S. Downs, England; forms part of Sussex, Surrey, and Kent; was formerly covered by Forest of Anderida; still wooded in places. Till 19th cent. noted for iron industry based on local ores.

Weald′stone, urb. dist., Middlesex, England, 1½ m. N. of Harrow; part of Greater London. Pop. 27,000.

Wear (*wēr*), riv., Durham, England, rises in Pennine Chain and flows into North Sea at Sunderland; length, 60 m.

Web′ster, town, Massachusetts, U.S.A., 16 m. S.W. of Worcester; manufactures cottons, woollens, and shoes. Pop. 13,000.

Wed′more, par. and vil., Somerset, England, 8 m. W. of Wells; makes Cheddar cheese. Treaty signed here (878) between Alfred the Great and the Danes. Pop. (par.) 2,400.

Wednesbury (*wenz′ber-i*), tn., Staffs, England, 7 m. N.W. of Birmingham; iron and coal mining centre; manufactures iron and steel ware, and pottery. Pop. 31,500.

Wednesfield (*wens′fēld*), urb. dist., Staffs, England; suburb of Wolverhampton; locks and keys; coal mining. Pop. 9,300.

Wee'don Beck, parish and vil., Northants, England, 8 m. w. of Northampton; has military barracks, powder magazines, and stores. Pop. 2,000.

Wei-hai-Wei (*wā-hī-wā'*), terr., N.E. coast of Shantung peninsula, China, extends 10 m. along Bay of Wei-hai-Wei, and includes several islands in bay; leased by Britain in 1898; restored to China in 1930; contains city of Wei-hai-Wei; has naval and coaling station; cereals, vegetables, and fruit are grown; exports groundnuts, oil, fish, eggs, sugar; excellent climate makes it a summer resort. Area, 285 sq. m.; pop. 154,000.

Weimar (*vī'mar*), cap. Thuringia, Germany, on R. Ilm; contains 15th cent. church, Liszt Museum, and Goethe-Schiller monument; book trade; manufactures cloth and leather. Pop. 46,000.

Weinheim (*vīn'hīm*), tn., Baden, Germany, 10 m. N.E. of Mannheim; manufactures leather, soap, machinery, wine. Pop. 16,000.

Weissenfels (*vī'sen-fels*), tn., Saxony, Prussia, on R. Saale, 20 m. s. of Halle; manufactures machinery, ironware, boots, paper. Pop. 37,000.

Well'and, city, Ontario, Canada, on Welland Canal, 40 m. S.E. of Hamilton. Pop. 10,000.

Well'and Canal, artificial waterway between lakes Erie and Ontario, Canada; cut (1824–29) to avoid Niagara Falls; reconstructed (1913–30); difference of level of lakes (326 ft.) overcome by 7 locks; length (Port Colborne to Port Weller), 25 m.; depth, 25–30 ft.; bottom width, 200 ft.; available for largest lake steamers.

Well'esley Province, British colony, Straits Settlements, w. coast of Malay Peninsula, opposite Penang I., to which it belongs administratively; rice, pepper, spices, tapioca, sugar, tobacco. Area, 270 sq. m.; pop. 116,000.

Well'ingborough, urban dist. and mkt. tn., Northants, England, 10 m. N.E. of Northampton; boots and shoes; iron smelting and brewing. Pop. 21,200.

Well'ington. (1) Cap. of New Zealand, in North I., on Cook Strait; seapt. with excellent harbour; seat of Victoria Univ. College; foundries, freezing works, soap and candle works, boot factories; important trade. Pop. 134,000. (2) Urb. dist. and mkt. tn., Shropshire, England, 10 m. E. of Shrewsbury; manufactures agricultural implements, wood ware, nails, brass and iron articles. Pop. 8,200. (3) Urb. dist. and mkt. tn., Somersetshire, England, 6 m. s.w. of Taunton; from it the Duke of Wellington took his title; druggets, serges, brick and tile works. Pop. 7,100. (4) College near Sandhurst (public school).

Wells. (1) Munic. bor. and mkt. tn., Somersetshire, England, at base of Mendip Hills; fine cathedral; theological coll. Bath and Wells form one bishopric. Named from holy springs where King Ina built a monastery (704). Pop. 4,800. (2) Port, N. Norfolk, England; brewing, rope making; machinery; oyster fisheries. Pop. 2,500.

Welsh'pool, munic. bor. and mkt. tn., Montgomeryshire, Wales, on R. Severn, 7 m. N. of Montgomery; trade in flannel, tweeds, woollen shawls, agricultural produce. Pop. 5,600.

Welwyn Garden City (*wel'in*), tn., Herts, England, 6 m. w. of Hertford; founded 1920 as first of Satellite Towns of London (21 m. distant). Pop. 8,600.

Wem, urb. dist. and mkt. tn., Shropshire, England, 10 m. N. of Shrewsbury; flour milling, tanning. Pop. 2,200.

Wem'bley, urb. dist., Middlesex, England, 10 m. from St. Paul's Cathedral; was site of British Empire Exhibition (1924–25). Pop. 48,500.

Wemyss (*wēms*), par., Fife, Scotland, on Firth of Forth; includes villages of Buckhaven, Methil, Innerleven, W. and E. Wemyss; coal mining. Pop. 25,000.

Wenchow', treaty port, Chekiang, China, on Wenchow Bay; formerly centre of Japanese trade with China; exports tea, timber. Pop. 90,000.

Wend'over, mkt. tn., Bucks, England, at foot of Chiltern Hills, 5 m. S.E. of Aylesbury. Halton, about 1½ m. distant, is a headquarters station of Royal Air Force. Pop. 2,400.

Wend'ron, vil. and par., Cornwall, England, 8 m. W. by S. of Falmouth; tin mines. Pop. (par.) 3,400.

Wener, LAKE. See VENER.

Wen'lock, munic. bor., Shropshire, England, on R. Severn; coal mines and ironworks. Pop. 14,200.

Werdau (*ver'dou*), tn., Saxony, Germany, 30 m. S. of Leipzig; cotton and wool spinning; machinery, paper, chemicals. Pop. 21,000.

Werden (*ver'den*), tn., Rhine Prov., Prussia, on R. Ruhr, 6 m. S. of Essen; woollen goods, paper, leather; coal mines. Pop. 13,000.

Wermelskirchen (*ver'mels-kĕrch-en*), tn., Rhine Prov., Prussia, 20 m. E.S.E. of Düsseldorf; textile industries; manufactures metallic wares and cigars. Pop. 16,000.

Wernigerode (*ver'ne-ga-ro'da*), tn., Saxony, Prussia, at N. foot of Harz Mts., 43 m. S.W. of Magdeburg; manufactures machinery, brandy, and cigars. Pop. 20,000.

Wesel (*vā'zel*), tn., Rhineland, Prussia, at junction of Rs. Lippe and Rhine; metal goods, cement, pottery, soap; annual fair. Pop. 24,000.

Weser (*vā'zer*), riv., Germany; rises as Rs. Werra and Fulda, which join at Münden; flows N. to Bremen and enters North Sea; navigable for 270 m. to Münden. Length, 440 m.

Wesermünde (*vā-zer-mün'da*), formerly LEHE, tn., Hanover, Prussia, at mouth of R. Weser; adjoins Bremerhaven; market gardening, brick making, and brewing. Pop. 72,000.

West Af'rica, general name for African coast territories belonging to various European countries, comprising: *British*: Nigeria, Gambia, Gold Coast, Sierra Leone. *French*: Senegal, French Guinea, Ivory Coast, Dahomey, French Sudan, Upper Volta, Mauritania, Niger, Dakar. *Portuguese*: Cape Verde Island, Portuguese Guinea, Angola. *Spanish*: Fernando Po, Rio de Oro, Spanish Guinea. Mandated regions of Togoland and Cameroons divided between Britain and France. See separate articles.

West Al'lis, tn., Wisconsin, U.S.A., 6 m. W. of Milwaukee; manufactures engines, steam pumps, tanks, machine tools, and steel castings. Pop. 35,000.

West Bridg'ford, urb. dist., Notts, England, 2 m. S.S.E. of Nottingham; here Grantham Canal joins R. Trent. Pop. 17,800.

West Bromwich (*brom'ich*), munic. and co. bor., Staffs, England, 6 m. N.W. of Birmingham; hardware manufacture; forges, iron and brass foundries; coal mines. Pop. 81,300.

West'bury, urb. dist., Wilts, England, 4 m. S. by E. of Trowbridge; ironworks; woollens; important rly. jn. Pop. 4,000.

West Calder. See CALDER.

West Ches'ter, residential centre, Pennsylvania, U.S.A., 23 m. W. of Philadelphia; market gardening, dairy farming; agricultural implements. Pop. 12,000.

West'erham, par. and mkt. tn., Kent, England, 21¼ m. S.E. of London, on N. Downs; birthplace of General Wolfe. Pop. (par.) 3,165.

West'ern Austra'lia, most W. state, Australia; coast deeply indented in N.W.; surface generally tableland, with mountain ranges on W. coast, reaching 4,024 ft. in Mt. Bruce; drained by Rs. Ord, Fitzroy, De Grey, Fortescue, Ashburton, Gascoyne, Murchison, Greenough, Swan, and other streams; climate dry, and very hot in N., Mediterranean in S.W.; large stretches of desert, but about three-fourths of surface suitable for grazing. Agriculture carried on in fertile parts, the chief crops being wheat, oats, and barley; fruit cultivated; horses, cattle, sheep, and pigs reared; minerals include gold (chief source of wealth), coal, lead, silver, copper, tin. Large forests, with much valuable timber, karri and jarrah in S.W. being two of most valuable hard woods known. Chief exports, wheat, flour, wool, gold, timber, hides, pearls, and fresh fruit. Cap. Perth. Area, 975,920 sq. m.; pop. 333,000.

Western Isles. See HEBRIDES.

West'field, town, Massachusetts, U.S.A., 8 m. W. of Springfield; machinery, bicycles, radiators, and pasteboard boxes. Pop. 19,000.

West'gate-on-Sea, wat.-pl., Kent, England, 2 m. S.W. of Margate. Pop. 5,000.

West Ham, munic. bor., Essex, England, on R. Thames, part of Greater London; manufactures iron, rubber; shipbuilding yards, sugar refineries, soap and jute works; contains Victoria Docks and part of Royal Albert Docks. Pop. 294,100.

West Hartlepool. See HARTLEPOOL.

West Hobo'ken, tn., New Jersey, U.S.A., adjoining Hoboken; manufactures artificial flowers, silk, and embroidered goods; flowers extensively grown. Pop. 40,000.

West'houghton, urb. dist., Lancs, England, 5 m. E.N.E. of Wigan; silk and cotton factories; collieries. Pop. 16,000.

West In'dies, islands to N. and E. of the Caribbean Sea; extend from Yucatan and Florida to Gulf of Paria, and along N. coast of Venezuela; comprise the Bahamas; the four large islands of Cuba, Jamaica, Haiti, and Porto Rico, known as the Greater Antilles; Leeward and Windward Islands, known as Lesser Antilles; and Trinidad, off Venezuelan coast. Of these, Cuba and Haiti are independent; Bahamas, Barbados, Jamaica, most of Leeward and Windward Islands, and Trinidad belong to Great Britain; Porto Rico and part of Virgin group to U.S.A.; Martinique and Guadeloupe to France, and Curaçao and dependencies to Holland. Many of islands mountainous in character; others of coral formation. Climate generally tropical and soil fertile. Islands produce sugar, bananas and other fruits, cotton, coffee, cocoa, ginger, sponges, arrowroot, tobacco; and asphalt from Trinidad. Area, 91,819 sq. m.; pop. 10,529,000. See separate articles.

West Kilbride', tn., Ayrshire, Scotland, 4 m. W. of Ardrossan; summer resort; hydropathic. Pop. 3,600.

West Kir'by, tn., Cheshire, England, included in urban dist. of Hoylake and W. Kirby; residential dist. and wat.-pl. Pop. 6,000.

West Lo'thian, formerly LINLITHGOWSHIRE, maritime co., S.E. Scotland; surface undulating; slopes from S. to Firth of Forth in N.; watered by Rs. Avon and Almond; chief industry, agriculture; cereals, dairy farming; coal, iron, oil shale, and fireclay are worked; paraffin oil and other shale products manufactured, also paper. Co. tn., Linlithgow. Area, 120 sq. m.; pop. 81,400.

West'meath, inland co., Leinster, I.F.S.; bounded by Cavan, Meath, Offaly, Roscommon, Longford; surface varied with hill, valley, and lake, interspersed with bog; drained chiefly by R. Shannon; Lough Ree is largest lake; occupations mainly agricultural, oats being chief crop; cattle rearing; limestone quarries. Co. tn., Mullingar. Area, 680 sq. m.; pop. 57,000.

West'minster, metropolitan bor., London; extending from banks of R. Thames to Hyde Park; includes within its bounds Hyde Park, St. James's Park, and Green Park, and contains Houses of Parliament, Westminster Hall, Westminster Abbey, Westminster Cathedral (R.C.), Cenotaph, Buckingham Palace, and St. James's Palace. In former times Westminster was separated from City of London by Temple Bar. Abbey is one of finest examples of Early English architecture; it is burial-place of eighteen sovereigns of England, and of the Unknown Warrior. Pop. 129,500.

West'morland, co., N. England; bounded N. and N.W. by Cumberland, W. and S. by Lancs, E. by Yorks and Durham. Surface generally hilly, with moorlands and deep valleys; highest points, Helvellyn and Bow Fell; drained by Rs. Eden, Kent,

Lune, Leven. Contains famous Lake Dist., with Ullswater and Windermere on the Cumberland and Lancs borders respectively, and Grasmere, Rydal Water, and others entirely within county. Lead, slate, graphite, granite produced. Chief crop is oats; largest part is pasture; sheep and cattle are reared. Co. tn., Appleby. Area, 789 sq. m.; pop. 65,400.

West New York, tn., New Jersey, U.S.A., on R. Hudson; connected by ferry with New York; large grain elevators; manufactures silk and rubber goods, pianos, cotton-seed oil. Pop. 37,000.

Weston-super-Mare, wat.-pl., Somerset, England, on Bristol Channel; Worlebury Camp, anc. British stronghold, is on hill above town. Pop. 28,600.

West Palm Beach, tn., Florida, U.S.A., on W. shore of Lake Worth, opposite Palm Beach; popular holiday resort. Pop. 27,000.

Westphalia (*west-fā'le-a*), prov., Prussia, bordering on Holland; surface largely hilly; Weser Mts. and Teutoburger Forest in E., Sauerland Mts. and Westerwald in S., whence they slope into N. German plain drained by Rs. Ems, Weser, Lippe, Ruhr, and other streams; large area forested; flax and hemp, potatoes, and cereals grown. Large deposits of coal and iron; one of greatest industrial states of Prussia; iron and steel and textile manufactures. Cap. Münster. Largest tns., Dortmund, Gelsenkirchen, and Bochum. Area, 7,803 sq. m.; pop. 4,811,000.

West Point, military post, New York, U.S.A., on Hudson R., 45 m. N. of New York; U.S. military academy; includes Constitution I., directly opposite.

West'port, urb. dist., port, and wat.-pl., co. Mayo, I.F.S., on Westport Bay; trade in agricultural produce and provisions. Pop. 3,500.

West'slade, urb. dist., Northumberland, England, 6 m. N. of Newcastle; coal mining. Pop. 7,700.

West Tar'ring, eccles. dist., Sussex, England, 1 m. N.W. of Worthing; remains of former palace of archbishops of Canterbury. Pop. 3,300.

West Virginia, S. Atlantic State of U.S.A.; bounded N. by Pennsylvania and Maryland, E. and S. by Virginia, W. by Kentucky and Ohio. Surface mountainous, esp. in E., where it is crossed by ranges of Alleghany Mts., reaching 4,860 ft. in Spruce Knob; drained by R. Ohio and tribs. Climate healthy and temperate. Agriculture specially important; chief crops, wheat, maize, oats, potatoes, tobacco; fruit cultivated; live-stock raised. Large area forested. Coal mining important; other minerals, petroleum, natural gas. Leading industries include steel, glass, leather, and pottery manufacture, lumbering; rly. workshops. Chief tns., Wheeling, Huntington, Charleston (cap.). Area, 24,170 sq. m.; pop. 1,724,000.

West'ward Ho, wat.-pl., Devonshire, England, on Bideford Bay; named from Charles Kingsley's novel; good bathing; golfing centre.

Weth'eral, par. and vil., Cumberland, England, on R. Eden; ruins of Benedictine abbey. Pop. (par.) 3,400.

Weth'erby, mkt. tn., W. Riding, Yorks, England, on R. Wharfe, 12 m. N.E. of Leeds. Pop. 2,100.

Wetter, Lake. See Vetter.

Wetzlar (*vets'lar*), tn., Rhineland, Prussia, 33 m. N.W. of Frankfurt-on-Main; cathedral; manufactures iron, gloves, optical instruments, chemicals. Pop. 13,000.

Wex'ford. (1) Maritime co., Leinster, I.F.S., bounded by Wicklow, Carlow, Kilkenny, Waterford; surface generally level; highest point, Mt. Leinster (2,610 ft.), in N.W.; watered by Rs. Slaney, Barrow, and other streams; excellent grazing and large export of agricultural produce, pigs, cattle, butter, poultry, eggs; valuable fisheries on coast. Area, 908 sq. m.; pop. 95,800. (2) Co. tn. of above, at mouth of R. Slaney; seapt.; shipbuilding; fisheries; trade in agricultural produce. Pop. 12,000.

Wey'bridge, urb. dist., Surrey,

England, at junction of Rs. Wey and Thames; Brooklands racing track here. Pop. 7,400.

Wey'mouth. (1) Or WEYMOUTH AND MELCOMBE REGIS, wat.-pl., Dorsetshire, England, on Weymouth Bay; boatbuilding; stone quarries; packet station for the Channel Islands. Pop. 22,000. (2) Tn., Massachusetts, U.S.A., 11 m. S.E. of Boston; manufactures boots and shoes. Pop. 15,000.

Wha'ley Bridge, vil., Cheshire, England, 10¼ m. S.E. of Stockport; collieries in vicinity. Pop. 6,000.

Wheel'ing, tn., W. Virginia, U.S.A., 60 m. s.w. of Pittsburgh; iron, steel, tin, glass, pottery, tobacco. Pop. 62,000.

Whick'ham, tn., Durham, England, 3½ m. s.w. of Gateshead; centre of coal-mining area; iron, steel, wine, and chemical works; roperies. Pop. 20,800.

Whip'pingham, par. and vil., N. Isle of Wight, England; church of St. Mildred contains memorials to Queen Victoria and members of the royal family. Pop. 2,000.

Whip'snade, hamlet, Beds, 3 m. s. of Dunstable. Famous zoological gardens.

Whit'burn. (1) Par. and vil., Durham, England, 3 m. N. of Sunderland; sea-bathing; coal and lime mines. Pop. (par.) 5,300. (2) Tn., West Lothian, Scotland, on R. Almond, 2½ m. s.w. of Bathgate: coal and iron. Pop. 2,400.

Whit'by. (1) Tn., N. Riding, Yorks, England, at mouth of R. Esk. Fashionable resort; ruins of Whitby Abbey. Caedmon died in monastery (680). Manufactures jet ornaments; fishing and boat-building. Pop. 11,400. (2) See ELLESMERE PORT AND WHITBY.

Whit'church. (1) Mkt. tn., Shropshire, England, 18 m. N. of Shrewsbury; malting and large cheese fairs. Pop. 6,000. (2) Par. and tn., Hants, England, on R. Test, 7 m. N.E. of Andover; has large trade in agricultural produce. Pop. (par.) 2,500. (3) Par. and vil., Glamorgan, Wales, on R. Taff, 1 m. N.W. of Llandaff; has large iron and tin works. Pop. (par.) 11,000.

White'chapel, 'East end' dist., London, included in metropolitan bor. of Stepney. Pop 54,000.

White'field, urb. dist., Lancs, England, 6 m. N.W. of Manchester; cotton manufactures. Pop. 9,100.

Whiteha'ven, port and mkt. tn., Cumberland, England; collieries, deposits of hæmatite iron ore; engineering works, shipbuilding yards, and breweries. Pop. 21,100.

White Plains, tn., New York, U.S.A., on R. Bronx, 22 m. N.E. of New York; residential town. Pop. 36,000.

White Russia, republic, U.S.S.R., N. of Ukraine and E. of Poland; level surface; swamps in s.; largely forested; drained by Rs. S. Dvina, Dnieper, and tribs.; flax, potatoes; live-stock. Cap. Minsk. Area, 48,940 sq. m.; pop. 4,984,000.

Whit'horn, royal burgh, Wigtownshire, Scotland, on Solway Firth; landing-place of St. Ninian, the first apostle of Scotland (4th cent.); ruins of cathedral. Pop. 1,000.

Whit'ing, tn., Indiana, U.S.A., on L. Michigan; oil refining. Pop. 10,000.

Whit'ley Bay, holiday resort, Northumberland, England, in urb. dist. of Whitley and Monkseaton, on coast, 2½ m. N.E. of N. Shields; lighthouse on St. Mary's I. Pop. (urb. dist.) 24,200.

Whit'stable, urb. dist. and wat.-pl., Kent, England, 6 m. N.W. of Canterbury; oyster-beds. Pop. 11,200.

Whit'tington, urb. dist., Derby, England, 10 m. s. of Sheffield; earthenware, bricks; coal mining and iron working. Pop. 8,000.

Whit'tlesey, or WHITTLESEA, urb. dist. and mkt. tn., Cambridgeshire, England, 5 m. E. of Peterborough; brick-making important. To N. is artificial cut forming new R. Nen. Pop. 8,300.

Whitwick (*whit'ik*), par. and tn., Leicestershir England, included in

Coalville; coal mining; hosiery. Pop. 4,500.

Whit'wood, urb. dist., W. Riding, Yorks, England, 4½ m. N.W. of Pontefract; coal mining. Pop. 6,200.

Whit'worth, urb. dist., Lancs, England, 3 m. N. of Rochdale; has cotton mills, coal mines, and slate quarries. Pop. 8,400.

Wich'ita, city, Kansas, U.S.A., on R. Arkansas; railway workshops, meat-packing establishments, flour mills; aeroplanes; centre for live-stock and grain. Pop. 111,000.

Wich'ita Falls, tn., N. Texas, U.S.A., on R. Wichita; great gas and oil fields in surrounding country; oil refineries. Pop. 44,000.

Wick, royal burgh and port, on North Sea, E. Caithness, Scotland; herring-fishing centre; manufactures fish guano, nets, boats. Pop. 7,500.

Wick'low. (1) Maritime co., Leinster, I.F.S.; lies along E. coast, between Dublin and Wexford; Wicklow Mts. cover practically whole surface (Lugnaquillia, 3,039 ft.); several lakes; watered by Rs. Liffey, Slaney, and other streams; agriculture limited; good sheep pasture; lead, copper, sulphur, granite occur; manufactures cordite; oyster-beds at Arklow in S.E. Area, 782 sq. m.; pop. 61,000. (2) Co. tn. of above, at mouth of R. Vartry; chemical works; good harbour; exports ores and grain. Pop. 3,200.

Wid'nes, tn., Lancs, England, on R. Mersey; manufactures soap and alkali; iron foundries; copper smelting, paint and locomotive works. Pop. 40,600.

Wieliczka (*vyā-litch'ka*), tn., Poland, Europe, 6 m. S.E. of Cracow; remarkable salt mines. Pop. 6,000.

Wiener-Neustadt (*vē-ner-noi'stat*), tn., Lower Austria, Austria, 26 m. S. of Vienna; manufactures locomotives, machinery, earthenware, leather, paper. Pop. 37,000.

Wiesbaden (*vēs'bä-den*), wat.-pl., S. Hesse-Nassau, Prussia; hot saline springs; surgical instruments, artificial manures, and chocolate. Pop. 152,000.

Wig'an, co. bor., Lancs, England, on R. Douglas, 18 m. N.W. of Manchester; collieries; cotton manufactures; forges; oil and chemical works. Pop. 85,400.

Wight (*wīt*), Isle of, isl., England, in English Channel, off coast of Hants, separated from mainland by Spithead and Solent; surface generally undulating; off extreme W. are high chalk pinnacles known as 'The Needles'; drained by R. Medina. Fine climate, favourite winter and summer resort and great yachting centre. Produces wheat; sheep raised; cement. Chief tns. are Newport, Ryde, Cowes. Area, 147 sq. m.; pop. 88,400.

Wig'ston Mag'na, urb. dist., Leicestershire, England, 5 m. S. of Leicester; railway workshops. Pop. 11,400.

Wig'ton, urb. dist. and mkt. tn., Cumberland, England, 12 m. S.W. of Carlisle; tanneries; jam making. Pop. 3,500.

Wig'town, co. tn., royal burgh, and port, Wigtownshire, Scotland, on Wigtown Bay. Pop. 1,300.

Wig'townshire, maritime co., S.W. Scotland; lies along Irish Sea and North Channel; coast broken by Loch Ryan and Luce Bay; surface generally low-lying and comparatively level, with low hills in N.; divided into the Rhinns, the peninsula formed by Loch Ryan and Luce Bay, the Machers, between Luce Bay and Wigtown Bay, and the Moors; drained by Rs. Luce, Bladenoch, Cree, and other streams; many lakes. Agriculture carried on; chief crops, oats and turnips; cattle and sheep raised; dairy farming is important, numerous creameries; no mineral wealth, and manufactures unimportant. Exports wool, cheese, live-stock. Chief tns., Wigtown, Stranraer. Area, 487 sq. m.; pop. 29,300.

Wilhelmshaven (*vil'helmz-hä-fen*), port, wat.-pl., Hanover, Prussia, on North Sea, in an enclave surrounded by Oldenburg; formerly station for German North Sea fleet; large dockyard; fine harbours; exports agricultural produce. Pop. 25,000.

Wilkes-Barre (*wilks'bar-i*), city, Pennsylvania, U.S.A., on N. branch of R. Susquehanna, 15 m. S.W. of Scranton; anthracite coal region; manufactures machinery, locomotives, iron, steel, and copper articles, silk and cotton goods. Pop. 87,000.

Wil'kinsburg, residential tn., Pennsylvania, U.S.A., 5 m. E. of Pittsburgh; planing mills and ice-plant. Pop. 30,000.

Will'enhall, urb. dist., Staffs, England, 3 m. E. of Wolverhampton; coal mining; iron and brass founding; bolts and locks. Pop. 21,100.

Will'esden, suburb of London, Middlesex, England, 7 m. N.N.W. of St. Paul's; large railway works. Pop. 184,400.

Will'iamsport, city, summer resort, Pennsylvania, U.S.A., on W. branch of R. Susquehanna; extensive lumber industry; manufactures fire and gas engines, sewing machines, rubber, silk. Pop. 46,000.

Will'iamstown, port, Victoria, Australia, at mouth of R. Yarra Yarra; suburb of Melbourne; shipbuilding, rly. workshops, and meat-freezing works.

Williman'tic, town, Connecticut, U.S.A., 30 m. E. of Hartford; manufactures thread, silk, woollens. Pop. 12,000.

Will'ington, urb. dist., Durham, England, 5 m. N. of Bishop Auckland; large collieries, whinstone quarries. Pop. 9,000.

Wil'mington. (1) Port, Delaware, U.S.A., on R. Delaware; manufactures leather, gunpowder, machinery, iron and steel goods; shipbuilding. Pop. 107,000. (2) Port, N. Carolina, U.S.A.; largest commercial city in the state; exports cotton, lumber, naval stores. Pop. 32,000.

Wilm'slow, urb. dist., Cheshire, England, on R. Bollin; cotton manufactures; residential outskirt of Manchester. Pop. 9,800.

Wil'no (*vil'no*), formerly VILNA. (1) Co., N.E. Poland, Europe; mainly plain, rising in S. to low uplands; many marshes and lakes, with much forest; drained by Rs. Dvina and Wilija; chief occupations are agriculture (rye and oats), and forestry. Chief tn., Wilno. Area, 10,814 sq. m.; pop. 1,006,000. (2) Cap. of above, on R. Wilija; cathedral, univ.; important rly. centre; manufactures buttons, gloves; exports timber and grain. Lithuania claims Wilno as its cap. Pop. 129,000.

Wils'den, par. and vil., Yorks, England, 5 m. N.W. of Bradford; manufactures worsted and worsted goods. Pop. (par.) 2,400.

Wil'ton, munic. bor. and mkt. tn., Wilts, England, on R. Wiley, 2½ m. N.W. of Salisbury; manufactures carpets. Pop. 2,200.

Wilt'shire, or WILTS, inland co., England; bounded N. by Gloucester, E. by Berks and Hants, S. by Dorset, W. by Somerset and Gloucester. Surface undulating; crossed by various ranges of hills, including the Marlborough Downs (highest point, Inkpen Beacon, 1,010 ft.). Drained by headwaters of R. Thames, and by Rs. Salisbury Avon, Bristol Avon, Kennet, and other streams; several canals. Agriculture carried on; chief crops, wheat and barley; cattle, sheep, and pigs reared; bacon curing and dairy farming are important. Manufactures include woollens, silks, carpets, railway material. Contains Stonehenge, and Salisbury Plain was acquired by government for military purposes. Co. tn., Salisbury. Area, 1,350 sq. m.; pop. 303,300.

Wim'bledon, munic. bor., Surrey, England, part of Greater London; Common was meeting-place of Rifle Association (1860–89); headquarters of English lawn tennis. Pop. 59,500.

Wim'borne-Min'ster, or WIMBORNE, urb. dist. and mkt. tn., Dorsetshire, England, at junction of Rs. Allen and Stour, 6 m. N. of Poole; noted minster and library with chained books; coach-building works. Pop. 3,900.

Winch'burgh, par. and vil., W. Lothian, Scotland, 12 m. W. of Edinburgh; oil works; brick and tile making. Pop. (par.) 2,000.

Winch'comb, tn., Gloucestershire, England, on R. Isborne, 6½ m. N.E. of Cheltenham; flour, silk, and paper mills; tanneries. Pop. 2,700.

Winch'elsea, par. and anc. tn., Sussex, England, 8 m. N.E. of Hastings; former Cinque Port. Old Winchelsea, an important seaport in Saxon times, was submerged in 13th cent. Pop. 150.

Win'chester, city, Hants, England, on R. Itchen; place of great antiquity; residence of Saxon kings, and for long cap. of country. Cathedral is longest in England, and has magnificent interior. Remains of old royal castle and Wolvesey Castle. Winchester College, famous public school, was founded (1387) by William of Wykeham. Pop. 23,000.

Windau. See VENTSPILS.

Win'dermere. (1) Lake, Westmorland and Lancs, England; shores much indented and generally low; wooded islets in centre; drained by R. Leven; largest lake in England; stretches 10½ m. N. and S., greatest breadth 1,610 yds. (2) Tn., Westmorland, England, on Lake Windermere, 7 m. N.W. of Kendal; picturesque scenery. Pop. 5,700.

Windhoek (*vind'hook*), cap. of S.W. Africa, 253 m. inland from Walvis Bay; alt. 5,600 ft.; hot springs; fruit culture; silver, copper, lead, and salt are found in vicinity. Pop. 8,000 (including 3,500 whites).

Windsor (*win'sor*). (1) Tn., Berks, England, on R. Thames. Contains Windsor Castle, a royal residence, with St. George's Chapel, containing many royal tombs. In park is mausoleum of Frogmore. Windsor is connected with Eton by a bridge across river. Pop. 20,300. (2) Port, Ontario, Canada, on R. Detroit; connected with Detroit by tunnel and train ferries; agricultural and fruit-growing region; salt industries; flour milling, and canneries. Pop. 61,000.

Wind'ward Islands, part of the Lesser Antilles, Brit. W. Indies; include Grenada, St. Vincent, St. Lucia, and the Grenadines; cotton, sugar, cocoa, spices, lime juice, fruits produced. Total area, 516 sq. m.; pop. 175,000. See separate articles.

Win'gate, par. and vil., Durham, England, 9 m. S.E. of Durham; coal mining and iron working. Pop. (par.) 11,425.

Win'nipeg ('murky water'). (1) Cap., Manitoba, Canada, at confluence of R. Assiniboine and Red R.; seat of provincial parliament; has two cathedrals, univ. In 1871 it had a pop. of 241, and was one of the trading posts of the Hudson's Bay Co., known as Fort Garry; now a centre of rail and river trade; chief grain market in world; fur auctions; great grain elevators and flour mills; machinery, confectionery, meat products; workshops of Canadian Pacific Rly. Pop. 202,000. (2) LAKE, Manitoba, Canada; drained by R. Nelson into Hudson Bay. Area, 8,555 sq. m. (3) Riv., Manitoba, Canada; issues from Lake of the Woods, and flows W. to Lake Winnipeg.

Winnipego'sis, lake in Manitoba and Saskatchewan, Canada; drains into L. Winnipeg. Area, 2,000 sq. m.

Wino'na, city, Minnesota, U.S.A., on R. Mississippi, 100 m. S.E. of St. Paul; medicines, furs, shoes, food products; large grain and lumber trade. Pop. 19,000.

Wins'combe, par. and vil., Somerset, England, 16½ m. S.W. of Bristol; finely situated in Mendip Hills. Pop. (par.) 2,000.

Wins'ford, urb. dist., Cheshire, England, 15 m. E. of Chester; important salt-producing dist. Pop. 11,000.

Wins'low, mkt. tn., Bucks, England, 6 m. S.E. of Buckingham; agricultural centre. Pop. 1,500.

Win'ston-Sa'lem, two continuous towns in N. Carolina, U.S.A., 60 m. W. of Raleigh; manufactures tobacco and cotton. Pop. 75,000.

Winterthur (*vin'ter-toor*), tn., Zurich, Switzerland, 17 m. N.E. of Zurich; great railway centre; important locomotive and machinery works; cotton goods, wine. Pop. 54,000.

Win'throp, town, Massachusetts,

U.S.A., on peninsula in Massachusetts Bay, 4 m. N.E. of Boston; summer resort. Pop. 15,500.

Wirks'worth, urb. dist., mkt. tn., Derbyshire, England, 12 m. N. by W. of Derby; lead mines, stone quarries; manufactures cotton, silk, hosiery, and tape. Pop. 3,900.

Wisbech (*wiz'bēch*), munic. bor., mkt. tn., and river port, Cambridgeshire, England, 21 m. N.N.E. of Peterborough, on R. Nen; manufactures agricultural implements, beer, oilcake; fruit extensively grown. Pop. 12,000.

Wisby. See VISBY.

Wiscon'sin, N. Central State, U.S.A.; bounded N. by Lake Superior, Michigan, E. by Lake Michigan, S. by Illinois, W. by Iowa and Minnesota. Surface an undulating plain with elevation of from 600 to 1,000 ft.; in S. are prairie lands; drained mainly by R. Mississippi on W. boundary, and its tribs. St. Croix, Chippewa, Black, and Wisconsin. Numerous lakes, largest Lake Winnebago, in E. Climate temperate, although winters are long and cold. Agriculture important; large crops of wheat, maize, oats, and barley, also potatoes, rye, sugar-beet, and tobacco are cultivated; dairying very important; cattle, sheep, horses, mules, and pigs raised in large numbers. Dense forests, with pine, oak, and other valuable timber trees. Chief mineral, iron. Principal manufactures are flour, butter and dairy produce, hardware, lumber products, agricultural tools, furniture, leather, paper, textiles; meat packing is carried on. Cap. Madison. Area, 56,066 sq. m.; pop. 2,953,000.

Wisconsin Rapids, formerly GRAND RAPIDS, tn., Wisconsin, U.S.A., on Wisconsin R., 100 m. N. of Madison; manufactures wooden goods. Pop. 6,500.

Wish'aw, tn., Lanarkshire, Scotland; amalgamated with Motherwell; rly. wagon works, blast furnaces, ironworks, engineering works, and coal mines. Pop. 19,000.

Wismar (*vis'mar*), port, Mecklenberg-Schwerin, Germany, on Baltic Sea; excellent harbour; shipbuilding; manufactures sailcloth, tobacco, paper; was an important Hanse town. Pop. 26,000.

Witham (*wit'am*). (1) Mkt. tn., Essex, England, 8 m. E.N.E. of Chelmsford; trade in agricultural produce; fine old church. Pop. 4,400. (2) Riv., England, rises in Rutland, flows generally N. to Lincoln, then S.E. to Wash. Length, 80 m.

With'ernsea, seaside resort, Yorks, England, 15 m. E. of Hull; fishing; sea rapidly encroaching on land. Pop. 4,300.

With'ington, tn., Lancs, England, 4 m. S. of Manchester, of which it is a residential suburb. Pop. 15,000.

With'nell, urb. dist., Lancs, England, 4 m. S.W. of Blackburn; cotton mills, bleach works. Pop. 3,000.

Wit'ney, mkt. tn., Oxfordshire, England, on R. Windrush, 11 m. W. by N. of Oxford; blankets, gloves, and woollen goods. Pop. 3,400.

Witten (*vit'ten*), tn., Westphalia, Prussia, 8 m. S.W. of Dortmund; iron and steel foundries, railway machine shops, glass works. Pop. 73,000.

Wittenberg (*vit'ten-berg*), tn., Saxony, Prussia, on R. Elbe, 55 m. S.W. of Berlin; manufactures machinery, cloth, leather; famous for its connection with Luther (1517); univ. united with that of Halle (1815). Pop. 23,000.

Wittenberge (*vit'ten-ber-ga*), town, Brandenburg, Prussia, 75 m. N.W. of Berlin; railway machine shops; manufactures textiles. Pop. 26,000.

Witu (*wē'too*), or VITU, sultanate in Tanaland prov. of Kenya Colony, at mouth of R. Tana; rubber is chief product. Cap. Witu. Area, 1,200 sq. m.; pop. 15,000.

Wit'watersrand ('white waters ridge'), popularly known as THE RAND, a rich gold-mining dist. in S. Transvaal, S. Africa. Chief tn., Johannesburg.

Wiveliscombe (*wils'cum*), mkt. tn., Somersetshire, England, 10 m. W. by N. of Taunton; agricultural centre; slate quarries. Pop. 1,300.

Wiv'enhoe, tn., Essex, England, on R. Colne; ship and yacht building; oysters. Pop. 2,200.

Wloclawek (*vlots-lă'vek*), tn., Warsaw prov., Poland, on R. Vistula; river port; breweries, ironworks, pottery, and chicory factories. Pop. 40,000.

Woburn (*woo'burn*). (1) Mkt. tn., Beds, England, 11 m. N.W. of Luton; Woburn Abbey, seat of Duke of Bedford, occupies site of Cistercian abbey. Pop. 1,200. (2) City, Massachusetts, U.S.A., 10 m. N.W. of Boston; boots, shoes, chemicals, glue. Pop. 17,000.

Wo'king, tn., Surrey, England, on R. Wey, 6 m. N. of Guildford; health resort; barracks. Pop. 29,900.

Wo'kingham, mkt. tn., Berks, England, 7 m. E.S.E. of Reading. Pop. 7,300.

Wolfenbüttel (*volf'en-boo-tel*), town, Brunswick, Germany, on R. Oker, 45 m. W. of Magdeburg; machinery, copper goods, cloth; has anc. castle, famous library. Pop. 18,000.

Wollin (*vol-ēn'*), island, Pomerania, Prussia, at entrance to Great Haff, opposite mouth of R. Oder; fishing and cattle rearing. Cap. Wollin. Area, 95 sq. m.; pop. 5,000.

Woll'ongong, coast tn., New South Wales, Australia, 48 m. S. of Sydney; centre of coal-mining and dairying region; coal exported. Pop. 7,600.

Wol'singham, par. and tn., Durham, England, 9 m. N.W. of Bishop Auckland; manufactures woollens, agricultural implements, tools; marble quarries. Pop. (par.) 3,500.

Wolstan'ton United, urb. dist., Staffs, England; in Potteries dist.; has also iron and steel works, silk and cotton mills. Pop. 30,500.

Wolverhamp'ton, co. bor., Staffs, England, 13 m. N.W. of Birmingham; centre of iron industry; manufactures electrical plant, motor-cars, zinc and tinwares, locks and keys. Pop. 133,200.

Wol'verton, urb. dist., Bucks, England, 10 m. N.E. of Buckingham; railway and printing works; practically continuous with Stony Stratford. Pop. 12,900.

Wombwell, tn., W. Riding, Yorks, England, 4 m. S.E. of Barnsley; coal mines, brickyards. Pop. 18,400.

Woo'burn, tn., Bucks, England, 4 m. S.E. of Wycombe; paper and millboard mills. Pop. 4,650.

Wood'bridge, urb. dist., mkt. tn., Suffolk, England, on R. Deben, 7 m. E.N.E. of Ipswich; river port. Pop. 4,700.

Wood'ford, urb. dist., Essex, England, 10 m. N.N.E. of St. Paul's, near S. boundary of Epping Forest; part of Greater London; residential and holiday resort. Pop. 23,900.

Wood Green, urb. dist., Middlesex, England, 7 m. N. of St. Paul's, London; part of Greater London; contains Alexandra Palace. Pop. 54,200.

Wood'hall Spa, tn., Lincolnshire, England, 7 m. S.W. of Horncastle; mineral spring. Pop. 1,400.

Wood'stock. (1) Tn., Oxfordshire, England, 8 m. N.E. of Witney; manufactures gloves; near by are Blenheim Park and Palace, granted to Duke of Marlborough. Pop. 1,500. (2) Tn., Ontario, Canada, on Cedar Creek, 78 m. S.W. of Toronto; manufactures woollen goods, agricultural machinery, musical instruments; electric power supplied from Niagara. Pop. 10,000.

Wool'er, par. and tn., Northumberland, England, near Cheviot Hills; has large cattle and sheep markets. Pop. 1,600.

Woolwich (*wool'ich*), tn., E. London, England, on R. Thames; royal arsenal and dockyard; contains factories for guns, gun-carriages, torpedoes, and ammunition; saddlery and harness departments; large storehouses; barracks and military hospital; headquarters of Royal Artillery; seat of Royal Coll. for Engineering and Artillery. Pop. 146,900.

Woon'socket, city, Rhode I., U.S.A., on R. Blackstone, 15 m. N.W. of Providence; cotton, woollen, and worsted mills; rubber goods. Pop. 50,000.

Woot'ton Bas'sett, mkt. tn., Wilts, England, 6 m. W. of Swindon; large cattle markets; trade in agricultural produce. Pop. 2,100.

Worcester (*woos'ter*). (1) Co. tn.,

Worcestershire, England, on R. Severn; has fine cathedral, several old churches, and two grammar schools of Tudor foundation; manufactures porcelain, vinegar, chemicals, gloves, iron goods; large hop market. Pop. 50,500. (2) Tn., Massachusetts, U.S.A., on R. Blackstone, 44 m. W.S.W. of Boston; univ.; railway centre; important manufactures of wire, boots and shoes, metal goods, machinery. Pop. 197,000. (3) Tn., Cape Prov., S. Africa, 62 m. N.E. of Cape Town; wine, raisins; tanning and wagon building; ostrich farming. Pop. 4,200.

Worcestershire, inland co. of W. central England; bounded by Shropshire, Stafford, Warwick, Gloucester, and Hereford; crossed by several ranges of hills; well wooded; watered by Rs. Severn, Avon, Stour, Teme, and other streams; agriculture and market gardening important; fruit in Vale of Evesham and hops in R. Teme valley; chief crops, wheat and barley; cattle and sheep raised. Minerals include coal, iron, salt, limestone; manufactures are iron and steel goods, china, carpets, glass, gloves. Co. tn., Worcester. Area, 716 sq. m.; pop. 420,200.

Work'ington, mkt. tn. and port, Cumberland, England, at mouth of R. Derwent; manufactures steel rails, boilers, motor vehicles, paper; shipbuilding; coal mined in vicinity. Pop. 24,700.

Work'sop, tn., Notts, England, 12 m. N.N.E. of Mansfield, on R. Ryton, near N. extremity of Sherwood Forest; coal mining, malting, woodwork; chemicals and agricultural implements. Pop. 26,300.

Worms (*vōrmz*), tn., Hesse, Germany, on R. Rhine; cathedral; important river trade; manufactures wine, chemicals, paints, tobacco, leather, machinery. Here Luther defended his position at Imperial Diet (1521). Pop. 47,000.

Wors'borough, urb. dist., W. Riding, Yorks, England, 3 m. S. of Barnsley; collieries, gunpowder mills, sawmills. Pop. 12,400.

Worsley (*wurs'li*), urb. dist., Lancs, England, 6 m. N.W. of Manchester; cotton, iron and brick works, coal mines. Pop. 14,500.

Worth'ing, wat.-pl., Sussex, England, 12 m. W. of Brighton; mackerel fishing; cultivation of greenhouse fruit and flowers. Pop. 46,200.

Wotton-under-Edge (*woo'ton*), par. and tn., Glos, England, 19 m. N.E. of Bristol; grammar school (1382) is oldest in England. Pop. (par.) 3,000.

Wrang'el Island, isl., in Arctic Ocean, N.W. of Bering Strait; mountainous in interior; claimed by U.S.S.R. Area, *c.* 2,000 sq. m.

Wrexham (*rex'am*), munic. bor., Denbighshire, Wales, 11 m. S.W. of Chester; malt, iron, terra-cotta works, tanneries, and breweries. Pop. 18,600.

Wrotham (*roo'tam*), urb. dist., Kent, England, 6 m. N.E. of Sevenoaks; fine church. Pop. 4,500.

Wuchang', cap., Hupeh, China, on R. Yangtze Kiang, opposite Hankow; contains mint, and cotton mills. Included in Hankow. Pop. *c.* 800,000.

Wuchow', tn., Kwangsi, China, on R. Sikiang, 125 m. W. of Canton; port of transhipment of sea-borne goods for the West; hides, oils, and sugar exported. Pop. 90,000.

Wuhu', treaty port, Anhui, China, on R. Yangtze Kiang; exports grain to the S.; coal, tea, silk produced in vicinity. Pop. 136,000.

Württemberg (*voor-tem-berg*), rep., S. Germany; bounded by Baden, Bavaria, and Switzerland. Surface undulating, rising to Black Forest in W.; drained by Rs. Danube, Neckar, and other streams; large area forested. Chief industry agriculture; wheat, oats, rye, potatoes, barley, and other crops cultivated; vines; livestock reared; minerals include salt, iron, limestone; manufactures textiles, paper, leather, hardware, beer, tobacco, spirits, firearms, gunpowder; Tübingen has univ. Cap. Stuttgart. Area, 7,530 sq. m.; pop. 2,580,000.

Würzburg (*voorts'boorg*), tn., Bavaria, Germany, on R. Main; dates from 7th cent.; famous cathedral, royal castle, univ. with celebrated medical school; breweries; mathematical, surgical, and musical instruments, machinery, printing presses; tobacco. Pop. 90,000.

Wurzen (*voor'tsen*), tn., Saxony, Germany, on R. Mulde, 16 m. E. of Leipzig; castle, cathedral; manufactures machinery, carpets, paper, leather. Pop. 18,000.

Wy'andotte, tn., Michigan, U.S.A., 12 m. S.W. of Detroit; chemicals and bleaching powders. Pop. 28,000.

Wycombe (*wik'um*), CHEPPING or HIGH WYCOMBE, mkt. tn., Bucks, England, on R. Wye, trib. of R. Thames; manufactures chairs, cabinet work, and furniture. Pop. 28,000.

Wye (*wī*). (1) Mkt. tn., Kent, England, 10 m. S.W. of Canterbury; grammar school. Pop. 1,400. (2) Riv., Wales and England; rises in Plinlimmon; joins estuary of R. Severn; famed for beautiful scenery; length, 130 m.

Wymondham (*wind'am*), tn., Norfolk, England, 10 m. S.W. of Norwich; brush making, brewing. Pop. 4,800.

Wyoming (*wī-ō'ming*), Mountain State, U.S.A.; bounded by Montana, S. Dakota, Nebraska, Colorado, Utah, and Idaho; traversed N. to S. by Rocky Mts. (Fremont Peak, 13,790 ft.), flanked on either side by plateaus from 7,000 to 8,000 ft.; watered by Rs. Green, Snake, Yellowstone, Big Horn, Powder, N. Platte, and other streams. Pine forests among the hills, and in N.W. is Yellowstone National Park. Climate temperate and healthy in lower districts; more severe in the mountains. Excellent grazing land, and large numbers of cattle and sheep raised; agriculture carried on by irrigation and dry farming, vegetables, fruits, and cereals cultivated. Mining most important industry; minerals include petroleum, coal, copper, iron, limestone. Chief towns, Cheyenne (cap.) and Casper. Area, 97,914 sq. m.; pop. 194,000.

X

Xanthe (*zan'the*), tn., N.E. Thrace, Greece, on R. Mesta; noted for tobacco. Pop. 25,000.

Xenia (*zēn'ya*), tn., Ohio, U.S.A., near R. Little Miami, 16 m. S.E. of Dayton; ropes, twine, boots and shoes. Pop. 9,000.

Xeres. See JEREZ.

Xingu (*shing-goo'*), riv., Brazil, S. America; rises in plateau of Matto Grosso; flows N., and enters R. Amazon at beginning of estuary; numerous waterfalls; navigable for 110 m. Length, 1,300 m.

Y

Y, or IJ (*ī*), S.W. arm of Zuider Zee, N. Holland, Holland; now largely drained; joined to North Sea by North Sea Canal; R. Amstel enters at Amsterdam.

Yablonoi', mt. range, Siberia; extending N.E. from Urga till it merges in Stanovoi Mts.; separates basins of rivs. Amur and Lena.

Yak'ima, tn., Washington, U.S.A., 165 m. S.E. of Seattle; centre of productive agricultural region, producing fruits, vegetables, live-stock, and grain. Pop. 18,000.

Yakutsk (*ya-kootsk'*). (1) Republic, U.S.S.R.; bounded N. by Arctic Ocean, W. by Siberian Area, S. and E. by Far Eastern Area. Surface level in N., mountainous in S.; drained by R. Lena and tribs.; numerous lakes; much forest; produces rye, barley; cattle and horses raised;

exports furs and ivory; chief mineral, gold. Area, 1,600,000 sq. m.; pop. *c.* 279,000. (2) Cap. of above, near R. Lena; wooden houses built on marshy plain; furs. Pop. 10,000.

Yalding (*yawl'ding*), par. and vil., Kent, England, 6½ m. s.w. of Maidstone; hops and fruit are largely grown. Pop. (par.) 2,600.

Yalu (*ya-loo'*), riv., Korea; for most of its course forms boundary between Korea and Manchuria. Upper basin richly forested; much timber floated down to Wi-ju, below which river is navigable; length, 300 m.

Yam'bol, tn., Bulgaria, on R. Tunja, 48 m. w. of Burgas; agricultural dist. Pop. 23,000.

Yanä'on, or YANAM, French possession, India; near mouth of R. Godavari; under govt. of Pondicherry. Area, *c.* 5 sq. m.; pop. 5,000.

Yang'tze Kiang', largest riv. and chief commercial highway of China; rises in mts. of Tibet; traverses central provinces of China, and after tortuous course of *c.* 3,000 m. through densely populated region, enters Yellow Sea near Shanghai; receives numerous tributaries; communicates by Grand Canal with Hwang-Ho R.; navigable to Ichang (1,726 m.).

Yan'nina, formerly JANINA, tn., N. Epirus, N.W. Greece, on L. Yannina; seat of archbishop; manufactures gold and silver embroidered goods. Pop. 21,000.

Yap, Japanese isl., Caroline group, N. Pacific Ocean; cable station to which U.S.A. has free access. Area, 79 sq. m.; pop. 7,500.

Yarkand', tn., Sinkiang, China, on oasis in R. Tarim basin; important trade centre; produces wheat, rice, beans, and fruit; manufactures leather, saddlery, carpets, textiles. Pop. *c.* 90,000.

Yar'mouth. (1) Or GREAT YARMOUTH, co. bor., seapt., and wat.-pl., Norfolk, England, at mouth of R. Yare; fine parish church; great centre of herring and deep-sea fishing; noted for Yarmouth bloaters; ship and boat building; manufactures ropes, nets. Yarmouth Roads is an anchorage off the port, protected by sandbanks. Pop. 56,800. (2) Small seapt., Isle of Wight, England, on Solent; yachting station. Pop. 900. (3) Seapt., s.w. Nova Scotia, Canada; shipbuilding; exports fish and lumber. Pop. 7,000.

Yaroslav'l, formerly JAROSLAV. (1) Prov., Russia; consists of broad depression traversed by Upper R. Volga; much marsh and forest; flax widely grown; important dairying industry. Area, 12,680 sq. m.; pop. 1,338,000. (2) Cap. of above, at junction of Rs. Volga and Kotorost, 150 m. N.N.E. of Moscow; 13th cent. cathedral; cotton, tobacco, leather, and linen. Pop. 112,000.

Yar'row Water, riv., Selkirkshire, Scotland; flows through Loch of the Lowes and St. Mary's Loch to enter Ettrick Water 2 m. above Selkirk; trout fishing; famous in Scottish song and legend. Length, 25 m.

Yassy. See JASSY.

Yea'don, urb. dist. and par., W. Riding, Yorks, England, 8 m. N.W. of Leeds; woollen goods. Pop. 7,700.

Yell. See SHETLAND ISLANDS.

Yellow River. See HWANG-HO.

Yellow Sea, or HWANG-HAI, inlet of Pacific Ocean, N. China, between Chinese coast and Korea; Pohai Gulf forms its N. extension; shallow owing to great deposit of silt received from Hwang-Ho or Yellow R.

Yellowstone National Park, N.W. Wyoming, U.S.A., region of cañons, cataracts, hot springs, geysers, and mud volcanoes; Yellowstone R. passes through Grand Cañon. Geysers are finest in world. Most of area thickly forested. Region was set apart as a national park (1872). Many species of animals which have elsewhere been exterminated have found refuge here. Area, 3,350 sq. m.

Yemen. See ARABIA.

Yenisei (*yen-e-sā'*), riv., Siberia; rises in N.W. Mongolia and flows N. through thinly populated country to Arctic Ocean; ice-bound in winter;

much flooding in spring; has many navigable stretches; length, 2,700 m.

Yeniseisk (*yen-e-sāsk'*), tn., Siberian Area, U.S.S.R., on Yenisei R.; gold-mining centre. Pop. 6,000.

Yeovil (*yō'vil*), mkt. tn., Somerset, England, on R. Yeo; 14th cent. church; manufactures gloves. Pop. 19,100.

Yetholm (*yet'um*), par. and double vil., Kirk-Yetholm and Town-Yetholm, on Bowmont Water, Roxburghshire, Scotland, 7½ m. S.E. of Kelso; formerly headquarters of a tribe of gipsies. Pop. 540.

Yezd, city, Persia, 160 m. S.E. of Isfahan; trading centre on several important caravan routes. Pop. *c.* 30,000.

Yezo. See HOKKAIDO.

Yiews'ley and West Drayton, urban dist., Middlesex, England, 2½ m. S. of Uxbridge; part of Greater London; brick making. Pop. 13,100.

Yochow', city, Hunan, China, on R. Yangtze Kiang; walled; opened to foreign trade (1900). Pop. *c.* 20,000.

Yokohama (*yō-kō-hä'ma*), seaport, Japan, on Tokyo Bay; large trade, chiefly in silk, silk goods, and tea. Practically destroyed by earthquake (1923); since rebuilt. Pop. 519,000.

Yokosu'ka, seaport, Japan, 12 m. S. of Yokohama; shipbuilding, dockyards, arsenals. Pop. 96,000.

Yola (*yō'lä*), prov., N. Nigeria, W. Africa; fertile; watered by R. Benue; rice, cotton, tobacco. Cap. Yola. Area, 16,000 sq. m.; pop. *c.* 300,000.

Yonk'ers, city, New York, U.S.A., on Hudson R.; residential suburb of New York; carpets, sugar, hats, rubber goods, photographic supplies. Pop. 135,000.

Yonne (*yon*), dep., France; hilly and undulating; forests in N.; drained by R. Yonne, trib. of R. Seine; very fertile, producing cereals, wine; forestry, mining, sugar refining, glass making. Cap. Auxerre. Area, 2,892 sq. m.; pop. 277,000.

York. (1) Co. tn., Yorks, England, at junction of Rs. Foss and Ouse; still has old walls and several old gateways ('bars'); Roman remains; archbishop's see; fine cathedral (minster), dating in part from 12th cent.; famous Five Sisters window, restored (1925); other interesting old churches, and ruins of Benedictine monastery; important railway and agricultural centre; manufactures flour, beer, hardware, glass, confectionery, leather, and artificial manure. Pop. 84,800. (2) City, Pennsylvania, U.S.A., 96 m. W. of Philadelphia; manufactures agricultural implements, cars, confectionery, tobacco. Pop. 55,000.

Yorkshire, largest co. of England; bounded by Westmorland, Durham, North Sea, Lincolnshire, Nottinghamshire, Derbyshire, Cheshire, and Lancashire. Undulating surface slopes W. to Pennine Chain. Centre of county is plain known as Vale of York; E. of this are two groups of hills, York Moors in N. and York Wolds in S.; drained by Rs. Hull, Derwent, Swale, Ure, Nidd, Yorkshire Ouse, Wharfe, and Aire (all of which belong to basin of R. Ouse, and by R. Don, both Ouse and Don entering Humber estuary; in N. a small portion drains to R. Tees. County is divided into three Ridings (from O.E. *thridding*, 'third part'); in E. Riding industries are mainly centred about Hull; in N. Riding there is coal, iron, salt, lead, barytes; and W. Riding has a large coalfield, with manufactures of woollens, linen, cutlery, hardware, as well as iron smelting. Agriculture is carried on, especially in E. Riding; chief crops are oats, barley, and wheat; horses, cattle, and sheep are raised; important fisheries. Chief tns., York (cap.), Leeds, Sheffield, Bradford, Huddersfield, Hull, Middlesbrough. Area, 6,071 sq. m.; pop. 4,304,700.

York'ton, tn., Saskatchewan, Canada, 105 m. N.E. of Regina; centre of agricultural dist. Pop. 5,150.

York'town, tn., Virginia, U.S.A., 10 m. above mouth of York R.; here Cornwallis surrendered to Washington (1781). Pop. 150.

Yosemite (*yo-sem'it-ā*), valley, in

w. slope of Sierra Nevada Mts., California, U.S.A.; enclosed by walls of rock rising 3,000–5,000 ft.; traversed by R. Merced; numerous cascades; magnificent scenery; discovered in 1851; established as a state park (1864); tourist resort.

Youghal (*yawl*), seapt. and wat.-pl., co. Cork, I.F.S., on Youghal harbour, at estuary of R. Blackwater; exports corn; fisheries; manufactures earthenware and bricks. Pop. 5,600.

Youngstown, city, Ohio, U.S.A., 65 m. S.E. of Cleveland; manufactures iron and steel. Pop. 170,000.

Ypres (*ēpr*), tn., W. Flanders, Belgium, 35 m. s. of Ostend; chief industries, manufacture of woollen goods, printed cottons, linens, and lace; tanneries and dyeworks. During Great War Ypres was centre of salient (1914–18), held by Brit. and French troops, and city, including famous Cloth Hall, was reduced to ruins; after the war town was rebuilt. The famous Menin Gate was opened (1927) as memorial to missing Brit. soldiers. Pop. 15,000.

Ystad (*us'tad*), seaport, s. Sweden, on Baltic Sea; flour, saw, and sugar mills. Pop. 11,000.

Yucatan (*ū-ka-tan'*), peninsula, Central America; includes Mexican states of Campeche and Yucatan as well as parts of Brit. Honduras and Guatemala; surface flat, with Sierra de Yucatan crossing centre; few rivers; produces maize, rice, cotton, tobacco, sisal hemp, sugar-cane; fine forests, with mahogany and other valuable trees. Area, 55,400 sq. m.; pop. *c.* 400,000.

Yugosla'via, kingdom, S.E. Europe; bounded N. by Austria and Hungary, N.E. by Romania, E. by Bulgaria, S. by Greece, W. by Albania, Adriatic Sea, and Italy. Comprises former states of Serbia, Montenegro, Bosnia and Hercegovina, Dalmatia, Croatia, and Slovenia. In W. are the Dinaric Alps; remainder mostly occupied by Rhodope Mts.; low-lying river plains are economically very important. Principal rivers are Danube, Drava, Sava in N., Vardar flowing to Ægean Sea. Apart from Karst lands in N.W., surface is mostly forest and grazing areas; live-stock reared and exported; agriculture widely practised, principal crops being wheat, barley, rye, oats, maize, grapes, and other fruits; tobacco and silk culture also important. Minerals undeveloped. Important industries are flour milling, brewing, distilling; cotton manufacture still in stage of early development. Yugoslavia suffers also from lack of seaports, but has access to Fiume and Salonica. Chief tns., Belgrade (cap.), Subotica, Sarajevo, and Novi Sad. Area, 96,134 sq. m.; pop. 12,017,000.

Yu'kon. (1) Terr., Canada, bounded by Arctic Ocean, N.W. Terrs., Brit. Columbia, and Alaska; created a Territory (1898) after discovery of gold in Klondyke; mountainous (Mt. Logan, 19,800 ft., highest mt. in Canada); drained by R. Yukon; gold, silver, and coal mining; abounds in big game; cap. Dawson. Area, 207,076 sq. m.; pop. 4,000. (2) Riv., Yukon and Alaska, formed by union of Rs. Lewes and Pelly at Fort Selkirk; flows N.W. into Alaska, then S.W.; empties by great delta into Bering Sea; chief tribs. are Stewart White, Selwyn, and Klondyke rivers; navigable from June till Sept. to L. Bennet, source of R. Lewes. Length, *c.* 2,300 m.

Yunnan'. (1) Prov., S.W. extremity, China Proper; central part consists of a lofty plateau sloping towards S.E. and studded with lakes; very mountainous in N. and W.; traversed by parts of Rs. Yangtze Kiang, Mekong, Salwin, and Songkoi; rich mineral resources include copper, coal, lead, zinc, and silver; agricultural products include rice, maize, buckwheat. Area, 146,680 sq. m.; pop. *c.* 10,000,000. (2) Cap. of above; walled and intersected by canals; increasing trade since opening of railway from Tongking; manufactures silk and leather goods. Pop. *c.* 45,000.

Yuzovka. See STALIN.

Z

Zaandam (*zan-dam'*), tn., N. Holland, on R. Zaan, 6 m. N.W. of Amsterdam; paper works, oil and saw mills; cement, colours. Pop. 32,000.

Zabern. See SAVERNE.

Zabrze. See HINDENBURG.

Zacatecas (*tha-ka-tā'kas*). (1) State, Mexico, belonging to the central plateau; cereals, sugar, and fruit grown; rich in minerals, silver, gold, iron. Area, 24,471 sq. m.; pop. 379,000. (2) Cap. of above; silver mines, pottery. Pop. 15,000.

Zaffarines. See CHAFFARINES.

Zagazig', tn., Nile Delta, Egypt; centre of cotton and grain trade. Pop. 53,000.

Zagreb, formerly AGRAM, chief tn., Croatia-Slavonia, N.W. Yugoslavia, on R. Sava; Gothic cathedral; univ.; linen, carpets, leather, tobacco. Pop. 108,000.

Zambe'zi, large riv., E. Africa; generally regarded as N. limit of S. Africa; rises in N.W. Rhodesia, near R. Congo: general course S.E.; flows through Portuguese W. Africa, Rhodesia, Portuguese E. Africa; enters Indian Ocean by several branches (most important Chinde). Length, 2,200 m.; navigable for *c.* 1,700 m. in three separate sections, navigation being interrupted by falls and rapids; most important falls, Victoria Falls, in Rhodesia. Principal tribs. are Lungwebungu, Kwando, Shiré. Discovered by Livingstone.

Zamboan'ga, tn., W. Mindanao, Philippine Islands; important commercial centre; chief products, timber, rice, copra, sugar, and tobacco. Pop. *c.* 44,000.

Zamo'ra. (1) Prov., Leon, Spain; drained by R. Douro; generally level; agricultural; wheat, wine. Area, 4,097 sq. m.; pop. 266,000. (2) Cap. of above; anc. walled city; fine cathedral; wine, coarse linen, wheat. Pop. 17,000.

Zanes'ville, city, Ohio, U.S.A., 54 m. E. of Columbus; pottery, textiles, machinery, railway material. Pop. 36,000.

Zan'te. (1) Isl., Ionian group, Greece; surface fertile plain with hills in W.; currants, olives; subject to earthquakes. Area, 277 sq. m.; pop. 40,000. (2) Cap. of above; manufactures carpets, gold and silver articles. Pop. 13,000.

Zanzibar'. (1) Isl., E. Africa, 20 m. from coast of Tanganyika Terr. Climate hot and moist. Staple product, cloves. Area, 680 sq. m.; pop. 115,000. (2) Tn. on W. coast of above; cap. of Protectorate; most important trade centre of E. Africa; excellent harbour; former great slave market; exports cloves, copra, soap, and ivory. Pop. *c.* 60,000. (3) PROTECTORATE, consisting of islands of Zanzibar, Pemba, and adjacent small islands; provides bulk of world's supply of cloves. Protectorate established (1890). Area, 1,020 sq. m.; pop. 217,000.

Zapor'ozhe, formerly ALEXANDROVSK, tn., Ukraine, U.S.S.R., on R. Dnieper; rly. jn.; motors; agricultural machinery. Pop. 55,000.

Zar'a, seapt., Italy, in enclave in Dalmatia, E. coast of Adriatic; manufactures maraschino, flour, wax, glass; cathedral (13th cent.); seat of Catholic archbishop and Greek bishop. Pop. 18,000.

Zaria (*za-rē'a*), prov., N. Provinces, Nigeria; cotton-producing region. Cap. Zaria, 87 m. S.W. of Kano. Area, 23,695 sq. m.; pop. 1,031,000.

Zatec (*zhat'ets*), formerly SAAZ, tn., N.W. Bohemia, Czechoslovakia, on R. Ohre; centre of hop trade; manufactures sugar and leather. Pop. 16,000.

Zea'land, largest isl., Denmark, between Kattegat and Baltic Sea; surface low-lying and undulating; fertile and well-cultivated; fine beech woods; on isl. is Copenhagen, the Danish cap. Area, 2,636 sq. m.

Zeebrugge (*zā-broog'e*), seaport, Belgium, 9 m. N. of Bruges, with which it is connected by ship canal; harbour is protected from silting by crescent-shaped mole, 1½ m. long and nearly 100 yds. wide. Steamer service to Harwich. During Great War was German submarine, destroyer, and seaplane base; destroyed by British (April 1918). Monument erected (1920) commemorates this exploit.

Zee'land, most S. maritime prov. of Holland; comprises six islands, with strip of land along W. bank of R. Schelde; surface flat and mostly below sea-level; protected by dikes; soil fertile; fishing. Cap. Middelburg. Area, 707 sq. m.; pop. 250,000.

Zeitz (*tsits*), tn., Saxony, Prussia, on R. White Elster, 23 m. S.W. of Leipzig; manufactures textiles. Pop. 35,000.

Zemun, formerly SEMLIN, tn., Yugoslavia, on R. Danube, opposite Belgrade; important transit trade in grain, fruit, and timber. Pop. 18,000.

Zenjan, cap. Khamseh Prov., Persia, 175 m. N.W. of Tehran; trade in carpets. Pop. 25,000.

Zenta. See SENTA.

Zerbst (*tserpst*), tn., Anhalt, Germany, on R. Nuthe, 27 m. S.E. of Magdeburg; manufactures jewellery, machinery, beer. Pop. 19,000.

Zermatt', vil., Valais, Switzerland, at foot of Matterhorn; tourist centre; alt. 5,315 ft. Pop. 800.

Zhitomir. See JITOMIR.

Zhob. (1) Dist., N.E. Baluchistan; hilly, intersected in S. by great valley of Zhob R.; dry, bracing climate; wheat, maize, fruits; asbestos, chromite, salt produced. Area, 9,626 sq. m.; pop. 57,000. (2) Riv. in above, flows N.E. to join R. Gomal after course of *c.* 240 m.

Zimbab'we, GREAT, collection of ruins, S. Rhodesia, Africa, 17 m. S. of Victoria; original purpose unknown, but may have been a stronghold and place for smelting and purifying ores; rediscovered in 1867.

Zin'der, tn., Niger Colony, French W. Africa, 135 m. N.E. of Kano; surrounded by earthen walls; trade in cottons, silks, ostrich feathers, salt, spices · military post. Pop. 6,000.

Zinovievsk (*zin-ov-ē-ävsk'*), formerly ELIZABETGRAD, tn., Ukraine, U.S.S.R., 140 m. N. of Odessa; smelting, distilling, and brewing; soap, bricks, tobacco. Pop. 65,000.

Zirian. See KOMI.

Zittau (*tsit'ou*), tn., Saxony, Germany, 50 m. S.E. of Dresden; damasks and woollen goods; lignite mines in vicinity. Pop. 38,000.

Zlatoust (*zlä-tō-oost'*), tn., Ural Area, Russia; in Ural Mts., 120 m. S. of Sverdlovsk; observatory; mining centre for gold and iron; ironworks and manufacture of machinery. Pop. 48,000.

Znojmo (*znoi'mo*) (German *Znaim*), tn., Czechoslovakia, 45 m. N. of Vienna; vegetables, especially cucumbers, grown; manufactures pottery. Pop. 21,000.

Zom'ba, cap., Nyasaland Protectorate, E. Africa, on slope of Mt. Zomba, at alt. of 3,000 ft.; tobacco and cotton cultivated. Pop. (whites) 250.

Zombor. See SOMBOR.

Zout'pansberg, mt. range, N. Transvaal, Africa; gold and copper mines.

Zug (*tsoog*). (1) Canton, Switzerland, N.E. of L. Lucerne; mountainous in S. and S.E.; watered by R. Reuss; inhabitants mainly German-speaking and R.C. Area, 92 sq. m.; pop. 32,000. (2) Cap. of above, on L. Zug; enamel and metal articles. Pop. 9,000.

Zuider Zee (*zoi'der zā*), shallow inlet of North Sea, Holland; originally a small inland lake; united to North Sea by inundations in 13th cent. Depth, 10 to 19 ft.; area, 1,428 sq. m. Dikes are in process of construction, separating the North Sea from the Zuider Zee, by which it is hoped to reclaim over 800 sq. m. of land, thus adding one-tenth to the cultivable area of Holland.

Zu'luland, N.E. dist. of Natal,

S. Africa. Surface mountainous, with low plains in N. and E. Drained by R. Tugela, which forms part of S.W. boundary. Climate unhealthy on coast. Produces cereals, sugar, coffee, tea, tobacco; cattle and sheep raised. Gold and coal exist, but are little worked. Area, 10,450 sq. m.; pop. 251,000.

Zurich (*tsoo-rich*). (1) Canton, N. Switzerland; contains large part of L. Zurich and several smaller lakes; belongs to basin of R. Rhine; surface hilly (highest point, 3,012 ft.); fertile valleys; manufactures cotton, silk; inhabitants mostly German-speaking Protestants. Area, 667 sq. m.; pop. 539,000. (2) Cap. of above, on L. Zurich; chief commercial and industrial city of Switzerland. Notable buildings include Grossmünster (Romanesque cathedral, begun 11th cent.); Wasserkirche (containing famous library); national museum; town hall and Pestalozzianum; univ.; fine bridges, etc. Chief industries are silk weaving, cotton spinning; manufacture of machinery and paper. Pop. 207,000. (3) Lake in above canton. Length, 25 m.; greatest width, 2½ m.

Zut'phen, or ZUTFEN, tn., Gelderland, Holland; tanneries, paper, and oil works; trade in grain, timber; Sir Philip Sidney killed here (1586). Pop. 19,000.

Zvenigorodka (*zvān-i-gor-od'ka*), tn., Ukraine, U.S.S.R.; 100 m. S. of Kiev; tobacco; trade in grain and agricultural produce. Pop. 40,000.

Zweibrücken (*tsvī'brook-en*), town, Rhine Palatinate, Bavaria, Germany, 48 m. N.W. of Strasbourg; manufactures machinery, leather, silk. Pop. 16,000.

Zwickau (*tsvik'ou*), tn., Saxony, Germany, 20 m. S.W. of Chemnitz; coalfields; machinery, chemicals, motors, glass, and wire goods; birthplace of Schumann. Pop. 80,000.

Zwolle (*tsvol'e*), tn., Overyssel, Holland; cotton; ironworks; boat building; important canal centre. Pop. 39,000.

DICTIONARY OF GEOGRAPHICAL TERMS

NOTE.—*Names printed in small capitals, and occurring in the course of an article, indicate that there is a special article under that head.*

Aborigines (*ab-or-ij'in-ēs*), the first inhabitants of any country, or those in possession of it at time of its discovery or colonization by civilized peoples. The adjective, *aboriginal*, is also applied to the original FAUNA and FLORA of any region.

Afforesta'tion, the planting of land with trees whether for timber or hunting grounds. In N. America, Scandinavia, New Zealand, and other timber-exporting areas the planting of young trees (*reafforestation*) accompanies cutting, so that future supplies of timber may be assured.

Agave (*ā-gā'vē*), a plant originally found in dry, tropical Americas; now cultivated also in E. Africa, the Philippine Islands, etc. It has thick, fleshy leaves with sharp edges and tips. The fibres of the leaves yield sisal hemp; in Mexico the fermented juice is a favourite drink called *pulque*. See SISAL.

Ainos (*ī'nōz*), or AINU, a rapidly dwindling race of people living in Hokkaido, Japan, and Sakhalin; probably a remnant of the aboriginal inhabitants. They are short of stature but strongly built, and their bodies are frequently covered with short, bristly hair; their features are European rather than Mongolian. Chief occupations are hunting and fishing; number *c.* 15,000.

Air Port. See PORT.

Air Routes. With the rapid development of aviation, both during and since the Great War, the question of routes suitable for aircraft has come to be of great importance. The chief factors to be taken into account are the surface of country flown over, mountainous or otherwise, and the weather conditions; in long-distance flights the direction of prevailing winds is as important as it was for sailing ships. Suitable sites for aerodromes and the provision of meteorological and wireless services must also be considered. See TRANSPORT.

Al'fa, or **Halfa,** the N. African name of *esparto*, a grass of Algeria, Tunis, and s. Spain, used chiefly in paper making.

Alfal'fa, the Spanish name for *lucerne*, and also known as Spanish trefoil or purple medic, is a Mediterranean fodder plant resembling clover. It is now widely cultivated, especially on irrigated lands in the temperate Americas, S. Africa, Australia, etc. By fixing nitrogen from the air the plant tends to enrich the soil.

Allspice. See PIMENTO.

Allu'vium, very fine particles of soil or sand (silt) carried by running water and deposited in river beds, along river banks during floods, in lakes and deltas, and on seashores; fertile plains may thus be formed (*e.g.* valley of R. Po).

Alpaca (*al-păk'ă*), an animal resembling a sheep, but with a long neck, found on the high plateaus of the Andes. It is of the camel family, and is closely related to the llama. The alpaca is domesticated for the sake of its soft, silky wool, from which fine cloth (alpaca) is made, especially at Saltaire, Yorks. See also LLAMA, VICUÑA.

Alumin'ium, a white, light, but strong metal, largely used in the motor-car industry, and essential in aircraft construction. It is extracted from its ore in countries with large water-power resources (*e.g.* U.S.A., Germany, Norway, France, Switzerland, Canada). See BAUXITE.

An'eroid. See BAROMETER.

Ango'ra Goat, a species of goat, a native of the steppes of Asia Minor, whence it was introduced (*c.* 1840) into S. Africa. Its wool, known as *mohair*, is noted for its long, fine, soft, silky qualities, and is used for making a cloth called *angora.*

Antarctic Circle. See LATITUDE.

An'thracite, a very hard variety of coal, with bright surface and free from dust, burning with little flame, but giving intense heat; it contains 90–95 per cent. of carbon. It is mined in S. Wales and E. Pennsylvania, U.S.A. Anthracite is burned in house-stoves in large cities (*e.g.* Paris, New York), and is used also for smelting iron.

Anticyclone (*an'ti-sī'klōn*), or HIGH, an area of high air pressure in which the ISOBARS form a series of roughly concentric rings, indicating a steady rise of pressure inwards towards the centre. Over the centre the descending air is cool and dry; it moves outwards as a gentle wind-whirl, blowing clockwise in the N. hemisphere, anticlockwise in the S. hemisphere. Anticyclonic weather is marked by clear skies with cool and misty mornings and evenings, between which the days are generally sunny and rainless in summer, but often dull and foggy in winter. Anticyclones usually persist for several days. See CYCLONE, WIND.

Antip'odēs, that part of the earth's surface which is diametrically opposite one's own country. In the British Isles the name is often used to mean New Zealand or Australia.

Archipelago (*ar-ki-pel'agō*), a group of islands. The name was at first given to the Ægean Sea, and was later applied to any large group of islands, or to a sea with many islands.

Arc'tic Circle. See LATITUDE.

Ar'eca Nut. See BETEL NUT.

Arête (*a-rāt'*), a roof-like ridge of steep rock above the snowline, formed by the action of frost. The term is mostly used in connection with mountaineering, particularly in Switzerland.

Ar'rowroot, a nutritious flour-like foodstuff prepared from the underground stems of the tropical American arrowroot plant; it is exported from Jamaica, Bermudas, India, etc.

Artesian Wells, wells bored to reach underground water which either rises by pressure or is pumped to the surface. Such wells may be as much as 5,000 ft. deep. The water varies in warmth according to the depth from which it rises, one deep well in Queensland, Australia, yielding water nearly boiling hot. Artesian water may also be either fresh or saltish; when pure it can be used for domestic, industrial, and agricultural purposes, but it is sometimes too saline for the irrigation of crops. Numerous wells have been sunk in Australia, the Sahara, U.S.A., etc.; the oldest known in Europe were in Artois (France), from which the name *artesian* is derived.

Artificial Silk. See SILK.

Asbes'tos, a whitish, lustrous, and fibrous mineral found in E. Canada (Thetford), Italy, and Russia. It is not affected by fire, and is used in making gas stoves, fireproof curtains, covering for steam-pipes, etc.

At'mosphere, the air surrounding the earth. It is composed mainly of a mixture of the gases nitrogen and oxygen, and is of the greatest importance. The oxygen is required to support human, animal, and vegetable life. Without the atmosphere, sound could not be carried, the sun's heat could not be retained, and wind, rain, etc.—the various things making up weather—would not take place. It can expand and contract, can carry varying quantities of water vapour, and exerts pressure (*c.* 15 lb. per sq. in.). The height of the atmosphere is at least 200 miles.

Atoll′. See CORAL.

Avalanche (*av′a-lansh*), a mass of snow, usually mixed with ice, soil, and stones, sliding at great speed down a mountain slope, often causing much damage to villages and forests.

Ax′is (of the earth), the imaginary line joining the N. and S. poles, and passing through the centre. Round this axis the earth rotates.

Az′tecs, the most important of the native N. American peoples, dominant in Mexico at the time of the Spanish invasion under Cortes in 1519; their tradition was that they came from N. The chief tribe had its cap. at Tenochtitlan, now the city of Mexico, and had founded the Empire of Mexico. They possessed a high degree of culture, but their religious rites were debased by human sacrifice. A few descendants, still speaking the ancient language, are to be found in outlying villages round the city of Mexico.

Bactrian Camel. See CAMEL.

Banan′a, the fruit of a plant grown everywhere in the tropics. The plant requires a deep soil with abundant heat and moisture. The fruit is largely exported from Central America and the W. Indies. A subtropical variety formerly obtained from the Canary Islands is now of less importance. The *plantain*, belonging to the same family, must be cooked before it is eaten.

Ban′tu, name applied to various tribes of Negroes, chief amongst whom are Kaffirs and Zulus, living in that part of Africa lying S. of 5° N. of the equator. Name is also used for the large group of languages and dialects spoken by these peoples.

Bar (of river), a bank of sand, gravel, or silt deposited at the mouth of a river where its current is checked by the sea, and forming a hindrance to navigation.

Barom′eter, an instrument for measuring the pressure or weight of the atmosphere. The mercury or Torricellian barometer was invented in 1643 by Torricelli. It consists of a glass tube about 34 in. long and sealed at one end. This is filled with mercury, inverted, and placed vertically in an open dish of mercury. The height at which the mercury in the tube remains above the level of the mercury in the dish indicates the pressure of the atmosphere on the surface of the open cistern, and this height is measured by means of a graduated scale. Normal pressure is *c.* 15 lb. per sq. in. Another form is the aneroid barometer, consisting of a thin metal box completely emptied of air. The shape of the box alters with different pressures, the alterations being shown on a dial by a pointer.

Barrier Reef. See CORAL.

Barter, exchange of articles without use of money or credit; *e.g.* cotton cloth or coloured beads for African native products, blankets for furs in Canada.

Basin (river), the area of land drained by a river and its tributaries. The term basin is also used to denote the area draining to one sea (*e.g.* Mediterranean Basin).

Basques (*basks*), people inhabiting certain provinces of N.E. Spain—Vizcaya, Guipuzcoa, and Alava (the Basque provinces), with part of Navarre—besides a small part of Department of Basses-Pyrénées, France. In Spain they remained independent till 1876, and in France till the Revolution. They are of good height and physique, fair-skinned and fair or dark-haired; brave, intelligent, ardent and enthusiastic, religious but full of prejudices and superstitions, and easily angered, especially where their pride is concerned; long famous as daring seamen. Their origin and race are unknown, and their language unrelated to any other known tongue.

Basu'tos, powerful nation of Bantu-speaking people inhabiting the Crown Colony of Basutoland, S. Africa, and composed of a large number of different tribes brought into union in the 19th century under the leadership of a famous chief, Moshesh. They are one of the most intelligent of coloured races, and are practically self-governing. They number *c.* 550,000.

Bathyorograph'ical. See MAP.

Bauxite (*bō'zīt*), clay containing alumina found at Les Baux, S.E. France (whence the name), Antrim, U.S.A., W. Indies, and elsewhere. From it ALUMINIUM is extracted in the very high temperatures available in electric furnaces at Niagara Falls, L'Argentière (France), Kinlochleven (Scotland), etc.

Beaches, RAISED, terraces of land at different heights above present sea-level which at one time were sea-beaches. They are due to the rising of the land or the sinking of the sea. Many raised beaches exist round the shores of Scotland, at 25, 50, 75, and 100 ft. above the level of the present beach.

Beasts of Burden. See TRANSPORT.

Bêche de Mer (*besh*), also called *trepang, sea-slug, sea-cucumber,* a soft, slimy worm-like animal, 6–24 in. long, found on coral reefs and in shallow tropical seas between E. Indies and N. Australia; when cooked and sun-dried it is a favourite dainty among the Chinese.

Bedouin (*bed'oo-ēn*), certain Arab tribes who lead a nomadic life in the deserts of Arabia and N. Africa. Their mode of life makes them fiercely independent and jealous of their liberty; extremely hospitable where their confidence is won; their love of warfare and of plunder makes them suspicious and treacherous. They are chiefly Mohammedans in religion, but acknowledge no authority except that of their own sheiks or chiefs.

Beet, the name for several varieties of a plant with large, broad leaves and a long tap-root. Common varieties are *mangold* or *mangel-wurzel,* grown as food for cattle; *red beet,* used as a vegetable; and *white beet* or *sugar beet,* widely cultivated for making beet-sugar in central Europe, U.S.A., and now also in Great Britain.

Belts, or ZONES, areas of the earth's surface within which certain types or conditions of climate (*e.g.* temperature, pressure, rainfall), vegetation, or human culture are most markedly seen. Such belts usually merge into one another, the most typical example of any condition or type being found near the centre of each belt.

Ber'bers, a people, numbering *c.* 10,000,000, originally occupying the part of Africa between the Mediterranean and the Sahara, and between Egypt and the Atlantic; but now, owing to Arab immigration, widely scattered and found chiefly in the Atlas Mountains and in desert areas to the S. They are a white race, of good physique, with dark hair and brown or hazel eyes; a warlike people constantly striving either with their neighbours or among themselves, Mohammedans in religion, and very superstitious. In many parts they are engaged in agriculture, following primitive methods, or in various industries, such as the working of iron and the manufacture of swords, guns, and gunpowder. The chief tribes are the Kabyle (Algeria), the Shelluh and Riffs (Morocco), and the Tuareg (desert regions).

Bergschrund (*bārg'shroond*), a great crack in ice or snow, often reaching down to the solid rock underneath, where a snowfield or a glacier leaves a gentle slope to move down a steeper mountainside. At the bottom of the crack are blocks of ice and large pieces of rock.

Be'tel Nut, the nut of the Areca palm, so called because the nut is rolled in a leaf of the betel, a variety of pepper plant, together with a little shell lime, and is then chewed in India and E. Indies. It is said to sweeten the breath, strengthen the gums, promote digestion, and act as a stimulant. It is an important article of commerce in the East.

Bise (*bēz*), a cold, dry, keen N. and N.E. wind which blows in s. France (Rhone Valley) and Switzerland. It is often accompanied by heavy cloud, and it shrivels up vegetation.

Black Earth, a dark-coloured, fertile soil covering parts of s. Russia, Hungary, and Romania, on which large crops of wheat and maize are grown. See also LOESS.

Boers (*bō'ers*), originally Dutch colonists of S. Africa engaged in agriculture and cattle farming; now, more widely, the whole Dutch population of S. Africa, especially of Transvaal and Orange Free State.

Bō'ra ('north wind'), a violent, cold, dry N.E. wind which blows over the KARST towards the Adriatic Sea, mainly in winter and spring, and usually during the daytime.

Bore, or EAGRE, a deep tidal wave which, when the tide begins to flow, rushes up the narrowing estuaries of certain rivers, especially during spring tides. It is well seen in the Rs. Severn, Trent, Seine (*Mascaret*), Ganges, Yangtze Kiang, Amazon, and in the Bay of Fundy.

Borough. See COUNTY BOROUGH, MUNICIPAL BOROUGH.

Boulder Clay. See GLACIER.

Boundary, the actual line of division between countries, states, provinces, counties, etc. It passes through the FRONTIER between countries, and is usually drawn in thinly-populated areas—*e.g.* highlands (where it follows line of crests or water-parting), marshes, upper river courses—as is the boundary between England and Scotland. In new countries it frequently follows lines of latitude and longitude (*e.g.* Canada, Australia), and the actual position on the ground must be determined by survey.

Brave West Winds, regular strong W. and N.W. winds which blow all the year round in the 'Roaring Forties,' *i.e.* between 40° and 50° s. lat. They are of much assistance to sailing vessels.

Bread-fruit, the fruit of a tropical tree native to the Pacific Islands, and also cultivated in W. Indies and tropical America. The fruit is a fleshy mass about the size and shape of a pineapple. When roasted, or sliced, dried, and ground into flour, it forms the staple food of the South Sea islanders. Cloth is made from the inner bark of the tree, and canoes from its trunk.

Bret'ons, a Celtic people inhabiting Brittany (Fr. *Bretagne*), an anc. province occupying the great N.W. peninsula of France. The Bretons are noteworthy for their attachment to old ways and customs, their loyalty to Church and State, their piety, and the great wealth of their traditional folk-tales and folk-songs, probably the finest in the world.

Buddhism (*bood'izm*), one of the great religions of the world, having a larger number of followers than any other faith except Christianity (*c.* 325,000,000). Buddhism, which is largely a religion of self-denial, was founded in India by Prince Siddhartha or Gautama, later called the Buddha, in 6th century B.C., and is now, in various forms, chiefly the religion of China, Japan, Further India, Nepal, and Ceylon.

Buffer State, a country, usually independent, situated between two or more powerful states, and useful as helping to lessen the chance of war between them (*e.g.* Belgium, with neutrality guaranteed by Britain, France, and Germany; Afghanistan, between India and U.S.S.R., but under British influence).

Bunker Coal, the fuel required for ships' furnaces and carried in their 'bunkers.' Such coal is available at coaling stations, which may be near coalfields—*e.g.* Cardiff, Durban, Norfolk (U.S.A.); it is transported, especially from s. Wales, to stations remote from coalfields (*e.g.* Port Said, Falkland Is.). See COALING STATIONS.

Burgh. See COUNTY BOROUGH, MUNICIPAL BOROUGH, ROYAL BURGH.

Bush, the name given, particularly in Australia, to uncultivated dists. covered with a wild growth of shrubs and small trees. Along the desert margins are tracts of *salt-bush* and *blue-bush,* whose grey fleshy leaves supply food for sheep or for rabbits.

Bushmen, aborigines of s. Central Africa, especially of Kalahari Desert, rapidly approaching extinction. They are of moderate stature, with complexion of dirty yellow; the head is small and flat, the nose broad, and the forehead bulging. Savage, fearless, and nomadic in habits, they are great hunters and very swift-footed. Gifted with considerable intelligence, they are very reliable when civilized. Crude drawings and sculpture have been found in some of the caves which they formerly inhabited, giving evidence of some artistic ability.

Butte (*būt*), the name applied in western U.S.A. to any flat-topped hill rising steeply from the surrounding plain.

Cables, SUBMARINE, consist of twisted strands of copper wire enclosed in insulating and protecting materials. Such cables are laid on the ocean floor to transmit telegraphic messages. The first successful cables were laid from S. Foreland to N. France in 1851, from s.w. Ireland to Newfoundland in 1866, from Vancouver (Canada) to New Zealand and Australia in 1902; a cable from Durban crosses the Indian Ocean to the Cocos Islands, whence others are laid to Java and to Perth (W. Australia). The total length of the world's cables is *c.* 310,000 m.

Cacao (*ka-kä'ō*), or COCOA (*kō'kō*), the seeds (30–40 in number) found in the fleshy fruits or pods (7–10 in. long) which grow on the trunk and branches of the evergreen cacao tree, a native of the deep soils of hot, wet, sheltered lowlands near the equator in S. America; it has been planted with much success in W. Africa, and in Ceylon and Java. W. Africa now produces half the world's supply. The seeds or beans are allowed to ferment before being dried in the sun They are shipped whole or broken (cocoa nibs) from the Gold Coast, Brazil, Ecuador, São Thomé, Trinidad, etc. Cocoa is consumed as a beverage or prepared as eating chocolate in Holland, Switzerland, Germany, Great Britain, France, U.S.A. It was known in England in the 16th cent., before either tea or coffee. *Cocoa butter,* extracted from the beans, is used in making soap and pomade. Distinguish cocoa carefully from COCONUT and COCA.

Camel, a large four-footed, cud-chewing animal used as a beast of burden in Asia, Africa, and Australia. The Arabian camel, or *dromedary,* with one hump, domesticated in Arabia and Egypt, is the speediest camel; it carries *c.* 400 lb. The *Bactrian camel,* with two humps, is a native of central Asia, named from Bactria, an anc. dist. between the R. Oxus and the Hindu-Kush Mts.; it is slow of movement, but can carry 700–1,000 lb. Camels arc especially fitted to transport goods in dry lands (*e.g.* Sahara and Sudan), for they carry a reserve of water (lasting 3–13 days) in their stomachs, and eat coarse, prickly plants or absorb the fat of their humps; their eyes are protected against flying sand, and their broad-spreading feet do not sink into the sand.

Camphor (*kăm'for*), a white substance with a strong, pungent smell, obtained mainly from the wood and leaves of a tree of the cinnamon family which grows in Japan, Formosa, central China, and the Malay Peninsula; also from the wood of a large tree in Borneo. It is used in medicine, as a disinfectant, and the wood is made into boxes which, like the commodity itself, preserve clothes from moths.

Cam'pos, the name for the level open plains of Argentina and E. Brazil.

Canal, an artificial waterway for draining land, for irrigation, and particularly for inland navigation by boats and barges (barge canals), or by ocean-going ships (ship canals). Originally constructed on flat plains, canals can, by the use of locks or lifts, be carried by a series of level reaches over hilly ground, or can be carried through a hill by means of a tunnel. Ship canals convert inland towns into ports (*e.g.* Manchester), shorten sea passages (*e.g.* Suez and Panama Canals), avoid dangerous rapids on navigable rivers (*e.g.* Welland and St. Lawrence Canals, Canada). Stretches of shallow rivers are made navigable by being canalized (*e.g.* Thames, Seine).

Cañon (*can'yon*), or CANYON, a deep valley with very high and steep sides, cut out by a river running through a dry region. The most famous example is the Grand Canyon of R. Colorado, Arizona, U.S.A., which is *c.* 300 m. long, from 5 to 15 m. wide, and in places the river is 5,000 ft. below level of plateau.

Car'damom, a spice prepared from the seeds of the reed-like cardamom plant which grows 6–10 ft. high in s. India and Ceylon, where the spice is largely used. It is employed as a remedy for certain stomach troubles, and also for seasoning sauces.

Car'ibs, an American-Indian race found by Columbus in many islands of the West Indies; either exterminated or expelled thence, they are now few in number, and are chiefly found along the shores of the Caribbean Sea from the Isthmus of Darien to the mouth of R. Amazon.

Car'ob, or LOCUST BEAN, the long, flat, dried pod or fruit of the carob tree which grows in Mediterranean coast-lands, especially in Cyprus. It is rich in sugar, which is extracted for use in preserving fruits. It serves as food for animals or even as fruit for human beings; it is called St. John's bread because it was mistakenly supposed to have been the food eaten in the wilderness by John the Baptist.

Carse, the Scottish name for a low-lying, fertile, alluvial plain drained by a river (*e.g.* Carse of Gowrie, Carse of Stirling).

Cassav'a, the starchy flour prepared from the underground stems of the manioc plant, a native of Brazil, now widely cultivated in the tropics. The root-like stems, *c.* 3 ft. long, are poisonous before the milky juice is removed. When dried and ground the flour is used for bread-making, or washed and dried to form *tapioca*, which is exported from W. and E. Indies.

Chart, a map of a portion of the sea showing coast outlines and prominent landmarks, rocks, shallows, depths of the sea (marked in fathoms or in feet). It enables a sailor to navigate seas and oceans, to lay his course from one place to another, to find his exact position, and to know what dangers to avoid.

Chicle (*chik'l*), the solidified milky juice (a form of rubber) of a tree of Mexico and Central America, especially Honduras. It forms the basis of chewing-gum. Nearly 12,000,000 lb. are annually imported by the U.S.A.

China-clay, or KAOLIN, a fine, white, greasy clay used in making porcelain. It results from the weathering of granite, when the felspar breaks up into a powder which, when wet, forms the clay. It is found in Cornwall, central France, Saxony, China, Japan, and U.S.A. The china-clay of Cornwall is transported to central England to be made into Wedgwood, Worcester, Derby, and other ware; that of Limoges is used in making Sèvres ware; that of Saxony for Dresden china.

Chinook', a dry wind, warm in winter and cool in summer, which descends the eastern slopes of the Rocky Mts., Canada. In spring and winter it rapidly removes snow from the western prairies, exposing grass for cattle ranching, and in autumn it makes natural hay of the grass. It also occurs in Montana and Wyoming, U.S.A.

Cinchona (*sin-kō'nă*), the name of *c.* 40 varieties of a tropical evergreen tree, native of the hot, wet E. slopes of the Andes between 7° N. and 22° S. lat., at alt. of 5,000–10,000 ft. The tree has been successfully transplanted in Himalayas, Nilgiri Hills, Sumatra, and Java. It is the source of Peruvian bark, from which is extracted *quinine*, used since 1638 as a remedy for malarial fevers and as a tonic. Java is the principal source of supply.

Cin'namon, the inner bark (ground or unground) of the branches and twigs of a tree native to favoured parts of Ceylon, which yields the bulk of the world's supply. The tree has been introduced into E. and W. Indies and S. America. It is used as a spice. Oil of cinnamon is used medicinally and in the preparation of liqueurs and perfumes.

Cirque (*sirk*), a semicircular depression hollowed out by ice action at the head of a valley in a mountain region. It has steep, high sides, and often contains a lake. The Scottish name is corrie. Examples: Cirque de Gavarnie (Pyrenees), Devil's Beef Tub (Dumfriesshire).

Citronel'la Oil, an oil prepared from a fragrant grass grown extensively in Ceylon. It is used in India as a cure for rheumatism, in Europe and America in making soap and scent, and as a preventive against insect bites.

Cit'rus Fruits, pulpy fruits, with a tough skin or peel, produced by varieties of evergreen citrus tree, which is a native of tropical Asia and thrives only in subtropical and Mediterranean climates. The principal fruits are the orange, lemon, tangerine, lime, kumquat, and grape-fruit, of which the first three grow most abundantly in Spain, Sicily, Algeria, W. Indies, Brazil, Paraguay, U.S.A., and S. Africa; the finest oranges are Maltese, Jaffa, St. Michael (Azores), and W. Indian. The lime is grown chiefly in Montserrat, the kumquat in Japan, and the grape-fruit in California, Florida, and W. Indies.

Climate, the average of weather conditions over a long period of years in any part of the world. The chief factors in climate are TEMPERATURE, RAINFALL, and WIND, and these depend mainly upon latitude, distance from the sea, relief, soil, and vegetation. As regards temperature, the world has been divided into the following belts: *Torrid,* between 23½° N. and 23½° S.; *N.* and *S. Temperate,* between 23½° N. and 66½° N., and between 23½° S. and 66½° S.; and *Frigid,* between 66½° N. and S. and the Poles. These divisions, however, give a very inadequate idea of the various climates of the earth, as they depend solely on latitude. A glance at a temperature map shows that ISOTHERMS do not coincide with lines of latitude. A more satisfactory classification of climate zones, which takes into account all the factors of climate, divides the earth into eight main belts, viz.: the *Tropical Rain Zone*; two *Dry Zones,* steppe and desert; two *Warm Temperate Zones,* including Mediterranean and monsoon areas; *Snow* and *Forest Zone,* with hot summers and cold winters, only found in N. hemisphere; two *Polar Caps.*

Types of climate may be classified as follows: *Marine* or *Oceanic,* in which, owing to the influence of the adjacent sea, the climate is equable, damp, and cloudy, weather is changeable, but seasonal changes are not great (*e.g.* British Isles); *Continental,* in which owing to distance from the sea's influence temperatures are high in summer and low in winter, the air is dry and clear, rainfall diminishes with distance from the sea, and weather changes are not abrupt (*e.g.* Siberia); *Desert,* an extreme form of continental climate in which are warm days often with high winds, and relatively cool and calm nights, rainfall being scanty or irregular (*e.g.* the Sahara); *Subtropical,* found at the tropical margins of temperate zones, and characterized by mild, rainy winters and hot, dry summers; best seen on the W. coasts and islands of continents in the warm temperate zones (*e.g.* Sicily); further inland there may be a tendency to spring and autumn rains (*e.g.* southern U.S.A.); *Monsoon*, depending largely on seasonal winds with summer rainfall (*e.g.* India); *Coast* or *Littoral*, in which owing to the influence of ocean currents and prevailing winds the climate is between marine and continental (*e.g.* Oregon, U.S.A.); *Mountain* or *Plateau*, where, owing to the influence of altitude, there are low temperatures, high winds, and dry, pure air (*e.g.* Tibet).

Climate plays a very important part in determining the distribution of plants, animals, and people over the earth's surface.

Cloud, a mist high above the level of the ground. It is formed by the condensation of the water vapour in the air into minute particles of water, the cores of which are specks of dust. These particles are sometimes frozen into minute crystals of ice and snow. The chief cloud forms are: (*a*) *Cirrus* ('a hair'), white and feathery, and composed of ice crystals; average height, 30,000 ft. (*b*) *Nimbus* ('rain cloud'), a thick, dark layer of cloud with ragged edges, from which rain is falling; average height, 6,500 ft. (*c*) *Cumulus* ('wool pack'), thick, woolly, with horizontal base and rounded domes at upper side; average height, 4,500 to 6,000 ft. (*d*) *Stratus* ('sheet'), a horizontal sheet of lifted mist; average height, under 3,300 ft. There are many intermediate forms, such as cirrostratus, cirrocumulus, stratocumulus, etc.

Cloves, the dried flower-buds of an equatorial tree belonging to the Spice Islands, and for long almost confined to Amboina, but now grown also in Zanzibar and Pemba, tropical America, and W. Indies. Zanzibar, the main source of supply, is being challenged by Java and Sumatra. Cloves are used as a spice because of their strong, fragrant odour and hot, sharp taste. Oil of cloves is extracted for use not only in cooking and the making of liqueurs, but also as a local anæsthetic by dentists and a cure for toothache by their patients.

Coal'ing Sta'tions, or FUELLING STATIONS, ports conveniently situated and equipped for storing and supplying fuel (coal or oil) to merchant or naval steamers. They are necessary because vessels cannot carry in their bunkers sufficient fuel for long voyages, or require the space for cargo. They include most large seaports of the British Empire, and are least numerous on the American Pacific coast, where there is none between San Francisco and Concepcion Bay (Chile). Important mid-ocean coaling stations are Honolulu, Samoa, Fiji, and Mauritius. See BUNKER COAL, ENTREPÔT, TRADE ROUTES.

Coast, the strip of land touching or adjoining the sea. The nature of the coast varies according to the kind of land bordering the sea, and may be: (*a*) *irregular*, with numerous bays, fiords, headlands, fringing islands, etc. (*e.g.* w. coast of Scotland); (*b*) *regular*, with few openings (*e.g.* s. coast of Australia).

Coast Erosion. See EROSION.

Coast'ing Trade, the trade carried on in small vessels from port to port round the coasts of a country, including the distribution of large cargoes brought to the great ports by ocean traders.

Co'ca, the dried leaves of the coca shrub, a native of the E. slopes of the tropical Andes, now also extensively cultivated in Java. The leaves are chewed by S. American Indians to prevent fatigue and hunger. *Cocaine*, used as a local anæsthetic, is extracted from coca leaves.

Cocoa. See CACAO.

Co'conut, the fruit of the coconut palm (60–80 ft. high), which thrives best on the sandy shores of tropical lands. From the fibrous husk *coir* is obtained. Inside the hard shell is a fleshy kernel which forms *copra* when dried in the sun, and *desiccated coconut* (much used in confectionery) when dried by artificial heat. *Coconut oil* is obtained both from the fresh kernel and from copra. The largest exporters of copra are the Dutch E. Indies, Philippine Islands, and Ceylon, while coconut oil is most largely exported from the Philippines. The chief importers of both are the U.S.A., followed by Germany and Holland. The timber of the palm is used in building; the leaves serve for thatching or basket-making; the fermented juice of the flower forms the drink called *arrack.* A large variety of coconut, weighing 40–50 lb. and containing usually four fruits, is a native of the Seychelles; it is known as *coco de mer* or *double coconut.* See Coir, Copra.

Cof'fee, the seeds or beans, usually two in number, enclosed in the pulpy berries ('cherries') of a tropical shrub which grows in the rich soils of well-watered slopes at alt. of 600–6,000 ft., but generally *c.* 2,000 ft. The beans are dried in the sun, separated from their covering coats, and exported in bags of *c.* 130 lb. The largest exporter is Brazil (cheap qualities); the best coffees come from Guatemala, Costa Rica, s. India (Mysore, Coorg), and Kenya; other sources are E. and W. Indies, W. Africa, and Arabia ('Mocha'). Coffee was introduced into England in 1652; the consumption per head is largest in U.S.A., Sweden, Denmark, and Holland.

Coir, the thick fibre forming the husk of the coconut. It is exported from Ceylon, India, and tropical islands, and is made into ropes, brushes, door-mats, stair-carpets, etc.

Col ('neck'), a narrow depression or pass in a mountain range allowing fairly easy passage from one valley to another. It is usually formed by the headwaters of streams wearing away the water parting from opposite sides.

Condensa'tion, the change or process by which invisible water vapour in the atmosphere is converted into liquid or solid form, such as dew, mist, rain, snow, hail. Condensation is brought about by cooling. Water vapour will not condense unless dust particles are present in the air.

Con'tinent, the name given to a large continuous mass of land on the earth's surface. The adjacent islands are reckoned as part of the continent. There are six continents, viz: Eurasia (Europe and Asia), Africa, N. America, S. America, Australia, Antarctica. In the British Isles 'the Continent' means the mainland of Europe.

Continent'al Shelf, Ledge, or Platform. The continents are fringed by a belt of shallow water where the sea bottom slopes gently from the shore line to a depth of *c.* 600 ft.; this is known as the Continental Shelf. Beyond this the slope is very much steeper. The shallow seas covering continental shelves are the richest fishing grounds in the world (*e.g.* Newfoundland Banks, North Sea).

Contour Lines (*kon'toor*), lines drawn on a map through points at the same height above sea-level. Such lines are drawn at fixed intervals, which vary according to the scale of the map. Where slopes are steep the lines lie close together, and where they are far apart it indicates that the slopes are very gentle.

Cool'ies, unskilled labourers, especially from India and China, usually employed in tropical countries other than their own, in various parts of the world. The need for such labour arose on the abolition of slavery, when it became impossible to secure an adequate supply of such workers locally. Coolies usually agree to serve for a certain number of years at a fixed rate of pay, and then return to their own country, their passage being paid both ways. Their employment has caused much trouble among the working-classes in certain countries, particularly America and Australia, owing to their being willing to work for very low wages.

Coomb, Combe, Cwm (*koom*), a short, steep-sided valley on the flank of a hill or running inland from an elevated coast. The term is used in parts of s.w. England and Wales.

Co'pal, a hard, clear resin obtained from many tropical trees, the best quality from E. Africa (Zanzibar). It is used in making varnishes and lacquers.

Cop'ra, the dried kernel of the coconut, exported from the Pacific Islands, etc. The oil extracted is used in margarine factories, especially at Hamburg and Marseilles.

Cor'al, a kind of rock formed from the hard, limy skeletons or frameworks of minute marine animals called coral *polyps*. Multitudes of these tiny creatures, chiefly *madrepores* and *nullipores*, attach themselves to under-water rocks and peaks, and, by the secretion of carbonate of lime from the sea, generations of polyps gradually build up the rocks till they reach the surface in the form of reefs or islands. This active building is carried on in the tropical seas between 30° N. and S. of the equator. There are three kinds of coral reef. If the reef is close to or attached to an island or part of the mainland it is called a *Fringing Reef* (common in E. Indies). If it runs roughly parallel to the mainland, from which it is separated by a navigable channel of considerable width, it is called a *Barrier Reef* (Great Barrier Reef, Australia, 1,200 m. long). The reef may take the form of an *Atoll*, an irregular ring-shaped island surrounding a central lagoon (many in Laccadive and Maldive Islands). Coral rock may be of many colours (green, red, blue, pink, yellow), which combine to give the reefs their beautiful tints. Coral polyps can only live in the warmer parts of the ocean, and in clear, very salt water, and they find most food and grow fastest on the seaward sides of reefs and atolls. They cannot live at a greater depth than 150 ft. The chief coral formations are found in the Gulf of Mexico and the w. coast of Florida, the western Indian Ocean, and particularly the western Pacific Ocean. The red or precious coral found in the shallow parts of the Mediterranean Sea along the coasts of Tunisia, Algeria, and Morocco and other parts, is much used for making jewellery and ornaments.

Cordillera (*cor-dil-yā'ra*), a Spanish name for a ridge or chain of mountains. It is now applied to any series of parallel ranges of mountains, such as the Andes in S. America and the Rocky Mountains in N. America.

Corrie. See CIRQUE.

Cot'ton, the fine hairs on the seeds of the cotton shrub. The shrubs are usually planted each year, but in some countries are left for a second year (ratoon cotton). They are cultivated in tropical, and especially in subtropical, climates, and require *c.* 200 days free from frost. They are subject to insect pests (*e.g.* boll-weevil in America). In India and China much of the cotton, and in Egypt the whole crop, is grown on irrigated fields. The seeds, which are like slightly flattened peas, are contained in a fruit or boll about the size of a small apple. The ripe bolls are hand-picked, and the fibres separated by a machine (the saw-gin). The quality is judged by the length (staple) of the fibres; long-stapled cotton has fibres of 1⅛ in. or more; the long-staples are W. Indian, Sea-Island, and Egyptian cottons; American uplands have a staple of 1⅛ in.; Indian, Russian, and Chinese cottons are short-stapled (¾–1 in.). The ginned cotton fibre is pressed into bales of *c.* 500 lb. for export. The principal producing lands, with production in millions of bales, are U.S.A. (Texas, Mississippi, Arkansas, Oklahoma, Alabama, Georgia) (15), India (5), China (1¾), Egypt (1½), U.S.S.R. (1¼), British Empire (excluding India) (½), world (30). Great Britain, U.S.A., Germany, France, India, Japan, and Italy are the chief cotton-manufacturing countries. Cotton seeds yield an oil used as salad oil, etc.; the refuse is made into cattle cake or used as manure on cotton fields.

Coun'ty Bor'ough, name applied since the passing of the Local Government

Act, 1888, to all English towns having a population of 50,000 and upwards. Previously these had been under the control of the county council of the county in which they were situated, but were then given full and entire control of their own local affairs. These boroughs number about a hundred, and include all the larger English towns. In their number are those towns which were counties of themselves before the Act of 1888, and which should, more properly, be called *counties of towns* or *of cities*. These were towns so important in old days that separate sheriffs were appointed to manage their affairs, as was done in the case of the counties themselves. London, Nottingham, Bristol, Gloucester are examples of such cities.

Crater. See VOLCANO.

Crevasse (*kre-vas'*), a deep crack or fissure in the ice of a glacier. It may run across or along the glacier, and is caused by the strain produced by unequal rates of movement or by the movement of the ice over an uneven surface. The term is sometimes applied to the cracks appearing in the LEVEES of the lower Mississippi.

Cur'rants. (1) Dried small seedless grapes, grown in Mediterranean climate of Greece, especially round the Gulf of Corinth, and exported from Corinth, from which the name (Corinths) is derived; now also prepared for export in E. Australia. (2) Small round fruits, resembling the above in size, grown on bushes in temperate climates, and named by colour—black, red, and white. They are made into jams and jellies.

Currents, OCEAN. See OCEAN CURRENTS.

Cyclone (*sī-klōn*), or LOW or DEPRESSION, area of low air pressure in which the ISOBARS indicate a steady decrease of pressure towards the centre. The isobars form a series of oval rings, generally close together at the broad end, near which the centre lies, but farther apart at the narrow end, which is the 'front' of the system. Air moves spirally inwards to the centre, over which it tends to ascend; the movement of such air or wind is anticlockwise in the N., clockwise in the S. hemisphere, and is strongest where the isobars are closest, *i.e.* where the gradient is steepest. Cyclones tend to move rapidly, and are accompanied by cloudy skies, strong and stormy winds, and heavy rains. See also WHIRLWIND.

Dam, an embankment or wall of earth or masonry built across a river valley to form a lake or reservoir. The water thus kept back may be used to supply towns (*e.g.* Talla Reservoir and Edinburgh, or Lake Vyrnwy and Liverpool), or to irrigate a stretch of land over which the amount of rainfall is uncertain, or insufficient for agriculture (*e.g.* Sennar Dam at Makwar on R. Blue Nile stores water for the irrigation of the plain of Gezira).

Date Line, or INTERNATIONAL DATE LINE, a 'time' line agreed upon at which the 'day' begins. It follows roughly the 180th meridian of longitude. The necessity for such a line arises thus. Two ship captains start from London to sail round the world, one called A. sailing eastward, and the other, called B., sailing westward. They meet at the 180th meridian, and on comparing notes find that A.'s watch is 12 hours fast as compared with Greenwich time, while B.'s watch is 12 hours slow. Moreover, A. declares that the date is, say, Tuesday, 15th March, while B. is sure that the date is Monday, 14th March. A whole day, or 24 hours, is thus 'lost' or 'gained' according as one completes an eastward or westward voyage round the world from London. To avoid this confusion due to difference of dates the 180th meridian was chosen as the longitude where sailors could change the day, backward if sailing eastward, forward if going westward. The date line is not straight, but is drawn in such a way that islands of any one group may be on the same side of the line. American possessions near the 180th meridian take the same dates as America, and certain Pacific islands take Australian dates. See TIME.

Dates, the fruits of the date-palm which thrives in the oases of hot deserts from N. Africa to India, and is cultivated under irrigation in Iraq. They form an important article of food in these lands, and are also exported. The finest qualities come from Algeria, Tunis, and Morocco, and large quantities reach European markets from Basra (Bussorah dates). In India sugar is extracted from dates.

Del'ta, a fan-shaped tract of coastal land composed of the fine silt brought down by a muddy river and deposited when the current of the river is checked by the sea or a lake. This at first forms a shoal or bar, and later an island dividing the river into two branches, and a similar process takes place at the mouths of these and other branches. It is bounded by the farthest apart branches or distributaries into which the river divides, and is traversed by numerous other branch streams. When tidal currents are very weak the delta grows seaward, thus adding new land to the local coast (*e.g.* deltas of Rs. Mississippi and Po). In a lake the delta sometimes grows as far as the opposite shore, and the lake is divided into two parts (*e.g.* Lake Thun, Switzerland). Deltas are usually very fertile and are thickly populated. The name of this formation was first given to the delta of the Nile, the triangular shape of which resembled the Greek letter delta (Δ).

Dēnudā'tion, the breaking up and carrying away of particles and fragments of rock and soil by running water, wind, etc. The chief agents in this work are wind, rain, running water, frost, glaciers, and the sea, and there are usually several of these agents acting together. In some dry regions wind hurls sand and grit against rock faces, which are thus worn away. Rain dissolves mineral matter in rocks, thus breaking up the solid texture of the rock and the smaller particles are washed away. Running water carves out valleys, gullies, ravines, etc., and also carries away the finer material to form plains, deltas, etc. Frost does much destructive work, particularly at high altitudes and in cold countries, by shattering or cracking rocks, and this greatly assists other denuding agents. Glaciers, in addition to carrying away large quantities of boulders, grind the underlying rock surface into fine soil, which is finally carried off by water. The sea pounds rocks into gravel and sand, both of which may be removed by currents and deposited at some distance. The rate of denudation varies according to the nature of the surface, the slope of the ground, and the climate.

Depression. See CYCLONE.

Des'ert, a barren tract of land with little vegetation and few, if any, inhabitants. Deserts are the result of very high temperatures along with very scanty rainfall, or of very low temperatures. In *hot* deserts (*e.g.* the Sahara) occasional areas of fertile land surrounding a spring of water are found (OASES), but in *cold* deserts (*e.g.* the TUNDRA of N. Siberia) only coarse mosses grow during the brief summer. In both types of desert animal life is scarce.

Dink'as, Negro tribes occupying districts on either side of the Bahr-el-Abiad or White Nile in the southern part of the Sudan. In appearance they are tall and very black, and in character brave and warlike.

Dol'drums, the belt of calms and light variable winds between the N.E. and S.E. Trade Winds. The belt is found over the ocean at or near the equator, and changes its position according as the sun 'moves' N. or S. to the Tropics of Cancer and Capricorn. The air is hot and steamy, rainfall is very heavy and frequent, severe thunderstorms occur, and winds are squally.

Drainage. See RIVERS.

Drift. See OCEAN CURRENTS.

Dry Farming, a system of cultivation of lands with scanty rainfall, otherwise too dry for agriculture. The land is deeply ploughed and the surface soil is kept loose, and thus forms a 'blanket' or 'mulch' which prevents the moisture from the damp earth underneath rising by capillary attraction and being evaporated. The subsoil is made compact to increase its water-holding capacity. Seeds (*e.g.* of wheat) are sown deep by drill plough. This system of farming is practised in dry regions where irrigation is not practicable, in Europe, India, w. U.S.A., w. Canada, Australia, and S. Africa.

Dunes, mounds or ridges of drifting sand heaped up and shaped by the wind. Dunes are formed where some small obstacle checks the speed of the wind, and allows some of the rolling or drifting sand grains to come to rest on the windward side of the obstruction. In this way dunes or sand hills are soon formed, which usually show a long slope on the wind side, and a shorter, steeper slope on the lee side. The dunes tend to advance in the direction of the prevailing wind, unless the sand is fixed by planting suitable vegetation. They are numerous along sandy seashores with prevailing onshore winds (*e.g.* Landes of France, Bay of Biscay), and in the low-lying areas of hot deserts (*e.g.* the Sahara). When they move forward much destruction results, whole forests, farms, and villages being buried. Sand dunes on the N. African coast are 600 ft. above the general ground level.

Durra (*doo'ra*), the African name for the great millet of India; also known as Guinea corn. See MILLET.

Dy'aks, or DAYAKS, aboriginal inhabitants of Borneo. They are akin to the Malays, being reddish-brown in colour, but are taller in stature, and more honest and trustworthy in character. They were long notorious for head-hunting, but that practice is now almost given up. Their weapons are the blowpipe, the sword, and the spear. Of considerable intelligence, they practise spinning, weaving, and other crafts.

Dyke (*dīk*), (*a*) in Scotland, a boundary wall of turf or stone; (*b*) name used in East Anglia for a natural or artificial trench filled with water; (*c*) an embankment to keep a river or the sea from overflowing the land (*e.g.* Lower R. Mississippi (LEVEES), and Holland); (*d*) a more or less vertical wall of volcanic rock filling a crack or fissure in the earth's crust. Such dykes sometimes show above the surface as the result of denudation, but most of them are under the surface; some are many yards broad, but more commonly they are only a few feet. See VOLCANO.

Eagre (*ā'ger* or *ē'ger*). See BORE.

Earth Pil'lar, a tapering column of earth on the top of which a large boulder is frequently perched. Such columns may be from 30 to 100 ft. in height, and are produced by the action of rain on the surrounding soft, stony clay, while the pillar itself is protected from erosion by the boulder or other hard material. They are common in regions where glacial moraines and boulder clay are found (*e.g.* the Tirol, Alps).

Earth'quake, a more or less violent shaking of the earth's crust, due to the fracture and movement of rocks below the surface. The point of origin is believed never to exceed 35 m. in depth. From that point the disturbance travels in wavelike motion and in all directions to the surface, decreasing in intensity as it proceeds. The shocks may be so gentle at the surface as not to be noticeable, or they may be so violent as to cause much destruction and loss of life and buildings. Landslips may occur, crevasses or cracks in the land surface may appear, and the whole drainage system of an area may be altered. When shocks originate under the sea near the shores of continents or islands great sea waves are produced which cause much damage. All shocks are preceded by slight tremblings, which are followed by more or less severe vibration which gradually dies away. In most cases the shocks last only a few seconds, but the tremblings may continue for days or weeks. Italy, Japan, China, and Peru are subject to frequent and destructive earthquakes. The earthquakes at Lisbon (1755), Messina (1908), and Tokyo, Japan (1923), are among the worst of which there are records. The study of earthquakes is called *Seismology*, and the recording and measuring instrument is a *Seismometer*.

Eclipse (*e-klips'*), the obscuring or darkening of a heavenly body by another, or by its shadow. An eclipse of the sun is caused by the moon passing between it and the earth; the moon is eclipsed when it passes through the earth's shadow. An eclipse is *total* when the whole face of the sun or moon is hidden, and *partial* when only a portion of the face is in darkness. When the moon leaves the outer rim of the sun exposed, the eclipse is *annular*. Stars and planets also suffer eclipse.

Entrepôt (*on'tr-pō*), a commercial centre, either seaport or inland town, at which goods are collected to be distributed over a large area or to be exported in bulk (*e.g.* Singapore). Many entrepôts are also important coaling stations. *Entrepôt Trade* is the collection at entrepôts of commodities from many different parts of the world for distribution to many other parts, and is naturally centred at seaports (*e.g.*London, Hong Kong). See TRADE ROUTES.

Equator. See LATITUDE.

Equinox, the time of the year when day and night are equal. This occurs twice each year all over the globe, when the sun is vertical over the equator on or about March 21 (the *Vernal* (Spring) Equinox), and again about September 22 (the *Autumnal* Equinox).

Erō'sion, the gradual removal or wearing away of portions of the earth's surface by natural agencies. Rain, ice, wind, etc., continually carry on this work, and the small fragments and finely broken material are removed by running water. The erosion of coast cliffs is mainly the work of sea waves dashing stones, rock fragments, and sand against the lower portions of the cliffs, causing them to be undermined; frost, rain, and the roots of vegetation attack the upper portions, and the masses of rock which are loosened and fall to the base are instruments of further erosion. The harder portions of the cliffs remain as capes and peninsulas. Rivers erode their channels and banks, especially in times of flood, and where the current is swift an enormous amount of erosion takes place in mountain chains.

Escarp'ment, a ridge of land or rock with a steep, abrupt slope on one side, the other slope being much more gentle. The escarpment is the outcrop of a tilted stratum of hard rock, the steep part being the face of the stratum and the gentle slope representing its surface.

Es'kimos, or ESQUIMAUX, aboriginal inhabitants of Greenland and the Arctic regions of N. America. They number *c.* 30,000, and, as they are very widely scattered, the number at any particular place is comparatively small, only some 20 or 30 families in a group. They are of short stature, have broad, fat faces and coarse black hair, bearing very close resemblance to the N. American Indians. They live by fishing, and hunting seals and whales, but the commercial hunting of these animals by traders has reduced their natural food supplies, and in Alaska, for example, reindeer have been introduced in order to provide better food supplies. In summer they live in tents near open water; in winter in huts of turf and snow, heated by oil-lamps. They are an extremely healthy and contented race, and are very conservative in habits, showing little inclination to adopt civilized ways of life. In 1912 the explorer

Stefannson discovered near Coronation Gulf, on the arctic shores of N. America, a community of white Eskimos with red hair and blue eyes who were probably descended from the old Norse Vikings who visited America from *c.* 1000 onwards.

Esparto. See ALFA.

Es'tūary, the part of a river mouth up which the tide flows. In the estuary of a river like the Thames the water becomes rapidly salter from the river to the sea, and the lower layers are much salter than the surface. If the river mouth is very large and wide, with no obstruction or bar (*e.g.* Firth of Forth), the saltness of the water is uniform in the seaward half, only the upper and narrower portion being really estuarine.

Eucalyptus (*ū-ka-lip'tŭs*), a family of plants, allied to the myrtles, native to Australia, where the trees are called 'gum-trees.' The species, numbering over 350, vary in size from forest trees to low-growing, stunted MALLEES, *c.* 15 ft. high, which form the scrub country of N.W. Victoria. The trees are classed as ironbarks (with a corrugated bark), stringy-barks (with a fibrous bark), and gums (with smooth bark); the gums are distinguished by the colour of their bark as blue gums, red gums, spotted gums, etc. Eucalypt timber is a strong and durable hardwood, generally red or brown in colour; the best-known woods are those of S. Swanland, W. Australia—*Jarrah* (used for street paving, railway sleepers, and piles for piers), *Karri* (for bridge building), *Tuart* (for framing), *Wandoo* and *York Gum* (for pit props). The *Tallow-wood* of New S. Wales is used for flooring, and the *Mountain Ash* of Victoria, which splits readily, is largely employed in making fences. *Eucalyptus oil*, extracted from the leaves, is used in making soap and disinfectants.

Evapora'tion, the process by which a solid or liquid is converted into an invisible vapour or gas. The conversion of ice and water into water vapour goes on constantly, not only over the sea but wherever there is moisture in the soil, except where the air is already *saturated*, or contains all the water vapour it can hold. As the capacity for holding water vapour is greater in warm air than in cold, it is in the warmer areas that evaporation is most extensive and rapid. Conditions favouring evaporation are *warm* and *dry* air which is not saturated; *wind*, which carries away the wet air, replacing it with drier air; and a *large water surface* over which there is high temperature.

Fall Line, the American name for the irregular line marking the junction of the Appalachian Mts. and the E. coastal plain. The rivers form waterfalls and rapids as they pass from the high ground to the plain. On their banks below the falls many important manufacturing cities have arisen (*e.g.* Philadelphia, Trenton) in which numerous industries are carried on by the help of water-power. A similar line is seen where the Italian Alps meet the Plain of Lombardy.

Fauna (*faw'na*), the native animals of any particular geographical region or any epoch of time.

Fertilizers, substances used to make soil more productive or to enable plants to withstand adverse conditions and thrive in spite of them. The following are the chief fertilizers: farmyard manure, guano or the droppings of sea-birds obtained from islands off Peru, S. Africa, etc., lime, limestone and chalk, nitrates, phosphates, and potassium salts. Nitrates are obtained from Chile, Norway, and Germany; phosphates from raw material obtained in N. Africa; and potassium salts from Stassfurt in Germany.

Fiord. See FJORD.

Firn. See GLACIER.

Fjord (*fē'ord*), a long, narrow arm of the sea between steep, high cliffs. Fjords are usually shallow at the mouth, with deep water inland. They are numerous on the W. coasts of Norway, Scotland, British Columbia, Chile, and S. New Zealand. Sogne

Fjord, Norway, is over 100 m. long and 4,000 ft. deep. In Scotland such openings are known as *Firths* or (sea) lochs.

Flax, or LINT, an annual plant with a tall, upright stem (*c.* 2 ft.), small leaves, and blue flowers. It grows through a wide range of climate, but is cultivated only on suitable soils where labour is abundant. It is grown either for its fibre or for its seeds. The fibre of the inner bark of the stem forms the flax of commerce, and is spun and woven into *linen*, a word derived from *Linum*, the Latin name of the plant. Russia exports large quantities of flax, but the best quality comes from the valley of the R. Lys in Belgium; some is produced in N. Ireland. The plants are pulled by the roots by hand labour, *rippled* by machines to remove the seeds, *retted* (rotted) in water or dew, dried in the open air, rolled by machines which break the wood of the stems, and *scutched* to separate the wood from the fibre, which is then *heckled* (combed); the short fibres form *tow*. The linen industry, which dates as far back as history and is widely carried on, is specially important in N. Ireland, w. Fife and s. Angus (Scotland), Westphalia, Bohemia, and Belgium. In Argentina, India, U.S.A., Canada, and Russia much flax is grown for its seed (linseed), which yields an oil used in making paints, varnishes, and printer's ink, while the crushed seeds are prepared as *oilcake* for feeding cattle. *New Zealand Flax* (*Phormium*) is the very strong fibre of a plant of a quite different species grown in New Zealand; it is made into ropes, mats, sailcloth, etc.

Flo´ra, plants native to any particular geographical region, or belonging to a particular period of time.

Föhn, a warm, dry wind which blows down the northern valleys of the Alps in winter and spring. It blows from the south; its moisture is deposited on the s. side of the mountains, and warm dry weather is experienced on the N. side. A similar wind blows over the Rocky Mts. from the w., and is known in Canada as the CHINOOK.

Forest, an area of land well stocked with trees, either of natural growth or planted by man. Such areas are found only where the rainfall and temperature are suitable. There are three main types of forests according to the nature of the wood produced—(1) *coniferous* or *softwood* forests, consisting chiefly of pines, spruces, firs, larches, etc., and found in the northern hemisphere, chiefly in Canada, U.S.A., Norway, Sweden, Finland, Russia, and Manchuria; (2) *temperate hardwood* forests, consisting chiefly of oaks, maples, birches, poplars, etc., and found in the northern hemisphere in the parts lying immediately s. of the coniferous areas mentioned above; (3) *tropical hardwood* forests, consisting chiefly of mahogany, logwood, rosewood, ebony, etc., found in their greatest extent in the tropical regions of America, Africa, and Asia. The first two kinds of forests are those most generally useful to man, and they are found chiefly in the north temperate zone, where the population is most dense, and the need therefore greatest. Tropical forests are not so useful because many of the trees do not provide suitable timber, but more because of the lack of easy transport and the difficulty of securing a sufficient supply of workers. Besides providing man with timber, forests are useful and important in other ways—they affect climate and direction of rivers, protect the soil from erosion, and sometimes act as barriers to the colonization and development of a country. At certain periods and in certain places the forest areas have been too ruthlessly cleared, and it has accordingly become necessary to replant areas of this kind and to protect existing areas against the ravages of man or of nature. See AFFORESTATION.

Fox Farming. See FURS.

Free Port, a port, or area within a port, exacting no customs duties on imports or exports from any vessel discharging or loading cargo. Such duties are payable only when goods are carried from the free zone into the HINDERLAND. A free port is usually an ENTREPÔT, *e.g.* Copenhagen serves the Baltic lands. By the establishment of bonded warehouses, in which taxable commodities may be stored duty-free till they are required for consumption, the privileges of free ports have become less valuable. Of European free ports Hamburg, Danzig, and Copenhagen are the most important; in the British Empire the largest free ports are Hong Kong, Singapore, and Penang.

Frontier, the area of separation (generally thinly populated) between two densely peopled areas whose inhabitants form distinct political groups (*e.g.* English Channel between England and France, Alps between France and Italy); it is known also as the *Marches* or *Borders.* Through it the *boundary* is drawn. It serves as a protection against surprise attacks by either people, and is usually fortified where routes cross it (*e.g.* Belfort, France). On the frontier are Customs stations to prevent smuggling, and medical centres to keep out people infected with diseases. The best frontiers are seas, deserts, mountains, forests, and swamps. The term is also applied to the area where one group of races, languages, climates, plants, or animals passes into another such group. See BOUNDARY.

Frost, a general name for the conditions when the temperature falls to 32° F., which is the freezing point of water, or to a lower degree. Frost is one of the active agents of denudation. Water enters the pores and cracks of apparently solid rocks. On freezing, this water expands and helps to break up or disintegrate the rocks. If not of too long duration, frost is of service to the farmer in temperate lands, as it breaks up the surface soil and makes the land easy to work in spring. Spring frosts may do damage to growing vegetation in May or June, and in some places autumn frosts are very injurious to ripening grain. *Hoar-frost* is the visible frozen vapour found on exposed surfaces.

Fu'lahs, or FULANI, a race of people distributed across Africa from the Upper Nile to Senegal. A white race, strong and well-built, with Caucasian features, they are frank and intelligent, trustworthy, and devout Mohammedans. They are industrious, practising agriculture, carrying on trade, working iron and silver, and weaving various fabrics. At the beginning of the nineteenth century they conquered their neighbours and founded great kingdoms in Nigeria, which still remain under British suzerainty.

Furs, the skins of certain animals, covered with fine, short, soft hair, through which long protective hairs (over-hair or guard-hair) protrude. Fur is used as clothing, especially in colder climates. Furs are mainly collected by trappers in temperate and arctic N. America and Eurasia, where the weasel family (stoat or ermine, marten, sable, mink, and skunk), and beavers, raccoons, foxes, musk-rats or musquashes, etc., are numerous. To these may be added Australasian rabbits, opossums, and wallabies; S. American chinchilla rats and coypus (nutria furs); and certain tropical animals. Furs are collected (*e.g.* by the Hudson's Bay Co.) for sale at the great auctions held in London, Leipzig, and New York. To maintain supplies some governments have established experimental farms where fur-bearing animals, especially foxes and rabbits, are bred in captivity (*e.g.* in New York state and California, U.S.A., Prince Edward I., Canada); and similar farms have been established (*fox farming*) as private enterprises in America, Europe, and even in Britain. To prevent extermination the fur seal and sea-otter are protected by U.S.A. and Canada.

Gap. See PASS.

Gauge, RAILWAY, the distance between the inner edges of the rails. The *standard* gauge (4 ft. 8½ in.) is that of British lines, which were the first to be laid down, and conformed to the earlier wooden wagon ways. This gauge was generally adopted on the continent of Europe, in Egypt, in N. America, and for the transcontinental line from Port Augusta to Kalgoorlie in Australia. *Broad* gauges are used in U.S.S.R. (5 ft.), Ireland (5 ft. 3 in.), and Spain and Portugal, India, and Argentina (5 ft. 6 in.); *narrow* gauges in Japan and S. Africa (3 ft. 6 in.), Kenya, Uganda, and India (partly) (metre), and generally for mineral and similar traffic (2–3 ft.).

Gauge, Rain, an instrument for measuring the amount of rainfall at any place. In its simplest form a rain gauge consists of a funnel, 5 or 8 in. in diameter at the wide end, fitted into a narrow glass jar which holds the collected water, the whole being enclosed in an outer cylindrical vessel, open at the top. When in use the instrument is firmly fixed in an exposed position, the rim of the outer vessel being horizontal and *one foot* above the level of the ground. To prevent the water from splashing over during very heavy rains, and also to collect snow during high winds, the rim of the funnel should be 4 in. below the rim of the outer covering. The collected water is poured into a graduated vessel, and the amount of rainfall for a stated period, say 24 hours, is measured in inches. An inch of rain means the amount of rain that would cover the ground to the depth of 1 in. if none escaped by evaporation or by sinking into the ground. 10 in. of snow are reckoned as equal to 1 in. of rain, but by melting the snow collected more accurate measurements are obtained.

Geyser (*gā'ser* or *gīz'er*), a natural fountain throwing up a column of hot water or steam at more or less regular intervals. It consists of a crater-like basin above ground and a narrow passage leading underground. Water accumulates in the passage or in its expansions, becomes gradually hotter until the pressure of the water overhead is overcome by that of the steam generated nearer the source of heat, and a column of hot water is shot up the tube into the air. This water falls back into the basin or around it, and on cooling or evaporating, deposits mineral matter which it has held in solution (mainly silica), and successive deposits form the basin. As geysers only occur in regions where volcanoes have been recently active, the source of heat is probably hot underground lava, and since geysers gradually cease working, the lava is probably cooling. The best known geysers are those of Iceland (near Mt. Hekla), Yellowstone Park, Wyoming, U.S.A., and North I. of New Zealand (near Lake Taupe).

Ghats (*gauts*), an Indian name used for mountain passes. The name is now applied by Europeans to the ranges of mountains running along the w. and e. coasts of India (W. and E. Ghats). Ghat is also used to mean a flight of stairs leading down to a landing-place on an Indian river (*e.g.* at Benares, on R. Ganges).

Ghee (*gē*), Indian name for butter clarified by boiling over a clear fire to resemble oil. The best quality is prepared from cow's milk, but buffalo-milk is also used. Ghee is a common article of diet among Indians, by whom it is also regarded as a valuable cosmetic and medicine, and a suitable sacrifice in religious ceremonies.

Ginger, an aromatic and pungent spice consisting of the sun-dried underground stems of the ginger plant, a native of s.e. Asia, now widely cultivated in tropical lands. It is yellowish in colour and fibrous in structure, and is exported in branched pieces, *c.* 3 in. long, from British E. and W. Indies and Sierra Leone. It is used for flavouring and for medicinal purposes, and when preserved in syrup (in the W. Indies and China) forms a popular sweetmeat.

Glacier (*glas'ier*), a mass of ice moving slowly down a valley. Above the Snowline great quantities of snow accumulate, forming *snowfields*. The snow in the lower layers is changed by pressure into *granular* ice, which is called *névé* (French) or *firn* (German), and is forced to move down the slope as a glacier, the granular ice, meantime, being transformed into blue crystalline ice. The rate of movement varies from a few inches to a few yards per day, but is not uniform, being fastest in the centre and slowest where the glacier meets the valley walls. The nature of the valley floor may also cause the lower layers of ice to move more slowly than the upper. This irregular movement causes cracks or CREVASSES to occur. During its progress the glacier smooths, scrapes, and scratches the rock over which it moves, and also the sides of the valley; the rocks thus treated are said to be *striated*. The glaciated valley becomes regular and usually U-shaped in section.

In the high altitudes, where glaciers are found, frost is very active in *disintegrating* or breaking up the rocks, and boulders and smaller pieces of rock which fall on a glacier are carried along with it. When this material is carried along the edges of the glacier it forms a *lateral moraine*. Some of the material which is pushed along the bottom of the glacier forms a *ground moraine*. When two glaciers join, two adjoining lateral moraines unite to form a thicker *medial moraine* down the centre of the resulting greater glacier. On reaching lower levels, where the sun is strong enough to melt the ice as fast as it advances, the glacier deposits its load as a *terminal moraine*, while the muddy water forms a river.

During the *Ice Age* a great part of N. Europe, including the British Isles, was covered by an immense sheet of glacier-like ice, or *ice cap*, 2,000 to 3,000 ft. thick. Parts of this ice sheet moved as glaciers in various directions according to the general slopes of the land. When the Ice Age passed, huge quantities of rock waste were thus left behind as moraines, and this soil is known as *boulder clay* or *till*. Where a mass of hard rock obstructed the flow of the ice, the obstructing face was ground into a steep cliff, and the ice, flowing round the sides, piled up the rubbish in a long slope behind. On the disappearance of the ice a formation known as *crag* and *tail* was exposed (*e.g.* Edinburgh Castle Rock and High Street).

Mountain glaciers are numerous in the Himalayas, Caucasus, Andes, Rockies, etc. Those of the Alps, though well known, are really very small. Ice caps cover Greenland and the S. polar continent.

Glen, the Scottish name for a long narrow valley. Glens are usually traversed by rivers, and form the best means of communication in mountainous areas. Glenmore extends for 100 m. from the Moray Firth in the N.E. to Loch Linnhe in the S.W. Through it runs the Caledonian Canal, which links up Lochs Ness, Oich, and Lochy.

Graphite (*graf'it*), also known as PLUMBAGO and BLACKLEAD, is a soft, greasy, black, opaque mineral, composed almost entirely of carbon. It is found in its purest form most abundantly in Ceylon, Madagascar, Bohemia, Japan, U.S.A., and Cumberland (England); it is produced artificially in U.S.A. It is used in the manufacture of lead pencils, as a polish lubricant for machinery, as a polish for grates, and in making crucibles, type-metal, and anti-rust paints.

Grasslands, the treeless, grassy plains in the interiors of continents, between the forest belts and the arid regions. They are most extensive in the cold Temperate Zones, and are generally unsuitable for cultivation. In S. and S.E. European Russia, and S.W. Siberia, they are called *steppes*, in N. America *prairies*, and in Argentina *pampas*. In these regions temperatures are extreme, and rain, which only falls in summer, is scanty (under 25 in.). For part of the year these lands provide good grazing, and in the steppes stock raising by nomadic tribes is important. In the steppes of s.w. Asia the growing season lasts only for a few weeks in spring and summer, but good crops of cereals, fruit, and vegetables are grown on irrigated land. In N. America much prairie land has been converted into farms, on which wheat and other crops are grown, but in the western parts, where rainfall is insufficient for crops, ranching is extensively carried on. The Argentine pampas are pasture grounds, but there are many fertile areas suitable for agricultural purposes. The Australian grasslands in the s.e. are great sheep-rearing grounds.

In subtropical regions, especially in Africa, grasslands are called *savannas*. The most extensive savanna land, a fine cattle country, stretches from Senegal to Abyssinia. Here during the growing season rainfall is adequate and temperatures are not so extreme as in the cold temperate grasslands. Grass is often 6 ft. high, clumps of trees occur like oases, and trees grow along the river banks. The *llanos* of the n.w. Orinoco Basin and of Colombia, and the *campos* of s.e. Brazil in S. America, are of a similar nature.

Great Circle, a circle whose plane passes through the centre of the earth. All meridians of longitude and the equator are great circles; parallels of latitude other than the equator are *small* circles. The shortest distance between two points on the globe lies along the arc of the great circle which passes through these points, and sailors take advantage of this by sailing along that great circle unless forced from it by land, ice, etc. In sailing due n. or s. the meridians are followed, but in going e. and w., except along the equator, great circles are followed which curve towards the n. and then towards the s. of parallels of latitude in the n. hemisphere, and towards the s. and then towards the n. in the s. hemisphere.

Ground Nut, Earth Nut, Monkey Nut, or Pea Nut, the fruit contained in the pod of a tropical plant of the pea family, native of S. America, but now widely cultivated on the light sandy soils of India, W. Africa, China, and s. U.S.A. When the flowers of the plant give place to the seed-pod the stem (*c.* 1–2 ft. high) bends over to allow the pod to enter the soil where the seeds ripen (hence the name). The nuts (seeds) are eaten, fresh or roasted, in the lands which produce them, and in U.S.A. pea-nut butter is a popular preparation; they are largely imported into France, Germany, Great Britain, and Holland, where the oil is extracted for use as a salad oil and for other food purposes.

Gulf Stream. See Ocean Currents.

Gunny Cloth, a cheap, coarse material woven from *jute* fibres, and used for making sacks—*e.g.* for coal, and as packing for cotton, coffee, and other transported products. The main seats of the industry are Howrah (Calcutta) and Dundee (Scotland), but factories have been erected in many European and N. American centres. The largest importers of gunny cloth are U.S.A., Canada, Argentina, and Brazil. See Jute.

Gurkhas (*goor'kaz*), the dominant race in Nepal, India. They are short and thick-set in build, and make very brave, faithful, and self-reliant soldiers. They rendered valuable service to the British in the suppression of the Indian Mutiny and during the Great War. Their national weapon is the kukri, a heavy curved knife.

Hachures (*hash'oor*), short lines drawn on a map to represent differences of slope. They are drawn from the highest point of a hill towards the base, and should cut contour lines at right angles. Short, dark hachures close together indicate a steep slope; longer, finer, and further apart hachures, a more gentle slope. The lines give the effect of shading on the map, but unlike contour lines they give no indication of height above sea-level.

Hanse Towns, the trading centres of

the Hanseatic League, or Hansa, a company of German merchants who almost monopolized the trade of N. Europe from the 13th cent. until the era of oceanic discoveries, and sank into insignificance during the Thirty Years' War (1618–48). During that long period the League maintained armed forces for checking piracy on the Narrow Seas and robbery on land, securing fair trade from neighbouring rulers, and obtaining commercial privileges from surrounding states. The headquarters of the Hansa were at Lübeck; among its principal depots were Wisby, Cologne, Brunswick, Danzig, Hamburg, Magdeburg, Halle, Frankfurt-on-Oder, and Thorn; and it maintained 'factories' at Bruges, London, Bergen, and Novgorod.

Harmat'tan, a hot, dry, dust-laden, northerly wind which blows from the Sahara to the Gulf of Guinea from December to March. It is harmful to vegetation.

Hausas (*houz'az*), an African people, of mixed Arab and Negro blood, living in Northern Nigeria between Lake Chad and R. Niger. They are agriculturists and very successful traders, using well-defined trade routes to the Mediterranean and Red Seas and the Gulf of Guinea. Among their manufactures are cloth, leather articles, and glass. Their language is the most important of the many languages of West and Central Africa, being used by more than 15,000,000 people all over Central Africa. In religion they are Mohammedans.

Head of Navigation, the highest point up a river to which a trading vessel can be safely navigated.

Hemp, fibre prepared from the bark of an annual plant, native of s. Asia, but cultivated on a large scale, under conditions of soil and climate suitable for flax, in Russia, Germany, Italy (which yields the finest quality), etc.; very little is raised in Britain. It is coarser and stronger than flax, and is used for ropes, cordage, and stout canvas (*e.g.* for sails). From the leaves of hemp grown in India and other warm lands intoxicants and narcotics such as *bhang* (India) and *hashish* (Arabia, Egypt) are prepared; the resin, prepared as *charas* in Kashmir, is also smoked in India. Hemp seeds are used as a bird food; from them an oil is extracted. *Manila hemp*, obtained from the *abaca*, a tree of the banana family, is a product mainly of the Philippine Islands. It is used for the best class of ropes; the finer fibres are woven into delicate fabrics (*e.g.* for curtains); and from old ropes strong *manila paper* is made. See FLAX, SISAL.

Hin'derland, or HINTERLAND, geographically the land which lies behind a seaport or seaboard, and to which it owes its size and importance as such. The hinderland provides the seaport with most of the goods to be exported from it, and provides a market in which the greater part of its imports will be distributed and sold. The size of the hinderland serving any port may depend to some extent on the ease of communication with the interior or the destination of the goods to be imported. Thus, although the W. Riding of Yorkshire is the hinderland of the Humber ports, it is also the hinderland of Liverpool for trade with America.

Hindus (*hin'dooz*), the name applied to *c.* 215,000,000 of the people of India, adherents of the religion called Hinduism, which was founded *c.* 1000 B.C. These people represent about a dozen different nationalities and speak some six hundred different varieties of language. The Hindu is earnest and devoted in the service of his gods, every detail of his life being ordered by his religion. A prominent feature of Hinduism is the caste system, by which all Hindus are divided into classes or groups (*c.* 200), according to trade, profession, etc.

Horizon, the line bounding our view of earth or sea where earth and sky seem to meet. On land the spectator sees this *visible* or *sensible* horizon as a more or less irregular circle;

at sea it is a perfect circle, of which the observer is the centre, the distance of the circumference depending upon the elevation of the observer.

Horse Latitudes, belts of high atmospheric pressure over the ocean, in the N. hemisphere between the N.E. Trade Winds and the S.W. Variables, and in the S. hemisphere between the S.E. Trade Winds and the N.W. Variables. These belts vary in latitude according as the sun 'moves' N. or S. to the Tropics of Cancer and Capricorn. Like the Doldrums, they are regions of calms and light variable winds, but, unlike the Doldrums, the weather is comparatively bracing and dry.

Hot'tentots, S. African aborigines (calling themselves *Khoikhoi*, Men of Men), now chiefly inhabiting the western part of S. Africa. They are closely allied to the Bushmen in physical characteristics and language, which, from its use of 'clicks,' caused early Dutch settlers to name them Hottentots or stutterers. They are of middle stature, yellowish-brown in colour, and have woolly hair. In habit they are a nomadic, pastoral people, living peacefully under a patriarchal form of government. In contact with white races they have been found to be cunning, lazy, and dishonest, and their character has become much degraded through intermarriage with the lowest types of white settler. They number *c.* 100,000.

Hydro-electric Power. See WATER POWER.

Ice, the solid form which water takes when it freezes. Ice is lighter than the water out of which it is formed, and therefore when lakes or seas freeze the ice floats on the surface, increasing in thickness as the cold continues. Along the shores of polar lands an *ice foot* is formed which rises and falls with the tide, and is driven by the waves against the shore, thus acting as a coast erosion agent. In the open polar seas slabs of *floe ice* are formed, which under the action of winds and currents are thrown together and frozen into a jumbled mass known as *pack ice*, which adds greatly to the difficulties and dangers of communication in these regions.

On land ice acts as a powerful denuding agent. See DENUDATION; GLACIER.

The manufacture of artificial ice has been of great service to commerce, as it enables foodstuffs to be preserved for long periods, and to be carried over long distances without becoming unfit for consumption.

Ice'berg, a huge mass of ice floating in the sea. In the N. hemisphere many glaciers reach the sea, where great irregularly shaped masses are broken off and carried southwards by the polar and Labrador currents to the W. Atlantic Ocean, where they are a great danger to ships. Round Antarctica the very thick, flat sheet of mingled ice and snow, forming a continuous glacier, is known as *barrier ice*. Immense blocks of this break off and form the *tabular* or flat-topped icebergs of the Antarctic Ocean. Only about one-ninth of the mass of an iceberg is visible above water. Arctic icebergs are often 200 to 300 ft. above water; many Antarctic icebergs are like huge islands, 200 ft. or more in height, and a mile or more in length.

Incas, an American-Indian tribe of Peru who claimed to be the Children of the Sun sent from heaven to subdue and instruct the other natives of the country. By their skill and prowess as soldiers they established a vast empire, stretching from Chile to Quito, and from the Pacific to Paraguay. They were a highly civilized people at the time of their conquest by Pizarro in 1533, being skilled as farmers, metal-workers, weavers, and potters, and had some knowledge of the arts and of astronomy. Centuries of oppression have much debased their character, though they still retain some of the virtues of their ancestors. Their language, called Quichua, is still spoken.

Indian Corn. See MAIZE.

Indians, natives of India; also, more commonly, the aboriginal inhabitants of America and the W. Indies. These were called *Indians* from the error of Columbus and other early explorers, who believed the newly discovered land to be near India. See HINDUS and RED INDIANS.

Irriga'tion, the artificial distribution of water from rivers or storage reservoirs for the growing of crops in parts of the world where farming is otherwise impossible owing to scanty rainfall. *Baling* water from wells by hand is probably the oldest method of irrigation, and is still practised in many parts of the world, particularly in India. Mechanical aids were soon invented, such as the shadoof in Egypt, consisting of a pole with bucket and counterweight, and the water-wheel used in Egypt and N. India. *Flooding* by the seasonal overflow of rivers, such as the Nile and the Ganges, provides what may be called a natural form of irrigation, and is very valuable because of the quantity of rich silt or alluvium so distributed. In the *reservoir system,* largely used in India, rain water is stored in tanks and distributed as required. Where rivers are available, reservoirs are formed by dams or barrages to store water at a constant level, and *irrigation canals,* with branches and distributaries, are led from them to supply large areas of level ground, a method largely in use in India, America, and Australia. An interesting method, employed in certain parts of England, is to flood fields with water in winter-time, the coldest and wettest part of the year, so as to protect the roots of grasses from the frost of winter. Such fields are called *water meadows.* Wherever irrigation is practised care must be taken to provide for adequate drainage, for if water is left stagnant in the soil it becomes more harmful than helpful to vegetation.

Islands, land areas surrounded by water. These occur in rivers, lakes, seas, and oceans. Some islands rise from a CONTINENTAL SHELF and are called *continental* islands (*e.g.* British Isles). Others rise from great ocean depths and are known as *oceanic* islands. If an island is volcanic in origin it is called a *volcanic* island (*e.g.* St. Helena). In the tropical seas some islands are built up by CORAL polyps and are called *coral* islands. Sometimes islands occur in chains (*e.g.* Japan) or as groups, known as ARCHIPELAGOS (*e.g.* Philippines). The island of Australia is so large that it may be called a *continent-island.*

I'sobar ('equal pressure'), a line drawn on a map to connect places which have the same average atmospheric pressure over a given period. Actual pressures are obtained by barometric readings, and corrections are made in order to reduce these to the corresponding pressures at sea-level. Reports of barometric pressure are received from stations in various parts of the country and from ships at sea, and from these weather forecasts can be made.

I'sobath ('equal depth'), a line drawn on a map or chart connecting places where the sea is of the same depth. The unit of measurement is usually the fathom (6 ft.).

Isohyet (*ī-so-hī'et*) ('equal rain'), a line drawn on a map to connect places with equal rainfall during a given period. The unit of measurement employed may be the inch or the millimetre.

Isoneph (*ī'so-nef*) ('equal clouds'), a line drawn on a map to connect places having the same average proportion of the sky obscured by clouds during a given time.

I'sotherm ('equal heat'), a line drawn on a map connecting places with the same average temperature for a given time. Thermometric readings are taken at various stations, and corrections are made in order to raise the readings for all elevations to what the corresponding figures would have been at sea-level. The most important isothermal maps are those showing average winter and average summer temperatures.

Ivory, the hard, white substance that composes the teeth or tusks of certain animals, such as the elephant, hippopotamus, walrus, narwhal, and S. African wart-hog. Elephant tusks, which form the largest source of supply, are obtained principally in tropical Africa; a small supply of mammoth ivory, obtained from the curved tusks of a prehistoric elephant, is still exported from arctic Asia. Ivory is used for making billiard balls, handles for cutlery and toilet articles, piano keys, etc.; the parings and chips are carved into ornaments or used in inlaid work; and the dust serves for polishing and for preparing Indian ink. The principal ivory markets are London and Antwerp. *Vegetable ivory,* prepared from the hard, white parts of the seeds of a S. American palm, is of much less value, and is made into buttons, toys, etc.

Jarrah. See EUCALYPTUS.

Jute, the fibre of the inner bark of two varieties of a slender-stemmed annual plant of the same family as the lime tree. The plant is a native of Bengal, where it grows 6–12 ft. high on the alluvial banks of the lower Ganges and Brahmaputra rivers. The fibre, which is weaker and less durable than flax or hemp, is prepared in much the same manner as flax, and exported, chiefly from Calcutta, in bales of 400 lb. With an annual production of *c.* 10,000,000 bales Bengal is still the greatest source of world supply. Jute is made into cordage, coarse cloth for gunny bags, and cheap carpets, the principal centres of manufacture being Calcutta and Dundee (Scotland). In Dundee jute yarns are also used in making Hessian canvas, coverings for furniture, and even velvets. See GUNNY CLOTH.

Kaffir, also spelt KAFIR and CAFFRE, an Arabic word meaning 'unbeliever' (*i.e.* not a Mohammedan), originally applied to the Bantu peoples of S.E. Africa. The name is much resented by them, and is properly falling into disuse. See BANTUS and ZULUS.

Kaolin. See CHINA CLAY.

Karri. See EUCALYPTUS.

Karst (Italian *Carso*), the term applied particularly to the limestone region of the Dinaric Alps, N.E. of the Adriatic Sea, and generally to any limestone region showing similar features—*e.g.* Causses (France), Ardennes, Pennines. In the Adriatic Karst the heavy rains disappear through fissures in the limestone and give rise to a system of underground streams, the surface being left dry and barren. The erosion caused by this subterranean drainage frequently leads to subsidence of the surface, and hollows are thus formed where surface water remains and rich soil collects; such fertile basins in Yugoslavia are called *dolinas* if of small extent, and *poljen* if more extensive. Below the surface great caverns or grottos are often formed in which are found the limestone formations known as *stalactites,* which resemble hanging icicles, and *stalagmites,* which seem to grow upwards from the ground to meet them. Both are formed by the slow dripping from the roof of water containing lime in solution. As this water evaporates the mineral matter is deposited both where the drops fall from the roof and where they reach the floor. Sometimes the upper and the lower formations grow till they meet, and thus form a pillar. The underground streams may find their way to the surface only at the coast or even under the sea.

Kauri (*kou'ri*), a species of pine which grows in the North I. of New Zealand to a height of 80 to 100 ft. It yields a strong, durable, and easily-worked timber greatly in demand for joiner-work, but now becoming scarce. Through the bark oozes a gummy fluid which hardens and falls into the ground. In Auckland this kauri gum is dug from the soils which were formerly covered with kauri forests, and is used in making varnishes.

Kham'sin (Arabic, 'fifty'), a hot,

dry, S.E. to S.W. wind, laden with sand and dust, which blows over Egypt for periods of two to three days during *c.* fifty days in spring. It causes discomfort, but is not usually dangerous to human beings.

Knot, a measure of speed (not of distance); 10 knots means a speed of 10 nautical miles *per hour*, a nautical mile being 6,080 feet or $\frac{1}{60}$ of one degree of latitude. In the days of sailing ships their speed was measured by dropping over the stern a 'log' attached to a reeled line which had knots at regular intervals; the number of 'knots' which ran off the reel in a certain time gave the number of nautical miles per hour which were being sailed by the ship.

Ko'la Nut, the brownish, bitter seed (about the size of a chestnut) of a tropical tree, a native of W. Africa, and introduced into the W. Indies and tropical S. America. The nut is chewed by Africans to relieve hunger and fatigue. It is exported from the Gold Coast and Sierra Leone; from it *caffeine* is extracted.

Kuro Shiwo. See OCEAN CURRENTS.

Lac, a dark-red resin produced by the action of an insect on the sap of certain trees in N.E. India. It is so named because of the infinite number (see next article) of insects required for its production. Twigs covered with this substance form *stick-lac*; from these the resin is removed by washing, and melted to form *shellac*, which is used in making varnishes, and is the principal ingredient of sealing-wax. Shellac is exported chiefly from Bengal. From lac a scarlet dye is also obtained.

Lac or **Lakh,** in India, a hundred thousand; *e.g.* a lac of rupees = 100,000 rupees.

Lacquer, a varnish prepared from shellac applied in Western lands to metals to give them lustre or prevent tarnishing, in Eastern lands to thin wooden wares for purposes of ornament. Lacquered wares are most largely imported from Japan and China; in appearance they rival highly glazed porcelain, and are often beautifully decorated with gold foil (Japan), or by cutting through successive layers of differently coloured lacquers (China).

Lagoon', a shallow stretch of salt, brackish, or even fresh water cut off from the sea, either partly or completely, by a spit of land. Lagoons are found inside atolls or fringing coral banks, and also on sea coasts where banks of sand, mud, or gravel have been formed which shut off bays or inlets from the sea. Lagoons which run parallel to the coast are found on the Baltic coast of Germany, where they are known as *Haffs*.

Lake (Scottish *Loch*; Irish *Lough*), a stretch of inland water occupying a depression of the earth's surface. Small lakes are called pools, ponds, tarns, etc. *Fresh-water lakes* are found in surface hollows, *e.g.* Loch Leven, in river expansions, *e.g.* Lough Derg, in rift-valleys, *e.g.* Lake Nyasa, or in volcanic craters, *e.g.* Crater Lake (Oregon, U.S.A.); they are often the result of glacial action, some lakes being formed by the blocking of valley mouths by morainic material, *e.g.* L. Garda, others by the collecting of water in CIRQUES, *e.g.* Glaslyn (Snowdon). Lakes which have no outlet become *salt lakes*. The river water which enters such a lake is removed by evaporation, but the small amount of salts which it holds in solution remains in the lake. The water of the lake thus becomes highly impregnated with salt, *e.g.* the Dead Sea, whose water is thirteen times as salt as that of the open ocean. The terms *loch* and *lough* are also applied to arms of the sea, *e.g.* Loch Linnhe, Lough Foyle.

Land and Sea Breezes, a form of periodic wind occurring daily on the sea coasts of countries. They are due to the unequal heating of the surface of the land and of the sea under the sun's rays. The surface of the land is quickly heated, and also loses its heat quickly. The sea heats more slowly and to a greater depth, and retains its heat longer. It follows that the air over the sea does not vary in temperature so much or so quickly as that over the land. Thus during the day, when the land surface becomes hotter than the sea surface, the air above expands and becomes lighter, and cooler air flows from the sea to the land as a *sea breeze*. Towards evening, the land surface becomes quickly colder than the sea surface. The air above the land also cools and becomes heavier than that over the sea, and this heavier air flows from the land to the sea as a *land breeze*. Such land and sea breezes are usually most strongly felt in tropical regions, but may not be felt at all if they are overpowered by some stronger wind due to different causes.

Landes (*lond*). See DUNES.

Latitude, the angular distance of any place on the earth's surface N. or S. of the equator, the equator being represented by 0°, and the angles calculated as at the centre of the earth. Places in the plane of the equator are therefore in lat. 0°, while the N. and S. Poles are in 90° N. and S. latitude respectively. A line passing through all places that are, say, 10° N. of the equator must be parallel to the equator, and all such lines are therefore called *Parallels of Latitude*. We speak of a place as having a *low* latitude if it is near the equator, and a *high* latitude if it is near the poles. While a degree of latitude is an angular measure, it has been possible to find its equivalent as a linear measurement on the earth's surface. Thus one degree corresponds to 68.7 m. Owing to the flattening of the earth's surface near the poles this distance increases slightly, and in the highest latitudes becomes 69.4 m. A traveller or navigator finds the latitude which he has reached by calculations based upon the altitude of the sun or of particular stars above the horizon.

Lava, rock-forming substances melted by heat and poured out from the earth's interior through volcanic vents; the name is also given to the rock when cooled and hardened. Many lavas break up into soils of great fertility, *e.g.* in Campania and Sicily (Italy), Java, Japan, N.W. U.S.A., S. Brazil, and Hungary. See VOLCANO.

League of Nations, an association set up by the leading nations of the world on January 10, 1920, as a part of the Treaty of Versailles which concluded the Great War, with the main object of preserving international peace. This it seeks to do by encouraging the reduction of armaments and the settling of disputes by arbitration or agreement. The peoples represented on the League have agreed not to enter into secret treaties with one another, and to observe justly and fairly all treaty obligations. In addition to this, the League has done valuable work for backward or uncivilized peoples by seeking to ensure that their lands shall be governed for the betterment and in the interests of the native inhabitants themselves. On this understanding certain territories, former overseas possessions of Turkey and Germany, have been handed over for government, under Mandate of the League, to different Allied countries. These governing nations are called *Mandatory Powers*, and the territory so handed over is known as *Mandated Territory*. The League also undertakes the protection of minorities, that is, of people living within a state the governing race of which outnumbers and is different from their own, seeking to ensure for them free exercise of their religious rights and the free use of their native tongue, with opportunities of education in their own language. It is also doing much for the improvement of the health of the world by its organization for the study of and methods of combating various widely-spread diseases. In 1930 the League of Nations included over fifty of the countries of the world.

Levee (*li-vē′* or *lev′i*), an embankment designed to keep the river Mississippi within its proper channel, particularly in its middle and lower reaches, where vast stretches of valuable arable land may be laid under water by floods. The necessity for levees is due to the quantity of silt which is carried down by the river, and by which its bed at many places has actually become higher than the surrounding country. The river itself, as it flows through its alluvial plain, also builds natural levees by the deposit of silt along its banks.

Lig'nite, a brown, woody coal showing traces of vegetable matter much less altered than in ordinary coal, and containing *c.* 70 per cent. of carbon. It is inferior in burning qualities to black coal, 9 tons of lignite being regarded as equivalent to 2 tons of black coal. It is produced most largely in Germany, Czechoslovakia, Austria, U.S.A., and Canada.

Llama (*lä'mä*), a woolly-haired, humpless member of the camel family, standing *c.* 3 ft. high, native of the Andes of S. America, where it is domesticated. It is a sure-footed beast of burden, carrying *c.* 100 lb., and is valued also for its wool. See ALPACA, VICUÑA.

Llanos. See GRASSLANDS.

Local Time. See TIME.

Loch. See LAKE.

Lo'cust, an insect of the grasshopper family, *c.* 2 in. long, travelling by jumps in its early stages, and flying when full grown. It breeds largely in treeless arid regions, especially of the hot temperate belt. 'From time to time they invade cultivated fields, where they arrive flying in thick solid masses, filling the air, darkening the sun, forming an immense, unbroken cloud which may take more than an hour to pass by, and when they settle, consuming every green thing to be seen, the working of their jaws meanwhile causing a sound that can be heard at a great distance' (Chisholm, *Handbook of Commercial Geography*. See also Joel ii. 1–11). Their ravages are most severe in E. Europe, W. Asia, N. and S. Africa, and Argentina. When the breeding grounds are known the eggs may be destroyed; during migration on foot trenches are dug to trap the swarms; and poisons are sprayed over vegetation by aeroplanes to reduce the flying army. In some countries locusts are prepared as a human food.

Lo'cust Bean, the fruit of the carob tree. See CAROB.

Lo'ess (German *Löss*), a yellowish, fine-grained soil found especially in the basins of the Rhine, Rhone, Danube, Missouri, and Hwang-Ho. It is a loam, or mixture of sand and clay, rich in lime, and has been borne by wind to its present situation. In N. China it is remarkably fertile under irrigation; the famous BLACK EARTH of Russia is of a similar formation.

Longitude (*lon'ji-tūd*), the angular distance of a place, measured in degrees, as at the earth's centre, E. or W. of a given point. In Britain Greenwich is taken as the fixed point from which longtitude is reckoned, and the meridian line through Greenwich is called the first or prime meridian and marked 0°. From this line longitudes are measured up to 180° E. or W. Some countries use a prime meridian of their own, but since 1884 there has been general agreement among other countries to use that of Greenwich. Owing to the relation between longitude and time it is possible for a traveller or navigator to determine his exact longitude by comparing the local time of midday with that of Greenwich as shown on his chronometer. See MERIDIAN and TIME.

Lough. See LAKE.

Lucerne. See ALFALFA.

Macaro'ni, a food prepared from a paste made, principally in Italy, from the flour of hard varieties of wheat, and generally forced through tubes which give it a pipe-like form. Smaller kinds of macaroni are known as *spaghetti* and *vermicelli*.

Magyars (*mod'yorz*), the predominant race in Hungary. They are a branch of the Mongolian family, and are closely allied to the Finns. They settled in Hungary in the 9th century, and although before the Great War they formed barely half the population of the country, they had for long dominated it, their language being the official language of Hungary, and the official name of the country being *Magyarorszag*, or country of the Magyars. They are a people remarkable for their energy and courage, their quick impulsive temperament, and their intense patriotism.

Maize (*māz*), or INDIAN CORN, the grain of a cereal which grows 6 to 18 ft. high in lands with a higher temperature and heavier rainfall than are suited for wheat. It is a native of the Americas, whence it has been introduced into all tropical and subtropical countries, except those with 'Mediterranean' climates, which are unsuited for the crop. It is most largely produced in U.S.A.; the greatest exporters are Argentina, U.S.A., Romania, and S. Africa; and Britain is the chief importing land. Maize supplies food for man as well as for beast; the unripe heads are cooked as a vegetable, and coarsely-ground maize is prepared as *hominy* and *mush* in U.S.A., as *tortillas* in Mexico, as *polenta* in Italy, and as *mamaliga* in Romania; some is ground as *cornflour* in U.K.; and it is the *mealies* of S. Africa. In most countries maize is fed to farm animals; and much is also used in breweries and distilleries.

Malaria, also called AGUE or INTERMITTENT FEVER, and, in its deadlier forms, YELLOW FEVER and BLACKWATER FEVER, an infectious disease commonest in the marshy districts of warm and tropical climates, and the cause of more sickness and of a greater number of deaths than any other disease. For this reason, and because of its weakening effects on those who do recover, it has had a marked influence in hindering the development of the tropical regions of the world, and until it has been conquered progress in trade, civilization, etc., in these regions must be very slow. The disease takes many forms, but is always due to the one source of infection, the mosquito, which carries the micro-organism of the disease from the blood of one affected person to the blood of another. Much has been done in the conquest of the disease by draining the marshes (breeding-place of the mosquito), by destroying the insects, and by educating the native population of tropical countries in the right measures to be adopted for cure and for safeguarding themselves from infection. Notable results have followed the adoption of such methods in Italy, Ismailia, the Federated Malay States, and, above all, the Panama Canal Zone.

Mallee (*măl'ē*), the name given in Australia to low-growing species of eucalyptus or gum tree. Such stunted gums form the scrub country of the lower basin of the Murray-Darling river system. Some mallees are of use for the strong oils distilled from their leaves; none yields timber of commercial value. Much mallee scrub has been rolled down by traction engines or other means and burned off to form wheat lands. See EUCALYPTUS.

Man'date. See LEAGUE OF NATIONS.

Man'grove, a tropical tree or shrub from whose trunk and branches aerial roots are sent downwards into the ground to form new trees. Such mangrove forests thrive in the salt marshes and the coastal muds of equatorial lands (*e.g.* Nigeria). The bunched roots serve to arrest soil and vegetable matter, and thus act as agents of reclamation in impenetrable, malarial areas. Mangrove bark is used in medicine, and yields the tanning material known as *cutch.*

Manila Hemp. See HEMP.

Man'ioc. See CASSAVA.

Maoris (*mou'rēz*), the aboriginal race of New Zealand. They form a branch of the great Polynesian race which inhabits the various islands of the east Pacific Ocean. A vigorous and intelligent people, they are generally brown in colour, with thick lips and straight black hair, and practise tattooing their bodies. They number *c.* 55,000, the majority of whom are found in North Island. While there was much fighting between the Maoris and the British settlers in the early years of the 19th century, they are now peaceable, loyal, and contented citizens of New Zealand, possessing full citizenship and sending representatives to parliament. The majority are farmers. The State provides them with free education, so that most of them can now speak and write English, though they still retain their Polynesian speech among themselves.

Map, a flat representation, on paper or other substance, of the surface of the whole or any part of the globe, to show physical, political, or other features or distributions. A collection of maps of various parts of the earth's surface is called an *atlas*. A *bathy-orographical* map shows depths of the oceans and heights of the land; a *political* map indicates the boundaries, chief towns, railways, etc., of countries; other maps show climatic phenomena, distributions of peoples, languages, products, etc. The most accurate maps are those prepared from actual measurements by the skilled surveyors of the *Ordnance Survey* Office of our own or other countries; maps of comparatively unknown areas (*e.g.* parts of Africa) are drawn from sketches made by travellers and explorers, but more accurate maps are now made by using aeroplane photographs of such parts For general use atlas and wall maps are prepared by drawing a network of lines of longitude and latitude according to some mathematical scheme (see PROJECTION), and marking the outline and other features in strict relation to such lines. It is important to note the *scale* of a map, and the method employed to show *relief* thereon. The scale is usually indicated by a representative fraction (R.F.) which states the number of units on the ground represented by one unit on the map—*e.g.* 1 : 1,000,000 means that one unit (inch, centimetre, etc.) on the map represents one million of that unit on the earth's surface. This scale of 1 : 1,000,000 has been selected for the International Map of the World. Relief is shown by contouring (see CONTOUR LINES), and slope by HACHURES. On certain maps contours are chosen (*e.g.* 500, 1,500, 3,000 ft., etc.), and the land areas between are distinctively coloured; ocean depths are indicated by a scheme of blue tints. Such maps are known as *layer* maps. *Relief* maps really represent models of the earth's surface; on them altitude is necessarily exaggerated. Any exact representation of the earth must be drawn on a globe; on it direction and distance, as well as area, may be most correctly determined. See CHART.

Masai (*maz'ī*), an African people residing mostly in the Great Rift Valley which lies E. of L. Victoria. They are an aristocratic people, warlike, of fine physique, well-built, tall and slender. The women and boys do all the menial work, while the men spend the prime of their lives as warriors, living apart from the rest of the tribe in separate kraals or villages. Their weapons are the spear, the knobkerry, and a kind of sword. Their staple diet consists of milk, blood, and meat.

Maté. See YERBA MATÉ.

Mediterranean Climate and Flora, the climatic conditions existing in lands bordering the Mediterranean Sea and the special type of vegetation resulting therefrom. Similar climatic conditions are found in the coastal areas of Central California, Central Chile, Cape of Good Hope region, S.W. and South Australia. This type of climate is marked by mild, humid winters and warm, dry summers. All the above areas lie between 30° and 40° N. or S. latitude on the fringe of the trade wind belts. Owing to the seasonal change in the position of the sun, the position of these belts also varies, moving S. as the sun moves to Capricorn, and N. as it moves to Cancer. In these areas trade winds prevail in summer, and these are dry winds because they blow over land and are moving to warmer latitudes, and can therefore hold more moisture. In winter, westerly winds, blowing off the sea, prevail and bring adequate rainfall. The resulting vegetation is of a type which can resist the summer drought, having small, thick, often thorny leaves to prevent too rapid evaporation, bulbous roots and watery fruits in which water is stored. Where conditions are favourable there are evergreen forests of cork-oak, cedar, mulberry, and chestnut trees. The typical fruit-bearing trees are the olive and the vine, along with the citrous group of oranges, lemons, limes, grape-fruit.

Meridian, one of the great circles on the earth's surface passing through the poles and cutting the equator at right angles—also called a line of longitude. Strictly speaking, a meridian is only half a great circle, lying between the North and South Poles, on which all places have noon at the same time; on the other half of the great circle all places have midnight at that time. At the equator the linear distance between any two meridians, corresponding to one degree of longitude, is 69.2 m., but as all meridians converge to pass through the poles, this distance diminishes gradually with the distance from the equator. Thus at 50° N. latitude the linear distance corresponding to one degree is only 44.6 m. See LONGITUDE and GREAT CIRCLE.

Merino (*me-rē'nō*), a fine-wooled sheep, native of N. Africa, whence it was introduced first into Spain and later into Saxony, England, Cape of Good Hope, Australia, U.S.A., and Argentina. Its abundant wool surpasses all other kinds in fineness; its mutton, however, is relatively poor in quality and quantity. The name merino is applied also to goods containing fine, soft wools.

Mese'ta, the extensive tableland of Spain, occupying *c.* three-fourths of the surface of the country, and composed of an ancient and much broken and eroded block of the earth's crust. It consists mainly of flat-lying strata, and descends abruptly to the plains of Andalusia in the S., and those of Aragon in the N.

Me'teorite, a mass of mineral or stony matter, generally containing iron and nickel, which falls to the earth from outer space. When a small meteorite traverses the earth's atmosphere it is heated by the friction of the air and becomes incandescent, and is therefore often called a *falling star*. When small they are disintegrated by the heat, but larger ones may strike the earth; in weight they may range from less than 1 lb. to over 70 tons.

Meteorol'ogy, the science of atmospheric phenomena in relation to weather and climate. It thus includes the study of *air temperature* and *pressure, wind,* and *precipitation.* Rays from the sun heat the earth's surface, whence the heat passes by radiation and convection into the atmosphere. Hence air temperatures are highest at the earth's surface, and decrease with altitude at a rate of about 3° F. per 1,000 ft. Owing to the curvature of the surface of the globe the same amount of sun-heat is distributed over a larger area towards the poles than within the tropics, so that average temperatures decrease from the equator polewards. The earth's rotation on its axis explains the variation of temperature from day to night. There is also a *seasonal* variation of temperature depending upon the earth's revolution round the sun. The temperature of the oceans is more constant than that over the lands.

As a result of gravity the atmosphere is densest at the earth's surface, where the mean pressure produces a barometric reading of 30 in. or 760 mm. This decreases with elevation, the rate of decrease being about 1 in. for each 1,000 ft. Owing to movements in the atmosphere, barometric pressure is constantly varying, and the barometer sometimes indicates readings of over 30 in., at other times pressures below that figure. Air moves outwards from a high pressure area (see ANTICYCLONE) to fill up areas of low pressure (see CYCLONE); such moving air is called wind.

As a result of evaporation over water surfaces the atmosphere contains a certain quantity of water-vapour. This capacity for water-vapour increases with a rise of air temperature until saturation point is reached. If the temperature of saturated air is lowered it cannot contain so much water-vapour, and some is precipitated. Hence rain falls when air temperatures fall, as they do when air moves upwards (*e.g.* over the Doldrums), or if the winds, which carry the water-vapour over the lands, blow towards the poles (*i.e.* from a warmer to a cooler area), or are forced to rise over mountainous areas where pressure is less and air expansion is accompanied by loss of heat.

In most civilized countries meteorological offices have been established to record all meteorological observations, and by preparing weather charts, to forecast the weather from day to day. See ATMOSPHERE, CLIMATE, CONDENSATION, EVAPORATION, RAINFALL, RADIATION, SEASONS, TEMPERATURE, WIND.

Midnight Sun, a phenomenon of high latitudes, at and near midsummer, during which the sun, though skirting the horizon, does not dip below it. At North Cape, in lat. 73¼° N., the sun is visible at midnight from 12th May to 29th July.

Migration (1) OF PEOPLES. The movement of peoples from one part of the earth to another. Such movements have taken place from the very earliest times. In primitive times, when man followed a pastoral life, his migrations were regulated by the necessity of finding fresh pasture for his flocks. By gradual stages this led to the peopling of the habitable earth. Sometimes the need for food for himself decided his migrations, as with the Eskimos to this day, who in winter move to the sea coasts to catch seals, and in summer may move inland to regions where they can hunt the reindeer or musk-ox. Decisive changes in climate will also cause the movements of large masses of people, as in the desert part of Central Asia, where we find the remains of former civilizations. In more modern times, while these causes still operate, others appear. The desire to obtain freedom, religious or otherwise, caused the migration of the Pilgrim Fathers to America, the Huguenots to Britain, etc. Religious enthusiasm led to the Mohammedan invasion of Europe and the foundation of the Moorish kingdoms of Spain and N. Africa. With the great geographical discoveries of the 15th century a new epoch in the history of migration began and a new motive operated. The vast new continents offered unlimited resources, and so a steady flow of people from the Old World to the New set in. These people were actuated by love of adventure or lust for gold, or desire to escape from the overcrowded old countries, with their attendant evils of unemployment, hunger, etc., to the newer, less congested lands.

(2) OF ANIMALS. Large numbers of animals, too, are remarkable for their periodic movements from one place to another. Speaking generally, these movements are determined by the supply of food or water, or by the need for obtaining suitable breeding-places in which the young may be reared in security. These movements are most general and are most easily observed among birds, practically all of which seem to be migratory to some extent. In Britain some birds, such as the swallow and the cuckoo, are summer visitors, while others, such as the fieldfare and the redwing, are winter visitors, coming from the north in autumn, remaining here throughout the winter, and returning to their northern breeding-places in spring.

There are also birds of passage which rest in this country for a little on their longer journeys farther north or south. These movements are seasonal, as are those of most mountain animals, such as the reindeer or the wild asses of the Asiatic Steppe, which alternate between one feeding ground and another as the seasons make one or another more suitable. More extensive and more definite are the migrations of certain aquatic mammals, primarily for the purpose of finding safe breeding-places. Thus the Alaskan fur seal in winter travels as far south as California, and returns in spring across the Northern Pacific to its breeding-place at the Pribilof Islands, a distance of *c.* 2,000 miles. Migrations of similar type occur among fish—the periodic movements of the salmon, the eel, herring, and mackerel being familiar examples.

Mil'let, the name given to several kinds of a cereal grass which yields a small-sized grain, used as food for human beings in Asia and Africa, and for fowls in Europe and America. Most important are the tropical millets, especially the *Great Millet*, extensively grown in India, where it is known as *Jowar*, and in Africa as *Durra* or *Guinea Corn*; and the *Spiked Millet*, called *Bajra* in India. Neither enters largely into world trade.

Mirage (*mir-äzh'*), an optical illusion in which an observer sees images of distant objects either apparently below the ground level or high up in the atmosphere. Thus, in hot climates, such as that of the Saharan desert, an observer often sees towards the horizon what appears to be a sheet of water shimmering in the sunlight; in Arctic regions, also, it is not uncommon for sailors to discover the proximity of other ships, which may be far beyond the horizon, by seeing the images of these ships reflected in the air. Sometimes double images of an object may be seen—the one that of the object itself, the other an inverted image of it much magnified. Sometimes distant coast-lines, as much as 50 miles away, can be seen across the sea with the greatest distinctness. The sailors' term for such appearances is 'looming.' Whatever forms the mirage takes they are all caused in the same way—by variations in the density of different layers of air, as a result of which the rays of light passing from any object are bent and present a distorted image to the observer.

Mis'tral, a north-westerly wind which prevails at certain seasons of the year, particularly from late autumn to early spring, on the south coast of France, being most marked in the Rhone delta, where Marseilles experiences it, on an average, on 175 days of the year. It is a strong dry wind, and is generally accompanied by cloudless skies, brilliant sunshine, and piercing cold. It is due to the unequal pressure of the air over the Mediterranean and that over the colder lands of the north. The lower pressure over the sea causes the heavier air from the north to flow towards the south.

Mohair. See ANGORA GOAT.

Mohammedanism, or ISLAM, one of the great religions of the world, with *c.* 175,000,000 adherents. Founded by Mohammed in Arabia in the 7th century, during his lifetime and for centuries afterwards the area of its influence was widely spread, chiefly through conquest, till now it is professed by large numbers in N. Africa, India, E. and S.E. Asia and Turkey. Its fundamental tenet is that 'there is no God but God, and Mohammed is His prophet.' It enjoins on its followers the importance of prayer, almsgiving, fasting, and pilgrimage.

Monsoons, seasonal winds that blow over the Indian Ocean and adjacent lands. In the winter months, from October to March, the monsoon blows from the N.E.; in the summer months, from April to September, from the S.W. The N.E. monsoon is the regular TRADE WIND of the N. hemisphere. In summer the great heat over S. Asia causes this area to be the heat equator for the time, and the air there to be lighter than that over the Indian Ocean. The air passes from the area of high pressure over the ocean to that of low pressure over the land. The S.E. trade wind of the S. hemisphere accordingly crosses the equator, but owing to the rotation of the earth is deflected and becomes the S.W. monsoon. The change from one monsoon to the other is accompanied by violent storms. Similar monsoon conditions prevail, though to a less marked degree, in the S. hemisphere, particularly in parts of Australia.

Moraine. See GLACIER.

Mother-of-pearl, a lustrous, iridescent substance forming the internal layer of the shell of many molluscs, especially the pearl oyster. It is exported from N. Australia, Ceylon, etc., and is used for inlaid work, cheap jewellery, and knife handles.

Mountain, an elevated mass of land, generally more than 2,000 ft. above sea-level. Mountains may be the result of earth movements, of EROSION, or of volcanic action. As a result of earth movements the earth's crust may be 'wrinkled' in parts and form *folded mountains*—*e.g.* in Eurasia nearly continuous lines of folds may be traced from the Atlas Mts., through the Alps and Caucasus, to the Himalayas and ranges of Malaya, with peaks rising to upwards of 20,000 ft. By erosive action, especially of water and ice on plateaus, the harder parts may be left as mountains while the less resistant rocks round about are removed. Such mountains are called *mountains of circumdenudation* (*e.g.* Ben Nevis, Table Mountain). Volcanic mountains are *mountains of accumulation*, built up of the lava and ash poured out through volcanic vents (*e.g.* Mt. Egmont); they generally have a conical form. Mountains have always been barriers to migrating peoples; they are generally thinly populated.

Municipal Borough, in England a town of less than 50,000 inhabitants, governed, since 1835, by a town council, consisting of a mayor, aldermen, and councillors elected by the citizens of the town. In Scotland the word *burgh* corresponds to the English *borough*, and the term corresponding to the above is *Parliamentary Burgh*, a Scottish burgh being governed by a provost, bailies, and councillors. See also ROYAL BURGHS.

Muskeg, a name of Red Indian origin applied to the boggy, waterlogged lands of N. and N.W. Canada.

Nautical Mile. See KNOT.

Neap Tides. See TIDES.

Negritos (*ne-grē'toz*), the name originally given by the Spaniards to the aboriginal inhabitants of the Philippine Islands, but now extended to include all similar peoples in S.E. Asia and Oceania. The Negritos are generally very dark in colour, have short, black, woolly hair, are short in stature (not more than 5 ft.), and have the flat nose and other physical characteristics of the Negro. They are at a very low stage of culture, as is indicated by the absence of fixed houses, of all arts, of religion, and of all weapons save the bow and arrow. The chief groups are the Aetas of the Philippines, the Semang of the Malay Peninsula, the Tapiro of New Guinea, and the Andamanese.

Negroes, the principal race inhabiting Africa. The name embraces, however, all the black races of the intertropical regions of the eastern hemisphere from West Africa to the Fijian Islands in the Pacific. The *Negro proper* is represented by those tribes that live in Africa between the Barbary States on the north and the Congo on the south. All others may be grouped under the term *Negroids*, and include the Bantu-speaking peoples, the Hottentots, the Bushmen, and the Zulus of Southern Africa, the Papuans of New Guinea, the Melanesians of the Solomon and Fiji Islands, and the Australian aborigines. The Negroes of the Sudan are the best representatives of their type. They are tall, have thick lips, short flat nose, woolly hair, and black skin. The skull is generally long and narrow. In their primitive state the Negroes represent a very low stage of culture, and it is uncertain what the possibilities of their development may be. The Negro is usually an agriculturist, an occupation which he diversifies with hunting, fishing, and, more rarely, cattle breeding. His diet is mainly vegetarian, the chief article being either manioc or mealies. Formerly cannibalism was widespread, but is now much less common. He generally lives in a community ruled by a chief, though in some parts, where conditions were favourable, kingdoms of considerable size have been formed. In certain crafts the Negro shows both aptitude and skill, such as iron smelting and working, carving, pottery, and weaving. His primitive religion takes many and varied forms. The foreign religion which has appealed most to the Negro is Mohammedanism.

Névé. See GLACIER.

Ni'trate, the commercial contraction for nitrate of sodium, potassium, or calcium. Nitrate of soda (*caliche*), a product of the Atacama Desert (Chile saltpetre), is used as a fertilizer, and in the manufacture of glass, soap, and nitric and sulphuric acid. Nitrate of potassium (potash), used in the making of gunpowder, glass, etc., is largely produced from the deposits at Stassfurt (Germany). Calcium nitrate, or lime saltpetre, prepared from atmospheric nitrogen, is used as a fertilizer and in making nitric acid.

Nomads, primitive peoples who have no settled habitation but move from place to place, generally in quest of food either for themselves or for their flocks and herds. People of this type are found in every large continental area. Thus in Europe there are the gipsies, in Asia the Khirgiz, in Africa the Bedouin and the Hottentots, and in Australia the aborigines. See MIGRATION.

Nutmeg, an aromatic spice consisting of the kernel of the fruit of an evergreen tree native of the Moluccas, where it is still widely grown, and now also cultivated in the Straits Settlements, India, and the tropical Americas. It is ground or grated for use in flavouring dishes. From small and inferior nutmegs *oil of mace* or nutmeg butter is extracted; from the coat or skin round the kernel another spice—*mace*—is prepared.

Oasis (*ō-ā'sis*), a place in a desert area rendered fertile by the presence of water. The best-known oases are those of the Sahara and the Libyan Desert of Africa. The water may come from outside the desert area, as in the case of the river Nile, which creates by its floods the great oasis of El-Khargeh in Egypt, or it may be derived from a spring. Oases may sometimes be created by the sinking of artesian wells, as has been done by the French in N. Africa. They vary greatly in size, some supporting a large and settled population, others serving merely as halting-places in the desert. The characteristic form of vegetation is the date-palm, in the shade of which cereals and other food plants are cultivated.

Ocean, the great, continuous sheet of salt water which surrounds the land masses on the earth's surface. This covers 72 per cent. of the surface of the globe, and is divided by the continents into large portions, each of which is also known as an ocean, viz., Atlantic (31,000,000 sq. m.), Pacific (64,000,000 sq. m.), Indian (29,000,000 sq. m.), and Arctic (5,400,000 sq. m.). Near the continents the floor of the oceans has a gentle slope, but beyond the continental shelf the depth quickly increases. The floor of the ocean is not a uniform plain, but, like the land surface, is diversified by ridges and deep valleys. The greatest known depth, 35,000 ft., is east of N. Mindanao, one of the Philippine Islands, and the average depth of the greater half of the ocean is over 12,000 ft. The surface temperatures vary from 80° F. near the equator to below freezing point near the polar circles. The *salinity* or saltness of the water also varies, being greatest where evaporation is most rapid, and least where there is a large supply of fresh water from rain, rivers, or ice. In all depths animal life is found.

Ocean Current, a movement of the surface water of the ocean. Currents are the result of prevailing winds, or differences of temperature, or differences of salinity. Currents which are caused by prevailing winds are known as *drift* currents. These follow the directions of the winds except when contact with islands, submarine ridges, coast-lines, or other currents forces them out of their paths. The rotation of the earth also alters their directions. A current is named from the direction in which it flows. Currents flowing from the N. or S. polar regions are *cold*; those from the equator are *warm*. Cold currents wash the *east* coasts of continents in the N. hemisphere, and the *west* coasts in the S. hemisphere; warm currents wash the *west* coasts of continents in the N. hemisphere, and the *east* coasts in the S. hemisphere.

The best-known drift current is the GULF STREAM. This is formed from the equatorial drift current which enters the Gulf of Mexico from the Caribbean Sea, flows round it, and finally leaves the Gulf by Florida Channel between Florida and Cuba; it then flows along the E. coast of the U.S.A. as far as Cape Hatteras, where it broadens out and, assisted by the prevailing S.W. winds, flows eastward across the Atlantic Ocean as the *Gulf Stream Drift*. About half-way across the Atlantic it divides into two parts, one portion proceeding E. and S. to skirt the W. coasts of Spain and N. Africa, the other portion flowing N.E. and continuing its course under the influence of the prevailing winds till it reaches the British Isles, Norway, and the Arctic Ocean. The Gulf Stream leaves the Gulf of Mexico as a river of very salt water *c.* 50 m. broad and 2,000 ft. deep, moving with a speed of *c.* 5 m. per hour, and having a surface temperature of 80° F. Speed and temperature gradually decrease, and the portion of the Gulf Drift reaching the British Isles has a speed of *c.* 4 m. per day and a surface warmth of 60° F. From this warm surface drift N.W. Europe largely derives its mild winter climate. The corresponding stream in the Pacific is the *Kuro Shiwo* ('black stream'), a warm current which washes the shores of Japan and reaches the W. shores of N. America.

Currents due to differences of temperature are called *convection* currents. From the equator warm surface water moves very gradually towards the poles, where it cools, sinks, and very slowly moves along the ocean floor towards the equator, where it rises to replace the large amount of water lost by evaporation and by the movement towards the poles. By this very important circulation the ocean deeps never become stagnant.

Currents arise from differences of salinity. As the Mediterranean Sea receives few rivers, has a small rainfall, and is subject to great evaporation, it is salter than the Atlantic Ocean in the same latitude. A fresher surface current enters from the Atlantic, while a salter under-surface current flows out into the Atlantic. If this were not so the Mediterranean would become exceedingly salt.

The numerous ocean currents can best be studied from a map of the world on which they are distinctly marked.

Oceanog'raphy, the science which deals with the ocean, its tides, currents, composition, temperature, depth, salinity, deposits, vegetable and animal life, and all other aspects. While it has always been comparatively easy to observe the surface features of the ocean, the scientific investigation of the unseen depths is of recent date, but has advanced rapidly by the help of intricate and delicate instruments which have been devised for various purposes, *e.g.* for taking SOUNDINGS, for recording temperatures and pressures and bringing up samples of water from different depths, and for measuring the speed and direction of currents. Nets of different kinds are used to trap the varieties of animals at all depths, and samples of the ocean floor can now be brought to the surface and studied. The most famous expedition for the observation of oceanic phenomena was that of H.M.S. *Challenger* (1872–1876), which circumnavigated the world and crossed and recrossed the oceans, recording innumerable observations and collecting enormous quantities of specimens. Since then numerous expeditions have been carried out by various European countries. The results of oceanography have supplied sailors with invaluable charts of soundings as well as information about tides and currents, meteorologists with important climatic data, and fishermen with facts about the food, distribution, and migration of fishes.

Oil-seeds, the fruits or seeds of a vast number of very different trees, shrubs, and plants, all of which yield oils which are used for the lubrication of machinery, the preparation of food, for lamp oils, and in the making of soap, candles, varnishes, etc. The most important oil-seeds are COTTON seeds, COPRA, GROUND NUTS, olives (from Mediterranean lands), palm nuts and kernels (from W. Africa), SOYA BEANS, sunflower seeds (from Russia), rape-seeds (from India) yielding *colza oil*, and sesame, a herb yielding an oil known in India as *jinjelly* or *til*.

O'pium, a brownish, strongly scented, bitter drug, prepared from the juice of the seed-pod of the white poppy. In India, China, Asia Minor, and Persia, where the poppy is cultivated, opium is eaten or smoked to stimulate the faculties or to induce sleep. In India the drug is a Government monopoly. The finest quality is obtained from Asia Minor, which supplies Britain. By dissolving opium in spirits of wine *laudanum* is obtained; the active principle of opium is known as *morphia*; both are employed in medicine to alleviate suffering.

Ordnance Survey. See MAP.

Outport. See PORT.

Oxbow Lake, water left in the abandoned meander of a river. Such lakes are found in the lower courses of rivers where they are flowing slowly through flat country. In their course they form many bends or meanders, the two ends of which may approach one another very closely. In a time of flood the river, instead of flowing round the meander, may cut across its neck and form a new channel. Owing to the deposit of silt at this point the meander may be cut off, forming a curved lake known as an oxbow.

Packet Station, a port of call for mail and passenger ships, such as Dover and Calais.

Paddy (Malayan *Padi*), the name given to growing rice and to the grain before the husks have been removed. In monsoon lands peoples store their rice as paddy, removing the husks only when the grain is to be used, in order that the nutritious flour round the grains may be preserved. See RICE.

Pam'pas, vast plains in Argentina, between 30° and 40° S. latitude, stretching from the Andes to the Atlantic. Formerly the bed of an ancient sea, they are covered, in their western part, by deposits of shingle and sand, and in the E. by estuary silt. The rainfall is scanty (10–15 in.), and occurs mainly in summer. The western area is mostly sterile, and is marked by large salty areas, brackish streams and lakes, and immense deserts. The eastern part is more fertile, and is covered by the typical pampas grass, tall and coarse-leaved, whose feathery spikes often attain a height of eight or nine feet. In this area alfalfa and other forage plants, which have been introduced by Europeans, support enormous numbers of horses, cattle, and sheep.

Pampero (*pam-pā'rō*), a cold, south-westerly wind that sweeps across the pampas of Argentina to the Brazilian coast. It usually follows in the wake of a barometric depression, and is similar to the thunderstorms of our own climate in its sudden onset and its displacement for the time being of the more regular winds.

Paraguay Tea. See YERBA MATÉ.

Pass, a depression or *col* or *gap* in a mountain range by means of which communication may be carried on between the one side of the range and the other. Where mountain systems intervene between populous countries, as the Alps do, the passes are of great importance and roads are constructed, carefully planned so that the gradient shall not exceed a rise of *c.* 1 in 20. Railways are also constructed, climbing the valleys in a series of curves and loops, while the last part of the ascent is usually avoided by tunnelling under the pass.

Pathans (*pa-tănz'*), the name applied in India to the Afghans, especially those settled in India or on its N.W. frontier. They number *c.* 3,000,000, and consist of many tribes, the best known being the Afridis, the Ghilzais, and the Mohmands. They are of fine physique, but untrustworthy in character, being vain, greedy, treacherous, and revengeful. They have given much trouble to the British Government of India, and since 1850 have been the object of no fewer than fifty punitive expeditions. In religion they are Mohammedans.

Pearls, the spherical, pear-shaped, or irregular lustrous bead-like pieces of mother-of-pearl material secreted by various molluscs. These are formed as a protection round irritating substances, *e.g.* a grain of sand or parasite, which have entered the shell. Pearls are obtained principally from the pearl oyster of tropical seas, in depths averaging 7–8 fathoms, especially off N. Australia, in the Gulf of Manar, Persian Gulf, E. Indian Archipelago, and Gulf of California; small pearls are found in mussels, *e.g.* in Scottish rivers. *Culture pearls* are obtained by the Chinese and Japanese, who introduce foreign substances into the pearl oyster to cause the formation of pearls. *Artificial pearls* are made by covering wax globules with a preparation of fish scales.

Pepper, a pungent spice, used to flavour food, made from the berries of a tropical climbing plant, native of s. India, Indo-China, and Malaya. It is exported to the U.K. chiefly from the Straits Settlements, Java, Siam, and French Indo-China, almost entirely through the port of Singapore. By quantity it is the most important spice imported by the U.K., where it is marketed either as whole berries, known as *pepper corns,* or as ground berries forming *black pepper* and *white pepper,* the latter made from berries which have been deprived of their outer coats. *Cayenne pepper,* or *red pepper,* consists of the ground pods of the capsicum plant, a native of S. America; the small pods of a variety of this plant are dried to form *chillies* which are used for pickling. See also PIMENTO.

Petro'leum ('rock oil'), mineral oil, formed in the interior of the earth's crust by the compression of hydrogen and carbon from muds containing the remains of plants and animals. It is found most abundantly in U.S.A., Russia, Venezuela, Mexico, Persia, Romania, Dutch E. Indies, and Colombia. It may either flow freely or may be pumped from wells sunk deep in the ground. By distillation petroleum yields light oils, *e.g.* petrol or gasoline and paraffin, various lubricating oils, fuel oils, and a residue containing asphalt, wax (used for candles), etc.

Phosphates, chemical salts containing phosphorus, formed naturally or obtained from the bones of animals, and used as fertilizers. Natural phosphates occur most abundantly in Florida (U.S.A.), N. Africa, and Nauru and other islands of the Pacific Ocean.

Pimen'to, ALLSPICE, or JAMAICA PEPPER, the unripe, dried berries of a tropical shrub cultivated chiefly in Jamaica. It combines the flavours of several spices, and is used to flavour food. From the fruit *oil of pimento* is distilled.

Plain, an area of flat or gently undulating land at a low level, usually not more than 1,000 ft. in its highest part; but the prairie region of N. America, which rises gradually from E. to W. to a height of 6,000 ft., is generally called a plain. Most of the great rivers of the world flow through plains which they have built up with ALLUVIUM transported from their upper courses (*e.g.* R. Ganges), and under favourable conditions of climate such plains are usually very fertile. On some plains in the temperate latitudes grass is the chief form of vegetation, and these form good grazing areas. In the far north little vegetation grows on the level stretches, which are almost uninhabited. The great plain of the Sahara, owing to lack of rain, is infertile, except where oases occur. Plains are known by different names in different parts of the world, *e.g. Steppes, Prairies, Pampas*.

Plateau, or TABLELAND, an area of level, or mostly level, ground occurring at a considerable elevation. It may have rivers, and even mountain ranges, running across it (*e.g.* Spain), and may be very high (*e.g.* Tibet, 13,000 ft.). The borders of a plateau may rise quickly from sea-level (*e.g.* Asia Minor), or the plateau may be shut in by high mountains (*e.g.* Plateau of Pamir, Asia). A submarine plateau is a steeply bordered elevation in the sea floor.

Po'lder, the Dutch name for a piece of low-lying land reclaimed from the sea or from a lake. Such land is first surrounded by a dyke and then drained by pumping, if natural drainage is impossible. Polder land is usually very fertile, and suited for agriculture or grazing (*e.g.* Haarlem Lake, 70 sq. m.). A great scheme is in progress to enclose and reclaim the greater part of the Zuider Zee, thus adding *c.* 850 sq. m. of fertile land to Holland.

Poles, a branch of the Slav race inhabiting Poland. Originally one of a number of tribes living between the Rs. Oder and Vistula, they eventually became predominant in that region. Their history has been very chequered, and their form of government has so often been changed that there has been little opportunity for the steady development of the people. The position of their country made it a battle-ground in the long strife between Teuton and Slav. Their forests were destroyed, their agricultural wealth confiscated, the peace of their country broken by marching armies, and their land itself divided in various ways among Germany, Russia, and Austria. After the Great War Poland became a free, self-governing state.

Porcupine Grass. See SPINIFEX.

Port, a town or place with a harbour, to which ships resort for the loading or unloading of goods. The most primitive are the *fishing ports*, established from the earliest times at convenient harbours along the coast. As ocean transport developed many of these harbours proved suitable for the larger vessels which came into use, and became of sufficient importance to be known as *seaports*. In many other cases the harbours had to be deepened and extended, or to be artificially protected by breakwaters. *River ports* are situated generally at the highest point to which the river can be navigated by vessels of a size suitable for transport. Ports for sea-going vessels situated far up rivers are preferable to those nearer the sea, as less railway transport is needed for their cargoes. The harbours of some seaports are not deep enough for the largest of modern vessels, and this has led to the creation of *outports*, at which these vessels discharge their cargoes into smaller vessels that can reach the original port. Thus Avonmouth has become the outport of

Bristol, and Tilbury of London. Seaports may serve special purposes along the ocean routes, as coaling or oiling stations, or as packet stations. With the development of aviation the term *Airport* has come into use, and is applied to an aerodrome on a recognized flying route, such as that between London and the Continent. These are usually situated at some easily accessible place near a great city, as Croydon at London.

Prairie, the vast tract of grassy plains in central N. America. In the United States they stretch from the foothills of the Rocky Mountains eastward to southern Michigan and western Ohio, and in Canada to near the Great Lakes. The prairie is not quite flat, but presents an undulating surface. Formerly it was almost treeless through the occurrence of prairie fires, but with the prevention of these, large areas of timbered ground are now being formed. The soil is generally productive, and where the rainfall is sufficient farming is carried on, the great wheat belt of Canada and the U.S.A. lying in this region. Near the Rocky Mountains, where the rainfall is scanty, sheep and cattle ranching replaces agriculture.

Precipita'tion, the fall from the atmosphere to the earth's surface of surplus water vapour in a condensed form, *e.g.* dew, mist, rain, snow, sleet, or hail, but chiefly in the form of rain. The term is also used to express the whole amount of water resulting from this fall for a given time on any area.

Pressure. See METEOROLOGY.

Projec'tion, the method of representing the whole or a part of the earth on a *flat* surface. The earth can only be truly represented by a globe, but a globe showing details of all countries of the world would be excessively large. A map projection is really a means of showing in a convenient form the network of the lines of latitude and longitude on which the details may be traced from the globe. Various methods of projection are employed, all of them depending upon the position of the observer's eye, as it is supposed to view through a transparent plane the part of the earth to be shown on the map. Since it is impossible to represent a curved body accurately on the flat, every projection must produce greater or less distortion either of size or shape, or of both, in the countries.

A very useful and common projection of the whole globe is *Mercator's*. In it the lines of latitude and longitude are both represented by sets of parallel straight lines drawn at right angles to each other. As the eye of the observer is supposed to be at the centre of the earth, and those lines are projected on a cylinder touching the earth at the equator, the parallels of latitude are farther and farther apart towards the poles, and meridians of longitude which should pass through the poles are all shown as straight lines. This results in very great distortion and exaggeration in the higher latitudes, but the projection is much used for sailors' charts, as they show true bearings of one place from another. Other projections are the *Orthographic*, *Stereographic*, *Globular*, and *Conical*, which cannot be easily understood apart from geometrical diagrams.

Pulses, a term applied to certain plants, *e.g.* pea, bean, lentil, producing pods of seeds which are used as food by man and domestic animals. Pulses are grown widely in the British Isles, and are also imported, usually preserved, from both temperate and tropical lands. Among these are SOYA BEANS, LOCUST BEANS, and GROUND NUTS.

Puna, lofty plateau in S. America, lying between the eastern and western divisions of the Andes in Peru, Bolivia, and Chile, at *c.* 11,000 ft. above sea-level. Cold and wind-swept, it is largely desert and scarcely habitable. The name is also applied to the intensely cold wind, the S.E. trade wind after crossing the E. Andes, which blows in this region at certain seasons.

Pygmies, people of diminutive

stature. The name is generally applied to such people inhabiting the equatorial forests of Africa. They are also called *Negrillos*, and except in stature have the general characteristics of the Negroes, though they are often lighter in colour and have a more rounded shape of head. The chief tribes are the Akkas of the Upper Welle, the Obongas of the Gabon, and the Batwas of the Congo. They represent a very low stage of culture.

Quebracho (*ke-brä'chō*, 'break-axe'), a S. American tree yielding a very hard wood, which grows in N. Argentina and Paraguay. The wood is exported as logs, but is much more largely used in the production of an extract for the rapid tanning of cheap leather.

Quinine. See CINCHONA.

Races of Mankind. Mankind may be divided into a comparatively small number of groups or types, each with certain common characteristics, physical and mental. Many methods of classification have been suggested, chiefly according to colour of skin or hair or shape of skull. The classification most commonly accepted is that which reduces all the races of mankind to three primary types—the Black or Ethiopic, the Yellow or Mongolic, and the White or Caucasic.

THE BLACK OR ETHIOPIC DIVISION is found chiefly in Africa, and in the Malay Peninsula, the Andaman Islands, the Philippines, New Guinea, and Tasmania. People of this race are distinguished physically by black, woolly hair, scanty beard, dark brown to black skin, long narrow skull, thick projecting lips, and broad, flattened nose. In character they are pleasure-loving and fitful, passing easily from joy to sorrow. Their religion is a form of Nature and ancestor worship, and is often debased by witchcraft and human sacrifice.

THE YELLOW OR MONGOLIC DIVISION is distributed throughout the greater part of Tibet, China, Japan, Korea, Formosa, Siberia, Indo-China, and the Malay Peninsula. In Europe they are found in Finland, Estonia, Hungary, and a great part of Russia. The American or Red Indians also belong to this stock. Distinguishing physical characteristics are straight, coarse black hair, scanty beard, yellow to brownish-yellow or copper-coloured skin, prominent cheek bones, small and narrow nose, and small, oblique, black eyes. The American Indians differ from the other branches of the race in greater stature and in shape of nose, which is generally large and aquiline. In temperament the Mongolic races are sluggish and morose, inclined to be indolent and lacking in initiative, but capable of great endurance under adverse conditions. In religion, except in America, the greater number are Buddhists and Mohammedans.

THE WHITE OR CAUCASIC DIVISION is distributed chiefly throughout Europe, N.E. Africa, Arabia, Persia, India, and Asia Minor. People of this race have wavy hair with full beards, skin varying from fair to olive or tawny in colour, skull long or oval in shape, nose large and straight or aquiline, cheek bones small and features regular. They are the most civilized of the races, and are enterprising and intellectual, having greater power of adjustment to their environment than others. Their religion, generally speaking, is of a purer and more ennobling type than that of the other races.

About the people of Polynesia, New Zealand, and Australia there has been much controversy, some including them under the Black or Ethiopic division, and others under the White or Caucasic division.

Radia'tion, the process by which any form of energy (*e.g.* heat) is emitted from a body. The sun sends out radiant energy, some of which comes in contact with the earth and is converted into heat. The heated surface of the earth then sends out invisible heat into the atmosphere by which the lower layers are warmed, particularly when water vapour or clouds are present to prevent the rapid dispersion of this radiated heat. High ground loses heat by radiation more quickly than low ground, because the layers of atmosphere above it hold smaller quantities of water vapour. In deserts, where the atmosphere is very dry, temperature at night falls very rapidly owing to there being no blanket of water vapour or cloud to confine the radiated heat to the lower layers of air.

Rain, condensed atmospheric water vapour falling to earth as separate drops of water. CONDENSATION always requires some solid particle as a nucleus, and the centre of each raindrop is a particle of atmospheric dust. So long as the particles can support their coating of moisture they remain in the air and form clouds or mist. When the coating of water becomes too heavy, or when several droplets join together, a raindrop falls.

Rainfall, the amount of rain which falls on a given area during a given time. This can be accurately measured by a RAIN GAUGE.

Well-marked types of rainfall are: (1) *Convectional,* in the equatorial belt of calms, particularly over the oceans, where highly heated saturated air rises, is cooled, and heavy rain falls daily, usually in the afternoon. (2) *Relief.* When moisture-bearing winds come to a range of mountains directly obstructing their path they are compelled to rise to a higher and therefore colder level in passing over the barrier. As cooling takes place rain falls, especially on the windward slopes, the leeward slopes receiving scanty supplies (*e.g.* w. Highlands of Scotland, S.E. Australia). (3) *Cyclonic.* Winds come in from all sides to fill up a centre of low pressure, are forced upwards, and rain occurs. Much of the rainfall of the E. of the British Isles is of this type.

Winds are the great moisture-carriers, and so a study of the World System of Winds will give in a general way the distribution of rainfall over the world, viz.: at the equatorial calms there is heavy rainfall diminishing N. and S. to a minimum over the Horse Latitudes, which is followed by an increase towards latitude 50°, to be succeeded by a diminishing quantity towards the poles. The greater amount of the rainfall of any area may fall during a particular and sometimes a short season of the year. In MONSOON regions and in the interiors of continents practically all the rain falls in the *summer* of those regions, while in 'Mediterranean' regions (35°–40° N. and S.) a *winter* rainfall is predominant. In countries exposed to S.W. and N.W. variable winds rain falls throughout the whole year, winter being rather more rainy than the other seasons. This winter rainfall usually includes SNOW.

The heaviest annual rainfall which has been measured (*c.* 500 in.) occurs at Cherrapunji, in the Khasi Hills, India; the driest known place is Copiapo, Chile, S. America.

Rain Gauge. See GAUGE, RAIN.

Raisins, dried grapes, exported chiefly from California, Australia, Asia Minor, and Spain (*muscatels*). From the seedless grapes of W. Asia Minor and its islands *sultanas* are produced. Still smaller seedless grapes, grown almost exclusively in the district near the isthmus of Corinth, are dried to form CURRANTS.

Ramie (*răm'ē*), or CHINA GRASS (Indian *Rhea*), the fine, strong, lustrous fibre prepared from the inner bark of two plants of the nettle family. The plants are natives of China, India, and Malaya, but are now cultivated also in Japan, Queensland, W. Africa, W. Indies, tropical Americas, and S. Europe. As the fibre is difficult to separate from the bark it is expensive. The silky fabric woven from it is made into light clothing by the Chinese; in industrial countries ramie is made into a wide variety of commodities, *e.g.* gas mantles, paper, ropes, canvas, and table linen.

Rattans' or RATANS', the stems of

many kinds of climbing palms, *c.* one inch in diameter, found in tropical Asia and exported from Singapore. They are used locally for house-building in China, and for foot-bridges, cordage, and fishing-lines in the Malay Archipelago; in manufacturing countries they are employed in wicker-work, and as walking sticks.

Raw Materials, all commodities imported into an industrial country for the purpose of being manufactured. These include not only such products as wheat grain, bales of cotton, and iron ores, but also partly manufactured goods, *e.g.* wheat flour, wood-pulp, cotton yarns, which are to be further used by manufacturers.

Red Indians, aboriginal inhabitants of America. They were called Indians by the original discoverers of America, who believed the newly-discovered land to be near India. They are generally classed as a Mongolian people, as their general characteristics agree with those of the Yellow Race—their copper-coloured skin, lank black hair, high cheek bones, prominent noses, and large deep-set eyes. They are in general tall, but vary in stature and physique. The finest specimens are found among the Patagonians of S. America and the Iroquois, Pawnees, and Sioux of the United States and Canada. Formerly they were skilled hunters, keen observers of Nature and natural phenomena, with extraordinarily acute senses. In temperament they were impassive, and capable of enduring great hardships and even torture without any outward show of emotion. They were cruel and relentless to their foes without respect of age or sex. Through long contact with civilization many of these characteristics have been lost or weakened. There are numerous tribes of Indians, and throughout America some sixty different Indian languages are spoken. In N. America they live in reservations set apart for them, but are not confined to these.

Reef, a ridge of rocks which is usually covered by the sea but may be visible when the tide is low. The most common are those formed by coralline deposit. See CORAL.

Refrigeration, a process by which foodstuffs can be kept in good condition for long periods of time by storing them in rooms or chambers maintained at a temperature below freezing point. By this means it is now possible to transport meat, fruit, etc., between the most distant parts of the world and through the heat of the tropics, and deliver it at its market in fresh condition. The overseas trade in frozen and chilled meat is now of very large dimensions, the chief countries engaged in it being Australia, New Zealand, the Argentine Republic, and other S. American states. *Chilled* meat is carried at a temperature of 30° F. and arrives at its market in soft condition, while *frozen* meat is carried at a temperature of 10° to 15° F., and must be thawed before it is used. Refrigeration is also used in the transport of poultry, fish, fruit, eggs, butter, cheese, etc. Thus English fish can be obtained fresh in the tropics, and in Rhodesia fresh fish, sent from Cape Town in blocks of ice, is sold.

Relief, the surface features of any part of the earth with regard to differences in elevation. Various plans are adopted in maps to show relief. A *Relief Map* is one on which the surface is actually raised on an exaggerated vertical scale. If this is photographed in a suitable light a *Photo Relief* map is produced, showing slopes by means of light and shade. *Contours*, *Hachures*, and the *Layer System* of colouring are also employed to represent relief. See MAP.

Ria (*rē'a*), a narrow bay or 'drowned valley' running into the land. When a subsidence of the earth's surface takes place along a mountainous coast where the mountains are not parallel to the sea, the lower parts of the river valleys are drowned and form rias (*e.g.* N.W. Spain, S.W. Ireland). These channels, unlike FJORDS, deepen steadily towards the sea. Frequently their landward ends have branches which receive as separate rivers what were formerly tributaries of that in the chief valley, and these branches usually form safe and sheltered anchorage for ships.

Rice, the principal grain crop of tropical and subtropical coast lands having heavy hot-season rains. While the plant is growing the soil must be covered with water, which is drained off just before harvest. Such conditions are most easily secured in river deltas, but may be obtained in suitable soils elsewhere by plentiful irrigation. Rice is grown most largely in the densely populated parts of China, India, Japan, Indo-China, Dutch E. Indies, Siam, and the Philippines, and the harvests are almost entirely consumed by the inhabitants. Only a small quantity enters the world's markets, chiefly from Burma, Indo-China, and Siam; and from these China is the largest importer. Rice is also grown in Africa (Egypt and Madagascar), s. U.S.A., S. America (especially Brazil), and Europe (Italy and Spain). A variety, known as *Upland* or *Hill Rice,* suited to drier soils, is cultivated on the terraced slopes of Ceylon and Java. For European and N. American markets the rice is husked and polished, making it less nutritious. See PADDY.

Rift Valley, a valley with steep walls formed by the sinking of a tract of land lying between two roughly parallel geological faults. Such valleys are long in proportion to their breadth. The chief example is the Great Rift Valley of E. Africa and Syria, stretching from Lake Tanganyika through Lakes Kivu, Edward, and Albert to Lake Rudolf, whence it runs through E. Abyssinia and the Red Sea to the Dead Sea and the R. Jordan. At Lake Rudolf it is joined by a branch which starts near the R. Zambezi and runs through Lake Nyasa. Other examples are the Central Lowlands of Scotland and the Rhine Valley between the Black Forest and the Vosges Mts.

River, a stream of fresh water flowing in a definite natural channel over the land from a higher to a lower level. A river may have its origin, or *source,* in a spring, a melting glacier, a lake, a marsh, or in a combination of tiny rills. On its way from its source to its *mouth* or entrance into a sea or lake a river gradually increases in size by the addition of other streams or *tributaries* which join it, the whole forming a *river system.* The path followed is called its *course,* and the total country drained by the river and its tributaries is its *drainage area* or BASIN. When an observer looks downstream the *right bank* is on his right, the *left bank* on his left. Generally a river's course can be divided into three parts, the *upper* in hilly or mountainous land where the flow is torrential, the *middle* in undulating country where the flow is fairly fast, and the *lower,* near its mouth, where the country is flat and the flow is a smooth and gentle glide. In the more rapid portions of their courses rivers are continually at work carrying rock fragments and sediment, with whose help they deepen their beds and erode their banks. In their lower courses, where the current is slow, they deposit sediment and build up beds, sandbanks, BARS, or DELTAS. Some rivers which flow over hot, arid areas receive no tributaries, and lose so much water by evaporation that they finally disappear as rivers before reaching a lake or sea. Such rivers, and those which discharge into a lake which has no outlet, are said to flow through a region of *inland drainage.*

The longest river in the world is the Missouri-Mississippi (4,200 m.).

River Port. See PORT.

Roaring Forties. See BRAVE WEST WINDS.

Royal Burghs, certain towns in Scotland, such as Edinburgh, Perth, etc., which in mediæval times were founded and had certain rights conferred upon them by *royal charter.* One of the most important of these rights was the grant of a monopoly of the trade in a particular district. At the time of the Union of Scotland and England in 1707 there were seventy of these burghs in existence, of which sixty-seven are recorded in the 1931 census.

Rubber, an elastic substance prepared from the milky juice or *latex* of many tropical trees, originally found in the forests of the Amazon basin, but now cultivated in plantations in Malaya, the Dutch E. Indies, Ceylon, India, Sarawak, Indo-China, and tropical Africa. When the trees are about five years old cuts are made through the bark, and the juice which flows from these is collected in small cups. The collected latex is treated with an acid which causes the rubber to become firm; it is then rolled out into thin sheets, and either hung up to dry as *crêpe rubber* or dried with smoke as *sheet rubber*. In these forms it is exported. When treated with sulphur rubber loses its stickiness; the uses of this *vulcanized* rubber are innumerable. The best qualities of rubber are known as *Para* and *Ceara*, names derived from Brazil, the original source of supply. Between 60 and 70 per cent. of world production goes to U.S.A., over 25 per cent. to U.K., France, Germany, and Canada, and the rest to Japan, Russia, Italy, etc. *Gutta-percha*, a variety of rubber obtained from certain E. Indian islands, is used to cover telegraph cables; still another variety, *balata*, comes from British Guiana.

Sago, a starchy foodstuff prepared from the pith of certain tropical palm trees, natives of the E. Indies, and from another variety of palm in the W. Indies. It is imported into the U.K., chiefly from Singapore.

Salin'ity, the saltness of the water in rivers, lakes, and oceans. River water is called fresh, but it contains a small amount of mineral salts dissolved from the land over which it flows. If a river flows through a lake, the lake water will also be very slightly saline. In the arid parts of the world certain lakes into which rivers flow have no outlet to the sea. The surplus water is evaporated from the surface, but the mineral salts remain in the lake, causing its remaining water to become *brackish* or definitely salt. The Dead Sea, for example, has *c.* 25 per cent. of salts in solution, while sea water, which holds many substances in solution, especially common salt, has an average salinity of only 3½ per cent. But the sea is not uniformly salt. Where evaporation is intense and rainfall is scanty the salinity increases (*e.g.* Mediterranean and Red Seas); where oceans receive much fresh water from rivers, rain, or melting ice the salinity decreases (*e.g.* Baltic, Equatorial, and Polar Seas).

Salt, a much-used and easily-prepared mineral product, obtained either from rock-salt mines or brine deposits, *e.g.* in Cheshire, or by the evaporation of sea-water, *e.g.* in Portugal. Only in wet tropical lands is there a shortage of salt, *e.g.* India; it is an important article of trade in the Sahara. The principal exporting countries are U.K., Spain, Germany, and Portugal. Salt is used for seasoning and preserving foods, and in the manufacture of washing soda, hydrochloric acid, etc.

Savan'na. See GRASSLANDS.

Sea Breezes. See LAND AND SEA BREEZES.

Sea-level, the level, or level agreed upon, from which heights and depths on the earth's surface are usually measured. Over the surface of the ocean generally there is much variation of level caused by winds, barometric pressure, and varying degrees of salinity. Mountains near the coast attract the sea, and where the coast region is high this raises the level of the sea. It is thus necessary to take a *mean sea-level* for the measurement of heights and depths. On the Ordnance Survey maps of Britain the datum level is the 'assumed mean level of the sea at Liverpool,' though this is lower than the average level round the country. On charts used for navigation the datum level taken is the average level of low water at spring tides.

Seaport. See PORT.

Seasons, periods of the year during which different types of weather prevail, the differences being due to the annual movements of the earth round the sun. In temperate regions there are four: spring, summer, autumn, and winter. In monsoon countries these are usually reckoned: cold, rainy, and hot. In tropical areas there are frequently two rainy and two dry seasons.

Selvas, the dense forested plains of the river Amazon in S. America. Owing to the excessive rainfall and the high temperature in this region growth is rapid and continuous, there being no seasonal leaf fall and flowering time. So dense is the growth of vegetation that it presents an almost impenetrable barrier to communication and commerce. Characteristic trees are the palms, mimosa, figs, and bamboos around whose base grows dense underwood and climbing plants. The whole area presents the most wonderful variety of different types of vegetation to be found anywhere.

Shotts, shallow salt lakes found in N. Africa in the states of Algeria and Tunis. A line of them extends for about 250 m. over the plateau between the Tell Atlas Mountains on the north and the Sahara Atlas Mountains on the south, hence called the Plateau of the Shotts.

Sikhs (*sēks*), originally a religious sect founded in the 16th century in India, near Amritsar, which has ever since been the holy city of the Sikhs. In the 18th century, under Guru Govind, the Sikhs organized themselves as a military power, and ultimately possessed an army of some 120,000 men trained in European methods of warfare under French officers. In 1845 and again in 1848 they came into conflict with the British, and, after defeat, their country, the Punjab, was annexed. Since then the Sikhs have been most loyal adherents of the British Crown, and rendered very helpful service during the Indian Mutiny. The Sikh is tall, well-built, and handsome, brave to the death, and submits readily to discipline. Loving war and adventure, many of them serve as soldiers in the Indian army. They also make excellent police, and are employed as such in several British colonies.

Silk, the very fine, soft, glossy threads spun round themselves for protection by certain kinds of caterpillars (the so-called silk-worms) in their chrysalis stage previous to their transformation into moths. The silky cases or *cocoons* thus formed are placed in very hot ovens or in dry steam to kill the chrysalis, after which the silk is unwound or 'reeled,' mostly by machines. One cocoon yields *c.* 400 yards of extremely fine thread, and 10 lb. of cocoons furnish about 1 lb. of raw silk. From 5 to 7 of these threads are twisted together to form the best silk thread of commerce; for coarser qualities up to 20 threads are required. The principal producing countries are China, Japan, India, Indo-China, Italy, and France, all of which have sufficiently hot climates for the silk-worms, and grow abundantly the mulberry trees of which the leaves form their favourite food, and also have an adequate supply of relatively cheap yet skilled labour to produce and prepare the thread at low cost. The chief manufacturing countries are U.S.A., France, Italy, and Switzerland, and Lyons, Krefeld, Zurich, and Basle are specially noted for the manufacture of satins and velvets. *Artificial silk,* or *rayon,* is prepared from cotton wool, sawdust, or wood-pulp. From these cheap raw materials liquid cellulose is chemically prepared and squeezed through very narrow glass tubes. From them it emerges as long, thin threads which are spun and woven in the same manner as real silk. Artificial silk is now produced in enormous quantities in the industrial countries of Europe and N. America.

Silt. See ALLUVIUM.

Simoom′, an intensely hot, dry, and suffocating whirlwind which blows chiefly in spring and summer in the Saharan, Arabian, and Baluchistan desert areas. It usually raises columns of sand, which sometimes overwhelm caravans and modify the form of the sand-dunes in its path.

Sirocco, or SCIROCCO (*sir-ok′ō*), a hot southerly wind experienced on the African coast of the Mediterranean Sea, and also in Sicily, southern Italy, Malta, and Greece. In southern Italy and Greece it is very hot (sometimes 110° F.) and dry, but as it passes northward it gathers moisture.

Sis′al, the fibre obtained from the leaves of sisal hemp or *henequen*, a variety of agave native to the arid, rocky soils of Yucatan, but now cultivated in Tanganyika Territory and elsewhere. It ranks next after manila hemp in the making of ropes and twine.

Slavs, one of the chief divisions of the Aryan race, forming the majority of the population of Europe. The original home of the Slavs was in the district N.E. of the Carpathian Mountains in the valleys of the Rs. Vistula, Pripet, and Dniester. From there they have spread over eastern Europe, and are represented now by the Russians, the Bulgarians, the Serbo-Croats and Slovenes of Yugoslavia, the Kashubes north-west of Danzig, the Poles, and the Czechs, Moravians, and Slovaks of Czechoslovakia. In all there are probably *c.* 150,000,000 Slavs in Europe. In general the Slav is broad-headed, short of stature, and of pale white to swarthy colour.

Snow, one of the forms of condensed atmospheric water vapour which falls to earth. When moisture is condensed at a temperature below freezing point it is changed into ice crystals, groups of which form snow-flakes. When the moisture is formed into drops before freezing it falls as hail, each hailstone consisting of several coats of frozen moisture.

Snowline, the limit of altitude above which perpetual snow lies, or below which all the fresh snow of winter is melted during the summer. This limit varies in different places, depending on latitude, steepness of slope, the amount of snowfall, and exposure to rain-bearing winds and the sun's rays. Near the equator the snowline is *c.* 18,000 ft. above sea-level, but in Spitsbergen it practically coincides with sea-level. In the Alps it is higher on the south side than on the north.

Soil, the loose material, primarily resulting from the decay of rocks, into which the roots of plants penetrate, and from which they derive moisture and food. Soils either lie upon the rock from which they have been formed, or are transported from a distance by running water, or by glaciers, or by the wind. The fertility of a soil depends chiefly on the nature of the particles of which it is composed, a sufficiency of plant food, and suitable climatic conditions. The particles composing it may be fine or coarse, and either porous or tenacious of water. In addition to such mineral particles soils must contain organic matter, mainly derived from decayed vegetable substances. This is known as *humus*, and not only contains plant food but helps to retain moisture in the soil. Where soil is continually cropped its stores of plant food become exhausted, and some means must be employed for the preservation of its fertility, either by the rotation of the crops grown, or by allowing it to lie fallow for a time, or by the use of fertilizers.

Solar System, the sun, and the planets with their satellites or moons which revolve round the sun, controlled in their courses by its gravitation. The planet nearest to the sun is Mercury (35,900,000 miles); that farthest distant is Pluto (discovered 1930; *c.* 3,800,000,000 miles); between these are Venus, Earth, Mars, Jupiter, Saturn, Uranus, and Neptune. The Earth with its satellite, the moon, is at an average distance of

92,870,000 miles from the sun. The diameter of the sun is 864,000 miles, or about 35 times that of the earth; its mass is equal to 332,000 earths. The sun radiates heat and light to the planets.

Solar Time. See TIME.

Solstice (*sol'stis*), the time in summer or winter when the sun, through the annual revolution of the earth, is vertical at its farthest distance N. or S. of the equator (23½°) and for a few days before moving in the reverse direction seems to stand still. In the N. hemisphere the *summer* solstice occurs *c.* 22nd June, which is the winter solstice in the S. hemisphere, and the *winter* solstice *c.* 22nd December, which is the summer solstice in the S. hemisphere.

Sounding, the process of finding out the depth of the sea. When the sea is fairly shallow a piece of lead weighing 7 lb. or more and attached to a rope marked at regular intervals is dropped overboard a vessel. When the lead strikes the bottom the shock is usually felt, and the length of line run out gives the depth. To sound great depths a steel wire with heavy sinkers is used, and there is a device by which the leads are detached on striking bottom. The most recent method of measurement is by *echo sounding*. A sound produced at the surface travels through water at a known rate. The time taken for such a sound to travel to the bottom and its echo to be reflected back to the surface is carefully noted, and from this the depth is accurately calculated. From the results of soundings seamen's CHARTS are constructed.

Soy'a Bean, or SOJA, or SOY, a leguminous plant, one of the PULSES, yielding a bean resembling a green pea, which is used for human food in E. Asia and for animal fodder in Europe and U.S.A. The plant thrives wherever maize or cotton can be grown, but its value was not realized in the U.K. till 1908, when the first shipment arrived at Hull from Manchuria, still the principal source of supply. Japan and S. China are large importers. The beans are rich in oil, and after the oil has been expressed, the residue forms a valuable cattle-food and fertilizer. See OIL-SEEDS.

Spices, fragrant or pungent products, obtained almost entirely from tropical plants, and employed to flavour foods. The principal spices of British commerce are pepper, ginger, cloves, and cinnamon (see separate articles). The very high value of spices in 16th-century England was due to the difficulties and dangers of the long voyages round the Cape of Good Hope; and one reason for the formation of the E. India Co. was the Dutch monopoly which raised the price of pepper from 3s. to 6s. per lb. Shakespeare mentions mace, nutmegs, and ginger as spices well known in Elizabethan England.

Spin'ifex, the name applied to two groups of thorny, salt-loving grasses which grow in arid parts of Australia. In the one group is *Hairy Spinifex* or *Spiny Rolling Grass*, which is found in S.E. Asia, Australasia, and the Pacific Islands, where it serves to bind the sand. The other group includes *Porcupine Grass*, also a sand-binder, which grows in round, isolated hummocks, 1 to 3 ft. high, formed of dense masses of needle-like prickles; above these rise blades of very coarse grass, sometimes 6 ft. high, which cause sores on the legs of camels and horses. When in seed the grass forms a food for horses; at other stages it is useless, except to kangaroos and rats, which feed on its roots. This plant is found over about one-third of Australia.

Spring Tides. See TIDES.

Stalactites and **Stalagmites.** See KARST.

Steppes. See GRASSLANDS.

Strath, Scottish name for a broad river valley. See VALLEY.

Sudd, a floating mass of vegetable matter that forms in the Upper Nile and obstructs navigation. It is composed of plants which cover the swamps on either side of the river.

When such plants are loosened and reach the main channel of the river they often lodge on some obstruction and form a dam or floating island, sometimes 25 m. in length and 20 ft. in thickness. In 1900–4 much of the sudd was removed and freedom of navigation secured.

Sugar, the sweet substance extracted from the stems of the sugar-cane and the root of sugar-beet. The *sugar-cane*, a native of E. Asia, now cultivated throughout the tropics, is a member of the grass family. It grows on moist soils in tropical and subtropical countries, its stems rising to 10 or 12 ft. The canes are crushed between rollers to obtain the juice, which is boiled. As it cools, the crystals separate out and form *raw sugar*; the thick syrup remaining is known as *molasses*, and from this *rum* is distilled, principally in the W. Indies. The raw sugar is refined in importing countries, *e.g.* U.K., and the by-products of *syrup* and *treacle* are obtained. The largest producers of cane-sugar are Cuba, India, Java, Brazil, Sandwich Islands, Philippines, and Porto Rico. The *sugar-beet*, a white variety of beetroot, is an annual plant widely cultivated in temperate Europe and U.S.A. The turnip-like roots are washed and passed through machines which reduce them to pulp. The juice is crystallized by boiling, and is then known as beet sugar. The principal producing lands are Germany, Czechoslovakia, France, Poland, U.S.S.R., U.S.A., Belgium, and Holland; the world production is more than half that of cane-sugar. In India some sugar is obtained from certain palm trees; in Canada some is made from the sap of the maple tree, obtained by tapping the tree.

Swahili (*swă-hē'lē*), the native inhabitants of Zanzibar and the coast lands opposite. They are of mixed Negro and Arab blood, and in colour range from pure black to tawny. They are a tall, strong, and handsome people, and owing to their intelligence and enterprise are in great demand in Central Africa as porters. Their language, Kiswahili, is one of the Bantu group of languages, and is widely used as a trade language.

Tableland. See PLATEAU.

Taiga (*tī'gă*), irregular belts of coniferous forest land in the N. hemisphere. These lie S. of the TUNDRA, and much of the land becomes flooded in spring by water from the head-streams of north-flowing rivers whose lower courses are still ice-bound. This renders the timber useless for commercial purposes. Population is scanty. Hunting and trapping fur-bearing animals are the chief occupations.

Tapioca. See CASSAVA.

Tariffs, duties imposed on foreign goods imported into a country either as a means of raising revenue for the Government, or for protecting its own manufactures from competition by those of other countries; also known as customs duties.

Tea, the cured leaves of the tea plant, a hardy, subtropical shrub, possibly native to Assam, which grows on the rich soils of well-drained mountain slopes in lands of hot-season rainfall. The leaves are picked by hand several times each year, the earliest picking yielding the best tea. After being sun-dried the leaves are rolled, and allowed to ferment in order to reduce the quantity of *tannin* they contain. They are again dried, and exported as *black tea*; in *green tea* no fermentation has taken place. The principal producing lands are China, India, Ceylon, the Dutch E. Indies (especially Java), and Japan. India and Ceylon are the largest exporters to the U.K., which is the chief importer; Japan sends green tea to the U.S.A.; from China *brick tea*, made by mixing inferior leaves, stalks, and dust with rice paste, is exported to the U.S.S.R., which also buys *tea-tablets* of the finest tea-dust compressed by machinery. Tea was first introduced into England in 1665, when it cost £3 per lb.; the consumption per head is largest in Australia, New Zealand, and the U.K.

Temp'erature, the degree of heat possessed by a body. This is measured by a THERMOMETER. On the earth's surface there is a steady diminution of temperature from the equator towards the poles. The slope of the land, nearness to the sea, the direction of mountain chains, the direction of prevailing winds, the nature of the soil, and the quantity of vegetation also modify land temperatures. Temperature decreases with altitude at the rate of *c.* 3° F. for every 1,000 ft. of ascent. The difference between the hottest and coldest part of a day is called the *Daily Range of Temperature,* while the difference between the average temperature of the hottest and coldest months is the *Annual Range.* See ISOTHERM.

Terrace Cultivation, a method of cultivating barren and steep hillsides. The slopes are cut into terraces which rise like stairs above one another. Walls from 5 to 15 ft. high are built round these patches, to retain moisture and prevent the soil which may have been carried to the fields from the valleys from being washed away. Such terraces are easily irrigated by mountain streams or artificially, and are common where cultivable land is scarce and rainfall irregular. By this method good crops are raised in parts of Arabia and the hilly regions of India, Ceylon, China, Spain, Italy, etc.

Thermom'eter, an instrument for measuring temperature. It consists of a glass tube of very fine, uniform bore, at one end of which is a bulb. Mercury, or some other liquid which expands with heat and contracts with cold, fills the bulb and a portion of the stem. On the stem is a graduated scale of units, called *degrees,* the two fixed points marking the freezing and boiling points of water. On the Fahrenheit thermometer freezing point is 32° and boiling point is 212°. On the Centigrade scale, mostly used for scientific purposes, these points are 0° and 100°.

Tides, the alternate rise and fall of the waters of the ocean twice in the course of nearly twenty-five hours. The rise is called the *flood,* and the fall the *ebb.* Tides are caused by the gravitational force exerted by the moon, and to a lesser degree the sun, on the earth. The tides do not always rise to the same height. At the time of new or of full moon, when the sun and moon are in a straight line with the earth, the tides rise higher and are then known as *spring tides.* Midway between new and full moon, when the sun and the moon are at right angles as to their direction from the earth, tides are at their lowest height and are then called *neap tides.* When a long and narrowing river estuary is subject to tides, the flood causes a BORE, which in turn causes exceptionally high tides far up the estuary. Thus, on the Severn, the bore has been known to cause at Chepstow, on the Wye, a tidal range of 47 ft. Where the tidal current rushes through a narrow channel we get what is called a *race,* as at Alderney in the Channel Islands, and if the channel be irregular may cause violent whirlpools such as the Maelstrom off the Lofoten Islands. Inland seas, like the Mediterranean, have a very small tidal range. The times at which high and low water occur vary from day to day, being about 50 minutes later each day; thus if it is high tide at 12 noon, it will be high water again about 25 minutes after midnight, and again the next day about 12.50 p.m. Low water occurs about half-way between two high waters.

Till. See GLACIER.

Time. The movements of the earth, or the apparent movements of the sun, are the standards by which we measure time. The *solar day,* or the time between midday and midday, is divided into hours, minutes, and seconds. All places on the same meridian A have the same *solar time, i.e.* noon occurs at the same time at all parts of the line, but, owing to the rotation of the earth from west to east, places that lie to the east or west of this line have a different solar time. Thus a place to the east of A will have the sun overhead at noon earlier than A, so that clock-time there will be ahead of clock-time at A; a place to the west of A will similarly have its clock-time behind that of A. As the earth rotates through 360° in 24 hours, there is a difference of 4 minutes of time for each degree of longitude. Thus the *local time* of any place on the earth's surface with reference to any other place can easily be calculated. In order to avoid the confusion of a number of places within a certain range of longitude keeping each its own local time, the local time of one convenient meridian of longitude is adopted for the whole range, and is known as the *standard time* for that area.

Tinplate, thin sheets of iron or steel coated with tin to protect them from rusting. Tinplates are most largely produced in the industrial centres of the s. Wales coalfield at Swansea and Cardiff. In the U.K. tinplate is made into biscuit tins, etc.; it is also exported, especially to the Americas and British Dominions, to be used in the form of containers in the meat, fruit, fish, and vegetable canning industries.

Tobacco, the prepared leaves of certain plants, native of the Americas, used for smoking or chewing, and, in the form of powder, for snuffing. The plant may be cultivated in both tropical and temperate lands, but the finest leaves are grown in Cuba, where they are made into cigars. The U.S.A. grows by far the largest tobacco crop. Tobaccos are named from their lands of origin, *e.g.* Virginian, Turkish, Egyptian, etc., and are blended to make smoking mixtures and cigarettes. Empire tobaccos come principally from N. and S. Rhodesia, Nyasaland, India, and British N. Borneo.

Tonnage, name used to indicate the carrying capacity of a vessel, and not the weight of the vessel itself.

Torna'do. See WHIRLWIND.

Towns, places where people congregate and live in houses either for social reasons, for mutual defence, or for convenience of trade. Where the number of people is small they are known as villages; where they are very large and the towns consequently important they may be called cities. Their position has generally been determined by a number of different factors. In Europe in the Middle Ages castles were erected by kings or nobles, and round these grew up towns which looked to the lord of the castle for protection, as at Stirling and Carnarvon. Towns also grew up round the great cathedrals, as at Durham. As trade developed, market towns arose where routes converged, but with greater facilities for transport lost much of their importance. As mining developed, mining towns arose in the mineral areas. With the development of manufactures came the rise of manufacturing towns, situated where most convenient for raw material, coal, or distribution of goods. Other special considerations may determine the site of a town, so that we find towns built at the end of a pass (Bologna), at important fords or bridges (Oxford and London), at the head of deltas or on one of their distributaries (New Orleans and Calcutta), at the head of navigation on a river (Montreal), at the junction of rivers (Allahabad), or where falls and rapids occur (Minneapolis). See also PORT.

Trade Routes. The early *land routes* of trade were *caravan* routes from E. and s. Asia, and across the Sahara, to the markets of s. Europe. Many of these are still used, but some have been superseded, in parts, by *railways*, *e.g.* Baghdad Rly., while others are developing into *motor* routes, *e.g.* between Damascus and Baghdad. The early *sea routes* were through the Mediterranean and Red Seas, or mainly *coasting* routes along the shores of the Old World. At a later period sailing routes, adapted to the winds, were more important. At present the busiest routes are those of the *steamship*, following arcs of GREAT CIRCLES whenever possible, but requiring fuelling stations, and utilizing ship canals. For the rapid transport of mails, passengers, and light freight, AIR ROUTES are now increasingly followed.

Trade Winds, constant winds, roughly between latitudes 30° N. and 30° S., that blow towards the equatorial region of calms or the DOLDRUMS, and so called because of their regularity and consequent value to navigators. Heated and moisture-laden air from the torrid zone rises upwards and flows off towards the poles, and cooler air from regions north and south of the equator flows in along the surface to take its place. If the earth were at rest a north wind would prevail north of the Doldrums and a south wind to the south, but the earth's rotation being most rapid at the equator, deflects these winds to the west, causing them to be north-easterly in the N. hemisphere and south-easterly in the S. hemisphere.

Train Ferry, a means of transport by which railway trains are carried across stretches of water, generally too wide for bridging, on vessels with rails on their decks. This saves the time required for the transfer of goods between train and ship, and is important where perishable goods are concerned or where a quick passenger service is considered essential.

Transport. The most primitive form of *land* transport is the carriage of goods by *human porters*, still common in tropical Africa and in monsoon Asia, where men also draw or push vehicles containing commodities. Animal transport is the most widely employed form, the *beasts of burden* most generally employed being the horse, the mule, the ass, and the ox; in dry deserts the camel; in S. America the llama; in Tibet the yak; in India the elephant; and in tundra lands the reindeer and dog (husky). Such animals may either carry the goods, *e.g.* pack-horse, or draw vehicles, much heavier loads being transported by the latter method, but the use of vehicles necessitates the laying of *roads*. In the late 18th century came the cutting of *canals* in Britain, especially for the cheap transport of coal. In the 19th century the invention of the steam and later of the electric locomotive brought about the *railway* age. The employment of *motor* vehicles has greatly increased the importance of road transport. Water carriage developed from simple *rafts* and *boats* propelled by oars to the *sailing vessel*, and later to the *steamship* driven by coal or oil; and a more recent development is the use of ships driven by motor or *internal combustion* engines. *Air transport* is still in its experimental stages, but mails are already being carried by aeroplane to India and S. Africa, as well as over many parts of Europe and America. In Australia there are regular air lines for the service of districts remote from railways. See TRADE ROUTES.

Treaty Ports. Certain Chinese ports which are open to international commerce are so called. Till the middle of the 19th century foreigners were allowed to trade at various Chinese ports, but under no formal permission. In 1842 trouble which arose at Canton in connection with the trade in opium led to a war between Britain and China in which the Chinese were defeated. By the treaty which followed, five ports—Canton, Amoy, Fuchow, Ningpo, and Shanghai—were thrown open to foreign trade. Since then, at various times, other ports have also been made available for foreigners, and there are now more than forty such ports.

Tro'pics (' turning points '), parallels of latitude 23½° N. (*Tropic of Cancer*) and 23½° S. (*Tropic of Capricorn*) of the equator. They mark the northern and southern limits of places on the earth that receive vertical rays from the sun at noon. The sun reaches Cancer *c.* 22nd June, our Summer Solstice; and Capricorn, our Winter Solstice, *c.* 22nd December; and appears to *turn* back after some days.

Hence the name Tropic. The name Tropics is also used to mean the whole area between the tropical lines, or the Torrid Zone.

Tsetse Fly (*tset'si*). About twenty kinds of tropical African blood-sucking flies are so named. The most common is slightly larger than the ordinary house-fly, and has a protruding mouth through which poisons pass into animals or men bitten by the insect. The bite of certain tsetse flies is fatal to domesticated animals; that of others infects human beings with the deadly *sleeping-sickness*; and still others spread less fatal diseases. The principal method of getting rid of the fly is to clear away the low vegetation among which the young develop. Tsetse flies are most troublesome in the lowlands of Tanganyika Territory, N. Rhodesia, and Nyasaland.

Tuareg, or TAWAREK, a nomadic Berber race living in central and western Sahara. Of S. European type, they are reddish-yellow in colour, have long, black, silky hair, and are tall and muscular in build. They are known to the Arabs as the 'veiled' people, from the fact that the men wear a veil day and night, though the women never do. Averse to manual labour, the Tuareg live by convoying caravans of traders, by raiding unprotected traders, sometimes by plundering Arab settlements. Formerly Christian, they are now Mohammedan in religion.

Tundra (*toon'drä*), swampy, low-lying lands in the N. hemisphere, round the shores of the Arctic Ocean. In winter the ground is snow-covered and frozen, but during the short summer mosses, lichens, and some stunted herbage and flowering plants appear. The tundra is a grazing ground for reindeer and caribou, and supports a scanty population of nomadic tribes who live by hunting and fishing.

Turks, an important people of Tatar origin, widely distributed throughout Asia and S.E. Europe, being found from the banks of the R. Lena on the east to the Bosporus in Europe. The most important branch is that which founded the Ottoman Empire in Asia Minor and S.E. Europe. Their first invasion of Europe took place in 1355, and their capture of Constantinople in 1453 marked an epoch in European history. As a people the Turks are industrious, sober, and brave, and are Mohammedans in religion. Other branches of the race include Yakuts, Kirghiz, and Turkomans.

Typhoon (*tī-foon'*). See WHIRLWIND.

Urban District, a district in a county which by reason of increase of population has acquired the character of a town but has not yet become a municipal corporation. These areas are proclaimed as such by special legislation or by orders of the Government Department concerned with county and local administration.

Valley, a long stretch of low land between two ridges of higher ground and with a fairly regular downward slope. Usually a valley has been carved out from the surrounding country by the river which traverses it. A valley which has been carved out by a glacier is U-shaped in section, while one produced by a river is more V-shaped. *Longitudinal* valleys run between and parallel to mountain ranges; *transverse* valleys cut across ranges; *lateral* valleys are those caused by the tributaries of the river flowing in a longitudinal valley. See CAÑON, CARSE, COOMB, GLEN, RIA, RIFT VALLEY, STRATH.

Valo'nia, the acorn-cups of the Mediterranean oak, imported into the U.K., mainly from Smyrna, for use in tanning, dyeing, and making ink.

Veld (*velt*), a name applied in the Transvaal, S. Africa, to more or less elevated grassy plains which form part of the great S. African plateau. It is divided into (1) the High Veld, stretching east and west across the southern Transvaal; (2) the Middle or

Bush Veld in the north; and (3) the Low Veld in the east. It varies in height from 6,000 to 3,000 ft. above sea-level, and consists generally of rolling, grass-covered, treeless downs.

Vicuña (*vi-koo'nyä*), a small, undomesticated member of the camel family found at altitudes of over 13,000 ft. on the plateaus of the Andes. It is hunted for its fine wool, of which only small quantities are available for the world's markets.

Volca'no, an opening in the earth's crust through which molten rock or lava, rock fragments, ashes, and steam are ejected from the hot interior. The ejection of material is called an *eruption*. The material forms a cone-shaped hill or mountain round the opening, with a *crater* or cup at the summit. Some of the lava may fill cracks or fissures in the walls of the volcano or underground, and when it cools and hardens it is known as a DYKE. *Pumice stone* is the solidified froth or scum of lava. The supposed flame of a volcano is merely the reflection of the red-hot rock within the crater on a cloud of vapour which forms above the mountain. At the base of some volcanic cones *sulphur* is found (Mt. Etna in Sicily). Volcanoes may be *extinct*, *dormant* (liable to break out), or *active*. The chief centre of volcanic activity is the line of weakness in the earth's crust surrounding the Pacific Ocean. Familiar examples of volcanic mountains are Vesuvius (Italy), Fujiyama (Japan), and the Peak of Teneriffe (Canary Islands).

Wallace's Line, a line passing N.N.E. between the islands of Bali and Lombok in the E. Indies, thence through the Strait of Macassar between Borneo and Celebes, and finally S.E. of the Philippine Islands. To the west of this line flora and fauna are of distinctly Asiatic character, while to the east and south Australian elements are predominant. This shows that the islands west of this line must at one time have formed part of the mainland of Asia, from which they were detached by subsidence, while those to the east formed part of the Australian mainland. Wallace's line indicates the deep channel which must have separated these continents in remote times. It is so called after Alfred Russel Wallace, the famous scientist, who first defined its course in his *Island Life* (1880).

Waterfall, or CASCADE or CATARACT, a sudden descent of water in the current of a river. Waterfalls are naturally commonest in a mountainous country, but some of the finest, such as the Niagara Falls on the St. Lawrence R., or the Victoria Falls on the Zambezi R., are in relatively flat country. This is due to rock strata of different degrees of hardness in the bed of the stream lying horizontally or dipping up-stream. When a hard layer lies over softer rock, the latter is more rapidly worn away, and a step or terrace formation results. As the hard layer also wears away, but more slowly, the position of the fall gradually moves up-stream, and a gorge is formed below it. The word '*cascade*' is often reserved for falls where the descent is made in a series of steps. *Rapids* are formed where these steps are small in height. Waterfalls interrupt navigation, but may be invaluable as a source of water power.

Water Power, energy derived from natural or artificial waterfalls, used directly for driving machinery by turning a water-wheel or turbine, or indirectly through electricity generated in dynamos worked by turbines.

Watershed, the slope down which a stream flows. The high ground separating two watersheds is called the *water parting* or *divide*, but in many cases the divide is really a level stretch of boggy ground from which water flows out at both sides. Such ground may occupy the highest part of a pass, as in the Great Divide of the Rocky Mountains in Canada.

Wattle, several kinds of Australian acacia varying in size from shrubs (*e.g.* mulga) to forest trees (*e.g.* ironwood). The bark of several varieties is valuable for tanning, and some of these, particularly the *black wattle*, have been introduced into Natal. The trees were called *wattles* because their long, pliant branches were used by early settlers to form the framework of their 'wattle-and-daub' huts.

Weather, the atmospheric conditions for a particular day, week, month, season, or year, as distinguished from CLIMATE, which takes account of the *average* conditions over the longest period under observation. See METEOROLOGY.

Weathering, the change produced on rocks by the action of the atmosphere, frost, and rain. See DENUDATION.

Wheat, one of the most important cereals, a member of the family of grasses. It is cultivated principally in temperate lands, but is grown also in lands of subtropical and tropical climates. The largest producers are the U.S.A., Canada, India, U.S.S.R., France, and Italy. The U.K., which produces less than one quarter of the wheat required by its population, is the largest importer, and, like Italy and Germany, purchases largely from Canada, U.S.A., Argentina, and Australia.

Whirlwind, a column of air rotating rapidly round its own vertical axis and at the same time moving forward with great speed. It is due to an atmospheric disturbance over a small area produced by a quick change in temperature and pressure. A whirlwind frequently assumes the shape of a long, narrow funnel, and is violent and destructive, but usually dies away before travelling very far. The chief whirlwinds are: the *typhoon*, which blows during August, September, and October over the China Sea; the *hurricane*, often experienced in the West Indies; the *tornado*, which occurs in the Mississippi Valley.

Wind, air moving more or less horizontally from a high-pressure area to a low-pressure area. A wind is always named from the direction in which it starts (*e.g.* a *west* wind is one which blows from the west). The rate of movement, or *force*, is measured in miles per hour, and may vary from a calm to over 100 miles per hour. Some winds are *constant*, or blow steadily all the year round in one direction (*e.g.* trade winds); others blow in particular places (*e.g.* harmattan), or at certain seasons (*e.g.* monsoon), or at a certain time of the day (*e.g.* land and sea breezes). See METEOROLOGY, BRAVE WEST WINDS, MONSOON, TRADE WINDS, WHIRLWIND.

Wine, the fermented juice of the fruit of the vine (grapes), used as a beverage as far back as historical records extend. The original home of the vine appears to have been in W. Asia or S.E. Europe; it thrives in lands of long, hot, sunny summers followed by warm autumns; its long roots favour its cultivation in 'Mediterranean' climates. France holds the first place for the quantity, the quality, and the variety of its wines (*e.g. claret, burgundy, champagne*), each of which comes from a different district. Italian wines, in quantity not far behind French, are not in so great demand abroad; Spanish *sherry* and Portuguese *port* are largely exported; other well-known wines are *Tokay* (Hungary) and *Moselle* (Germany). British Empire wines from Australia and S. Africa are now marketed in increasing quantity in the U.K. The spirit of wine is distilled as *brandy*, of which the finest quality comes from Cognac (France).

Wood-pulp, a material prepared from soft-wooded trees (*e.g.* spruce, fir, pine, hemlock), increasingly employed in the making of paper since its introduction about 1880. *Mechanical* wood-pulp is prepared by reducing the wood to pulp on grindstones; its inferior quality makes it suitable for only cheap papers (*e.g.* newsprint). *Chemical* pulp made by treating small chips of wood with soda, sodium sulphate, or sulphurous acid and lime or magnesia, yields finer and stronger pulp. The principal producing countries are Canada, U.S.A., Sweden, and Finland.

Wool, the hairy covering of many animals, particularly the sheep, goat, llama, alpaca, vicuña, and camel. Sheep thrive on the grasslands of cool, dry climates; goats are reared on mountain slopes. The principal sources of sheep wool, of which *merino* is the finest, are Australia, Argentina, U.S.A., S. Africa, and New Zealand. The scoured wool is spun into yarn before being woven into cloth. The grease that is removed by washing the wool, known as *lanoline*, is used in making toilet soaps. Of goat wools, *mohair* is exported from S. Africa, and *cashmere*, the fine undercoat of the Kashmir goat, from Himalayan lands. *Camel's hair* comes from China and Turkestan. France, U.K., U.S.A., and Germany are the largest importers of wool.

Yak, a large kind of ox or bison, with long hair hanging from its lower body, found wild in Tibet, where it is also domesticated as a sure-footed beast of burden. Its wool is made into clothing, and the cow yields milk.

Yer'ba Maté (*mä'tā*), or MATÉ, or PARAGUAY TEA, the prepared leaves of a small tree of the holly family which grows wild, and is also cultivated in plantations in tropical and subtropical S. America. From the leaves a beverage is prepared like tea, which has a stimulating effect on fatigued persons, and is much used in S. American countries.

Zones. See BELTS.

Zulus, a S. African native people, one of the branches of the BANTU race, living in the N.E. part of Natal. Physically they are a fine race, and in character are brave and warlike, intelligent and independent. They live mainly by cattle farming, and such arts as they have developed are very primitive. They care little for trading. In the early 19th century, under their great chief Chaka, they developed into a warrior nation, establishing complete supremacy over other native races from Cape Colony to the Zambezi. Though their warlike proclivities have been much curtailed since their defeat by the British in 1879, they still retain a strong sense of nationality.

STATISTICS OF THE

	Area in Sq. Miles.	Pop. in 1,000's.
BRITISH ISLES:		
England and Wales	58,340	39,948
Scotland	30,405	4,843
Northern Ireland	5,240	1,256
Irish Free State	26,601	2,972
Isle of Man	221	49
Channel Islands	75	93
	120,882	49,161
EUROPE:		
Gibraltar	2	21
Malta (with Gozo and Comino)	122	231
	124	252
ASIA:		
Indian Empire	1,805,332	318,942
Ceylon	25,332	4,504
Aden and Dependencies	9,000	55
Bahrein Islands	250	100
Straits Settlements	1,600	884
Federated Malay States	27,506	1,325
Other Malay States	22,855	1,162
British Borneo (three jurisdictions)	81,106	857
Hong Kong	391	1,076
Cyprus	3,584	311
*Iraq	143,250	2,849
*Palestine	19,000	757
	2,139,206	332,822
AFRICA:		
Union of South Africa	471,917	7,100
Basutoland	11,716	496
Bechuanaland	275,000	153
Swaziland	6,704	113
*South-West Africa	322,768	259
Southern Rhodesia	149,000	996
Northern Rhodesia	287,950	1,270
Nyasaland	37,890	1,307
*Tanganyika Territory	374,000	4,139
Zanzibar	1,020	217

* Administered under Mandate of the League of Nations.

BRITISH EMPIRE

	Area in Sq. Miles.	Pop. in 1,000's.
Africa (*continued*):		
Kenya	225,000	2,892
Uganda	94,204	3,157
Anglo-Egyptian Sudan	1,008,100	5,484
Somaliland	68,000	345
Gambia	4,130	210
Sierra Leone	31,000	1,541
Gold Coast	80,000	2,300
*Togoland	12,600	188
Nigeria	335,700	19,409
*Cameroons	34,236	687
Mauritius	720	385
Seychelles	156	27
St. Helena and Ascension	81	4
	3,831,892	52,679
America:		
Canada	3,685,000	9,934
Newfoundland and Labrador	152,734	270
Bermuda	19	31
British Honduras	8,598	45
Bahamas	4,404	59
Barbados	166	168
Jamaica and Dependencies	4,674	954
Trinidad and Tobago	1,976	420
Leeward Islands	715	122
Windward Islands	516	175
British Guiana	89,480	308
Falkland Islands and South Georgia	7,300	4
	3,955,582	12,490
Australia, New Zealand, and Oceania:		
Australian Commonwealth	2,974,581	6,263
Papua and *Territory of New Guinea	166,500	1,023
New Zealand	103,569	1,474
Fiji	7,083	177
Pacific Islands, including *Nauru and *Western Samoa	12,710	312
	3,264,443	9,249
Total	13,312,129	456,653

* Administered under Mandate of the League of Nations.

MISCELLANEOUS FACTS AND FIGURES

THE EARTH

Area, 196,550,000 sq. miles (Land, 55,500,000 sq. miles; Water, 141,050,000 sq. miles).
Population, *c.* 19,000,000,000.
Diameter at Equator, 7926.7 miles; Polar Diameter, 7,900 miles.
Circumference at Equator, 24,902 miles.
Mean distance of Earth from Sun, 92,900,000 miles.
Mean distance of Moon from Earth, 238,840 miles.

LENGTH IN MILES OF A DEGREE OF LATITUDE AND OF LONGITUDE

	At Equator.	At Lat. 15°.	At Lat. 30°.	At Lat. 45°.	At Lat. 60°.	At Lat. 75°.	At Poles.
1° of Latitude .	68.70	68.75	68.88	69.05	69.23	69.36	69.41
1° of Longitude .	69.17	66.83	59.96	49.00	34.67	17.96	0.00

HIGHEST MOUNTAINS

In British Isles . . . Ben Nevis (4,406 ft.).
In Europe . . . . . Mont Blanc (15,782 ft.).
In Asia . . . . . . Mount Everest (29,140 ft.).
In Africa . . . . . Kilimanjaro (19,324 ft.).
In N. America . . . Mount McKinley (20,464 ft.).
In S. America . . . Aconcagua (22,868 ft.).
In Australia . . . . Mount Kosciusko (7,336 ft.).

GREATEST OCEAN DEPTHS

Pacific Ocean . . . . Off Mindanao, 35,433 ft.
Atlantic Ocean . . . Off Porto Rico, 27,972 ft.
Indian Ocean . . . . Off Sunda Islands, 22,968 ft.

LARGEST CITIES IN THE WORLD

1.	London	8,202,818
2.	New York	6,981,927
3.	Berlin	4,024,154
4.	Chicago	3,375,329
5.	Paris	2,871,429
6.	Shanghai	2,674,447
7.	Moscow	2,412,300
8.	Osaka	2,114,804
9.	Buenos Aires	2,030,700
10.	Tokyo	1,995,567
11.	Philadelphia	1,964,430
12.	Vienna	1,857,000
13.	Leningrad	1,614,008
14.	Detroit	1,573,985
15.	Tientsin	1,388,747
16.	Calcutta	1,327,547
17.	Peking	1,297,718
18.	Sydney	1,238,660
19.	Los Angeles	1,233,561
20.	Bombay	1,175,914
21.	Rio de Janeiro	1,158,000
22.	Warsaw	1,109,478
23.	Montreal	1,098,000
24.	Glasgow	1,088,417
25.	Hamburg	1,079,126
26.	Cairo	1,064,567
27.	Melbourne	1,018,200
28.	Budapest	1,004,699
29.	Birmingham	1,002,413

LARGEST TOWNS IN THE BRITISH ISLES

England and Wales (Census, 1931)

1.	London— Administrative County and City of London	4,396,821
	Outer Ring	3,805,997
	Greater London	8,202,818
2.	Birmingham	1,002,413
3.	Liverpool	855,539
4.	Manchester	766,333
5.	Sheffield	511,742
6.	Leeds	482,789
7.	Bristol	396,918
8.	Hull	313,366
9.	Bradford	298,041
*10.	West Ham	294,086
11.	Newcastle-upon-Tyne	283,145
12.	Stoke-on-Trent	276,619
13.	Nottingham	268,801
14.	Portsmouth	249,288
15.	Leicester	239,111
*16.	Croydon	233,115
17.	Cardiff	223,648
18.	Salford	223,442
19.	Plymouth	208,166
20.	Sunderland	185,870
*21.	Willesden	184,410
22.	Bolton	177,253
23.	Southampton	176,025
24.	Coventry	167,046
25.	Swansea	164,825
*26.	Tottenham	157,748
27.	Birkenhead	147,946
28.	Brighton	147,427
*29.	East Ham	142,460
30.	Derby	142,406
31.	Rhondda	141,344
32.	Oldham	140,309
33.	Middlesbrough	138,489
34.	Wolverhampton	133,190
*35.	Walthamstow	132,965
*36.	Ilford	131,046
*37.	Leyton	128,317
38.	Norwich	126,207
39.	Stockport	125,505
40.	Blackburn	122,695
41.	Gateshead	122,379
42.	Southend-on-Sea	120,093
43.	Preston	118,839
*44.	Ealing	117,688
45.	Bournemouth	116,780
*46.	Hendon	115,682
47.	Huddersfield	113,467
48.	South Shields	113,452
49.	St. Helens	106,793
50.	Walsall	103,102
51.	Blackpool	101,543

* Part of Greater London.

Scotland (Census, 1931)

Town	Population
1. Glasgow	1,088,417
2. Edinburgh	438,998
3. Dundee	175,583
4. Aberdeen	167,259
5. Paisley	86,441
6. Greenock	78,948
7. Motherwell and Wishaw	64,708
8. Clydebank	46,963
9. Kirkcaldy	43,874
10. Coatbridge	43,056
11. Kilmarnock	38,099
12. Hamilton	37,863
13. Ayr	36,784
14. Falkirk	36,565
15. Dunfermline	34,954
16. Perth	34,807
17. Airdrie	25,954
18. Rutherglen	25,157
19. Dumfries	22,795
20. Stirling	22,593
21. Inverness	22,582
22. Dumbarton	21,546

Northern Ireland (Census, 1926)

Town	Population
1. Belfast	415,151
2. Londonderry	45,159
3. Bangor	13,311
4. Lurgan	12,500
5. Lisburn	12,406
6. Newry	12,226
7. Portadown	11,991
8. Ballymena	11,873
9. Newtownards	10,149

Irish Free State (Census, 1926)

Town	Population
1. Dublin—	
County Borough	316,693
Four adjoining Urban Districts	102,288
	418,981
2. Cork	78,490
*3. Rathmines and Rathgar	39,984
4. Limerick	39,448
*5. Pembroke	33,383
6. Waterford	26,647
*7. Kingstown (Dun Laoghaire)	18,987
8. Galway	14,227
9. Dundalk	13,996
10. Drogheda	12,716
11. Wexford	11,879
12. Sligo	11,437
13. Tralee	10,533
14. Kilkenny	10,046

* Urban District adjoining Dublin.

FOREIGN AND COLONIAL MONEY

Countries.	Chief Coins.	Approximate value in British money. s.	d.
Argentina	Peso (paper) = 100 centavos	1	8
	„ (gold) = „ „	4	0
Austria	Schilling = 100 groschen	0	7
Belgium	Franc = 100 centimes	0	1½
	Belga = 5 francs	0	7
Brazil	Cruzeiro = 4 milreis	2	0
	Milreis (paper) = 1,000 reis	0	6
B. Honduras	Dollar (gold) = 100 cents	4	1
Bulgaria	Lev = 100 stotinki	0	0½
Canada	Dollar (gold) = 100 cents	4	1
Ceylon	Rupee = 16 annas	1	6
Chile	Peso (gold) = 100 centavos	0	6
China	Tael (dollar) = 100 coppers	2	8
Cuba	Peso (gold) = 1 dollar (U.S.A.)	4	1
Czechoslovakia	Krone	0	1½
Denmark	Krone = 100 öre	1	1½
Egypt	Egyptian £ = 100 piastres	20	6½
Finland	Markka = 100 penni	0	1¼
France	Franc—100 centimes	0	2
Germany	Reichsmark = 100 pfennige	0	11¾
Greece	Drachma = 100 lepta	0	0½
Holland	Florin or Gulden = 100 cents	1	8
Hungary	Pengo = 100 filler	0	8½
India	Rupee = 16 annas	1	6
Italy	Lira = 100 centesimi	0	2½
Japan	Yen = 100 sen	2	0½
Mauritius	Rupee = 16 annas	1	6
Mexico	Dollar (gold) = 100 centavos	2	0½
	Peso (gold) = 50 cents (U.S.A.)	2	0½
Newfoundland	Dollar (gold) = 100 cents	4	1
Norway	Krone = 100 öre	1	1½
Peru	Libra = 10 soles	20	0
Portugal	Escudo (gold) = 100 centavos	4	5¼
Romania	Lëu = franc = 100 bani	0	0¼
Russia	Rouble = 100 copecks	2	1½
Spain	Peseta = franc = 100 centimes	0	9½
Straits Settlements	Dollar (silver)	2	4
Sweden	Krona = 100 öre	1	1½
Switzerland	Franc = 100 centimes	0	9½
Turkey	Lira = 100 piastres	18	0
United States	Dollar (gold) = 100 cents	4	1
Uruguay	Peso (gold) = 100 centimes	4	3
Yugoslavia	Dinar = 100 paras	0	9½